Early Christianity

Early Christianity: A Textbook for African Students, a significant contribution, is very timely in addressing a broader readership of Christians and Muslims interested in understanding an important common heritage of contemporary Africans. A substantive resource for students.

Tite Tienou, PhD
Research Professor, Theology of Mission,
The Tite Tienou Chair of Global Theology and World Christianity,
Dean Emeritus, Trinity Evangelical Divinity School,
Deerfield, Illinois, USA

Wendy Helleman and Musa Gaiya provide an indispensable resource for the study of early church history. Building on the work of Bediako, Kalu and other African scholars, they take seriously Africa's contribution to world Christianity – the text itself is anything but Afrocentric however. It plumbs the depths of the great minds of early African Christianity, placing them in the context of the larger church and the theological, political, social and cultural issues early Christianity in general faced. This is the kind of Christian history text African Christians have been waiting for.

Joel C. Elowsky, PhD
Professor of Historical Theology,
Director of the Study of Early Christian Texts,
Concordia Seminary, St Louis, Missouri, USA
Research Fellow, Centre for Early African Christianity

This significant history of the early church by two scholars who have lived in Africa is long awaited. It is in-depth, up-to-date and comprehensive. Highly recommended.

Timothy Palmer, PhD
Former Professor of Biblical Studies,
Theological College of Northern Nigeria,
Bukuru, Plateau State, Nigeria

This textbook gives a comprehensive account of the history and thought of early Christianity, particularly in Africa, making it easy to understand the trends and dynamics of present-day African Christianity. Written in simple English, it is useful for students, lecturers, Christians and Muslims.

Rev Thomas A. Oduro, PhD
President,
Good News Theological Seminary, Accra, Ghana

This book provides a concise summary of the history of the church from the Jewish backgrounds of early Christianity until the fall of the Roman Empire. It proceeds to provide the reader with an explanation of a selection of the most influential events within this time period. With its introductory level content, the book's goal is to be an overview of early church history and not an exhaustive text. It serves as an informative source for an undergraduate theology student or any student in need of accessible, introductory material regarding early church history.

Retief Muller, PhD
Associate Professor of Church History,
Stellenbosch University, Stellenbosch, South Africa

Early Christianity

A Textbook for African Students

Wendy Elgersma Helleman
and
Musa A. B. Gaiya

GLOBAL LIBRARY

© 2019 Wendy Elgersma Helleman and Musa A. B. Gaiya

Published 2019 by Langham Global Library
An imprint of Langham Publishing
www.langhampublishing.org

Langham Publishing and its imprints are a ministry of Langham Partnership

Langham Partnership
PO Box 296, Carlisle, Cumbria, CA3 9WZ, UK
www.langham.org

ISBNs:
978-1-78368-568-4 Print
978-1-78368-569-1 ePub
978-1-78368-570-7 Mobi
978-1-78368-571-4 PDF

Wendy Elgersma Helleman and Musa A. B. Gaiya have asserted their right under the Copyright, Designs and Patents Act, 1988 to be identified as the Authors of this work.

All rights reserved. No part of this publication may be reproduced, stored in a retrieval system or transmitted, in any form or by any means, electronic, mechanical, photocopying, recording or otherwise, without the prior written permission of the publisher or the Copyright Licensing Agency.

Requests to reuse content from Langham Publishing are processed through PLSclear. Please visit www.plsclear.com to complete your request.

All Scripture quotations, unless otherwise indicated, are taken from the Holy Bible, New International Version®, Anglicised, NIV®. Copyright © 1979, 1984, 2011 by Biblica, Inc.® Used by permission. All rights reserved worldwide.

Qur'an, The Holy. 1946. Text (English) trans. and commentary by Abdullah Yusuf Ali. 3rd ed. New York: Hafner Pub. Co.

British Library Cataloguing-in-Publication Data
A catalogue record for this book is available from the British Library

ISBN: 978-1-78368-568-4

Cover & Book Design: projectluz.com

Langham Partnership actively supports theological dialogue and an author's right to publish but does not necessarily endorse the views and opinions set forth here or in works referenced within this publication, nor can we guarantee technical and grammatical correctness. Langham Partnership does not accept any responsibility or liability to persons or property as a consequence of the reading, use or interpretation of its published content.

CONTENTS

List of Figures xv
List of Maps xviii
Preface and Acknowledgements xix
Abbreviations xxvii

Section I: Issues in the History of Early Christianity

1 Background to Early Christianity 3
    A. The Jewish Background (537 BC–AD 135) 4
        A.1. Introduction 4
        A.2. Second Temple Judaism under the Persians 6
        A.3. The Greek Period and Hellenization of the Jews 9
        A.4. The Hasmonean Period 12
        A.5. The Roman Period 13
        A.6. Jewish Religious Groups Important for
            Early Christianity 16
    B. The Roman Political, Cultural and Religious Background
       (63 BC – AD 410) 20
        B.1. Size of the Empire 21
        B.2. Roman Government and Emperor Worship 22
        B.3. Roman Religious Syncretism 24
        B.4. Mystery Religions 27
    Questions for Discussion and Review 30
       The Jewish background (537 BC – AD 135) 30
       The Roman political, cultural and religious background
          (63 BC – AD 410) 31
    Further Reading 31

2 The Rise and Spread of Christianity to AD 325 33
    A. Factors in the Geographical Expansion of Christianity 34
        A.1. Background 34
        A.2. The Admission of Gentiles into the Church 37
        A.3. The Jerusalem Council 40
        A.4. Rabbinic Judaism and Jewish Christianity 41

	B. Early Expansion of Christianity to the West, the Far East and Africa..44
	B.1. Christianity in Other Parts of the Roman Empire.......46
	B.2. Syrian Christianity 47
	B.3. Persian Christianity................................49
	B.4. Arab Christianity 50
	B.5. Christianity in the Far East 52
	Questions for Discussion and Review 53
	Further Reading 54
3	Monasticism and Missions 55
	A. Eastern Monasticism....................................57
	A.1. Early Asceticism: Anthony (ca. 250–356)..............58
	A.2. Cenobitic Monastic Organization: Pachomius (ca. 290–346)..62
	A.3. Monasticism in Ethiopia 65
	A.4. Syrian Monasticism: Symeon the Stylite (ca. 390–459)...66
	B. Spread of the Monastic Ideal............................69
	B.1. Athanasius and Basil of Caesarea 69
	B.2. Monasticism and Women 70
	C. Monasticism in the West................................73
	C.1. Martin of Tours (ca. 325–400) 73
	C.2. Jerome (ca. 342–420) 74
	C.3. John Cassian (ca. 360–435).........................75
	C.4. Patrick of Ireland (b. ca. 389) 76
	C.5. Cassiodorus (ca. 485–582).........................78
	C.6. Benedict of Nursia (ca. 480 – ca. 547) 79
	C.7. Monastics as Missionaries..........................80
	Questions for Discussion and Review 81
	Monasticism and Missions 81
	Further Reading 81
4	Persecution and Martyrdom: From Nero to Valerian (AD 64–260)..83
	A. Persecution of Christians 85
	A.1. The New Testament Witness........................86
	A.2. From Nero to Decius 87
	A.3. From Decius to Valerian 95
	B. Response of the Apologists..............................98
	B.1. Causes of Persecution and Martyrdom 99

        B.2. Strategies of Response. 100
        B.3. Justin Martyr (d. ca. AD 165) 103
    C. The Impact of Persecution and Martyrdom on Early
        Christianity. 109
        C.1. The Sympathy of Pagans. 110
        C.2. Martyrs and Lapsed Christians. 110
        C.3. Martyrdom as a Baptism of Blood 111
        C.4. Martyrs as Saints. 112
        C.5. Women Martyrs receive Special Status as
        "Confessors" 113
        C.6. Lingering Effects of Persecution. 114
    Chapter Appendix 4.1: The Persecution in Lyons and Vienne. . . 115
    Chapter Appendix 4.2: Key Dates for Early Christian
        Persecution 117
    Chapter Appendix 4.3: Important Apologists. 117
    Questions for Discussion and Review:
        Persecution and Martyrdom from Nero to Valerian
        (AD 64–260). 118
    Further Reading 120

5   Church and State in the Roman Empire (AD 260–380). 121
    A. Introduction 122
    B. From Persecution to the Triumph of Christianity
        (AD 64–313) 124
        B.1. Diocletian and the Reorganization of the
            Roman Empire 124
        B.2. The "Great Persecution" of the Church, AD 303–324 . . . 126
        B.3. Church and State under Constantine. 129
        B.4. Christian Writers on the Persecution. 131
        B.5. Constantine as *Pontifex Maximus*. 133
        B.6. The Sons of Constantine. 138
        B.7. Julian "the Apostate" (360–363) 139
    C. Church and State in East and West 140
    Questions for Discussion and Review 141
        Church and State in the Romans Empire, 260–380 141
    Further Reading 142

6   The Early Church in North Africa. 145
    A. Introduction 146
    B. Early Expansion of Christianity in Northern Africa. 149

  B.1. The Donatists.................................152
  B.2. Christianity among the Berber People...............156
 C. The Egyptian Church 159
 D. The Ethiopian Church................................164
 E. The Nubian Church 170
 Questions for Discussion and Review 173
  The Early Church in North Africa 173
 Further Reading 174

Section II: Christian Belief and Teaching

7 Jesus Christ as Son of Man and Son of God: The Challenge of Judaism and Docetism 177
 A. Who Is Jesus Christ? 178
  A.1. The Historical Jesus 179
  A.2. Jesus in the Gospels 180
  A.3. Early Christianity in Conflict with Judaism 184
  A.4. Was Jesus Divine?...............................186
  A.5. Docetism 188
  A.6. Apostles and Apostolic Fathers.....................190
 B. The Divine Jesus: Philosophical Aspects..................192
  B.1. Socrates (d. 399 BC) 193
  B.2. Plato (427–347 BC).............................194
  B.3. Aristotle (384–322 BC)..........................196
  B.4. Stoicism......................................197
  B.5. Philo of Alexandria (ca. 20 BC – AD 40)..............198
 Chapter Appendix 7.1 200
  Old Testament Prophecy of Jesus as the "Messiah" 200
 Chapter Appendix 7.2 203
  New Testament Passages on "Jesus as Lord"...............203
 Questions for Discussion and Review 204
  Jesus Christ as Son of Man and Son of God:
   The Challenge of Judaism and Docetism 204
 Further Reading 205

8 Second-Century Gnosticism and Its Impact 207
 A. Gnosticism 208
  A.1. Gnostic *gnôsis* 211
  A.2. Gnostic Leaders: Valentinus and Basileides 213
  A.3. Marcion (AD 85–160) 220

      A.4. Other Important Gnostic Groups 221
      A.5. Summary of Shared Features of Gnostic Groups 222
   B. The Response to Gnosticism: Irenaeus, Clement of
   Alexandria, and Tertullian 225
      B.1. Irenaeus (ca. AD 115–200) 225
      B.2. Clement of Alexandria (d. AD 215) 229
      B.3. Tertullian (ca. 160–225) 231
   C. Apostolic Succession, Ecclesiastical Structures and Creeds .. 233
      C.1. Apostolic Succession 234
      C.2. Apostles and Fathers............................ 238
      C.3. Early Creeds................................... 239
      C.4. Irenaeus, Tertullian, and the "Rule of Faith" 241
   Chapter Appendix 8.1 243
      Writings of the Apostolic Fathers....................... 243
   Chapter Appendix 8.2 243
      The Apostles' Creed 243
   Questions for Discussion and Review 244
      Second-Century Gnosticism and Its Impact............... 244
      The Response of Early Christian Fathers to Gnosticism 245
      Apostolic Succession, Ecclesiastic Structures and Creeds.... 245
   Further Reading 246

9   The Biblical Canon and Alternative Gospels 249
   A. The "Canon" 251
   B. The Scriptures of the Jews 253
      B.1. Use of the Old Testament in the New................ 256
      B.2. Christian Rejection of the Old?..................... 257
      B.3. Interpretation of the Old Testament................. 258
   C. Formation of the New Testament 259
      C.1. Factors Influencing the Formation of the "Canon" 261
      C.2. Acceptance of Four Gospels 263
   D. The Canon in the Making............................. 264
   E. Alternative Gospels and Apocryphal Books................ 267
      Conclusions 271
   Chapter Appendix 9.1 273
      Dan Brown on Jesus, Paul and Women 273
   Chapter Appendix 9.2 280
      Origen's Writings on Scripture 280
   Chapter Appendix 9.3 282

   Eusebius on Categories of New Testament Writings 282
  Questions for Review and Discussion 283
   The Biblical Canon and Alternative Gospels. 283
  Further Reading 284

10 Arianism and the Trinity: The Ecumenical Councils of Nicea
  and Constantinople (AD 325–381) 287
  A. The Nicene Council of AD 325 289
   A.1. Background 289
   A.2. The Councils: Organizational Aspects. 292
   A.3. Theological Background for the Nicene Council. 295
   A.4. Arius and the Nicene Council. 305
  B. The Second Ecumenical Council of Constantinople of 381 . . . 312
   B.1. Athanasius 313
   B.2. Reconciliation of Nicene Supporters and Homoians 313
   B.3. "Ousia" and "Hypostasis" Once Again 314
   B.4. The Cappadocian Fathers. 316
   B.5. The Council of Constantinople (381) 317
  Questions for Discussion and Review 320
   Arianism and the Trinity: Ecumenical Councils of Nicea
    and Constantinople (AD 325–381) 320
  Further Reading 322

11 The Person of Jesus: Five Ecumenical Councils (AD 431–787). 323
  A. The Councils of Ephesus (431) and Chalcedon (451):
   On the Human and Divine Natures of Christ 324
   A.1. The Council of Ephesus 324
   A.2. The Council of Chalcedon (451). 329
  B. The Last Three Ecumenical Councils: Monophysites,
   Monothelites, and Iconoclasm 333
   B.1. The Fifth Ecumenical Council of Constantinople, 553 . . 333
   B.2. The Sixth Ecumenical Council of Constantinople
    (680–681): Monophysites and Monothelites 340
   B.3. The Seventh Council at Nicea (787) 343
  Chapter Appendix 11.1 345
   Summary of the First Seven Ecumenical Councils 345
  Chapter Appendix 11.2 346
   Obstacles in Understanding the Early Councils. 346
  Questions for Discussion and Review 353

  The Person of Jesus: Five Ecumenical Councils
   (AD 431–787)..353
  Further Reading 355

12 The Golden Age of Early Christian Thought: Outstanding
  Fourth-Century Leaders 357
  A. Alexandrian Theology...................................360
   A.1. Athanasius (ca. 295–373)..........................360
   A.2. Cyril of Alexandria (ca. 372–444) 361
  B. The Cappadocians 362
   B.1. Basil of Caesarea (ca. 330–379)....................362
   B.2. Gregory of Nazianzus (ca. 330–390)................363
   B.3. Gregory of Nyssa (ca. 335–395) 364
  C. Syrian Antioch 365
   C.1. John Chrysostom (354–406).......................365
  D. The Latin West 367
   D.1. Ambrose (ca. 340–397) 367
   D.2. Jerome (ca. 342–420) 370
   D.3. Augustine of Hippo (354–430).....................372
  Questions for Discussion and Review 381
   The Golden Age of Early Christian Thought: Outstanding
    Fourth-Century Leaders............................381
  Further Reading 382

Section III: Epilogue

13 The Disintegration of the Roman Empire......................385
  A. Invasions and Other Factors in the Collapse..............388
  B. The Influence of Christianity 392
  C. Augustine's Contribution in *The City of God* 394
  Questions for Discussion and Review 397
   The Fall of the (Western) Roman Empire 397
  Further Reading 398

Appendix I: From Patristics to the Study of Early Christianity 399
  A. Renaissance and Reformation 399
  B. Seventeenth- and Eighteenth-Century Developments.......401
  C. The Nineteenth Century: Historical Criticism 403
   Adolf von Harnack....................................405
  D. The Twentieth Century.................................408
   Archaeological Work 410

>   Patristics in the Modern University Context 412
>   New Directions: Women in Early Christianity............ 414
>   Sociology and Anthropology Impact Early
>   Christian Studies 416
>   E. Conclusion 418

Appendix II: Four Important Early Church Historians................ 421
   A. Eusebius of Caesarea 421
   B. Socrates (ca. 379–440)..................................... 424
   C. Sozomen (d. ca. 450) 425
   D. Theodoret (ca. 393–460).................................... 426

Appendix III: Historiography of Early Christianity in Africa........... 429
   Groves: *The Planting of Christianity in Africa* 429
   Postcolonial Studies of African Christianity.................... 429
   Verstraelen on Historiography of Christianity in Africa......... 431
   Finneran: The Archaeological Contribution.................. 433
   Four Recent Authors on Early Christianity in Roman
      North Africa 433
      Joseph Cuoq.. 434
      Robin Daniel 435
      François Decret 435
      J. Patout Burns Jr (et al.)............................ 436
   Shaw: The Kingdom of God in Africa 437
   Dominique Arnauld: The First Seven Centuries of
      Christianity in Africa................................... 437
   Oden: How Africa Shaped the Christian Mind 438
   The Center for Early African Christianity.................... 440

Glossary of Important Terms.. 443

Bibliography... 453

Annotated Guide to Sources for Studies in Early Christianity 475

Index of Subjects 485

Index of Names 499

List of Figures

Figure 1.1. Alexander the Great at the battle of Issus (333 BC) 9
Figure 1.2. Cave of the Dead Sea Scrolls 17
Figure 1.3. Ruins of living quarters at Qumran 18
Figure 1.4. Roman Trireme 22
Figure 1.5. Emperor Caesar Augustus 23
Figure 1.6. Ruins of the great temple of Artemis in Ephesus 25
Figure 1.7. The goddess Demeter blessing Metanira, the queen of Eleusis 28
Figure 1.8. Emperor Caesar Augustus as *Pontifex Maximus* 29
Figure 2.1. Aerial view of the Great Theatre of Ephesus 38
Figure 2.2. The Etchmiadzin Cathedral in Armenia 48
Figure 2.3. Ring-stone from Dhofar (Yemen) 51
Figure 2.4. Tenth-century Persian cross 52
Figure 3.1. Church of the Cross and Resurrection at the Monastery of St Anthony 60
Figure 3.2. The nine saints of Ethiopia 65
Figure 3.3. Symeon the Stylite 67
Figure 3.4. St Martin shares his cloak with a beggar 73
Figure 4.1. The martyrdom of St Polycarp 84
Figure 4.2. The Emperor Nero and his mother Agrippina 89
Figure 4.3. Martyrdom of Ignatius of Antioch 94
Figure 4.4. The Colosseum 95
Figure 4.5. The catacomb of Callistus (Rome) 100
Figure 4.6. Blandina 116
Figure 5.1. Emperor Galerius's *Edict of Toleration* (AD 311) 128
Figure 5.2. Constantine and Sol Invictus 130

Figure 5.3. The Emperor Constantine dedicates Constantinople as imperial capital 135
Figure 6.1. The ancient North African Cyrene (East Libya) 149
Figure 6.2. Mark in the Coptic church 160
Figure 6.3. The Coptic Orthodox Church of Amman (Jordan) 164
Figure 6.4. Bet Giyorgis, Ethiopia's famous rock-hewn church 166
Figure 6.5. Surface view of Bet Giyorgis 166
Figure 6.6. The Ezana Tablet 168
Figure 6.7. Yared and his disciples before King Gebre Meskel (AD 525–539) 169
Figure 6.8. Empress Theodora 171
Figure 7.1. The raising of Lazarus 181
Figure 7.2. Jesus's compassion for women 182
Figure 7.3. Christos Pantocrator 187
Figure 7.4. Head of Plato 195
Figure 7.5. The Arabic Aristotle 196
Figure 8.1. The Jung codex of the Gospel of Truth 210
Figure 8.2. The Valentinian Pleroma 213
Figure 8.3. Irenaeus among the Church Fathers 226
Figure 8.4. Ignatius 234
Figure 9.1. Ezra the scribe 255
Figure 9.2. The Shrine of the Book (Jerusalem) 257
Figure 9.3. Christ and the four living creatures 264
Figure 9.4. Codex Sinaiticus (ca. AD 350) 265
Figure 9.5. Liturgical Codex 273
Figure 9.6. Pompeiian fresco celebrating literacy 276
Figure 10.1. The council of Nicea (AD 325) 307
Figure 10.2. Hagia Irene, site of the First Council of Constantinople (381) 318
Figure 11.1. Palm Sunday procession of Nestorians 328

Figure 11.2. Ephesus, site of the Ecumenical Council of 431 330

Figure 11.3. Major branches of Christianity after the Council of Ephesus (431) 331

Figure 11.4. Justinian as emperor 334

Figure 11.5. Hagia Sophia, exterior 336

Figure 11.6. Justinian, Hagia Sophia and Constantinople 336

Figure 11.7. Interior of the Hagia Sophia 337

Figure 11.8. The Council of Nicea (787) 344

Figure 12.1. Gregory of Nyssa 364

Figure 12.2. John Chrysostom 366

Figure 12.3. Ambrose, bishop of Milan 368

Figure 12.4. Jerome in his study 370

Figure 12.5. Augustine's conversion 376

Figure 13.1. St Martin leaving the imperial army to seek baptism as a Christian 396

List of Maps

Map 1.1. The Persian/Achaemenid Empire at its maximum extent under Darius I and Xerxes (around 500 BC) 7

Map 1.2. The Ptolemaic Empire, 200 BC 11

Map 1.3. The Roman Empire under Augustus Caesar (AD 14) 21

Map 2.1. Palestine: The Decapolis 35

Map 2.2. The early days of Christianity: Distribution of population in the early Roman Empire 39

Map 3.1. Spread of Christianity AD 300–800 77

Map 4.1. The Roman Empire at its greatest extent in AD 117 92

Map 5.1. The Roman Empire under Diocletian (after AD 299) 125

Map 6.1. Pre-colonial African civilization, groups North and South 157

Map 6.2. Map of Ancient Egypt and Nubia 159

Map 11.1. Extent of the Byzantine Empire under Justinian AD 555 339

Map 11.2. Spread of Syriac Christianity to the Orient 340

Map 11.3. Age of the Caliphs AD 622–750 341

Map 13.1. Migration and invasion in the Empire, AD 100–500 389

Preface and Acknowledgements

Christianity has experienced an unprecedented expansion in Africa during the past number of decades. The history of Christianity in Africa is typically divided into three unequal periods. The first takes Christianity from its earliest days in the first century through some seven centuries of development in North Africa (the Maghreb), Egypt, Ethiopia and Nubia. The second period follows on the Arab conquests, to recognize the work of Portuguese missionaries in the fifteenth century, especially in coastal regions and major river estuaries of the Congo, Guinea, Angola and lower Zambezi; this lasted about two hundred years. The third and most recent period dates from the late eighteenth century and colonization of Africa by European powers. Extensive missionary efforts of Protestant denominations and societies resulted in a renewed presence of Christianity, which has not dissipated with the post-war years of independence and the push toward indigenization of the faith. On the contrary, it appears that the exit of colonial powers stimulated the search for a "non-Western" identity. Church groups began the work of addressing properly African concerns, and reflecting a truly African experience in religion. Churches continued to grow, and many new charismatic groups have emerged.

Historians of Christianity in Africa typically minimize or ignore the first of these three phases, on the assumption that this period is already covered well enough in the general study of early Christianity in the Roman Empire as such. Indeed, North Africa, from east to west, was incorporated in what was then the Roman (and later the Byzantine) Empire, and might therefore rightly be considered part of the Mediterranean world, with its orientation to the Mediterranean Sea and Europe, rather than to the Sahara desert in the south, and beyond. However, from the beginning, Egypt itself was recognized for a more complex identity compared with the western provinces, since the Nile and the Red Sea encouraged trade routes and convenient travel to Yemen, as well as more southern regions, Ethiopia and Nubia. Such means of travel also facilitated the spread of the Christian gospel; we know specifically of early travel to the kingdom of Aksum, also designated as "India" at the time.

Postcolonial African scholars have been especially concerned to document the history of African Christianity or the history of religion in general from a point of view not dictated by colonial/western rulers, or a missionary presence. This concern was valid, for religion has a very important role in African societies, a role often underestimated by western historians, especially those working from a secularist outlook. For Africans, religion is no private or individual matter, relegated to the privacy of home and family. Historiography cannot ignore that role, and certainly not when these societies experience large-scale conversion from traditional religion to Christianity.

The historiographical work of indigenous Africans in recent decades has certainly done much to address issues pertaining to specific regions or periods of history, especially the more recent history for which scholars can call on living memory. Using methods appropriate for a postcolonial, post-missionary era, they have turned to oral history and oral tradition to study the growth of the indigenous African church, its leaders and evangelists. At the same time, it is far less common for Africans to focus on the history of Christianity in the entire continent of Africa, or to encompass that history from its very beginning. For such large-scale projects, African scholars still work under serious handicaps.[1]

Even so, a sense of the continuity of Christianity in Africa from those earliest years, and recognition of the significance of that early period for its later history, is now emerging. New interest in the roots of Christianity in (northern) Africa has actually surfaced as Christians have recognized the need for an indigenous identity. Christianity had to free itself from its image as a western import, or even a remnant of the colonial era. Study of the earliest years of Christianity in the North African Roman and Byzantine world clearly demonstrates that Christianity cannot be dismissed as a colonial imposition. Its roots are equally Eastern and Western. Two important modern African authors who have devoted serious attention to these issues are the Ghanaian theologian Kwame Bediako (who died in 2008), and Gambian Lamin Sanneh, professor of history with Yale University in the USA (until his recent death, January 2019).[2]

Nevertheless, few publications have been devoted specifically to the study of early Christianity in Africa, and the number of those written in English is far less. Robin Daniel's work, *This Holy Seed*, François Decret's *Early Christianity in North Africa* (now in English), and J. Patout Burns's *Christianity in Roman Africa: The Development of Its Practices and Beliefs*, take the history of early African Christianity up to the Vandal and Arab invasions, but are all restricted

---

1. In his bibliographical survey Frans Verstraelen recognized that African scholars could take on projects like the 1970 UNESCO *General History of Africa* (published in 8 volumes, 1981–1993) when these were well-funded, but they often lacked the resources or opportunities to pursue large-scale research. See Verstraelen, *History of Christianity in Africa*, 3, and 32–33.

2. These emphases can be noted in Kwame Bediako's *Christianity in Africa*, and Lamin Sanneh's *West African Christianity*.

to the North African provinces of the empire. Of two recent works in French, Joseph Cuoq's *L'Eglise d'Afrique du Nord du IIe au XIIe siècle* (*The North African Church from the Second to the Twelfth Century*) is similarly restricted to the north-western African provinces, while Dominique Arnauld's *Histoire du Christianisme en Afrique: Les sept premiers siècles* (*A History of Christianity in Africa: The First Seven Centuries*) has the broader scope, including the Coptic, Ethiopian and Nubian Christian church.[3] Aside from these, we note the initiative of Thomas Oden in exploring early Christian African texts. In his work on the first five centuries of Christianity in Africa, *How Africa Shaped the Christian Mind: Rediscovering the African Seedbed of Western Christianity*, Oden argues for Africa as the true "cradle" of Christianity, particularly on the basis of significant theological discussion initiated by the North African Christian church.

The contribution of individual early North African Christians like Tertullian, Origen and Augustine is readily acknowledged in work on early Christianity. While the present study of early Christianity is not limited to North Africa, it has adopted a specifically African perspective in presenting that history, and devotes special attention to the role of North Africa and African church leaders in earliest Christianity. Significant aspects of the early history of Christianity are based on African soil. Major early discussions of Gnosticism, Donatism, Arianism and Monophysitism arose in the African context, and many important early leaders were African. Indeed, if one were to select a single early Christian leader, thinker and writer as the most brilliant, dynamic and prolific of all the church fathers of the time, it would be the African Augustine of Hippo (present-day Annaba in Algeria). His work continued to be influential for hundreds of years after his death; this was recognized in 2001 by Algeria's President Bouteflika, who initiated an international conference to honour "Augustinus Afer."[4]

The present work is focused on the period from the beginning of Christianity to the fall of the Roman Empire in the West. But some attention is also given to the continuing influence of Christianity in the East, including the period of Muslim dominance in the Middle East. This context is important for understanding the last three ecumenical councils, and especially the

---

3. For further discussion of these publications, see appendix III, "Historiography of Early Christianity in Africa."

4. This conference was held at Alger-Annaba in early April 2001, and organized by the *Haut Conseil Islamique Algérie* in collaboration with the Swiss University of Fribourg; for the subsequent publication, *Augustinus Afer* (in two volumes), see Pierre-Yves Fux, *Augustinus Afer: Saint Augustin*.

repudiation of iconoclasm at the Council of Nicea (AD 787). From its capital in Constantinople (the modern Istanbul) as the centre of Orthodox Christianity, the Greek-speaking Byzantine (eastern) Roman Empire would have a considerable impact on the religious character of North African churches in (Coptic) Egypt, Ethiopia and Nubia. Although the Coptic Orthodox Church survives to the present, the major turning point for these regions came with the mid-seventh-century Arab invasions of Egypt, with the tenth-century attacks on the Nubian kingdom, and the mid-sixteenth-century Muslim attacks on Ethiopia.

In medieval Europe, Latin Christianity continued to be a major influence, both religiously and politically. Again, the important transitional figure is the North African Augustine, who maintained a significant profile in medieval Europe, though he was never well known in the Byzantine church. The fall of Rome and the demise of the western Roman Empire in the fifth century may therefore be considered a reasonable turning point for the transition from early to medieval Christianity. Again, for early Christianity in North Africa, a major watershed came first with the fifth-century invasion of the Vandals, and again later, with the late seventh-century Muslim invasion of North Africa.

In the present study, these periods of early Christianity will be covered in two ways. The first part provides an overview of historical development and historical factors important to that development, especially missionary effort and expansion, monasticism, persecution, martyrdom and church-state relations. The second part examines Christian belief and teachings, with attention to cultural, religious and philosophical issues, particularly as these affect the early development of Christianity. The focus is on the question, "Who is Jesus?" and the different answers given by Gnostics and Arians. These chapters also examine how the Christian church developed its settled theological positions with the help of intellectual giants like Tertullian, Origen and Athanasius. Special attention is devoted to a series of ecumenical and empire-wide church councils which responded to the major philosophical and theological challenges of gnostic and Arian interpretation of the Scriptures.

Publication of this work was initially motivated by the need for an adequate textbook to support the course in Early Christianity in the Department of Religious Studies and Philosophy at the University of Jos (Nigeria); both Christian and Muslim students take this course. Available textbooks typically assume a Christian audience; they also assume considerable knowledge of Christianity and the terminology familiar to Christians. The present text does not make such assumptions on familiarity with terms and thought patterns characteristic of Christianity. This is also why the glossary, included at the end of the text, provides a basic explanation of all-important terms. This is helpful particularly because significant terminology and titles commonly used by early Christians still reflect their roots in the Greek or Latin language of the time.

Both the historical survey and the introductory chapter on Christian beliefs include considerable information and explanation to help students understand the beginning of Christianity from the New Testament. Although this material cannot take the place of independent study of the New Testament, it is included primarily to avoid any confusion on relevant issues for those who are not familiar with the biblical account. Similarly, this work includes some discussion of Eastern Orthodox Christianity. Indeed, the Roman Empire did not fall in the East until 1453, when Constantinople fell to the Turks – a fact of considerable importance in the history of Islam.

Undoubtedly, Muslim students who take a course in early Christianity will approach the material with a perspective shaped by accounts of early Christianity given in the Qur'an and the Hadiths. At various points in the discussion, this work addresses such concerns by contrasting a Christian theological position (as on the crucifixion of Jesus) or an early Christian understanding of a text, with the Islamic perspective on the story. In this connection, we have taken into account the contribution made by Muslim historians on Christianity. Outstanding among them is Abd Al-Jabbar, the Grand Qadi of the city of Rayy (now Teheran), who published a revisionist history of Christianity (AD 995) when he sought to prove that Prophet Muhammad was a true prophet of Allah.

This work includes an appendix on the history of the study of early Christianity from the time of the Renaissance and Reformation. This historical survey serves primarily to orient students to figures like Adolf von Harnack, whose seminal work on early Christianity continues to be cited and retains its influence in scholarship on the history of Christianity. The appendix provides an introduction to significant issues, particularly by giving the scholarly background of the modern profiling of Gnosticism (after the 1945 discovery of the Coptic Nag Hammadi library). This survey highlights the empirical shift in the venue of teaching early Christianity from seminaries to theological faculties and departments of religion in the contemporary university. It also helps to explain the modern fascination with heretical figures and the considerable body of scholarship attempting to rehabilitate these figures. Finally, the survey can help the students in navigating the contemporary bibliography on important issues like the role of women in early Christianity.

The final two appendices are historiographical. The first surveys four early historians to whom we are indebted for basic information on events and developments in early Christianity for the years studied in this text. Of course, this information can be supplemented from other sources, whether in the apologetic or theological writings of church leaders, in contemporary historical literature or the witness of archaeology; in that connection we note particularly J. Stevenson's *A New Eusebius*, and his *Creeds, Councils and Controversies*, as useful collections of such additional witness to early Christianity. The second historiographical appendix highlights recent publications noteworthy for specific attention to earliest Christianity on African soil, or to the nature of the African factor in that early history. As such, this appendix reflects the growing concern to document earliest Christianity in North Africa, particularly in affirming the truly indigenous character of Christianity for Africa. Even so, as noted above, very few English publications cover both the entire period of early Christianity and the entire North African context, East to West. A number of recent studies have focused more particularly on the western region of North Africa, as the Maghreb, but none of these are written by authors who are themselves African. This survey therefore highlights the need for indigenous African writers to turn their attention to this early period. It also reveals the urgency of providing a text like the present one, devoting specific attention to issues of early North African Christianity as an important part of the history of early Christianity.

As a further aid for the student in studying and understanding the given historical material, a series of questions for review and suggestions for further reading are provided for each chapter. For citations from the Bible, unless otherwise stated, the NIV version is used throughout. For the Qur'an, the translation of Abdullah Yusuf Ali has been used. All citations from the church fathers, unless otherwise stated, are based on translations in *The Ante-Nicene Fathers* and *The Nicene and Post-Nicene Fathers*. For most of these citations the language has been updated for intelligibility.

The present syllabus is a cooperative effort of Dr Wendy E. Helleman and Dr Musa A. B. Gaiya, both of the Department of Religious Studies and Philosophy of the University of Jos (Plateau State, Nigeria). Chapters 1 through 5 represent a joint effort. Chapter 6 has been written by Gaiya, with limited revision by Helleman. The second section on belief and teaching (chs. 7 – 12), written primarily by Helleman, includes additions and revision by Musa Gaiya. The concluding section on the disintegration of the Roman Empire (ch. 13), appendix I on the transition from Patristics to study of early Christianity, and appendices II and III on historiography (at the end of the book), represent the contribution of Helleman.

The authors express their appreciation to the students at the University of Jos and other universities where they have taught this material. Through their questions and comments, the students who have used this material over the years have been helpful in giving shape to the text as it appears in this publication. We also acknowledge the help of libraries, with a special word of thanks to the Classics Department of the University of Toronto, which facilitated access to the University of Toronto libraries; use of its holdings was particularly significant in the final stages of preparation of the manuscript. To conclude, we also wish to express our deep appreciation for the cooperation and support toward the completion of this work given by our respective spouses, Adrian Helleman and Pamela Gaiya.

Wendy E. Helleman
Musa A. B. Gaiya
University of Jos,
Jos, Plateau State, Nigeria

Abbreviations

AD	*Anno Domini* (i.e. "in the year of our Lord")
ANF	*Ante-Nicene Fathers* (A. Roberts and J. Donaldson eds. 1994 [1867–1872])
Apol.	*Apology* (Justin Martyr/Tertullian)
b.	born
bp.	bishop
BC	before Christ
ca.	*circa* (approximately)
Chr	Chronicles (OT)
Cor	Corinthians (NT)
CSEL	*Corpus Scriptorum Ecclesiasticorum Latinorum* (Vienna, 1866)
d.	died
Deut	Deuteronomy (OT)
Dial.	*Dialogue with Trypho the Jew* (Justin Martyr)
Ep.	Epistle
Eph	Ephesians (NT)
fl.	*floruit*, or "flourished" (used in calculating a person's years from date of active work)
Gal	Galatians (NT)
Gen	Genesis (OT)
GCS	*Graecorum Corpus Scriptorum* (Berlin, 1897–)
HE	*Historia Ecclesiastica* (Eusebius, *Church History*)
Heb	Hebrews (NT)
Kgs	Kings (OT)
Macc.	Maccabees (Septuagint)
Matt	Matthew (NT)
Neh	Nehemiah (OT)
NPNF	*Nicene and Post-Nicene Fathers* (H. Wace and Ph. Schaff eds. 1994 [1867–1872])
NIV	New International Version
Phil	Philippians (NT)
Prov	Proverbs (OT)

Pet	Peter (NT)
Rev	Revelation (NT)
Rom	Romans (NT)
Thess	Thessalonians (NT)
Tim	Timothy (NT)

Section I

Issues in the History of Early Christianity

1

Background to Early Christianity

> The mother was especially admirable and worthy of everlasting remembrance. For she witnessed her seven sons all die in a single day, and bore it courageously because of her hope in the Lord. Filled with a noble spirit she encouraged each of them in the language of their ancestors, reinforcing her womanly arguments with manly courage, saying, "I do not know how you came to be in my womb; it was not I who gave you breath and life, nor was it I who shaped your every part. It is the Creator of the universe who ordains the beginning of humankind and presides over the origin of all things. And he, in his mercy, will surely give you back both breath and life, because you now disregard your own existence for the sake of his laws."
>
> 2 Maccabees 7:20–23

We do not know the name of this brave "mother in Israel" who was arrested along with her seven sons. Their crime? The refusal to violate the law of Moses and defile themselves by eating pork, as demanded by the Hellenistic ruler, the Seleucid Antiochus IV Epiphanes (175–164 BC). One by one the brothers were cruelly tortured. But with the encouragement of their mother they were, each in turn, ready to die rather than abandon the laws of their ancestors. In response to malicious taunts they affirmed, "It is better for us to meet death through human hands, while we rely on God's promise that we shall be raised up again by him" (2 Maccabees 7:14).[1] With these words they provided one of the very early indications of the hope for the resurrection

---

1. See also 2 Macc. 12:43–45, "He (Judas) then took up a collection . . . to provide for an expiatory sacrifice for sin. This was an altogether excellent and noble act, for he had the resurrection in mind; if he had not expected the fallen to rise again, it would have been

from the dead of those who die a holy death, the very hope which would also prove to be central for early Christianity.

After six of the sons died, Antiochus addressed the mother herself, asking her to convince her youngest that he would be favoured with high office and become a rich man, if he would only abandon the tradition handed down from Moses. The mother responded by turning to her son, encouraging him rather to become worthy of his brothers by facing death nobly. This he did, offering his body and life, "trusting wholly in the Lord."

This story is recorded in the second book of Maccabees, written late in the second century before Christ. The book sought to commemorate the early second century BC struggles of the Jews for independence from their Hellenistic rulers, particularly the Seleucid Antiochus. Although the story of this courageous mother in Israel was not recorded in the canonical Scriptures accepted by the Christian church, her courageous stand for Jewish law and custom was well known to early Christians, and remained an encouragement for Jews and Christians alike to remain steadfast in the face of persecution, and ready to suffer for the truth.

A. The Jewish Background (537 BC–AD 135)

A.1. Introduction

The present chapter introduces the significant influence of Jewish, as well as Greek and Roman, religion and culture in shaping early Christianity. The above story from 2 Maccabees provides an important example of the debt which Christianity owes to Judaism. We realize that Christianity grew as a branch from its religious roots in Judaism. Indeed, it is impossible to understand New Testament Christianity without understanding the Jewish religious milieu that gave birth to it. This has not always been recognized. The history of Christianity provides many examples of anti-Semitism, or hatred of the Jews as a race. The outstanding modern example is that termed the "holocaust" during World War II, when about six million Jews were tortured and executed in Germany under the Nazis.

A different kind of anti-Semitism, or rather, anti-Judaism, based on an interpretation of Scripture, can be traced back to the second-century gnostic Christian Marcion, who lived and taught in Rome from AD 140 to 155 and attracted many disciples for his cause. Marcion did not recognize common

---

superfluous and foolish to pray for the dead. Since he did this with regard to the splendid reward awaiting those who met their end in godliness, it was a holy and pious thought."

ground between Christianity and Judaism; he disputed the dependence of the New Testament on the Old. According to Marcion, Christianity and Judaism represent two separate and quite unrelated religions, worshipping two different gods. The God of Christians (the Father of Jesus) is good, kind and forgiving; the God of Judaism is cruel, violent, evil and vengeful. This theme also surfaces in Christian/Muslims relationships in Nigeria, for Christians have taken a similar approach in describing the relationship between the (Christian) God and Allah.

But Marcion's position was clearly at odds with more widespread perception during the first centuries of Christianity. More typically, Christians maintained the connection between the Old Testament and the New as one of deep intertwinement. Christianity is greatly indebted to Judaism. Historians have designated Christianity as the most important "Messianic Sect" of Judaism.[2] Even though Christianity and Judaism would go their separate ways in history, and Christians did accuse the Jews of killing Jesus Christ (as a form of "deicide"), Marcion's approach on the Jews and Judaism was soundly rejected by the Catholic church.[3] While the challenges of reconciliation remain an ongoing concern, the papal encyclical, *Nostra Aetate* (*In Our Time*), may be cited as a Catholic declaration on interfaith relations which recognizes the deep roots of Christianity in Judaism and the Hebrew Bible as a basis for mutual respect and dialogue.

From the beginning, the influence of Judaism on Christianity also introduced a significant degree of Hellenization, especially because post-exilic Judaism in Palestine was itself already Hellenized, that is, influenced by Greek culture ("Hellene" was the name Greek people use for themselves).[4] And *Hellenism* would continue as a major cultural influence on the Jews, even when the Romans ruled Palestine. Greek culture continued to permeate the entire Roman Empire; Roman rulers even encouraged Hellenization as a civilizing factor, to foster cultural unity. Culturally, the period of Roman rule from the

---

2. This is recognized in the work of Jean Daniélou, *The Theology of Jewish Christianity*; and Martin Hengel, *Judaism and Hellenism*, and *The 'Hellenization' of Judaea in the First Century after Christ*. See also Christopher Rowland, *Christian Origins*.

3. For further discussion of Marcion, see ch. 8, §A.3.

4. "Hellenization," broadly defined, refers to the influence of Greek culture particularly in language and literature, but it is also extended to political, religious, cultural and philosophical factors. The great patristic scholar Adolf von Harnack (1851–1930) is noted for his discussion of Hellenization as a significant factor in understanding early Christianity. The outstanding contemporary discussion of Hellenization as a factor in post-exilic Judaism is that of Martin Hengel; see note 2 above, and appendix I on the history of patristic scholarship.

collapse of the Greek (and Macedonian-Greek) states as independent political units is also called the Greco-Roman period.

Because of the substantial influence of Judaism on its early development, Christianity too would be thoroughly *Hellenized*. We should not be misled by protests against the Hellenization of Christianity from the North African Tertullian and his colleagues in the second century AD. Tertullian is well known for his rhetorical question, "What has Athens to do with Jerusalem? What has the Academy to do with the Church? Away with all attempts to produce a Stoic, Platonic or dialectic Christianity!"[5] As we know, even Tertullian could not escape the influence of Stoic philosophy in his development of Christian teachings.[6]

A.2. Second Temple Judaism under the Persians

We begin this discussion by turning to post-exilic Judaism under Persian rule as a significant prelude for Second Temple Judaism and the subsequent emergence of Christianity. In 538/37 BC, after a long period of exile in Babylon (from 597 BC), the Israelites from Judah in the Southern Kingdom were given permission by Cyrus, the Persian ruler, to return to their Palestinian homeland.

The policy of Cyrus was totally different from that of the Assyrian and Babylonian rulers (see 2 Kgs 17 and 24–25), who regarded Jews as notoriously rebellious and preferred to keep them in exile. Cyrus ordered the Jews to return and rebuild the temple in Jerusalem (2 Chr 36:22–23; Ezra 1:1–4). We refer to this period as *post-exilic Judaism* because it followed on the exile in Babylon; it is also called *Second Temple Judaism* because at this time Jews began to reconstruct the temple built by Solomon, which was destroyed by the Babylonians at the time of exile.[7]

---

5. Tertullian, *Praescriptio haereticorum* [*The Prescription of Heretics*], 7; the passage is quoted in Kwame Bediako, *Theology and Identity*, 117. On this treatise see ch. 8, §B.3. For Tertullian, the city of Athens represented Greek culture at its best, just as Jerusalem represented Judaism. On the school of Plato, the Academy, see ch. 7, §B.2; on the Stoics, see ch. 7, §B.4.

6. For further discussion of Tertullian, see ch. 8, §B.3 and §C.4, and ch. 10, §A.3. On Tertullian's famous question, see also W. E. Helleman, *Hellenization Revisited*, 361–381.

7. First Temple Judaism (referring to the temple built by King Solomon, from ca. 950 BC) ended with the Babylonian Captivity in 586 BC.

Background to Early Christianity   7

Map 1.1. The Persian/Achaemenid Empire at its maximum extent under Darius I and Xerxes (around 500 BC). Map "The Achaemenid Empire at its Greatest Extent" by Mossmaps / CC SA 4.0.

Not all Jews returned from Babylonia to Judea. A significant number stayed in Babylon, continuing as an influential sector of post-exilic Judaism.[8] The Bible introduces a number of these Jews: Daniel, Mordecai, Ezra and Nehemiah. Many others joined the large number of Jews in diaspora, or "dispersion," for they were *scattered* throughout the world around the Mediterranean Sea.[9] Equally important is a large group of Jews who fled to Egypt and settled there after the Babylonian invasion of Judea. Through their role in the development of Hellenized Judaism in Egypt they would influence the future of Judaism, and eventually also impact emerging Christianity.[10]

Under Persian rulers the Jews who returned to Judea (in 537 BC) were allowed a degree of autonomy. But they encountered significant opposition from "the people of the land," particularly the Samaritans (2 Kgs 17), who remained estranged from the Jews even in New Testament times (John 4).[11] In spite of such opposition the Jews were able to rebuild the temple and dedicate it in 515 BC. This marks the beginning of what is called the Second Jewish Commonwealth. Under the strong leadership of the scribe Ezra the returning exiles renewed their commitment to the law (Neh 8), and put away the non-Jewish wives they had married (Ezra 9–10). Even the Persian king Artaxerxes instructed Ezra, "to teach any who do not know them (i.e. the laws)" (Ezra 7:25).[12] Ezra was especially concerned that the Jews not fall back into the idolatrous practices for which their ancestors were punished (with exile). His efforts were effective. Indeed, as we shall see, the Jews would now be ready to fight to maintain observance of the law.

---

8. On the role of Babylonian Judaism after the fall of Jerusalem, see also below, §A.5.

9. On Diaspora Judaism see §A.5.

10. For further discussion of the Jews in Egypt and their role in the Hellenization of Judaism, see §A.3 and A.5.

11. Most Samaritans lived north of Jerusalem in Samaria (the former Northern Kingdom); see Everett Ferguson, *Backgrounds of Early Christianity*, 534–536. See also F. F. Bruce, *Israel and the Nations*, 110–111, 170–171. Samaritans and Jews were of the same ancestry, differing in religion, but not in origin. Even so, Samaritans and Jews had much in common in religious matters: belief in one God, a hatred for idolatry and devotion to the law of Moses. Of the Old Testament, Samaritans accepted only the five books of Moses. They rejected the Jerusalem priesthood (as did the Essenes); they also rejected the idea of the resurrection of the dead (as did the Sadducees). But the most serious difference was on the issue of temple worship, for the Samaritans had their own priests who maintained worship on Mount Gerizim, as a rival to the temple in Jerusalem. This angered the Jews, who destroyed the temple on Mount Gerizim during the rule of John Hyrcanus (134–104 BC); see Ferguson, *Backgrounds*, 535.

12. On Ezra and Nehemiah, see Bruce, *Israel and the Nations*, 99 and 105; on their role in determining the OT canon, see ch. 9 §B.

A.3. The Greek Period and Hellenization of the Jews

The relative freedom of Jews in Judea under the Persians did not last long. The epic battles between the Greek/Macedonian Alexander the Great and the Persians quickly involved the Jews in their sweep of the region.

Alexander conquered Palestine in 332 BC.[13] Macedonian rule brought the introduction of Greek culture, and with that an era of Hellenization of Palestine.[14] Greek architecture began to appear in Jewish cities, and public festivals would be celebrated in the style of the Greeks. Even by 300 BC Greek influence in Palestine was so deep that the Greek traveller Hecataeus noted that, through their contact with Greek civilization, the Jews "had greatly altered the ordinances of their forefathers."[15]

Figure 1.1. Alexander the Great at the battle of Issus (333 BC). He is portrayed riding his famous horse Bucephalus. The Yorck Project. Public Domain.

---

13. On the significant career of Alexander the Great, see Ferguson, *Backgrounds*, 10–15.

14. As noted above, the term "Hellenization" refers to the influence of Greek/Hellenic culture, particularly with the spread of that culture after the conquest of Alexander the Great, from the fourth century BC through the period of the Romans. Since it was impossible to separate culture and religion in the ancient world and Greek culture was decidedly pagan in origin, for both Jews and (later) for Christians the term "Hellenization" would almost inevitably represent a type of "paganization" or "secularization." On the issue of Hellenization, see Helleman, *Hellenization Revisited*, 429–484, particularly 429–434, 442 and 444–452.

15. On the observation of Hecataeus, see Hengel, *Judaism and Hellenism*, 255–256; also W. H. C. Frend, *The Early Church*, 16.

Greek influence on the Jews was strongest in use of the Greek language, although Aramaic remained the lingua franca, or common everyday language of Jews in Palestine.[16] The Hebrew language of the written Scriptures also remained in use, but in a more limited way, as it was used mainly in synagogue worship. Greek was the language of culture and education. Sophisticated Jews would rather speak Greek than Aramaic. Many of the Jews who left Palestine at this time for other cities of the Hellenistic kingdoms came to settle in Egyptian Alexandria, the city built by Alexander the Great as capital of Hellenistic Egypt. Here the Jews prepared the first Greek translation of the Old Testament, the Septuagint (typically designated simply as LXX).[17]

When Alexander the Great died in 323 BC, his kingdom was divided among his generals. Egypt came under the Ptolemies; Syria was ruled by the Seleucid kings; and Asia Minor (modern Turkey) and Greece came under the authority of Antigonus. These Hellenistic rulers struggled to control Palestine in turn. The first to take over Palestine was Ptolemy I (323–305 BC), whose rule brought peace and prosperity.

---

16. On Aramaic as the common language of the Babylonian exiles, see Elias J. Bickerman, *The Jews in the Greek Age*, 51–65.

17. LXX is the Roman number, and *septuaginta* the Latin for "seventy"; the Septuagint translation received its name from the seventy Jewish scholars who allegedly prepared it, all of them working independently, and all supposedly in full agreement on the established translation. On the Septuagint as a translation completed late in the third century BC, see Ferguson, *Backgrounds*, 432–438; on the significance of this OT translation, see Bickerman, *Jews in the Greek Age*, 101–116. For its important role in the formation of a biblical canon, see the discussion of the Septuagint in ch. 9, §B.

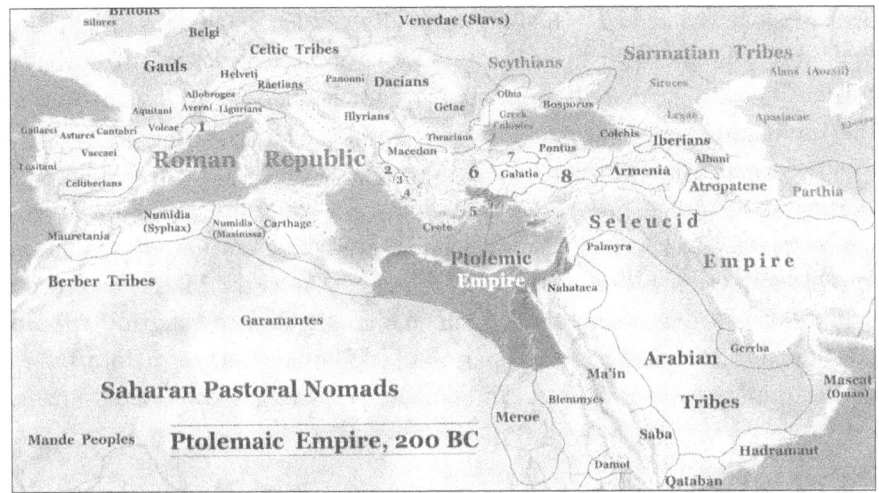

Map 1.2. The Ptolemaic Empire, 200 BC.
"Ptolemaic-Empire 200 BC" by Thomas Lessman / CC SA 3.0.

With the encouragement of the Egyptian rulers, even more Jews migrated to Egypt, where they were welcomed as a buffer between the indigenous Coptic population and the Greek colonizers.[18]

But in 216 BC the Syrian king Antiochus III took Palestine from the Egyptians. While the Jews had no alternative but to accept the Syrian rulers, their presence introduced a difficult period for the Jews in Palestine. It was not long before the Syrians encouraged a more extreme form of Hellenization of the Jewish society. While some "Hellenizers" supported this process, many turned against them; the latter were called the "Hasidim" or Hasideans (i.e. "pious" ones). Antiochus III relaxed the policy of Hellenization when the Jews assured him of their loyalty, but his son Antiochus IV Epiphanes (taking over in 176 BC) reinforced Hellenization by appointing as chief priest a leading Hellenizer, Jason. With his support Greek statues and pagan rites were introduced into the temple; and Jewish young men accepted the nudity of Greek games which were celebrated in the temple courtyards. Finally, the sacrifice of a pig on an

---

18. By the first century AD, it is estimated that they formed up to 15% of the population of Egypt, and dominated two of the five quarters of Alexandria. Such a role would not have endeared them to the native Egyptian population, and tensions were never far below the surface. These boiled over in serious attacks on the Jews in AD 58, and reprisals in 73; see also Elizabeth Isichei, *A History of Christianity in Africa*, 16. For a helpful analysis of the political role of the Jews and the challenges faced in Egypt, see Pedar Borgen, *Early Christianity and Hellenistic Judaism*, 71–102.

altar in the Jewish temple (168 BC) was, as Everett Ferguson describes it, "the supreme insult to Judaism."[19] But this was not all. Antiochus also forbade celebration of the Sabbath, prohibited circumcision, ordered the burning of the Torah and instituted a cult of prostitution in the temple.

These acts led to widespread rebellion against the Syrian rulers. The Jews, especially the "pious" ones, organized themselves into a resistance movement led by Judas Maccabaeus.[20] Using guerrilla tactics in a war for religion, Judas and his men were able to oust the Syrian rulers. Under the Maccabeans (also called *Hasmoneans*, based on the family name), the Jews in Palestine enjoyed considerable independence for a period of more than 100 years, from 167 to 63 BC, until they once more became subject to a foreign power, the Romans.

A.4. The Hasmonean Period

Under Judas Maccabaeus and his colleagues the Jews achieved remarkable success.[21] Once they forced Antiochus IV to withdraw from Palestine (not long after 165 BC), temple worship was restored and all forms of Greek idolatry were eradicated. The desecrated altar was removed; a new altar was built and dedicated. This dedication came to be included in the Jewish festal calendar as *Hanukkah*, the Feast of Dedication. The high priest appointed by the Syrian Greek rulers was replaced in 143 BC when Judas appointed Simon, the last of his Maccabean brothers and one of the "pious" ones, to this role. Simon, who was also commander of the army, was assassinated in 134 BC. He was replaced as both king and high priest by his son, John Hyrcanus, who led the Jews from 134–104 BC. Hyrcanus managed to expand the Jewish nation, subjugate the Idumeans (or Edomites, descendants of Esau), and force circumcision on them. The Hasmonean Alexander Jannaeus, ruling from 103 to 76 BC, further expanded the kingdom to include the territory once ruled by Solomon.

But the period of Hasmonean rulers was not without problems. The sharp division between Hellenizers (led by Sadducees) and those committed to the law (led by the Pharisees) became more pronounced during the reign of Jannaeus. To support their cause, the rulers were tempted to appeal to non-

---

19. See Ferguson, *Backgrounds*, 406; on this "abomination," see also Bruce, *Israel and the Nations*, 142. The story of the Maccabean mother at the opening of the present chapter can be dated to that period of persecution. Such incidents convinced the Jews that Hellenization was no innocent cultural matter but had deep religious roots. As we know, they reacted sharply and bravely to the imposition of idolatry by the Seleucids.

20. On the accomplishments of the Maccabees, see Ferguson, *Backgrounds*, 407–411; also Bruce, *Israel and the Nations*, 144–158.

21. On the Hasmonean rulers, see Bruce, *Israel and the Nations*, 169–178.

Jewish kings for assistance. Many Jews lost their lives in the resulting civil wars. At the time of the conquest of Syria, the Roman army under Pompey took advantage of civil unrest to the south, and entered Palestine in 63 BC.[22] In fact Aristobulus II, a rival to the throne, had invited the Romans to help resolve the ongoing internal dispute. And the Romans used their leverage to assign the throne to Aristobulus, demoting Hyrcanus II, the current ruler.

A.5. The Roman Period

Conquest of Jerusalem by the Roman general Pompey that year effectively brought the Jews under Roman rule. For his victory parade Pompey took many Jews back with him to Rome as slaves. These slaves would eventually form a significant Jewish community in Rome. By the time the apostle Paul visited the city (about AD 60) their number had increased substantially.

Under the Hasmoneans, the Jews of Palestine had strengthened the sense of national pride which emerged from their experience of exile in Babylon. It is important to remember that in Palestine the distinctive features of Judaism were more than the functions of religion; circumcision, Sabbath observance and the Torah became strong symbols of national pride. Recognizing this, the Romans wisely abstained from interfering with Jewish religious practice. They did not impose cultural change beyond what was required for the exercise of political power. In that respect they were quite unlike the Seleucids and more like the Egyptians. Accordingly, the religious Jews initially regarded Romans as liberators. But they were taken aback by Pompey's decision to enter the temple; this they recognized as an inexcusable defilement of the holy place. And the Romans did not eliminate the influence of Greek culture in Palestine. In fact emperors like Augustus and Hadrian adopted the Greek god Zeus Olympios as the equivalent of Jupiter, and supreme deity for the Greco-Roman world. But the Jews won important concessions on emperor worship; recognizing that the Jews would not accept emperor worship as it was introduced in other provinces, the emperors allowed them a special exemption.[23]

Even so, the Jews were unhappy with the local rulers imposed by the Romans, especially with their use of the Idumean (Edomite) family of the Herods, who served as "client" kings for Rome. Herod the Great, appointed king of the Jews in 40 BC, became the effective ruler in 37 BC when he replaced

---

22. See Ferguson, *Backgrounds*, 25 and 411–412, on the role of Pompey.

23. On the relationship between Jews and the Roman administration, see Ferguson, *Backgrounds*, 411–412 and 427–430.

the last of the Hasmonean kings, Antigonus. Jesus's birth occurred during the reign of this Herod (37–4 BC),[24] and the NT Gospels reflect how unpopular he was with the (religious) Jews, especially those expecting the Messiah, a King who would truly free them from foreign rule. Herod did use projects like the elaborate expansion of the temple in Jerusalem to appease his subjects.[25] He also tried to improve the economy of Palestine through development of agriculture; and the port city of Caesarea, named in honour of Emperor Caesar Augustus, was built to enhance international trade.

Recognizing the resentment of pious Jews, Herod further supported his position through an alliance with the Hasmoneans. He married one of the royal daughters, Mariamne.[26] But he was prepared to deal decisively with any threat to his throne, even if it came from members of his own family.[27] The story of his massacre of infants in Bethlehem, recorded in the Gospel of Matthew, shows the extent of Herod's jealousy.

On Herod's death (4 BC) the kingdom was divided among his children.[28] One of his sons, Archelaus, turned out to be a poor ruler and was deposed by the Romans in AD 6. At this time Roman governors were posted to take charge of Judea, Samaria and Idumea (the domain of Archelaus). Of these governors, Pontius Pilate is well known for his role in presiding over the trial of Jesus. The Roman governors lived in Caesarea, coming to Jerusalem only occasionally. In Jerusalem itself Roman soldiers were kept permanently in a garrison, to insure peace.

Even so, under what is known as *Pax Romana* (the peace brought by the Roman emperors), Judaism developed and was strengthened. Three important factors (or factions) influenced the character of post-exilic Palestinian Judaism: (1) *Babylonian Judaism*, or adherence to the traditions by Jews who remained in Babylon after 537 BC, loyal to Parthian rulers; (2) *Palestinian Judaism* itself, representing the strong influence of Jews who had returned to Palestine and benefited from the leadership of Nehemiah and Ezra; and (3) *Diaspora Judaism*, representing the influence of those Jews who were integrated within the Greco-Roman world outside of Palestine, whether as traders, artisans or professionals

---

24. For a survey of the Herods, see Ferguson, *Backgrounds*, 413–419. On Herod as king, see Bruce, *Israel and the Nations*, 190–196.

25. On Herod's temple, see Ferguson, *Backgrounds*, 562–563.

26. Mariamne (the Hebrew form for "Mary") was granddaughter of Hyrcanus II; Ferguson, *Backgrounds*, 414.

27. On suspicion of disloyalty Herod killed two of his own sons, as well as Mariamne. Augustus is reported to have said that he would rather be Herod's pig than his son; see Ferguson, *Backgrounds*, 414.

28. On Herod's sons, see also Bruce, *Israel and the Nations*, 197–211.

in different fields. Many of them were freed slaves.[29] This group would also include those Gentiles who had converted to Judaism. As such, the diaspora Jews were typically designated as "Hellenist" (as in Acts 6:1). While the first two of the above-mentioned groups would be deemed conservative, the third tended to be more liberal in its outlook on life, mainly from a need to survive in a competitive world. They were also regarded with a degree of disdain by Palestinian Jews, mainly because of their more liberal attitude to the traditional religious scruples of the Jews, especially in matters of obedience to the laws of Moses. Of course, the type of Judaism under which Jesus was born had already been subject to a process of Hellenization;[30] it is just that in Palestine, particularly in Jerusalem, the influence of conservative Judaism was felt more strongly.

If both Babylonian and Diaspora Judaism influenced the religious character of Palestine, both groups would certainly influence early Christianity. The influence of Babylonian Judaism on Palestinian (or Second Temple) Judaism can be detected in the expectation of bodily resurrection and an apocalyptic understanding of history, expecting God's decisive intervention in judgement at the end of time. Such elements, which characterize especially the New Testament book of Revelation, can already be found in teachings of the Pharisees and Essenes.

Familiarity with the Greek language and culture was the outstanding distinctive of Diaspora Judaism. We have already alluded to growing use of the Greek language as it raised a need for the Septuagint translation of the Scriptures among the Jews of Alexandria.[31] It is not clear whether the Alexandrian Philo Judaeus (ca. 20 BC – AD 50) even knew Hebrew when he used the Septuagint in preparing extensive commentaries on the Scriptures. Philo's exegetical work is another important facet of the Hellenization of Judaism, and would continue to influence biblical studies in the Christian era.[32]

In Roman-occupied Palestine the ongoing influence of Hellenization could be seen in matters of topography, with cities built by Greeks and bearing Greek names: Gadara, Gerasa (Jerash), Tiberias, or Sepphoris. The story of Jesus

---

29. On Diaspora Judaism, see above §A.2. See also Frend, *Early Church*, 30–43, and 44 (for significant bibliography). See further Frend, *The Rise of Christianity*, 18–22; and A. von Harnack, *The Mission and Expansion of Christianity*, 1–9.

30. See Ferguson, *Backgrounds*, 403; on this point he follows Hengel's groundbreaking work on Judaism and Hellenism. See further, G. Vallée, *The Shaping of Christianity*, 42. On "Hellenization," see also notes 4, 6, 14 and 19 above.

31. On the Septuagint, see also note 17 above.

32. On Philo of Alexandria, see further discussion of his work in ch. 7, §B.5; also Ferguson, *Backgrounds*, 478–485.

sending the evil spirits into pigs in Gerasa (Luke 8:26–39) is better appreciated if one realizes that the city was Greek, not Jewish.[33] And wealthy Jews of Jerusalem appreciated a Greek lifestyle as a matter of status and evidence of progress.

To summarize, it is clear that Hellenization cannot be limited to the issue of Greek colonization of Palestine; Palestinian Judaism was deeply influenced by the Greco-Roman world, as well as the earlier Babylonian context. Under the first Hellenist colonizing rulers Judaism was still focused on temple worship, and it was nationalistic; such nationalism accounts for the remarkable triumph of the Jews under Maccabean and Hasmonean rulers. Nationalism remained vigorous when the Jews submitted to the Romans. Zealous Jews openly expressed their strong expectation of the Messiah. Their opposition forced the Romans to expend more effort in suppressing rebellion than in administering the region. In that context the Romans astutely granted the Jews considerable autonomy in the practice of religion. For everyday matters the Jews were ruled by their own religious council, the *Sanhedrin*, whose seventy-one members included Pharisees and Sadducees working together with the high priest.[34] This body combined the work of a senate and supreme court; their role was comparable to that of the Islamic *Ulama*. Even so, most Jews hated the Romans as an idolatrous occupying power, no better than the Greeks before them.

A.6. Jewish Religious Groups Important for Early Christianity

The political, cultural and religious struggles of this period made a deep impact on the various religious groups that emerged. They would continue to influence Second Temple Judaism, and later, Christianity:[35]

- *Sadducees* – politically prominent, they formed the aristocracy as it controlled the priesthood and maintained contact with the Roman government.[36] They represented the wealthy Jews, and were despised by the Essenes for liberal tendencies in religious matters. As long as Sadducees dominated the priesthood, the Essenes avoided temple worship.

---

33. The story can be found in Matt 8:28–34, Mark 5:1–17 and Luke 8:26–39.

34. The name is based on the Greek *sunedrion*, meaning "council." Other designations, as the *gerousia* or *boulê* (using Greek political terms), would have encouraged Jews to regard this council as a Greek, and thus a foreign institution; see Ferguson, *Backgrounds*, 567–570.

35. On the ongoing importance of these groups for early Christianity, see Vallée, *Shaping of Christianity*, 30–33; and H. Chadwick, *Early Church*, 13–15.

36. Ferguson, *Backgrounds*, 519–520; and K. S. Latourette, *The First Five Centuries*, 51–52.

- *Herodians* – they represented a political faction in support of Roman indirect rule for Palestine.[37] They worked hand in hand with the Sadducees to support the Idumean dynasty, disregarding the antagonism of many Jews.
- *Essenes* – also called the "Covenanters of the Scroll" or "Holy Society," and the "Sons of Zaddi," or "Elect of Israel"; in their dissatisfaction with the leadership of the high priest they separated themselves from the religious rites of Jerusalem. We know more about this group (or a similar group) from the Dead Sea Scrolls, documents recovered only a number of decades ago from the caves

Figure 1.2. Cave of the Dead Sea Scrolls. It is not far from the location of the Qumran community, on the West Bank of the Jordan River, close to the Dead Sea.
Photo "Qumran Caves" by Grauesel / CC SA 3.0.

---

37. Ferguson, *Backgrounds*, 533.

Figure 1.3. Ruins of living quarters at Qumran.
Photo by Mark A. Wilson. Public Domain.

of Qumran.[38] The Essenes living in caves in the Qumran desert near the Dead Sea were strictly disciplined in an ascetic lifestyle. Venerating a "teacher of righteousness" (rather than the high priest), they regulated individual and community activities according to strict rules, and regarded themselves as a faithful remnant, as it were. Expressing strong expectation of the coming Messiah, they are rightly regarded as one of the most important messianic groups of post-exilic Judaism. Entry to the group was marked by baptism, through immersion in water, while a sacramental meal of bread and wine was the highlight of community celebrations. Combining piety with zeal for the law, the Essenes shared a hatred of all forms of idolatry; they went so far as to consider any association with pagan Romans as a type of idolatry. Communities established by Essenes may be regarded as forerunners of later monastic communities.

---

38. On Essenes, the Qumran community and these Dead Sea scrolls, see Ferguson, *Backgrounds*, 521–530. Modern discovery of these documents would provide a significant witness to the Hebrew OT, especially for the quotations from Isaiah. They also demonstrate the prominence of apocalypticism in Hellenistic Judaism of the time; see Bart Ehrman, *Truth and Fiction in the Da Vinci Code*, 26–35. We note that contemporary scholarship has questioned the identification of the Essenes described in Josephus's work with the group represented in the Dead Sea Scrolls; see Steve Mason, *Josephus, Judea, and Christian Origins*, 239–279, especially 276–277.

- *Zealots* – this group originated with the Essenes; one of them, Simon, became a disciple of Jesus.[39] The Zealots were essentially freedom fighters, prepared to use any means to drive out the Romans, even at the cost of their lives. The Jewish rebellion of AD 66, which precipitated the destruction of Jerusalem, was carried out by Zealots called *Sicarii* or "knife men," a group which may be compared to the *Yan Tauri* in Northern Nigeria. They carried knives in their clothes, and would stab anyone suspected of collaborating with the Romans. Zealots tended to support messianic religious leaders. They may have formed a part of the Qumran community, the group from whose writings (i.e. the Dead Sea Scrolls) we have acquired a clearer picture of early Second Temple Judaism.[40] If so, these Zealots may also have been included among the "pious" ones (also called *hasayya* or *Hasideans*), the group that flourished during the Hasmonean period.
- *Pharisees* – although the gospels tend to present a negative picture of Pharisees (or "separatists"), Christianity actually owes more of a debt to the Pharisees than to any of the other groups. This is mainly because, as teachers of the law, the Pharisees were strict in preserving Jewish traditions. In many aspects their views overlapped with those of the Essenes; and their beginning as a faction may possibly be traced also to the "pious" ones.[41] But unlike the Essenes, Pharisees lived within a normal social context. They formed a vocal group within early Christianity; the early church in Jerusalem may well have been controlled by Jewish Christians from among the Pharisees. Positions taken by Pharisees were typically the opposite of those taken by Sadducees. While the Sadducees may be regarded as modernizing, making efforts to integrate modern ways of life and thought (like the Nigerian *Yan Izala*),[42] the Pharisees would have been anti-modernist (as are present-day *Darika*, a conservative Islamic group in Nigeria). Only Pharisaic Judaism survived the Jewish rebellions of AD 66 and 135.[43]

---

39. On the Zealots, see Ferguson, *Backgrounds*, 532–533.

40. Ferguson, *Backgrounds*, 523. According to Vallée, they may also have been recruited from the Pharisees (*Shaping of Christianity*, 32–33).

41. Ferguson, *Backgrounds*, 514; and Latourette, *First Five Centuries*, 16–17.

42. For discussion of the modernization thrust of the *Yan Izala* in Northern Nigeria, see Ousmane Kane, *Muslim Modernity in Postcolonial Nigeria*.

43. See ch. 2, §A.4; also Ferguson, *Backgrounds*, 515.

- *Scribes* – this group may be considered a branch of the Pharisees, for they were particularly concerned with the interpretation of the law. In New Testament writings they are closely linked with the Pharisees. This is because scribes helped Pharisees in their interpretation of the law. Rejecting Sadducee interpretation for its restricted appeal to *written* Torah, the Pharisees emphasized the additional authority of *oral* law. On this matter they depended on scribes to provide an authentic interpretation by applying a principle of analogy (like that called *Qiyas* by Islamic scholars), to develop laws based on Torah, though not specifically found in Torah. Jesus referred to such additions to the laws as the "tradition of men" (Mark 7:3–4, 8).

By the time that Christianity was recognized as a religious group distinct from Judaism, about AD 50, Judaism itself had spread widely throughout the Roman Empire. Jews were well known as a stubborn people. The Romans certainly knew of Judaism as a prominent contender for monotheism in religion, and the religious practices of the Jews were treated with considerable tolerance. Because the Roman Empire was the dominant context for early Christian expansion, the next section will take a closer look at Roman society, politics and culture.

B. The Roman Political, Cultural and Religious Background (63 BC – AD 410)

As noted above, the Maccabean rulers lost their power in Palestine in 63 BC, when the Roman army won a decisive victory under the powerful general Pompey. At the time of Jesus's birth, Jerusalem was ruled by Herod the Great (37–4 BC), but by the time of his crucifixion Palestine had become one of the many provinces of the empire, ruled by Pontius Pilate as governor (*procurator*) on behalf of the Romans.[44] In the Gospels the accounts of this period reflect the prominent role of the Roman army, especially its leading centurions (Matt 8:9; Luke 7:8; Acts 10). The imperial presence was considered oppressive especially because the Roman system of tax collection allowed for extortion; this is reflected in the very negative reputation of the "publicans" who typically collected far more than was their due according to contract. We know this especially from the story of Zacchaeus (Luke 19:2–10).

---

44. For a general account of the presence of Rome in the Mediterranean, see Frend, *Early Church*, 4–14; on socio-political conditions, see also Harnack, *Mission and Expansion*, 19–23.

B.1. Size of the Empire

The Roman Empire of the first century AD rivalled the Persian Empire and the domain conquered by Alexander the Great; it included enormous stretches of land, from Germany in the north, the old Persian Empire in the east, North Africa to the south, and Spain and the Atlantic in the west, all of it centred on the Mediterranean Sea.

In Europe, the Rhine and Danube rivers served as important markers for its border. At this time Rome had already been a centre of power in Italy for some 750 years, but on a smaller scale and with a different political structure, namely that of a *republic*. By the year 256 BC, it controlled the Italian peninsula; over the next 200 years the Romans managed to conquer further territories through a series of wars.[45] The Punic wars (262–146 BC) resulted in the acquisition of west Mediterranean territories formerly under the control of Carthage in North Africa, as well as Carthage itself and territories along the African shores of the Mediterranean.

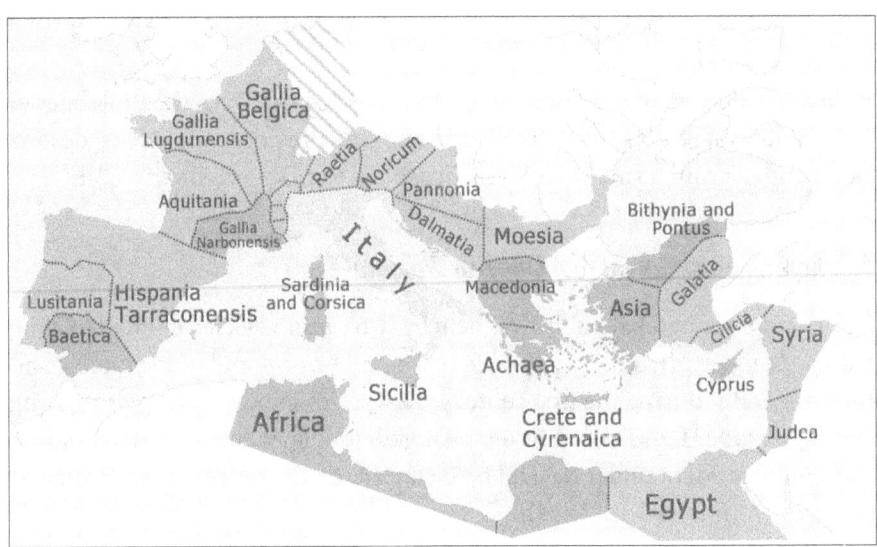

Map 1.3. The Roman Empire under Augustus Caesar (AD 14).
Map by Homoatrox / CC BY-SA 4.0.

The Macedonian wars (214–148 BC) ended with the defeat of Hellenistic Macedonian rulers and Greek city states (like Athens and Corinth) under their control. The Romans were soon involved in political intrigue with other

---

45. On the expansion of Rome in Italy and neighbouring countries, see Ferguson, *Backgrounds*, 20–22; on expansion in the east, Ferguson, *Backgrounds*, 23–24.

Figure 1.4. Roman Trireme. With the Mediterranean as its center, travel by water was a significant means of transportation, and the trireme the common mode of sailing. Photo "Romtrireme" by Maciej Szczepańczyk / CC SA 3.0.

Hellenistic powers of the Middle East, the Seleucids of Syria, the Ptolemies of Egypt and smaller kingdoms like Pergamum. As previously noted,[46] Palestine came under Roman rule when Syria became a Roman province in 63 BC.

B.2. Roman Government and Emperor Worship

Ultimate power in the republic was held by two *consuls* elected annually, ruling with a strong army, and responsible to a number of popular assemblies and the senate. But during the first century BC a series of power struggles among leading Roman families led to a prolonged civil war; this chaotic situation was finally brought under control by Octavian, or Caesar Augustus (ruling as emperor from 31 BC – AD 14).

Caesar Augustus is well known in the New Testament for imposing the census mentioned in Luke 2. To give his new status a semblance of legality, he kept the old republican political structures intact; even so, real power rested with this one man, the emperor, especially because he controlled the army, based on his chief function as *Imperator*, or chief military officer.[47] The

---

46. See above, §A.3.

47. Both terms "emperor" and "empire" are based on the Latin *imperium*, representing "authority based on military power." On this role, see also Ferguson, *Backgrounds*, 26–31.

title accorded him, *Augustus* (meaning "awesome"), is also reflected in his assumption of the title *divi filius* (Latin for "son of a god"), taken on because he was, in fact, the adopted son of his uncle, the "deified" Julius Caesar, the first of the Roman rulers to take up the pretence of eastern rulers in considering themselves divine. Julius Caesar had become sole ruler (in 48 BC), after he defeated Pompey in Thessaly, but enjoyed this position only four short years, for he was assassinated by defenders of the republic in 44 BC.[48]

Taking over in 31 BC, Caesar Augustus was astute in consolidating his position; he enjoyed a rule of more than forty years. Roman poets were exuberant in their praise of this first emperor, especially because he managed to bring an end to the century of infighting and civil war. The rule of Caesar Augustus was extended by four other emperors of the Julian family: the reclusive Tiberius (AD 14–37); the more popular but foolish Gaius Caligula (AD 37–41); the learned Claudius (AD 41–54), of whose expulsion of Jews from Rome we read in Acts 18:2;[49] and finally the notorious Nero (AD 54–68), last of the Julio-Claudian emperors, whose rule marked the first serious public persecution of Christians at the time of the fire in Rome (AD 64).[50]

Figure 1.5. Emperor Caesar Augustus. This statue is dated 30–20 BC. Photo "Caesar Augustus" by-Marie-Lan Nguyen / CC BY 2.5.

The peace established by Caesar Augustus, popularly labelled the *Pax Romana*, lasted about two hundred years. Its main virtues were stability, security, safe travel and the economic prosperity which followed on these benefits.[51] The city of Rome, located midway in Italy, on the seven hills along the Tiber river, remained the centre of the empire until the late third century with Diocletian, who established Byzantium (later known as Constantinople, or the present Istanbul) as a second major imperial capital. Although the

---

48. This crucial event is dramatized as a turning point in Roman history with William Shakespeare's well-known play, *Julius Caesar*.

49. See Ferguson, *Backgrounds*, 31–33.

50. Nero's role in persecution is discussed in ch. 4, §A.2; on Nero, see also Ferguson, *Backgrounds*, 33–35, and Paul McKechnie, *The First Christian Centuries*, 59–64.

51. On the significance of *Pax Romana* for the growth of Christianity, see Latourette, *First Five Centuries*, 21–22.

imperial borders never extended far beyond the territory already controlled by Caesar Augustus, the empire managed to incorporate varied races and peoples, showing remarkable flexibility in absorbing groups of different cultural and religious character. Roman rulers were typically recognized for applying the law in an evenhanded manner.

B.3. Roman Religious Syncretism

Roman traditional religion was polytheistic, worshipping many gods. As in most ancient cultures, Roman religion was an important part of state affairs. In the years before the birth of Jesus, religion was closely intertwined with political and public life in the empire. The state religion of the empire had its own divinities, priests and priestesses.

The chief gods of the Romans were paralleled in the Greek pantheon in what is called *syncretism* (literally, a growing together, or mixture) of Roman and Greek religion: Jupiter was considered the Roman equivalent for Zeus; Juno for Hera; Minerva for Athena; and Ceres for Demeter.[52] The numerous deities were distinguished according to the region where they were principally worshipped and for which they functioned as patron deity. Athena was closely associated with Athens, and Zeus was particularly associated with Olympia in Greece (home of the Olympic games); Jupiter was especially connected with the Roman Capitol, the heart of the city of Rome. Deities were also distinguished according to function. Like Zeus, Jupiter was god of the thunderbolt and guardian of hospitality; Juno, his wife, was goddess of marriage, while Ceres protected grain. Numerous deities represented natural forces; Poseidon, the Greek equivalent to the Roman god Neptune, was god of the seas, while Diana (Greek Artemis) protected wildlife.

But there were also many woodland spirits, daemons or nymphs, as well as countless lesser deities overseeing aspects of the household and home, the hearth or storerooms; others could be called on for help in marriage, childbirth, or sicknesses of various kinds. In fact the early imperial period witnessed considerable interest in minor deities, the daemons (good or bad). Similarly, we note a strong interest in angels and demonic powers among the Jews of Jesus's time.

---

52. On important Greek gods, see Ferguson, *Backgrounds*, 153–154; on Roman acceptance of their equivalents, 167; and on civic cults, 182–199. On "syncretism," see Harnack, *Mission and Expansion*, 15 and 24–35; Latourette, *First Five Centuries*, 123–125; and Vallée, *Shaping of Christianity*, 60–64. See also the discussion of syncretism in connection with Gnosticism in ch. 8, §A.

Figure 1.6. Ruins of the great temple of Artemis in Ephesus. Artemis was goddess of wildlife and abundance. Her temple was once acknowledged as one of the Seven Wonders of the ancient world and the center of cultural and religious life in this part of Asia Minor. It was also a significant source of revenue for its silversmiths, enough to cause a riot when they thought their livelihood threatened by the new gospel preached by Paul (Acts 19). In the background one sees a Byzantine castle, the ancient Church of St John and a 14th-century mosque.
Photo "Turkey-2827" by Dennis Jarvis / CC BY-SA 2.0.

The Roman state supported a priesthood of outstanding citizens. Special days were appointed for festivals dedicated to the gods; parades and public games were held in their honour. What is new in the time of Emperor Caesar Augustus is the introduction of rites of worship for the emperor himself, or more precisely, for his divine *genius* (spirit).[53] Citizens of the empire throughout the provinces were required to offer as little as a pinch of incense on the altar of the deified emperor, and pour out a libation of wine. In these rites the emperor was recognized as the source of peace, prosperity and justice, in short, the final appeal for help in a troubled world. Such rites would also be used as a test for loyalty to the empire, and be required as a show of support

---

53. On the ruler cult as a focus for imperial loyalty, receiving far more attention in the provinces than in Rome itself, see Ferguson, *Backgrounds*, 199–212.

for the emperor. Failure to comply with such requirements at the imperial altar could be considered treason. The rites of worship for the emperor became an important means of reviving public religion, unifying the ethnically and religiously diverse empire, and fostering a sense of patriotism focused on its ultimate ruler.

Indeed, by this time the older gods as we know them from traditional Greek and Roman literature and mythology had lost much of the appeal they once enjoyed.[54] As noted above, a process of syncretism or amalgamation of religious traditions from various ethnic origins marked the new kingdoms arising after the premature death of Alexander the Great (323 BC).[55] While the territories ruled by Alexander's generals (Seleucids in Syria, and Ptolemies in Egypt) were united at least superficially by use of Greek language, these generals had also encouraged the spread of Hellenistic culture and introduction of traditional Greek deities in these territories. Moreover, the Hellenistic period is marked by considerable movement of peoples around the Mediterranean; with movement came exposure to new cultures and religions which led, in turn, to a degree of borrowing, especially when similarities in the types of deities worshipped were acknowledged. This is evident, for example, in the parallel list of major deities of Greeks and Romans (as indicated above). Indeed, once the Romans had conquered many of the Hellenistic kingdoms (by the first century BC), the religious practices characterizing these regions began to arrive in Rome itself, along with the peoples from such provinces.

As we have already noted in the case of the Jews, the Roman governors were relatively tolerant with respect to religious observance of their subject peoples.[56] Jews were exempt from the requirements of sacrifice to the emperor; the Romans knew that they would not tolerate such an idolatrous abomination. Jews were also allowed exemptions in matters like Sabbath observance. Although the ruling Sanhedrin in Palestine was subject to the final authority of Romans on matters like capital punishment, they maintained considerable autonomy in both civil and religious matters, even for matters which affected the diaspora Jews, scattered throughout the Empire.

---

54. On the many reasons for this, see the discussion of philosophy in ch. 7, §B.

55. See Justo L. Gonzalez, *The Early Church to the Dawn of the Reformation*, 15–16; Harnack, *Mission and Expansion*, 15 and 24–35; and Ferguson, *Backgrounds*, 230–231.

56. On the tolerance of the Romans, see also H. Chadwick, *The Early Church*, 25.

B.4. Mystery Religions

Important among the new religions surfacing at this time were mystery religions, as a type of secret cult.[57] It is important to devote some attention to these especially because pagan outsiders often understood Christianity in its early years as a mystery religion. Coming from the provinces, these new movements and cultic practices were not received without question in Rome itself. Romans were suspicious of the (political) intent of the practitioners of these religions, especially because magic and prophetic power could be implemented to the detriment of their rulers. Like schools of philosophy which used astrological calculation (such as the Stoics), the cults might be suspect as potential centres of intrigue and opposition to the emperors.[58]

While the popularity of traditional public rites was waning in Rome, the newer cults were quite successful in appealing to the general populace, satisfying a deep religious longing and giving much needed hope. The cults gave adherents a sense of having a closer relationship with divine power, and a better means of communicating with the deities who truly controlled their life, the community and larger world.[59] In that regard, the magical arts, promising to manipulate the gods or minor deities to act in one's favour, drew much interest. Although Christianity may have been regarded as simply one more phenomenon of popular religious interest, it was also thought to be more dangerous because of a degree of secrecy, meeting in private homes, and thereby raising suspicion of seditious and antisocial practices.[60] When Christianity was recognized as distinct from Judaism, its adherents became objects of fear, hatred and persecution within the Roman Empire, far more than adherents of other popular cults.

Outstanding among mystery religions, and representative for many others, was that practised at Eleusis, some kilometres outside of Athens, and established there long before the fifth century BC. This was not a state or public

---

57. The tradition of studying ancient mystery religions (as far back as Casaubon in 1614) was inspired by scholarly attempts to link Catholic ritual and liturgy with aspects of ancient mystery religions; treatment of the issue is summarized in B. M. Metzger, "Considerations of Methodology," 1–20. Evaluating the similarities, Metzger ("Considerations of Methodology," 8, and 11–20) accents profound difference in terminology, especially in the degree of secretiveness and role of myth.

58. Ramsay MacMullen, *Enemies of the Roman Order*, 46–162, examines the roles of philosophers, magicians and astrologers in the empire from that perspective.

59. On the mystery cults in general, see Vallée, *Shaping of Christianity*, 62–64; and Frend, *Early Church*, 12–14. On Orphism, see Ferguson, *Backgrounds*, 162–164. For a useful summary of the literature on ancient mystery religions, see Marvin W. Meyer, *Ancient Mysteries*, 13–14.

60. On such public antagonism to Christianity, see ch. 4, §B.1.

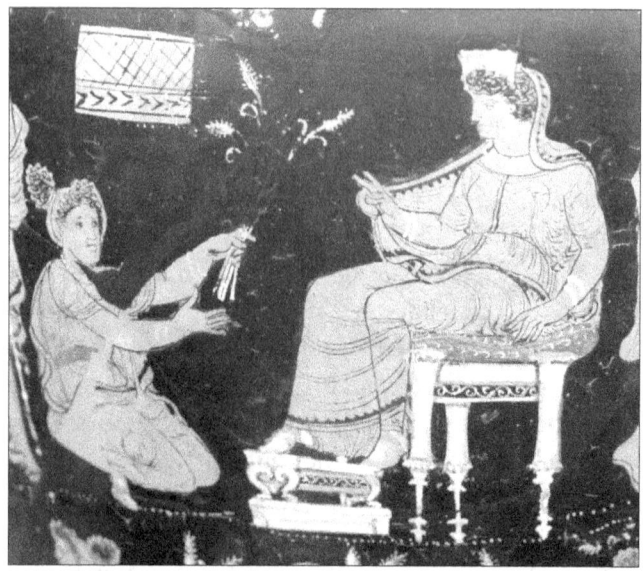

Figure 1.7. The goddess Demeter blessing Metanira, the queen of Eleusis.
Metanira offers a sheaf of wheat, the symbol of the Eleusinian mysteries. This portrayal decorates a 4th-century BC red-figured water jug.
Photo by Bibi Saint-Pol. Public Domain.

cult to which one belonged simply by being a citizen of that region. Rather, one became a member through a process of *initiation*, usually through cultic rituals of purification, participation in a meal of fellowship, and a solemn promise not to share with outsiders what happened or was seen on the night of the festival. The Eleusinian cult was older than most extant mystery religions, and had its roots in agricultural patterns of planting and harvest, closely connected with both Demeter, goddess of grain, and with Dionysus, god of the vine.[61]

We know that initiates undertook elaborate preparatory rites of purification, usually by bathing in the sea, after which they dressed in special clothing. Initiation involved nightly procession through difficult terrain, perhaps through caves. At the end a "revelation" (perhaps the showing of a head of new grain) served to give the initiate a sense of hope for personal salvation or rebirth. It appears that initiates were encouraged to think that their own life might parallel that of the god (of agriculture) who was thought to die, be buried and disintegrate, but then, with the cycle of the grain crops, to rise to new life. It must not be forgotten that these were truly *secret* rites, and that any information

---

61. On the Eleusinian mysteries, see Ferguson, *Backgrounds*, 254–259. For significant texts on the mysteries of Demeter, see M. Meyer, *Ancient Mysteries*, 15–46.

in the literature which has come down to us does not necessarily present the full story; witnesses who spoke of the rites may even have tried to mislead the overly curious. But adherents did report a sense of joy experienced at these rites, a sense of cleansing, of fellowship and new hope in overcoming death and attaining to happiness. Initiates concluded rites by dedicating their lives in the service of the deity at the heart of the respective mysteries; they continued to experience a special bond with fellow initiates.

The Roman Empire at this time witnessed the introduction of various mystery rites, like those celebrating Cybele, the Great Mother goddess,[62] who was introduced with great pomp and ceremony on her arrival in Rome from Asia Minor. Similarly, the rites for Isis and Osiris (or Serapis) from Egypt emphasized regeneration and new life.[63] The rite for Mithras, a cult with Persian roots, rose to prominence in the third century. It focused on the sacrifice of a bull and cleansing through a bath in its blood. The rite was connected with worship of *Sol Invictus*, the Unconquered Sun, and was extremely popular in the army, providing a sense of brotherhood among its members.[64]

Figure 1.8. Emperor Caesar Augustus as *Pontifex Maximus*. The statue represents the emperor as chief high priest of state religion. Photo by Ryan Freisling (2007). Public Domain.

In spite of the proliferation of so-called "foreign" religious practices, it is important to remember that throughout the period being studied in this text (the first four centuries of Christianity), popular religious experience remained deeply intertwined with state occasions and festivities. The older gods never disappeared, though they were certainly eclipsed by new rites. And the emperor

---

62. On Cybele, see Ferguson, *Backgrounds*, 281–287.

63. Ferguson, *Backgrounds*, 266–276, especially 269 and 271; for literature on these Egyptian mysteries, see M. Meyer, *Ancient Mysteries*, 155–196.

64. On the sources for the mysteries of Mithras see M. Meyer, *Ancient Mysteries*, 197–222. On *Sol Invictus*, see ch. 5, §§B.2, B.3 and B.5.

maintained a special role in religion, whether as a deified character, or in his role as chief high priest of state religion (*Pontifex Maximus*).[65]

Such a special role did not disappear with the acceptance of Christianity under Constantine early in the fourth century. In fact, it is impossible to explain the involvement of Constantine in fourth-century Christianity, especially his role in calling and presiding over the Nicene council, the first ecumenical gathering of church leaders, without recognizing that special religious role of the emperor.[66]

Questions for Discussion and Review

The Jewish background (537 BC – AD 135)

1. What are the important contributions of Ezra for Second Temple Judaism?

2. Which major contributions to Hellenistic Judaism were made by Jews under the Ptolemies in Egypt?

3. What are the outstanding aspects of the Hellenization of the Jews in the post-exilic period? How did the Seleucid Antiochus try to hasten the process of Hellenization? And in what sense might Hellenization still be an issue for contemporary Christians?

4. Why did Jews of Palestine typically look down on Jews from the diaspora?

5. How did Babylonian Judaism influence Judaism in Palestine?

6. How would you describe the major achievements of the Hasmoneans during the period of their rule in Palestine?

7. How did the Romans manage to enter Palestine and occupy the territory as part of their growing empire?

8. Which religious policies did the Romans implement with respect to the Jews?

9. For which major accomplishments did the Jews have to thank Herod (even though they hated him)?

---

65. See also the discussion of religion and the state, ch. 5, §B.5.
66. On the emperor as *Pontifex Maximus*, especially in the context of the Nicene debates, see chs. 5, §B.5 and 10, §A.1.

10. Why did Roman governors rule Palestine more directly after the death of Herod?

11. How did nationalism express itself among Palestinian Jews? Which major uprisings were caused by this kind of nationalism?

12. Which important aspects of (Hellenized) Judaism help us understand early Christianity? To what extent was early Christianity based on Judaism?

The Roman political, cultural and religious background (63 BC – AD 410)

1. Why was the introduction of emperor worship significant for the Roman provinces, and especially for the Jews of Palestine?

2. Give an account of the extent of the Roman Empire at the time of the birth of Jesus; find a map and locate Palestine, as well as major regional centres like Athens, Alexandria, Jerusalem, Antioch, Rome and Carthage.

3. How can the appeal of mystery religions in the Roman Empire be explained?

4. What were some important advantages of religious expression in the mysteries over traditional polytheistic religious practice?

5. Why might Christianity have been confused with a mystery religion?

Further Reading

Benko, Stephen. *Pagan Rome and the Early Christians*. London: Batsford, 1984.
Bickerman, Elias J. *The Jews in the Greek Age*. Cambridge, MA: Harvard University Press, 1988.
Borgen, Peder. *Early Christianity and Hellenistic Judaism*. Edinburgh: T&T Clark, 1998.
Bruce, F. F. *Israel and the Nations: The History of Israel from the Exodus to the Fall of the Second Temple*. Revised by David F. Payne. Grand Rapids, MI: Eerdmans, 1997.
———. *Paul: Apostle of the Heart Set Free*. Grand Rapids, MI: Eerdmans, 2000.
Burkert, W. *Ancient Mystery Cults*. Cambridge, MA: Harvard University Press, 1987.
Ferguson, E., ed. *Early Christianity and Judaism*. New York: Garland, 1993.
Levine, L. I. *The Synagogue in Late Antiquity*. Philadelphia: The American Schools of Oriental Research, 1987.
MacMullen, Ramsey. *Enemies of the Roman Order: Treason, Unrest and Alienation in the Empire*. London: Routledge; Cambridge, MA: Harvard University Press, 1992.
Martin, L. H. *Hellenistic Religions*. Oxford: Oxford University Press, 1987.

Mason, Steve. *Josephus, Judea, and Christian Origins: Methods and Categories*. Peabody, MA: Hendrickson, 2009.

McKechnie, Paul. *The First Christian Centuries: Perspectives on the Early Church*. Leicester: Apollos, 2001.

Meeks, Wayne. *The First Urban Christians: The Social World of the Apostle Paul*. New Haven: Yale University Press, 1983.

Meeks, Wayne, and Robert L. Wilken. *Jews and Christians in Antioch in the First Four Centuries of the Common Era*. Missoula, MT: Scholars Press, 1978.

Meyer, Marvin W., ed. *The Ancient Mysteries: A Sourcebook*. San Francisco: Harper & Row, 1987.

Neusner, Jacob. *The Rabbinic Traditions about the Pharisees before 70 AD*. 3 vols. Leiden: Brill, 1971.

———. *From Politics to Piety: the Emergence of Pharisaic Judaism*. Englewood Cliffs, NJ: Prentice-Hall, 1973.

———. "The Rabbinic Traditions about the Pharisees before 70 CE." In *In Quest of the Historical Pharisees*, edited by J. Neusner and Bruce D. Chilton, 297–312. Waco, TX: Baylor University Press, 2007.

Sanders, E. P. *Paul and Palestinian Judaism*. Philadelphia: Fortress, 1977.

———. *Judaism: Practice and Belief 63 BCE – 66 CE*. London: SCM Press, 1992.

Segal, A. *Rebecca's Children: Judaism and Christianity in the Roman World*. Cambridge, MA: Harvard University Press, 1986.

Simon, Marcel. *Verus Israel: A Study of the Relations between Christians and Jews in the Roman Empire (135–425)*. Oxford: Oxford University Press, 1986.

Vallée, Gérard. *The Shaping of Christianity*. New York: Paulist Press, 1999.

VanderKam, J. C. *The Dead Sea Scrolls Today*. Grand Rapids, MI: Eerdmans, 1994.

2

The Rise and Spread of Christianity to AD 325

> Those [Jewish Christians] who are called Ebionites agree that the world was made by God.... They use only the Gospel according to Matthew, and reject the apostle Paul, maintaining that he was an apostate from the law. As for the prophetical writings, they are inclined to explain them in a unique way, for they practice circumcision, and maintain observance of those customs which are required by the law, and according to their Judaic style of life. In fact, they adore Jerusalem as if it were the house of God.
>
> Irenaeus, *Against Heresies* 1.26.2

The Ebionites (whose name is based on the Hebrew term *ebion* for "the poor"), are important for our story because they made up the majority of Jewish Christians who fled to the Transjordan region when the Jews fled persecution in the rebellion of AD 66–70, and that of Simon ben Kochba, AD 135. Compared to extensive evidence on Christians who converted from pagan beliefs as "Gentiles," we know far less of what happened to Jews who accepted Christ, but wished to maintain a traditional Judaic lifestyle. There are a few brief references to Jewish Christians in early Christian writers like Justin Martyr and Jerome.[1] And we know of Jewish Christian Elkesaites because Mani, the third-century founder of Manichaeism, emerged from this group. The information about the Jewish Christian Ebionites is not extensive.[2]

---

1. On the sources for Jewish Christianity, see Vallée, *Shaping of Christianity*, 33–34.
2. See J. Stevenson, *A New Eusebius*, 99. Our sources do not indicate clearly whether the term represents physical or spiritual poverty.

Due to the complexity and indirect witness of the sources, much uncertainty remains about the nature of the Ebionite community and beliefs.³ Yet the report of Irenaeus (as given above) appears reliable enough and is supported by later evidence which indicates that Ebionites denied the ongoing validity of Old Testament passages about sacrifices, but continued practices like Sabbbath keeping, circumcision and acceptance of dietary regulations. They respected Jesus as the Messiah, but viewed him as a prophet like Moses: highly regarded for his righteous life, but no more than a man. On this point they would come into serious conflict with the settled position of the church long before that was finally determined at the fourth-century Nicene council.

The present chapter is focused on the expansion of Christianity beyond Palestine. It also recounts the beginning of Christianity as a global religion. Unlike other world religions, Christianity is undeniably plural and maintains a plural character from its beginnings within the Jewish context. In our time we certainly do not experience Christianity in a single form; rather, we find world Christianities. Initially the Christian faith adapted to the Greco-Roman context. The two significant early branches are those of the Latin (or Roman) Catholic church and the (Greek) Eastern Orthodox church. From an African perspective we also note the significant emergence of the Coptic, Syriac and Asian Christian Churches. Today we talk about Western Christianity, Indian Christianity, Chinese Christianity and African Christianity; and in Africa we further distinguish Nigerian Christianity from South African Christianity. None of this diversity would have been possible without the important decision taken at the Jerusalem Council of AD 50 (Acts 15), to remove cultural and religious stumbling blocks for the Gentiles turning to God in Christ. The council thereby effectively provided the base for Christianity as a global religion.

A. Factors in the Geographical Expansion of Christianity

A.1. Background

Jesus was born in the Greco-Roman world, where Palestinian Jews were influenced culturally by the Greeks, while politically they were under the influence of Rome.

In the present section we trace the story of the beginnings of Christianity from Palestine to its spread throughout the Greco-Roman world, from its

---

3. Ferguson, *Backgrounds*, 615–616.

beginning as a "sect" of Judaism dominated by those of Jewish religious background, until it emerged as a world faith.[4]

Map 2.1. Palestine: The Decapolis.
Map by Nichalp / CC BY-SA 2.5.

Jews had not hidden their disdain for the Greeks, or for Syrian collaborators; they certainly did not hide their hatred for the Romans. In this context they were looking for a liberator such as they had found with the Maccabeans,[5] one who would bring an end to the Roman domination and pollution of their ancestral "Holy Land." Such a liberator was called a "Messiah" (literally, an *anointed* leader, a term used for the priests and kings of Israel and close to that for the Islamic *Mujadadi*); this messianic leader would initiate confrontation

---
4. The formative work of Harnack (*Mission and Expansion*) is known for accenting "the fullness of time" in explaining political and historical factors affecting the period of Christ's coming in the Roman Empire; on this theme see also Gonzalez, *Early Church*, 7–17.
5. On the Maccabeans (Judas and his brothers) see ch. 1, §A.3 and §A.4.

and even full-scale war to gain victory and independence for the Jews.[6] Many leaders, especially from among the Zealots, had already claimed this title.[7] Notable among such messianic figures is Judas of Galilee, who had led a revolt against Roman taxes in AD 6. In the Acts of the Apostles, Luke mentions Theudas as such a liberator (Acts 5:34–40). But these leaders were unsuccessful; the Romans were merciless in crushing such rebellion.

In this tense religious and politically charged atmosphere Jesus emerged from an obscure background; his name, the Greek equivalent of the Hebrew "Joshua" (i.e. "the Lord saves") already points to his role as Messiah. Though he might be known as the "son of a carpenter," Jesus had popular support from the beginning. He was heralded as a Messiah also through the courageous and straightforward preaching of his cousin, John the Baptizer, who may well have been a member of the Essenes. But Pharisees and Zealots were disappointed to note that Jesus did not subscribe to their type of nationalism. He seemed unwilling to deal decisively with the Roman menace and did not call for war. His advice even appeared to encourage loyalty to the Romans: "Give to Caesar the things of Caesar and to God the things of God" (Matt 22:21). Disappointed Jewish leaders, even those with hitherto opposing interests, united to have him killed as a traitor to the Roman state, thinking that this would mean the end of the impostor Messiah.

Within a few days after Jesus's death, a rumour circulated in Jerusalem that he had come back to life, and had been seen by some of his friends. Seven weeks later his closest friends were publicly and boldly proclaiming that Jesus had been raised from the dead. For the Jewish religious leaders this preaching had a frightening effect, for thousands of Jews were joining the small group of Jesus's followers, the "Messianic sect." This included diaspora or Greek-speaking Jews, most of whom would have had little first-hand knowledge of Jesus's life. They were joined by Jewish religious leaders, including the Pharisees (even if some may have joined just to keep the group in check). The disciples of Jesus, now called *apostles* (i.e. those who are sent, based on the commissioning of Matt 28:19–20),[8] took on the responsibility of teaching and explaining the meaning of Jesus's role as the true Messiah for new converts, particularly for diaspora

---

6. On the term "Messiah," the Hebrew equivalent for the name "Christ," or "the Anointed One," see chapter appendix 7.1.

7. On the role of the Zealots in Palestine at this time, see ch. 1, §A.6 above; also Bruce, *Israel and the Nations*, 221–223.

8. The term "apostle" is based on the Greek verb *apostellō*, meaning "I send away"; in his "Great Commission" (Matt 28:19–20), Jesus told his followers, "Go and make disciples of all nations."

Jews. Jesus was not the political figure expected by the Jews, but a spiritual reformer in the line of Old Testament prophets. Such was the beginning of the early church.

A.2. The Admission of Gentiles into the Church

If the Christian church was initially comprised of both Palestinian and Greek-speaking diaspora Jews, this changed dramatically by the end of the first century when the majority of Christians were Greek-speaking Jews or Gentiles. Diaspora Jews used their numerical strength effectively in spreading a Christian interpretation of the Old Testament, with a broad understanding of its universal implications, somewhat analogous to the interpretation of the Pentateuch given by Philo in Egyptian Alexandria. We can see the effect of this in Stephen's defence before the Sanhedrin (in Acts 7), and more importantly, in decisions of the Jerusalem Council in AD 50 (Acts 15).

Just as Jews of Alexandria in Egypt had translated the Jewish Scriptures into Greek (ca. 270 BC), diaspora Jews also needed to present the teachings of Jesus in an idiom more familiar to those they designated as "Gentiles."[9] Recognizing the "foreign" character of the term "Messiah" for Jesus, they would use a more common Greek title for deity, *Kurios* (i.e. Lord or Master). While this might recall the name "Lord" applied to the Syrian god *Baal* (literally, "Master"), *Kurios* was also used for the deified Roman emperor. Early Syrian converts to Christianity may well have accepted the gospel message through familiarity with a term like *Kurios*. The very next church group to be established after the congregation in Jerusalem, that of Syrian Antioch on the Orontes, where followers of Jesus were first designated as "Christian," was also the first multi-ethnic church. Already at this stage we witness what Andrew F. Walls has called the "cross-cultural diffusion" of Christianity.[10]

Gentiles were soon an influential presence alongside Greek-speaking Jews in the Syrian Church of Antioch. This church is important because it was the first to send missionaries to other diaspora Jews.[11] And its earliest missionaries

---

9. The designation "Gentile" is based on the Latin *gentili* for "nations"; the equivalent in Hebrew, *goyim*, was the (disparaging) name by which Jews referred to non-Jews (in this respect it is similar to Muslim reference to an "unbeliever" or "infidel" as *kafir*). The strong distinction came from the fact that Jews saw themselves as God's chosen race. One could be incorporated into the Jewish nation only by birth, by circumcision and obedience to the law of Moses.

10. Walls, *Cross-Cultural Process*, 32.

11. Jenkins recognizes the ongoing stature of this church as due to traditions connecting its origin with Mary and Joseph, Jesus's own family, and its significant location as terminus of the ancient trade route connecting the Roman world with the central Asian and Persian empires

used the Greek language to preach Jesus to both Jews and Gentiles. One of them, Saul (better known by his Greco-Roman name, *Paul*), acquired the title of "apostle to the Gentiles"; he recognized that God had called him to preach to the Gentiles.

Figure 2.1. Aerial view of the Great Theatre of Ephesus. It remains one of the best-preserved theatres from the ancient world. Seating as many as 25,000, and richly decorated with columns and statues, it is still noted for its fine acoustics. It was the site of the riot incited by silversmiths of the city, who felt threatened by the preaching of the Apostle Paul (Acts 19).
Photo "Great Theatre, Ephesus" by Austrian Archeological Institute / CC BY-SA 3.0.

The immediate apostles of Jesus, all of them Palestinian Jews, apparently did not envision the global nature of Jesus's teaching as seriously as did Paul and the new Christian converts among the Gentiles. With James, a younger brother of Jesus, some initially regarded Christianity as another "sect" of Judaism. This may reflect the influence of the Pharisees, who were inclined to maintain Jewish traditional laws along with acceptance of Jesus. Indeed, we know of Jewish Christians who continued to accept Old Testament laws, customs and rituals like circumcision, as a necessary basis for admission of non-Jews or Gentiles

---

(Jenkins, *Lost History of Christianity*, 52 and 84). These factors certainly facilitated its missionary task in the eastern regions.

into the new faith.[12] But the more global diaspora understanding of the gospel, such as we find in Stephen's defence of the gospel of Jesus (in Acts 7), especially for Greek-speaking Jews, could not accept such restrictions.

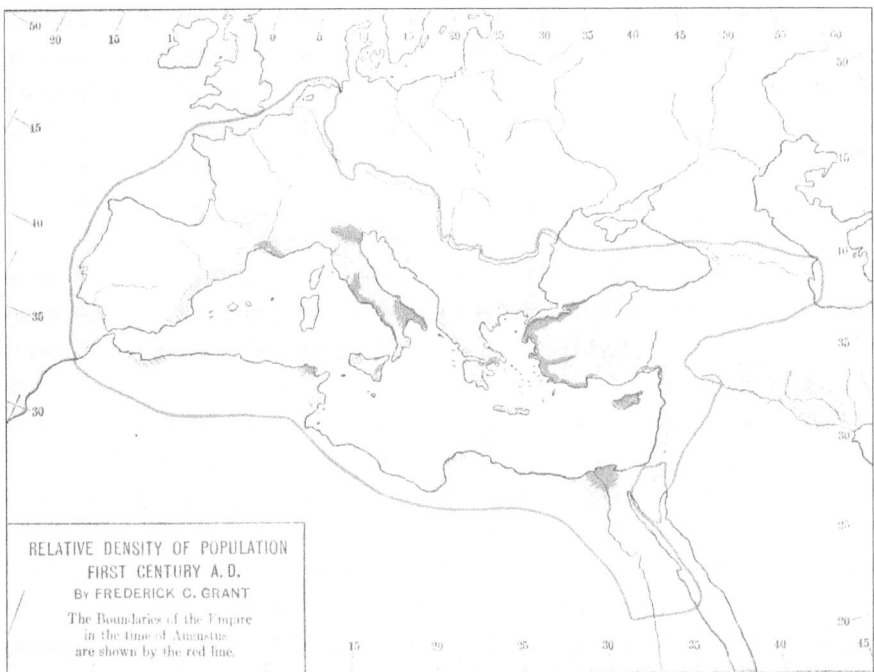

Map 2.2. **The early days of Christianity: Distribution of population in the early Roman Empire.** Public Domain.

Peter, a Palestinian Jew and leader among the apostles, was actually compelled by a dream-vision to visit a Gentile, the Roman centurion Cornelius and to baptize him and the members of his family (Acts 10). When he did, the results were amazing. Every member of the family received the Holy Spirit. Conservative Jewish Christians in Jerusalem (also called the *Circumcision Party*)[13] were reluctant to accept such a turn of events. Members of this party even went to the church in Syrian Antioch, where many adherents of Christianity came from a Gentile background, to instruct such converts that

---

12. Before this time, any non-Jew who wished to worship the God of the Jews in Jerusalem had to be circumcized and agree to obey the law of Moses fully. Those of the diaspora who found Judaism and synagogue worship attractive, but did not wish to take the final steps for membership were recognized as "God-fearers"; on their role, see further below, at §B.

13. According to Vallée (*Shaping of Christianity*, 35–36) their views resemble those of the Christians whom the church came to recognize as Judaizers.

they must be circumcized and obey the law of Moses before being admitted into the church.

This position brought them into sharp conflict with the missionary leaders of this church, Paul and Barnabas (Acts 15:2). Not many Gentiles wished to subject themselves to the more demanding Jewish religious scruples, particularly the practice of circumcision.[14] The issue was critical to the missionary efforts in the expansion of Christianity, and warranted a full discussion at a council of the "mother" church in Jerusalem.

A.3. The Jerusalem Council

The Jerusalem meeting represents a watershed moment in the history of the Christian church in its infancy. The spread of Christianity would have been hindered greatly if it were regarded as no more than another form of Judaism, representing the Jewish cultural matrix. A compromise position was needed, allowing for adaptation so that Gentiles could accept the new faith without undue barriers.

The council was led by the "apostles and elders" and may well have been chaired by James, the brother of Jesus (also called "James the Just"). The discussion evidently came to a conclusion on the basis of his arguments from the Old Testament prophets (Acts 15:13–21). The debate was undoubtedly heated and the writer of Acts has given only a summary of the proceedings in this chapter. The final decision was both a reinterpretation of the Messianic mission and a compromise. Greek-speaking Jews argued their position by spiritualizing the coming of the Messiah to save all mankind from sin and complete damnation. Diaspora Jews would have argued that Jews and Gentiles both need this deliverance. Because salvation was not based on merit, they asked Palestine Jews not to make demands on Gentile believers beyond adherence to the teachings of Jesus.

Members of the "circumcision party" also made their contribution by asking that Gentiles observe the covenant of Noah, a covenant with implications for diet, sexual behaviour and the idol worship that was so contemptible to Jews (Gen 9:8–17). These requirements were traditionally imposed on all non-Israelites who wished to worship with them. The decisive position given in the letter to the Gentile churches (Acts 15:23–29) shows that there was a limit to adaptation. More positively, Christianity would no longer be bound by the

---

14. See Chadwick, *Early Church*, 11.

strings of Jewish religious culture. It had the freedom to spread throughout the Roman Empire.

A.4. Rabbinic Judaism and Jewish Christianity

Jewish Christians, particularly Palestinian Jews, continued to uphold Jewish religious traditions, observing the ceremonies and performing all the rituals even after the Jerusalem Council. They tended to look down on Christians who did not engage in all such religious activities. Jewish hostilities toward Gentile Christianity and their restrictions on table fellowship meant that very few Jews would join in church worship with Gentiles. Traditional antagonism between Jewish and Gentile Christians was heightened after the wars of AD 66–70, and finally led to the separation of the two groups, with Gentile Christianity becoming increasingly more popular by the second century.

Palestinian Jews revolted against the Romans from AD 66–70. Roman reaction was vicious and unrestrained.[15] The Qumran community was destroyed in AD 68. When Roman soldiers entered Jerusalem, Jewish resistance was strong, but the temple was destroyed in AD 70. The final resistance was given by the Essenes, who would rather commit suicide than be killed or surrender to the Romans. As a result, the stronghold of the Essenes at Masada was totally destroyed by the Romans in AD 74.

Temple worship ceased with the destruction of the temple in Jerusalem. Without the temple, the priesthood had lost its meaning. As a place for worship the synagogue now took the place of the temple. The Rabbis emerged as leaders of Judaism and as successors to the Pharisees and the Sanhedrin. They were now recognized as the final authority in the study of the Torah. According to Jewish tradition, the Rabbis, led by Johanan ben Zakkai, met in Palestinian Jamnia (or Jabneh) to regroup and determine strategies for the future. This marks the beginning of Rabbinic Judaism.[16]

Jewish resistance was not yet at an end. Skirmishes of rebellion continued to occur among diaspora Jews (AD 115–117), and also in Palestine. When Emperor Hadrian decided to turn Judea into a Roman colony and rebuild Jerusalem, he gave it a new name, Aelia Capitolina, and established a temple

---

15. On these revolts and the consequences for Judaism, see Bruce, *Israel and the Nations*, 220–227.

16. On Pharisees and Rabbinic Judaism, outstanding scholarly work in the past decades has been done by Jacob Neusner. See his, *Rabbinic Traditions about the Pharisees*; *From Politics to Piety*; "The Rabbinic Traditions about the Pharisees before 70 CE," in *In Quest of the Historical Pharisees*, etc. This work is recognized by Ferguson, *Backgrounds*, 423 and 572–73.

for the worship of Jupiter (Zeus). This angered the Jews; tempers flared and they rebelled once more (AD 135), defending their religion just as they had resisted the Syrians under the Maccabees. The instigator of this rebellion was Simon ben Kochba ("son of a star"), who was declared a messiah by Rabbi Akiba of the Jamnia academy.[17] But once more the Jews were driven from Jerusalem. Some moved to Galilee, while many others, especially the Rabbis, fled to Babylonia. With the collapse of Palestinian Judaism, Babylonia would become the new strong centre of Judaism. However, the Romans eventually recognized the Jamnia academy as legitimate successor to the Sanhedrin and thus a vehicle for official representation of the Jews in the empire.

Gentile Christians came to reside in the Roman Aelia Capitolina (Jerusalem), and established a church there. This church was never strong, certainly not before the fourth century when Helena, the mother of Emperor Constantine, began to acquire traditional holy sites for the church and initiate pilgrimage to Jerusalem. Under its first bishop, Marcus, the church had a serious rival in neighbouring Caesarea, where Origen, Eusebius (the church historian) and Pamphilus would be instrumental in establishing a theological school and library. Caesarea became the more important centre, second only to Alexandria for articulating Gentile Christianity.

Once the temple had been destroyed, Jews and Christians found that they had little in common to foster an ongoing relationship. Christian Jews, even if they continued to undergo circumcision and adhere to features of the law of Moses, including observance of the Sabbath and other Jewish feasts, had already been expelled from the synagogues after AD 70. In the ongoing conflict between Romans and Jews, these Christians maintained their neutrality, taking refuge at a place called Pella, in the Decapolis (in the Transjordan region), and in Kochaba in Arabia, where Ebionites and Nazarenes also lived.[18] The Jews did not take kindly to Christian neutrality and failure to provide support, and in subsequent years they would continue to harass Christians. This continued until 312, when the situation was reversed under Constantine, although it is true that we have no evidence of Christian harassment of Jews until the late fourth century. But these events did serve to put an end to any lingering cordial relationship between Jews and Christians, including Jewish Christians.

---

17. Ferguson, *Backgrounds*, 423–425. According to Vallée, this revolt also marks the occasion for the Christian church to separate itself more decisively from Judaism and the Jewish element in the Gentile church (*Shaping of Christianity*, 36).

18. Ferguson, *Backgrounds*, 421.

Three groups of early Jewish Christians

It would appear that Judeo-Christianity was neglected by the mainstream of Christianity once the latter was dominated by the Gentiles. Although we have little information about the further development of Jewish Christianity, this early form of Christianity seems to have splintered into several groups.[19] Historians have identified one of these early Jewish Christian sects, the *Elkesaites*, which arose toward the end of the second century and is associated with Apamea in Syria.[20] The sect took its name from the prophet Elkesai, who received a vision of an angel and a book.[21] Elkesaite practice resembled that of the Ebionites (see below). And we know that this sect influenced the development of Manichaeism in the third century.[22]

Another Jewish Christian sect, the *Nazarene* (also called Nazorean or Nazraye/Nasara [in Hausa]) was named after Jesus himself, as he was called "Jesus of Nazareth."[23] This group accepted Gentile Christians and did not require them to keep the law of Moses, although they did insist on Jewish members keeping the law (as to circumcision, or Sabbath observance), as both a cultural and religious duty.[24] They taught that Jesus was the Messiah, the Son of God and that his teaching surpassed that of Moses. The majority of the Nazarenes fled to Pella with the resumption of hostilities between the Romans and Jews under Simon ben Kochba in AD 135.

A third group of Jewish Christians has been identified as the *Ebionites* or the "poor" (based on the Hebrew, *ebion*). Ebionites were less flexible on Old Testament requirements.[25] Like the Circumcision Party they insisted

---

19. For a thorough treatment of Jewish Christianity including the various sects, theological or organizational concerns and writings, see J. Daniélou, *Theology of Jewish Christianity*. Chadwick (*Early Church*, 21–22) recognizes an ongoing presence of Jewish Christians in Syria right up to the fourth century, when Jerome translated a "Gospel according to the Hebrews" into Latin for such a group; but Chadwick also notes confusion of Jewish Christians with the Ebionites, on whom see below.

20. See Ferguson, *Backgrounds*, 614; also Harnack, *Expansion of Christianity*, 287.

21. Daniélou (*Theology of Jewish Christianity*, 65–66) notes similarity between this vision and that of the Shepherd of Hermas.

22. Ferguson, *Backgrounds*, 614. In this connection we note the conclusion of Daniélou, who locates the origin of the earliest Christian heresies, particularly Gnosticism, at the intersection of Jewish Christianity, heterodox Judaism and Christianity (*Theology of Jewish Christianity*, 73).

23. Ferguson recognizes some confusion with Ebionites in the sources representing this group (*Backgrounds*, 614–615). Chadwick regards "Nazarene" as a name used by Jews for Christians (*Early Church*, 16 and 21).

24. Daniélou, *Theology of Jewish Christianity*, 56.

25. On documents for our acquaintance with the Ebionites, see Daniélou, *Theology of Jewish Christianity*, 55–64.

that every convert to Christianity must keep the law of Moses as the highest expression of God's will. The Ebionites also adopted use of the ritual bath, reminiscent of the Essenes. Like the Essenes, they rejected blood sacrifice and temple worship.[26] They believed that Jesus was a great prophet who became the Messiah by perfectly fulfilling the law. If Jesus was the Son of God, however, he was regarded as such only through "adoption" as son, as a reward for his righteousness.[27] Although they accepted the Gospel of Matthew, they rejected the letters of Paul.

The Ebionites were suppressed during the Roman conquest of Jerusalem and were later branded as heretical for their unacceptable teaching.[28] At the time they were living alongside the Jordan River and remained there until AD 400 and perhaps even much later. The Christians with whom early Muslim traders had contact may well have been Ebionite Jewish Christians.[29]

B. Early Expansion of Christianity to the West, the Far East and Africa

Christianity was first spread through the Pentecost pilgrims and expanded in a series of phases.[30] According to Luke (in Acts 2:5–11), there were more than fifteen nations present in Jerusalem on Pentecost. Upon return to their homes throughout the empire and beyond (witness the Ethiopian eunuch of Acts 8), these pilgrims would have related to their countrymen what they experienced in Jerusalem. The second phase of expansion came with missionaries who travelled throughout the Roman world. They were able to do so freely thanks to the peace achieved by a stable Roman government, the good roads of the

---

26. Daniélou, *Theology of Jewish Christianity*, 64.

27. See Daniélou, *Theology of Jewish Christianity*, 57 and 63; also Ferguson, *Backgrounds*, 615. Such an understanding of Jesus's sonship resurfaces in later christological discussion; see ch. 10, §A.3, on dynamic monarchianism, or adoptionism.

28. In his discussion of the Ebionites, Irenaeus links them with the heretical groups of Cerinthus and Carpocrates; see the relevant quotation in Stevenson, *New Eusebius*, 99.

29. This could help explain the numerous parallels with Jewish thought and practice in early Islam. Jenkins (*Lost History of Christianity*, 188–189) gives an alternative explanation for the phenomenon from early Muslims who fled to Ethiopian Aksum when they faced persecution in Arab territories. Here they made contact with a form of Christianity which continued to incorporate many Judaic practices; on Ethiopian Christianity, see ch. 6, §A and §D.

30. The story of the "sweep across the Greco-Roman world" is well told in Latourette, *First Five Centuries*, 67–108. Among the numerous reasons for the spread of Christianity, Chadwick focuses on Christian charity, particularly the generosity of Christians to the poor (*Early Church*, 54–60, especially 56).

empire, safety in travel ensured by the government and use of Greek as a universal language.³¹

Paul was the outstanding missionary of the early church, but he was not alone. By the time of his death, most probably in Rome (ca. AD 68), Paul had preached and organized churches in almost all the cities in Asia Minor, in Greece and also in Rome, the capital of the Roman Empire.³² Paul planned to visit Spain, but it is not clear whether he actually achieved that; Spanish Christianity claims its origin in the apostle James. In every city visited, the Jewish synagogue would be a first port of call. Jews had spread throughout the Mediterranean world and synagogues were a common feature of diaspora Jewish communities.³³ It was therefore reasonable for Paul and members of his team to begin by visiting the Jews in their own synagogue, before turning to the Gentiles.³⁴

Diaspora Judaism was comparatively tolerant of Christianity and was able to offer it some cover in the first century.³⁵ Both Judaism and Christianity practised proselytism among Gentiles. Gentiles who were attracted to Judaism, but considered Jewish religious scruples (especially circumcision) humiliating, would certainly be attracted to Christianity. In many cities and provinces, like Bithynia in Asia Minor, Christianity spread through the conversion of Gentiles who were already admirers of Judaism, called "God-fearers." But by AD 130 the relationship between Christians and Jews had become quite embittered. From that time, the Jewish *Shema* (recited in worship) contained curses on Christians. From the side of Christianity we have the (apocryphal) *Epistle of Barnabas* (written ca. AD 100), with a bitter attack on Judaism.³⁶ This situation changed only late in the fourth century, once the situation had been reversed under Constantine, and Jews began to suffer persecution as those accused of crucifying Jesus.

In Rome itself, the capital city and centre of the empire, we know of a significant number of Christians right from the beginning. As the centre,

---

31. On proselytizing by Jews in the Greco-Roman world, see Simon (*Verus Israel*, 369, 375 and 383); also Harnack (*Mission and Expansion*, 9–13), who recognized that the work of Christian missionaries was anticipated by Jewish missionary zeal, particularly that of the Pharisees. On the second phase of missionary outreach by apostles, prophets and teachers, see Harnack, *Mission and Expansion*, 319–368.

32. On the missionary role of Paul, see Latourette, *First Five Centuries*, 68–74; also Frend, *Rise of Christianity*, 86–117.

33. On Diaspora Judaism, see also the above discussion, ch. 1, §A.3 and §A.5.

34. For an assessment of Paul's achievement, see Chadwick, *Early Church*, 19–21.

35. Frend, *Early Church*, 35.

36. Frend, 36–37. For further discussion of the apocryphal gospels see ch. 9, §E.

Rome was the choice destination for Christians travelling in the empire; as the saying goes, "All roads lead to Rome." In fact, Rome would rival Bithynia in its concentration of Christians. From the time of his imprisonment, Paul reports the presence of Christians even "in Caesar's household" (Phil 4:22). As religious centre of the empire, Rome was pluralistic, welcoming a great variety of sects and religious groups including the various branches of Christianity which developed in the first centuries: Montanists, Marcionites, Modalists, and several branches of Gnostics, alongside (mainline) Catholic Christianity.

B.1. Christianity in Other Parts of the Roman Empire

Christianity evidently continued to spread along the trade routes of the Roman Empire and beyond its borders. In the first century Christian preachers could be found preaching in public.[37] But after the persecution under Nero, public preaching would have been more risky. From the mid-first century the spread of the Christian message was more likely to occur in private, particularly in private homes.[38] It is understandable that in such a private context, women had far more liberty to exercise the kind of leadership which is indicated, for example, by the role of Lydia in Acts 16.

Christian apologists who wrote in defence of Christianity were also great preachers. We know of numerous Christians who were converted through arguments for the integrity and consistency of Christianity as it was presented by Christian apologists like Justin Martyr.[39] Some apologists became missionaries. One of them, Pantaenus, is described by Eusebius:

> He was renowned for great learning, trained as a philosopher. Later he taught at the Christian school at Alexandria. . . . Now it is said that he showed such burning enthusiasm for the divine Word that he was appointed herald of the gospel of Christ to the nations of the East and traveled as far as the land of the Indians.

---

37. For early Christian practice in matters like baptism, see the *Didachê* (*Teaching of the Twelve Apostles*), quoted in Stevenson, *New Eusebius*, 9–14. On the significance of this early document, see also Latourette, *First Five Centuries*, 117–118; and Chadwick, *Early Church*, 46–48.

38. An interesting account of Christians meeting in the first century in Rome, is given in Banks, *Going to Church in the First Century*.

39. The Apologists are discussed more fully in ch 4, §B.

... And he found that people there, who had come to know Christ, already had Matthew's Gospel.[40]

Further expansion of Christianity to the north, south and west of the Mediterranean Sea would take place more effectively after the peace afforded by Constantine (from AD 313).[41] Before that time, the only region around the Mediterranean Sea where Christianity might have been considered predominant was Asia Minor (approximately the geographical extent of present-day Turkey). The apostle Andrew, however, came to be known as the apostle to the Black Sea communities in the northern regions later incorporated in the Ukraine (and Russia). In most provinces of the empire, Christianity was regarded as a minority religion, an illegal faith group, or even a cult; Christians were often subject to persecution.

Before AD 313, the number of Christians in Egypt was not significant. Although we know little of a Christian presence before the late second century, Christianity was probably introduced with the first apostles. According to tradition, Mark was the first missionary to visit Egypt, either in AD 48 or 55–61; he was probably martyred in AD 68 and is regarded as the first patriarch of the Coptic church.[42] But the first substantial reports of Christians martyred in this region of North Africa come with the episcopacy of Demetrius (AD 180). Much more is known of Christianity in the late second and early third century from the work of Clement of Alexandria. Egyptian Alexandria had been a centre of Greek learning from the time of the Ptolemies and it is perhaps not surprising that the city was an early base for Christian educational institutions, if not also for the spread of Gnosticism.

B.2. Syrian Christianity

Through the missionary work of Jesus's disciples (or apostles), it took less than a generation for Christianity to reach places outside Palestine. The church in Antioch had a significant role in the spread of the gospel in Mesopotamia,

---

40. Eusebius, *Ecclesiastical History* 5.10.1–3; the passage is quoted in Foster, *First Advance*, 42; and in Stevenson, *New Eusebius*, 179. In subsequent citation this work of Eusebius will be abbreviated *HE*, according to its Latin title: *Historia Ecclesiastica*. The reference to "India" in this passage may actually refer to Ethiopia; the regions were often confused by ancient authors not well acquainted with the geography.

41. The role of monastic movements in missionary work is discussed in the next chapter. Further discussion of early expansion of Christianity in North Africa can be found in ch. 6. On the spread of Christianity and its causes see also Latourette, *First Five Centuries*, 104–108.

42. Kalu, "The Golden Age of Christianity in Africa," 41. On further development of Christianity in Egypt, see ch. 6.

Persia, Armenia and Georgia, right up to the fourth century.[43] Tradition has it that Thaddeus brought Christianity to the city of Edessa, the capital of the kingdom of Osrhoene. The king of Edessa became a Christian and was the first king to do so. According to legend, King Abgar of Edessa wrote to Jesus himself for a cure of his leprosy, inviting him graciously to share his kingdom: "I have a very little city, but comely, which is sufficient for us both."[44] This city, near a caravan route in use since the time of Abraham, came to have the first Christian church in Osrhoene.[45]

Figure 2.2. The Etchmiadzin Cathedral in Armenia. This sketch represents the mother church of the Armenian Apostolic Church, with roots going back to the 4th-century. Sketch from John M. Neale (1850), *A History of the Holy Eastern Church: General Introduction*, Vol. 1:290.

---

43. Harnack recognized Antioch as the "strong-hold of Eastern Christianity" (*Expansion of Christianity*, 285); on the significance of Antioch, see also note 11 above.

44. See Isichei, *History of Christianity in Africa*, 18, also Jenkins, *Lost History of Christianity*, 84.

45. Frend, *Rise of Christianity*, 295; see also Jenkins, *Lost History of Christianity*, 84–86.

Edessa was the home of the hymn writer Bardaisan,[46] and the theologian Tatian, a student of Justin Martyr and author of the *Diatesseron*, a work by which he sought to harmonize the four canonical gospels in the Syriac language (ca. 170).[47] Tatian thus prepared the way for the translation of the New Testament, and eventually the entire Bible into Syriac (the *Peshitta*).[48] In later centuries this Eastern type of Christianity maintained significant contact with Coptic Christians in Egypt, Nubia and Ethiopia; these links were strengthened after the rise of Monophysite Christology (after Chalcedon, AD 451).[49] Syrian Christianity would also be transferred to Asia and China.

Armenia, a country formerly under the control of the Parthian Kingdom, was the first kingdom to accept Christianity as a national religion.

This occurred under the Armenian prince Gregory, who was converted in Cappadocia, a province in Asia Minor with a very strong Christian presence. Gregory, in turn, won over the Armenian king Tiridates (AD 274–314).[50] The New Testament was translated into Armenian in AD 410.[51]

B.3. Persian Christianity

From Edessa Christianity spread to the Parthian kingdom (Persia, now Iran) under the Sassanid dynasty. The centre of Christianity here was Adiabene, five hundred kilometres east of Edessa, across the Tigris. But Christians were a minority in the midst of an overwhelming majority of adherents of the Zoroastrian religion. Especially from AD 339 to 420 these Christians were severely persecuted by Persian rulers for refusal to accept Zoroastrianism, the national religion; as Christians, they were suspected of a treasonous alliance with the Roman Empire, the arch-enemy of the Persian kingdom.[52] To show national loyalty, the church was forced to sever its relationship with Rome. But Christianity survived, and the church in Persia was able to send missionaries

---

46. Chadwick, *Early Church*, 61.
47. Chadwick, *Early Church*, 62; and Jenkins, *Lost History of Christianity*, 87. On Tatian's *Diatesseron* see ch. 9, §C.2.
48. Jenkins, *Lost History of Christianity*, 87.
49. Isichei, *History of Christianity in Africa*, 18, 29–30.
50. Frend, *Rise of Christianity*, 445; and Jenkins, *Lost History of Christianity*, 54.
51. See also the report on the Synod of Ashtishat (AD 365) in Stevenson, *Creeds, Councils and Controversies*, 87–88.
52. On the persecution, see the excerpt from Theodoret in Stevenson, *Creeds, Councils and Controversies*, 294; see also Latourette, *First Five Centuries*, 99–100 and 103–104.

(mostly monks) to the Far East; Nestorian Christianity was significant for the beginnings of Christianity in China, Tibet and Mongolia.[53]

B.4. Arab Christianity

Fourth-century Arab Christianity was strongest in Yemen.[54] With the presence of a significant population of Jews, Christianity in Yemen may well have its origin with converts from Judaism. These regions were never conquered by the Romans, and Christianity here was less influenced by Hellenism. In his *Ecclesiastical History*, Eusebius records distinctive views on the divinity of Christ and the mortality of the human soul as characteristic of Arab Christians but not acceptable to other churches.[55] The issues were significant enough to warrant a synod, and Origen was among those sent to these churches to discuss and correct the matter.[56] Eusebius reports that these Christians were certainly open to such correction.

Yemen was on a sea route from Alexandria through the Nile and the Red Sea, into the Arabian Sea and the Indian Ocean and from here to Asia and the Far East. Christian influence in these regions came from both north and south.

From the north, it was Roman Christianity and from the south, it was Persian Christianity.[57] Most of the missionaries who came to Arabia were monks; foremost among these was a leader called Moses.[58]

Arab Christians also faced opposition from various groups, especially from Jews, although these were not the traditionalist Jews who would oppose Muslims in the sixth century. From the fourth to the sixth century the Himyar (or Himyarite) Kingdom of Yemen had rulers who were converts to Judaism

---

53. On Nestorius and his role in fourth-century theological debates, see ch. 11, §A.1.

54. Arabia, as such, represents a large region, which may include the southern districts of Palestine, areas around Damascus (as the area to which Paul retreated, according to Gal 1:17), and even Mesopotamia; see Harnack, *Expansion of Christianity*, 300.

55. According to Eusebius (*HE* 6.33.1–3) the bishop of Bostra in Arabia, Beryllus, taught that before his incarnation, Jesus did not have an individual existence of his own. And his divinity came only through the indwelling of the Father; it was not his own divinity. Again, Arab Christians held to the teaching that at the time of death the human soul dies with the body; even so, both body and soul will come back to life at the resurrection (*HE* 6.37). On these discussions, see also Stevenson, *New Eusebius*, 195–196. The mortality of the soul, a position held by modern Seventh-Day Adventists, has remained a subject of debate among evangelical scholars. See further, Hick, *Death and Eternal Life*; Edwards and Stott, *Essentials*; and Marshall, *The Devil Hides Out*, 101–110.

56. On Origen's role in these theological discussions, see ch. 10, §A.3.

57. Latourette, *First Five Centuries*, 80 and 104.

58. On the significance of monasticism for the spread of Christianity in the East, see the next chapter, especially §C.7.

and are known for persecuting Christians. Unlike Muslims, the Jews killed both Christian men and women. The prayer of the women and girls who were about to be killed in Najran (an Arab city in Yemen close to Aden) has been preserved:

> O God, come to our aid!
> O Lord Jesus Christ, behold our oppression,
> And turn us not away, but grant us the power to walk our way to martyrdom,
> that we may reach our men-folk who died for Thy sake.
> Forgive us our sins,
> And receive the sacrifice of our lives as acceptable in Thy sight.[59]

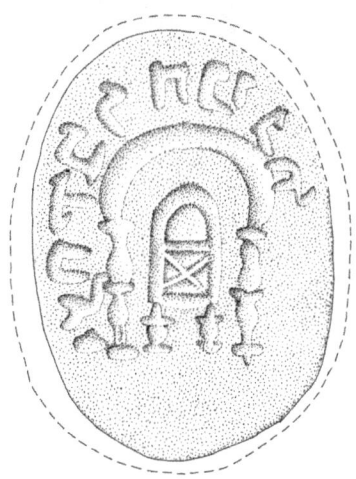

Figure 2.3. **Ring-stone from Dhofar (Yemen).** The Aramaic name Yishak bar Hanina and an image of a Torah shrine are engraved.
Portrayal by Paul Yule / CC BY 3.0.

Had it not been for the intervention of the Ethiopians, who had already embraced the Christian faith as a national religion at this time, the Christians in Najran could have suffered total annihilation.[60] Since Christianity in Africa as a whole is the focus of a subsequent chapter (ch. 6), we will not pursue discussion of the condition of Christianity in Ethiopia at this point.[61] In spite of persecution of Christians by Jews, Arab Christianity did not die out. We know of Arab bishops in both Aden and Cana. And in Najran Christianity survived until the time of Muhammad (seventh century). Indeed, the dialogue between the Christian community in Najran and Muhammad in Medina cited in the Qur'an (Sura 3.33–64), indicates a reasonable beginning for Muslim-Christian dialogue.

---

59. On the slaughter of the Christians of Najran (AD 523), see Jenkins, *Lost History of Christianity*, 189. The prayer is quoted in J. Foster, *First Advance*, 112.

60. The Ethiopian ruler who intervened even colonized Yemen for Ethiopia for a short period of time. Judaism survived in Yemen; in the nineteenth century some 150,000 Jews were left, but most of them migrated to Israel by 1960. See Isichei, *History of Christianity in Africa*, 17; also Latourette, *First Five Centuries*, 104.

61. See ch. 6, §D, below.

Figure 2.4. Tenth-century Persian cross. It is portrayed at the Valiya Pally, the prominent church of Kottayam, a centre for Syrian Christians in Kerala State, India. Photo taken in The Syrian Church in India by George Milne Rae. Public Domain.

B.5. Christianity in the Far East

A strong tradition claims that the apostle Thomas brought Christianity to India (or southern Arabia) in AD 50.[62] According to the tradition, Thomas died in India and was buried there.

European travellers who visited India in the thirteenth and fifteenth centuries claim to have visited his grave there. But there is also convincing evidence that Nestorian Christianity spread to India from the Syro-Persian church in the fourth century. Christianity certainly reached India in the late third or early fourth century. We know that in AD 350 Pallivanavar, the king of Malabar (now Kerala) in south India, was Christian. At the council at Nicea in 325 the Bishop of Persia appears to have been responsible for representing India as well; the record indicates that John the Persian signed the Nicene document "on behalf of [the churches] in the whole of Persia and in the great India."[63] Asian Christianity continued to grow. Philip Jenkins has noted that, "[a]s late as the eleventh century, Asia was still home to at least a third of the world's Christians..."[64] And the language of these churches in Asia was neither Greek nor Latin, but Syriac, Persian, Turkish, Arabic, Chinese and Indian.

---

62. Latourette, *First Five Centuries*, 80 and 104. On the travels of Thomas and legendary missionary journeys of apostles like Andrew, James, John and Philip, see Chadwick, *Early Church*, 17–18.

63. J. Foster, *First Advance*, 113. On representation of Christian bishops at the great council of Nicea (AD 325), see ch. 10, §A.4.

64. Jenkins, *Lost History of Christianity*, 4.

Questions for Discussion and Review

1. Why were the Jews looking for a Messiah at the time of the Roman occupation?

2. How did the Jews understand the coming of the Messiah? In which important respects did Jesus not meet their expectations?

3. Which distinguishable groups of Jews joined the Christian church from the beginning?

4. In what sense can a process of Hellenization be noted from the beginning of Christianity?

5. Which important factors led to the dominance of Gentiles in the early Christian communities?

6. How does the Jerusalem Council (Acts 15) mark a significant turning point in the first-century history of Christianity?

7. What is the significance of the destruction of the temple for Judaism, and for relations between Jews and Christians?

8. How did further rebellion of Palestinian Jews against the Romans affect the relationship between Jews and Gentile Christians?

9. Which significant groups of Judeo-Christians are known from the early history of Christianity? Which restrictions did these groups impose on continuing observance of Jewish tradition?

10. Why is it significant that the Christians with whom early Islam had contact may well have been the Ebionites?

11. How would you describe Paul's missionary strategy as he travelled through the Roman Empire at this time?

12. Why were Gentiles who were already attracted to Judaism more ready to accept Christianity?

13. Which important factors influenced the spread of Christianity in the Roman Empire, and beyond, from the first through the fifth century?

14. Why did relations between Christians and Jews continue to deteriorate during these centuries?

15. Why is early acceptance of Christianity in Edessa and Armenia significant?

16. Why did Christians of the fourth and fifth centuries suffer persecution in the Persian Empire?

17. How and where did Christianity spread among the Arabs at this time?

18. How did Christianity first come to India?

Further Reading

Daniélou, J. *The Theology of Jewish Christianity*. The Development of Christian Doctrine before the Council of Nicaea, vol. 1. Translated by J. A. Baker. London: Darton, Longman & Todd, 1964.

Ferguson, Everett. *Early Christianity and Judaism*. New York: Garland, 1993.

Frend, W. H. C. *The Early Church*. London: Hodder & Stoughton; Philadelphia: Fortress Press, 1982.

———. "Early Christianity and Society: A Jewish Legacy in the Pre-Constantinian Era." *Harvard Theological Review* 76 (1983): 53–71.

Gonzalez, Justo L. *The Early Church to the Dawn of the Reformation*. The Story of Christianity, vol. 1. San Francisco: Harper & Row, 1984.

Harnack, A. von. *The Mission and Expansion of Christianity in the First Three Centuries*. James Moffatt trans. of vol. 1 of the 1908 edition. Gloucester, MA: Peter Smith, Harper Torchbook; London: Williams & Norgate, 1972 (1963, 1908).

Latourette, K. S. *The First Five Centuries*. History of the Expansion of Christianity, vol. 1. Revised edition. New York: Harper & Row, 1975.

Levine, L. I. *The Synagogue in Late Antiquity*. Philadelphia: The American Schools of Oriental Research, 1987.

Meer, F. van der, and C. Mohrmann, eds. *Atlas of the Early Christian World*. London: Nelson, 1958.

Neusner, Jacob. *The Rabbinic Traditions about the Pharisees before 70 AD*. 3 vols. Leiden: Brill, 1971.

———. *From Politics to Piety: the Emergence of Pharisaic Judaism*. Englewood Cliffs, NJ: Prentice-Hall, 1973.

Walls, Andrew F. *The Cross-Cultural Process in Christian History*. New York: Orbis, 2002.

3

Monasticism and Missions

> When the mother had arranged excellent marriages for the other sisters, such as was best in each case, Macrina's brother, the great Basil, returned after a long period of education, already a practiced rhetorician. He was far too much puffed up with the pride of oratory, and looked down on other dignitaries, for in his own estimation he excelled all the men of leading and position. Nevertheless, Macrina took him in hand, and speedily drew him also toward the mark of philosophy. As a result he forsook the glories of this world and despised the fame gained by speaking; he deserted public affairs for this busy life where one toils with one's own hands. His renunciation of property was complete, lest anything should impede the life of virtue.
>
> Gregory of Nyssa, *The Life of St Macrina*, 6

Gregory of Nyssa's account of the life of his sister Macrina was written shortly after her death and also the death of his brother Basil; it was a time when he was assuming a significant role in reaffirming the Nicene position on the deity of Christ at the Council of Constantinople (AD 380). Macrina, the oldest daughter in the large family, had once been prepared to marry, but her fiancé died before the wedding and she rejected any further proposals of marriage. Together with her mother she began to live the simple life of ascetic renunciation marked by virginity, toiling with her own hands and showing generosity in sharing with the poor and needy. At the same time she began to turn the family estate into a monastic establishment for female virgins. It became a place of refuge for many.

Several features of this short section of the *Life* are important for highlighting the inversion of traditional values which Christianity, and especially Christian asceticism, brought with it. We note first that Macrina brings her "great" brother down to earth. From being "puffed up" with pride in public speaking he comes down to a life marked by working with his own hands. By the fourth century such a lifestyle of Christian asceticism, as a life of "virtue," was commonly designated as the "mark of philosophy."[1] It is noteworthy, in this connection, that the Greek term for virtue, *aretê*, was the word traditionally associated with the ideals of the aristocracy, as their lives were marked by significant possessions (especially in land), public status, education, leisure and slaves.

Gregory uses only a few words to depict how Basil's life gets turned upside down. As an accomplished speaker, he could have attained to fame and glory in public life; as the elder brother in charge of the family estate, he would have been awarded much public respect. But under Macrina's guidance, Basil begins to work with his own hands, highly unusual for aristocratic landholders. His possessions are given away, and the slaves are freed. In this way all the traditional sources of public wealth and status for this family are undermined, and a totally new definition of the "life of virtue" emerges.

But the real climax of this series of events is not stated in so many words, though it would have been clear enough to any ancient reader. Basil's conversion to the ascetic life comes through a woman, his older sister.[2] Gregory's *Life of Macrina* provides one small but highly significant window on the wholesale redefinition of aristocracy and family life brought about by the monastic movement as it affected leading families in fourth-century Cappadocia.

Contemporary Sub-Saharan African churches are not very familiar with the monastic model of Christian life. Few monasteries have survived in the current African landscape. Yet in the fourth and fifth centuries, a formative period of growth and change for Christianity, monasticism was considered a "normal," and even an ideal practice of Christian commitment and devotion.[3] Monastic centres served as hospitals, hostels and schools. Throughout the

---

1. While Tertullian and the monk, Anthony, might denounce philosophy as the source of heresy, a favourable appreciation of philosophy already characterized the second-century work of Justin Martyr (d. ca. AD 165); on this topic see also ch. 4, §B.3. On the role of philosophy in arguments against Christians in the "great persecution" of Diocletian, see ch. 7, §B. That challenge would be answered by Christianity referring to itself as the true philosophy. The passage above shows how the designation "philosophy" was applied to the ascetic life practiced by Christians at this time. See also Helleman, *Feminine Personification of Wisdom*, 59–94.

2. On the significant roles taken on by women in early Christianity, see §B.2 below, and chapter appendix 9.1.

3. This is especially true of eastern Christian practice; see Jenkins, *Lost History of Christianity*, 72. On the various forms of early ascetic Christian piety, see Frend, *Rise of Christianity*, 567–569.

European Middle Ages, monastic orders were responsible for maintaining a degree of civilization, and fostering advance in unlikely preoccupations like animal husbandry and agricultural method. They were also instrumental in preserving literature and the accumulated wisdom of ancient civilizations in various branches of knowledge: music, grammar, architecture, politics or philosophy. In a time of chaos and upheaval, monasteries provided a degree of stability as centres of culture and education. The monks boldly went beyond the walls of their establishments to serve as missionaries, advancing the gospel among people groups who had never heard of Jesus. The conversion of Europe was accomplished largely with the support of monastic orders.

A. Eastern Monasticism

Even before the rise of Christianity, elements of ascetic practice were known from Judaic communities like the Essenes, the Qumran community (represented by the Dead Sea Scrolls), or the *Therapeutae*, whose communal life in the proximity of Alexandria is described by Philo of Alexandria. Members of these groups were known for sharing their belongings.[4] The simple lifestyle of the Essenes was focused on agricultural work. They denied themselves many accepted pleasures in the use of clothing and food; most members were celibate.[5] From the New Testament we know of John the Baptist spending time in the wilderness when he was preaching and baptizing (Mark 1:1–8). Jesus also sought such a solitary place for prayer (Mark 1:35). And from the letters of Paul we know of vigorous debate in the early Christian community in Corinth on reasons for rejecting marriage (1 Cor 7).

Certainly, the earliest Christian congregations imposed strict demands on their members. While many regarded baptism (correctly) as the washing away of sin, they also thought (incorrectly) that after baptism no further repentance for sins was possible, an assumption which led many early Christians to postpone baptism until late in life. In the second century we have examples of those who followed the apostle Paul himself in foregoing the comfort of having a wife, rejecting marriage to devote himself wholly to the Lord in a life of prayer and service. But the earliest accounts of regular, disciplined Christian monastic life come from the Coptic Christians of Egypt. According to local tradition, the first Christian to retreat from community life in favour of the life

---

4. On the Essenes, see ch. 1, §A.6, and E. Ferguson, *Backgrounds*, 521–531; on the *Therapeutae* see §B.2 below.

5. Latourette, *First Five Centuries*, 17.

of a hermit in the desert was Abu Bolos, or "Father Paul" of Upper Egypt. He fled the persecution of Decius in 250, and remained in the desert as a solitary ascetic until he died, some ninety years later.[6] His example was followed by many who sought to escape the socio-political stress of persecution by adopting the precarious solitary life of a hermit in the desert.[7]

A.1. Early Asceticism: Anthony (ca. 250–356)

Far more is known about monastic life in the fourth century, especially through widespread acquaintance with Athanasius's account of Anthony. Born along the Nile in Upper Egypt, Anthony was left an orphan by wealthy parents.[8] While attending his village church in Heracleopolis he heard the gospel account of Jesus's instruction to a wealthy young man, to sell all of his possessions if he would be perfect, and so have treasure in heaven (Matt 19:21). Anthony took it to heart. He sold his property and distributed the proceeds to the poor, making provision for his younger sister by sending her to join a house of virgins (*parthenôn*, or *parthenaion*).[9] He began his ascetic discipline by apprenticing himself to an older hermit (also called an anchorite),[10] and spent about fifteen years living in the loose community of hermits. At that point he sought greater solitude and moved further into the desert east of the Nile, to live a solitary life of dedication in caves and among tombs. His was a simple subsistence lifestyle, with a few meals consisting of bread, salt and water, and a regime of frequent fasting to discipline his body against temptation and demonic attack.[11] Throughout this time Anthony experienced many encounters with demonic forces; one of these attacks is reported by Athanasius:

> The demons came inside, taking the shape of wild beasts and reptiles in a nightmare. Suddenly the place was filled with the illusory shapes of lions and bears and leopards and bulls and male and female serpents and wolves; and each one came toward him

---

6. L. A. Thompson, "Christianity in Egypt before the Arab Conquest," *Tarikh* 2, no. 1 (1967): 8.

7. See Frend, *Rise of Christianity*, 422 on the papyrus fragments revealing questions put to an oracle by the peasant-farmers of the area: "Shall I flee?"; "When shall my flight end?"; "Am I to become a beggar?"

8. Latourette, *First Five Centuries*, 225–226.

9. Frend, *Rise of Christianity*, 423 and 574–576.

10. The term "ascetic" is based on the Greek *askein*, to train, as for athletic contests; the term "hermit" comes from the Greek *erêmos*, alone, or deserted, while "anchorite" comes from Greek *anachorein*, to retire, or retreat.

11. Pelikan, *Emergence of the Catholic Tradition*, 135–137.

with a loud roar and hissing, according to its kind. The roaring lions wanted to leap upon him; the bull acted as though it would gore him; the snake struck, but did not reach him; and the wolf stalked towards him.

Anthony responded by mocking them:

> If you had any power over me, just one of you would be enough against me, but because the Lord has destroyed your power, you attempt to terrify me with a mob. But you show your weakness because you imitate the forms of animals . . . If you are able and have authority over me, don't stop, but attack right now. If you are not able, why do you bother me in vain? For our seal and purity and wall of protection is our faith in our Lord Jesus.[12]

Anthony's solitude was also disturbed by a stream of human visitors, especially the sick and troubled who came for advice and healing. His response to such attention was to keep retreating further into the desert; but people still came. Finally he withdrew into an abandoned fort in Pispir, where he remained alone and unseen for some twenty years, until the "great persecution" under Emperor Diocletian (303).[13] Eventually he gathered a number of ascetic disciples about him, younger monks who wanted to learn the discipline of fasting, prayer and contemplation. With these he made an arrangement to live in a loose-knit community. His followers kept to their own cells, but they also enjoyed a degree of fellowship in a common life (*coenobium*). Anthony took on the role of teacher, mentoring ascetic discipline for them. Such a grouping of monks who are essentially hermits, yet joined in semi-monastic fellowship, has come to be called a *laura* (or *lavra*).[14] During the illness of the last years of his life Anthony did allow two monks to attend to him.

The accomplishments of Anthony were popularized in the biographical account of Athanasius (ca. 295–373, bishop of Alexandria from 328), who describes Anthony's visit to Alexandria during the worst of the Diocletian persecution. Although prepared to suffer martyrdom, Anthony was not chosen for that. Instead, he encouraged others. During the Arian controversy, which came to a head soon after Christianity was legalized in 313, he came to Alexandria once more to address false rumours that he, Anthony, favoured

---

12. Athanasius, *Coptic Life of Anthony*, 42.
13. Latourette, *First Five Centuries*, 226.
14. The Greek term *laura* originally meant an alley, or narrow lane in a city; it came to represent a monastery consisting of groups of caves or cells for hermits, united through a common church or refectory; see Latourette, *First Five Centuries*, 226.

the Arian interpretation of the life of Jesus; he responded by denouncing the role of (Greek) philosophy as the source of all heresy. Athanasius became acquainted with him at this time, and relates how Anthony, himself unlearned and ignorant of Greek literature, spoke with great conviction and wisdom to oppose the Arian position.[15] At his death Anthony left his cloak to Athanasius, though he gave instructions that his burial place be kept secret, for he did not wish it to become a cult centre.

Figure 3.1. Church of the Cross and Resurrection at the Monastery of St Anthony.
This church belongs to one of the world's oldest monasteries (at Coma, Egypt, about 200 miles southeast of Cairo). Established by followers of Anthony, it was prominent among contemporary monasteries and the source of numerous patriarchs of the Coptic Orthodox Church.
Photo "Monastery of Saint Anthony, Egypt" by Berthold Werner / CC BY-SA 3.0.

---

15. See Athanasius's *Life of Anthony*, 72, 74 and 77. According to Chadwick (*Early Church*, 179), Athanasius was motivated to write the *Life* to show that Anthony subscribed to orthodox views; in spite of a reputation for intense ascetic practice, Anthony respected the church, its liturgy and its sacraments.

Athanasius's account of the ascetic lifestyle of Anthony was highly instrumental in popularizing the monastic life for Christians in Egypt.[16] We know that Anthony's story could have been multiplied many times, for both men and women. We have accounts of two other outstanding ascetics, Amun and Macarios, who established similar monastic communities in the desert west of the Nile.[17] Amun had been married, but he finally separated from his wife of many years through mutual agreement (in 325); at that time his wife established a convent for women.[18] The monastery established by Amun grew in just a few years to include some five thousand monks. Indeed, for this period there are reports of thousands of "Desert Fathers" and "Desert Mothers" living as hermits far from civilization, seeking retreat from the dangers of "worldly" life in cities and villages. They kept themselves alive by simple enterprise, planting vegetables or weaving baskets.

Much time was spent in prayer, memorization of Scripture and recitation of the Psalms. Ascetics focused on self-denial, abstaining from unnecessary foods like meat or wine and from ordinary comforts, especially those of marriage. They held a minimum of possessions, just one or two pieces of clothing and a mat to sleep on. For these achievements they were admired by others who would come to them, seeking their wisdom on a range of issues from politics and war to personal conflict. Written records collecting the proverbial wisdom of these early Desert Fathers have survived as *Desert Sayings of the Fathers* (*Apophthegmata Patrum*).[19] Among these ascetics we find no emphasis at all on literacy or the use of books.[20] Nor were their acts of ascetic abstinence constrained by normal social conventions; the zeal and devotion of the desert

---

16. Athanasius's account had a remarkable influence, as in the story of Augustine's conversion. Augustine was moved by the account of Ponticianus, an imperial officer who happened upon a small Christian ascetic community and found a copy of *Life of Anthony*. Upon hearing the story, he immediately joined the community. Ponticianus's example led Augustine to the critical moment of his life-changing breakdown in the garden (*Confessions*, 8.5); see below §B.1, and ch. 12, §D.3.

17. Thompson, "Christianity in Egypt," 8–9.

18. Frend, *Rise of Christianity*, 576.

19. These *Sayings of the Fathers* from fourth- and fifth-century Egyptian monks were highly appreciated by western monastics; for excerpts from the *Apophthegmata Patrum*, see Stevenson, *Creeds, Councils and Controversies*, 197–199.

20. On Anthony's disparaging of Greek culture and philosophy, see also Frend, *Rise of Christianity*, 423.

monks did make them prone to a certain fanaticism and extremism in acts of self-denial.[21]

Such monasticism represents a lay movement for the most part. Very few monks were ordained as priests and thereby incorporated into the regular structures of the church. Sometimes churches were built near dwellings of the hermits, who then gathered there for services on Saturdays or Sundays. But many monks went for long periods without participating in the eucharistic liturgy. The independence of their ascetic practice inevitably led to tension and conflict with priests and bishops of nearby cities.[22] Widespread appreciation of hermits as "holy men" could be taken to imply that the regular clergy or church members were somehow inferior in rank, less worthy. And social separation of the monks could lead to weakening of the "ordinary" congregation, which was left with fewer active participants to help care for the sick, prisoners, orphans and widows. In the early years of the ascetic movement, bishops typically regarded ascetic exploits with distrust, as overly separatist or individualistic.[23]

A.2. Cenobitic Monastic Organization: Pachomius (ca. 290–346)

"Monasticism" as such refers to the practice of ascetic discipline with a *solitary* focus; the term *cenobitic* (based on the Latin *coenobium*) refers to monastic discipline in a communal context.[24] Drawbacks of the solitary life, even within a loose-knit community like the *laura*, led another Copt named Pachomius (Pakhôm) to organize hermits into a more closely-knit community regulated by strict rules and discipline. Pachomius is recognized for his initiative in establishing cenobitic monastic life.

Pachomius was born in Upper Egypt near the Thebaid; he became a Christian while serving in the Roman army (at about the age of 20). Moved by the love and companionship of Christians, he decided to become a hermit when discharged from the army. He withdrew to the desert and submitted to the discipline of Palaemon, an older hermit. But he preferred to practice

---

21. Feats of asceticism were recorded by Palladius (ca. 367–430); he speaks of the monk Macarius staying awake for twenty consecutive days, and standing upright throughout the entire Lenten period (see Frend, *Rise of Christianity*, 576). On Macarius, see also Stevenson, *Creeds, Councils and Controversies*, 196–197.

22. Frend (*Rise of Christianity*, 576, 579) recognizes some monastic groups who did submit to episcopal authority.

23. Chadwick, *Early Church*, 176–177.

24. The term "monasticism" is based on the Greek *monos*, meaning "alone"; the English term *cenobitic* (*coenobium* in Latin), is based on the Greek *koinos bios*, meaning a "common life." See also Frend, *Rise of Christianity*, 576–577; and Latourette, *First Five Centuries*, 227–228.

asceticism in community with others. When his brother joined him, they decided to establish a communal monastery on the east bank of the Nile at Tabennesi.[25] They built an enclosure and recruited members to join them in a life of work and prayer, contemplation and mutual support. For this form of monasticism they used the organizational model with which they were familiar, that of Roman military life.

Through Jerome's Latin translation of the *Rule of the Holy Pachomius* we have considerable information about this establishment. The monastic enclosure had a single entrance. It contained a number of buildings: a church, a bakery, library, dining hall, workshops, store houses and living quarters for members of the various occupations. Each cell was occupied by at least two monks. Members were asked to renounce personal property and to promise obedience to their superiors in ascetic practice; full membership came after a trial period of three years.[26] Dress was very simple. Chastity and poverty were basic principles. If discipline was strict, extremism in devotional practice was discouraged.

Each monastery held about three hundred monks. Life within the monastery was strictly organized with a regimen like that of military service. The daytime hours of the monks were regulated, with specific hours for activities like eating, sleeping, work and worship. Monks were to work with their hands to support the community, so that the monastery could be self-sufficient through industry and agriculture. Major tasks, from hospitality to baking or gate-keeping, were distributed among the monks; each was expected to take up a line of work, whether as carpenter, smith, tailor, shoemaker, weaver, scribe, maker of books or agricultural labourer. Food was simple; the diet did not include meat. Items produced by the community were sold in local markets, and proceeds given as alms for the poor or for needy travellers.[27]

All members participated in obligatory prayer and recitation of Scripture. Every morning and evening the entire community gathered for Scripture reading, song and prayer. Literacy would certainly have a greater value for such a community, in comparison with the monastic model pursued by Anthony. Literate monks were expected to teach the illiterate. These monastic groups were known for their interpretation of the Scriptures; they were also responsible for writing and translating Christian literature into the Coptic language.[28]

---

25. See Stevenson, *Creeds, Councils and Controversies*, 190.
26. Latourette, *First Five Centuries*, 227.
27. Thompson, "Christianity in Egypt," 9–10.
28. Thompson, 10.

At first these groups experienced challenges in finding the appropriate level of ascetic rigour. If the regime was too strict and demanding, discipline became a problem. Pachomius set a good example by taking on lowly jobs himself. Final authority within the monastery was assigned to the abbot, or to the *archimandrite* for a group of monasteries;[29] monks vowed obedience to him and to his successors as these were chosen before his death. Monks rarely took on any regular ecclesiastical offices, though they might join the services at a nearby church or have a priest administer communion in their own church. From the perspective of the church, such disciplined communal monastic life was a positive move in restraining the irresponsible excesses to which solitary asceticism was prone.

The pattern set by Pachomius and his community was soon copied by others, and nine other communities were established, each with several hundred monks. Pachomius's *Rule* influenced ascetic patterns adopted by Cappadocian Basil, by Cassian and Benedict of Nursia. When Jerome visited the region (ca. AD 390), he found an assembly of some fifty thousand monks coming together to celebrate Easter.[30] Pachomius's sister Mary had also established a communal monastery (or convent) for women who joined the movement. Its members, the nuns, used an organization similar to that of the men. The nunnery was also under the supervision of the *archimandrite*, or superior-general of the community, but provisions were made to keep a strict separation between men and women; indeed, articulation of fear of the opposite sex could get a little excessive.[31] Nevertheless, it is important to remember that the *Desert Fathers* had an important complement in the *Desert Mothers*.

Monasticism remains an important aspect of the Coptic church, and some scholars regard this as the distinctive Coptic contribution to world Christianity. Monks still live in desolate parts of Egypt and survive by receiving alms. And they still have an influential role in selecting the patriarch (or pope) of the Coptic church. The patriarch, given the title *Qodsak* (Your Holiness), is appointed through the casting of lots by nine monks of the Convent of St Antonius.

---

29. The title "abbot" is based on the Aramaic *abba*, "father," as the supervisor of a monastery. "Archimandrite" is based on the Greek *archimandritēs*, literally, "leader of the sheepfold" (*mandra* represents an enclosure, or monastery). In Eastern Orthodox Church context the archimandrite was the senior abbot, typically appointed by the bishop to supervise other abbots.

30. For Jerome's description of life in the monastery (from the preface to his translation of the *Rule* of Pachomius), see Stevenson, *Creeds, Councils and Controversies*, 192–194; also Frend, *Rise of Christianity*, 577.

31. Latourette, *First Five Centuries*, 228.

A.3. Monasticism in Ethiopia

Christianity in Ethiopia would hardly have prospered without the monks. Some of these monks came from Egypt. Others, like Libanos, who was of noble birth, came from Rome. He had already given up his wealth and his wife to take up a monastic life in Egypt, but in his travels he came to Ethiopia and settled in Bakla. Libanos is noted for his work on the translation of the Gospel of Matthew into Geʾez, the Ethiopian branch of an ancient Semitic language, related to Amharic. He is also known for spreading the gospel message to Seraye and beyond, making converts and building churches. Yohani, another Egyptian monk who worked in Ethiopia, arrived with a group of monks and settled in Bogos. Yohani is credited with establishing the famous convent of Debre Syna.

Aside from these noteworthy monks, many hermits, monks, nuns and priests arrived in Ethiopia in AD 502. Drawn from different parts of the Byzantine Empire, all were trained in Egypt. Nine of them are significant for their piety and their role in the expansion of Christianity in Ethiopia: Liqanos, Yimata, Tsihma, Gubba, Pantalewon, Aregawi, Alef, Aftsie and Gerima.

Figure 3.2. The nine saints of Ethiopia. This portrayal is found at the Abba Pentalewon Monastery near Aksum (Tigray Region, Ethiopia). Photo "Nine Saints" by Ondřej Žváček / CC BY-SA 3.0.

For their valuable contribution to the Ethiopian church they were designated as "saints" and given the title *Abba*. These men have been recognized for their role in transforming Ethiopia from paganism to become one of the strongest centres of early Christianity. They took over pagan temples and converted these into churches; Abba Aftsie is noted for turning the ancient temple at Yeha into a church.[32]

These nine saints settled in various locations and built monasteries, each with the disciples they had acquired; most famous is Debre Damo, established by Aregawi. These monasteries, some with churches attached, became a distinctive mark of Ethiopian Christianity. As such they held a significant role in education, religion and politics, and functioned as an important source of wise counsel for the kings of Ethiopia. In fact, when King Caleb abdicated his throne, he enrolled as a monk at the monastery founded by Abba Pantalewon near Aksum. The monasteries had a critical role in translating the Scriptures and in liturgy; the great Ethiopian musician Yared was an important beneficiary of monastic education. When substantial tracts of land were donated to monasteries by Ethiopian rulers, these establishments also became important centres for agriculture.

A.4. Syrian Monasticism: Symeon the Stylite (ca. 390–459)

We know less about the origins of early Syrian and Mesopotamian monasticism compared with that of Egypt, but it is clear that the monastic model spread quickly throughout the Christian world from its base in Egypt. Ascetic practice in Syria is mostly associated with the feats and regimes of individual anchorites. This may be a reflection of the Palestinian tradition of the solitary prophet, using a wilderness context to give authority to his preaching.[33] Church historians like the fifth-century Sozomen have provided us with accounts of some rather bizarre kinds of restraint which the monks imposed on themselves.[34] We know of monks who mortified their bodies with the use of heavy iron collars on their necks, or chains around their body. Others fasted for days on end; the *Boskoi* tried to live just on grass.[35]

The outstanding mid-fourth-century teacher of Syrian ascetics, Ephraem (d. 373), is known for the beauty of his Syrian Christian poetry; he was a native of Nisibis, but moved to Edessa when this city was taken by the Persians (365).[36] Here he was visited by Basil of Caesarea, who admired him and his

---

32. Tafla, "Establishment of the Ethiopian Church," 32–34.
33. Frend, *Rise of Christianity*, 567.
34. The church historian Sozomen (d. ca. 450) speaks of the Syrian Aones introducing the practice of the anchorites in Syria, just as Anthony had introduced this in Egypt; see his *Ecclesiastical History* 6.33. On Sozomen, see also appendix II, §C.
35. See Frend, *Rise of Christianity*, 578.
36. See Stevenson, *Creeds, Councils and Controversies*, 88–89.

fellow monks for their hard work, self-control and life of prayer.³⁷ But most well known for excessive austerity is Symeon (or Simeon) the Stylite, who lived on top of a column for some thirty-six years, chained there with a leg iron.

Figure 3.3. Symeon the Stylite. A 16th-century Polish icon.
Photo taken in the Historical Museum in Sanok, Poland by Przykuta. Public Domain.

His own explanation was that it kept him from wandering, while it also kept his mind fixed on the heavens above.³⁸ Symeon's example won admiration and respect. As with Anthony, many came to visit the saintly monk, seeking his advice on all kinds of questions, including the thorny issues raised by the ecumenical councils of Ephesus and Chalcedon (AD 431 and 451, respectively).³⁹

---

37. J. Foster, *First Advance*, 152–153.

38. For this account, Frend (*Rise of Christianity*, 578) cites the fifth-century church historian Theodoret's *History of the Monks*. On Theodoret, see also appendix II, §D.

39. Chadwick, *Early Church*, 180. To explain the attraction, Peter Brown developed the conception of the holy man as a new type of "patron" for late ancient society in transition and in a crisis of leadership; see Brown, *Society and the Holy in Late Antiquity*, and Vallée, *Shaping of Christianity*, 135–136.

The Syriac churches continued to foster solitary "stylites" or "pillar saints," at least until the end of the eighth century. Following the model of Symeon, we note other "holy men" like Daniel (AD 409–493), who lived on top of a pillar in Constantinople for thirty-three years; he was visited by officials, priests, patriarchs and even emperors seeking advice on matters of state.[40] We also know of the late sixth-century hermit, Theodore of Sykeon (born in Galatia, Asia Minor), who followed a similarly stringent ascetic regime. After some time travelling to Jerusalem and Palestine, he returned home to enclose himself in a small cage suspended from a rocky cliff, fasting and singing psalms. Once again, many were attracted to his model of dedication and devotion; he became famous for miracles of healing and exorcism, for ending a plague, and for moral and spiritual advice.[41] Such extreme ascetics were awarded the title "athlete for God." Monks of Syriac Christianity only began to establish communities living together under a monastic rule in the sixth century, with Abraham of Kashkar (Mesopotamia) (502–596).[42]

These Syrian monks from Edessa and Persia had a very important role in the eastward expansion of Christianity, carrying the faith all the way to India and China. For this work the monks used the Syriac language and Christian literature developed in Edessa. In the context of the Roman Empire the Latin language, together with Greek (and Aramaic), would dominate theological discussion after the fourth century, but in the third and fourth centuries Syriac represented a significant third international language for the church.

It is quite possible that Muhammad became familiar with the practices of these Syrian hermits from the time of his trade expeditions in the region. It is clear that he began to implement aspects of such a lifestyle on his annual retreats to the mountains. Indeed, he received his first revelation at night on one such retreat on Mount Hira. A strong Islamic tradition speaks of this as the "night of destiny."[43] Aspects of the type of rigorous self-restraint exercised by Muhammad may be understood in terms of practices which were not unusual for that time, as we know from the accounts of the Syrian hermits.[44]

---

40. Latourette, *First Five Centuries*, 298.
41. Latourette, 298.
42. J. Foster, *First Advance*, 153–154.
43. Kenny, *Early Islam*, 16, 17. On the Christian context of Muhammad's world, see further Jenkins, *Lost History of Christianity*, 187–189.
44. Kenny, 19.

B. Spread of the Monastic Ideal
B.1. Athanasius and Basil of Caesarea

As bishop of Alexandria, Athanasius knew and visited Pachomius, but we have noted his biographical *Life of Anthony* as particularly important for the spread of the ascetic ideal beyond Egypt. Moreover, Athanasius used the various periods when he was exiled from Egypt to share his own appreciation of Egyptian asceticism with Christians in other areas, especially in the western empire. Also important were Jerome's Latin translations of the *Rule* for the Pachomian monastery.[45] Jerome's colleague Rufinus provided further accounts (in Latin) of the Desert Fathers of Egypt.[46] These writings were critical to the spread of the monastic ideal to Italy, and from there to France, Spain and North Africa. From Augustine's *Confessions* we know how he, for one, was deeply moved by Athanasius's *Life of Anthony* (*Conf.* 8.6.14–15). After his conversion and return to North Africa (386–387), Augustine settled with friends on the family estate, establishing a celibate community based on the household model.[47]

In Asia Minor, Basil of Cappadocian Caesarea was deeply influenced by the monastic ideal; after his conversion he travelled to Egypt to observe the Pachomian communities in action (358).[48] Upon his return to the family estate he gathered a few friends and colleagues, and settled on a remote corner of the property. In the years before being called to serve as bishop, he devoted his time to this community, reading Scripture and devotional literature; in this context he began collecting well-loved readings, especially from the work of Origen, in the *Philokalia*.

The monastic establishments founded by Basil focused on deeds of mercy in service to the community, with special attention to the needy, the sick, orphans and outcasts (as was noted in the introduction to this chapter on the work of his sister Macrina). New members of the community were invited for an initial period of trial (or "novitiate"), and were sworn to obedience to their superiors. Basil was himself well-educated, and the study of Scripture was

---

45. On Jerome's own ascetic practice, see Frend, *Rise of Christianity*, 716; also Latourette, *First Five Centuries*, 232–234. On the ongoing influence of Pachomius, see Frend, *Rise of Christianity*, 631.

46. See Chadwick, *Early Church*, 182.

47. On the role of Anthony's *Life* in Augustine's conversion, see also above, note 16; for further discussion of Augustine's contribution, see ch. 12, §D.3.

48. On the contribution of Basil and his Cappadocian colleagues to fourth-century Christianity, see ch. 10, §B.4 and ch. 12, §B.

given prominence in these monasteries; his monastic regime valued intellectual efforts as much as any other kind of work. For the life of the community Basil sought a balance of work, study and prayer. When young boys were admitted to be educated they were housed in an establishment separate from the monks. Basil's *Rule* is also unique in its insistence on respect for the authority of the local bishop; his model is noted for integrating the monastic movement within the normal life of the church.[49]

By the end of the fifth-century monasticism had become an accepted part of Christianity; in both the east and west the bishops would typically be drawn from the monasteries.[50] To this day, the pattern established by Basil remains the basis for monastic life in the Eastern Orthodox church. The eighth-century revival of Byzantine monasticism under Theodore the Studite was based on the writings of Basil.[51] And Basil's influence would be marked in the west in the writings of the fifth-century Cassian and sixth-century Benedict of Nursia.[52]

B.2. Monasticism and Women

Although much of the literature on the spread of monasticism has focused on the role of men, we have considerable information on women who were prominent in the movement. Even from New Testament accounts we know of women, like the widow Anna who was always seen in the temple, worshipping, fasting and praying (Luke 2:36–38).[53] It is quite possible that mention of special honour for *widows* in the New Testament provides an early reference to those later renowned in the congregations as "virgins."[54] Thus it would appear that later feminine ascetic and monastic developments can be traced to earliest Christianity. In fact it may be traced back further to Judaism of the Hellenistic

---

49. Chadwick, *Early Church*, 178–179.

50. Latourette (*First Five Centuries*, 222) notes that the very able sixth-century Pope Gregory I was called to this position from the monastery; on this pope, see further below, §C.7.

51. On the reform of monastic life by Theodore the Studite, at the time of the iconoclast controversies (on which see ch. 11, §B.3), see Latourette, *First Five Centuries*, 294–295.

52. Latourette, 230.

53. On Tabitha (or Dorcas), see Acts 9:36; and on proper recognition for widows, 1 Tim 5:3–5 and 9–10. These passages demonstrate that early asceticism, certainly for women, was typically practiced within the household setting.

54. Laurie Guy (*Introducing Early Christianity*, 183–184) quotes the reference (in Ignatius' letter to Polycarp 5.2, and the letter to Smyrna 12.2), designating "virgins" who are also called "widows."

period, since we know of the *Therapeutae*[55] as ascetic women associated with the Essenes, and perhaps also with the Qumran community.[56] The apostle Paul gave significant encouragement to those women who chose to remain virgins:

> Now about virgins . . . Because of the present crisis I think that it is good for you to remain as you are. . . . An unmarried woman or virgin is concerned about the Lord's affairs. Her aim is to be devoted to the Lord in both body and spirit. (1 Cor 7:25, 34)

We also know of women who pioneered ascetic communities before the well-known developments of the fourth century. Before Anthony himself withdrew as a solitary anchorite, we know that he made provision for his sister, placing her in a house of virgins; and the account appears to take the existence of such homes for granted.[57] A similar account is given for the wife of Amun, and for Pachomius's sister who established a feminine counterpart of the monastery established by her brother.

From the fourth century we know of a number of Roman women of noble birth who were encouraged by Jerome to take up an ascetic lifestyle: Albina and her daughter Marcella,[58] Marcellina (sister of Bishop Ambrose), the two Paulas, Blaesilla, Lea, Demetrias, Poimenia, Melania the Elder, Melania the Younger and Eustochium, to name a few.[59] Some of these ladies were already widows, and some virgins, while others were still deeply involved in the demands of life of the upper classes of Roman society. Jerome encouraged them to apply

---

55. Philo's *The Contemplative Life* describes the ascetic community of *Therapeutae* (or "healers") near Lake Mareotis (lower Egypt). Its members, both men and women, renounced property and family life; they were also known for severe fasting (Ferguson, *Backgrounds*, 530–531). According to the church historian Eusebius of Caesarea, who himself regarded asceticism as the "true philosophical life" and the goal of authentic Christianity, the Therapeutae were actually Christian (*HE* 2.17).

56. Although Philo of Alexandria spoke of Essenes forbidding marriage, Josephus knew of Essenes who allowed marriage; and Ferguson recognizes that the Qumran scrolls did not forbid marriage (*Backgrounds*, 523). Women's bones have been discovered at Qumran (although it is possible that these were introduced from more recent burials).

57. Athanasius calls this residence a *parthenôn*, namely, a house of virgins; see his *Life of Anthony*, 3.

58. Marcella was an important sponsor of asceticism in Rome. When she died (AD 410), Jerome wrote an account of her life (*Ep.* 127); for excerpts, see Stevenson, *Creeds, Councils and Controversies*, 229–232.

59. Guy (*Introducing Early Christianity*, 138–140 and 183–185) refers to the outstanding work of Elizabeth Clark on these Roman women of the upper classes (see Clark, *Jerome, Chrysostom and Friends*; *The Life of Melania the Younger*; and *Ascetic Piety and Women's Faith*); even as they renounced marriage, these aristocratic women probably maintained servants (women) to attend to their needs. For current scholarly discussion of these women, see appendix I, §D; see further, Frend, *Rise of Christianity*, 717–718.

ascetic Christian principles to their own particular circumstances. Paula (d. 404) and her daughters Eustochium and Blaesilla accompanied Jerome in his travels to Palestine and set up a convent in Bethlehem, alongside Jerome's own monastic establishment. Under Jerome's tutelage these women learned both Hebrew and Greek, and were able to help him in the work of translation.[60]

In Antioch we know of Olympias as the confidante of John Chrysostom. In Cappadocia, Macrina, the elder sister of Basil and Gregory of Nyssa, was instrumental in establishing a convent for women on the family estate, as an establishment parallel to that of Basil for men.[61] In fact, as noted above, Gregory's *Life of Macrina* clearly suggests that she encouraged Basil in the kind of monasticism adopted on the estate. And she provided exemplary leadership for the community of women in caring for orphans, the sick and the poor. Within the Eastern Orthodox tradition Macrina is honoured as the founder of female monastic life.

Monasticism within the context of the Syriac churches is also noted for spiritual mothers, *ammas*, alongside the "fathers," although their accomplishments were rarely included in the historical records.[62] In this connection it is important to recognize that such monastic practices were even more countercultural for women than they were for men, since women were expected to marry and bear children.[63] But their commitment to virginity was respected in the Christian communities. They were regarded as a "third sex," and as "manly" women; they were thought to "transcend the weakness of their sex," and they certainly exceeded traditional (stereotypical, or misogynistic) expectations of the capabilities of women. Even if these terms do not appear particularly complimentary to modern ears, it is clear that the women were respected as such.[64]

---

60. Frend, *Rise of Christianity*, 717. On these ascetic women, see also Vallée, *Shaping of Christianity*, 191.

61. On her accomplishments, celebrated in Gregory of Nyssa's two essays in her honour, *The Life of the Holy Macrina*, and *On the Soul and the Resurrection*, see Helleman, *Feminine Personification*, 59–93.

62. See Jenkins, *Lost History of Christianity*, 73–74.

63. Guy, *Introducing Early Christianity*, 184–185. We note in passing that contemporary analysis regards these practices as a welcome "freedom" for women, and an escape from oppressive social constraints accompanying marriage, along with the dangers of pregnancy and childbirth; see Burrus, *Chastity as Autonomy*.

64. Guy, *Introducing Early Christianity*, 185–186.

C. Monasticism in the West

C.1. Martin of Tours (ca. 325–400)

Martin was serving in the Roman army in Northern Gaul one cold day when he decided to share his coat with a beggar. That night he had a dream in which he recognized Christ clothed with the coat he had given away.

Figure 3.4. St Martin shares his cloak with a beggar. As a soldier in Gaul (France), Martin met a beggar outside the city walls and cut up his own cloak to keep the man warm. A dream of Jesus accepting this act of kindness led him to request baptism. This 14th-century fresco was painted by Simone Martini for the Chapel of St Martin in the Lower Church (San Francesco, Assisi). The Yorck Project. Public Domain.

The dream inspired him to resign from the army as soon as possible and seek baptism (ca. AD 360). For some time he joined himself to the well-known theologian Hilary (ca. 315–367, and bishop of Poitiers from ca. 350). Not long after this Martin determined to live as a hermit in Gaul, not far from Tours.[65]

There Martin attracted other monks, and organized them in a semi-monastic community.[66] When appointed Bishop of Tours, Martin continued to live the life of a hermit in a cell outside the city; other bishops expressed dismay at his appearance, but he continued to dress simply.[67] Aside from

---

65. Latourette, *First Five Centuries*, 230–231.

66. See the description of monastic life, from Sulpicius Severus's *Life of Martin* 10, in Stevenson, *Creeds, Councils and Controversies*, 183–184.

67. See Sulpicius Severus's *Life* (*Vita S. Martini*) 13.9.

responsibilities as bishop, Martin focused his attention on the pagan population of the area, destroying ancient shrines and replacing pagan worship patterns by organizing new believers into a parish system.

Martin's life and work, and especially the miracles attributed to him (recorded by Sulpicius Severus), soon became popular in the western provinces of the Roman Empire. This was certainly helpful in establishing a positive profile for monastic life in the region. As Frend has recognized, Martin's example served as an influential model for "an authentically Christian civilization in which mission, theological learning, dogmatic discussion, church building and the cult of saints and martyrs with their relics and legends all had a place."[68]

C.2. Jerome (ca. 342–420)

In his support of monasticism Jerome was totally different from Martin. Not only was Jerome well-educated; he was probably the most learned scholar of his time, matching in Latin the erudition of Origen in Greek.[69] After baptism in his mid-twenties (369), he was deeply attracted to the ascetic life. After spending some time in Rome, where a monastic calling was still regarded with some suspicion, and even seen as a possible cover for Manichean thought, Jerome travelled to Antioch to observe Syrian ascetic practice.[70] Disappointed in what he found, Jerome was ordained a priest by the rigorous Nicene Evagrius,[71] after which he travelled through Palestine to Constantinople, where he became a friend of Gregory of Nazianzus.[72] Once more back in Rome (382–385), Jerome became secretary to Pope Damasus,[73] who encouraged him to provide a new translation of the Scriptures in Latin.

In Rome Jerome assumed an austere lifestyle and dressed like a hermit. Yet, as noted above, he was invited to give spiritual counsel to women of the highest social classes (including the aristocratic Aemilii), advising them in their

---

68. Frend, *Rise of Christianity*, 709. Frend also notes how the influence of Martin extended to Roman Britain through his disciple Ninian, whose successful mission work was marked by combining episcopacy with asceticism. Ninian's life and accomplishments were noted by the English historian Bede (d. 732), whose *Ecclesiastical History* 3.4 is quoted in Stevenson, *Creeds, Councils and Controversies*, 433–434.

69. On Jerome, see also ch. 12, §D.2.

70. Frend, *Rise of Christianity*, 716.

71. On Jerome's desert experience (AD 374–378), see Stevenson, *Creeds, Councils and Controversies*, 207–208.

72. Latourette, *First Five Centuries*, 232.

73. Damasus was pope from AD 366–384.

attraction to asceticism.[74] He even taught some women the ancient languages, Greek and Hebrew, so they could help him in the work of translation.[75] When Pope Damasus died, Jerome left for Palestine and eventually settled in Bethlehem, where he built a monastery. Paula followed some time later and established a convent, as well as a hospice for pilgrims. Jerome would spend the last thirty-four years of his life here, focused on the work of a new Latin translation of the Bible.

Jerome's unrelenting advocacy of monastic life provided a strong stimulus for the movement in the West.[76] Especially important were his arguments in support of celibacy against Helvidius (384/385), who denied Mary's perpetual virginity, arguing that she led a normal married life after the birth of Jesus. His tract *Against Jovinian* was similarly influential in establishing asceticism as the norm for Christian life. A former monk, Jovinian had argued that after baptism ascetic practice was not necessary, for human sin would be washed away upon true repentance. Jerome argued that if Jovinian was right one could sin with abandon, confident that repentance would bring restoration of divine favour.[77]

C.3. John Cassian (ca. 360–435)

Cassian's origins were Scythian, but his ascetic training took him to Palestine (ca. 392) and Egypt. He also travelled to Constantinople, where he was ordained a deacon by Chrysostom (399). When Chrysostom was exiled from that city, Cassian moved to Rome (404). He finally settled in Marseilles, southern Gaul (ca. 415), where he was ordained presbyter; here he established monastic communities for men and women on the eastern model.[78]

In a number of writings Cassian detailed the life of these communities, advising a monastic practice marked by moderation. A simple diet would consist of bread and vegetables; sleep could be restricted to three or four hours. Work on copying manuscripts was as important as agricultural work. In the *Institutes* (ca. 426), Cassian adapted the *Rule* of Pachomius to prescribe a degree of moderation in matters of habit and liturgical offices; his twenty-

---

74. See §B.2 above. For his advice to a virgin, see his *Ep.* 22, quoted in Stevenson, *Creeds, Councils and Controversies*, 214–216.

75. Frend, *Rise of Christianity*, 717.

76. An excerpt from Jerome's description of the monastic life (*Ep.* 22.34–35) is given in Stevenson, *Creeds, Councils and Controversies*, 192–194.

77. Frend, *Rise of Christianity*, 718.

78. On Cassian, see also C. Stewart, *Cassian the Monk* (New York: Oxford University Press, 1998).

four *Conferences* (ca. 429) feature well-known ascetics from Egypt in a number of discourses.[79] The pattern of common worship featured five daily "offices": *Laudes* at dawn, *Terce* (9 a.m.), *Sext* (noon), *None* (3 p.m.) and *Vespers* (at nightfall), with an added long vigil on Saturdays from Vespers to the crowing of the cock at dawn. The goal of monastic life was to defeat sin while working to ascend the ladder of prayer toward union with God.[80] Cassian's influence was established particularly through Benedict's adoption of his monastic rules; the Benedictine monks also adopted his *Conferences* as meal-time reading.

C.4. Patrick of Ireland (b. ca. 389)

Irish Christianity was also deeply influenced by monasticism as it was introduced by Patrick.[81] Such monastic practice had a missionary focus, and featured a blend of the ascetic patterns from both Anthony and Pachomius. Patrick was born of Christian parents in Roman Britain, but was captured by (Scottish) raiders from Ireland at the age of sixteen (ca. 405); enslaved, he tended flocks for about six years. Hardship strengthened his faith, and led him to develop a routine of prayer.[82] Eventually he broke free and made his way back to Britain, but he soon sensed a call to return to Ireland to establish Christianity there (ca. 432).

Patrick was not himself a monk, but a consecrated bishop; as such he would seek the conversion and baptism of the Irish, and ordain clergy for the growing church. Wanting to bring civilization to a barbarian people whose gods drove them to violence and destruction, he preached a gospel of love balanced with judgement. Under his leadership the traditional religion of the Druids was undermined, and strong foundations were laid for a growing Christian church.[83]

By the sixth century the church in Ireland was flourishing.

---

79. Chadwick, *Early Church*, 181–182.
80. Frend, *Rise of Christianity*, 720.
81. On the life and work of Patrick, see Frend, *Rise of Christianity*, 793–795; also Latourette, *First Five Centuries*, 101–102.
82. See Patrick's *Confession*, 16, quoted in Frend, *Rise of Christianity*, 793; also in Stevenson, *Creeds, Councils and Controversies*, 434–439.
83. Frend, *Rise of Christianity*, 794.

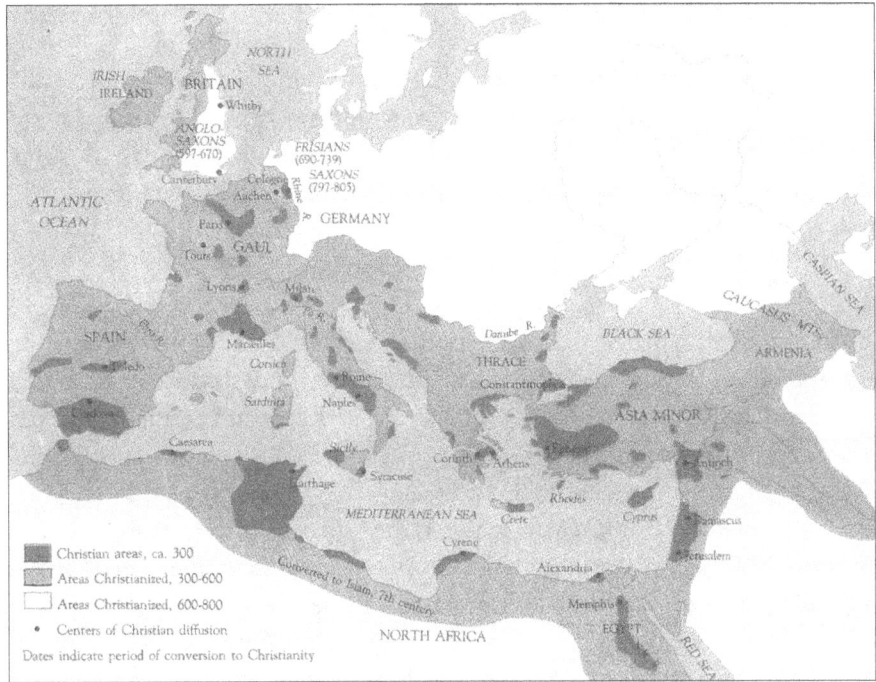

Map 3.1. Spread of Christianity AD 300–800.
Map by Agur / CC BY-SA 3.0.

For the most part, the island had been spared the violent invasions which troubled the rest of western Europe at the time. Monasticism was well-established. Many prominent Irish had adopted monastic Christianity, and monasteries were known as important centres of learning, focused on the Scriptures. In the chaotic and violent context of early medieval Europe, Irish monks were noted for excellence in education, maintaining strong levels of literacy.

Apart from routine duties in the monasteries and provision of social services, Irish monks were engaged in Bible translation, writing commentaries, preaching and teaching the Bible to those outside the monasteries. The monasteries became famous for beautifully copied and illuminated manuscripts of Latin Christian authors. Before the printing press, the Irish were also foremost in preserving knowledge from antiquity on topics such as architecture, philosophy, rhetoric and grammar, agriculture, and political thought; they were acclaimed for copying relevant books and accumulating these in their libraries.

From Ireland the monks travelled widely to evangelize northern England and Scotland. Particularly important in these efforts are Columba (521–597), who introduced the monastic tradition to Scotland, and Columbanus (540–615), who introduced the rigorous, austere Christianity of central Gaul to northern Italy. Within two hundred years after the death of Patrick (ca. 461), Irish monasticism had spread throughout England and western Europe.

C.5. Cassiodorus (ca. 485–582)

Born of a distinguished family in south-eastern Italy, and provided with a traditional education in rhetoric and philosophy, Cassiodorus assumed a number of significant legal and political roles in Italy from an early age, even attaining to the honour of becoming consul in 514. In these capacities he served the Ostrogoth rulers, and started his career by writing works of history, the *Chronicon* and *Gothic History*. When the Ostrogoths were overthrown by Justinian (538), Cassiodorus retired to his estates in southern Italy, and founded a double monastic establishment: one part for those following the solitary life of a hermit, and the other a house (named *Vivarium* [or *fishpond*]) for scriptural and theological studies. In addition, he built baths along the river bank on his estate as a refuge for the sick, the poor and travellers. Thus the monastery would provide both for those with a sense of social obligation and for those seeking solitary retirement in their quest for union with God. His aim was to establish a theological school to rival that of Alexandria or Syrian Nisibis.[84]

Cassiodorus was active in instructing the monks, but did not himself assume monastic life. His role was one of collecting manuscripts and writing commentaries on them. He also wrote a treatise *On the Soul* and a *Commentary on the Psalms*. The monastery followed the rule of Cassian, although it did not exclude the liberal arts for the study of Scripture; rather, in his *Introduction to Divine and Human Readings* (*Institutiones divinarum et humanarum lectionum*) Cassiodorus aligned himself with Augustine's work, *On Christian Teaching* (*De Doctrina Christiana*). In an age of violence and warfare, when such interests were diminishing, Cassiodorus's house of learning served as an important encouragement for scholarly work, especially translation, commentary, preservation and transmission of ancient literature. The centre was well-equipped with a library of traditional Greek and Latin authors, as well as Christian literature. These books were copied, and new books were written.[85]

---

84. Chadwick, *Early Church*, 251.
85. Latourette, *First Five Centuries*, 332.

C.6. Benedict of Nursia (ca. 480 – ca. 547)

Benedict of Nursia, a contemporary of Cassiodorus, came from a region to the northeast of Rome. Already in his teens he took on the life of a hermit; later the monks of a nearby monastery invited him to become their abbot. He was too strict for them, and soon returned to the solitary life of the hermit. Once more he became famous and attracted disciples who sought him out for training. Over the years he established twelve monasteries, each with twelve monks and a superior.

The monastery for which Benedict is famous, that on Monte Cassino between Rome and Naples, was established ca. 528. For this growing centre Benedict developed a *Rule* which came to have enormous significance for later monasticism in Europe. While Benedict incorporated elements of the *Rules* of Pachomius, Basil of Caesarea and John Cassian, he also used his own experience to develop an ascetic discipline for a cenobitic community well-suited to the local conditions of (southern) Europe. In comparison with others regimes, Frend has described it as "better-structured, more institutionalized and more humane."[86] Each monastery would be self-contained and self-supporting, and follow the pattern of a well-regulated spiritual life in which prayer, worship, manual work and study were balanced.

The various communities were independent of one another, and monks were not free to move about; they became members of a communal monastic "family," and membership was for life. Benedict's *Rule* gives clear directions for developing the spiritual life alongside daily routines of the monastery. His form of monastic organization reveals the genius of the Romans for administration. It was also based on the ideal community of the early Christians in Jerusalem who held their possessions in common; upon entry, the monks submitted to the superior and surrendered all private property.[87] Three vows (of chastity, poverty and obedience) formed the core ascetic commitment. The abbot governing the community had final authority, but was required to consult with the members in all-important matters.

The ascetic regime was not excessively severe. Life in the community was regulated by a schedule of work, sleep, meals and worship; the goal was for all monks to grow in humility, in love for God and for each other.[88] The same was

---

86. Frend, *Rise of Christianity*, 881.
87. See Latourette, *First Five Centuries*, 333–334.
88. For significant passages on the character of monks and abbots, the need for obedience and humility, the frequency of divine service and regulations on food, sleep, work and possessions, see Tierney, *The Middle Ages*, 74–82. On the *Benedictine Rule*, see also Latourette,

true of establishments for women (convents, or nunneries) on the Benedictine model. Unlike most monastic groups of the east, these monasteries would eventually be noted as centres of education; indeed, such monasteries would form the nucleus of the future universities of Europe.

The *Rule* established by Benedict (ca. AD 530) came to be copied in many other communities, especially in France and England. While public life remained disorderly and unpredictable, the Benedictine monasteries were centres of orderly, regulated life. The ideals for monastic life would not always be achieved, and the monastic movement certainly experienced periods of decline; but we also know of periods of revival, like the Cluny movement of the tenth century, bringing a return to basic rules and an austerity of discipline.[89] In later centuries, Cluny would motivate new monastic movements: the Cistercians, Franciscans, Dominicans and Jesuits.

C.7. Monastics as Missionaries

Even though monasteries were essentially centres of retreat, drawing citizens away from the normal patterns of society into a new form of fellowship, we have noted the significant role of the monks and monastic orders in the missionary work of western Christianity. Irish monks took an important initiative in bringing Christianity to western Europe. Pope Gregory the Great sent a group of forty Benedictine monks, led by Augustine of Canterbury, as missionaries to England (in 596).[90] And Boniface (675–754) spread Roman and Benedictine Christianity to Germany. The same can be said for the spread of Christianity in the East, to the Persian Empire and on to India and China, as well as for medieval Christianity in eastern Europe. In thirteenth-century Russia, at the time of the Mongol conquest, the monastic life attracted many. At that time the monks and hermits made their way into the forests of the far north, where they established monasteries which would become schools for Christianity and foster agricultural advance. Like their western counterparts, these monks were instrumental in clearing the land, building roads, and improving methods of cultivating the soil, while they were also teaching the faith and converting the indigenous population.[91]

First Five Centuries, 333–336.
    89. Latourette, *First Five Centuries*, 418–419.
    90. See also Chadwick, *Early Church*, 254.
    91. Latourette, *First Five Centuries*, 401 and 581–584.

Questions for Discussion and Review
Monasticism and Missions

1. What is the origin of monasticism? What motivated people to withdraw as hermits or in monastic communities?

2. Where did monasticism first begin?

3. What are the basic features of the life of the hermit in Egypt?

4. What kind of monastic organization is represented by the *Rule* of Pachomius? What was the function of the *Rule*?

5. What are the important differences between the Anthonian and Pachomian forms of monastic life?

6. Why was Symeon the Stylite respected in his time? Might you have consulted him on any question?

7. Explain why the role of Athanasius was crucial in the spread of monasticism.

8. How did Basil modify monasticism and its goals?

9. Why is it important to recognize the role of women in the monastic movement?

10. What significant contributions were made, respectively, by Martin of Tours, Jerome and Cassian, in developing monasticism for the western Roman Empire?

11. What is the significance of Irish monasticism for European Christianity?

12. If Cassiodorus was not himself a monk, why is his life important for the development of monasticism?

13. How did Benedict influence monasticism in the European context?

Further Reading

Athanasius. *The Life of St Anthony*. Translated by R. T. Meyer. New York: Newman Press, 1987.
———. *The Coptic Life of Anthony*. Translated by Tim Vivian. London: International Scholars Publications, 1995.
Brown, Peter. *The Cult of the Saints: Its Rise and Function in Latin Christianity*. Chicago: Chicago University Press, 1981.

———. *Society and the Holy in Late Antiquity*. Berkeley: University of California Press, 1982.

———. *The Body and Society: Men, Women and Sexual Renunciation in Early Christianity*. New York: Columbia University Press, 1988.

Chitty, D. J. *The Desert a City*. Crestwood, NJ: St Vladimir's Seminary Press, 1966.

Elm, Susan. *Virgins of God: The Making of Asceticism in Late Antiquity*. New York: Oxford University Press, 1994.

Jenkins, Philip. *The Lost History of Christianity: The Thousand-Year Golden Age of the Church in the Middle East, Africa and Asia*. Oxford: Lion, 2008.

Rousseau, Philip. *Ascetics, Authority and the Church in the Age of Jerome and Cassian*. Oxford: Oxford University Press, 1978.

———. *Pachomius: The Making of a Community in Fourth-Century Egypt*. Berkeley: University of California Press, 1985.

Schüssler Fiorenza, Elizabeth. *In Memory of Her: A Feminist Theological Reconstruction of Christian Origins*. New York: Crossroad, 1983.

Stevenson, J., ed. *Creeds, Councils and Controversies. Documents Illustrative of the History of the Church AD 337–461*. Revised by W. H. C. Frend. London: SPCK, 2012.

Stewart, C. *Cassian the Monk*. New York: Oxford University Press, 1998.

Thompson, L. A. "Christianity in Egypt before the Arab Conquest." *Tarikh* 2, no. 1 (1967): 4–15.

4

Persecution and Martyrdom

From Nero to Valerian (AD 64–260)

> Polycarp was brought before the Proconsul, who asked him if he were Polycarp? He said, "Yes." The Proconsul tried to persuade him to deny his faith, urging him, "Have respect for your old age," and similar words which they would use: "Swear by the genius of Caesar; change your mind; say, 'Away with the atheists!'" Then Polycarp looked solemnly at the crowd of lawless pagans gathered in the stadium, waved his hand at them, looked up to the heavens with a groan, and said, "Away with the atheists!" The Proconsul continued insisting, saying, "Swear, and I will release you; curse Christ." But Polycarp said, "Eighty-six years I have served him, and he has done me no wrong. How then can I curse my King who saved me?"
>
> "The Martyrdom of Polycarp," 9[1]

During the mid-second century the Christian community in Smyrna (modern Izmir) was challenged by accusations of undermining traditional worship and sacrifices to local deities. A number of Christians had already been arrested, some of them tortured with whips and others placed before wild beasts. They could have walked away unharmed if only they offered a pinch of incense and proclaimed Caesar as *Kurios* (Lord). Initially the congregation of Smyrna encouraged their elderly bishop Polycarp to hide; he was known

---

1. For this excerpt of the letter from the congregation in Smyrna to other Christian communities, sharing the death of Polycarp (dated to February of 156, or 155), see Stevenson, *New Eusebius*, 23–30.

Figure 4.1. The martyrdom of St Polycarp. This 6th-century mosaic of Polycarp holding the martyr's crown is part of the "Procession of the Holy Martyrs" in the Basilica of Sant' Apollinare Nuovo in Ravenna (Italy). The Yorck Project. Public Domain.

as an outstanding teacher, with Irenaeus among his disciples. They wanted to protect him as their leader. But eventually he was tracked down by officials, willingly gave himself up for arrest and was taken to the Proconsul for interrogation and punishment.

The letter quoted above explicitly mentions both Jews and Gentiles inciting the crowd to let wild animals loose on Polycarp. But the hunting season was already over, so the animals were not available. They asked instead that he be burned alive. In this way Polycarp received the "crown of immortality." When it was over, Christians were able to take away his bones to commemorate his martyrdom as a victory in the great contest. This is also why the church in Smyrna composed the letter to share with other Christian congregations how Polycarp was put to death, seeking to encourage those who would face a similar trial in the future. The letter gives the very first account, after the New Testament period, of martyrdom in the Christian congregations. It would become a model for a new genre of literature documenting Christian martyrdom.

Such letters typically included an eye-witness account of the pursuit, arrest, trial and execution, sometimes with vivid detail of cruelties inflicted. The letter on Polycarp's trial and death is particularly interesting for portraying him as a fearless defender of Christ, unflinching in a series of challenges to his Christian faith. It is also important for revealing underlying tensions around Christian profession of the Lordship of Jesus Christ as it came into conflict with the "Lordship" of the emperor. And it documents a popular conception of Christians as "atheist" because they would not support the gods considered essential to the well-being of the Empire.

A. Persecution of Christians

Early Christianity experienced persecution in more or less severe forms for a period of nearly three centuries, from the very earliest days until the important reversal of its legal position within the empire when Constantine sought to legitimize Christianity (AD 313). The present chapter will focus on the various ways that persecution shaped the early church, especially in her theology and understanding of the Christian life. In the crucible of suffering the church was sorely tested, but it was also moulded. And such suffering ultimately constituted a significant cause of growth. Tertullian's claim that, "The blood of the martyrs is the seed of the church," was certainly true of the first centuries.[2] The historical record of persecution clearly undermines allegations of Muslim scholars like Abd Al-Jabbar, alleging a first-century treaty between Romans and Christians, that they would adopt Roman gods in exchange for their freedom and protection in the empire.[3]

At the same time we note that scholarly assumptions on the issue of persecution have long attributed the cause of persecution to the Christians themselves, accusing them of an unhealthy attraction to martyrdom. For more than two centuries this approach has characterized discussion of persecution, particularly since the critical historical approach of the Enlightenment historian Edward Gibbon (1737–1794) in his work on the decline and fall of the Roman Empire.[4] The term "martyrdom" has its root in the Greek term *martus*, meaning a "witness." Recognition of that core meaning helps us to understand why early Christians might have held "a passionate attachment to martyrdom," to make a sacrifice in the defence of their faith.[5] Christians had before them the example of Jesus's own suffering; that account is prominent in each of the four gospels. If their Lord had suffered, should they expect anything less, as they followed

---

2. Tertullian, *Apology* 50.13. For the text see *ANF* 3.55; and Chadwick, *Early Church*, 29.

3. Stern, "Abd Al-Jabbar's Account of How Christ's Religion Was Falsified," 134–135 and 138.

4. For further discussion of Gibbon's work, see ch. 12, §A and §B below. A variant on Gibbon's thesis can be found in Perkins ("Apocryphal Acts of the Apostles," 211–230), discussing martyrdom and the second-century *Apocryphal Acts of the Apostles* (John, Peter, Andrew, Thomas). She suggests that those who accepted martyrdom positively thereby confirmed an antisocial worldview, rejecting traditional social relationships, as in the ascetic repudiation of marriage. And such an attitude, in turn, would fuel even more local persecution ("Apocryphal Acts," 211–212). Perkins cites literary evidence like Justin Martyr's citation of the angry husband seeking to arrest his wife after she converted and left him (216–219; the account is given in Justin's *Second Apology* 2; *ANF* 1.188–189). Guy recognizes such early Christian rejection of society for being evil and hostile, as motivated by their experience of public rejection of the church (*Introducing Early Christianity*, 76).

5. See Ferguson, "Aspects of the Early Christianity in North Africa," 25.

in his footsteps? Beyond suffering, they could already perceive the crown of new life, in resurrection with their Lord.[6] Even so, their own acceptance of martyrdom cannot possibly be the true cause of the suffering which Christians experienced at this time.

The onslaught on Christians and the specific reasons for these attacks varied significantly throughout these centuries and in the various regions affected. It is important to note that in the first two centuries accusations against Christians were typically a local matter, with charges on an individual basis, not as an identifiable group. So it is necessary to distinguish various types of persecution and the specific impact of martyrdom according to the periods: (1) early Christianity, when it was distinguishing itself from Judaism; (2) persecution in the Empire from Nero to Decius (AD 64–250); (3) the period in which churches and leaders were targeted, from Decius to Valerian; and (4) the "great persecution" under Diocletian and his successors, until Constantine put an end to it in AD 312/313. The present chapter will examine persecution in the first three periods; chapter 5 addresses the last and most severe period of persecution.

A.1. The New Testament Witness

In the book of Acts we read that Christians, when they were forbidden to preach in the name of Jesus, responded by claiming a prior obligation to obey God, rather than men (Acts 4:17). Severe persecution followed Stephen's defence of his understanding of Jesus (Acts 6–7). This caused a scattering of Christians from the centre in Jerusalem; such scattering in turn resulted in gospel preaching in Samaria, in Gaza (to an Ethiopian eunuch), and in Caesarea (to the Roman centurion). The church in Antioch also sent out its missionaries to go further abroad, to Cyprus and Asia Minor.

Saul, better known as Paul, had consented to the stoning of Stephen and the persecution that followed. After his conversion he would suffer serious persecution himself, especially on missionary journeys to Asia Minor, Macedonia and Greece. New Testament writings, like Hebrews, reflect on the reality of public abuse and oppression that included confiscation of property (Heb 10:33). Such persecution was initially motivated by Jews who opposed the message of Jesus as the long-awaited Messiah.[7] In the first years of Paul's missionary journeys we find problems typically arising from his policy of

---

6. On this approach to martyrdom, see Latourette, *First Five Centuries*, 86.
7. Frend, *Rise of Christianity*, 101.

visiting the synagogues before striking out to preach to Gentiles. After the fall of Jerusalem in AD 70 Christians were expelled from the synagogues, and definitively excluded by AD 84. But this did not mean the end of involvement of Jews in the persecution of Christians. This much is clear from the accounts of the martyrdom of Polycarp and Ignatius in the second century, where we hear of Jews actively involved in pursuing Christians.[8]

We know that the Jews (and Jewish Christians) were particularly angered by Paul's inclusion of Gentiles as Christians without imposing conditions like circumcision. As we have also noted, Jews were afraid that their special exemption from the universal requirement of emperor worship might be taken away.[9] This was an important motivation for their demand that converts be circumcised and obey the Mosaic ceremonial laws with respect to food. The Jerusalem Council (Acts 15) gave the initial response; the Christian position was further defended by Paul's strongly worded argument in the letter to newly converted Christians of Galatia.[10]

A.2. From Nero to Decius

In the decades after Jesus's death and Paul's missionary work the imperial authorities only gradually realized that Christians were a group distinct from Jews. Aside from the fact that Jews might be wealthy and influential in their communities, they were easily identified by the distinctive characteristics of their religion. Christians were by no means so readily distinguished. They represented the mainstream of people in the empire, the lower classes, freed slaves and those still enslaved; not many came from higher social classes, certainly not in the first centuries.[11] The inclusion of slaves and women as members meant that the congregation would be regarded as a group of ignorant, foolish people, unworthy and uncultured. If Stoic philosophers throughout the empire accepted slaves or women as equal with any others, not many would have followed them on this point.[12]

---

8. On persecution in the time of Polycarp and Ignatius, see Frend, *Rise of Christianity*, 138–139 and 181–183.

9. See ch. 1, §A.5.

10. On the Jerusalem Council (Acts 15), see ch. 2, §A.3.

11. On common misconceptions about Christians, and corresponding accusations, see especially §B.2 below; and Frend, *Rise of Christianity*, 181.

12. On Stoic social views, see ch. 7, §B.4.

The issue of obligatory sacrifice to the deified emperor continued as a serious point of contention.[13] In a context where proper sacrifice and worship of state deities, and especially the deified emperor, was considered vital to the well-being of the empire and its citizens, any dissenter could be singled out and held responsible for public misfortunes.[14] As we have seen, the Roman rulers allowed for exemption from these rites for Jews, recognizing Judaism as a legitimate religious association (*religio licita*). At first Christians would have benefited from that exemption; but this changed when they were recognized as a group separate from the Jews, not observing the distinctive practices of Judaism. Yet they also had strong scruples against making public sacrifice. Their confession, "Jesus is Lord (*Kurios*)," effectively proclaimed Jesus as a rival to the emperor as *Kurios*.[15] Christians were committed not to a man, but to Jesus as Lord and God. Of these two "lords," the emperor was praised as a victorious warrior, a conqueror, with the power of exacting burdensome taxes from all dependents; Christians gloried in a crucified king. For Christians, true life meant following that king, even to the point of dying for him. The believers in effect turned the values of the Greco-Roman world upside down. But Christianity was not a religion approved by imperial authorities. Theirs was a *religio illicita*: unlawful and not to be tolerated; believers were granted no exemption from emperor worship.[16]

In the beginning Christian communities were relatively small and obscure. Without church buildings, Christians met in the homes of fellow members. In commemoration of the resurrection, they transferred celebration of the Jewish Sabbath (Saturday) to the first day of the week (Sunday) as their day of rest; but Christians could not expect to be released from work on that day. So they met at night, or early in the morning for what they called the "Love Feast," the gathering for which outsiders accused them of immorality.[17] Fear of persecution led Christians to conduct worship services behind closed doors. In

---

13. In his study of martyrdom among Christians, Frend ("Early Christianity and Society," 53–71, especially 56–57) focused on continuity in attitudes from Jews who were prepared to die for adherence to Torah (citing Josephus, *Contra Apion* 29.192). The link is that of "righteous suffering" in the Maccabean tradition of 2 and 4 Maccabees, which is cited for Christians in Cyprian's *Epistle* 58.6 (Frend, "Early Christianity and Society," 56). Frend also cites Philo of Alexandria's *The Embassy to Gaius*, as a precedent for those who (like Eusebius, later) would regard the emperor in messianic terms, as the guardian of peace for mankind ("Early Christianity and Society," 56–57; see also his *Martyrdom and Persecution*, 31–78).

14. Chadwick, *Early Church*, 28–29.

15. Latourette, *First Five Centuries*, 84 and 140–141.

16. Ferguson, *Backgrounds*, 429.

17. Pliny's correspondence with Emperor Trajan indicates that such gatherings were common practice; the letter (cited below, at note 29) is quoted in Stevenson, *New Eusebius*, 19.

Rome they met in the *catacombs*, the extensive system of underground tunnels which had been dug as a place of burial under the city.[18] And secrecy in turn led to nasty rumours about Christian behaviour and worship. Calling each other "brother" and "sister" fed into rumours of incest. Outsiders understood such language as representative of cult activity, and gave a highly negative interpretation of what the Roman historian Tacitus (ca. 58–116) called "their abominations."[19]

The general populace clearly did not understand Christians; nor did they wish to make allowances for people who took such strange views seriously. Grossly misunderstood, Christians were always liable to persecution in the first few centuries of the faith.[20] These conditions remained in force until the early fourth century; a simple charge, along with an affirmation of Christian identity, was enough for condemnation. Accusation could lead to interrogation and condemnation, a public defence in court, and execution. Numerous records of such trials have survived in the *Acts of the Martyrs*.

We have no evidence of involvement of imperial authorities in persecution of Christians before the time of Nero.[21] The first record, provided by Tacitus, reports how Christians were targeted when fire levelled much of the city of Rome in July AD 64.

Figure 4.2. The Emperor Nero and his mother Agrippina. This gold coin (from ca. AD 54) reflects the youth of Nero and the early strong influence of Agrippina (along with that of his tutor, the Stoic philosopher Seneca).
Photo by Classical Numismatic Group (http://cngcoins.com) / CC BY-SA 3.0.

Strong winds fanned the fire, so it spread rapidly and was not brought under control for six days. Thousands were left homeless. To vent their anger, they accused Nero of setting the fire to allow for radical change in the architecture and layout of the city. Nero in turn blamed the Jews for this fire;

---

18. In the catacombs Christians took advantage of Roman tolerance of burial societies, as one of the private associations (*collegia*) regarded as legitimate/legal (*licita*). Thus in Rome, famous for its catacombs, we find Christians meeting under such a guise. For Jerome's comments on the catacombs, see Stevenson, *Creeds, Councils and Controversies*, 171–172.

19. See J. Foster, *First Advance*, 68.

20. On general reasons for persecution, see also Latourette, *First Five Centuries*, 81–83.

21. On persecution under Nero, see Frend, *Rise of Christianity*, 109–110; and Latourette, *First Five Centuries*, 85.

and Jews refocused the accusation on Christians. Although very few in Rome understood clearly what Christians believed, they would now be recognized as distinct from Jews. For Nero Christians provided a convenient scapegoat, and they suffered badly.

Tacitus gives a full report of this unfortunate turn of events:

> Consequently, to get rid of the report, Nero fastened the guilt and inflicted the most exquisite tortures on a class hated for their abominations, called Christians by the populace. Christus[22] [that is Jesus Christ], from whom the name had its origin, suffered the extreme penalty during the reign of Tiberius at the hands of one of our procurators, Pontius Pilatus, and a deadly superstition,[23] thus checked for the moment, again broke out not only in Judea, the first source of the evil, but also in the City, where all things hideous and shameful from every part of the world meet and become popular. Accordingly, an initial arrest was made of all who confessed [to being Christians]; then, upon their information, an immense multitude was convicted, not so much of the crime of arson, as of hatred of the human race. Mockery of every sort was added to their death. Covered with the skins of beasts, they were torn by dogs and perished; they were nailed to crosses, or they were doomed to the flames. These served to illuminate the night when daylight failed. Nero had thrown open his garden for the spectacle, and was exhibiting a show in the circus, while he mingled with the people in the dress of a charioteer or drove about in a chariot. Hence, even if they were considered criminals who deserved extreme and exemplary punishment, a feeling of compassion arose for the victims; for it was not, as it seemed, for the public good, but to glut one man's cruelty, that they were being destroyed.[24]

In pointing to such public animosity for the "abominations" of Christians, Tacitus clearly classifies them with the "riffraff" seen to flow into Rome from the provinces of the empire, especially from Judea. People were ready to accept the worst rumours because, like Jews, Christians were uncompromising on religious principles. They would not participate in public worship of traditional

---

22. This is the first time a secular historian mentions the name of Jesus Christ.
23. Tacitus refers to the resurrection of Jesus.
24. For this quotation from Tacitus's *Annals* 15.44.2–8, see Frend, *Early Church*, 30–31; also Stevenson, *New Eusebius*, 2–3.

deities, leaving them open to the charge of "hatred of the human race," that is, being antisocial. Still, it is remarkable that Tacitus tempers a very negative view of Christians with a recognition that such punishment aroused public sympathy for the unfortunate victims of the emperor's excessively cruel treatment.

It is thought that two key apostles died in this wave of persecution under Nero; Peter was crucified, and Paul, a Roman citizen, was beheaded. Clement of Rome gives the following report in his first epistle (ca. AD 100):

> But, not to dwell on these ancient examples, let us come to the spiritual athletes of the recent past. Let us take the noble examples given from our own generation. Through jealousy and envy the greatest and most righteous pillars [of the Church] were persecuted and put to death. Let us set before our eyes the heroic Apostles like Peter, who through unrighteous envy endured not one or two but many labours, and so, having borne the witness of martyrdom, departed to his due place of glory. Through envy and strife Paul also obtained the reward of patient endurance. After seven times in captivity, driven into exile or stoned, he went on to preach in both the East and the West and gained a noble reputation for his faith; he taught righteousness to the whole world and, after reaching the far limits of the West, suffered martyrdom before the rulers. Then he was removed from the world and went to the holy place, having shown himself the greatest example of endurance.[25]

Persecution under Nero was limited to Rome.[26] There is no record of widespread local persecution on this scale until some 130 years later. More typically there were sporadic mob attacks on Christians, following on accusations of the practice of cannibalism, ritual murder, incest, witchcraft or magic.

The reign of Domitian (AD 81–96) is known for the widespread persecution in Asia Minor which affected the apostle John; he was exiled and assigned to hard labour on the island of Patmos where he wrote the book of Revelation.[27] At this time Domitian also brought charges for "Judaism" and "atheism" against Roman senators, including his cousin Clemens. He even charged his own wife Domitilla. It is possible that these accusations were a cover for suspicions of a treasonous conspiracy to overthrow his imperial power.

---

25. The letter is quoted in Frend, *Early Church*, 31–32.
26. Frend refers to it as "police action" (*Early Church*, 33).
27. Chadwick, *Early Church*, 26–27; and Stevenson, *New Eusebius*, 6.

In provinces like Bithynia in Asia Minor, where there was a strong concentration of Christians, persecution was more frequent and aimed at reducing their number and influence. We know of a serious wave of persecution during the reign of Trajan (AD 98–117).[28]

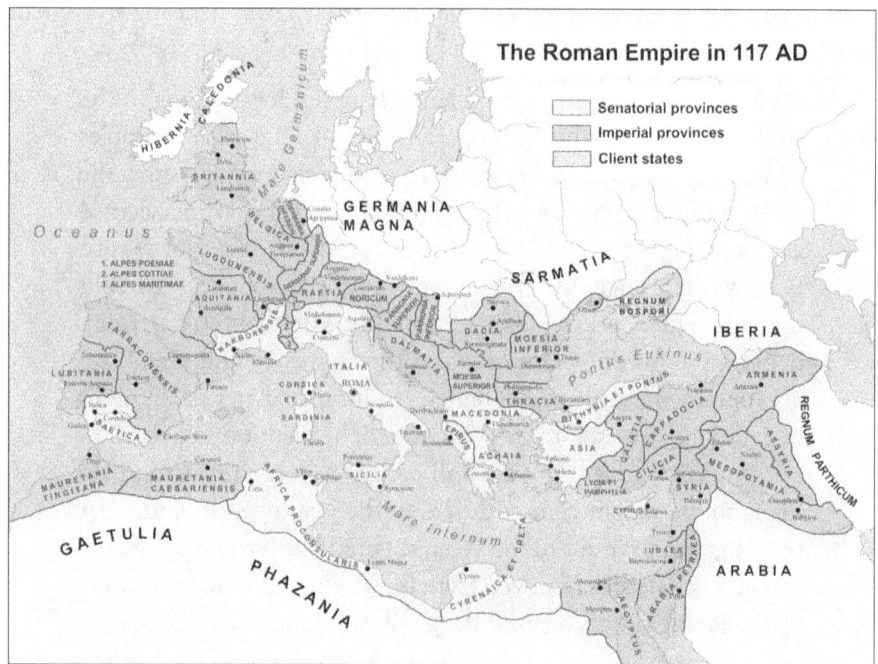

Map 4.1. The Roman Empire at its greatest extent in AD 117.
Map by Andrei Nacu. Public Domain.

The governor of Bithynia, Pliny the Younger, corresponded with the emperor, asking for advice on treatment of Christians who would not renounce the faith, invoke the traditional gods, or sacrifice to the emperor and curse Christ, even under the threat of execution. And these Christians were so numerous that the ancient temples were deserted and pagan rites abandoned:

> (T)his is the course I have taken with those who were accused before me as Christians. I asked them whether they were Christians, and if they confessed, I asked them a second and third time, with threats of punishment. If they kept to it I ordered them for execution; for I assumed without question that whatever it was to which they admitted, obstinacy and unbending perversity

---

28. Latourette, *First Five Centuries*, 84.

deserve to be punished. There were others of a like insanity; but as these were Roman citizens, I noted them down to be sent to Rome...

They maintained that the amount of their fault or error had been this, that it was their habit on a fixed day to assemble before daylight and recite by turns a form of words to Christ as a god; and that they bound themselves with an oath, not for any crime, nor to commit theft or robbery or adultery. They would not break their word, and not deny a deposit when demanded... The contagion of that superstition has penetrated not the cities only, but the villages and the countryside. (Pliny, *Letter* 10.96)[29]

Trajan's advice to the governor was that Christians were not to be sought out; nor should he respond to anonymous charges.[30] Once Christians were properly accused, however, he should encourage them to renounce the faith and make the appropriate sacrifice to the image of the Roman emperor; otherwise they should be punished to the full extent of the law, which meant execution. Evidently, the profession of being a Christian could bring instant death. If they were Roman citizens, and maintained their convictions, however, they were to go to Rome for trial.[31]

The policy outlined by Trajan was maintained by most second-century emperors and determined how Ignatius of Antioch, Polycarp of Smyrna, Telesphorus of Rome (all bishops), Perpetua of Carthage and believers of neighbouring Scillium, among others, would be executed.[32] It appears that a major source of accusation was suspicion of disloyalty to the emperor.

We hear of martyrdom in Rome under Hadrian (117–38) and the Antonines (138–161).[33] The persecution of AD 177 that broke out in Lyons and Vienne (modern France) under the Stoic philosopher-emperor and author of the well-known *Meditations*, Marcus Aurelius (ruling AD 161–180), was particularly vicious.

---

29. See Stevenson, *New Eusebius*, 18–19.

30. Stevenson, 20–21.

31. On the correspondence, see Chadwick, *Early Church*, 27–28.

32. Musurillo gives the report (in Latin, with English translation) of the martyrdom of Perpetua and Felicitas (*Acts of the Christian Martyrs*, 106–131); it is in part an account given by Perpetua herself. For an interesting recent discussion of the significance of Perpetua's account, see S. Parvis, *Early Christian Thinkers*, 100–110. On the martyrs of Scillium (AD 180), see Stevenson, *New Eusebius*, 44–45.

33. Latourette, *First Five Centuries*, 85–86.

Figure 4.3. Martyrdom of Ignatius of Antioch. This anonymous medieval painting depicts Ignatius, Apostolic Father and Bishop of Antioch, attacked by wild beasts in Rome. Tradition dates his death to AD 108. Image found in the Menologion of Basil II, Vatican Library Rome. Photo by pravoslavie.ru. Public Domain.

It began with mob violence against Christians and ended with the brutal torture of those hunted out, in an attempt to get them to renounce the faith.[34] Here too we find the scapegoat motif in the charges against Christians for the disasters of the time: famine, flooding, an outbreak of plague, as well as the invasion of barbarians at the Danube border.

The reign of Septimius Severus (AD 193–211) is noted for the very first decree by an emperor forbidding anyone to convert to either Christianity or Judaism.[35] The persecution which followed was especially severe in Egypt, as we know from the death of Origen's father. From this period we have the noteworthy accounts of the martyrdom of the catechumens in Carthage, which included the free-born lady Perpetua, who faced persecution bravely alongside her slave girl, Felicitas.[36] After this the church enjoyed a number of decades of peace and growth, until persecution resumed under Decius.

---

34. For excerpts from Eusebius's account of the event, see chapter appendix 4.1. For a detailed study of the Lyons persecution, see Frend, *Martyrdom and Persecution*, 1–30; also Chadwick, *Early Church*, 29.

35. Latourette, *First Five Centuries*, 86.

36. On the account, see note 32 above.

Figure 4.4. The Colosseum. This is the building where, according to tradition, Ignatius suffered martyrdom as a public spectacle. Built near the Roman Forum (1st century AD), the oval amphitheatre could hold up to 80,000 spectators. Even in ruins the Colosseum remains an important tourist destination.
Photo "Colosseum in Rome" by Jakub Halun / CC BY-SA 4.0.

A.3. From Decius to Valerian

An especially severe persecution began in 250, during the reign of Emperor Quintus Mesius Decius (AD 249–251); it lasted ten years. This came at a difficult time for the empire, for Decius faced aggressive invaders on more than one front along the eastern and northern borders.[37] As the empire appeared to be losing its greatness, Romans looked about for the cause of such decline and once more found a scapegoat. A significant increase in the adherents of Christianity at this time led to a noticeable decrease in public worship of the pagan gods to whom the Romans had traditionally appealed for the safety of the empire; as a result, Christians were accused of contributing to "so much sedition."[38] Christians serving in the armies were suspected of undermining

---

37. See Latourette, *First Five Centuries*, 87–88; and Frend, *Rise of Christianity*, 318–324.
38. J. Foster, *First Advance*, 74.

state (pagan) prayers for relief. But if they did not serve in the army, they were suspected of disloyalty.[39]

The significant growth in the number of Christians throughout the empire, particularly in the cities, was clearly an underlying cause for persecution in the third century. So significant was this growth, that some regarded the Christian community as a "state within the State."[40] Indeed, the Christian church had set up some social institutions parallel to those of the state. For instance, Christians typically brought disputes among their members not to Roman civil courts, but to the bishops. Congregations also set up charitable organizations to minister to the needs of the poor, Christian and non-Christian alike. The entire Christian body acted as one family; when Christians travelled to neighbouring cities where there were churches, they would carry letters of introduction and be received warmly, as members of the family of faith.

Fear of Christianity as a rival power of the Roman state led Decius to punish Christians for their part in the decline of Rome. He decreed a single religion for the entire empire. State edicts targeted Christians for neglect of the Roman gods; in a time of invasion, plague, epidemic and seemingly endless calamity, adherence to Christianity was tantamount to treason.

The Decian persecution proceeded in two phases. Initially attention was focused on church leaders, especially the bishops who were backed by strong allegiance from the Christian population. The rulers demanded that they show loyalty by offering their sacrifice to traditional state deities, or face execution. Although in Carthage Cyprian remarked that Decius feared these bishops and "would rather face a rival for the throne than a successor to the bishop,"[41] many bishops were arrested and killed. These include Fabian of Rome, Babyllas of Antioch and Alexander of Jerusalem. Others would have suffered the same fate had they not gone into hiding.[42]

The second phase affected every Christian. All citizens were required to sacrifice to state gods and obtain a certificate (*libellus*) to verify their participation in these public rites. Because of the severe measures taken against those who refused to sacrifice, many Christians compromised. Their compliance with the order became an embarrassment and source of friction, causing even further persecution for their communities. Some found friends to sacrifice on their behalf and others bought the certificates, without themselves making the

---

39. On significant factors affecting the persecution of Christians at this time, see Chadwick, *Early Church*, 117–118.
40. J. Foster, *First Advance*, 74.
41. Frend (*Early Church*, 97) quotes a comment given in Cyprian's *Epistle* 55.9.
42. Chadwick, *Early Church*, 118–121.

sacrifice. Christian communities were damaged by such action; those who sacrificed broke trust with those who refused. Procurement of a certificate under false pretence in effect also meant betrayal of the faith. In Carthage alone an entire congregation came out to offer the sacrifice.[43] It seemed as if Christianity had come to an end. At least forty-three certificates (*libelli*) issued to those who sacrificed to the gods have survived.[44] The documents were constructed in such a way that they could hardly be forged. One of them reads:

> To the commission chosen to superintend the sacrifices at the village of Alexander's Isle. From Aurelius Diogenes, son of Satobous of the village of Alexander's Isle. Aged 72 years, with a scar on the right eyebrow. I have always sacrificed to the gods, and now in your presence in accordance with the edict I have made sacrifice and poured libation.[45]

This is not the whole story. Many Christians refused to perform the sacrifice; in prison they were tortured in an attempt to get them to recant. At this time public executions were rare; there were few orders to have Christians sent "to the lions!"[46] Officials recognized that public sentiment opposed such open cruelty. In Carthage bishop Cyprian initially went into hiding, as did other bishops.[47] In Palestinian Caesarea the great biblical scholar and theologian Origen was cruelly tortured and finally released, but he died shortly afterwards from the wounds inflicted.[48] Such persecution would not easily attain its goal of eradicating Christianity, since ordinary Christians would lay low when state authorities were hunting for them; as soon as the authorities were out of sight, they returned to the churches.

Decius soon discovered that Christianity could not be exterminated by force. The waves of attack were finally interrupted by an external threat, that of the Gothic tribes who lured Decius into the marshes of modern Bulgaria and killed him (in 251). Gallus (251–253) continued Decius's policy of persecution only sporadically, as did his successor Valerian (253–260), who had been Decius's censor.[49] The severe plagues of the year 257 were specifically

---

43. Stevenson, *New Eusebius*, 216–217.
44. See Stevenson, *New Eusebius*, 214–215 for translation of such certificates.
45. See Frend, *Early Church*, 98 for this quotation from certificates discovered in Fayoum, Egypt, and published by Knipfling, "The Libelli of the Decian Persecution," 345–390.
46. As in Tertullian's *Apology* 40.2, quoted in Stevenson, *New Eusebius*, 158.
47. For Cyprian's reflections on going into hiding, see Stevenson, *New Eusebius*, 221.
48. For a recent assessment of Origen's life and work, with special attention to the important themes developed in his theological writings, see Rebecca Lyman, "Origen," 111–126.
49. See Latourette, *First Five Centuries*, 88–89; and Frend, *Rise of Christianity*, 324–328.

attributed to the "atheism" of Christians. Bishops were targeted and deacons and priests were also asked to sacrifice or suffer exile. Many church leaders were ruthlessly executed and church property was confiscated to fund the war against the Persians. Christian civil servants were condemned to death and Christian members of the imperial family subjected to enslavement. Valerian's edict went so far as to determine specific penalties for clergy, for Christians of senatorial rank and for employees of the imperial household. At this time Cyprian, beloved bishop of Carthage, was beheaded; he was the first African bishop to face martyrdom.

But as the external threat increased, the emperors found that persecution and killing of Christians became counterproductive, particularly in the East where Christianity was very strong. Persecution raised unfortunate tensions as it also depleted the population. In 261 persecution was abandoned and church property returned. After Valerian, the church enjoyed decades of peace (from 261 to 302) and expanded rapidly.[50] It appears that Christians had enough confidence during these years to build church structures and assemble in a far more public manner. By the year AD 303 there were two hundred and fifty bishoprics throughout the empire, in both the cities and rural areas. The reign of Diocletian would witness the last and most vicious wave of persecution; that period will be discussed in chapter 5.[51]

B. Response of the Apologists

Apologists are "defenders of the faith" who gave a public response to persecution suffered by Christians, covering the period from the early second century to about AD 250.[52] Their response also served to encourage Christians, and assure them of the ultimate victory of the church. In this respect they could appeal to the book of Revelation (the Apocalypse of John), written toward the end of the first century, as a source of comfort for Christians experiencing severe repression. In this struggle Apologists warned Christians against taking the law into their own hands, as also Christ had commanded them not to use physical force to resist evil (Matt 5:39). These words remain as good advice for Christians today and especially the Christian religious leaders of Nigeria who find themselves in similar situations.

---

50. Latourette, *First Five Centuries*, 89–90.

51. See ch. 5, §B.2.

52. On the Apologists, see Frend, *Rise of Christianity*, 231–250; and Latourette, *First Five Centuries*, 83–84.

The term "apology" comes from the Greek *apologia*, a specific term used for a legal defence in response to accusation in a court of law. The most celebrated use of this term in antiquity was that of Plato's *Apology*, in which he presented Socrates defending himself against his accusers (in the late fifth century BC); indeed, many Apologists overtly or indirectly compared their work with that of Plato on behalf of Socrates.

B.1. Causes of Persecution and Martyrdom

It is important to note that the response of the Apologists was closely related to the kinds of accusations made against Christians. In the first two centuries, as noted above, accusations were made against Christians typically on an individual basis, not as a group. Much of our information about the specific charges comes from Apologists like Justin Martyr, Tertullian and Irenaeus in their defence of Christians. These Apologists addressed the direct public accusation, that of simply bearing the name "Christian."[53] They also went further to deal with underlying causes, the rumours of cannibalism or incest,[54] arising from Christians embracing each other as "brother" and "sister" at "love feasts" where they "ate the body" and "drank the blood" of Christ.[55]

We have already considered the reluctance of Christians to participate in public festivities and state occasions because these typically involved them in what they regarded as idolatrous acts of worship and sacrifice. In the first centuries Christians excluded themselves from civil positions, especially the army; as a result, they were accused of being unpatriotic, antisocial and atheist.[56] Failure to support the cult of the emperor led to charges of subversion and sedition. Christians were considered unreasonable in their approach.[57] Why could they not simply do both: honour Christ and also respect the Roman

---

53. On such accusations, see especially Pliny's letter, quoted above at note 29.

54. The three charges against which the Apologist Athenagoras defended himself include: atheism, Thyestian feasts (cannibalism) and Oedipodean intercourse (incest); see Stevenson, *New Eusebius*, 66–67.

55. Stephen Benko has attempted to explain the accusations sympathetically from a pagan perspective; see Benko, "Pagan Criticism of Christianity," 1055–1118, giving a collection and translation of passages which mention Christians. See also his discussion of the charges connected with the name "Christian" (Benko, *Pagan Rome*, 1–29), especially charges of immorality or cannibalism (54–78), and the kiss of fellowship (79–102).

56. On Christian refusal to serve in the army, see Latourette, *First Five Centuries*, 253. On the charge of atheism, see the record of the martyrdom of Polycarp (AD 155/6), noted in the introduction to this chapter; also in Stevenson, *New Eusebius*, 23–30, especially 24–25.

57. On public hostility, see Frend, *Rise of Christianity*, 181; and Chadwick, *Early Church*, 68.

gods together with any other gods of the pantheon?[58] As bishop Polycarp was asked, why not simply claim the emperor as *Kurios*, and save your life?[59]

Particularly problematic was one major result of these attacks: worship services would be held in private quarters, in secret.[60] Were Christians then truly seditious; did they practice magic, especially illegal black magic, against community members and political leaders? These are the criticisms addressed in the apologetic works.

Figure 4.5. The catacomb of Callistus (Rome). This 3rd-century painting of a festive Eucharistic meal decorates the wall of the catacomb. Photo: akg-images / © André Held.

B.2. Strategies of Response

Christian writers and speakers developed a number of specific strategies to set the record straight and deal with accusations. One important aspect of their work was to encourage Christians themselves, reminding them that not all emperors were equally negative to Christianity; there were even some secret Christians among them. In his *Apology* Tertullian wrote fiercely against the

---

58. In his thorough review of the legal basis of early condemnation of Christians, Barnes ("Legislation," 32–50) largely discounts as evidence for what happened at such trials the early witness of martyrs in the *Acta Martyrum*, certainly from the period before Decius (44). He does highlight the important correspondence between Pliny and Trajan (48), indicating the kinds of accusations on which magistrates acted, particularly because Christians repudiated established traditions in religion (the *mos maiorum*, 50).

59. Rahner, *Church and State*, 9.

60. Frend (*Rise of Christianity*, 233) notes that Justin Martyr responded clearly to suspicion of what went on behind closed doors, by giving a detailed explanation of Christian worship (in *Apology* 1.65–67).

Roman state, but he acknowledged that only a few emperors had persecuted the church. Like Lactantius (in the late third century), he noted Nero and Domitian as especially bad emperors, while Tiberius and Marcus Aurelius had "directly and indirectly protected Christians."[61] Furthermore, those who persecuted Christians were inspired by demonic powers:

> If the Christians, by every means of persuasion and pressure and under pain of death, are to be compelled to sacrifice, they know who has instigated the pagans to do it. The spirit of demons and evil angels is the enemy of the Christians, because they have deserted him who envies them God's grace. He drives the pagans to their perverse trials and their unjust cruelty towards the Christians.[62]

The second-century Christian Apologist Melito focused on Nero and Domitian for persecuting the church, saying that they did so in ignorance, and were motivated by evil advisers.[63] Such an argument recalled the words of the apostle Paul in Ephesians 6:12, "For our struggle is not against flesh and blood, but against the rulers, against the authorities, against the powers of this dark world and against the spiritual forces of evil in the heavenly realms." Justin Martyr similarly spoke of the persecution of Christians as the work of evil demons (represented by Roman gods). Justin argued that these demons had resisted even Socrates, the respected philosopher, who was not a Christian, and when Socrates wanted to show up the demons for the deceivers they really are, the demons succeeded in having him killed as an atheist and a violator of religion (*Apol.* 1.5.1–2).[64] Apologists urged Christians to persevere in the face of persecution, the handiwork of the devil, even if it led to death. Tertullian encouraged Christians to stand fast in their confession, and not to avoid persecution through flight.[65]

Apologists also urged Christians to pray for their government, as a command from the Scriptures (Rom 13 and 1 Pet 2:13–17). Athenagoras told the emperor,

> We pray for your sovereignty, so that the son may succeed the father in the only right way, so that your sovereignty may increase

---

61. See K. Aland, "Relation between Church and State," 118; also Stevenson, *New Eusebius*, 157–158, quoting Tertullian's *Apology* 5.5–8.
62. This is Kurt Aland's summary of Tertullian's argument, *Apology* 27.3–5 (K. Aland, "Relation between Church and State," 119).
63. Frend, *Rise of Christianity*, 240–241.
64. See also K. Aland, "Relation between Church and State," 119.
65. See K. Aland, 122.

and extend, bringing the whole world into subjection.... That is of advantage to us too, in that we can lead a quiet, secure life and cheerfully carry out all instructions.[66]

Cyprian wrote in a similar vein; and even Tertullian affirmed, "We pray also for the emperors, their officials and magistrates, for the preservation of the world, for peace in the state, for the delay of the end of the world (*Apol.* 39.2)." Elsewhere he writes,

> We pray from the heart – we are ever making intercession for all the emperors. We pray that they may have a long life, a secure rule, a safe home, brave armies, a faithful Senate, an honest people, a quiet world – and every thing for which a man and a Caesar can pray. (*Apol.* 30.4)[67]

And indeed, Christians prayed sincerely *for* the emperors, while they resisted with their blood the idea of praying *to* the emperor. Their loyalty to the emperors as political leaders was not to be questioned, but emperor worship was unacceptable.

Apologists also found it helpful to share with the Roman public some basic information about Christian congregations, their practice in worship, and standards of ethical behaviour.[68] Beyond that, these Apologists made clever use of low popular appreciation of the pagan gods, even among pagans themselves; they would turn the tables on religious issues, showing that supposedly preferable pagan practices did not reflect a higher standard when compared to those supported by Christians. And finally, they appealed to rulers themselves to address the unfairness of accusations against Christians who were persecuted simply for the name and label of being Christian, not for any crime they might have committed. These various strategies are all evidenced in the work of Justin Martyr, and we examine his work in greater detail, as representative of other apologists.

---

66. Athanagoras, *Leg.* 37, quoted in K. Aland, "Relation between Church and State," 123; see also Tertullian's *Apology* 31. On Athenagoras as Apologist, see further Stevenson, *New Eusebius*, 66–67.

67. The quotation from Tertullian's *Apology* 30.4 is given in Stevenson, *New Eusebius*, 161; also K. Aland, "Relation between Church and State," 123.

68. See Justin Martyr, *Apology* 1.66–67 (and note 60 above).

B.3. Justin Martyr (d. ca. AD 165)

Justin was born in Samaria of Gentile parents, who may well have served there on behalf of the Roman government, since the name (Justinus) is typically Roman.[69] The status of the family is also noted from the good education which Justin received, not just in the more elementary subjects of grammar and literature, but in rhetoric and even philosophy. We meet him in one of his earlier writings (*Dialogue with Trypho the Jew*) as he describes his travels upon completion of his training as an orator, ready to turn to an education among the philosophers. In this, as he explains, he was searching for reliable knowledge about God, guidance for the soul and for truth about the virtuous and happy life.[70] As such his goals were not out of line with those of his contemporaries. The answers he found, however, took him in a direction that was by no means typical.

Justin had already made the round of well-known philosophical schools, the Stoics, Aristotelians and Platonists. But none of the answers given there satisfied him, until he met an old man on the outskirts of the city (Ephesus or Corinth) and heard of wisdom much older than that of the philosophers, a wisdom handed down by prophets and finally represented by the Christ. At that point Justin speaks of a flame of love for these teachers enkindled in his heart; from that time he regarded such teaching as the true philosophy.[71] Even as a Christian, Justin Martyr continued to wear the cloak, carry the leather satchel and grow the beard which identified him as a philosopher.[72]

Aside from the *Dialogue* (noteworthy for lengthy passages with typological interpretation of the Old Testament),[73] the important works are his two *Apologies*, written to defend Christians against accusations typical of the time. It is noteworthy that Justin used strategies already developed by Jews to defend themselves against typical accusations. Like other apologists, Justin addressed his apologetical works to influential leaders, particularly to Emperor Antoninus

---

69. For a recent introduction to Justin, see P. Parvis, "Justin Martyr," 1–14. On Justin as Apologist, see Frend, *Rise of Christianity*, 237–240; and Chadwick, *Early Church*, 74–79.

70. Chadwick, *Early Church*, 66–67 and 74–75.

71. Frend, *Rise of Christianity*, 238. On the significance of referring to Christian truth as "the true philosophy," see ch. 3, note 1.

72. Chadwick, *Early Church*, 75.

73. Throughout the *Dialogue* Justin refers to OT passages given in the Septuagint translation and used by Christians for their prophetic messianic character; his discussion reflects clearly how Christians were reading such passages to affirm Christ as the long-awaited Messiah who was to come and set the Israelites free. On typological interpretation, see ch. 9, §B.3. On the debate with Trypho, see also Frend, *Rise of Christianity*, 239–240.

Pius. Moreover, his words are certainly not characterized by what we might consider a self-deprecating "apologetical" tone.

Justin's apologetical arguments

After a few introductory words of address to the emperor Antoninus Pius and his philosopher sons, Justin challenges them: if they are truly to be considered devout, or *pious* men and philosophers (playing on the Latin "*pius*" as part of the emperor's name) and thus guardians of justice and lovers of learning, it will be evident soon enough whether that reputation is deserved.[74] He asks them to make a thorough, balanced examination of accusations against Christians and the Christian faith; he also challenges them not to execute Christians for the name alone, but to discover if they really have committed crimes that are deserving of barbarous forms of persecution and execution:

> As far as we (Christians) are concerned, we believe that no evil can befall us unless we be convicted as criminals or be proved to be sinful persons. You indeed may be able to kill us, but you cannot harm us. (*Apol.* 1.2)

And he reminds them that once the truth has been discovered, they will certainly "be without excuse before God," if they do not implement justice (*Apol.* 1.3).[75]

In this way Justin skillfully turns the tables on his opponents. If Christians are accused of madness, he will demonstrate that they are reasonable people (*Apol.* 1.13). But he goes further to show that their accusers have not themselves

---

74. Chadwick, *Early Church*, 75.
75. He continues, in *Apology* 1.4:
    If we are convicted as evil-doers, we would not think it just to beg to be acquitted on account of the name. On the other hand, if we are found to have committed no offence, either in the matter of thus naming ourselves, or of our conduct as citizens, surely you should very earnestly guard against incurring just punishment yourselves, for unjustly punishing those who are not convicted. For neither praise nor punishment could reasonably spring just from a "name," unless there is actual proof of something excellent or base in action. And you do not punish those among yourselves who are accused before they are convicted; but in our case you receive the name as proof against us; and you do this although, so far as the name goes, you ought rather to punish our accusers. For we are accused of being Christians, and to hate what is *excellent* (Greek: *chrêstian*, a pun on *Christian*) is unjust. Again, if any of the accused denies the name, and says that he is not a Christian, you acquit him, thinking that you have no evidence against him as a wrongdoer; but if any one acknowledges that he is a Christian, you punish him on account of this acknowledgment. Justice requires that you inquire into the life both of him who confesses and of him who denies; for by his deeds it will be apparent what kind of man each is.

acted with right reason, for they listen to gossip and allow emotions to get the better of reason![76] Accusations against Christians are false, based on nothing more than rumour. On the contrary, Christians set high moral standards and conditions for their lifestyle. Justin explains how they worship and how they encourage and support one another.

Justin also recognizes that if Christians are accused of atheism and impiety, they are in good company, for Socrates too was accused of such things. However, after Plato's *Apology* for Socrates, everyone recognized that indictment for what it was (*Apol.* 1.5, 6, and 2.10). As for the charge of atheism, Justin allows that he may be an "atheist" with respect to the pagan gods, but "not with respect to the most true God" (*Apol.* 1.6). Thus Justin refutes the charge by arguing that the God worshipped by Christians is more worthy than pagan gods. On the offensive, Justin goes on to criticize pagan practice, especially the portrayal of immorality and base behaviour by pagan gods in mythical tales.[77]

Throughout the *Apology* Justin makes effective use of examples of noble pagans like Socrates, whose lives are widely regarded as exemplary; he even compares them favourably with the lives of Christians.[78] In a discussion of Greek mythology he points to stories of suffering, death and resurrection for Greek gods like Dionysus, and asks why Christian accounts of Jesus's special birth, persecution, death and resurrection, should raise questions when there are clear parallels in the pagan stories. Where Greek myths reveal distortion of truth and immorality, Justin notes the work of demons or evil spirits who have twisted the stories to lead people astray. And indeed, he would say the same of those who are foolish enough to believe all the rumours about the life and behaviour of Christians.

---

76. See *Apol.* 1.3, 5: "You do not investigate the charges made against us. Instead, led by unreasonable passion and at the instigation of wicked demons, you punish us inconsiderately, without trial." See also *Apol.* 1.12.

77. See *Apol.* 1.9:
> For why should we need to tell you, who already know, into what forms the craftsmen fashion the materials as they carve and cut, cast and hammer? And often by merely changing the form, and making an image of the requisite shape, they make what they call a god, using vessels of dishonour. And this we consider not only senseless, but to be even insulting to God. In this way his name and his ineffable glory and form get attached to things that are corruptible, and require constant service. And you know only too well that these craftsmen are intemperate, and, not to enter into particulars, that they practise every vice; they corrupt even their own girls who work along with them.

78. Chadwick, *Early Church*, 75–76.

Apologetical use of the "Logos"

The most sophisticated aspect of Justin's defence is his discussion of Jesus as Logos (the Word), the title for Jesus featured in the Gospel of John 1:1, "In the beginning was the Word, and the Word was with God, and the Word was God." The term was well known among the philosophers, who used it for the revelation of a *higher divine principle* acting on a lower level of being.[79] Justin speaks of Christ as Logos especially in the sense of his being the entire and full revelation of God, the Father. As "full" or "complete" Logos, or Word, Jesus also represents the complete Truth. As such, Justin recognizes that the word of God was already present and active before its revelation in Jesus. In the Old Testament God spoke first in creation, but later he spoke through the patriarchs and prophets. The New Testament represents this Word as incarnate, appearing bodily in Christ.

Justin recognizes that pagan philosophers and teachers had given similar accounts of a Logos:

> We know that those who follow Stoic doctrines were hated and put to death. They were honourable at least in their ethical teaching, as the poets also were, at least in some respects; and this is due to the seed of reason (*logos*) implanted in the entire race of mankind. Among these we could mention Heraclitus, as we have stated already, and among those of our own times, Musonius and others. For the demons always saw to it that all those who would strive in any small way to live in accordance with (right) reason (*logos*), and avoid vice, would be hated, as we have indicated. And it is not surprising that the demons are shown to be the cause of much greater hatred for those who do not live in accordance with *a part of* the seminal word (*spermatikos logos*), but by knowledge and contemplation of *the entire* Word (*logos*), which is Christ. But these demons shall suffer their just punishment and retribution once they are confined to everlasting fire. (*Apol.* 2.8)

According to Justin then, Socrates's critique of deity (as commonly understood), and his teaching about God (as Plato reports it),[80] represented a partially correct insight. Stoic teachers too could be appreciated for high ethical standards. Justin notes that they had *glimmerings* of the truth, or *seeds* of the

---

79. Latourette, *First Five Centuries*, 141–142; and Chadwick, *Early Church*, 77. As can be noted from the quote below, the term logos also represents the reasoning power of the mind, as in the English derivative "logic" for a process of reasoning.

80. For further discussion of Plato, see ch. 7, §B.2.

true Logos implanted in their souls, even as pagans. Such seeds, however, left them with only *partial insight*; they had only a small share in the Logos, not the complete Truth. As a result, they ended up contradicting one another:

> Surely, therefore, our teachings are far more grand than any human teaching, because the whole rational principle (*to logikon*) became Christ, who appeared on earth for our sakes, and was human with respect to body, reason (*logos*) and soul. Whatever philosophers and legislators discovered and expressed well, they accomplished from their discovery and contemplation of their share of reason. But since they did not have complete knowledge of the reason (*logos*) which is Christ, they often affirmed things that are contradictory. (*Apol.* 2.10)

Justin recognizes that the crimes of which Socrates was accused (i.e. introducing new deities), were not unlike those attributed to Christians; and Socrates also repudiated deities whose deeds were shameful. Even so, Socrates had limited insight on the highest deity, for he could only affirm (as in Plato's *Timaeus*) that the Father and Maker of all is difficult to find and to explain to others. But Justin continues by arguing that the Creator and Father was indeed fully revealed in Jesus Christ and his teachings may be accepted by all, high or low, educated or uneducated. So much so that Christians, unlike followers of Socrates or other philosophers, are even willing to die for it:

> No one trusted in Socrates enough to die for what he taught. But even ordinary workers, all of them scorning glory and fear and death, trusted in Christ. And they were totally uneducated, not just philosophers and scholars. Even Socrates had a partial knowledge of Christ, for He was and is the *Logos* who is present in every person; and He predicted that which was to come about, first through the prophets and then in person when He assumed our human nature and taught us these things. Indeed his power is that of the ineffable Father and not that of the instruments of human reason (*anthropeios logos*). (*Apol.* 2.10)

So we see that Justin's arguments draw on pagan teachings and the model of an honoured leader like Socrates, to convince pagans from their own words. He wanted to show that the portrayal of Christians as ignorant, despicable or shameless is unwarranted. Through faith in Christ, Christians have access to the full Truth. With his courageous defence Justin tried to raise the profile of Christian teachings, to have the same respectability that was accorded the profession of philosophy. And with his treatment of the Logos, Justin laid the foundation for discussion of a theme which was to become critical for later theological discussion of Christ as Son of God; it was equally important for the development of Christian scholarship on the relationship between faith and reason.[81]

Even if the emperor did not himself hear the addresses of Justin, or personally respond to the arguments addressed to him, we know that two well-educated writers of the time did reflect a degree of respect for Christians as "philosophers." Galen, the medical writer sympathetic to Platonism (ca. AD 129–199), wrote positively of Christians, admiring them for their courage in the face of persecution.[82] And Celsus, the second-century Platonist who wrote a substantive work attacking Christianity and Christian practice from a philosophical point of view (finally answered by Origen in the third century as the *Contra Celsum*), also seems to have been well-acquainted with the arguments of Justin Martyr's *Apology*.[83] It is certainly possible that Celsus's *Alêthês Logos* (*The True Word*, from ca. AD 180), was written as a direct response and desire to overturn Justin's argument on the Logos.

Celsus went further than any earlier attack on Christianity. In addition to the usual slander about secrecy and immorality, his work presented a relentless and more refined onslaught, coming from the perspective of a philosophical critique of Christian beliefs. Celsus compares Christian faith unfavourably with Judaism, claiming that the Jews at least adhered to laws that had the respectability of antiquity. Christians were accused of introducing *new* teachings which could not boast the support of a venerable tradition. With respect to an issue which would long exercise Christians, that of the role of faith with respect to reason, he accused Christians of taking advantage of the naiveté of innocents, of unreasoning children and women.[84]

Although this work of Celsus was finally given a serious response by Origen in the third century, we also recognize that Origen's response is the source of much of our information of its content.[85] But in antiquity, Celsus's attack was equalled only by the Neoplatonist Porphyry's fifteen books *Against*

---

81. Vallée, *Shaping of Christianity*, 55.

82. On Galen see Benko, *Pagan Rome*, 140–147; and Stevenson, *New Eusebius*, 136–137.

83. On Celsus, see Benko, *Pagan Rome*, 147–162; Frend, *Rise of Christianity*, 177–180; and Chadwick, *Early Church*, 68–69 and 117.

84. Stevenson (*New Eusebius*, 134 and 135) quotes Origen, *Against Celsus* 1.9 and 3.55. For a contemporary presentation of Celsus's accusations (culled from Origen's response in the *Contra Celsum*), see the translation of R. Joseph Hoffmann, *On True Doctrine*.

85. Key quotes from Origen's work are given in Stevenson, *New Eusebius*, 131–136; see also Chadwick, *Early Church*, 111.

the Christians (ca. AD 290).[86] Porphyry gave detailed analysis of Scripture in an attempt to demonstrate that the texts on which Christians placed their hope were not reliable.[87] And with this we note that the lines of contention between Christians and pagans were drawn even more firmly in the sphere of philosophy.

C. The Impact of Persecution and Martyrdom on Early Christianity

Why is it important to reflect on martyrdom experienced by Christians during these first centuries? As mentioned above, scholarship of recent centuries has witnessed a trend to minimize persecution as a significant factor in early Christianity. Certainly, we should not over-emphasize martyrdom as a characteristic of early Christianity; indeed, for most of the early years persecution was localized and incited by individuals (Jew or pagan, personal or official) who took it upon themselves to make an accusation.

But persecution was a crucial factor in shaping the life of the church in its formative years.[88] Even if we regard second-century heretical teachings, like Gnosticism, as posing an even greater threat, it must not be forgotten that anyone making the decision to become a Christian in these first centuries could expect all kinds of opposition, from outright persecution, imprisonment, torture and death, to less obvious forms of rejection, economic discrimination and social exclusion. Christianity was regarded with suspicion as a "state within the State," and a rival to the true power of the Roman Empire, especially because its members confessed a Lord (*Kurios*) other than Caesar. In spite of numerous attempts to wipe it out, however, Christianity seemed only to grow.

---

86. On Porphyry, see Frend, *Rise of Christianity*, 441–444; for his concern about the spread of Christianity (as witnessed in property owned by congregations, or the role of educated women in Christianity), see Frend, *Rise of Christianity*, 443.

87. On Porphyry's critique of the Scriptures, see Stevenson, *New Eusebius*, 269–271; and Chadwick, *Early Church*, 116–117.

88. In his discussion of the martyrs of Lyons, Frend speaks of a "theology of martyrdom," and highlights the evident desire to imitate Christ, also in suffering and death (Frend, *Martyrdom and Persecution*, 15–16). He notes social factors in this persecution: the recently established Rhone valley congregations may well have represented recent immigrants or itinerant traders whose presence was resented for other reasons (*Martyrdom and Persecution*, 2–5). But Frend concludes that Christians would have been treated in much the same way that authorities dealt with claims of Judaism (*Martyrdom and Persecution*, 22); on this theme see also note 13 above.

C.1. The Sympathy of Pagans

Christians at first suffered from rumours and a bad reputation; public opinion regarded the violent treatment of Christians as no more than they deserved.[89] But over the years a change can be noted; audiences at the public games where Christians were tortured began to recognize the fearlessness of Christians as they confronted wild animals, and asked themselves, where could these ordinary men and women have obtained such courage in the face of extreme danger? When pagan friends and neighbours realized that these people had committed no crime or atrocity, and were being punished unfairly, persecution sometimes had a reverse effect. We hear of outright sympathy for the victims among spectators at the theatrical games; this might even have led to conversions.

The second-century Platonist Galen gives us a rare glimpse into the reaction of pagans to persecution, witnessing the compassion with which Christians were known to care for and encourage one another, in the face of danger.[90] This led the populace to take a renewed interest in Christianity for offering something they did not find in pagan society and customs. That is also the source of the saying, "The blood of the martyrs is the seed of the church." It is an important reason why, from the time of Emperor Decius, authorities reversed the decision to execute openly those who confessed the name of Jesus. Instead they imprisoned them, removing them from public view; out of sight they tortured them cruelly in an effort to get them to recant.

C.2. Martyrs and Lapsed Christians

It is clear that the martyrs came to have an important impact on the development of Christianity in the congregations. It remained the policy of Christians not to give themselves up voluntarily for martyrdom. The church dissuaded people from actively offering themselves; members and certainly the leaders were encouraged to go into hiding (as Cyprian did), to avoid the worst. The reason was that no one could predict what would happen, how far anyone could stand up under cruel torture. Those who were overhasty did not always stand up well under pressure to recant. Those who weakened under pressure and recanted, often under the strain of terrible weapons of torture, might be pressed to pass on names of other members, putting these at great risk. They could even

---

89. Chadwick, *Early Church*, 68.
90. On Galen's positive reports on Christianity, see also Ferguson, *Backgrounds*, 601.

be pressured into passing on property of the congregation, especially when authorities asked that precious copies of the Scriptures be handed over.

Eventually the status of those who lapsed under persecution and wanted to remain within the church became a source of considerable trouble.[91] Under what conditions were they to be taken back when persecution ceased? How could they be forgiven, and reinstated as members? The serious problems of Christianity in North Africa raised by the Donatists have their roots in this very issue, namely, the status of those who had been pressured into betraying the church by handing over (Latin: *traditor*; in English: traitor) property and documents. The fact that they were priests and leaders made it worse. Could the church forgive them, and go on as if nothing had happened?[92]

At the other end of the spectrum were Gnostics who saw no problem in the "material" token required when sacrificing at the altar of the deified emperor. For Gnostics the true content of faith was a secret, not to be disclosed publicly.[93] Their negative view of the body and of life in the context of this evil world allowed them to take a path of syncretism in religious practice, and regard an act done "in the body" as insignificant.[94] This led to public confusion regarding the faith of Christians, and discouragement among Christians who suffered for their faith.

C.3. Martyrdom as a Baptism of Blood

Those who died as martyrs formed an honour roll, as it were, within the church. Tertullian explains that martyrdom was regarded as a second baptism. The first was by water; the second baptism by blood had the power to wipe away all sins committed after baptism.[95] Martyrdom was even regarded as a substitute baptism, especially for those who had not yet been baptized at the time of death; the third-century Hippolytus (ca. AD 170–235) speaks of martyrs being

---

91. See Latourette, *First Five Centuries*, 216–217; also Chadwick, *Early Church*, 30 and 118–119. For Cyprian's letter on the issue, see Stevenson, *New Eusebius*, 219, 220 and 222.

92. Recognition of the extent of the problem leads Chadwick (*Early Church*, 120 and 122–124) to accent the issue of schism as internal division in the church.

93. On gnostic views, see ch. 8, §A.2 and §A.5.

94. Chadwick, *Early Church*, 31.

95. Tertullian based his view of baptism on Jesus's own reference to his coming suffering as a baptism (Luke 12:50). See Tertullian, *On Baptism* 16 (*ANF* 3.677); also *Scorpiace* 6 (*ANF* 3.639); and *Apol.* 50. Tertullian regarded martyrdom as an effective cleansing for post-baptismal sin, on the assumption (common at the time) that all one's sins were washed away at baptism, and there would be no other occasion afterward to wash away sins; see Guy, *Introducing Early Christianity*, 58.

"baptised in their own blood."[96] In his essay *On the Dress of Virgins*, Cyprian speaks of the heroic status of the martyrs, as a prestige matched only by those who have committed themselves to perpetual virginity.[97] The letter sent by survivors in Lyons to fellow Christians in Asia Minor speaks of a crown of glory for the martyrs who sealed their witness with death, as the ultimate sacrifice;[98] for them the faith was more important than life itself.

The letter from Lyons alludes to the underlying meaning of the name: *martyr*, as one who gives a true witness (from the Greek *martus*, a "witness") and remains unwavering in that witness to the very end. Indeed, Christians were called to faithful witness, following Jesus to the ultimate sacrifice (Heb 12:1–3; 1 Pet 2:18–25; Rev 20:4–5). Their witness was a witness unto death. Jesus had not avoided the death sentence imposed by the Roman authorities, and these martyrs followed the example of Jesus all the way on the path of his passion and suffering.[99] To die as he had died – this was the final step to the sure knowledge of the new life, the resurrection which he had prepared for his followers. Martyrdom itself was thus regarded as a supreme consecration of the Christian life, a reward not to be grasped at (lest it be removed), but to be meekly accepted, as did the old Pothinus, who prayed that he would not die of the complications of his old age before the final confrontation in the amphitheatre (Eusebius, *Ecclesiastical History* 5.1.29–31).[100] The final fight would bring him face to face with Satan, the Anti-Christ. In facing him Christians knew they had nothing to fear, for Christ himself had already overcome this enemy on their behalf; Satan could have no power over them.

C.4. Martyrs as Saints

Martyrs were honoured as saints, and were venerated, for the church knew that, inasmuch as they had maintained their witness to the end, their souls would be taken immediately into heaven (based on Rev 20:4–5); through their

---

96. See Hippolytus's *Apostolic Tradition* 19.2, quoted in Guy, *Introducing Early Christianity*, 58.

97. On Cyprian's essay *On the Dress of Virgins*, 3–4, and 21–22 (*ANF* 5.431–6), see Guy, *Introducing Early Christianity*, 138.

98. See the quotation of Eusebius's *Ecclesiastical History* 5.1.41–42, in chapter appendix 4.1.

99. On martyrdom as an imitation of Christ, see the report of the persecution of Christians in Lyons in Eusebius's *HE* 5.2 (on which see chapter appendix 4.1; also the quotation in Stevenson, *New Eusebius*, 46).

100. On the martyrs of Lyons, see also Guy, *Introducing Early Christianity*, 67–68.

life blood they would unlock the key to Paradise.[101] Thus the martyrs became a source of appeal in intercessory prayer, and the date of their martyrdom an occasion of celebration with song and liturgy for the day of their "translation" to heaven.[102] This movement fostered the collection of bones and relics and any other remains of their bodies. Such remnants were regarded as the point of contact between heaven and earth.[103] They also became the prized possession of the respective churches, assuring them of special guardian saints, as it were, to protect the members.

C.5. Women Martyrs receive Special Status as "Confessors"

Those who maintained their faith under pressure and survived torture, were given an honourable status in the church, that of "confessor."[104] The title refers to the fact that they had "confessed the faith" without succumbing in the face of great opposition. For this reason confessors were regarded as having an especially close link with heaven; as such, they received direct vision and divine revelation. Because martyrdom made no distinction of gender, class or social rank among its victims, the status of confessor, when attained by women, gave them a special role in the congregation.

When women survived martyrdom, their perceived closeness to God further enhanced their profile in the community. Their prayers and advice had special value, and they would be approached to convey forgiveness for those convicted of sins, even those as serious as lapse under torture. This is evident from the early third-century account of Perpetua and Felicitas, for Perpetua recognized that she was "privileged to speak with the Lord," and receive a special revelation.[105] In this way even women could take on a quasi-priestly status within the congregation.[106] In some cases recognition of such status led

---

101. See Tertullian, *On the Soul* 55 (*ANF* 3.232), quoted in Guy, *Introducing Early Christianity*, 57.

102. See Tertullian's observation on the celebration of the death of the martyrs, his essay *On the Crown* 3 (*ANF* 3.94), and *Scorpiace* 7 (*ANF* 3.639). See also Guy, *Introducing Early Christianity*, 58–60; and Frend, *Martyrdom and Persecution*, 257.

103. On this phenomenon, see Brown, *Cult of the Saints*.

104. On the distinction between confessors and martyrs, see Eusebius *HE* 5.2.2; also Latourette, *First Five Centuries*, 216.

105. See the *Passion of Perpetua* 1.3 (*ANF* 3.700), quoted in Guy, *Introducing Early Christianity*, 60; on the martyrdom of Perpetua and Felicitas, see also Guy, *Introducing Early Christianity*, 68–70, and above, note 32.

106. See Guy, *Introducing Early Christianity*, 60–61, who quotes Hippolytus's *Apostolic Tradition* 10.1; also Tertullian, *To the Martyrs* 1 (*ANF* 3.693).

to a conflict of authority within the church, and consequent problems for the bishop. In that regard, Cyprian sought to qualify assumption of priestly roles for confessors as a disturbance of right order.[107]

C.6. Lingering Effects of Persecution

Christian analysis and response to persecution continued to have an impact even in the years when persecution as such had come to an end. The language of combat continued to be used to describe the faith, particularly in the various ascetic movements which were coming to prominence in the late third century.[108] When the challenge of outright persecution was no longer an issue, a witness to the commitment of faith could be given through ascetic practice; monasticism in many ways sought to fulfil the role of martyrdom under different circumstances.

In the long run, we realize that whatever were the intentions of the persecutors, their goals were not realized, certainly not in any major way. From the beginning we note the paranoia of emperors who regarded any group that met as a freewill organization as potentially subversive of their supremacy. That attitude drove Christians even further underground, without accomplishing the goal of prohibiting their meetings. Under these circumstances we realize that the kinds of church councils which met later, as at Nicea (AD 325), were not yet possible. But we know that decisions from one part of the church were being communicated to Christians in other geographical locations. Even under regimes which persecuted them, Christians maintained considerable freedom of movement. They organized themselves through the offices of bishops, elders, and deacons, and threatened the state with an "alternative state" within its bosom. Only one of these "states" would survive, and few Roman citizens of the time realized that the one to survive would not be imperial Rome.

---

107. See Guy, *Introducing Early Christianity*, 61–62, where she refers to Cyprian's *Ep.* 27 (*ANF* 5.306). On the problem, see also Frend, *Rise of Christianity*, 322–323; and Stevenson, *New Eusebius*, 217. See further below, ch. 6, §B.1.

108. On use of the title "athlete of God" for outstanding ascetic achievement, see ch. 3, §A.4.

Chapter Appendix 4.1

The Persecution in Lyons and Vienne

The following are passages from a letter from persecuted Christians in Lyons to fellow Christians in Asia Minor, recorded by Eusebius in his *Ecclesiastical History* 5.1 (see also Stevenson, *New Eusebius*, 34–44):

5.1.4–5: They begin their account as follows: The greatness of the tribulation in this region, and the fury of the pagans against the saints, and the sufferings of the blessed witnesses, we cannot recount accurately, nor indeed could they possibly be recorded. For with all his might the adversary fell upon us, giving us a foretaste of his unbridled activity at his future coming.

5.1.11–12: Some finished their confession with all eagerness. But some appeared unprepared and untrained, weak as yet, and unable to endure so great a conflict. About ten of these . . . caused us great grief and sorrow beyond measure, and impaired the zeal of the others who had not yet been seized, but who, though suffering all kinds of affliction, continued constantly with the witnesses and did not forsake them. Then all of us feared greatly on account of uncertainty as to their confession; not because we dreaded the sufferings to be endured, but because we looked to the end, and were afraid that some of them might fall away.

5.1.17–19: But the whole wrath of the populace, and governor, and soldiers was aroused exceedingly against Sanctus, the deacon from Vienne, and Maturus, a late convert, yet a noble combatant, and against Attalus, a native of Pergamos where he had always been a pillar and foundation, and Blandina, through whom Christ showed that things which appear mean and obscure and despicable to men are with God of great glory, through love toward him manifested in power, and not boasting in appearance. For while we all trembled, and her earthly mistress, who was herself also one of the witnesses, feared that on account of the weakness of her body, she would be unable to make bold confession, Blandina was filled with such power as to be delivered and raised above those who were torturing her by turns from morning till evening in every manner, so that they acknowledged that they were conquered, and could do nothing more to her. And they were astonished at her endurance, as her entire body was mangled and broken; and they testified that one of these forms of torture was sufficient to destroy life, not to speak of so many and so great sufferings. But the blessed woman, like a noble athlete, renewed her strength in her confession; and her comfort and recreation and relief from the pain of her sufferings was in exclaiming, "I am a Christian, and there is nothing vile done by us."

Figure 4.6. Blandina. Viciously martyred in Lyons (France) in the 2nd century, she is honoured by the work of Lucien Bégule in this stained glass window (of 1901) in the Église Saint-Irénée of Lyons. Photo by Gérald Gambier. Public Domain.

5.1.29–31: The blessed Pothinus, who had been entrusted with the bishopric of Lyons, was dragged to the judgement seat. He was more than ninety years of age, and very infirm, scarcely indeed able to breathe because of physical weakness; but he was strengthened by spiritual zeal through his earnest desire for martyrdom. Though his body was worn out by old age and disease, his life was preserved that Christ might triumph in it. . . . Being asked by the governor, Who was the God of the Christians, he replied, "If you are worthy, you shall know." Then he was dragged away harshly, and received blows of every kind. Those near him struck him with their hands and feet, regardless of his age; and those at a distance hurled at him whatever they could seize; all of them thinking that they would be guilty of great wickedness and impiety if any possible abuse were omitted. For thus they thought to avenge their own deities. Scarcely able to breathe, he was cast into prison and died after two days.

5.1.37, 41–42: Maturus, therefore, and Sanctus and Blandina and Attalus were led to the amphitheatre to be exposed to the wild beasts, and to give to the pagan public a spectacle of cruelty, a day for fighting with wild beasts being specially appointed on account of our people . . . But Blandina was suspended on a stake, and exposed to be devoured by the wild beasts who should attack her.

And because she appeared to be hanging on a cross, and because of her earnest prayers, she inspired the combatants with great zeal. For they looked on her in her conflict, and beheld with their outward eyes, in the form of their sister, him who was crucified for them, that he might persuade those who believe on him, that every one who suffers for the glory of Christ has fellowship always with the living God. As none of the wild beasts at that time touched her, she was taken down from the stake, and cast again into prison. She was preserved thus for another contest, that, being victorious in more conflicts, she might make the punishment of the crooked serpent irrevocable; and, though small and weak and despised, yet clothed with Christ the mighty and conquering Athlete, she might arouse the zeal of the brethren, and, having overcome the adversary many times might receive, through her conflict, the crown incorruptible.

Chapter Appendix 4.2
Key Dates for Early Christian Persecution

Crucifixion of Jesus	AD 30/33
Nero's persecution in Rome	64/65
Persecution under Domitian	ca. 95
Martyrdom of Ignatius	ca. 110
Correspondence Pliny/Trajan	ca. 112
Martyrdom of Polycarp in Smyrna	156
Martyrdom of Justin	165
Persecution in Lyons	177
Martyrdom of Perpetua (Carthage)	202–203
Persecution under Decius	249–251
Persecution under Valerian	257–259
The "Great Persecution" under Diocletian	303
Cessation of persecution in West	305
Cessation of persecution in East	311
Constantine puts end to persecution	312/313[109]

Chapter Appendix 4.3
Important Apologists

Quadratus (ca. AD 125), under Emperor Hadrian
Aristides of Athens (ca. 140) under Emperor Antoninus Pius
Justin Martyr (d. ca. 165), also associated with Emperor Antoninus Pius
Tatian, from Assyria (ca. 120–175), student of Justin; author of *Address to the Greeks* and a *Diatesseron* (*Harmony of the Gospels*)

---

109. See Guy, *Introducing Early Christianity*, 51. On the events which led to this agreement, announced in the West in 312 and effected for the entire empire in 313, see below ch. 5, §B.3.

Melito, bishop of Sardis (fl. AD 180), addressing the *Apology* to Emperor Marcus Aurelius

Athenagoras, of Athens (fl. ca. 180), writing a *Plea for the Christians*, also addressed to Emperor Marcus Aurelius

Tertullian, of Carthage (ca. 160–220) writes an *Apology* and polemical treatises

Minucius Felix, Roman lawyer (fl. ca. 200), author of *Octavius*, an *Apology*

Origen (ca. 185–254), *Contra Celsum*

Questions for Discussion and Review

Persecution and Martyrdom from Nero to Valerian (AD 64–260)

1. What initially led the Jews to attack the Christians? What tactics were used, according to the book of Acts? What were some of the immediate results for the church?

2. Which major disagreements between Paul and the Jews sparked accusations against Paul? What was the real fear of Jews in these encounters?

3. How did Roman authorities finally determine that Christianity was different from Judaism? What were the repercussions of these differences for adherents of Christianity?

4. How did Roman authorities understand the Christian confession, "Jesus is Lord"?

5. What does it mean to consider Christianity a *religio illicita*? What were the reasons for this designation? And what were the repercussions for Christian life and worship?

6. Why were Christians persecuted under Nero? What kind of accusations led to persecution and martyrdom?

7. Which problems in religious practice were encountered by Pliny as governor in Bithynia? How did Emperor Trajan advise Pliny to deal with Christians there?

8. What is the significant new feature of persecution under Septimius Severus? Which regions of the empire were most affected by this wave of persecution?

9. How did imperial policies with respect to persecution change in the time of Emperors Decius and Valerian?

10. Why did the emperors try to get Christians to renounce their faith? What was the biggest concern of Christians with respect to those who did recant?

11. Who are the most important Apologists; and what kind of writings have they left us?

12. Why was the role of Apologists so crucial for the development of Christianity in the second century?

13. What strategies were developed by Apologists to answer typical accusations against Christians at this time?

14. What is the significance of Justin Martyr's education as a philosopher, and his ongoing use of the philosopher's cloak?

15. Justin Martyr addressed his *Apologies* to the emperor, and uses names of the emperor and his family members as part of the argument in defence of Christianity. Can you explain his reasons for such an approach? Why was he convinced that the emperor was "without excuse" for his harsh treatment of Christians?

16. Justin used Socrates as an example at various points in his argumentation. Explain the significance of Socrates for Justin's case in defence of Christianity.

17. Justin's apologetical work is remembered particularly for use of the term Logos for Christ. What is the significant difference between Christians and non-Christians in knowledge of God through the Logos? Why did Justin emphasize *partial access* to the Logos for philosophers like Socrates or Musonius?

18. What are some important ways in which the life of the early church was shaped by the factor of persecution?

19. Why did public persecution of Christians have the reverse effect, of arousing sympathy for them?

20. Which problems were presented by the attitude of (some) Gnostics to persecution?

21. How were the martyrs honoured within the Christian community? How did the church honour those who were persecuted and survived the ordeal?

22. Which ongoing features of the Christian church can be identified for having an origin in the persecution and martyrdom of the early centuries?

Further Reading

Aland, Kurt. "The Relation between Church and State in the Early Times: A Reinterpretation." *Journal of Theological Studies* 19, no. 1 (1968): 115–127.

Barnes, T. D. "Legislation against the Christians." *Journal of Roman Studies* 58 (1968): 32–50.

Benko, Stephen. *Pagan Rome and the Early Christians*. London: Batsford, 1984.

Frend, W. H. C. *Martyrdom and Persecution in the Early Church: A Study of Conflict from the Maccabees to Donatus*. Oxford: Basil Blackwell, 1965.

MacMullen, Ramsay. *Enemies of the Roman Order*. Cambridge, MA: Harvard University Press, 1966.

Musurillo, Herbert. *The Acts of the Christian Martyrs: Introduction, Text and Translations*. Oxford: Clarendon, 1972.

Stevenson, J. *A New Eusebius: Documents Illustrating the History of the Church to AD 337*. Revised by W. H. C. Frend. London: SPCK, 1987.

Wilken, R. L. *The Christians as the Romans Saw Them*. New Haven, CT: Yale University Press, 1984.

5

Church and State in the Roman Empire (AD 260–380)

The mother of Galerius, an exceedingly superstitious woman, was devoted to the gods of the mountains. Since that was her character, she made sacrifices with sacred banquets almost every day, and feasted her servants on the meat offered to idols. However, the Christians would not partake of these offerings. While she feasted with Gentiles, Christians would continue their fasting and prayer. This is why she fostered hatred against the Christians. With womanly complaints she incited her son, who was no less superstitious than herself, to destroy these Christians. So, during the entire winter Diocletian and Galerius took counsel together. . . . The older man long opposed the fury of Galerius . . . Yet he was not able to restrain the madness of that headstrong man.

Lactantius, *On the Deaths of the Persecutors*, 11

Lactantius, like Eusebius, is one of our best sources for developments in Christianity at a critical turning point in its history, the period of persecution which began in AD 303 under Diocletian. These years witnessed a series of events which seemed to portend the end of the world as it was known at the time. There has been much speculation on the reason why Diocletian initiated this very severe persecution of the church. Modern scholars have proposed the role of recent military success, or Galerius' own political ambitions.[1]

---

1. For a recent variant on Diocletian's motivation, see the argument of Elizabeth DePalma Digeser (*Threat to Public Piety*), which points to rivalry among politically influential NeoPlatonist philosophers and pagan priests as the spark which ignited this fierce persecution.

Lactantius, who would enjoy a distinguished career at the court of Constantine as tutor to his sons, gives his own interpretation from hindsight: Diocletian destroyed church buildings and sacred manuscripts and enslaved or imprisoned outstanding Christian leaders at the instigation of Galerius. And even Galerius might not have acted, had it not been for his mother's irritation with her Christian servants; they refused to join the feasts she provided as she sacrificed to gods to whom she had turned as the source of her good fortune. Perhaps this reason given by Lactantius is as good as any other.

A. Introduction

In the previous chapter we noted the variety of forms of opposition experienced by Christians under the Roman emperors. There were considerable periods of time when they were left at peace; then again, persecution would flare up with hardly any clear motivation. While some emperors were openly opposed to Christianity, some even showed sympathy for Christians and others maintained a neutral stance. Christians might recognize the emperor as himself the Anti-Christ, or an agent of Satan and understand the opposition of the emperors as an expression of the controlling power of demons. Nevertheless, they accepted the biblical injunction to respect the government and its officers as an authority instituted by God (Rom 13:1–7; 1 Pet 2:13–17).[2] Christians also prayed for the Roman state, asking that evil rulers experience a change of heart and that positions of power in government be occupied by righteous leaders.

In this discussion it is important to remember that from the beginning, the Roman state was itself deeply religious, not secular.[3] State religion, intermingled with state functions, was enforced as widely as the empire itself, if only as an act of patriotism. When Christian citizens would not worship state gods, many Romans wondered why they would not show such patriotism. After all, the *pax deorum* (i.e. the peace of the gods), guaranteed by constant sacrifice, was considered critical to the survival of the empire. Only such divinely given peace could ensure the success of the Roman Empire as a viable political entity. Jews still enjoyed special exemption, but when Christians refused to worship state gods they were regarded as opponents of the state itself.

Muslims adopted an integration of religion and the state from the beginning, but Christians have never adopted a truly uniform or consistent attitude toward politics and the state. The history of Christianity shows

---
2. See Latourette, *First Five Centuries*, 252.
3. Vallée, *Shaping of Christianity*, 101.

considerable variety in the relationship of church and state. Some Christians have asked, "What has the emperor do with the church?"[4] And in some modern contexts (as in the USA) the constitution designates a pointed separation between the state and religion in its organized forms; the original intention was the protection of religious liberty and to ensure freedom from state interference in church matters. Such a policy of separation also influenced the constitutions of numerous African states, including Nigeria. On the other hand, there are (Christian) nations like Germany or Britain, as well as the Scandinavian countries like Sweden, Denmark, Norway or Finland, where the Christian church has been incorporated as the state church; the church may even be regarded as an arm of government. The European Middle Ages witnessed endless battles for supremacy between powers of church and state. For the most part Christians recognized the superiority of the church; the state was to be "subservient to her demands."[5]

Such inconsistency among Christians has some roots in the attitude which Jesus himself demonstrated with respect to the Roman rulers of his time. While he proclaimed the kingdom of God, Jesus never formed an opposing government or political party. Moreover, when asked to comment on the taxes owing to the despised Roman rulers, he responded, "Give to Caesar what belongs to Caesar, and to God what belongs to God" (Matt 22:21). While not refusing to pay taxes owing to temporal rulers, Christians also recognize the more all-encompassing claims of the God who created our world and everything in it!

The present chapter covers the period after AD 260, to discuss the most serious wave of persecution by the Roman state and examine how early Christians fared under the repression of the early fourth century. When it was over, they were faced with a very different situation in the empire under Constantine. This chapter examines how events of that time led to the "triumph" of Christianity (after 312), when the church was recognized as a legitimate institution, and Christianity a *religio licita*, finally even becoming the official religion of the empire under Theodosius (AD 380). Christians were no longer persecuted; they were free to worship as they wished.

At the same time the state regarded the church as the source of unity based on a new religion. Rome still had a state religion; the emperor did not give up his control of religious affairs. Christians soon discovered the implications of that new role, as the state made very different demands of the church. In that

---

4. See §B.5 below on the complaint of Donatus.
5. K. Aland, "Relation between Church and State," 116.

regard we also note the beginnings of an entirely different relationship between the church and state in the conditions of the East and the West. While in the East, in the Byzantine Empire, the church was virtually an arm of the state, the church maintained a greater degree of independence in its relations with the rulers in the West.

B. From Persecution to the Triumph of Christianity (AD 64–313)

Initially Christian communities were relatively small and obscure. As a religious group Christianity was marginal; the people attracted to it came from the lower classes of society, both men and women, many of them slaves, or former slaves. As such, the state was hardly aware of the presence of a new faith group. When it was noticed, Christianity was first regarded as a sect within Judaism and, as such, would enjoy the tolerance given to Judaism by the Roman government. Christians could travel freely without hindrance, as indeed Paul travelled throughout the empire on his missionary journeys. They worked alongside non-Christians as artisans in the market, in offices, or the imperial service. The new faith did not attract much notice because Christians met in the homes of fellow members, and did not use distinctive buildings.

All of this changed after Nero first used Christians as scapegoats (in AD 64) for the burning of Rome.[6] Serious accusations were motivated by totally baseless rumours of incest or cannibalism, as we discovered from the historian Tacitus's reference to "their abominations."[7] Periods of persecution came and went. The rule of Decius (249–251) and Valerian (257–259), meant a very difficult time, for Christianity was considered the enemy. But the last and most harsh of all the waves of persecution came in the period 303–313, under Diocletian, his allies and successors.

B.1. Diocletian and the Reorganization of the Roman Empire

Diocletian did not initiate persecution of Christians until the nineteenth year of his rule as emperor. The first decades of his reign (AD 285–305) are noted for the reorganization of the empire. He transferred the administrative centre from Rome to Nicomedia (capital of the imperial province of Bithynia) in Asia Minor, not far from the ancient trade centre of Byzantium.

---

6. See ch. 4, §A.2.

7. J. Foster, *First Advance*, 68; see also the discussion in ch. 4, §A.2 and §B.1.

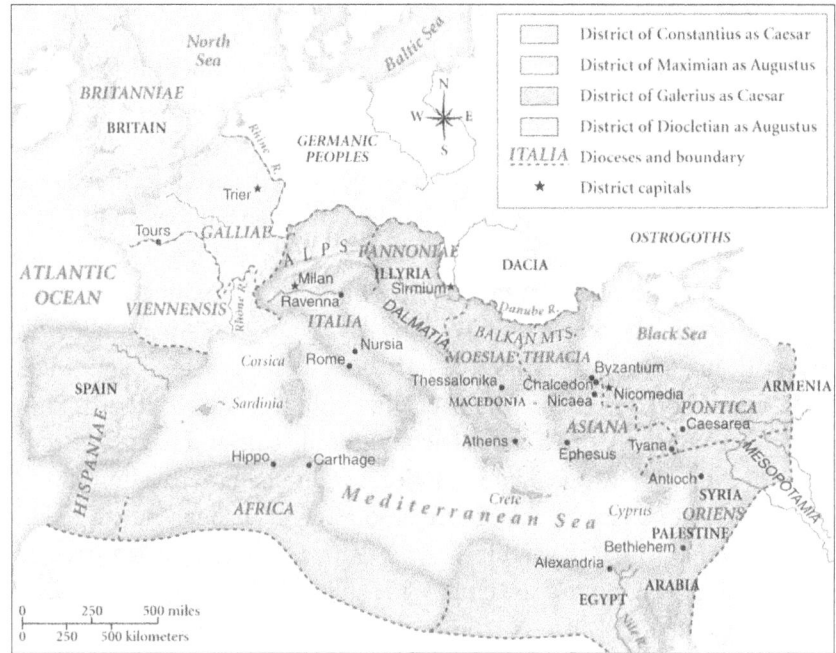

Map 5.1. The Roman Empire under Diocletian (after AD 299).
Map "Roman Tetrarchy Map" by Coppermine Photo Gallery / CC BY-SA 3.0.

This new capital would give emperors more effective control over the troubled eastern frontiers.[8] Since the serious defeat of Marcus Aurelius on the Danube, the army had weakened; the soldiers were typically mercenaries. Yet the army continued to exert significant control over the choice of each new emperor. Between AD 180–284 twenty-one (of twenty-five) emperors were murdered to end their rule.

To gain control of steadily deteriorating economic, social and political conditions and to strengthen his own position as emperor, Diocletian increased the size of the army. He also divided the empire into a western and eastern part, each with its own Augustus (supreme ruler) and Caesar (second-in-command, and successor upon the death of the Augustus). Diocletian himself maintained ultimate power, directing affairs from Nicomedia, the new centre in the East, which was also the more prosperous and stable part of the empire. From this time the city of Rome no longer functioned as the controlling centre of the empire. In fact, the western empire was now controlled effectively not from Rome, but from Milan, in northern Italy.

---

8. See Frend, *Rise of Christianity*, 452–456; and Chadwick, *Early Church*, 121.

B.2. The "Great Persecution" of the Church, AD 303–324

Numerous members of Diocletian's own family were sympathetic to Christianity at this time; both his wife and daughter were known to be Christian.[9] And by now the army and civil service included many Christians. The same can be said of the staff of the imperial court, where Christians even occupied senior positions. It is clear that, as Frend claims, "the church had now established itself as a political and religious force to be reckoned with."[10] It has been estimated that by AD 300 Christians numbered five million, approximately a tenth of the population of the whole Empire, and they rivalled Jews in number.[11] The growth of Christianity itself may well have been a major factor in igniting this last vicious period of persecution. Diocletian's co-regent Galerius was known to be vehemently anti-Christian, as Lactantius indicates, and it is assumed that it was Galerius who instigated persecution of Christians at this time.[12]

Other factors played a role. Persecution may have been motivated by a serious external threat, particularly from Persia. Public opinion attributed the vulnerable condition of the empire to the introduction of new (mystery) religions like that of Mithras. The cult of *Sol Invictus* (*Unconquered Sun*) had been introduced in the third century in an attempt to unite the empire under one deity. By ordering Christians to respect and worship the Roman gods, Diocletian may have wanted to appease the traditional gods and secure the empire's future by eliminating "centrifugal sects" that fostered diversity rather than unity. By obeying this order Christians would demonstrate loyalty to the state as the basis for duty in the army and the civil service.[13] Such a demonstration would be important especially in the eastern part of the empire, where the concentration of Christians was greatest, for these Christians might easily be influenced to betray Roman interests by supporting Christians among

---

9. This is clear from the name of one of his daughters, *Anastasia* (resurrection). See J. Foster, *First Advance*, 78; also Frend, *Rise of Christianity*, 450; and Latourette, *First Five Centuries*, 90–91.

10. Frend, *Early Church*, 107. To explain the harsh treatment of Christians after the considerable period of relatively comfortable co-existence within the empire (from 260–303), Frend examines Diocletian's programme of religious renewal (with its emphasis on deities to guarantee the safety of the empire), from its prelude, the "propanda war" (Frend, "Prelude to the Great Persecution," 3–4). He also recognizes Porphyry's efforts in undermining Christianity through his *Philosophy from Oracles*, and *Against Christianity*, to negate the veracity of the Scriptures and abuse the character of Jesus (Frend, 10–13).

11. Vallée, *Shaping of Christianity*, 107.

12. Frend, *Rise of Christianity*, 456–457.

13. Erwin W. Lutzer (*The DaVinci Deception*, 11–12) recognizes that Christians were challenged not so much by the request to forsake (the worship of) Jesus, but to worship *both* Jesus *and* Caesar. Emperor worship focused on the rite of burning incense and declaring, "Caesar is Lord."

its enemies to the east, especially the Persians, or those of the officially Christian kingdom of Armenia.

The first decree of 303 prescribed the burning of Christian books and destruction of Christian buildings.[14] Another edict ordered the arrest of clergy, and many of them were subjected to harsh labour. Some church leaders were imprisoned. Christians of noble standing were demoted. Even members of the imperial family were subject to enslavement.[15] The emperor ordered a purging of all Christians from the army. An edict of 304 ordered all Christians to sacrifice to the traditional gods of the Roman state, or be subject to execution. The severity of persecution led Christians to despair of an answer to their prayers for a change of heart in their rulers, calling for righteous leaders in positions of power.

Persecution was not as severe in the western part of the empire, for we know that the Augustus in the West, Constantius Chlorus (Constantine's father), did not enforce the edicts in Gaul,[16] and when Constantius died in 306, his son continued the policy of non-persecution. But in the East, persecution was more intense than at any previous time, and continued sporadically even beyond 311. Much pressure was put on Christians to recant. Few were actually executed; many were maimed and/or sent to the mines for hard labour. Church property was confiscated. There was some backsliding, even among the clergy, but the persecution caused even more to join the church, moved by the show of courage by Christians in the face of death.[17] Diocletian and his colleagues discovered that Christians could not be cowed into worshipping Roman gods like *Sol Invictus*, Jupiter, or the deified Caesar. One might say that the victory of Christianity over imperial politics was assured even then, whether or not Constantine saw a vision of the cross a decade later.

By 310 it seemed impossible to crush the church. Diocletian had fallen sick and had abdicated his position in 305, passing imperial power to Galerius.[18] Although Galerius tried to continue Diocletian's policy of persecution, he

---

14. Chadwick, *Early Church*, 121.

15. According to Vallée, persecution "involved the destruction of churches and scriptures, confiscation of property, prohibition of worship, cancellation of legal and civil rights, arrest of clergy, and orders to sacrifice to the gods on pain of death, torture and execution" (*Shaping of Christianity*, 104). See also Frend on the decree as it affected the clergy (*Rise of Christianity*, 457–460), and an exchange between the mayor of Cirta and its bishop (459).

16. Chadwick, *Early Church*, 121–122.

17. Vallée, *Shaping of Christianity*, 105–106.

18. Chadwick, *Early Church*, 122. On Galerius, see also Frend, *Rise of Christianity*, 461–463 and 479–480.

Figure 5.1. Emperor Galerius's *Edict of Toleration* (AD 311). This modern plaque in front of the Church of St Sofia (Sofia, Bulgaria) publishes the text in three languages (Latin, Greek and Bulgarian). It recognizes the historic importance of the edict for officially ending the persecution of Christians initiated under the Emperor Diocletian. Photo "Galerius Edict Sofia Plaque" by Miko / CC BY-SA 3.0.

too was struck with what appears to have been cancer and had to change his religious policy. In 311 Galerius issued his *Edict of Toleration*:

> In consideration of our most mild clemency, and of the unbroken custom whereby we are used to grant pardon to all men, we have thought it right in this case also, to offer our speediest indulgence. Christians may exist again, and may establish their meeting houses provided that they do nothing contrary to good order. . . . [It is] their duty to pray [to] their god for our good estate, and that of the state, and their own, that the commonwealth may endure on every side unharmed, and they may be able to live securely in their habitations.[19]

---

19. For this edict as reported by Lactantius (*On the Deaths of the Persecutors*, 34; also quoted in Frend, *Early Church*, 121), see Stevenson, *New Eusebius*, 280.

Galerius died the same year. His successor Maximin Daia discovered that he too could not pursue the course of persecution for long and published another edict of toleration, giving Christians freedom to rebuild their churches and to worship as they pleased.[20] Christians had won a victory, not by the sword, but by sheer resilience. The emperors were now even courting Christian support, months before Constantine's accession to power. Christianity had, as it were, become a political force, and that largely in response to state-sponsored persecution.

B.3. Church and State under Constantine

Constantine (b. 288), son of Constantius Chlorus and his first wife Helena, was already prominent as "son of an Augustus" when still a young Roman general. In 305, when Diocletian stepped down, his father had been promoted as Augustus. And when his father died the next year (306), Constantine himself was readily proclaimed an emperor by soldiers in York (Britain). Ambitious to rule the entire western part of the empire, he quickly took control of his father's territory.[21] At this time Constantine consulted the shrine of Apollo (at Autun) which also honoured the Sun God, *Sol Invictus*.

There he received omens of victory, and accordingly inscribed coins with *Soli invicto comiti* (i.e. to my companion, the Unconquered Sun). To establish supremacy in the West, however, he needed a victory over his rival, Maxentius, son of Maximian, co-regent with Diocletian and former Augustus of the western empire. At that point (in 312) Constantine received an important sign assuring him of victory, a vision with the words: *in hoc signo vinces* (i.e. "in this sign you will be victorious"). Later Constantine testified to the church historian Eusebius that while

> he besought his father's god in prayer . . . he saw with his own eyes the trophy of a cross of light in the heavens, above the sun and an inscription, "Conquer by this" attached to it. . . . And while he continued to ponder and reason on its meaning, night overtook him; then in his sleep the Christ of God appeared to him with the sign which he had seen in the heavens, and commanded him to make a likeness of this sign as he had seen it in the heavens,

---

20. Chadwick, *Early Church*, 122.
21. On Constantine's political role and his conversion, see Latourette, *First Five Centuries*, 91–93.

and to use it as a safeguard in all engagements with his enemies.[22]

According to Lactantius,

> Constantine was directed in a dream to mark the heavenly sign of God on the shields of his soldiers and thus to join battle. He did as he was ordered and with the cross-shaped letter X, with its top bent over, he marked Christ on the shields. (On the Deaths of the Persecutors, 44.3–6)[23]

Figure 5.2. Constantine and Sol Invictus. This gold medallion, minted in AD 313, foregrounds the "Unconquered Constantine," with a bust of Sol Invictus in the background. Photo by Marie-Lan Nguyen. Public Domain.

Armed with the sign which incorporated the Greek letters "chi" and "rho" (as the first two letters for the Greek name, "Christ"), Constantine and his army engaged the enemy. On October 28, 312, Maxentius was routed, and Maxentius himself drowned in the Tiber. The next day Constantine entered Rome.[24] The following year Constantine met the Augustus of the East, Licinius (also his brother-in-law), in Milan. Here the two rulers agreed to a new edict of toleration, the *Edict of Milan*, which placed Christianity on an equal basis with other religions. According to this edict, Christianity would be tolerated legally in the Roman Empire; it was no longer regarded as an illegitimate or illegal religion (*religio illicita*).[25] Church property was restored and churches which had been destroyed were rebuilt with state assistance.

Persecution should have ended completely when Constantine established his rule in the West and published the edict jointly with Licinius. In fact, persecution continued for some years in the East, until Licinius also saw a vision and was given a prayer to the *Summus Deus* (Supreme God) by an angel. With this prayer Licinius defeated his rival Maximin, who abandoned Asia Minor and fled to Tarsus, where he died. When Licinius finally published the

---

22. From Eusebius, *Life of Constantine*, 1.28–29 (quoted in Stevenson, *New Eusebius*, 283–284).

23. Quoted in Frend, *Early Church*, 123; see also Stevenson, *New Eusebius*, 283.

24. See Chadwick, *Early Church*, 125–126; and Frend, *Rise of Christianity*, 481–482.

25. Frend, *Rise of Christianity*, 483; and Stevenson, *New Eusebius*, 284–286 (quoting Lactantius).

text of the *Edict of Milan* in Nicomedia, eleven years of persecution came to an end. But the full intent of the edict came into force only when Constantine entered Nicomedia in 324, and defeated his brother-in-law to become the sole ruler of the whole empire, east and west.[26] As sole ruler, Constantine took up residence in Byzantium, close to Nicomedia. He named this city after himself, Constantinople; it would serve as a "New Rome" and reunite the empire.[27]

B.4. Christian Writers on the Persecution

The first of the Christian authors of this period to be considered is Lactantius, an African orator and Apologist who served as tutor at Diocletian's court in Nicomedia. He became a Christian ca. AD 300, and was considered "the Christian Cicero" because of his skill in public speaking. His important work, *On the Deaths of the Persecutors* (*De mortibus persecutorum*), reflects the belief that God was punishing wicked emperors through the way their lives ended.[28] On the basis of his appreciative reflection on the special role of Constantine, we might categorize his work as that of a political theologian. While he demonstrated considerable hatred for Roman emperors who persecuted the church, and deep sympathy for Christians, Lactantius's understanding of the reasons motivating persecution is of special interest. Like other Apologists, he understood persecution primarily as the work of demons, or the devil, the Anti-Christ. This approach is rooted in New Testament writings like the Apocalypse (Revelation),[29] which presents Babylon and the Beast (or Dragon) waging war against the saints; the book prophesies the eventual collapse of Babylon and victory over the Beast by the Ancient of Days.

Lactantius saw the hand of God in Nero's death, describing him as the "first of all who persecuted the servants of God" (*On the Deaths* 2.6).[30] But the remains of "this monster" were so totally obliterated that even his tomb could not be found.[31] Many thought that Nero might make a reappearance, in anticipation of the devil's own appearance at the end of time, to destroy the earth. Lactantius also regarded the first-century emperor Domitian as a tyrant, for "by instigation of demons, he went to the length of persecuting the

---

26. Chadwick, *Early Church*, 129; and Frend, *Rise of Christianity*, 484–488.
27. Frend, *Rise of Christianity*, 501–504.
28. Frend, 450–451 and 485–486.
29. Hemer, "Archaeological Light," 70.
30. For the Latin text, *De mortibus persecutorum*, see *CSEL* 27, 172.
31. See K. Aland, "Relation between Church and State," 116.

righteous people" (3.2). Domitian received the punishment he deserved, for he was killed in his own palace and his memory obliterated.[32] Many years later Decius appeared as another "abominable beast" who oppressed the church; but he too was "killed in battle by the barbarians," and was left naked on the battlefield, as food for birds and wild animals, "as becoming an enemy of God" (4.1 and 3). Valerian also "stretched his wicked hands against God and shed much righteous blood in a short time" (5.1); as a result, he was taken prisoner by the Persians, and suffered the shameful life of a slave. Aurelian (AD 260–265) was quite unable to carry out his wicked plans, for he was murdered by his own friends before he could do so (6.1).

Lactantius did acknowledge the rule of many good emperors; aside from the five persecutors, there were another twenty-five who did no harm to the church; at worst they were neutral in their attitude (*On the Deaths* 3.4).[33] With such rulers the empire enjoyed peace, and the church grew. In this way Lactantius continued the approach of earlier Apologists. Tertullian's *Apology* also examined the emperors who actively persecuted the church; but he recognized that both Tiberius and Marcus Aurelius had in some ways protected Christians, while other emperors had not enforced the laws against them (*Apol.* 5.2 and 6). In all this Tertullian recognized the paradoxical position of Christians who detected the work of Satan in the persecution of the church by the emperors, while they also encouraged prayer for the empire and its leaders so that, with all inhabitants of the empire, they might live in security and peace. Loyalty to the emperor and the empire was not in question. As Donata, one of the martyrs of Scillium (180), expressed it, "I honour Caesar because he is Caesar, but worship can be given only to God."[34] Christians certainly prayed *for* the emperors, but refused to pray *to* the emperor.[35]

Such loyalty to good emperors helps us to understand the Christian attitude to Constantine and other pro-Christian emperors before him. They were considered secret Christians and messengers of God, even when they were not visibly members of the church. In this capacity Constantine was called "God's instrument on earth." Christian Apologists recognized the accomplishments of Constantine as a fulfilment of the prophecy of Ezekiel on the revival of the valley full of bones (Ezek 37:1–14). In his reaction to events of 313, Lactantius wrote:

---

32. K. Aland, 116.
33. See also K. Aland, 117.
34. See *Acta Scilitanorum* 9 (quoted in Rahner, *Church and State*, 13).
35. See ch. 4, §B.2.

Behold all your enemies are crushed. Now peace has returned to the earth. The church not long before beaten to the ground has now risen again; God's temple, which the evildoers had destroyed, has been rebuilt in even grander style by God's mercy. The Lord has raised up a ruler who abolished the criminal and bloody decrees of tyrants and has had mercy on the human race. Now all hearts rejoice in this treasured and glorious peace. (*De mortibus persecutorem* 1)[36]

B.5. Constantine as Pontifex Maximus

Constantine took on two important roles as emperor: the supreme command of the army, and that of chief high priest of state religion.[37] Although himself a "catechumen" (preparing for baptism), clearly sympathetic to Christianity and growing as a believer, Constantine could not abandon the traditional aspects of his imperial role. After all, his imperial powers extended over a vast region, embracing people groups of many different backgrounds and religious beliefs, including those charged with upholding the traditional rites of state religion. So the image of the Sun God, *Sol Invictus*, was not obliterated at this time.[38] The imperial policy remained pluralist with respect to religion for many years after 313; there was no iconoclastic war on pagan images. Rather, Constantine decreed, "No one should disturb another; each ought to believe and act as his heart desires. . . . No one ought to injure another on the basis of religious conviction. To enter freely into the struggle for immortality is one thing; to have it imposed by constraints is another."[39] Indeed, the Christianizing of the empire was a process which would take many decades.[40]

To understand this period of history, it is important to note once more that there was no sharp line demarcating matters of religion and politics, church and state. This was a condition familiar to the pagan Roman Empire, but entirely new for Christians, who were used to being considered as outcasts, and in opposition to the state. As noted above, Constantine did attempt to make restitution to the Christian communities for the loss of church buildings and

---

36. For the Latin text, see *CSEL* 27, 172, 1.7 (quoted by Rahner, *Church and State*, 42).
37. Latourette, *First Five Centuries*, 94.
38. Frend, *Rise of Christianity*, 491–492.
39. Eusebius, *Vita Constantini* 2.56 (GCS 1, 64.8); cited by Rahner, *Church and State*, 44.
40. Vallée (*Shaping of Christianity*, 108) acknowledges that bishops were now assigned judicial functions and some worked in the civil service.

properties.[41] In this connection he took responsibility for erecting or rebuilding at public expense a number of churches in major cities. He also allowed legal privileges for clergy, much like those allowed for priests of official pagan cults. Sunday was declared a public holiday in 321.[42] With his mother, Helena, Constantine embarked on a project of Christianising Palestine, and especially Jerusalem, as the Holy Land and the Holy City. Recognition of Christian holy sites meant that these would become destinations for Christian pilgrimage, particularly for Christians from the West.[43]

For religious matters Constantine had a special adviser, the bishop from Cordova (Spain), Hosius (or Osius).[44] In his ongoing role as *Pontifex Maximus*, Constantine saw himself not only as representative of the Christian God on earth but also as "bishop extraordinary" or bishop of those outside the church. Constantine himself declared this new position: "You are bishops, whose jurisdiction is within the church: I also am a bishop, ordained by God to overlook those outside the church."[45]

In the East, where Constantine had taken up residence (at Byzantium, renamed Constantinople), he received considerable respect from bishops who were ready to acknowledge him as the "earthly manifestation of the Divine Logos," and to regard his success as a sign of divine approval.[46]

Here Constantine made a relatively smooth transition from being *Pontifex Maximus* to being regarded as virtually "the equal to the apostles," as also he was acclaimed by Bishop Eusebius at the celebration of the thirtieth anniversary of his becoming emperor:

> He it is – the Word of God proceeding above all things, and through all things, and in all things, both visible and invisible – who is the Lord of all the Universe; from whom and through whom the king . . . the beloved of God, receives and bears the image of His Supreme Monarchy, and steers and directs, in imitation of his

---

41. Frend, *Rise of Christianity*, 487; on grants to Christian communities in North Africa to compensate them for losses, see also Stevenson, *New Eusebius*, 287–288.

42. Frend, *Rise of Christianity*, 488.

43. This led to a battle for sacred space, and the destruction of pagan sacred places first built by Emperor Hadrian in 135 AD; see Chidester, *Christianity*, 113.

44. Frend, *Rise of Christianity*, 482–483 and 497.

45. For this quotation from Eusebius's *Life of Constantine* 4.24 (GCS 1, 124, 9.11) reflected also in his statement in the *Life* 2.17, see Rahner, *Church and State*, 45; it is true that the basic meaning of the NT Greek term for bishop, *episkopos*, is "overseer."

46. Frend, *Martyrdom and Persecution*, 545. Eusebius's *Ecclesiastical History* finishes with elaborate praise of the emperor.

Figure 5.3. The Emperor Constantine dedicates Constantinople as imperial capital. This 11th-century mosaic in the Hagia Sophia, the great cathedral church, marks the dedication of the well-fortified city, Byzantium/Constantinople on the Bosphorus (modern Istanbul) to the Virgin Mary and her Son. The city remained the capital of the Empire in the East.
Photo by Myrabella. Public Domain.

Superior, the helm of all the affairs of this world. As there is one God, so there is one Ruler.[47]

Certainly in the East, Constantine was recognized for having supreme power over both the secular and religious spheres. Of course, it is ironic that the very ruler who asphyxiated his wife, Fausta, and also killed his own son and heir, Crispus, on suspicion of treason, could be regarded as the "thirteenth apostle." But at the time it seemed expedient to give such honour to an emperor who was outstanding in his sympathy for the Christian church. Constantine himself was baptized on his deathbed (in 337), a move which was politically expedient because of his ongoing role in a religiously diverse empire. Of course, such a late baptism was not uncommon at the time, as Christians feared the wrath of God for backsliding after baptism. It was thought prudent to wait as long as possible.

For the church, this was the beginning of a totally new era. Under new and peaceful conditions, the church could begin to develop in ways impossible in earlier years, especially in terms of buildings and architecture, liturgy and social programmes. But it also had to learn to relate to its environment very differently, acknowledging the new expectations of the state. The emperors looked to the unity of the church for help in assuring the unity of empire. But real peace and unity were elusive. Aside from the newly emerging fierce debates over the Arian subordinationist view of Jesus, there were debates over practical matters like the treatment of those who had fallen away under persecution, the conditions of penitence and ordination of bishops.

---

47. See Eusebius, *Oration in Praise of Constantine*, 1.6 and 3.5–6 (translation *NPNF* modified).

The Arian controversy

As "bishop extraordinary," or more properly, the "supreme pontiff," Constantine was shocked to find that Christians in Byzantium (which had a strong Christian presence) engaged in one theological controversy after another over what he considered minor differences, no more than quibbling over words. He was determined to do what was needed to maintain peace; at the same time he wanted to support and encourage the orthodox Catholic faith and thereby secure the approval of the almighty God for the Roman Empire. Indeed, Constantine felt that he would be neglecting his duty if he allowed such divisive activity to go unchecked. Such a sentiment is clearly reflected in the letter he sent to the Christian official Aelafius:

> I consider it absolutely contrary to the divine law that we should overlook such quarrels and contentions whereby the Highest Divinity may perhaps be moved to wrath not only against the human race, but also against me, to whose care He has by his celestial will committed the government of all earthly things, and that He may be so far moved as to some untoward steps. For I shall really fully be able to feel secure and always to hope for prosperity and happiness from the ready kindness of the most mighty God, only when I see all venerating the most Holy God in the proper cult of the Catholic religion with harmonious brotherhood of worship.[48]

The most serious controversy at the time concerned the Arian view of the relationship between Jesus (as the Son) and God (the Father). It was to be resolved at a church council meeting in the city of Nicea, not far from Byzantium. The controversy itself will receive more adequate attention in chapter 10, but we note here the specific role of Constantine, as it represents a significant turning point in the relationship of church and state.[49] The conclusions of the Nicene council, too, would have enormous implications for church and state relations in both east and west.

---

48. This letter of the emperor is quoted by Frend from a nineteenth-century collection of sources pertaining to the Donatist problem (Frend, *Martyrdom and Persecution*, 543). Rahner notes that such a sentiment clearly prepared the way for Justinian's strong role in the church (*Church and State*, 45).

49. Frend, *Rise of Christianity*, 492–501. On the Arian controversy as a theological issue, see ch. 10.

When Constantine called a meeting of all Christian bishops in AD 325 to secure unity over issues raised by the Arians, at least 220 attended.[50] Those bishops who opposed Arius argued for equality of divine stature for the Son and the Father. When the discussion was at a deadlock, Constantine encouraged his adviser Hosius to introduce a crucial term, *homoousios* (i.e. consubstantial, or the same in [divine] essence); the term helped settle the matter at the time, but would lead to considerable controversy in the future.[51]

It should be noted that the settlement did not try to *prove* that Jesus was God, only to determine the precise relationship between the Father and Son. The divinity of Jesus, as such, was taken for granted by all, including Constantine, when he introduced the term which he hoped would settle disputes among the bishops on the relationship of Jesus to his Father. The bishops were sensitive to the emperor's desire to arrive at a constructive conclusion; but when it came to an attempt to influence theological interpretation of God's Word, they were also protective of their own role as guardians of truth.

It was not long after the Nicene council that Arians, under Eusebius of Nicomedia, managed to influence Constantine to modify its conclusions. Constantine accordingly sent a stern message to bishops and synods that they comply with his new orders.[52] Arians, including Arius himself, were recalled from exile and opponents like Athanasius were now exiled. For the rest of his life Constantine would remain a supporter of the Arians. On his deathbed he was baptized by the Arian Eusebius of Nicomedia.

Constantine and the Donatists

Not long after the Nicene council Constantine was asked to bring the power of the state to bear on other church problems. The most celebrated of these is the North African division between Donatus and the Catholic church.[53] Already in 316 Constantine had supported Caecilian as legitimate Catholic bishop of Carthage, against Donatus.[54] To force the followers of Donatus into submission,

---

50. Hastings estimates the number at two hundred and thirty bishops (Hastings, "150–550," 37).

51. On Constantine's introduction of the term at the council, and its meaning, see ch. 10, §A.4

52. See Rahner, *Church and State*, 48, quoting Eusebius's *Vita Constantini*, 4.42 (GCS 1. 134.30–135.4).

53. Frend, *Rise of Christianity*, 488–492. On the origin of the schism, see the report of Optatus, quoted in Stevenson, *New Eusebius*, 298–301.

54. Ongoing resentment to state persecution in the early fourth century added to suspicion of state interference in Constantine's support for Caecilian (see Frend, "Early Christianity and Society," 69–70; and Stevenson, *New Eusebius*, 308–309). In numerous publications Frend has

he embarked on the persecution of Donatists in 317. Donatus responded to the severity of this reaction by asking, "What has the emperor to do with the church?" Donatus's successor, Lucifer, would make similar statements; both saw themselves as successors to the Maccabees.[55] Their complaint should be understood against the background of the *Edict of Milan*, which affirmed the Roman Empire as a pluralistic society, tolerating all groups. Donatus and his followers were dismayed at the breach in the emperor's policy, expecting that freedom would still be extended to minor religious groups. Indeed, until 381, all other religious cults were tolerated.

B.6. The Sons of Constantine

When Constantine died in 337 the religious unity he had hoped to introduce in legalizing Christianity was further splintered by the varying allegiances held by his sons (and successors): Constantine II, Constans and Constantius. At this time the struggle for the church to maintain a degree of independence in theological matters also came to a head.[56] Two of the sons, Constantine II and Constantius, clearly favoured the Arian cause and promoted doctrinal positions which the church considered heretical. It appears that these rulers were more comfortable with an Arianizing subordinationist approach on the sonship of Christ, allowing for a "Lord-Satrap" relationship, with a clear demarcation of superiority and subordination between Father and Son. They argued that the kingdom of the Son (the church) must be subordinate to the kingdom of the Father (the empire), just as the Son was subordinate to the Father. Orthodox Catholic bishops (i.e. those supporting the decision of the Nicene council of AD 325), on the other hand, claimed that the Son was consubstantial (quoting the Nicene term, *homoousios*) with the Father; the kingdom of the Son (the church) must also be regarded as equal in dignity with the kingdom of the Father (the empire). The analogy drawn by the bishops, claiming equality between the

---

examined the Donatist controversy (of what is today east-central Algeria), particularly in terms of social and economic aspects of protest, not just as an ecclesiastical (schismatic) concern. See Frend, "Donatist Church," 70–84, especially 73 and 80–81, where he notes Lancel's publication (in *Sources chrétiennes*) of the *Acta* of the Carthage conference of 411 to settle the Donatist issue; Frend recognizes such scholarly work as a vindication of his own interdisciplinary approach. Frend's work has been fundamental in showing the significance of archaeological research on material culture, alongside work on relevant texts, for understanding these disputes in North Africa; on the significance of his work see appendix I, §D.

55. Frend, *Martyrdom and Persecution*, 557–558.

56. On Constantine's sons, see Frend, *Rise of Christianity*, 528–543; also Latourette, *First Five Centuries*, 93–94.

emperor and church leaders, may reflect somewhat the suspicions maintained by the bishops from the very beginning of "toleration," regarding the intentions of those in political leadership. Even though Christians recognized the role of Constantine as "supreme pontiff," they would try to maintain a degree of independence for the church with respect to the state. And that measure of independence (if not superiority) of the church would remain a preoccupation of Christian leaders in the West, far more than for those in the East.

Of the three brothers only Constans, ruling in the West (Italy, North Africa and Illyricum), had supported the Nicene position. Constantius, who ruled in the East from 337–350 (Macedonia, Greece, Thrace, Asia Minor, Palestine, Syria and Egypt), and became sole ruler on the death of Constans (in 350), favoured the Arian position. While he ruled alone (350–361), an Anomoian, or subordinationist creed was introduced; it stressed the "unlikeness" of the Son with respect to the Father, as the opposite of the *homoousion* creed.[57]

In exile, leaders like Athanasius influenced the western segment of the church and the bishop of Rome in their support of the Nicene formula, even modifying it to allow for wider acceptance. Their position would not be implemented for a number of decades. Meanwhile two abortive councils (Sardica in 343, and Sirmium in 357) appeared to assure a complete victory for the Arian formula of "unlikeness" (*anomoios*) between Father and Son. In fact, the controversy served to reinforce divisions between eastern and western parts of the empire on the issue of the respective roles of church and state.

B.7. Julian "the Apostate" (360–363)

Successors in imperial power, especially in the West, followed Constantine's policy of toleration; the outstanding exception is Julian, also called "the Apostate" for his anti-Christian legislation.[58] Julian became emperor in 360 on the death of his cousin Constantius II. He had become disillusioned with Christianity because of the squabbles he witnessed in Byzantium; his own point of view as a philosopher also led him to follow Porphyry in questioning Christian belief and interpretation of the Scriptures. Accordingly, when he became emperor, he took upon himself the task of restoring Hellenism and traditional worship of the Roman gods.[59] Privileges which Christians had

---

57. For further discussion of the involvement of the sons of Constantine in supporting the Arian position, see ch. 10, §B.

58. Frend, *Rise of Christianity*, 594–609; and Latourette, *First Five Centuries*, 94–95.

59. For documents and letters on the changes initiated by Julian, see Stevenson, *Creeds, Councils and Controversies*, 66–80.

assumed from the time of Constantine were now reversed. Julian tried to promote what he considered true religious pluralism, giving equal recognition especially to anti-Catholic groups, including schismatic elements like the Donatists. He was motivated by an expectation that the mutual antagonism of various sectors of Christianity would quickly lead them to "tear themselves to pieces in their deadly hatred of one another."[60]

But Julian's attempts were short-lived. He was soon forced to acknowledge that Christianity had taken deep root in the lives of people of the empire. The two short years of his reign could not reverse the process. When he died in battle in Persia, Christian emperors once more took control of the state. As emperor (in 380), Theodosius went much further in developing the religious policy initiated by Constantine. The religious toleration declared by Constantine in 313 became a thing of the past. Theodosius declared Christianity the official religion of the Roman Empire. Non-Christian cults were now declared illegal. Theodosius II followed this by explicitly forbidding pagan sacrifice. Even more significant for the development of Christianity was his declaration that heresy in doctrinal matters was considered a crime. Indeed, scholars like Vallée have concluded that, "more Christians were persecuted as heretics than had been persecuted as Christian by the pagans."[61]

C. Church and State in East and West

Bishops in the East tended to favour a cooperative relationship with the emperor. Except for Athanasius of Alexandria, all the bishops of the East had endorsed positions favoured by the sons of Constantine. Matters were a little different in the West. The vacuum in power created by the centre of government departing from Rome to Constantinople meant a real opportunity for the church to be more assertive in its relations with imperial rulers. Here Ambrose (ca. 340–397), as bishop of Milan (from 373), stood up to Emperor Theodosius and demanded penance for the massacre of 7,000 men, women and children in Thessalonica.[62] The western popes typically resisted emperors who supported Arianism; and bishops of the West questioned a totalitarian emperor. Also important for the West is the much earlier collapse of imperial power there; from 410 the entire western flank of the empire was subject to

---

60. For this quote from the pagan historian Ammianus Marcellinus, reflecting his contempt for Christianity, see Hastings, "150–550," 40.

61. Vallée, *Shaping of Christianity*, 113.

62. See Stevenson, *Creeds, Councils and Controversies*, 160–162; also Frend, *Early Church*, 183. On the role of Ambrose, see ch. 12, §D.1.

barbarian invasions. The imperial court could hardly make its presence felt in the midst of such social upheaval caused by attacks of the barbarian tribes.

The eastern part of the empire managed to maintain its core until 1453. In the East the emperor was seen more or less as "God on earth," as Eusebius had said of Constantine. There the church more readily accepted a degree of subordination to the state. The imperial court determined conditions for the church; bishops were punished and sometimes banished when they used a style of preaching which the imperial court found unacceptable. In the West, state and church existed as "two powers," and were commonly regarded as *two equal powers*, with the result that both were continually caught in a struggle for dominance. The Middle Ages would witness fierce struggles between emperors and church leaders, each competing for (temporal) power.[63] Such a phenomenon was not typical of the church in the East. Here only one power was accepted, that which was represented by and concentrated in the person of the emperor. Emperors could depose patriarchs with impunity, as when Emperor Anastasius challenged the pope in 514.

The emperor rising highest in imperial ascendancy was Justinian (527–565), who pursued a policy of "one empire, and one church, both led by one emperor."[64] During his reign the church was made truly subservient to the state.[65] Such a relationship between church and state continued for a thousand years, until the collapse of the Byzantine Empire with the attacks of the Muslim Turks in 1453. But even after the disintegration of the Byzantine Empire, church and state relationships have continued along these lines in Greece to the present day, and in Russia until the Revolution of 1917.[66]

Questions for Discussion and Review

Church and State in the Romans Empire, 260–380

1. How did Christians typically show respect for the Roman government and the emperors? Why was this not accepted or appreciated by the Roman rulers?

2. How would you describe the basic difference between Muslims and Christians in their view of the relationships of the church (or mosque) and the state?

---

63. Such a pattern is marked especially from the papal rule of Gregory VII (1073–1085) and of Innocent III (1187–1191).

64. Vallée, *Shaping of Christianity*, 118. On Justinian's role, see also ch. 11, §B.1.

65. Latourette, *First Five Centuries*, 283.

66. K. Aland, "Relation between Church and State," 126.

3. Which important structural changes were introduced for the government of the Roman Empire by Diocletian?

4. Which obstacles prevented the emperors from carrying on persecution as fully as they planned?

5. What role may be assigned to Constantine's vision of the sign, in terms of his becoming supreme ruler in the West?

6. When and how did persecution of Christians finally come to an end?

7. How did Christian writers like Lactantius interpret the role of the emperors in persecution? How did they encourage Christians under siege?

8. What is the significance of Constantine's office as *Pontifex Maximus* (chief high priest) of state religion?

9. How did Constantine seek to accommodate Christianity in the early years after the edict of toleration of 312?

10. What kind of honours were Christian bishops of the eastern empire willing to bestow on Constantine? What motivated them?

11. How would you describe the role taken by Emperor Constantine in the Arian controversy?

12. Which policies of the empire were enforced in using state resources against the Donatists?

13. How did Julian attempt to turn back the clock? Why was he not successful?

14. What were some of the important differences in the relationship between church and state in the eastern and western parts of the Roman Empire?

Further Reading

Barnes, T. D. *Constantine and Eusebius*. Cambridge, MA: Harvard University Press, 1981.

———. "Legislation against the Christians." *Journal of Roman Studies* 58 (1968): 32–50.

———. *The New Empire of Diocletian and Constantine*. Cambridge, MA: Harvard University Press, 1982.

Baynes, N. H. *Constantine the Great and the Christian Church*. London: Oxford University Press, 1972.
Ferguson, Everett, ed. *Church and State in the Early Church*. New York: Garland, 1993.
Frend, W. H. C. "Church and State: Perspectives and Problems in the Patristic Era." *Studia Patristica* 18 (1982): 38–54.
———. *The Donatist Church: A Movement of Protest in Roman North Africa*. Oxford: Clarendon, 1971.
———. "The Donatist Church – Forty Years On." In *Window on Origins: Essays on the Early Church*, edited by C. Landman and D. P. Whitelaw, 70–84. Pretoria: University of South Africa, 1985.
Greenslade, S. L. *Schism in the Early Church*. London: SCM, 1964.
Lane Fox, R. *Pagans and Christians*. Harmondsworth: Penguin; New York: Knopf, 1987.
Momigliano, A., ed. *The Conflict between Paganism and Christianity in the Fourth Century*. Oxford: Clarendon, 1963.
Rahner, H. *Church and State in Early Christianity*. Translated by L. D. Davis. San Francisco: St Ignatius, 1992.

6

The Early Church in North Africa

The boys [Aedesius and Frumentius] were found studying under a tree and preparing their lessons, and, preserved by the mercy of the barbarians, were taken to the king [King Ella Amida]. He made one of them, Aedesius, his cupbearer. Frumentius, whom he had perceived to be sagacious and prudent, he made his treasurer and secretary. Thereafter, they were held in great honour and affection by the king.

The king died, leaving his wife with an infant son [Ezana] as heir to the bereaved kingdom. He gave the young men liberty to do what they pleased but the queen besought them with tears, since she had no more faithful subjects in the whole kingdom, to share with her the cares of governing the kingdom until her son should grow up; she besought especially Frumentius, whose ability was equal to guiding the kingdom. . . .

While they lived there and Frumentius held the reins of government in his hands, God stirred up his heart and he began to search out with care those of the Roman merchants who were Christians and to give them great influence and to urge them to establish in various places religious buildings to which they might resort for prayer in the Roman manner. He himself, moreover, did the same and so encouraged the others, attracting them with his favour and his benefits, providing them with whatever was needed, supplying sites for buildings and other necessities, and in every way promoting the growth of the seed of Christianity in the country.

Rufinus, *Ecclesiastical History*, 10.9

The late fourth-century historian of Christianity, Rufinus, perhaps better known for his translation of the writings of Origen, provides this account of the amazing events which led to the formal introduction of Christianity in Ethiopia, then known as the Aksumite kingdom. It is a story given him by an important source who had first-hand knowledge of the events, Aedesius himself, who was the bishop of Tyre at the time. As a boy, he and Frumentius had accompanied Meropius of Tyre, a philosopher and teacher, who may have been their uncle, sailing with him to explore the world beyond the Roman Empire. They ended up on the shores of Ethiopia, then known as the Aksumite kingdom.[1]

Unfortunately, the Aksumite rulers had broken off relations with the Romans. When the ship entered port within their kingdom, presumably to replenish supplies, it was attacked, and everyone on board slaughtered. Fortunately for the two boys, they had already left the ship by the time it was attacked. They were captured alive to serve at the royal court of the king, Ella Amida.

Christianity was not unknown in Ethiopia at the time, having been introduced by merchants and traders from the Roman Empire. Other possible sources of Christian influence were the Christian community among the Jewish exiles who took refuge there, and Yemen/Sabaea across the Red Sea, a region with a strong Jewish population.[2] The presence of Aedesius and Frumentius at the Aksumite court provided an important opportunity for Christianity to impact the life of the kingdom at the highest political level. Their role in support of the queen at this time marked a turning point in the history of Ethiopia, which led to the embrace of Christianity.

A. Introduction

Africa has some of the oldest Christian communities, and the Ethiopian Orthodox church (also known as the Tewahedo church), must certainly be appreciated among them as the oldest indigenous religious body in Africa. This church community enjoys deep roots, whether we consider its connection with Judaism from the time of the Queen of Sheba (recorded in 1 Kgs 10:1–13),[3] or its formal adoption (around AD 350) of Egyptian Coptic Christianity.

---

1. The text refers to "India" as their destination, but "India" and "Ethiopia" were often confused in antiquity; see Mayerson, "A Confusion of Indias."

2. On the strong presence of Jews in Yemen, see ch. 2, §B.4.

3. On this encounter, celebrated in the fourteenth-century Ge'ez account of Ethiopian emperors tracing their lineage back to Solomon, the *Kebra Nagast*, see §D below.

In Ethiopia Judaism and Christianity became intertwined to form a unique branch of Christianity which managed to avoid the rivalries and conflicts between Jews and Christians that were experienced in the Roman Empire. Even today Ethiopia continues to celebrate both Saturday (as Sabbath) and Sunday (as day of resurrection) as public holidays. But the earliest recorded history of Christianity in Africa is not based in Ethiopia; it is the account of the persecution of Christians in Scillium (now Tunisia), in AD 180.

The continent of Africa got its name from the northern part, now Tunisia, where a local tribe called the "Afri" gave their name to the Roman province of "Africa," the name which would eventually be used for the entire continent.[4] So it is ironic that many North Africans, including Tunisians, now prefer to be considered "Arab" rather than "African." They are clearly not aware of what should be a source of pride for North Africans and indeed all Africans, Muslim and Christian alike. Important historical figures like Emperor Septimius Severus (AD 193–211) and the late second-century Pope Victor I (189–199), as well as noted writers and thinkers like Tertullian (ca. 155–240),[5] Cyprian (ca. 200–258),[6] Lactantius (ca. 250–325),[7] Didymus the Blind (313–398),[8] Optatus (mid-fourth-century Numidian bishop of Milevis), Athanasius (ca. 296–373),[9] Augustine (354–430),[10] and Verecundus (mid-sixth-century bishop of Junca, in the African province Byzacena), to name a few, were all Africans, even if not all of them had dark skin or lived within the confines of the Roman Empire. Aside from the common languages of the time, Latin and Greek, these North Africans spoke the Berber (or Imazighen), Punic, Numidian, Libyan (or Cyrenaic) and Coptic languages.

This chapter examines the historical development of early Christianity in Africa. The specific African contribution to early Christianity is often neglected in western scholarship. As Thomas Oden has recognized, the omission can be blamed in part on the influence of nineteenth-century Hegelian German

---

4. Lacroix (*Africa in Antiquity*, 285) explains that the term *Afri* was first widely used for the native population of North Africa by the Romans after they had conquered the Punic province of Carthage. It was later applied more widely.

5. On Tertullian, see also ch. 8, §B.3 and §C.4, and ch. 10, §A.3.

6. On Cyprian, see §B.1 below.

7. On Lactantius, see also ch. 5, §B.4.

8. Didymus the Blind followed Origen as head of the catechetical school of Alexandria. Blind from birth, he is said to have invented a method by which the blind could read. Didymus wrote numerous works, and influenced both Jerome and Gregory of Nazianzen; see Isichei, *History of Christianity in Africa*, 23.

9. On Athanasius, see §E below, and ch. 10, §B.1, and ch. 12, §A.1.

10. On Augustine, see §B.1 below, and ch. 12, §D.3.

idealism,[11] which fostered the problematic assumption that anything of intellectual importance occurring around the Mediterranean base would be assigned to the "European" tradition, and not rightly attributed to Africa's own tradition in religion and theology.[12] Of course, the Mediterranean world was part of what would become "Europe," but it is a mistake to assume that leaders and writers from the African part of the Mediterranean simply copied the ideas and conclusions of their "European" counterparts.

African theological reflection was certainly influenced by local cultures, and at significant junctures in time African leaders held positions at considerable variance with those of the church of Rome. Although the city of Carthage was colonized by Rome after 146 BC, Christians there stood their ground in opposing the church of Rome on the question of lapsed Christians.[13] Even more important is the distinctive African Christianity that originated in Egypt (with the Coptic church), and spread from there to Ethiopia and Nubia. Coptic Christianity managed to survive centuries of Muslim dominance and today counts more than six million adherents in Egypt alone. And certainly the Donatists, whether as rebels or founders of a new religious movement, made their mark on fourth- and fifth-century Christianity. These movements demonstrate that European or Greco-Roman Hellenism, so important to the birth and early spread of Christianity, was Africanized through the medium of the Nilotic languages, especially in southern Egypt, Ethiopia and northern Nubia.

Even a cursory review of early Christianity reveals that African leaders were responsible for formulating some of its core teachings, positions which would prove to be critical for western theology. We note Tertullian's formulation of a basic Trinitarian position with his introduction of the term *trinitas*,[14] or Clement of Alexandria and Athanasius on the theme of *theôsis* (i.e. Christians becoming like [or participating in] the divine), as well as the strong christological arguments through which Athanasius opposed Arius and

---

11. Important exponents of Hegelian Idealism include Friedrich Schleiermacher, Adolf von Harnack, Walter Bauer, Rudolf Bultmann and Paul Tillich; for further discussion of the significance of these scholars for the history of patristic studies, see appendix I. On the impact of their views, see Oden, *How Africa Shaped*, 9–18.

12. On Oden's efforts to correct this approach, see appendix III.

13. Frend, *Early Church*, 103. See §B below.

14. For a helpful introduction to Tertullian's life and writings and particularly his contribution in the development of theological themes like the Trinity, see E. Ferguson, "Tertullian," 85–99.

Figure 6.1. The ancient North African Cyrene (East Libya). It was once a thriving port city on the Mediterranean and early centre of Christianity in these Roman provinces. Photo by Maher27777. Public Domain.

his followers. Thomas Oden also posits the influence of African thinkers on Cappadocian theologians, especially in biblical exegesis.[15]

B. Early Expansion of Christianity in Northern Africa

Christianity entered Egypt, and probably also Cyrene, or Cyrenaica (now eastern Libya),[16] much earlier than it arrived in any part of the Maghreb (the Arab term for the western regions of North Africa).

Still it is important to start with Carthage (now in Tunisia), because the earliest accounts of Christianity in the continent of Africa concern the church in that city. Carthage was a major port city on the southern shores of the

---

15. Oden, *How Africa Shaped*, 47.

16. It is commonly accepted that mention of Rufus and Alexander as sons of Simon of Cyrene (in Mark 15:21) means that these men would be known in the early Christian community. For mention of Cyrene, see also Acts 2:10; men from Cyprus and Cyrene are further noted for sharing the gospel with the Greek community (Acts 11:20; see also Acts 13:1 regarding Lucius of Cyrene). We know that Greek colonists settled among the Berber population of Cyrenaica, where there was a reasonable livelihood for pastoral farming; see Isichei, *History of Christianity in Africa*, 15.

Mediterranean, a colony founded ca. 800 BC by the Phoenicians (from the eastern Mediterranean). Over the years control of this city was contested by both Greeks and Romans. It was completely razed to the ground with the Roman conquest of 146 BC. But eventually the city was resurrected to become the heart of the Roman province of "Africa," which also became a major source of grain, olive oil and wine for Rome itself. Roman soldiers were assigned substantial land grants, and many of them settled in the region. Urban centres were built on the Roman plan, and use of the Latin language was common (alongside Greek, Punic and Berber).

Christianity may have come to Carthage before the mid-second century, and spread from there to areas like Numidia and Mauretania Sitifensis to the west, and Tripolitania to the east. The earliest account of Christianity in Carthage reports the arrest and martyrdom of seven men and five women from Scillium, not far from Carthage (July 180). They all bore (Latinized) African names: Speratus, Nartzalus, Cittinis, Veturius, Felix, Aquilinus, Laetantius, Ianuaria, Generosa, Vestia, Donata and Secunda. For African women we have the elaborate account of the trial and death of the well-born Vibia Perpetua and her slave girl Felicitas, martyred in Carthage some twenty years later (March 203).[17]

Throughout the second century, Christianity spread among the poorer classes, especially in rural areas, giving these people new hope. At first not many were converted from the (urban) upper classes. We also know that the Christian church continued to grow rapidly. At the beginning of the third century there were seventy bishoprics in Carthage; by the mid-third century this number had grown to ninety. By the end of the century the number of bishops who gathered for a council session in Carthage had risen to two hundred and fifty. By this time Christianity was well represented in urban areas, and in such numbers that, according to Tertullian, Christians could almost claim a majority there.[18] There are a number of explanations for the rapid expansion of Christianity in North Africa. Among the most important is the witness of the martyrs. Tertullian affirmed a strong connection between martyrdom and growth in the development of the church.

---

17. On Perpetua's prison journal, her own account of detainment and preparation for martyrdom, see Isichei, *History of Christianity in Africa*, 34–35. The text is one of only four surviving documents of early Christianity written by women. Perpetua describes the despair of her pagan father as he tried to save her from death; she also recounts the visions which sustained her, with a ladder to heaven and herself treading on the head of a dragon as she ascended. In another vision she fought as a successful male gladiator. See ch. 4, §A.2 above and notes 32 and 105 there.

18. See Tertullian, *Ad Scapulam* 2; and J. Ferguson, "Aspects of the Early Christianity," 19.

The second factor in explaining the growth of Christianity is the attraction of Roman culture; by the fourth century, Christianity came to be closely identified with the Roman imperial presence. Several parts of the Bible were translated into Punic, the original language of Carthage (as a colony of Phoenicia);[19] Christianity was also adopted by a significant Berber community in "Africa" and Numidia (present-day Algeria). Even so, the North African church took on a strong Latin character, particularly in its literature. Use of Latin would have had an appeal as the gateway to an education and the means of acquiring status, especially in the cities. We know that those who were looking for an education in Latin did embrace the church; by the fourth century there were so many African students in Rome that a rule was made to limit the number of Africans who could attend a Roman theatre or all-night party.[20] In fact, Latin language and literature experienced a remarkable revival in Africa during these years. Scholars of North African Christianity have gone so far as to affirm Africa, not Rome, as the origin of Latin Christianity; they point to outstanding writers like Tertullian of Carthage.[21]

A third factor in the expansion of Christianity is its "puritanical" character. This is connected with the first factor as this character was shaped by persecution in ways peculiar to the North African region. This "puritanical" Christianity had able exponents like Tertullian and Cyprian, both associated with the century prior to Donatus. In troublesome times, especially during the third and fourth centuries, when the impact of external threat made the empire less secure, the church was recognized as a place to which people were drawn for refuge. For some rebel groups it might also serve as a refuge from persecution by the Roman state. Emerging from the experience of martyrdom, this "puritanical" character fed into stringent requirements of holy living, evident from the numerous treatises in which Tertullian advised Christians on how to live austerely in a deeply flawed and corrupt world. Concern for the purity of the church was clearly evident in the controversy between the Donatists and its Catholic (Roman) counterpart.

---

19. On the role of language among factors determining the indigeneity (and relative strength of a church community), see §B.2, note 49 below.

20. For the citation from the *Theodosian Codex* 14, 9.1, see J. Ferguson, "Aspects of the Early Christianity," 17.

21. This position, more recently supported by Thomas Oden (see §A above), can be traced back to Wilmot Blyden (1832–1912, quoting Dean Milman) that, "Africa, not Rome, gave birth to Latin Christianity." See Blyden, *Christianity, Islam and the Negro Race*, 165; and Ellis, "In Defence of Early North African Christianity," 162.

Such concerns are also rooted in the strong ecclesiology introduced in the North African church by Cyprian, the third-century bishop of Carthage.[22] Cyprian was a wealthy lawyer who experienced a dramatic conversion to Christianity and gave away all his possessions to the poor. He showed his deep concern for the church when he claimed that, "One cannot have God as father, when one does not have the church as mother."[23] Even more pungent is the statement, "One can no more escape judgment outside the doors of the church than the people of Noah's time could escape the flood, unless they entered the ark."[24]

B.1. The Donatists

The North African church had a strong nationalistic strain. Under the charisma of Donatus, the fourth-century church opposed both the Roman church and the Roman imperial government in North Africa. From about AD 340 a more extreme wing of Donatus's supporters, the Circumcellions, appeared as a type of "peasant revolt," motivated by economic grievance to take up arms against the imperial forces. Focused on the rich inhabitants of cities like Carthage (whose primary allegiance was with the imperial Roman government), the Circumcellions sought the cancellation of debt and freedom for slaves. In his studies of the Donatist church, W. H. C. Frend interpreted these efforts of the Donatists as a form of nationalism and a means of redressing the socio-economic imbalance between the rural and urban, or between the poor and wealthy sectors of the population.[25]

Because of the significance of the Donatist church in the history of early African Christianity, some detail on the development and impact of this wing of the church is helpful. Regarding their teachings, the Donatists were as orthodox as the Catholic church. In their views on the purity of the church, however, they formed a protest movement against the Catholic church. Since the fourth century the Catholic church had enjoyed the support of the imperial

---

22. A recent introductory article on Cyprian by Patout Burns accents Cyprian's concern for the purity and unity of the church; see Burns, "Cyprian of Carthage," 127–140.

23. Cyprian, *On the Unity of the Catholic Church* 6; the passage is quoted in Tennent, "Challenge of Churchless Christianity," 121; and Stevenson, *New Eusebius*, 230.

24. See Stevenson, *New Eusebius*, 230; also Needham, *2000 Years of Christ's Power*, 133.

25. See especially the important work of Frend, *The Donatist Church*. His interpretation was not universally accepted. The respected historian of the Roman Empire, A. H. M. Jones, took exception to his understanding of heresy as a disguise for social or nationalist movements; Peter Brown also sought to modify his understanding of local culture. See further, Isichei, *History of Christianity in Africa*, 37–38.

government; and it is important to note that the imperial powers valued unity in the face of division and sectarian tendencies.[26] As the "church of the martyrs," the Donatists traced their protest back to second-century Montanism, a "pentecostal" movement in Phrygia (Asia Minor) founded by Montanus, who went about preaching in the company of two women prophetesses, Priscilla and Maximilla.[27] The Montanist message proclaimed the approaching millennium as an event preceded by war, earthquake and catastrophe. They conveyed a message from the Holy Spirit that Christians should prepare for martyrdom, doing so by stringent abstinence and fasting.[28] Montanist theology had an able theological exponent in Tertullian of Carthage, who posed the question, "Does God desire man's blood?" And the answer was, "Yes!"[29] Martyrdom was seen as a way of purifying the church.

On this theme Tertullian was followed by Cyprian, who argued that the true church is not the church of sinners but of the pure and holy ones. This was the reason why Cyprian, as bishop from AD 248, refused to readmit to the church those who had succumbed to the persecution of Decius (AD 249–251), and surrendered the Scriptures to the authorities. These Christians were considered "traitors," based on the Latin term *traditor* for "one who hands over." In this position Cyprian opposed the influence of "confessors" who sought lenience.[30] Instead, he affirmed the final authority of the bishop in reinstating those who lapsed under persecution. At the council of Carthage (AD 256) he proclaimed that, "every bishop has the free use of his liberty and power, and has the right of forming his own judgment."[31] For *traditores*, Cyprian demanded

---

26. On political aspects of the Donatist case, see also ch. 5, §B.5.

27. For general discussion of Montanism as a rigorist apocalyptic movement, see Frend, *Rise of Christianity*, 253–256; also Latourette, *First Five Centuries*, 128–129. The movement represents an apocalyptic strain within Christianity as it experienced a time of persecution. Appealing to special revelations given him in Phrygia (ca. 155), Montanus prophesied the imminent return of Christ. Aside from teaching on moral restraint (to the point of forbidding marriage), the movement is considered schismatic, not heretical. It reflected dissatisfaction with complacency in the lifestyle of many Christians. Like the later Donatists, Montanists resented acceptance back into the church (with only minor indication of penitence) of those who renounced their faith under the pressure of persecution. Though repudiated by the church, the Montanist movement maintained its existence into the sixth century. Its rigorist attitudes are certainly reflected in North African Donatism.

28. See Tertullian, *On Fasting*, 9; and Frend, *Saints and Sinners*, 69.

29. Tertullian, *Scorpiace* 6–7; also quoted in J. Ferguson, "Aspects of the Early Christianity," 25.

30. That is, those who maintained their confession of "Jesus as Lord" under duress of persecution and lived through the experience; on the role of "confessors," see also ch. 4, §C.5.

31. See Stevenson, *New Eusebius*, 243–244.

sincere repentance and submission to a second baptism. When opposed on this issue by Stephen, the bishop of Rome, Cyprian refused to give in.[32]

Thus Cyprian encouraged the puritan wing of the church in its claim that, regardless of the position taken by the church of Rome, lapsed clergy could not be restored to ministry, even after confession. Sacraments served by such clergy were considered invalid, and a danger to the eternal welfare of the recipients.[33] Leaders in the church of Rome demanded that the North African "rebels" recant. Using his authority as bishop of Rome, Stephen even threatened Cyprian with excommunication, and had him exiled for his refusal to submit. When Stephen died Cyprian was recalled to Carthage, but not long after that he was charged by the provincial authorities, tried before the imperial Proconsul and executed as "ringleader of an unlawful association" (AD 258).[34] His martyr death only added to the appeal of Cyprian's views among his followers.

Donatism itself would become one of the serious consequences of the early fourth-century "great persecution" under Diocletian. The severity of persecution occasioned lapse in faith, even among bishops and clergy. But such persecution also produced many "confessors." In AD 304 some forty-seven martyrs from the small village of Albitina, when imprisoned in Carthage, declared that Christians who supported lapsed clergy would not share in the "joys of Paradise."[35] Their stringent view on reinstatement of the lapsed was challenged by Caecilian, the non-puritan archdeacon of Carthage, who responded by cutting off visitors to the prisoners. But in 311, when Caecilian was consecrated as bishop of Carthage on the death of Mensurius, his consecration was challenged by the puritan element which had supported the Albitanian "confessors." They argued that the consecration was accomplished before the arrival of the bishop of Numidia; more seriously, they accused Felix of Aphthungi, one of those who had consecrated Caecilian, of being a "traitor." For the puritan faction, this rendered Caecilian's consecration invalid, and they insisted that Caecilian be deposed. Donatus of Casae Nigrae, a Numidian priest and leader of the puritan cause, was declared bishop in his place and consecrated in 313. The church of North Africa was now divided into two factions; Caecilianists, or Catholics who supported the consecration of Caecilian, and were opposed to the Donatists; and puritans, who supported the consecration of Donatus. The latter were considered schismatic by the Catholics. The Donatists were in the

---

32. See Isichei, *History of Christianity in Africa*, 36.
33. Frend, *Saints and Sinners*, 100.
34. Frend, 102.
35. See Frend, 103; also Isichei, *History of Christianity in Africa*, 37.

majority and thought of themselves as the true Catholic church. Many of them came from the rural areas of Numidia. But ordinary people in Carthage also joined the Donatists.

The Catholics sent an appeal to Emperor Constantine, asking him to intervene.[36] The emperor, in turn, referred the matter to Miltiades, the bishop of Rome and an African, who sided with the Caecilian faction. A subsequent interprovincial council held at Arles (314) also supported Caecilian and rejected second baptism.[37] As a result, Donatists were branded as schismatics and also as "heretics" for their insistence on rebaptism. Persecuted by the Catholics and later by the state as well, the Donatist faction continued to grow. Their popularity was largely due to the charisma of Donatus, who was seen by his followers as a *Mahdi* (a religious reformer). Jerome tells us that Donatus nearly succeeded in mobilizing the whole of North Africa for the puritan cause.[38] On the basis of his research Frend has compared their popularity with the nineteenth-century revival movement, remarking that "chapels sprang up in Numidian villages in a manner reminiscent of Methodist and Baptist chapels in Wales and northern England in the nineteenth century."[39] As noted above, Frend himself recognized Donatism as a socio-economic protest of the poor and rural (Berber) peasants against the urbanized church, associated with wealthy landowners and imperial power. Their appeal to a social and nationalist conscience assured them the moral upper hand, religious enthusiasm and continued widespread popular support.

The influence of Donatism did not wane after Donatus was exiled to Gaul (in 346); Donatists prided themselves on being a select and chosen body. Among Donatus's successors were a number of learned and highly skilled leaders: Parmenian (who consolidated Donatism), the scholarly Tyconius, Petilian of Constantine, Emeritus of Caesarea and Primian of Carthage, all significant theologians in their own right. The Catholic church, however, benefited from a more solid and well-organized ecclesiastic structure.[40] And in support of its cause, we note the skill and eloquence of the bishop of Hippo Regius, Augustine (396–430), rallying the North African church as part of the wider Christian community within and beyond the empire.[41] In a sermon

---

36. See ch. 5, §B.5.
37. Frend, *Rise of Christianity*, 490–491.
38. See Jerome, *De Viris Illustribus*, 93; and Frend, *Saints and Sinners*, 105.
39. Frend, 107.
40. J. Ferguson, "Aspects of the Early Christianity," 24.
41. For further discussion of the life and work of Augustine, as well as his interaction with Donatists, see ch. 12, §D.3.

attacking Augustine personally, however, Petilian went so far as to cast doubt on the story of Augustine's conversion, claiming that the bishop had never fully given up adherence to the semi-gnostic Manichean religion of earlier years.[42] Petilian noted the claim of puritans in Numidian Constantine that two of their bishops who were friends of Augustine were still Manichee. Donatist leaders countered the case against them at every point, but Augustine's arguments would win the day. Against the rigorous position of the puritans, his vision of the church recognized "tares" mingled with the "wheat"; only with the final day of judgement would there be a full separation.[43] Augustine himself recognized that in terms of an austere and puritan viewpoint the two groups were really not that far apart. But Donatism maintained a strong and widespread presence in North Africa.[44] Indeed, it was so deeply rooted that it survived persecution by the Roman government and the Vandal invasion, lasting up to the time of the Muslim jihadists, whom Donatists would greet as African nationalists.

B.2. Christianity among the Berber People

Aside from its Latin (and puritanical) character, the North African church was also characterized by a distinctively Berber culture. Among the common people Christianity was accepted as somehow a continuation of Berber religion, for symbols typically associated with their ancient god Ba'al (identified in turn with the Roman god Saturn), such as the rosette, palm, dove, lion and crown, were used in the churches.

Christians adopted formulae which were popular among the Berbers, like "*bonis bene*" (i.e. "for those who are good, it is well"). The title of the Berber god *Senex* (lit. "elder") was also used for Christian bishops.[45] In continuity with traditional Berber religion, extreme human passion, implacable jealousy and desire for vengeance were attributed to God. To think of God as less than fearsome would be regarded as heresy.[46] The tradition of human sacrifice among the Berbers, perhaps a survival from Punic worship of Ba'al,

---

42. On Petilian's accusation in the *Ad Augustinum*, 3, see Frend, *Donatist Church*, 256. Augustine responded to these charges on numerous occasions and perhaps most eloquently in the account he gave of his life before ordination in the *Confessions*; on the context of such accusations, see ch. 12, §D.3.

43. See Augustine's *Enarrationes in Psalmos* CXIX [Vulgate] 7.72; also CXXXVIII 27; and his *Tractatus XI in evangelium Iohannis*, 12.

44. On the claim that members, and even some of the clergy of Bishop Augustine's church at Hippo were becoming Donatists, see Frend, *Donatist Church*, 240 and 272.

45. J. Ferguson, "Aspects of the Early Christianity," 24–25.

46. J. Ferguson, 25.

has been considered a factor in the appeal of martyrdom.[47] Consulting seers and magicians was not uncommon among the Berbers. We hear of one of Augustine's parishioners claiming, "Oh yes, I go to idols; I consult seers and magicians, but I do not abandon God's church. I am a Catholic."[48]

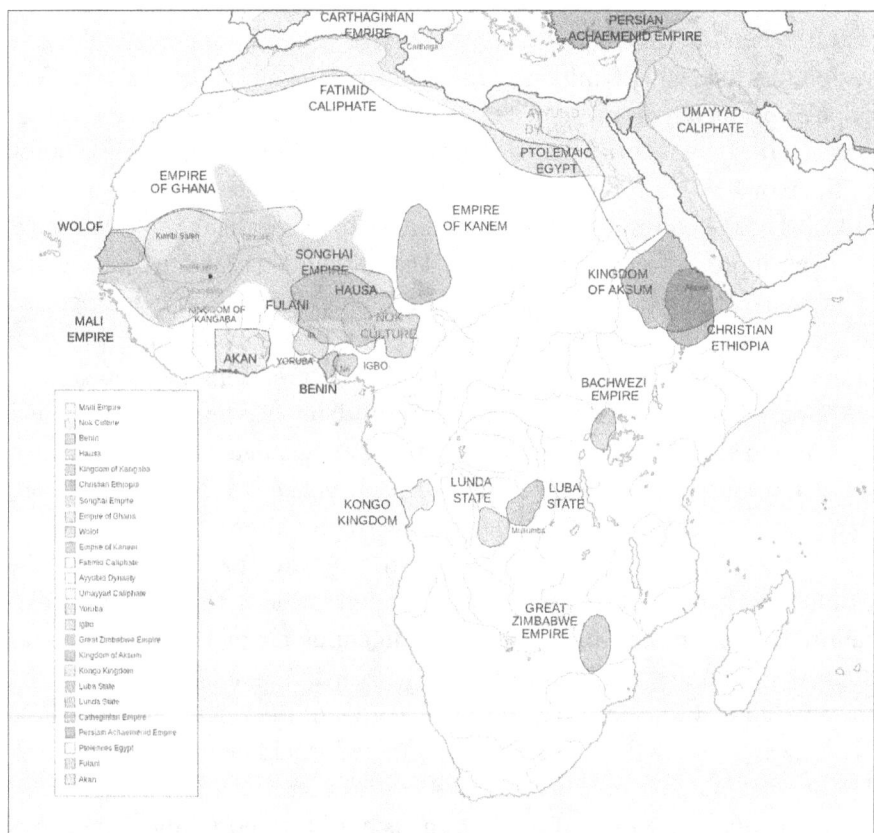

Map 6.1. Pre-colonial African civilization, groups North and South. "Diachronic map showing pre-colonial cultures of Africa" by Jeff Israel / CC BY-SA 3.0.

When Muslim forces invaded North Africa some centuries later, conquering Byzantine Africa between 670–705, Christianity had already been weakened significantly by persecution, conflict and internal crisis. Gothic Vandals had invaded and settled in modern Tunisia in 429. As Arians, they persecuted Catholic and Donatist Christians without distinction, imposing their own

---

47. See J. Ferguson, 25. Tertullian also thought God was pleased with the sacrifice of human blood (*Scorp.* 6–7), see note 29.
48. Augustine, *Sermon*, 2.4; the passage is quoted in J. Ferguson, "Aspects of the Early Christianity," 25–26.

Arian Christian views on the churches. These Gothic invaders were eventually overthrown by Justinian (AD 533), but Byzantine hold on power in the region was no longer reliable by the seventh century.

The collapse and almost total eradication of Christianity in North Africa has drawn considerable scholarly attention; it is often compared negatively with the persistence of Coptic Christianity in Egypt, Ethiopia and Nubia, a region in which Christianity had a significant rural and monastic base. One popular perspective represented by the nineteenth-century Liberian Wilmot Blyden (1832–1912) has focused on inadequate indigenization of Christianity in the North African regions, the failure to incorporate the languages and cultures of the common people, and failure to evangelize the hinterland.[49] Blyden's approach reflects the dissatisfaction with African Christianity as a European missionary import that prevailed in his time, and is now recognized as a considerable oversimplification of a complex set of circumstances.[50] Of course, the geography of North Africa is quite different from the regions along the Nile; while the Sahara presented a formidable barrier, the Nile invited exploration into the upper regions.[51] And the strong monastic tradition, which did so much to hold together the Christians of Egypt and the Nile communities, had never taken such deep root in the western provinces.

So the collapse of North African Christianity may have been an inevitable result of internal conflict and weakness; it cannot be attributed simply to a failure of Christianity to assume an indigenous character. As Frend has suggested, some remaining factions of the North African church may even have welcomed Muslim invaders, as did some of their counterparts in the Near East, thinking the religion they promoted would be more egalitarian.[52] Unfortunately, Christians who refused to convert to Islam were relegated to servile *dhimmi* status. At present one is hard pressed to find indigenous Christians in the Maghreb. Though their numbers have increased somewhat in

---

49. Blyden expressed great appreciation for the ancient African contribution to Christianity and attributed the resilience of Coptic and Ethiopian Christians to their success in incorporating the language and culture of the common people; see Ellis, "In Defence of Early North African Christianity," 161–162. See also appendix III on historiography of early African Christianity, where the issue is noted as a perennial concern.

50. For recent critical discussion of Blyden's position, using evidence from archeological excavation, see Ellis, "In Defence of Early North African Christianity," 157–158; see also Sawyer and Youssef, "Early Christianity in North Africa," 71–72.

51. Although Jenkins expressed some sympathy for Blyden's approach, he also recognized the significance of geographic factors for differences between Christianity in the Maghreb and the Coptic Christian world; see Jenkins, *Lost History of Christianity*, 228–230 and 236–240.

52. Frend, *Donatist Church*, 335; and Ellis, "In Defence of Early North African Christianity," 160.

recent years, the established Christian churches in Morocco, Algeria, Tunisia and Lybia are still attended almost exclusively by members of the expatriate community.

C. The Egyptian Church

In Egypt Christianity eventually moved into the rural south of the country, where it was "de-Hellenized" by the monks. In fact, after the persecution under Diocletian, the church in southern (or Upper) Egypt appears to have distanced itself from that of Alexandria in the Nile Delta. It took skillful negotiation by Bishop Athanasius to win back the monks from the south and reunite the two sectors of the Egyptian church. The indigenous Coptic church emerged from this union.[53] Egyptians succeeded where other North Africans failed, perhaps because the strong opposition suffered by indigenous Donatists in North Africa under the Roman government did not characterize the Egyptian context.

As noted in chapter 2, little is known about Christianity in Egypt before the late second century,[54]

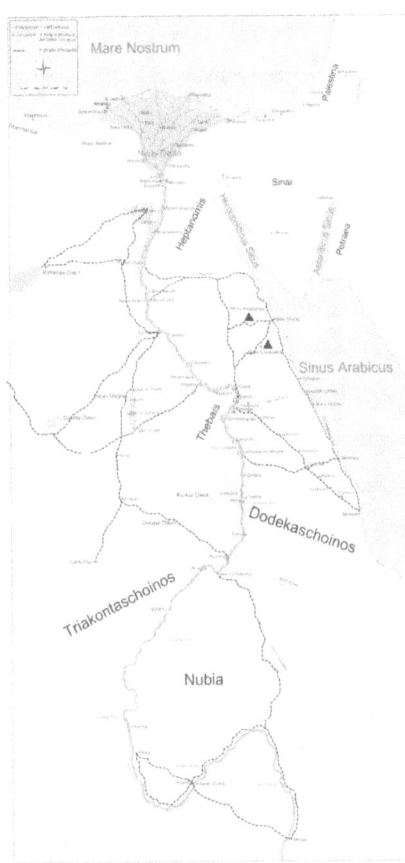

Map 6.2. Map of Ancient Egypt and Nubia.
Map "Map of Ancient Egypt, showing the Nile up to the fifth cataract, and major cities and sites of the Dynastic period (c. 3150 BC to 30 BC)" by Gigillo83 / CC BY-SA 4.0.

---

53. The term "Coptic" was originally used for the Egyptian language written with the Greek alphabet. "Coptic" actually has the same root as the term "Egyptian" (Greek *Aigyptos*), based on the ancient designation for Memphis as "House of Ptah." Coptic writing succeeded other forms: hieroglyphs, hieratic and demotic/cursive. Most of the Nag Hammadi documents were written in the Coptic language which was typically used also for Christian literature. Eventually Arabic took over for most common purposes, but Coptic remained the language and script of the liturgy. See Isichei, *History of Christianity in Africa*, 26.

54. The substantive work of Otto Meinardus, *Christian Egypt Ancient and Modern* (Cairo: American University in Cairo Press, 1977) devotes little attention to the early period, before the Arab conquest (1–7), with but sporadic attention elsewhere. The lacuna is filled admirably

Figure 6.2. Mark in the Coptic church. Depicted in this medieval (15th century) Ethiopian Gospel Book, the gospel writer Mark was highly regarded in the Coptic churches as a close associate of the apostles and first bishop of Alexandria. Digital image courtesy of the Getty's Open Content Program.

although Alexandria would presumably have been an important centre of Christianity well before that time.

The court of the Ptolemies had ruled from this city for three centuries, until Egypt was incorporated into the Roman Empire.[55] Alexandria was cosmopolitan; it boasted the most important port in the Mediterranean, and was acknowledged as the second city in the Roman Empire after Rome. Alexandria also had a large population of Jews, estimated to be as high as one third of its total population in the early imperial period.[56] According to Philo of Alexandria, the number of Jews in the whole of Egypt at this time may have been as high as one million, out of a total population of approximately eight million. Jews served as soldiers and civil servants; many were employed

---

by Arnauld, *Histoire du Christianisme en Afrique*.

55. On the significance of Alexandria for the Hellenistic and Roman empires, see ch. 1, §A.3 and §A.5.

56. A significant number of Jews had been encouraged to settle in Alexandria under the Ptolemies, but we note also the migration of Jews to Egypt and Kush from the time of the Babylonian exile, mentioned in Isaiah 11:11 and 18:1–2; Jeremiah 44; and Zephaniah 3:10. On this background, see also Isichei, *History of Christianity in Africa*, 16.

as tax collectors, while others were engaged in agriculture, as artisans, in shipbuilding, trade and merchandizing.[57] The Hebrew Scriptures were first translated into Greek in Alexandria, as Jews of that time were typically no longer conversant with Hebrew.

Throughout the centuries the Christian church in Egypt has taken comfort in the fact that Mary and Joseph took the child Jesus to Egypt when Herod sought to take his life (Matt 2:13–15). Its traditions also claim Mark as the first apostle to Egypt and its first bishop. Mark is believed to have been martyred in Alexandria.[58]

But long before the rise of Christianity, Alexandria was known as a centre for Greek scholarship. So it is not surprising that Alexandria became the home of the early catechetical school led by Pantaenus, preparing the way for more famous teachers like Clement of Alexandria and Origen; through their work the school had a profound influence on the development of western theology.

Alexandria also played an important role in the rise of Gnosticism. At least two outstanding leaders of Gnosticism in the second century, Valentinus and Basileides, came from Alexandria. Since the well-known analysis of Gnosticism by Adolf von Harnack as "acute Hellenization of the gospel," the gnostic factor has typically been explained in terms of the prominence of Greek culture and philosophy, which certainly characterized the Alexandrian context.[59] The pervasive gnostic influence in Egypt is clearly reflected in the Nag Hammadi documents, discovered (in 1945) as the remains of a library in Upper Egypt, north of Luxor. Gnostic influence is also evident in the theological response of the two important early Christian scholars connected with Alexandria, Clement and Origen;[60] both writers engaged Gnosticism in an attempt to reconcile Christian teachings with Greek ideas, while they also sought to reconcile their understanding with Old Testament writings and Jewish worship, as the foundation of early Christianity.

Unlike Alexandria and the Nile Delta region, which were highly Hellenized and culturally sophisticated, life in Upper (or the southern areas of) Egypt was rural, traditional and simple. When Demetrius was bishop of Alexandria (ca. AD 200), he sent missionaries to this southern area; the fruits of these efforts can be seen in the number of Christians who were brought to Alexandria from both Upper and Lower Egypt to be executed during the Severan persecution

---

57. Smallwood, "Jews in Egypt," 113.
58. See Isichei, *History of Christianity in Africa*, 17, where she cites Eusebius *EH* 2.16.
59. On Gnosticism see ch. 8. On Harnack, see appendix I, §C.
60. Frend, *Early Church*, 51. For a more extensive discussion of Gnosticism, see ch. 8.

of 202. Clement of Alexandria also attests to the fact that Christians could be found in any town or village of Egypt at this time.[61] The display of courage by these martyrs may well have been a significant factor in the expansion of Christianity, for after this wave of persecution Christianity spread even further in Upper Egypt, especially among the peasant population. These Christians were certainly stubborn in resisting further persecution and even tended to fanaticism in the exercise of their faith. This is evident from reports of persecution under Diocletian, and especially under Maximin (AD 311–312).[62] In fact, the Coptic Christian calendar dates "from the era of the martyrs," the time of Diocletian (AD 284), and does not calculate events with the Catholic church, which uses the designation *Anno Domini* (AD), counting from the birth of the Lord Jesus. In that respect the monks of Egypt may be compared with the Circumcellions of the western regions of North Africa, as they resisted secular authority. The Egyptian monks, however, gradually became loyal subjects of the Coptic church. Even the schismatic faction of the Meletians, rooted in factors similar to those which led to Donatism, never enjoyed the widespread support given Donatus in the West.

The introduction of the gospel to the rural population of Upper Egypt presented linguistic challenges. The important local languages were: Sahidic, spoken in the Upper Nile; Boharic in the Nile Delta; and Basmuric in the Middle Nile region.[63] Missionaries to these districts initially used interpreters, but were also ready to study the local languages, and significant portions of the Scriptures were soon translated into these languages. Later the entire Bible was translated, written with the Greek script. By the fourth century there was already a considerable amount of Coptic literature in circulation. Within a short period of time Coptic Christians were making a major contribution to Egyptian Christianity.

The Christian monastic movement may also be traced back to early Coptic Christianity; from those origins it would exercise a major influence on the development of worldwide Christianity.[64] Much like Donatism, Egyptian monasticism represented a puritanical movement. It aimed at purifying the church of the Egyptian cults that had crept in. Coptic resistance to Hellenization and a further reaction of the (ruling) Latin- and Greek-speaking elements to a

---

61. For citation of Clement, see Thompson, "Christianity in Egypt," 7.

62. For details of the gruesome forms of torture applied, see Eusebius's *Ecclesiastical History*, 7.6–9.

63. Kalu, "Golden Age of Christianity," 41.

64. On the role of African leaders in monasticism, see also the discussion in ch. 3, §A.1 and §A.2.

decidedly Coptic Christianity, in turn, could have led to theological crises, as it did in other parts of North Africa. In Egypt the situation was different, thanks to the mature intervention of leaders like Athanasius, reconciling the two sectors of the church and encouraging cooperative efforts. Such conciliatory efforts would shape the theology of the united Egyptian church, providing theological arguments against Arianism which would still be defended in later doctrinal controversies with Constantinople. In his determination to defend the Nicene Creed, Athanasius suffered ongoing persecution under the so-called Christian emperors and bishops of this time. Had he not continued his efforts to support the Nicene Creed, however, Christianity might well have been overwhelmed by Arianism.[65]

The union of the Alexandrian and Coptic churches led to the adoption of certain Egyptian cultural practices. Inasmuch as the church was not Greek, but Coptic, its archbishops adopted a role like that of the Pharaohs of old; they were called *Qodsak* (i.e. "Patriarch," or "Your Holiness").[66] In Egypt the Monophysite controversy also took on a distinctively African flavour, for adherents used a typically African understanding of spirit-possession in understanding Jesus's divinity.[67] They considered him "one with God" because he was possessed by the Holy Spirit.

The struggle for supremacy between Egypt and Constantinople continued until the invasion of the Persians (in 616) and of Arabs (639–641). Although the Copts might have rejoiced at the appearance of these invaders, expecting freedom from the oppression of the "Melechite" (imperial) Christians of Egypt and Byzantium, in fact, they did not welcome them; the Coptic bishop lamented that God had abandoned them and delivered them without mercy to the invading peoples.[68] They were at the mercy of the weakened Byzantine troops of the time. After the conquest many Copts did become Muslim. There is an account (from 1345) claiming that six hundred Copts converted to Islam in one day! During the seventeenth-century Coptic ceased to be the language of common usage, functioning only as a biblical language and in liturgical settings. Arabic was adopted as the official language for everyday use. Today approximately ten percent of Egyptians are Christian; the Coptic church in Egypt is marginalized, but has not disappeared.

---

65. On Athanasius's role, see ch. 10, §B.1, and ch. 12, §A.1; also Noll, *Turning Points*, 55.
66. Davis, "Coptic Christianity," 51.
67. On the Monophysite position, see ch. 11, §B.1 and §B.2.
68. Thompson, "Christianity in Egypt," 14.

Figure 6.3. The Coptic Orthodox Church of Amman (Jordan). This imposing structure witnesses to the ongoing life of the Coptic Church in Middle Eastern countries. Photo "Coptic Church, Amman, Jordan" by Shannon Hobbs / CC BY-SA 2.0.

D. The Ethiopian Church

We have already noted the Ethiopian church as one of the oldest and most significant institutions in this region, drawing from three religious traditions: the indigenous religion, Judaism and Christianity. Historically Ethiopia hosted a large Jewish community; a sense of identity with its Jewish heritage is a feature unique to the Ethiopian church.[69] In fact, the Falasha, who know and obey the Jewish law of Moses from the Pentateuch and keep the Sabbath, claim to be descendants of these Jews.[70] The Amharic language of Ethiopia also betrays the Jewish connection, as it is Semitic.

---

69. See Ward, "Africa," 197. For a brief introduction to Christianity in Ethiopia, see Ward, "Africa," 197–200.

70. The Falasha, who are Ethiopian and black, call themselves the "House of Israel" and claim roots in Judaism; they also appear to be descended from the Agaw, for they use the ancient Kushite language, Agaw, as the language of liturgy. They may have been influenced by Judaism in southern Arabia. Even so, the Falasha appealed to their Jewish roots when they sought to escape the famine in Ethiopia of the 1970s; at that time they were recognized by the state of

Indeed, the Ethiopian church takes pride in a historic connection with Judah, rooted in the story of the Queen of Sheba's visit with King Solomon (recorded in 1 Kgs 10 and 2 Chr 9). In the biblical account this royal encounter appears to reflect the queen's acceptance of faith in the God of Israel, for she tells Solomon, "Praise be to the Lord your God, who has delighted in you and placed you on his throne as king to rule for the Lord your God . . . to maintain justice and righteousness (2 Chr 9:8)." And Jesus referred positively to the faith of this queen (Matt 12:42). The story of king Solomon and the Queen of Sheba forms the basis of the fourteenth-century Ethiopian *Kebra Nagast*, affirming a connection with Solomon as the origin of a royal dynasty and the foundation of Ethiopian national identity.[71] From medieval times the kings of Ethiopia have claimed descent from Menelik I, born of that visit. Even so, we realize that the biblical Sheba may refer to *Sabaea* in southeast Arabia (Yemen), a region closely associated with Ethiopia from about 600 BC, when Arabs crossed the Red Sea to settle in northern Ethiopia. They brought with them the Semitic language and alphabet that is the ancestor of Ge'ez, and of the modern Amharic language.

The very architecture of the Ethiopian Orthodox Tewahedo churches reflects this continuity from Judaism of Solomon's time; some churches have been designed to resemble Solomon's temple in Jerusalem and include replicas of the ark of the covenant (the *tabod*).[72] As noted above, the Ethiopian church keeps both the Sabbath (on Saturday) and Sunday as public holidays. The Ethiopian liturgical calendar adopted the Coptic calendar of twelve months with thirty days each, and an extra thirteenth month consisting of the remaining five days.[73]

The New Year is celebrated on the feastday of John the Baptist; the flight into Egypt is commemorated in October; Christ's birth and baptism in January; Lent in February and March; Holy Week and Easter in April; Christ's Ascension and Pentecost in May and June; and the Assumption of Mary is celebrated in August.[74]

There is a legend that the apostle Matthew preached in Ethiopia; and the Acts of the Apostles (Acts 8:26–40) tells of the conversion of an "Ethiopian" eunuch, though he may well have been a Nubian from the royal court of

---

Israel, and allowed to migrate to a new homeland in Palestine. See Isichei, *History of Christianity in Africa*, 17.

71. See Isichei, 15.
72. Ward, "Africa," 197.
73. See Merahi, *Christianity in Ethiopia*, 32.
74. Merahi, 37.

Figure 6.4. Bet Giyorgis, Ethiopia's famous rock-hewn church. This magnificent *hypogea* church from the post-Aksum era (6th–7th century), cut from rocky local sandstone, is dedicated to Ethiopia's patron saint, Saint George. Located in Lalibela (southern Ethiopia), the church became a Unesco World Heritage Site. Photo "Bet Giyorgis" by Katie Hunt / CC BY 2.0.

Figure 6.5. Surface view of Bet Giyorgis. Photo by Katie Hunt / CC BY 2.0.

Meroe (in present-day Sudan).⁷⁵ Indeed, before the fourth-century arrival of Frumentius and Aedesius at the Ethiopian royal court, Christianity was relatively well-established, if not well-organized. The early Christians appear to have been traders or soldiers; we also know of Christians coming to Ethiopia to escape persecution elsewhere.

Even so, formal introduction of Christianity at the Ethiopian court is traditionally associated with the early fourth-century arrival of the brothers Frumentius and Aedesius from Syria (recounted above). The ship on which they had accompanied their teacher Meropius had stopped at the Ethiopian port of Adulis on the Red Sea when it was attacked by Ethiopians who thought it represented an enemy.⁷⁶ While all those on board were killed, Frumentius and Aedesius had already disembarked and were resting under a nearby tree. Their knowledge of Greek, the trade language of the region, may well have been key to their survival, making them useful to the regime. Taken to the royal court in Aksum, the young men clearly made a good impression and were given various responsibilities. The Emperor Ella Amida died shortly afterwards. Ruling on behalf of her son Ezana until he could assume power, the queen asked the two young Syrians to help her in administering the kingdom.⁷⁷ Frumentius used his role as tutor to influence the young heir to the throne in support of Christianity. When Ezana himself became king, the two Syrians were given their freedom and returned home. By that time there were thriving churches in Ethiopia.

It appears that Christianity became the official state religion in Ethiopia with the mid-fourth-century reign of King Ezana.

He became known as the "Constantine" of Ethiopia, and unity of the church with the royal court remained a feature of Ethiopian Christianity from that time. In affirmation of the story of Aedesius and Frumentius, there is evidence that King Ezana had already accepted Christianity when he came to the throne. In an extant declaration he attributes success (in the conquest of Nubian Meroe) not to the Ethiopian war-god Ares, but to the God of heaven. The inscription opens with the phrase, "By the power of the Lord of heaven, who in heaven and upon earth is mightier than everything that exists."⁷⁸

Aedesius returned to Tyre to continue his studies, but Frumentius travelled to Alexandria, where he asked Patriarch Athanasius to appoint a bishop for the Christians in Ethiopia. Athanasius could think of no better person for

---

75. See §E below.
76. On the prominence of Adulis as an Aksumite port on the Red Sea at the time, see Seland, "Early Christianity in East Africa," 640–641.
77. Davis, "Coptic Christianity," 63.
78. Tafla, "Establishment," 31.

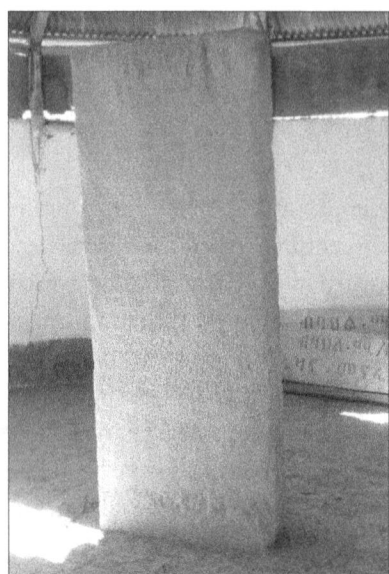

Figure 6.6. The Ezana Tablet.
With this multilingual inscription, Emperor Ezana recorded his victory over neighbouring peoples. The Greek side is shown in this photo; the inscription is also given in the Ge'ez and Sabaic languages. Photo "Enzana Stone" by Rajesh Singh / CC BY 2.0.

the task than Frumentius himself, and so consecrated him bishop of Ethiopia. The Ethiopian church honoured that first consecration by the Patriarch (*Abuna*) of Egypt and maintained a strong link with the Egyptian church right into the twentieth century (to 1958). When Frumentius returned to Ethiopia, his work resulted in the country becoming a Christian kingdom. The Ethiopians have revered him, calling him *Abba Salama* (Father of Peace).

The fifth-century arrival of Syrian missionaries, known as the "Nine Saints," further motivated the conversion of Ethiopia. These may well have been Monophysite monks fleeing persecution;[79] their work also served to affirm the Monophysite character of Ethiopian Christianity. With the encouragement of the state they founded monasteries and strengthened the church. The work of these monks in translating the Scripture into the local languages, particularly into Ge'ez (which would remain the language of ritual), was particularly significant for the integration of Christianity with Ethiopian culture. Yared, one of these monks, laid the foundation for Ge'ez poetry.[80] Old temples were converted into churches.

The Christian church in Ethiopia came to influence many facets of public life: the economy, literacy, education and politics. Before the twentieth century, when the Marxist regime came to power in Ethiopia, there was no separation between religious and secular powers.

With the coming of Islam, the relationship between Ethiopia and the growing Islamic empire was cordial at first. In obedience to a directive from

---

79. This is the suggestion of Isichei (*History of Christianity*, 33); as Monophysites, they may have been fleeing persecution after the council of Chalcedon. On Monophysites, see ch. 11, §B.1.

80. On the contribution of the monks, see ch. 3, §A.3.

Figure 6.7. Yared and his disciples before King Gebre Meskel (AD 525–539). This depiction of the singing saints decorates the walls of Hotel Remhai (in Axum). Photo "Yared An [sic] His Disciples" by A. Davey / CC BY 2.0.

the Prophet Muhammad, no jihad was declared against Ethiopia, especially because Ethiopians had provided refuge for Muslims when they fled from Mecca to escape persecution, just before the *hijra*. But once the Muslims enjoyed widespread success in the Middle East and were determined to build a global empire (like the Greeks, Macedonians and Romans before them), they felt they had no option but to attack Ethiopia as well. From 1529 to 1543 the Muslim general nicknamed (Ahmed) Gran of Gragn ("left-handed") devastated the Christian highlands of the Ethiopian kingdom, destroying many churches and monasteries.[81]

Without the timely intervention of the Portuguese king, Ethiopia would have been crushed. Portuguese support established a relationship between the Ethiopian church and Roman Catholicism. This link did not last; there were sharp theological differences between the two branches of Christianity. Like the Coptic church of Egypt, the Ethiopian church had rejected the decision of the Council of Chalcedon (AD 450) on the two natures of Jesus Christ.[82] Nevertheless, Catholics were instrumental in the survival of the Ethiopian

---

81. Ward, "Africa," 199.
82. For further discussion of the issues facing this council, see ch. 11, §A.2.

church. Because of its historically central role in the history of Ethiopia, the church continues to serve as a public archive, and no history of Ethiopia can be written without due consideration of records maintained through the Christian church.

E. The Nubian Church

There are many unknowns in the early history of Nubia, the ancient kingdom of Kush (now the Sudan). Its known history goes back to the dominance of Meroe (from ca. 300 BC to AD 300).[83] Most scholars believe that the Ethiopian eunuch encountered by Philip (recorded in Acts 8) was actually an official at the court of Candace, as Queen Mother of Meroe. A queen with that name did fight the Romans at the time of Augustus Caesar.[84] If this is true, the eunuch would have to be recognized as the first Nubian Christian. As in Ethiopia, Christianity may have arrived initially with traders doing business in the region.

The Nubian kingdom was created from what was left of Kush after the war with Ethiopia was won by the Aksumite Ethiopians under Ezana. The new kingdom consisted of three semi-autonomous states: Nobatia, with its capital in Ballana and Faras, to the north; Alodia, with its capital in Soba (near modern Khartoum) in the south; and Makuria, with its capital at Old Dongola, between the two kingdoms.[85]

At this time the Nubians would have become acquainted with Christianity through contact with Ethiopia; Christian influence also came from Egypt. After the Council of Chalcedon (451), persecution of adamantly Monophysite Christians resulted in the flight of numerous Egyptians, especially monks, to Nubia. A more formal introduction of Christianity to Nubia would also come from Constantinople under Justinian, who sent missionaries at the request of the Nubian King Silko (AD 540).[86] But differing theological positions of Emperor Justinian and his wife, Empress Theodora, translated into significant differences among the missionaries who were sent.

---

83. Isichei, *History of Christianity in Africa*, 30.
84. See Tafla, "Establishment," 30.
85. Hevbare, "Christianity in Nubia," 53.
86. In a thorough discussion of the introduction of Christianity in ancient Nubia, Faraji (*Roots of Nubian Christianity*) argues that mid-fifth-century military campaigns of the Nubian King Silko were very significant in the Christianizing of Nubia and prepared the way for the sixth-century Byzantine missionaries (*Roots of Nubian Christianity*, 69). Critical evidence comes from an inscription at the temple of Mandulis at Kalabsha, where King Silko recognized that "God gave me the victory" (*Roots of Nubian Christianity*, 85–177).

Justinian held to the Chalcedonian duophysite understanding of Christ (affirming two natures, human and divine), while Theodora adhered to the Monophysire position (maintaining only one nature for Christ, with the divine overshadowing the human).[87] On learning of Justinian's plan to send Orthodox duophysite missionaries, Theodora managed to block them until her own men, the (Monophysite) monks Julian and Longinus, got to Nubia. When the Emperor's missionaries finally arrived, Monophysite emissaries had already successfully spread their understanding of Christianity in Nobatia and Alodia, leaving only the central state of Makuria for Justinian's duophysite missionaries.

Figure 6.8. Empress Theodora. This 6th-century mosaic, a section from a larger portrayal of the empress surrounded by her court, is located in the Basilica of San Vitale (Ravenna, Italy). Detail from 6th century mosaic "Empress Theodora and Her Court." Photographic reproduction by Szilas. Public Domain.

In spite of these obstacles and the significant entrenchment of traditional religion among the Nubians, the three regions were converted to Christianity before the end of the sixth century. Ongoing contact with Coptic Christianity remained important, although it was inevitably diminished after the Arab conquest of Egypt (639–641). Nubian Christians under King Cyriacus of Alodia actually marched to Egypt to defend the Patriarch of Alexandria against Muslim invaders (in AD 737). By then Christianity had taken over the important central traditional shrine in Philae, once devoted to Isis. Upon destruction of the temple, the central statue of the goddess was removed and sent to Constantinople. In Makuria alone there were seven dioceses, many churches and also many monasteries. The influence of Nubian Christianity was felt, in turn, in regions to the south, in Kordofan, Darfur, Ennedi and even in the region of Lake Chad.[88]

Although it was predominantly Coptic and Monophysite, Nubian Christianity developed a distinct identity through use of its own Nubian

---

87. For further discussion of Justinian, the Monophysites and the Orthodox "duophysite" position, see ch. 11, §B.1 and §B.2.

88. Ward gives evidence for black Nubian priests and monks from mural representations on walls of the churches along the banks of the Nile ("Africa," 196). See also Hevbare, "Christianity in Nubia," 57.

language, written with the Greek alphabet. This language was used in the church to strengthen Nubian national identity in the face of the threat of Islam. Some of the beauty of Nubian culture was discovered in the 1960s when archaeological excavation of the region uncovered the cathedral of Faras, revealing walls that were richly decorated with regal figures, biblical characters and saints.[89]

Arab Muslims invaded the kingdom within a hundred years of the introduction of Christianity; they attacked Dongola between 651 and 652. Churches were burned, but the peace treaty (*baqt*) that was imposed allowed corn, oil and clothes for Christians. In return they were made to pay an annual tribute of 360 slaves. In 985, Muslims crushed both Makuria and Alodia, destroying the alliance between them. Philae was captured in 1172; churches were looted and the bishop tortured. An order was given "for the Muslim call to prayer to be sounded from the dome of the church" at Philae.[90]

Even so, written records and religious textual fragments attest to the continuing presence of Christianity. Immigration of Muslim Arabs into the area, however, meant a gradual shift in the population, with Nubian Christians being left as a minority.[91] In 1317 the cathedral of Dongola became a mosque. The southern kingdom of Alodia survived at least in some form until the year 1500. But there was no other nation to come to its defence against the military campaign of the Muslim (Negro) Amara Dunkas (in 1504).

If Nubian Christianity finally collapsed completely, one must not underestimate the resistance of the Christian population, which was put down with great ferocity during these crises. This much is clear from the reconstruction of churches as fortresses. The inexorable advance of Islam met with strong national resistance on the part of the Nubians.[92] Christians who fled the region may have come as far as Chad, northern Cameroon and present-day Nigeria, even if there are few traces of an ongoing presence of Christianity in these regions.

---

89. Isichei recognizes the cultural vitality evident in paintings on the church walls; she also notes the distinguished tradition of Nubian pottery decorated with realistic natural designs (*History of Christianity in Africa*, 31).

90. Hevbare, "Christianity in Nubia," 59.

91. Isichei, *History of Christianity in Africa*, 32.

92. Ward, "Africa," 196.

Questions for Discussion and Review

The Early Church in North Africa

1. Why has the history of early Christianity in Africa suffered neglect to date?

2. Which outstanding achievements of early African Christians make their work worthy of attention?

3. Why are the earliest records of martyrdom of Christians in Carthage significant?

4. What is the significance of the use of the Latin language by the North African church?

5. Who are the Donatists? And why is their contribution significant?

6. Which aspects of traditional Berber culture are evident in the early North African church?

7. Why is the city of Alexandria so important for the history of Christianity in Egypt?

8. How did persecution and martyrdom affect the Egyptian church?

9. What is the significance of the translation of the Scriptures into the languages of Upper Egypt?

10. Which important contributions were made by Coptic Christians in the development of monasticism? How did Egyptian monks serve the development of Christianity in the region?

11. Why might Coptic Christians have welcomed the invasion of the Muslims?

12. What are the distinctive features of Ethiopian Christianity?

13. What significant roles did Frumentius and King Ezana play in the introduction of Christianity in Ethiopia?

14. How did the coming of Islam impact Ethiopian Christianity?

15. How was Christianity introduced to Nubia?

16. How did the Monophysite controversy impact the development of Nubian Christianity?

17. How did use of the indigenous language in the church strengthen Nubian Christians? Why was the use of indigenous languages in the church significant for its confrontation with Islam?

Further Reading

Davis, A. J. "Coptic Christianity." *Tarikh* 2, no. 1 (1967): 43–52.
———. "The Orthodoxy of the Ethiopian Church." *Tarikh* 2, no. 1 (1967): 62–69.
Ellis, Ieuan. "In Defence of Early North African Christianity." In *New Testament Christianity for Africa and the World*, edited by Mark Glasswell and Edward Fashole-Luke, 157–165. London: SPCK, 1974.
Ferguson, John. "Aspects of the Early Christianity in North Africa." *Tarikh* 2, no. 1 (1967): 16–27.
———. *Clement of Alexandria*. New York: Twayne Publishers, 1974.
Frend, W. H. C. "Church and State, Perspectives and Problems in the Patristic Era." *Studia Patristica* 18 (1982): 38–54.
———. *The Donatist Church*. Oxford: Clarendon, 1971.
———. "The Donatist Church – Forty Years On." In *Window on Origins: Essays on the Early Church*, edited by C. Landman and D. P. Whitelaw, 70–84. Pretoria: University of South Africa, 1985. (Found also in Frend 1988, section XV.)
———. *The Early Church*. London: Hodder & Stoughton; Philadelphia: Fortress Press, 1982.
———. *Martyrdom and Persecution in the Early Church: A Study of Conflict from the Maccabees to Donatus*. Oxford: Basil Blackwell, 1965.
———. "Nationalism as a Factor in Anti-Chalcedonian Feeling in Egypt." In *Religion and National Identity: Studies in Church History* 18, edited by Stuart Mews, 21–38. Oxford: Blackwell, 1982.
———. *Saints and Sinners in the Early Church: Differing and Conflicting Traditions in the First Six Centuries*. London: Darton, Longman & Todd, 1985.
Hevbare, J. A. "Christianity in Nubia." *Tarikh* 2, no. 1 (1967): 53–61.
Kalu, Ogbu U. "The Golden Age of Christianity in Africa? Early Christianity in North Africa Revisited." *Nsukka Journal of Religious Studies* 1, no. 1 (1996): 34–49.
Noll, Mark A. *Turning Points: Decisive Moments in the History of Christianity*. Grand Rapids: Baker, 1997.
Oden, Thomas C. *How Africa Shaped the Christian Mind: The African Seedbed of European Christianity*. Downers Grove, IL: InterVarsity Press, 2007.
Tafla, Bairu. "The Establishment of the Ethiopian Church." *Tarikh* 2, no. 1 (1967): 28–42.
Thompson, L. A. "Christianity in Egypt before the Arab Conquest." *Tarikh* 2, no. 1 (1967): 4–15.
Ward, Kevin. "Africa." In *A World History of Christianity*, edited by Adrian Hastings, 192–237. Grand Rapids: Eerdmans, 1999.

Section II

Christian Belief and Teaching

7

Jesus Christ as Son of Man and Son of God

The Challenge of Judaism and Docetism

> Stop your ears, therefore, when any one speaks to you in a manner at variance with [what we know of] Jesus Christ, who was descended from David, and was the child of Mary; who was truly born, and ate and drank. He was truly persecuted under Pontius Pilate; He was truly crucified, and [truly] died, in the sight of beings in heaven, and on earth, and under the earth. He was also truly raised from the dead, His Father raising Him to life, in the same manner that His Father will also raise up us who believe in Him by Christ Jesus, apart from whom we do not possess the true life. . . .
>
> But if it be, as some that are without God [i.e. the unbelieving] say, that He only seemed to suffer (they themselves only seeming to exist), then why am I in bonds? Why do I long to be exposed to the wild beasts? Do I therefore die in vain? Am I not then guilty of falsehood against [the cross of] the Lord?
>
> Ignatius, *Epistle to the Trallians*, 9.1–2, and 10.1

Like Polycarp and other Apostolic Fathers, Ignatius wrote a number of letters to the churches when he was on his way to Rome to die a martyr's death there (ca. AD 107–110). In this letter to the Trallians (a tribal group of Thracian or Illyrian ancestry, in Asia Minor) Ignatius reflects his concern about Docetism, especially the belief that Jesus suffered only as a phantom, not in reality. He only *seemed* to suffer. While Judaizers, knowing that Jesus did suffer in the trial and crucifixion under Pontius Pilate, assumed that he could not have been divine, believers from a Greek background, particularly Docetists and Gnostics, found his crucifixion problematic and a real stumbling block for belief in Jesus as their Saviour; for them divinity and suffering were not compatible. If they were to accept Jesus's divinity, they could not accept a divine being who could also suffer.

According to Ignatius, an approach which does not accept Christ's suffering reflects unbelief. And he continues his elaboration by drawing an interesting connection between the Docetist position and the acceptance of a martyr's death. For he asks, if Jesus did not really suffer [on the cross], then why are Christians persecuted? Any real basis for the confession, "Jesus is Lord," is taken away and with it, the source of their condemnation. Moreover, if Jesus did not really die, he also would not truly have risen from the dead. And if Christ has not been raised, as the apostle Paul reminds early Christians, their faith is nothing more than a delusion; all who have died in Christ are lost (1 Cor 15:12–19).

A. Who Is Jesus Christ?

In this second major section of our study of early Christianity we examine issues of Christian belief and teaching, especially as these were shaped in the context of the Greco-Roman world, the world of peoples and nations whom the Jews had always designated as *goyim* or "Gentiles," that is the "nations" excluded from the special relationship with God which Jews claimed through the covenant with Abraham. The most serious controversies of early Christianity pivot on a clear understanding of the person of Jesus Christ.

The question of Jesus's identity and nature can be answered from a "historical" perspective, by telling the story of his life and deeds; and we do need to give some attention to basic historical factors. But that is only the beginning of the real answer. While the gospels clearly present Jesus as human, it is also evident from his power over nature, especially as it was revealed in healing and other miracles, that he was no ordinary human being. Peter confessed that Jesus was the Christ, the son of the living God (Matt 16:16), thus recognizing that he was the *Messiah* whose coming had been foretold in the Scriptures of the Jews. Even so, it is clear from reports of encounters with Jesus before his death, that the disciples did not yet fully recognize the meaning of that confession.[1]

A.1. The Historical Jesus

It is impossible to understand who Jesus is without taking into account the original Jewish context of his life. We note his names: *Jesus* (*Yesua* in Arabic), or *Joshua* – which means "Saviour," a name chosen consciously from the Old Testament Joshua, who followed in the footsteps of Moses and led the Israelites into the promised land.[2] He is also called the *Christ*, the one "anointed" (Greek, *Christos*), just as Old Testament priests and kings were anointed for their special work. This name is the Greek equivalent of *Messiah*,[3] the one long-expected to lead the Israelites, to set them free once more as a people. Though the Jews expected him to provide freedom primarily from political oppression within the Roman Empire; Jesus saw his own task as liberation from spiritual slavery, bondage to sin and evil.

For Christians these names for Jesus Christ are central for understanding his role within Judaism and Christianity. They designate him as the Messiah prophesied in the Old Testament and the Saviour who is to redeem people from sin, undoing the damage caused by the disobedience and sin of the first human parents, Adam and Eve. Indeed, the New Testament refers to Jesus as the "second Adam," and the "Son of Man."[4] When Jesus is also designated as "Lord," it reflects his authority and power to save people from sin and its inevitable consequence, death. The New Testament Gospels and Pauline Epistles give a clear account of how human beings can find and benefit from this saving power, as it effects a reconciliation with the God whom they have offended by

---

1. After his confession of Jesus as the Messiah, Peter was actually rebuked because he was not ready also to accept Jesus's prediction of the suffering and death that awaited him as Messiah, based on the prophet Isaiah's description of the suffering servant, a man of sorrows (Isa 53). Jesus told Peter, "You do not have in mind the things of God, but the things of men" (Matt 16:23).

2. Jesus's name was assigned with the angel's announcement to Joseph: ". . . do not be afraid to take Mary home as your wife, because what is conceived in her is from the Holy Spirit. She will give birth to a son, and you are to give him the name Jesus, because he will save his people from their sins" (Matt 1:20–21).

3. On the designation, "Messiah," and messianic expectation, see Ferguson, *Backgrounds*, 552–553. On prophecies and names for Jesus as the Messiah, see chapter appendix 7.1 at the end of chapter 7.

4. See 1 Cor 15:45–49, "So it is written: 'The first man Adam became a living being; the last Adam, a life-giving spirit.' . . . As was the earthly man, so are those who are of the earth; and as is the man from heaven, so also are those who are of heaven."

their sin: the key is faith in Jesus, believing the scriptural account of who he was and what he accomplished.

The title by which Jesus often referred to himself: "Son of Man," emphasizes his humanity. Like all human beings, Jesus was ultimately descended from Adam and shared fully in humanity, or human nature. He was also designated "Son of David" because from both parents, his mother Mary and (supposed human) father, Joseph, he was not of priestly lineage, or Aaronic descent, but traced his ancestors to the royal family of David and Solomon.[5] In this way he represented a fulfilment of Old Testament prophecies of a special deliverer who was to come from this lineage.[6] Jesus was also regarded as king of the Jews, although he made it clear to Pontius Pilate that his kingdom was not of this world (John 18:36).

A.2. Jesus in the Gospels

It is important to note that Jesus did not himself write down the story of his life.[7] Nor did he write down the message proclaiming good news, announcing the imminent arrival of the kingdom of God, or the kingdom of heaven (Mark 1:14–15).[8] We know about the life and death of Jesus from four documents, the *Gospels* of Matthew, Mark, Luke and John, written by his disciples and close associates, as trustworthy witnesses to these events.[9]

These gospels were written within the first sixty years after Jesus's death and resurrection; they testify to his life, birth, teaching, miracles and prophetic sayings.[10] The word *gospel* (in Greek, *euangelion*) means "good news." So these gospels are not primarily historical works; nor were they specifically written as biography, or even a type of hagiography. All four devote a large proportion of

---

5. For the full account of Jesus's lineage, right back to Adam, both on the side of his mother Mary and his father Joseph, see Matt 1:1–17 and Luke 3:23–37. In terms of priestly roles, we note that Hebrews 7:17 recognizes Jesus as a priest in the order of Melchizedek; this is based, in turn, on messianic interpretation of Psalm 110:4, "You are a priest forever in the line of Melchizedek."

6. We note the prophecies of Isaiah, as in Isa 11:1–10, "A shoot will come up from the stump of Jesse; from his roots a Branch will bear fruit. The Spirit of the LORD will rest on him – the Spirit of wisdom and of understanding, the Spirit of counsel and of power, the Spirit of knowledge and of the fear of the LORD."

7. For a historical survey of the life of Jesus, see Frend, *Rise of Christianity*, 54–74.

8. Mark 1:14–15, "After John was put in prison, Jesus went into Galilee, proclaiming the good news of God. 'The time has come,' he said, 'The kingdom of God is near.'"

9. While the gospels provide a primary source and witness, much has been written about that witness; see the bibliographical note of Frend, *Rise of Christianity*, 74–77.

10. The last of the gospels written, that of John, is typically dated by AD 90; see ch. 9, §C and §D.

their account to events surrounding Jesus's death and resurrection. Although there were many more "gospel" accounts in circulation at the time, these are the four accepted by the early Christian church as true and reliable.[11]

The story of Jesus's life begins with the record of his unusual conception and birth.[12] Little is known about his childhood and early adulthood. Luke is the only one of the canonical gospels to include a story from Jesus's childhood, his attendance at the festival in Jerusalem, with his parents, at the age of twelve (Luke 2:46–49). This account gives us some indication of his special, precocious understanding, even as a child. Other gospel narratives have tried to fill in the gap in Jesus's life, but the stories they tell have been judged fanciful, and are regarded as "apocryphal."[13]

Figure 7.1. The raising of Lazarus. This 6th-century mosaic in the Basilica of Sant' Apollinare Nuovo (Ravenna, Italy) depicts one of the most dramatic of Jesus's acts of healing, raising Lazarus from death (John 11:38–44). The gospel of John makes a direct connection between this miracle and the plot of the Jews to kill Jesus (John 11:45–53). Photographic reproduction by Testus. Public Domain.

---

11. Early Christians considered the other gospels spurious, based on fiction. On the choice of four gospels for the canon of Scripture, see ch. 9, §C.2.

12. For the announcement of the angel Gabriel to Mary, see Luke 1:35, "The angel answered, 'The Holy Spirit will come upon you, and the power of the Most High will overshadow you. So the holy one to be born will be called the Son of God.'"

13. On "apocryphal" writings, see ch. 9, §E.

Figure 7.2. Jesus's compassion for women. This depiction of Jesus healing the woman with a flow of blood was found on the walls of the catacomb of Marcellinus and Peter (Rome). She was healed simply by touching Jesus's cloak (Luke 8:40–48). This was not just an innocent act, for Jews felt contaminated when in contact with a woman experiencing a flow of blood. Without condemning her, Jesus assured her that she had been healed by her faith in him. "The healing of a bleeding woman, Rome." Photo: akg-images / © André Held.

The canonical gospels give a clear picture of Jesus from the beginning of his public ministry at the age of thirty (after he was baptized by John),[14] showing that he was no ordinary religious teacher (*rabbi*). Aside from the miracles of healing (both spiritual and physical),[15] the disciples witnessed his authority

---

14. See Luke 3:21–23, "When all the people were being baptized, Jesus was baptized too. And as he was praying, heaven was opened and the Holy Spirit descended on him in bodily form like a dove. And a voice came from heaven: 'You are my Son, whom I love; with you I am well pleased.'"

15. Matthew 8:16–17, "When evening came, many who were demon-possessed were brought to him, and he drove out the spirits with a word and healed all the sick."

over the forces of nature,[16] casting out demons,[17] and even raising people from death itself (John 11).

His teaching presented a new interpretation of the law of Moses, to lighten the burden imposed by the Pharisees, the teachers of the day, with their impossibly strict interpretation of the law (Matt 5–8); he also provided a new perspective on traditional interpretation of laws, for example laws on Sabbath observance, or loving one's enemies. The gospels reflect clearly his mission to seek out and save the lost, beginning with the lost of Israel, so that through them all of mankind could receive his salvation.

When the people of Galilee recognized Jesus as Messiah, and wished to crown him their King, Jesus refused (John 6:15, 26–27). But the traditional religious leaders were deeply offended when Jesus called God his Father, as it were placing himself on an equal footing with God. They accused him of blasphemy and became his fierce opponents (Mark 14:1–2; John 7:1).[18] They despised him for his association with "sinners," tax collectors (or publicans) and Gentiles (Luke 15; Matt 8:5–13). And his compassion for women raised their ire.[19] These leaders finally found a way to hand him over to the Roman rulers. So he was arrested, interrogated by the Jewish leaders and by Pontius Pilate (since only the Roman governor had the authority to carry out the death sentence), falsely condemned, flogged and crucified.

The gospels focus on the climax of this conflict at the Passover, the festival at which Jews traditionally sacrificed a lamb to atone for human sin.[20] Christians only later came to recognize that Jesus had presented himself as that sacrificial lamb, ready to die as an atonement for the sins of his people, and thus a fulfilment of the meaning of his name "Jesus" (Matt 1:21). The gospels witness to the fact that Jesus himself truly died on the cross. His place was not taken by someone else (Simon of Cyrene, or Judas Iscariot);[21] nor was it only

---

16. Mark 4:39, "He got up, rebuked the wind and said to the waves, 'Quiet! Be still!' Then the wind died down and it was completely calm. . . . They were terrified and asked each other, 'Who is this? Even the wind and the waves obey him!'"

17. Luke 8:29, "For Jesus had commanded the evil spirit to come out of the man." See also Luke 9:42, "But Jesus rebuked the evil spirit, healed the boy and gave him back to his father."

18. For Jesus's claim that, "I and the Father are one," see John 10:29–33. When the Jews want to stone him for blasphemy, they explain their anger, "because you, a mere man, claim to be God." On the resulting conflict with the Pharisees, see Latourette, *First Five Centuries*, 50–52.

19. Frend calls his relationship with women nothing short of "revolutionary" (*Rise of Christianity*, 67). The issue of women who accompanied Jesus in his ministry and were the first to witness the resurrection, receives further attention in chapter appendix 9.1.

20. Luke 22:7, "Then came the day of Unleavened Bread on which the Passover lamb had to be sacrificed." On this last phase of Jesus's life, see Frend, *Rise of Christianity*, 71–74.

21. On variant interpretations of the crucifixion, as in the view of Basileides, see ch. 8, §A.2.

the phantom of a person who died on the cross. We hear that his legs were not broken, because he was already dead. When his side was pierced, water flowed out, mingled with blood.[22]

On the night of his crucifixion (Friday), Jesus's body was taken down and placed in a new tomb by his friends. Nothing further could be done to prepare the body for burial, for the day after his death was the Sabbath. So the women who had accompanied him to the cross came to anoint the body on the third day. But they were surprised to find the tomb already open and the body gone. At first they thought the body had been stolen, but Mary Magdalene was confronted by Jesus himself, risen from death (John 20:1–18). And Jesus appeared to many others in the forty days between his resurrection and ascension. He assured them that he must leave them, but he would send the Holy Spirit, as "comforter," to lead them in all truth. During these days Jesus also took time to explain the Scriptures (the Torah, or Old Testament) for his followers, to show them that his life was a fulfilment of Old Testament promises (Luke 24:13-27, and 44–47). He made it clear that what he accomplished was for their benefit.[23] The anger of God against human sin had been averted through his death as the sacrificial lamb; faith in that accomplishment would be the new basis for forgiveness of sin.[24]

A.3. Early Christianity in Conflict with Judaism

Although Thomas had addressed the risen Jesus as "my Lord and my God," the full meaning of that confession would become more apparent in the early church after the outpouring of the Holy Spirit at Pentecost. From the account of Luke in the Acts of the Apostles it is clear that one of the central tasks of the apostles in preaching was to convince the Jews of the good news that Jesus was indeed the "Christ," the long-awaited Messiah. And we know that

---

22. John 19:33–35, "But when they came to Jesus and found that he was already dead, they did not break his legs. Instead, one of the soldiers pierced Jesus' side with a spear, bringing a sudden flow of blood and water. The man who saw it has given testimony, and his testimony is true. He knows that he tells the truth, and he testifies so that you also may believe."

23. See Luke 24:13–35, especially 26–27, "Did not the Christ have to suffer these things and then enter his glory? And beginning with Moses and all the Prophets he explained to them what was said in all the Scriptures concerning himself."

24. Luke 24:44–48, "He said to them, 'This is what I told you while I was still with you: Everything must be fulfilled that is written about me in the Law of Moses, the Prophets and the Psalms.' Then he opened their minds so they could understand the Scriptures. He told them, 'This is what is written: The Christ will suffer and rise from the dead on the third day, and repentance and forgiveness of sins will be preached in his name to all nations, beginning at Jerusalem. You are witnesses of these things.'"

early believers, when they called Jesus "Saviour," regarded him as both "Son of God" and "Son of Man." When Mark begins his gospel by speaking of the account of Jesus Christ, the "Son of God" (Mark 1:1), it is clear that he is not presenting Jesus as Son of God in a literal or human sense, that is as John was the son of Zechariah and Elizabeth. Mary was indeed his human mother, but his conception was a special work of the Spirit of God. So Jesus's divine "Sonship" was also to be understood in a spiritual sense. They also claimed him as *Kurios*, or Lord, the title which reflects early Christian acceptance of his deity.[25] This was a bold claim, for the Greek word represents the title given by Jews to God himself, *Adonai*.[26]

The sermons recorded in the book of Acts reveal the growing insight of the disciples into the life and work of Jesus as the Christ (Acts 5:42; 18:28; 26:7). The twelve disciples had been appointed by Jesus himself during the early years of his ministry (on the model of the twelve tribes of Israel). As his followers they were to succeed him in that task after his death. None of these disciples were highly educated and particularly skilled for the work; in Acts 4:13 Luke acknowledged that, "they were unschooled, ordinary men."[27] They were certainly no match for the philosophers of the time. Even Paul himself was no philosopher, though he certainly had a reasonable acquaintance with the subjects of a good general education; we know that, as a Pharisee, he had gone as far as possible in that kind of education in Judaism (Phil 3:5-6).[28]

Even if the disciples had limited insight into the work and mission of Jesus during his life time, their understanding of his life, death and teachings, clearly had grown considerably in the period between Jesus's resurrection and ascension. In their preaching they now recognized Jesus's crucifixion and death as a fulfilment of prophecy on the suffering of the Messiah (Acts 2:22-36; and 17:3); it was not just a terrible tragedy and travesty of justice. They

---

25. 1 Cor 12:3, "Therefore I tell you that no one who is speaking by the Spirit of God says, 'Jesus be cursed,' and no one can say, 'Jesus is Lord,' except by the Holy Spirit."

26. The Jews were afraid of committing blasphemy, and even refused to call God by his proper name, "Yahweh" (symbolized by the *tetragrammaton* YHWH). See Latourette, *First Five Centuries*, 140-141.

27. Acts 4:13, "When they [leaders of the Sanhedrin] saw the courage of Peter and John and realized that they were unschooled, ordinary men, they were astonished, and they took note that these men had been with Jesus."

28. See Phil 3:4-9, "If anyone else thinks he has reasons to put confidence in the flesh, I have more: circumcised on the eighth day, of the people of Israel, of the tribe of Benjamin, a Hebrew of Hebrews; in regard to the law, a Pharisee; as for zeal, persecuting the church; as for legalistic righteousness, faultless." Paul's education was certainly evident to the Roman governor, Festus, when he responded to Paul's defence (in Acts 26:24), "Your great learning is driving you insane!"

acknowledged Jesus as the sacrificial lamb who had to die so that the sin of Adam could be undone; forgiveness for sin was thereby made possible because the barrier to God's grace had been removed. This was also Paul's message as he preached the kingdom of God and taught about Jesus Christ as Lord and Son of God (Acts 9:20; 13:33; 26:6 and 23; 28:31). And when the disciples preached in the name of Jesus they preached with boldness, without fear of the inevitable opposition, urging all men to repent and to put their faith in him as Lord and Saviour, so that their sins might be forgiven (Acts 2:38; 3:19; 4:12; 13:38; 17:30). In Jesus's name they also performed miracles, including acts of healing (Acts 3:16; 14:3), and even raised the dead to new life (e.g. Peter with Dorcas or Tabitha, Acts 9:40; and Paul with Eutychus, Acts 20:9-10).

Such preaching inevitably brought the church into conflict with Judaism. The ruling Pharisees and Sadducees reacted angrily when they heard the disciples preaching in Jesus's name (Acts 4:2, 18). If they had been ready to stone Jesus himself for blasphemy in calling God his Father (John 10:29-33), they certainly could not accept Christians who affirmed him as Son of God, and insisted on his deity.

Jewish writers of the first and second centuries typically referred to Christians as those who posit a "second God." Before the end of the first century they insisted on the exclusion of Christians from the synagogue. It is interesting to note at this point that their concerns anticipate later Muslim accusations of Christians worshipping three (or four) gods: God the Father, God the Son, God the Holy Spirit (and Mary as the Mother of God).[29] Rabbinic sources would go further in denigrating Jesus's stature with the people, referring to him as a deceiver who exercised powers of magic, and one whose unwarranted additions to the law led people astray. For them his shameful death on the cross revealed the curse of God; it was no more than he deserved. As noted above, the accounts of persecution of Christians in the first centuries reveal the critical role of Jews in making accusations which led to the arrest of believers.[30] Jews saw the growing Christian church in the first two centuries as a direct threat to their own status in the Roman Empire.

A.4. Was Jesus Divine?

For the Jews, as we have seen, Jesus's claim to being the Son of God was nothing less than blasphemous, deserving death by stoning. Throughout history,

---

29. See the Qur'an, Sura 5.76 and 119 (translation Abdullah Yusuf Ali).
30. See ch. 4, §A.1 and §A.2.

Figure 7.3. Christos Pantocrator. This 12th-century mosaic from the Hagia Sophia (in Constantinople), depicting the victorious Christ, represents his victory over sin and death, and leaves no doubt regarding his divine nature. Photo by Mark Ahsmann / CC BY-SA 3.0.

theologians and religious authorities of various persuasions have followed the Jews in questioning the deity of Jesus. The first major Christian contender was Arius. We will examine his "adoptionist" position in chapter 10, for it became the focus of the first major Christian ecumenical council.[31]

Similarly, Islam, while it accepts Jesus as a great prophet, born of a divine spirit, rejects Christian recognition of Jesus as divine, as the Son of God; such honour they regard as a perversion of Jesus's own teachings.[32] Indeed, the presentation of Jesus in the Qur'an assumes that Jesus did not himself claim that he was divine; it also assumes that he did not teach a Trinitarian understanding of God. In corroborating the Qur'anic rejection of Jesus's divinity, Muslim scholars like to quote passages like John 17:3, "Now this is eternal life: that they may know you, the only true God, and Jesus Christ, whom you have sent." Similarly, John 8:40, "As it is, you are determined to kill me, a man who has

---

31. On the council, see ch. 10, §A.3 and §A.4.
32. Qur'an, Sura 19.34–35; 6.101–102; also 5.75, and 119–120.

told you the truth that I heard from God."³³ They point to passages highlighting Jesus's humanity, his weakness, and human need. Questioning why Christians hold him to be divine, they typically assume that the records have been forged, or otherwise falsified over the ages.³⁴

It should be noted at this point that texts like Mark 10:18, where Jesus attributes goodness to God alone, not to himself,³⁵ were used already by the fourth-century Arius to claim that Christ was not the Son of God from all eternity. This indicates that important issues which have arisen in the dialogue between Islam and Christianity over the centuries had already been addressed very early in the history of Christianity, especially in disputes with Gnostics (who recognized only a spiritual Jesus) and Arians (who recognized Jesus as primarily human).³⁶

A.5. Docetism

The views of Gnostics were anticipated by Docetists whose interpretation of the identity of Jesus was quite different from those of the Jews. Their position arose in the Greco-Roman Gentile communities where the church was growing. Here a typically pagan understanding of deity made its own impact on Christian understanding of Christ. Traditional pagan conceptions regarded the gods as more powerful than men; gods did not die, and were not subject to the normal human restrictions of time, place or change.

---

33. In his arguments against Jesus's divinity, the tenth-century Muslim scholar, Abd Al-Jabbar, uses these and other passages, like John 5:30, "By myself I can do nothing; I judge only as I hear, and my judgment is just, for I seek not to please myself but him who sent me"; John 14:24, "These words you hear are not my own; they belong to the Father who sent me"; Mark 13:32, "No one knows about that day or that hour, not even the angels in heaven, nor the Son, but only the Father"; Mark 10:45, "For even the Son of Man did not come to be served, but to serve, and to give his life as a ransom for many"; John 17:6, "I have revealed you to those whom you gave me out of the world. They were yours; you gave them to me and they have obeyed your word"; Mark 12:32, "'Well said, teacher,' the man replied. 'You are right in saying that God is one and there is no other but him'"; Luke 12:13–14 [and John 11:41], "So they took away the stone. Then Jesus looked up and said, 'Father, I thank you that you have heard me'"; Luke 22:44, "And being in anguish, he prayed more earnestly, and his sweat was like drops of blood falling to the ground." On this discussion of Jesus's humanity and his divinity, see Stern, "Quotations from Apocryphal Gospels," 34–57, especially 35–36.

34. On such Muslim arguments of Al-Jabbar, see also Stern, "Abd Al-Jabbar's Account," 128–185.

35. In Mark 10:18 (as in Matt 19:17 and Luke 18:19) Jesus asks, "Why do you call me good? No one is good, except God alone."

36. We turn to these disputes in much greater detail in subsequent sections, and in chapters 8 and 10.

Popular understanding of deity was further influenced by philosophical notions based on a type of *dualism* which characterized Platonism and other philosophical schools of the empire.[37] These views made a sharp distinction between things material and bodily (as subject to corruption and decay) and that which was immaterial and incorporeal (as more perfect). Regarding human beings, the ancient Greek philosophers showed great appreciation for the spirit, or soul and its intellectual powers; however, the material reality of the body, or flesh was much lower on their scale of values. They went so far as to regard the human soul (or at least its highest powers of reasoning) as close to the divine realm. Being spiritual and immaterial, it was also considered impassable (i.e. not subject to suffering), and (the source of) good. The body, on the other hand, as part of the world of matter, was mortal and corruptible (i.e. subject to disease, decay and death), and therefore less valuable, if not actually the source of human evil.

These views already characterized much older religious movements of antiquity, especially mystery religions like Orphism.[38] We also know that a strong form of dualism, with a sharp division between powers of good and evil in perpetual warfare (as forces of light and darkness), characterized Persian Zoroastrianism, a religion which would strongly influence the semi-gnostic Manicheism of the fourth and fifth century.[39] The divine (as spiritual) was typically contrasted unfavourably with the mortal and bodily which were subject to decomposition, disintegration and death.

From this perspective the question arises: How could the Christ, if he is truly God, possibly have lived a human life, using a human body? How could Jesus have been born of a human mother? How can one seriously accept that he lived as a human being, becoming tired and hungry like everyone else? How could he have truly experienced the suffering of death – especially a cruel and shameful death on the cross? If he truly died on the cross, how could he have experienced a bodily resurrection? These are the questions which led many who regarded Jesus as their Saviour, to claim that he could not have been born in a normal human way. If he was truly the Redeemer sent of God, he could not have been polluted by the taint of the flesh, and contaminated by what is material and evil. They concluded that he only *seemed* to be a man; he only *appeared* to have a body,[40] and what was seen was actually only a *phantom*.

---

37. For further discussion of these schools and their significance for Christian theology, and for more on Plato see §B of this chapter.
38. Ferguson, *Backgrounds*, 162–164.
39. On fourth-century Manicheans and Augustine's interaction with them, see ch. 12, §D.3.
40. Latourette, *First Five Centuries*, 127.

The Greek word for "seem" is *dokein*; those who interpreted Christ in this way were named *Docetists*.[41]

The early church wrestled with these questions: Did Jesus suffer in the flesh? Was he truly crucified? If he was truly divine, how could he have suffered in that way? Was his suffering real? In Greek thinking, passion (and passivity, or suffering) had deep-seated negative connotations, indicating weakness, impotence and imperfection. And they expected the gods to be powerful above all others. Divinity could not easily be regarded as the subject of passion, or suffering. These questions would make a deep impact on discussion of the identity of Jesus in the first centuries of Christianity. The answers emerged over a period of more than two centuries, although in essence they had already been given by Ignatius of Antioch.

A.6. Apostles and Apostolic Fathers

The disciples were called apostles because they were "sent out"; the title "apostle" is based on the Greek *apostellô*, "I send away." Even before the end of his ministry, Jesus had sent out his followers to the villages, to preach the coming of the kingdom of God (Luke 10:1–20). After he ascended to heaven the disciples were sent further abroad, beyond the confines of Judea (Matt 28:18–20).[42] We hear of their travels especially in the time of persecution after the death of Stephen (Acts 7 and 8).[43]

The term *Apostolic Fathers* refers to early leaders in the Christian congregations who represent the *second generation* of leaders after the apostles. The most important of these Apostolic Fathers are:

- Clement, an early bishop of Rome (fl. AD 93–97)
- Ignatius, bishop of Antioch (living ca. AD 35–117)
- Polycarp, disciple of Ignatius, and bishop of Smyrna (martyred at 86, ca. AD 155)
- Hermas of Rome (fl. AD 100–104)
- Barnabas (of [Alexandria], known from AD 131)
- The second Clement (fl. AD 160–170)

---

[41]. The issue is reflected in Ignatius's letter given at the introduction of this chapter; he asks why he is now in bonds, if Jesus only suffered as a *phantom*? See also Stevenson, *New Eusebius*, 14–15.

[42]. Matt 28:18–20, "Then Jesus came to them and said, 'All authority in heaven and on earth has been given to me. Therefore go and make disciples of all nations, baptizing them in the name of the Father and of the Son and of the Holy Spirit, and teaching them to obey everything I have commanded you.'"

[43]. On early travels of the apostles, see also the introduction to ch. 2, and §B above.

These Fathers are remembered for their leadership and writings, but they were respected primarily because their teaching directly passed on what they had received from the apostles themselves. Many of them met a martyr's death. Their teachings are reflected in an important anonymous document of this period, the *Didachê*, or *Teaching of the Twelve Apostles*, which probably originated in Syria (ca. AD 100).[44] The treatise provides valuable insight into the early organization and growth of congregations, matters of leadership and worship, use of the sacraments and other issues, like the practice of fasting.

Problems of leadership and issues of division in the congregations were an important concern for the Apostolic Fathers. At that time the churches were taught by "prophets," many of them wandering from place to place and dependent on the hospitality of congregations. The *Didachê* addressed the issue of impostors among them, who might take advantage of that hospitality. Both Clement and Polycarp sent letters to sister congregations like Corinth, to address issues of leadership. Ignatius's *Letters* focused on unity in the congregations. In *The Shepherd*, Hermas of Rome shared visions of the heavenly character of the church and teachings concerning the Christian life. The *Letters* of Barnabas, on the other hand, reflect contemporary figurative (or allegorical) interpretation of the Old Testament. "Clean" animals of the Old Testament, for example, are taken to represent purity of life (as in Peter's vision, Acts 10 and 11:1–18). Discernment and approval of the teachings given by wandering prophets became the task of the *bishop* as "overseer" (the literal meaning of the Greek title, *episkopos*). These writings thus witness to growing restrictions on leadership, even before the second-century threat of Gnosticism.

How did the Apostolic Fathers address questions regarding the deity and lordship of Jesus Christ? In his letters Ignatius calls Jesus "our God" made manifest as "man" (i.e. God incarnate).[45] As we have already noted, Justin Martyr discussed Christ as the Logos (from the Gospel of John): the divine

---

44. Holmes has recently (1999) republished the writings of the Apostolic Fathers (with translation), including the *Didachê*. This provides a new edition of the classic publication of these texts by J. B. Lightfoot and J. R. Harmer (*The Apostolic Fathers*, 1891). On the significance of the nineteenth-century discovery of the *Didachê* and other writings of the Apostolic Fathers for the dating of the New Testament (by Lightfoot), see appendix I.

45. See Ignatius's *Letter to the Ephesians*, 18.2, "Where is the boasting of those who are styled prudent? For our God, Jesus Christ, was, according to the appointment of God, conceived in the womb by Mary, of the seed of David, but by the Holy Ghost." Also at 7.2, "There is one Physician who is possessed both of flesh and spirit; both made and not made; God existing in flesh; true life in death; both of Mary and of God; first possible and then impossible, even Jesus Christ our Lord."

Word and first-begotten of God, who was also God.[46] He speaks of Jesus as God's offspring, his child and unique son.[47] For Justin, Christ was the "reason" or "wisdom" and "mind" of God, his "thought"; for him this meant that God was never without his Son. And as such, the Son was part of God's own being, and therefore not limited to time.

Further discussion of the precise identity of Jesus takes us to the great controversies of early Christianity: Gnosticism and Arianism. These will be discussed in chapters 8 and 10, as we continue the study of belief and teachings of the early Christian church. Before doing so, however, we take a detour to examine more closely religious and philosophical issues arising from the Greco-Roman background, particularly as these were raised by Docetists. Commonly accepted views on things human or divine would greatly impact subsequent discussions of the deity of Jesus Christ.

B. The Divine Jesus: Philosophical Aspects

Within the Roman Empire polytheistic religion had an enemy even stronger than the varied eastern cults (discussed in chapter 1) which eventually found a home in Rome. The challenge came from philosophical schools; from the beginning, their positions were often associated with critique of the pagan gods.[48] In terms of numbers, the adherents of schools of philosophy never constituted a significant threat. Philosophy was the pursuit of a small group, but one that had pretensions out of all proportion to its size, as a cultural elite; it would make a significant impact on Greek and Roman culture from the time of Socrates and Plato (fourth century BC). In the Hellenistic world, philosophy came to be regarded as the capstone of a fully rounded education, giving the finishing touches to an education based on grammar, literature and rhetoric.[49] As such, philosophy never outlived its elitist profile. The Romans inherited

---

46. See ch. 4, §B.3; also Justin's *Apol.* 1.63.15, "But so much is written for the sake of proving that Jesus the Christ is the Son of God and His Apostle, being of old the Word [Logos]."

47. See Justin's *Apol.* 1.21.1, "And when we say also that the Word, who is the first-born of God, was produced without sexual union, and that He, Jesus Christ, our Teacher, was crucified and died, and rose again, and ascended into heaven, we propound nothing different from what you believe regarding those whom you esteem sons of Jupiter." See also his *Dialogue*, 62.4, "But this Offspring, which was truly brought forth from the Father, was with the Father before all the creatures, and the Father communed with Him." And *Dial.*, 105.1, "For I have already proved that He was the only-begotten of the Father of all things, being begotten in a peculiar manner Word and Power by Him, and having afterwards become man through the Virgin, as we have learned from the memoirs."

48. Ferguson, *Backgrounds*, 321.

49. Ferguson, 110–111.

their educational ideals from the Greeks. Many Greek teachers who had been captured and enslaved in the wars of Roman conquest ended up serving as tutors in leading Roman families.

Throughout the Roman Empire, the appeal of traditional pagan deities and rites was gradually undermined by philosophy. By the third century AD, philosophers would also turn their attention to the truth claims of Christianity. The Platonist philosopher Porphyry (ca. AD 230–305) provided an entire arsenal of arguments to be used by Emperor Diocletian in support of his persecution of Christians.[50] By the fourth century the challenge of philosophy would be answered by Christianity referring to itself as the true philosophy. It is therefore imperative that we examine relevant issues in Greek philosophy as the background to the difficult discussions which occupied Christians as they tried to match their understanding of the divine Jesus with understandings of deity common in the Greco-Roman world.

B.1. Socrates (d. 399 BC)

Before Socrates, philosophers of the Greek world, especially in trading centres like Miletus (on the Aegean coast of Asia Minor), had speculated on the nature of the universe. They attempted to reduce reality from the four major elements (fire, air, water and earth), to one dominant aspect. Socrates was not interested in such speculation. He followed the lead of wandering teachers, the Sophists, who sought to understand human nature and virtue.[51]

Socrates focused particularly on the need for *self-knowledge*. He was challenged by the question: What makes a man noble? The question was urgent in the context of an emerging democracy, where every citizen had the right to contribute in ruling the state. But who is best equipped to do so? Sophists taught rhetoric, the art of persuasive speech, so that one could get the better of an opponent in the courts or political debate. Socrates was unhappy with the opportunistic attitude of such teachers. Is virtue (Greek *aretê*) a matter of influencing others through rhetorical skill? Does it depend on aristocratic lineage? Wealth? Property? Or fame?

In trying to understand *human nobility*, Socrates looked to that aspect of human nature which he considered to be most like the gods, namely the *soul*. Of the three major "parts" of the soul, he was interested in its highest faculty, the power of *reason*, or *logos*, which he rated higher than emotion, or desire and

---

50. On Porphyry's role under Diocletian, see ch. 4, §B.3 (at the end).
51. Ferguson, *Backgrounds*, 327–330.

appetite. According to Socrates, "Virtue is knowledge," and "right knowing" is the key to "right action."

B.2. Plato (427–347 BC)

Socrates did not write down his own teachings; these come to us from the *Dialogues* of Plato, his most famous pupil. In fact it is very hard to separate the teachings of Socrates from those of Plato. The dialogue which best introduces Socrates in action is Plato's *Apology*, presenting Socrates's defence against accusations of corrupting the youth by introducing new deities.[52]

Plato goes beyond Socrates in his focus on Ideas and an Ideal World; his teaching is often characterized as *Idealism*. The Ideas represent *concepts*, or conceptual realities found in the definitions by which we identify things (i.e. the immaterial *concept* of a tree, that by which it is defined, as a "perennial tall woody plant with a trunk and numerous branches," rather than the concrete *material* tree which can be seen). But Plato's concepts also represent *ideals*, which are normative. So the Idea of a "tree" included the precise *definition* of a tree and also represented the *perfect* tree, or the tree at its best, as a model for others.

Plato ranked the Ideas according to a hierarchy of values. At the top of the list are Ideas of the "true," the "good," and the "beautiful." Because these Ideas would represent perfection, Plato insisted that, in order to make proper judgements on goodness, truth, or beauty as we find these in our world, we must know the Ideas; how, after all, can we know the truth of a particular matter if we do not know what "truth" is itself, or "truth" as such? The Ideas are considered to be models or archetypes of how things should be, with *goodness* as the pinnacle of the hierarchically arranged set of Ideas which constitute a perfect "world." In fact, the "tree" as we find it in our world of material things, gives us no more than a poor copy, or imitation of the Idea, because trees as we know them can become diseased, decay, or fall apart. True Ideal trees (or fields, buildings, people), are those which remain unseen, immaterial and eternal.

Knowledge of Ideas, according to Plato, is based on direct vision of these Ideal conceptual entities, as spiritual realities in that Ideal world; this was possible only in a pre-incarnate life, through the disembodied existence of our soul (before its "birth" in a [human] body). Plato taught the immortality of the soul, but he also accepted the reincarnation of the soul from one body into another. Through the process of birth and embodiment that original knowledge

---

52. For a general introduction to Plato, see Ferguson, *Backgrounds*, 330–338.

was lost; but Plato thought that the mere sight of embodied copies would be sufficient to "recall" our memory to the true original (spiritual) reality which it once knew directly.

In separating invisible Ideas of "goodness" from those visible "good things" in which they are embodied, Platonism is considered to be *dualistic*. Plato considered the world of experience, as we know it, to be quite separate and imperfect, compared to that other Ideal world. In the world of daily experience we find material reality, stamped by form or shape, as a union of the Ideas with imperfect matter. Particularly the material base is regarded as the source of imperfection and all kinds of evil. In the dialogue *Timaeus*, Plato proposes a mythical demiurge (Craftsman) as a creator figure who wished to create our world by looking to that Ideal World as model; but as he imposed perfect Ideas upon the imperfect material base, the Creator did not even come close to achieving perfection in copying that world. Plato speaks of the resistance of matter as the explanation of evil and other imperfections. This is also why human beings, as a combination of soul and body, should welcome death as a release of the soul from bodily restrictions, allowing for return to a previous condition, in which it will once more be at home in the world of Ideal reality.

Figure 7.4. Head of Plato. A marble fragment copying an original statue of Silanion (ca. 370 BC) for the Academy, Plato's school in Athens. Photo "Copy of Silanion" by Marie-Lan Nguyen / CC BY 2.5.

These positions were also the basis of Plato's strong critique (in the *Republic*) of shameful deeds attributed to the traditional gods of Greek mythology: cruelty, cheating and deception. His concern was justified, because such mythical tales formed the core of the education of the young (based on Homeric epic poetry, the *Iliad* and *Odyssey*). How can children be taught honesty, he asks, when the highest gods are portrayed as cheating and lying? Thus begins a discussion which is significant in the history of theology for its examination of the essential attributes of deity: goodness, honesty, purity and truth. Plato measured divinity by the ideals of the unseen and perfect immaterial world of Ideas, the world of abstract spiritual reality, as a world of goodness and perfection. He tended to blame all the imperfections and sorrows of our world on its embodied, material condition.

Figure 7.5. The Arabic Aristotle. This 13th-century manuscript of the *Kitāb naʿt al-hayawān* (possibly from a Mesopotamian monastery, and attributed to Jabril ibn Bukhtishu) portrays Aristotle as a teacher, and reflects the extent of his fame in the Arabic world. Photographic Reproduction by Laura Scudder. Public Domain.

B.3. Aristotle (384–322 BC)

Aristotle was the most important of Plato's students, but his understanding of reality differed significantly from that of his teacher, for Aristotle had a much greater appreciation of natural scientific knowledge.[53] Indeed, he may be regarded as the exemplary scientist of the ancient world, particularly for his description of plant and animal life in marine biology.

In this respect his name has remained paramount, right up to the nineteenth century, with the discoveries of Darwin. Because Aristotle had

---

53. See Ferguson, *Backgrounds*, 338–342.

been a tutor to Alexander the Great, his work would be the major inspiration for the first great university library and museum of Alexandria.

Aristotle did not fully accept Plato's view of the Ideas. According to Aristotle the Ideas cannot be found in an Ideal world beyond the present world of bodies and matter; rather, they are embedded in material reality as its *forms* (i.e. the shape, figure, condition or quality of a thing). As such, forms constitute one of the major factors in explaining things (alongside material, efficient/shaping, and teleological/final causes). Aristotle's thought tended to monism, and supported monotheism, for he posited a hypothetical single first cause, the Unmoved Mover, as the pinnacle of the world of stars and planets, the cosmos. This First Cause represents ultimate divine reality; it represents the first power moving all that is subordinate to it, but it remains itself unmoved by anything else. It acts like a magnet, a powerful force attracting all else to itself, while it is not itself moved or changed in the process.

B.4. Stoicism

Important representatives of Stoicism from the third century BC include Zeno (d. ca. 264) as founder; Cleanthes (301–232 BC); and Chrysippus (280–207 BC). Stoicism flourished in the Roman Empire, with Seneca (d. AD 65) as an important proponent, and also Emperor Marcus Aurelius (AD 121–180).[54] Stoic thought was focused on ethical issues and questions of human conduct. Stoics emphasized high standards for a lifestyle of virtue, namely, austerity, self-mastery and self-restraint. Although they regarded virtue as fourfold (wisdom, courage, moderation and justice), any one of the four virtues was thought to include the rest.

The Stoics developed Aristotle's thought, but they were more consistently materialistic in cosmology. For Stoics spiritual reality has no separate existence; it is integrated with the material reality of the world. God (or "the divine") is himself the material "soul" which governs the cosmos, as his body. Stoics posited (a divine) Logos as the guiding principle of the universe, penetrating all things and shaping them. Even so, they regarded this Logos as a material component, both living and divine, present in all things, much like the presence of warmth in warm air. The Logos is not transcendent, but immanent, indwelling the cosmos; its correlate, our individual logos is a "part" of that divine Logos, regarded as a "god within." So, ultimately there is but one law

---

54. Everett Ferguson gives a useful introduction to Stoicism; Ferguson, *Backgrounds*, 354–369.

governing the universe and all individuals within it. Human beings are to follow the guidance of the Logos in all actions.

In religion and critique of the gods the Stoics were more conservative than Platonists. Stoicism wished to maintain the traditional gods as they were presented in literary tradition, like the epic poems of Homer. Even so, Stoics used an *allegorical method* to interpret these gods, adapting them to fit a new understanding of the cosmos. For instance, they identified the highest Olympian deity, Zeus, with the Logos as ruling principle of the universe; his wife Hera represented the equally important element, "air."

In social thought Stoics were known for being egalitarian. For Stoics, "All men are brothers." Slaves were not excluded, if only they would follow the demands of the Logos, and restrain the passions. Even so, Stoicism was hardly a "popular" school of thought. Conditions demanded of the sage were very strict, if not impossible. But as a school, Stoicism remained influential for its high ethical standards.

B.5. Philo of Alexandria (ca. 20 BC – AD 40)

Syncretism or eclecticism, which marked religious movements of this time,[55] also influenced the Hellenistic schools of philosophy. Although Stoicism was initially influenced by Aristotelian views, it later came to accommodate Platonic Idealism, choosing those elements it found congenial. Philo of Alexandria, whose contribution in allegorical interpretation of the Old Testament we have already noted, represents such eclecticism as he incorporated basic theological positions of Hellenized Jews.[56]

Philo came from a politically prominent family in the Jewish community of Alexandria, a city where Jews may have comprised as much as one third of the population. Under Emperor Augustus the Jewish community enjoyed a degree of autonomy through its own council of elders (*gerousia*).[57] Like many Jews of this city, Philo shows the influence of Hellenization in language and thought. Much of his writing consists of commentaries on Old Testament Scriptures, especially the Pentateuch, although we are not certain that he even knew the Hebrew language; his work is based on the Septuagint translation. His commentaries seek to interpret the Old Testament laws originally given to an

---

55. On syncretism as it characterized religion at this time, see ch. 1, §B.3.

56. Philo of Alexandria is introduced briefly in ch. 1, §A.5 above. See also Ferguson, *Backgrounds*, 478–485.

57. Borgen, *Early Christianity*, 93.

agricultural sheep-herding society, and apply them to contemporary life in a city. Throughout, Philo highlights Moses as the greatest teacher of Judaism; he assumes that Moses would not have required obedience to the law in matters which are impossible or repugnant to his followers. This leads Philo to use philosophical concepts in *allegorizing* the commandments, in an attempt to harmonize Scripture with Platonic and Stoic teaching.

Philo's explanation of the creation (in Genesis) gives a clear example of his practice of allegorical interpretation as an integration of philosophical thought with the biblical account. While Philo accepts one God, he realizes that the transcendent God is far removed from that which he has created. Thus, for the work of creation, Philo posits the role of intermediate *powers*, namely angels, or spirits, to work on his behalf. The angels implement God's plan (understood by Philo as a type of blue-print, based on the Platonic world of Ideas) by giving shape or form to the material base of our world. Philo recognized the *word of God*, or the *Logos*, as the highest of these mediating powers. This was the *Word*, spoken at the creation, through which everything in the cosmos was called into being.

Philo also recognized humanity as the pinnacle of the creation. According to Philo, the human being mentioned in the first account of the creation of man was the perfect, exemplary human (Gen 1:20–31). All other human beings are but poor copies, relatively speaking, of that first perfect model. He advised that human imperfections be corrected by following the Logos, as found in the creation and in God's ongoing revelation, through teachers and prophets.

Philo never abandoned the essentials of Judaism: monotheism, Sabbath keeping, circumcision, keeping of Torah and avoidance of pork or unclean animals; and it is clear that the Jews in Alexandria at this time maintained the right to live according to the traditional Mosaic laws and celebrate the major festivals like the Passover. Philo upheld Moses as greater than any pagan teacher, even the wise Plato. He argued that as Moses lived many years before Plato, any similarities in their teachings shows that Plato must have learned from Moses, and not vice versa. In this approach we note a degree of "one-upmanship" on behalf of Judaism.

Philo is of great importance for our understanding of Hellenistic Judaism as practised at the time of Christ, particularly outside of Palestine itself. He also gives important information about contemporary groups like the Essenes, as a "brotherhood" of Jews;[58] mid-twentieth-century discovery of the Dead Sea

---

58. On the Essenes, see ch. 1, §A.6. They were also mentioned by the first-century Jewish historian Josephus; see Ferguson, *Backgrounds*, 485–490.

Scrolls at Qumran, and other significant new information about the Essenes, has stimulated contemporary interest in the group. Because the Essenes emphasized rites of purification, including baptism, it is thought that John the Baptist may have been closely associated with them.[59]

Chapter Appendix 7.1
Old Testament Prophecy of Jesus as the "Messiah"

Christians recognize the significance of Jesus being called the "Messiah" or "Anointed One" as it is based on many Old Testament passages in prophetic literature, for example, Daniel 9:26: "After the sixty-two 'sevens,' the *Anointed One* will be cut off and will have nothing. The people of the ruler who will come will destroy the city and the sanctuary."

Other terms for this Messiah occur in Isaiah 9:6–7:

> For to us a child is born, to us a son is given, and the government will be on his shoulders. And he will be called Wonderful Counselor, Mighty God, Everlasting Father, Prince of Peace. Of the greatness of his government and peace there will be no end. He will reign on David's throne and over his kingdom, establishing and upholding it with justice and righteousness from that time on and forever.

Isaiah 42:1–4 gives a further profile of the Messiah:

> "Here is my servant, whom I uphold, my chosen one in whom I delight; I will put my Spirit on him and he will bring justice to the nations. He will not shout or cry out, or raise his voice in the streets. A bruised reed he will not break, and a smoldering wick he will not snuff out. In faithfulness he will bring forth justice; he will not falter or be discouraged till he establishes justice on earth. In his teaching the islands will put their hope."

Early Christians recognized that the Messiah would come from the royal line of David and would rule his people with righteousness. They cited Isaiah 9:7 (above), and Micah 5:2–4:

> "But you, Bethlehem Ephrathah, though you are small among the clans of Judah, out of you will come for me one who will be ruler

---

59. On Qumran, the Essenes and Dead Sea scrolls, see further Ferguson, *Backgrounds*, 521–531.

over Israel, whose origins are from of old, from ancient times." Therefore Israel will be abandoned until the time when she who is in labor bears a son, and the rest of his brothers return to join the Israelites. He will stand and shepherd his flock in the strength of the LORD, in the majesty of the name of the LORD his God. And they will live securely, for then his greatness will reach to the ends of the earth.

See also Psalm 110:1–2:

> The LORD says to my Lord: "Sit at my right hand until I make your enemies a footstool for your feet." The LORD will extend your mighty scepter from Zion, saying, "Rule in the midst of your enemies!"

Christians also knew from Old Testament prophecies that the Messiah would face suffering to atone for our sins, as in Daniel 9:26 (above), and Isaiah 53:5–12:

> But he was pierced for our transgressions, he was crushed for our iniquities; the punishment that brought us peace was upon him, and by his wounds we are healed. We all, like sheep, have gone astray, each of us has turned to his own way; and the LORD has laid on him the iniquity of us all.
>
> He was oppressed and afflicted, yet he did not open his mouth; he was led like a lamb to the slaughter, and as a sheep before its shearers is silent, so he did not open his mouth. By oppression and judgment he was taken away. Yet who of his generation protested? For he was cut off from the land of the living; for the transgression of my people he was punished. He was assigned a grave with the wicked, and with the rich in his death, though he had done no violence, nor was any deceit in his mouth.
>
> Yet it was the LORD's will to crush him and cause him to suffer, and though the LORD makes his life an offering for sin, he will see his offspring and prolong his days, and the will of the LORD will prosper in his hand. After he has suffered, he will see the light of life and be satisfied; by his knowledge my righteous servant will justify many, and he will bear their iniquities. Therefore I will give him a portion among the great, and he will divide the spoils with the strong, because he poured out his life unto death, and was numbered with the transgressors. For he bore the sin of many, and made intercession for the transgressors.

In Jesus's own time the Jews were looking for the coming of the Messiah, for they asked each other, as in John 7:31:

> "When the Messiah comes, will he perform more signs than this man?"

See also John 7:40–42:

> On hearing his words, some of the people said, "Surely this man is the Prophet." Others said, "He is the Messiah." Still others asked, "How can the Messiah come from Galilee? Does not Scripture say that the Christ will come from David's descendants and from Bethlehem, the town where David lived?"

Similarly, John 10:24:

> The Jews who were there gathered around him, saying, "How long will you keep us in suspense? If you are the Messiah, tell us plainly."

The gospels record Jesus's own confirmation that he was the Messiah, as in John 4:25–26:

> The woman said, "I know that Messiah" (called Christ) "is coming. When he comes, he will explain everything to us." Then Jesus declared, "I, the one speaking to you – I am he."

See also Matthew 16:16–17:

> Simon Peter answered, "You are the Messiah, the Son of the living God." Jesus replied, "Blessed are you, Simon son of Jonah, for this was not revealed to you by flesh and blood, but by my Father in heaven."

Also Mark 14:61–62:

> But Jesus remained silent and gave no answer. Again the high priest asked him, "Are you the Messiah, the Son of the Blessed One?" "I am," said Jesus. "And you will see the Son of Man sitting at the right hand of the Mighty One and coming on the clouds of heaven."

Similarly, Matthew 26:63–64,

> The high priest said to him, "I charge you under oath by the living God: Tell us if you are the Messiah, the Son of God." "You have said so," Jesus replied. "But I say to all of you: From now on you will see the Son of Man sitting at the right hand of the Mighty One and coming on the clouds of heaven."

Chapter Appendix 7.2

New Testament Passages on "Jesus as Lord"

Acts 8:36–37 – As they traveled along the road, they came to some water and the eunuch said, "Look, here is water. What can stand in the way of my being baptized?" Philip said, "If you believe with all your heart you may." The eunuch answered, "I believe that Jesus Christ is the Son of God."

Acts 16:30–31 – He then brought them out and asked, "Sirs, what must I do to be saved?" They replied, "Believe in the Lord Jesus, and you will be saved – you and your household."

Romans 10:9–10 – If you declare with your mouth, "Jesus is Lord," and believe in your heart that God raised him from the dead, you will be saved. For it is with your heart that you believe and are justified, and it is with your mouth that you profess your faith and are saved.

1 Corinthians 8:6 – Yet for us there is but one God, the Father, from whom all things came and for whom we live; and there is but one Lord, Jesus Christ, through whom all things came and through whom we live.

1 Corinthians 15:3–4 – For what I received I passed on to you as of first importance: that Christ died for our sins according to the Scriptures, that he was buried, that he was raised on the third day according to the Scriptures.

Philippians 2:10–11 – That at the name of Jesus every knee should bow, in heaven and on earth and under the earth, and every tongue acknowledge that Jesus Christ is Lord, to the glory of God the Father.

1 Timothy 2:5–6 – For there is one God and one mediator between God and mankind, the man Christ Jesus, who gave himself as a ransom for all people. This has now been witnessed to at the proper time.

1 Timothy 3:16 – Beyond all question, the mystery from which true godliness springs is great: He appeared in the flesh, was vindicated by the Spirit, was seen by angels, was preached among the nations, was believed on in the world, was taken up in glory.

2 Timothy 2:8 – Remember Jesus Christ, raised from the dead, descended from David. This is my gospel.

1 John 5:1 – Everyone who believes that Jesus is the Christ is born of God, and everyone who loves the father loves his child as well.

Questions for Discussion and Review

Jesus Christ as Son of Man and Son of God: The Challenge of Judaism and Docetism

Who is Jesus Christ?

1. How did Jesus's disciples learn about the true meaning of his lordship and divine status?

2. How did the disciples come to understand the meaning of his crucifixion?

3. What is the significance of the title *Kurios* for Jesus as it was used in early Christian congregations?

4. Why did Jesus choose twelve disciples? What was his plan in "sending them out"?

5. Why did the Jewish authorities attempt to stop the disciples preaching in the name of Jesus? Why did they finally expel Christians from the synagogue?

6. What explanation does Judaism give for Christian belief in Jesus Christ? Why did the Jews emphasize the human and historical aspects of his life?

7. How does Docetism explain the life and death of Jesus? Why does Docetism emphasize the spiritual character of his life?

8. Who are to be included among "Apostolic Fathers"? What is the significance of this group of leaders for early Christianity?

9. What important information is given by these Apostolic Fathers regarding the deity of Christ?

The Divine Jesus: Philosophical aspects

1. How did philosophy function in Greek culture, especially as a challenge to traditional worship of the gods?

2. What did Socrates attempt to accomplish through his emphasis on human self-knowledge? Which important questions was Socrates answering in his discussion of true "virtue" (*aretê*)?

3. What is the significance of Plato's appeal to an Ideal World, as basis for our understanding of "this world" of matter? In what sense did his explanation of that world contribute to *dualism*?

4. Why did Plato critique the traditional mythical accounts of the gods? How did such critique provide the foundation for the scholarly work of "theology"?

5. Why is Aristotle often considered the first modern "scientist"? How did Aristotle modify Plato's theory of Ideas in terms of "forms"?

6. What was the Stoic understanding of the Logos? How did they explain human responsibility with respect to that Logos?

7. Why is Philo of Alexandria significant for our understanding of early Christianity?

8. What is meant by *allegorical interpretation* of the Scriptures? Why did Philo use allegorical interpretation of Old Testament passages? To what extent did he follow the lead of Stoicism in this approach?

Further Reading

Armstrong, A. H. *An Introduction to Ancient Philosophy.* Totowa, NJ: Rowman & Allanheld; London: Methuen, 1983.
Borgen, Peder. *Early Christianity and Hellenistic Judaism.* Edinburgh: T&T Clark, 1998.
Chadwick, H. *Early Christian Thought and the Classical Tradition.* Oxford: Oxford University Press, 1966.
Dillon, John. *The Middle Platonists: Study of Platonism 80 BC to AD 220.* London: Duckworth, 1977.
Frend, W. H. C. *The Rise of Christianity.* London: Darton, Longman & Todd, 1984.
Hatch, Edwin. *The Influence of Greek Ideas on Christianity.* New York: Harper & Brothers, 1957.
Hengel, Martin. *Judaism and Hellenism: Studies in Their Encounter in Palestine during the Early Hellenistic Period.* 2 vols. Minneapolis: Fortress, 1974.
Jaeger, W. *Early Christianity and Greek Paideia.* Cambridge, MA: Harvard University Press, 1962.
Markus, R. A. *Christianity in the Roman World.* London: Thames & Hudson, 1975.
Rist, J. M. *Stoic Philosophy.* London: Cambridge University Press, 1969.
Stead, G. C. *Divine Substance.* Oxford: Clarendon, 1977.
———. *Philosophy in Late Antiquity.* Cambridge: Cambridge University Press, 1994.

8

Second-Century Gnosticism and Its Impact

> Valentinus had expected to become bishop because he was able, both in genius and in eloquence. So he became indignant when another obtained that position of honour by reason of a claim given by confessorship. As a result Valentinus broke with the church of the true faith. Just like the restless spirits which can be roused by opposition and are inflamed with a desire for revenge, he applied himself with all his vigour to exterminate the truth. Upon finding the by-way of a certain old opinion, he set out on a highway with all the subtlety of a serpent.
>
> Tertullian, Against the Valentinians, 4

Among the challenges facing Christianity in the first centuries of its existence, Valentinus provides the outstanding example of a serious threat to the church from within. As Tertullian tells the story, Valentinus came from well-educated circles in Alexandria, arrived in Rome (ca. AD 140), and made a good impression with his learning and ability in public speaking. He came very close to being elected as bishop of Rome, a position of great authority within the Christian church, certainly in the western sectors of the empire. But he was also ambitious. Tertullian attributes his "going astray" into the ways of the Gnostics as a reaction to disappointed hopes and ambitions. His pursuit of what came to be designated as Gnosticism is portrayed as a type of revenge for missing the opportunity of taking on leadership.

Although Tertullian's point cannot be corroborated from other sources and appears motivated by his polemics here, we do know that followers of Valentinus considered themselves Christian. While we have little information about the actual gnostic communities, we also know that they continued to hold the church in high regard, to the extent of designating one of the *Aeons* (the "eternal beings" recognized by them) as the church (*ekklêsia*), produced from the Word (*logos*) and Life (*zoê*). And these factors are extremely significant for understanding the hostility expressed by Irenaeus and Tertullian, the church leaders who responded to the Gnostics; these leaders are called "heresiologists" by virtue of that response to "heresy."

A. Gnosticism

As we take a closer look at Gnosticism, the question: "Who is Jesus Christ?" remains in the foreground. Judaism acknowledged only the human, historical Jesus. We have seen that the disciples increasingly recognized Christ as fully divine, with the confession of Jesus as Lord (*Kurios*); this is evident in the earliest sermons proclaiming that lordship.[1] Docetism also recognized Jesus as divine, but did not allow for his life in an ordinary human body; they could not account for him as fully human.

The docetic approach in explaining Christ's divinity was taken further by the Gnostics.[2] Like Docetists, Gnostics found it difficult to accept a divine Saviour who suffered and died. Most Gnostics had some alternative explanation for what happened on the cross. They speculated that someone else, perhaps Simon of Cyrene, was actually crucified in his stead.[3] At worst Jesus suffered only as a "psychic" person, while his higher divine (spiritual) identity was left untouched. But this approach also raised new questions for Christians about the basis of their salvation: how could the life, death and resurrection of Jesus have validity for human salvation if he did not truly suffer and die as an historical human being; did these events have only a "mythical" character?

At issue was an ancient understanding regarding the relationship between flesh and spirit, between body and soul. Even more, it was a question of the relationship between what is divine (or spiritual) and what is human (and bodily). These issues, which we explored in the previous chapter, also raise questions of the relationship between time (or history) and eternity.[4] Of

---

1. See ch. 7, §A.4; also chapter appendix 7.2 at the end of chapter 7.
2. See Rudolph, *Gnosis*, 157–158.
3. See the citation of Basileides on this theme (from Irenaeus, *Against Heresies* 1.24.4) in §A.2 below.
4. A brief introduction on these issues, based in Greek thought, is given in ch. 7, §B; see also Latourette, *First Five Centuries*, 122–123.

course, these are *philosophical* questions, but they are also essentially *religious* questions. In that context, Christianity inevitably had to address itself to such matters. Key Christian beliefs affected by the docetic/gnostic approach are the incarnation of Jesus, his crucifixion, death, and resurrection to a new body.

As a movement of the first few Christian centuries, Gnosticism was highly *syncretistic*;[5] and it was certainly not limited to attempts to incorporate itself within Christianity. It took elements from eastern religions, especially Persian Zoroastrian thought with its strong dualism of light and dark, of good and evil.[6] Among the philosophers, Pythagoreans were known for such dualism.[7] While Platonism was also dualistic, especially to the extent that it accepted basic premises of the Pythagoreans, later followers of Plato, like the third-century Plotinus, manifested another strain, with a monistic approach, and a correspondingly more positive appreciation of matter and the body. In terms of its understanding of the heavenly spheres and the archons, Gnosticism was clearly indebted to Ptolemaic astronomy. At present there are serious scholars of Gnosticism who surmise that this movement may even have origins within the Judaic communities, or its fringe groups. Gnosticism itself, in turn, would influence numerous other groups and philosophical schools of thought.

It is also clear that Gnosticism was not tightly organized as a single specific school of thought, but spread through charismatic teachers and their adherents. Throughout the second century it had the character of a loose spiritual movement. With different leaders, it showed itself in different forms.[8] Gnostics often attached themselves to Christian churches and infiltrated the leadership, making considerable use of Christian language and terminology,

---

5. See ch. 7, §B.5.

6. Scholars like Richard Reitzenstein and Hans Jonas accented an origin for Gnosticism in eastern religions; see Rudolph, *Gnosis*, 32–33, also appendix I, §D. Other scholars have presented compelling arguments that Gnosticism did not arise before the Christian period; see Edwin Yamauchi, *Pre-Christian Gnosticism*, and Simone Pétrement, *Separate God*.

7. Attributing the origin of Gnosticism to Greek philosophy already characterized the approach of early Christian Fathers like Hippolytus of Rome (170–235 AD), particularly in his *Refutation of All Heresies*. For a brief recent discussion of the numerous questions raised by Hippolytus's life and work, see Volf, "Allah and the Trinity," 141–153. This view of the origin of Gnosticism was also promoted by Tertullian (on whom, see §B.3 below), and is the well-known position of Adolf von Harnack, who spoke of Gnosticism as the "acute secularising of the gospel"; see Rudolph, *Gnosis*, 31–32. On the influence of Harnack on modern study of Gnosticism, see appendix I, §C and §D.

8. For a general introduction to Gnosticism, its history, main ideas and sources, see Rudolph, *Gnosis*. For a useful introduction to the important contemporary source of Gnosticism, the Nag Hammadi scrolls, see also Ehrman, *Truth and Fiction*, 36–49. On the great diversity of groups which may be characterized as "gnostic," see Ferguson, *Backgrounds*, 300–313, especially 301.

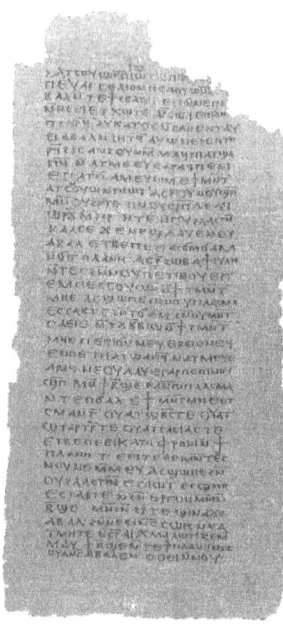

Figure 8.1. The Jung codex of the Gospel of Truth. This page gives a Coptic translation of the (mid-2nd century) Greek Valentinian document (mentioned in Irenaeus, *Against Heresies* 3.11.9). The manuscript survived in relatively good condition, as part of the first codex of the Nag Hammadi Library (discovered in 1945) to be sold to a Belgian antique dealer. It came into the possession of the renowned psychologist Carl G. Jung in 1951 and is named after him. Photographic reproduction by Hēsykhía. "Codex I, papyrus page 17. Gospel of Truth. The Nag Hammadi Library." Public Domain.

while in fact presenting a very different understanding of salvation.[9] In this way it would present a serious challenge to the church.

Before the significant discovery of the Nag Hammadi documents, our main source of information about Gnosticism came from second-century "heresiologists" like Irenaeus and Tertullian,[10] who confronted Gnosticism as a "heretical" development within Christianity. But even before that discovery, non-Christian gnostic documents like the Hermetic *Poimandres* were available. During the nineteenth century two documents – *Pistis Sophia* and the two *Books of Jeu* – aroused new interest in Gnosticism,[11] as did an old manuscript which included the gnostic *Apocryphon of John* and *Sophia Jesu Christi*.[12]

---

9. See Irenaeus, *Against Heresies* 1.27.4,
   They set forth, indeed, the name of Christ Jesus as a sort of lure, but in various ways they introduce the impieties of Simon [Magus of Samaria]; and thus they destroy multitudes, wickedly disseminating their own doctrines by the use of a good name, and, through means of its sweetness and beauty, extending to their hearers the bitter and malignant poison of the serpent, the great author of apostasy.

10. For a survey of relevant "heresiological" literature, see Rudolph, *Gnosis*, 9–25.

11. Rudolph, *Gnosis*, 27–28.

12. This is the 1896 document known as *Papyrus Berol* 8502, acquired in Berlin and finally published in 1955; see Rudolph, *Gnosis*, 28–29.

Also available late in the nineteenth century were the *Odes of Solomon* and the *Song of the Pearl*, documents associated with the later Mandaean Persian community which was affiliated with Gnosticism in thought.[13]

Modern understanding of Gnosticism was greatly enhanced by the significant twentieth-century (1945) discovery of Coptic manuscripts at Hag Hammadi, along the Nile in Upper Egypt. Here a whole library of gnostic manuscripts, forty-eight in all, had remained hidden in clay pots, placed there probably late in the fourth century by a local monastic community. Most of the documents were in Coptic, but the find included some treatises translated from Greek originals. These documents first appeared in English translation as *The Nag Hammadi Library* (1977), edited by James M. Robinson.[14]

A.1. Gnostic gnôsis

The name of this movement is based on the Greek term *gnôsis* (*knowledge*); this does not represent scientific or factual knowledge, but an intuitive knowledge characteristic of "knowing" people, or knowledge gained through insight, knowledge of the heart.[15] The title *gnostic* refers to the person who "knows" the way of redemption for humanity. Knowledge is the key in eluding enslavement to the powers of this world, expressed in terms of a dangerous ignorance.[16] Thus *gnôsis* represents soteriological knowledge through enlightenment, or illumination.[17] It is also esoteric, a *secret* knowledge, not commonly available; and it is given supernaturally, as a guarantee of salvation for those who are properly initiated. The Gnostics emphasized experiential and intuitive knowledge, the kind that can be obtained on a personal spiritual quest. One of the best indications of the knowledge given occurs in an explanation of baptism by the gnostic Theodotus:

> It brings us knowledge of our former state, and of what, through baptism itself, we have now become; knowledge of where we were,

---

13. Rudolph, 29.

14. For the fourth revised edition, see J. M. Robinson, *Nag Hammadi Library*. For a list of the documents, see Rudolph, *Gnosis*, 44–48. For the dramatic story of the discoveries in the Egyptian desert, and their identification, often told, see Ferguson, *Backgrounds*, 301–306; also Rudolph, *Gnosis*, 34–44. For photos of the location and the codices, see Rudolph, 123–130.

15. On the meaning of this term, see Pelikan, *Emergence of the Catholic Tradition*, 81–82; Rudolph, *Gnosis*, 55–56; and Latourette, *First Five Centuries*, 124.

16. On the significance of knowledge and ignorance for the Gnostics, see Rudolph, *Gnosis*, 55; see also passages quoted in Stevenson, *New Eusebius*, 68–70.

17. Rudolph accents the equivalence of ignorance with darkness; similarly, knowledge is equated with light (*Gnosis*, 113–114).

or came from, of whither we are heading and from what we have been redeemed, of the meaning of birth and rebirth.[18]

For Gnostics the theme of *salvation* or *redemption* was as important and central as it was for Christians.[19] According to gnostic teachings, the true self is not the body, or even the soul of the person, but the spiritual, pneumatic element, the divine fragment or spark, which derives from the heavenly realms.[20] This divine spark has become imprisoned within the body, or the lower world of nature, and is now exiled from its true home in the spiritual realms. In order to be released from its state of "sleep," a divine messenger, or Redeemer figure from that realm must come down to awaken the spiritual element. Through knowledge (*gnôsis*) communicated in initiation, those who are truly spiritual can be released from the human body, and guided on a path of return to their home in the world above.[21]

Accurate "self-knowledge" became a key theme for Gnostics. They took very seriously the *evil* character of this world; it is not a safe or good place in which to live. God is far away, if not absent. In fact, the *highest God* is not only transcendent; he is both unknown and *unknowable*.[22] Moreover, the present world as we know it owes its origin to a foolish or ignorant and second-rate deity, the demiurge. In this world we are surrounded by evil powers; and the path of freedom, the way of return to our divine origin is blocked by evil cosmic powers, *archontes*.[23] If the soul is to get past them on its journey to the heavenly spheres, where it belongs, it must know the all-important passwords, as the key to overcoming the power of these evil forces.[24] This too was a significant part of the esoteric knowledge imparted to the initiate.

---

18. For citation of fragment 78 of Theodotus (preserved by Clement of Alexandria), see Stevenson, *New Eusebius*, 68.

19. Ferguson, *Backgrounds*, 309–311.

20. On gnostic groups who took baptism of the Holy Spirit very seriously, see Stevenson, *New Eusebius*, 70.

21. This is very close to the summary of gnostic teachings given in standard theological discussions like that of Rudolf Bultmann in the German encyclopedia, *Die Religion in Geschichte und Gegenwart* (*Religion in History and the Present*); see Neill, *Interpretation*, 167–168. Neill himself recognized that such a neat summary is nowhere to be found in gnostic documents; it is constructed by bringing together elements from various sources into a single myth (*Interpretation*, 177). On basic beliefs common to many gnostic groups, see §A.5 below; also Ehrman, *Truth and Fiction*, 42–44.

22. For this theme in Basileides, see Stevenson, *New Eusebius*, 73; for Valentinus, see Stevenson, *New Eusebius*, 79–80. Such an approach to deity evidences basic elements of a negative theology.

23. Rudolph, *Gnosis*, 177–179 and 187.

24. See Rudolph, *Gnosis*, 183.

Second-Century Gnosticism and Its Impact 213

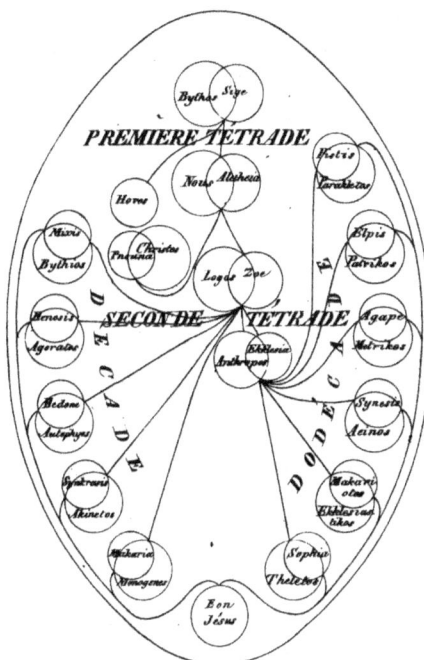

Figure 8.2. The Valentinian Pleroma.
This sketch is taken from Jacques Matter (1826), *Histoire critique du Gnosticisme*, Vol. II, Plate II. Public Domain.

Accurate knowledge about the cosmos and supra-cosmic realms, the *Pleroma*, the spiritual beings called "aeons," the nature of our world and its rulers – much of it provided in the form of myth, tantra and magical sayings – was equally important.[25]

Such knowledge also represents power, for it provides a roadmap that not only reveals our present condition, but points the way ahead, the way of ascent, by overcoming hostile opponents. Only such knowledge can provide peace of mind for this life, and the ability to face death with tranquillity. For the source of this knowledge Gnostics turned to the Redeemer, whom they identified as the Christ, as the one who descended from the *Pleroma* to reveal the mysteries and communicate the vital secrets.

A.2. Gnostic Leaders: Valentinus and Basileides

From the perspective of Christianity, the views of Valentinus represent what is probably the most important example of Gnosticism. The Valentinian school has also been described as "the most coherent of the gnostic movements."[26] Compared with other gnostic groups, the communities associated with Valentinus and Basileides were characterized by a teacher-student relationship more typical of a philosophical school, than a religious cult.[27] As two important representatives of second-century Gnosticism, both are well documented in

---

25. The key to such speculation is the Ptolemaic view of the cosmos typical of the period; it recognized the earth at the centre, surrounded by a series of spheres of the sun, moon and planets, beyond which are found the ethereal spheres. See Rudolph, *Gnosis*, 67–70; and Martin, *Hellenistic Religions*, 8–9.

26. Martin, *Hellenistic Religions*, 137–143, particularly 138.

27. Rudolph, *Gnosis*, 215.

the work of Irenaeus. Valentinus came from Alexandria to Rome (ca. AD 140), and attached himself to the Christian church there. He was an eloquent speaker but, as noted above, we know that he lost an election for bishop.[28] His teachings presented novel insight on central beliefs of Christians, especially the role of Jesus and the way of salvation.[29] For this he was accused of leading believers away from the traditional gospel presentation, and was finally denounced by the church.

Valentinus's mythical account of the soul

Valentinus taught that the ultimate origin of all was the Father (Unbegotten Monad, or *Bythos* [depth]), as the perfect *Aeon* (eternal spiritual being), and utterly transcendent. His companion is *Sigê* (silence) which is the Father's *Ennoia* (thought). Three further sets of aeons proceed from the original pair: *Nous* (*Monogenês* [only-begotten]) and *Alêtheia* (truth); *Logos* and *Zoê* (life); *Anthrôpos* (man) and *Ecclêsia* (church). This provides the first *Ogdoad* [set of 8] of the *Plerôma*, namely the "fullness" of the heavenly realms.[30]

A further five sets (i.e. a decad [ten]) of aeons proceed from *Logos* and *Zoê*; a set of six (a dodecad [twelve]) proceeds from *Anthrôpos* and *Ecclêsia*. Thus we have the first thirty aeons forming the *Plerôma*, or spiritual realm; the names and number of aeons vary in the different accounts, giving as many as 365.

Sophia

The last of this series of aeons is Sophia, and her role is pivotal to the story. While only *Monogenês* (*Nous*) can know and reveal the Father, Sophia possesses (or conceives) a curiosity, or desire (in Greek, *Enthymêsis*) to see him, to know him intimately and directly. She is stopped by *Horos* (limit), the guardian

---

28. On Valentinus, see also Frend, *Rise of Christianity*, 207–208; and Stevenson, *New Eusebius*, 79.

29. Of the Nag Hammadi documents which are specifically Valentinian, we note *A Valentinian Exposition* (see J. M. Robinson, *Nag Hammadi Library*, 481–489), the *Prayer of Paul* (J. M. Robinson, 27–28), the *Gospel of Truth* (J. M. Robinson, 38–51), and the *Gospel of Philip* (J. M. Robinson, 139–160). The *Valentinian Gospel of Mary* (J. M. Robinson, 523–527) was discovered in Cairo in 1896; see Witherington, *Gospel Code*, 81–85. For further discussion of these documents see ch. 9, §E below.

30. For the teaching of Valentinus on "aeons," see Rudolph, *Gnosis*, 318–322. On the Valentinian gnostic understanding of cosmic redemption, see also Pelikan, *Emergence of the Catholic Tradition*, 81–97, especially 84.

of the *Plerôma* (or alternatively, by *Stauros* [the Cross]) who explains the unknowability of the Father.³¹

Sophia can remain within the Pleroma only if she discards or aborts her "passion." But the orderly character of the Pleroma has been disturbed; to remedy this *Nous* and *Alêtheia* produce Christ and the Holy Spirit as a new set of aeons, to instruct all the aeons about proprieties in the Pleroma. The result is the birth of Jesus as Saviour.³²

Sophia's *passion* takes on a life of its own, expelled, or exiled outside the Pleroma; she is known as *Achamoth* or Lower Sophia.³³ Her unhappy wandering results in the birth of matter (the *carnal/choic* element). Her desire for Christ results in the birth of the *psychikon* (soul) element or substance. Christ takes pity on her, descends by way of the cross, and impresses form on her formlessness.³⁴ Then he returns. This allows Achamoth to give birth to *pneumatic* (spiritual) substance.³⁵ These three elements (choic, psychic, and pneumatic) provide the basis for the creation of the world as we know it.

Sophia begins by forming the creator, or demiurge (i.e. the Old Testament Creator God) from psychic substance, making him into a (false) image of the Father. The demiurge in turn creates the heavens and the earth, and finally also creates mankind. He first makes the "earthly" man, breathing his own psychic substance into him. But Achamoth outwits him by implanting the *pneuma* of her own spirit into the souls of some.³⁶

This explains why some human beings desire God, and seek liberation from the earthly bonds, although the lower elements hold them down. How are they liberated? This is explained as the work of Jesus the Saviour. He cannot save the carnal or materially-minded. Those who are *psychic* can be saved

---

31. For an account of the myth of Sophia based on writings of the church Fathers, see Stead, "The Valentinian Myth of Sophia," 75–104 (though written before the Nag Hammadi documents were published). Stead notes important connections with the work of Philo of Alexandria. Stevenson (*New Eusebius*, 68–69) gives the account of Sophia in the *Apocryphon of John* (see J. M. Robinson, *Nag Hammadi Library*, 104–123), which also receives attention in Rudolph, *Gnosis*, 76–83. For the Valentinian account in Irenaeus (*Against Heresies* 1.2.2-4), see Stevenson, *New Eusebius*, 80–82.

32. For the account of the heavenly Christ in Valentinian thought, see Rudolph, *Gnosis*, 155–156.

33. Achamoth is called Yaltabaoth in the Apocryphon of John; Stevenson, *New Eusebius*, 69.

34. Rudolph, *Gnosis*, 155; on the role of Christ, see also the quote from Irenaeus, *Against Heresies* 1.2.5-6, given in Stevenson, *New Eusebius*, 82.

35. Rudolph, *Gnosis*, 156.

36. The above gives a simplified version of more complex accounts found in various documents. The account of the origin of the world, based on the *Gospel of Philip* and *Gospel of Truth*, features similar themes: ignorance, error and failure on the part of the maker; see Rudolph, *Gnosis*, 83–84.

through knowledge and imitation of Jesus, while the *pneumatic* (or elect) are redeemed by listening to the teachings of Jesus.[37] Those who are to be saved are awakened, as from a drunken stupor; they are dazed and uncertain, until esoteric knowledge, given by way of a secret password, enables the elect to overcome the evil cosmic powers and make the journey of ascent through the heavenly spheres.

Jesus assumes a very specific role in this account, as the messenger from the Pleroma to pass on secret knowledge to his disciples, specifically, to explain the origin of evil and the way of salvation. He presents his Father as the unknowable and wholly transcendent deity who has generated a series of emanations to mediate between himself and the world; the latter was finally created, demonstrably as a mistake, or the result of a mistake. Gnostics used this account to explain evil in our world. Our visible, material world is not created to be good; it is essentially evil. Its creator, the demiurge, did not know what he was doing, and did a poor job of it. So the good Creator God of Genesis is demoted to an inferior deity, and characterized by harsh justice and jealousy. He is contrasted negatively with God the father of Jesus, the perfect God, the God of love and mercy.

But even more critical than Jesus's role is that of Sophia, as she represents the outstanding example of a series of feminine figures dominating the gnostic mythical accounts, like Norea, Pronoia, Epinoia, and Zoê (Eve). Such names typically indicate a personification, or even hypostatizing of a concept, like "wisdom," "forethought" or "life." Christian accounts of Sophia, rooted in OT texts like Proverbs 8, (deutero-canonical) Wisdom of Solomon 6–10, and Sirach 24, understood her role as God's agent in creation, with Jesus as the pre-existent Logos. We note the gnostic understanding of Sophia having an even more crucial role in forming the creator of the heavens and the earth.

Also noteworthy in gnostic documents is the considerable interest shown in the issue of gender, evident especially from the gendered pairing of aeons in the Valentinian *Pleroma*. The prominence of feminine imagery and the critical role of the feminine Sophia has drawn feminist scholars to these texts, leading them to suggest that women had greater prominence among Gnostics than was possible at this time in the orthodox Christian church.[38] Irenaeus's complaint that Marcus, one of Valentinus's disciples who settled in Lyons,

---

37. On gnostic anthropology and these three grades of humanity, see Stevenson, *New Eusebius*, 72 and 84–85; also Rudolph, *Gnosis*, 91–92.

38. See King, *Images of the Feminine in Gnosticism*. The bibliography on the topic only grew in subsequent years; Kraemer, "Women and Gender," 465–492, gives a useful survey of recent publications on these issues.

allowed women to celebrate the Eucharist, appears to affirm such roles for women.[39] The mythical character of gnostic documents, however, indicates the need to use extreme caution in examining these for reliable answers on (historical) questions regarding the place of women, or the specific roles they might have taken in gnostic communities.

It is clear that Gnostics like Valentinus interpreted the Christian writings according to their own insights, emphasizing the carnal/spiritual distinction in the writing of Paul. They claimed that only a few of Jesus's disciples had been part of an inner circle, and received secret teaching. And they regarded only a few Christians as truly *spiritual,* while most are thought to remain *carnal*; these were condemned to be destroyed with the cosmos in the final judgement. There was a third category, *psychic* Christians, those who had "faith," and for whom there was more hope than for "carnal" believers.

Basileides

Basileides, a disciple of Menander (who was in turn thought to be a disciple of Simon the Samaritan), lectured in Alexandria and Rome (ca. AD 120–140). His views, overlapping with those of Valentinus, featured a *graded order of existence* emanating from the ineffable and altogether transcendent Father; an *opposition* between the highest, transcendent God and the God of Jews or Jehovah; the *creation* of the universe and human beings by inferior powers, especially *Nous* (Mind) and *Logos* (Word); and *redemption* through a series of lower powers to release spiritual elements bound in human bodies.[40]

According to Basileides, as he is presented in Hippolytus's *Refutation of All Heresies,* the "non-existent" Father, the original cause of all else, projected

---

39. Eusebius, *EH* 1.14.1; see also Tertullian's *Praescriptio Haereticorum*, 41, on which see further below §B.3.

40. On Basileides, see Frend, *Rise of Christianity,* 205–207; and Daniélou, *Theology of Jewish Christianity,* 75–76. Rudolph notes the considerable difference in the report of his thought as given by Irenaeus or Hippolytus (Rudolph, *Gnosis,* 309–311). For representative views of Basileides given by Irenaeus, see his *Against Heresies* 1.24.5,
> Salvation belongs to the soul alone, for the body is by nature subject to corruption. He [Basileides] also declares that the prophecies were derived from those powers who were the makers of the world, but the law was specially given by their chief, who led the people out of the land of Egypt. He attaches no importance to [the question regarding] meats offered in sacrifice to idols, thinking them of no consequence, and makes use of them without any hesitation. And he holds the use of other things, and the practice of every kind of lust, a matter of perfect indifference. These men, moreover, practise magic; and use images, incantations, invocations, and every other kind of curious art.

a seed with the germinal power of a universal seed (*panspermia*).⁴¹ A triple sonship resulted: the first is like light, and rises in return to the Father; the second only attains to a middle region (*methorion*); the third remains mingled with *panspermia*. The *archontes* (cosmic rulers) are born from the presence of the third sonship, to create our world.⁴² Accordingly, the world as we know it has affinities with the upper world, but is also clogged with lower beings. The *pneumatikoi* (spiritual ones) reveal the presence of the third sonship in *panspermia* (*Refutation* 7.13).

According to Irenaeus, Basileides's discussion of the crucifixion questioned the reality of the death of Jesus:

> But the father without birth and without name . . . sent his own first-begotten Nous [mind], who is called Christ to provide deliverance from the power of those who made the world for those who believe in him. Thus he appeared on earth as a man, appearing to the nations of these powers, and performed miracles. This is why he himself did not suffer death, but Simon of Cyrene was compelled and bore the cross in his place. Simon was also transfigured by Christ, that he would be thought to be Jesus. Through ignorance and error Simon was crucified, while Jesus himself received the form of Simon and, standing by, laughed at them. For he was an incorporeal power, and the Nous [mind] of

---

41. See Hippolytus, *The Refutation of All Heresies*, 7.9–15; on the idea of *panspermia* (lit. "all seed"), see §7.9,

> And by the expression "world" . . . [I mean] the seed of a world. The seed/germ of the world, however, had all things in itself. . . . In this way, "non-existent" God made the world out of nonentities, casting and depositing some one Seed that contained in itself a conglomeration of the seeds of the world.

See also Stevenson, *New Eusebius*, 73.

42. Hippolytus, *Refutation* 7.10,

> There existed, he says, in the Seed itself, a Sonship, threefold, in every respect of the same Substance with the non-existent God, [and] begotten from nonentities. Of this Sonship (thus) involving a threefold division, one part was refined, [another gross,] and another requiring purification.

See also 7.11,

> While, therefore, the firmament which is above the heaven is coming into existence, the Great Archon [and] Head of the world burst forth, and was begotten from the cosmical Seed, and the conglomeration of all seeds . . . [I]magining Himself to be Lord and Governor and a wise Master Builder, He turns Himself to [the work of] the creation of every object in the cosmic system.

And 7.12,

> The third Sonship still remains in the (conglomeration of) all seeds . . . Now, we who are *spiritual* are sons, he says, who have been left here to arrange, and mould, and rectify, and complete the souls which are so constituted according to nature as to continue in this quarter of the universe.

the unbegotten father; so he [Christ] transfigured himself as he pleased, and thus ascended to him who had sent him. He derided his enemies, inasmuch as he could not be laid hold of, and was invisible to all. Those who know these things have been freed from the principalities who formed the world. Thus we are not to confess him who was crucified, but him who came in the form of a man, and was thought to be crucified, and was called Jesus, and was sent by the father, that by this dispensation he might destroy the works of the makers of the world.[43]

It is certainly possible that this account of the crucifixion was not original with Basileides, but was adapted by him from the docetic interpretation of the death of Jesus as he knew it, for Docetists too assumed that Jesus, if he were truly God, could not have died.[44] In this connection we note that, where the Qur'an denies the reality of Jesus's death by crucifixion, doing so in polemic with Judaic claims to have killed the one said to be the Messiah, it also speaks of the *appearance* of his being slain.[45] Although Muslim scholars like the ninth-century Al-Jabbar may have thought they were quoting the canonical gospels when they transmitted such accounts of the crucifixion, their version can actually be traced back only to apocryphal gospels which accented gnostic themes;[46] it would appear that the true source of the crucifixion account transmitted in the Qur'an is to be traced to such apocryphal gospel accounts.[47]

---

43. Irenaeus, *Against Heresies* 1.24.4. The quote is also given in Stevenson, *New Eusebius*, 96–97.

44. See Rudolph, *Gnosis*, 164–165.

45. See the Qur'an, Sura 4.156–157. See further, Stern, "Quotations from Apocryphal Gospels in Abd Al-Jabbar," 34–57, especially 40–50, for the argument of mistaken identity in Judas Iscariot's betrayal of Jesus to the guards; allegedly the guards did not recognize the man as Jesus. When Judas later asked them what they had done with the man, he exclaimed, "This is innocent blood" (Matt 27:3); these words are said to reflect Judas's own conclusion, that they had crucified the wrong man.

46. These apocryphal gospels (literally, "hidden" [or esoteric], which are equivalent, in practice, to those called "deutero-canonical") receive more attention in chapter 9. According to Philip Jenkins, Muslim groups like the Shi'ite Alawites of Syria were probably dependent on such gospels for typically gnostic language in referring to true believers as a people of light in the midst of a world of darkness (Jenkins, *Lost History of Christianity*, 190–191).

47. Stern ("Quotations from Apocryphal Gospels," 42–45, especially 45) concludes that Muhammad adopted a teaching like that of Docetists, assuming that another had been crucified in Jesus's place, or that Jesus, when crucified was not a true bodily human being, only a phantom. Stern realizes that Muslim scholars typically accept the former interpretation, supposing that Simon of Cyrene (or Judas) took the place of Jesus on the cross. He quotes al-Tabari (of mid-to-late ninth century) for the account which assumes that God had lifted Jesus up to himself; only a phantom was crucified (Stern, 46). The story can be traced back to an earlier author, Wahb b. Munabbih (d. 728/29), who is known to have shared Christian accounts with Muslims. Other

A.3. Marcion (AD 85–160)

Marcion shared some aspects of gnostic teachings, but was more closely integrated with the Christian church.[48] He came from a wealthy family of ship builders in Pontus, Bithynia, where his father was a bishop. When Marcion arrived in Rome (ca. AD 139), he was influenced by the gnostic Cerdo. His influence in the church came from a large donation he made, worth thousands of dollars in modern currency.

Marcion's understanding of Jesus reflects gnostic positions diametrically opposed to those accepted by the Jews. He characterized Jehovah of the Old Testament as a harsh judge and an inferior creator God, while God the father of Jesus is presented as kind, merciful and forgiving.[49] In fact, Marcion proposed a radical *rejection of the Old Testament* or Torah, as Law, in favour of the New Testament, as gospel.[50] To justify this approach, he accepted a very limited canon of Scripture, rejecting any connection between Jesus and the promises of the Old Testament; nor could the Old Testament Jehovah God be regarded as Jesus's Father. Of New Testament books, Marcion was partial to the writings of Luke and Paul, rejecting references to the Old Testament as too Jewish; he also made use of allegorical interpretation to fit his own understanding with the actual wording of the biblical text.[51]

---

versions of the crucifixion given by Stern present an apostle volunteering to take Jesus's place, and turning into his likeness.

48. On Marcion, see Rudolph, *Gnosis*, 313–316; Frend, *Rise of Christianity*, 212–217; and Latourette, *First Five Centuries*, 125–128. Adolf von Harnack devoted a massive work to Marcion (1921), and drew parallels with Paul and Luther, virtually ignoring Marcion's gnostic teachings; see also B. Aland, "Marcion," and Balás, "Marcion Revisited."

49. See Latourette, *First Five Centuries*, 126; this view was more widespread among Christian Gnostics like Cerdo, who "taught that the God proclaimed by the law and the prophets was not the Father of our Lord Jesus Christ. For the former was known, but the latter unknown; while the one also was righteous, but the other benevolent." (Irenaeus, *Against Heresies* 1.27.1)

50. For an example of his critique of the Old Testament, we note the sceptical question of Marcion's disciple Apelles regarding Noah's ark, asking how it could possibly have contained all those animals. The implication was that if it sounds so unbelievable, it must be false (Stevenson, *New Eusebius*, 98).

51. Irenaeus reports Marcion's approach in formulating his own "canon" of Scripture,
[H]e mutilated the gospel which is according to Luke, removing all that is written respecting the generation of the Lord, and setting aside a great deal of the teaching of the Lord, in which the Lord is recorded as most dearly confessing that the Maker of this universe is His Father. . . . In like manner, too, he dismembered the Epistles of Paul, removing all that is said by the apostle respecting the God who made the world, to the effect that He is the Father of our Lord Jesus Christ; he also removed the passages where the apostle quotes from the prophetical writings to teach us that they announced the coming of the Lord beforehand. (*Against Heresies* 1.27.2)

Like most Gnostics, Marcion taught a rigorous ethic of denial of the body and of bodily functions, with rejection of marriage and the eating of meat. He regarded life in the body as an obstacle for the true spiritual self, and detrimental in reinforcing the power of the inferior demiurge who formed us as bodily creatures. With such a radical dualism of spirit and matter, Marcion taught a thorough rejection of the material world. Accordingly he denied the incarnation of Jesus, his true humanity, real death and resurrection. For these views Marcion was excommunicated in AD 144. At that point he formed his own church, a group that survived to the fifth century.

A.4. Other Important Gnostic Groups

We have devoted some attention to Valentinus, Basileides and Marcion because their lives and work were closely integrated with second-century Christianity. While these figures were important, they were not the only gnostic thinkers known at that time. An important initial role has been assigned to Simon of Samaria, or Simon Magus (whom we know from Acts 8).[52] His disciples were Menander of Samaria (also known for use of magic),[53] Saturninus of Antioch (an ascetic),[54] and Carpocrates (an antinomian, i.e. rejecting the validity of law).[55] Heracleon (fl. AD 175)[56] and Ptolemaeus (d. ca. 180)[57] are known to have been students of Valentinus.

Among identifiable gnostic groups of this period, Irenaeus mentions the *Encratites* as a group practising strict celibacy.[58] The *Perates* focused on the serpent as a mid-point between the Father and unformed matter in the cosmos. The *Naassenes* likewise regarded the serpent (of Gen 3) as a regenerative

---

In this way Marcion motivated the church to clarify its own position on which books constituted the "canonical" Scriptures.

52. On Simon, see Rudolph, *Gnosis*, 294–298.
53. Rudolph, 298.
54. Rudolph, 298.
55. Daniélou (*Theology of Jewish Christianity*, 84–85) speaks of Carpocrates as a Jewish Christian whose views of Jesus (as no more than a prophet) resemble those of the Ebionites. As "antinomian," Carpocratians are known for what Daniélou calls "moral indifferentism," condoning indulgence in vices for its adherents as a way of freeing themselves from the control of the archons (*Theology of Jewish Christianity*, 85). See also Rudolph, *Gnosis*, 299.
56. Rudolph, *Gnosis*, 323–324.
57. Rudolph, 323.
58. On Irenaeus's inclusion of Tatian among the Encratites, see Stevenson, *New Eusebius*, 100–101.

principle (*nahas* is Hebrew for "serpent").⁵⁹ *Sethians*, who may have been a sub-group of the Naassenes, also took a special interest in the role of the serpent. Their name is based on an appeal to Adam's son Seth as a revealer and spiritual father. Sethian documents like the *Gospel of the Egyptians*,⁶⁰ noted for a focus on philosophical ideas,⁶¹ are well represented among Nag Hammadi manuscripts.

An important later group identifiable as a powerful sequel to the Gnostics, the Manicheans, originated with the second-century Persian *Mani*, whose views overlapped with those of second-century Gnostics in many aspects.⁶² Manicheans became an influential group in Carthage; as a student there, Augustine was attracted to Manichean teachings. Both in Carthage and Rome he remained a lower-ranking member of the group, but even before his conversion to Christianity Augustine began to refute Manichean teachings.⁶³

A.5. Summary of Shared Features of Gnostic Groups

a. Most Gnostics were dualist, making a sharp distinction between the spiritual and material worlds, as between good and evil.⁶⁴

b. The material world originates with a lesser (if not ignorant) God or demiurge (sometimes identified with the Old Testament Jehovah);⁶⁵ this demiurgic is distinguished from the highest deity and original Father. Accordingly, a (pre-creation) fall is assumed as the source of evil in our world.

c. Salvation, as an escape from evil, is accomplished through a redeemer, or saviour figure, an aeon, or pure spirit who descends

---

59. See Daniélou, *Theology of Jewish Christianity*, 82; based on their use of Genesis and other OT texts, Daniélou traces the Naassenes back to Jewish Christianity (*Theology of Jewish Christianity*, 83).

60. See J. M. Robinson, *Nag Hammadi Library*, 208–219. For *The Three Steles of Seth*, see J. M. Robinson, *Nag Hammadi Library*, 396–401; also Rudolph, *Gnosis*, 138–139.

61. Witherington, *Gospel Code*, 84.

62. See Rudolph, *Gnosis*, 326–342; also Latourette, *First Five Centuries*, 95–96.

63. See Augustine's *Confessions*, books 3–5; on Augustine and the Manicheans, see also ch. 12, §D.3.

64. On the significance of cosmological and anthropological dualism for Gnosticism, see Rudolph, *Gnosis*, 57–67.

65. Rudolph, *Gnosis*, 91.

from the heavens for this purpose.[66] His role is to reveal esoteric knowledge as the key to salvation.[67]

d. Privileged revelation of *gnôsis* (knowledge), given in a process of initiation (as in the mystery religions), provided those who are "spiritual" the knowledge they needed to free themselves from enslavement to matter, and return to their true home. Such knowledge was restricted to initiates, and was to be kept secret.

e. Those who were thus characterized by the spiritual element, or spark from the spiritual realm, were considered an elite, or elect group, elevated beyond the majority of simpler believers, who relied on faith (in Greek, *pistis*).[68]

f. Gnostics tended to syncretism, easily combining their views and teachings with those of more well-established religious groups or schools of thought, whether from Greek popular thought, mystery religions, dualistic Persian Zoroastrianism, astrology, Hermetism, Orphism, or positions of (heterodox) Hellenistic Judaism.[69]

g. Gnostic groups outside the Christian church are known to have used special rites resembling those of mystery cults.

h. The gnostic attitude to Scripture minimized its historical character, and tended to view the narrative of redemption as a type of mythical account. As a result, Gnosticism fostered allegorical interpretation of the Scriptures.

i. Gnostics explained their own particular version of the gospel accounts in terms of a secret transmission of the teachings of Jesus, handed down orally through an inner circle of apostles.

Especially important among such characteristically gnostic views of our world is the virtual *coincidence of the creation and fall*, most clearly seen in gnostic understanding of the creation of man. According to the Valentinian and Ptolemaic understanding, the creation of our world resulted from a serious

---

66. See Rudolph, 113–131.
67. On the central role of such a "revelation" for the Gnostics, see Rudolph, *Gnosis*, 132–134.
68. Rudolph, *Gnosis*, 214.
69. Rudolph recognizes that gnostic documents often feature elements ridiculing Judaism and a traditional understanding of its Scriptures (*Gnosis*, 147); they also critique OT figures like Abraham or Moses. This pattern is especially clear in the *Second Logos of the Great Seth*, on which, see J. M. Robinson, *Nag Hammadi Library*, 362–371.

mistake, involving the work of a lesser divine power, the demiurge. Three kinds of substance were in existence: material, psychic and spiritual. The demiurge formed human beings by breathing the psychic element into the body; but he was ignorant, and did not know what he was doing. Those ensouled in this way remain feeble; only the spiritual spark sown in the soul can prepare it for union with the Logos and true church.

Gnostic thinkers, integrating popular philosophical positions with their own views, typically presented Paul as if he too accented a strong dualistic disjunction of spirit and matter. Marcion is but one example. At this point we note that the Scriptures make a very different distinction between what is spiritual and what is carnal (i.e. of the flesh), between the divine and the human, between good and evil. The apostle Paul does refer to the "carnal" in us, at war with the "spiritual" (as in Rom 6 and 7). That which belongs with the flesh and is "carnal" is that *human* aspect which is inclined to sin and temptation, while the "spiritual" is that *human* aspect which is governed and directed by the Spirit of God. Here a careful reading of God's work in creation is essential. The canonical account of Genesis makes a clear distinction between the Creator and the creature. The first chapter of Genesis presents the creation as proclaimed good when it had come into being; its later fallen and sinful condition, caused by human fall into sin (Gen 3), is the source of evil and sorrow in our world.

The first chapters of Genesis were of considerable interest for Gnostics. Reading Genesis mythically, Gnostics posited a pre-creation fall (among the angels) as the explanation of the creation and the unhappy condition of humanity as we now know it. This meant a considerable change in appreciation of the role of Eve. In the gnostic accounts she is portrayed somewhat like a mythical figure in Greek drama, confronting the highest powers, seeking wisdom and trying to be like God in "knowing good and evil." In fact, the mythical lady Sophia is often cast in the role of Eve. The serpent is also given a crucial role but, unlike the biblical account, is portrayed positively by the Gnostics, as the source of wisdom. Gnostic diagrams of the serpent present him as a circular figure, with his mouth eating the tail; in this way the serpent symbolized eternity. Reading the early chapters of Genesis in this way inverted the meaning commonly accepted by Christians, for whom the temptation in the primeval garden and subsequent fall into sin was understood as a catastrophe.

B. The Response to Gnosticism: Irenaeus, Clement of Alexandria, and Tertullian

It should be clear from the above description that early Christianity was profoundly challenged by these movements. The gnostic approach to the gospel accounts was at the opposite end of the spectrum from that of the Jews. While Gnostics, like Docetists, accented the divinity of Jesus, they could not accept his incarnation and suffering as a human being. Viewing the creation as the work of an inferior and ignorant deity, they had a negative appreciation of matter and bodily reality. Denigration of matter also meant an inability to accept Jesus Christ having true humanity and ordinary bodily human life.

Such teachings were presented by gnostic leaders like Valentinus and Marcion, who were well-educated and intelligent. These teachers were skilful in sharing a message which appeared to have Christian contours; they incorporated their presentation of the gospel in terms of popular philosophical positions, and in a format which attracted wider audiences. The response from the Christian congregations would have to be equally eloquent. We know that Justin Martyr responded to Gnosticism as he knew it in his time, but his writings on the theme have not survived. By far the most substantive work in response to Gnosticism by Christians of the second century comes from three early Christian Fathers: Irenaeus, Clement of Alexandria and Tertullian.

B.1. Irenaeus (ca. AD 115–200)

Irenaeus was a disciple of Polycarp of Asia Minor.[70] He had moved to Lyons in France, where there was a strong Greek-speaking trading community, and served as presbyter in the church.

Sent to Rome as part of a delegation (ca. AD 177), he encountered the new teachings of Gnostics in Rome and recognized their interpretation of Scripture as unacceptable. His concern for those believers who might not be able to discern such incorrect teachings, and be deceived by them, motivated him to respond, writing two major works which are still available to us: *Against Heresies: The Refutation of So-Called Gnosis* (ca. 180–185), and *The Demonstration of Apostolic Preaching* (ca. 185).[71] For centuries these were our major source of information about gnostic teachings.

---

70. For a general introduction to Irenaeus, see Minns, "Irenaeus," 36–51; also Frend, *Rise of Christianity*, 244–250; and Chadwick, *Early Church*, 80–83.

71. Irenaeus's work *Against Heresies* focuses on Marcion and Valentinus; see Chadwick, *Early Church*, 80.

Figure 8.3. Irenaeus among the Church Fathers. The 2nd-century Bishop of Lyons and defender of the faith against the Gnostics, is the first (far left) depicted in this iconographic portrayal of Church Fathers for the apse of the Holy Ascension Orthodox Church (Albion, Michigan). It includes the 6th-century Gregory Dialogos (or St Gregory the Great), the Cappadocians Gregory of Nazianzen and Basil of Caesarea, and John Chrysostom. Photo "Irenaeus and Church Fathers" by Andrew Gould / CC BY-SA 2.0.

Central to his response to Gnosticism was Irenaeus's claim that there was nothing secret about the teachings of Jesus. There were no special teachings or revelations given only to a select group of disciples, and passed on secretly. None of the apostles had promoted an elitist approach to salvation by preaching such a "more perfect" way; and no secret knowledge had been given for that purpose. Nor had secret oral teaching been used to pass along a message to a few of the disciples, one that differed substantially from the public teaching of Jesus in Palestine.

Irenaeus affirmed the four genuine gospel accounts (Matthew, Mark, Luke and John) received by the churches as authentic records, written by two disciples, Matthew and John, and by two close associates of the disciples, Mark (with Peter), and Luke (with Paul). At the time there were numerous "gospels" in circulation, many of them introduced by Gnostics; but these rival gospels introduced speculative and fanciful stories, and most of them had been written well after the four widely accepted gospels. Had these "secret" gospels been available from the beginning, Irenaeus argued, they would have been entrusted by the disciples and passed down to their immediate followers, namely leaders close to the disciples in the churches established by the disciples themselves.[72] Aside from his concern about the gospel accounts, Irenaeus also affirmed baptism as a rite of the church which is not secret; nor does it provide a type of secret initiation. It is a public sacrament, and the means through which new Christians are incorporated, by faith, into the church as the body of Christ.[73]

This led Irenaeus to challenge believers to reflect on the churches which were first established by the disciples in major centres, cities like Rome, Antioch, Smyrna or Ephesus. They should check in these places for any signs of a tradition passing on the kind of gospel teachings proclaimed by the Gnostics, and to discover whether there were any remaining traces of a secret teaching supposedly handed on alongside the more public teaching of Christ Jesus.[74] Irenaeus's appeal came in the late second century, when leaders in these churches were only one or two generations removed from the work of the apostles themselves. Therefore there would certainly still be members alive who had received information directly from successors of the apostles, or who remembered the apostles.[75] Here we note the origins of the Christian position which would come to be known as the principle of "apostolic succession," to determine truth in writings that were transmitted within the Christian community.

Gnostic teaching about the *creation* of the world was a special concern. Irenaeus first affirmed the Old Testament God as the very God who also is the Father of Jesus Christ.[76] And he affirmed God's work in creation as a work of love and joy; God did not create the world out of necessity or ill-will, or even as a punishment for fallen spirits. The human being, the crown of that creation, is free and is given responsibility to live in a way that conforms to God's will as he has revealed it from the beginning. Irenaeus did recognize a degree of immaturity in humanity in its early stages, indicating the need for responsible leadership. In the church, congregations need a shepherd figure, so that all believers may grow in communion with God.[77] Accordingly, he

---

72. Irenaeus's defence of the four true gospels has come to be accepted as a classic statement on the matter – comparing these with the four points of the globe, and the four winds; on these gospels, see the introduction for ch. 9, and §C.2, notes 33 and 34.

73. See Irenaeus, *Against Heresies* 4.32.1.

74. In his analysis Frend focuses on the issue of "authority" in the churches as the underlying concern (*Rise of Christianity*, 245). On this aspect of the discussion, see §C below.

75. Chadwick, *Early Church*, 81–82.

76. Frend, *Rise of Christianity*, 246.

77. Chadwick focuses on Irenaeus's understanding of salvation as a progressive education of mankind (Chadwick, *Early Church*, 80–81); see also Frend, *Rise of Christianity*, 247.

highlights the role of the bishops as they succeed Christ, as a true shepherd, restoring and caring for that which was lost since the fall of Adam, "He became what we are, so that he could lead us to be like Himself."[78] In this way Irenaeus expressed succinctly what has come to be accepted as the teaching of "recapitulation": as the second Adam, Christ "recapitulated," or gathered up into himself all the experience of humanity, to enable him to inaugurate the new redeemed humanity.

Irenaeus was also clear on Jesus's *incarnation*, that it was not a result of sin, or even an indication of sin or evil.[79] Through the incarnation of his Son Jesus Christ, God was pleased to fulfill his purpose in history, to lead his people to fuller communion with himself. Israel was the people chosen by God to bring forth the Messiah, the Christ. His was the crucial role in salvation, as the second Adam, to do what the first Adam failed to do, namely to keep perfect obedience. Thereby the second Adam was to defeat Satan, and to prepare the way for deliverance and new freedom for mankind. Similarly, Mary took on the role of a new Eve, so that she might "by a virgin's obedience undo and put away the disobedience of a virgin."[80]

Impact of the work of Irenaeus

Irenaeus's arguments helped to support the leadership role of the bishop within congregations and in the church as a whole. In the beginning the church groups were not well-organized; nor was it possible to organize more strictly under given conditions. Congregations were subject to persecution, and members often had to go into hiding. Irenaeus encouraged local congregations to formulate the succession of leaders and teachers from the beginning, so that the positions taken by their leaders could be traced back through bishops and/or Apostolic Fathers to the apostles, and to Christ himself.

Another important result of Irenaeus's work was its impact on the formulation of a creed, or statement of faith, as a standardized "rule of faith" (Latin, *regula fidei*).[81] This creed was already developing on the basis of the confession made at the time of baptism. It was focused on the statement of "Jesus as Lord," but also affirmed God the Father as Almighty Creator,

---

78. See the preface of chapter 5 in *Against Heresies* 5.1.1.

79. On a positive understanding of incarnation, see Stevenson, *New Eusebius*, 119 (quoting Irenaeus, *Against Heresies*, 3.18.7).

80. See Stevenson, *New Eusebius*, 120, quoting Irenaeus, *Demonstration of the Apostolic Preaching*, 33. On Mary as the new Eve, see also Frend, *Rise of Christianity*, 247.

81. Frend, *Rise of Christianity*, 245; and Chadwick, *Early Church*, 44–45. On the "rule of faith," for more on this see §C.3 and §C.4 below.

and affirmed the work of the Holy Spirit in building the church. The most elaborate part of the creed was that concerning Jesus Christ, as conceived of the Holy Spirit and born of the Virgin Mary, suffering under Pontius Pilate, and rising from the dead. Such statements almost invariably represented a response to (current) heretical teachings, and accordingly, could be used as a test of "orthodoxy" or correct teaching. The creed was used at baptism, but also implemented when church leaders, presbyters or bishops, took up their positions, as a form of subscription or agreement, and a promise to uphold correct teaching while in office.

B.2. Clement of Alexandria (d. AD 215)

Clement was born in Athens, but spent much of his life teaching in Alexandria, where he was converted.[82] At that time he was looking for a guide to lead him into truth; he found Pantaenus, a convert from Stoicism and former evangelist to "India," then teaching in the *catechetical school* to prepare new converts for baptism and membership in the church.[83] When Pantaenus died (ca. 190), Clement took over as teacher, and stayed until driven away by serious persecution in AD 202. His writings, especially in his response to the Gnostics, show the marks of a teacher (while those of Irenaeus are noted more for pastoral concern). Clement developed his views in the tradition of Philo of Alexandria; his work also evidences wide reading, based on the availability of a good library and an intellectually stimulating environment. As we have noted, the city was located at the crossroads of the ancient world, where many cultural and religious groups met and exchanged ideas. Syncretism also flourished. Indeed, many gnostic groups were identified as having their roots in Alexandria.

Clement's work may be ranked with that of the *Apologists*, for one of his main works, the *Exhortation to the Pagans* (*Protrepticus*) was aimed at encouraging belief.[84] Somewhat like Justin Martyr, Clement used Platonic and Stoic teaching as a support for Christian faith. He wanted to show that Christianity was intellectually respectable; it was not just a religion for ignorant and foolish people. His *Paidagogus* (*The Teacher*), featured Jesus as

---

82. For a brief recent assessment of Clement, his life, work, and major themes addressed in his writings, see Kovacs, "Clement of Alexandria," 68–84; see also Chadwick, *Early Church*, 94–100; and Frend, *Rise of Christianity*, 252–253 and 369–373.

83. On Pantaenus, see ch. 2, §B.1, quoting Eusebius, *EH* 5.10; also Stevenson, *New Eusebius*, 179. We note that the reference to "India" in antiquity could also represent Ethiopia.

84. See Frend, *Rise of Christianity*, 286.

the outstanding teacher, and focused on Christian moral teaching; another work, the *Stromata*, or *Miscellany*, a collection of essays and shorter pieces on religion, theology and philosophy, sought to demonstrate how Christ, as the Logos, perfects human knowledge to become true *gnôsis*.[85] From this it is clear that Clement used gnostic terminology to argue that the Logos, as teacher and lawgiver, actually saves us by educating us to obtain eternal life. Like Irenaeus, Clement claimed that "He [Jesus] became human, so that we might become divine."

Praeparatio evangelica

Clement responded to gnostic teachings by developing what he called a *Christian Gnosticism*; he used the term to refer to a Christian view of Truth, culminating in Christ.[86] Indeed, he recognized different approaches to the Truth, and used the term *praeparatio evangelica* (preparation for the gospel) to allow for a variety of preparatory stages in receiving the good news of salvation.[87] On the one hand, the Jews had the Torah as their teacher, to prepare them to accept Christ. Similarly, the Greeks had philosophy as a teacher and preparation to accept the truth in Christ. Somewhat like Justin, Clement spoke of Christ as the Logos incarnate, who guides all humanity in faith to accept full knowledge of God as the Christian condition of blessedness. As Logos, Jesus represents the thought, or mind of God. By knowing Jesus Christ, Christian Gnostics would know God, and combine faith with a philosophical understanding of God. Knowledge of God is also the key to virtue, and virtue in turn means being "like God," which implies a recovery of the image of God that was lost (or distorted) through the fall into sin. Clement concludes that true Christians are also true Gnostics.

With his understanding of the *praeparatio evangelica*, Clement gave a clear argument to repudiate gnostic attitudes to the Old Testament, for he affirmed it as a (historically valid) preparation, albeit one that needs fulfilment in Christ. For Christians, he affirmed faith as the primary avenue for truth. But he allowed for the role of reason and knowledge in elaborating the faith when he also affirmed the preparatory value of *Greek philosophy*; and thereby he allowed

---

85. Frend, *Rise of Christianity*, 370–371; and Latourette, *First Five Centuries*, 147.

86. On this theme, see Frend, *Rise of Christianity*, 371–373; Chadwick, *Early Church*, 96–97; and Stevenson, *New Eusebius*, 184–185.

87. Clement could rely at least in part on Paul's arguments, as in Romans 2:14–15, "Even when Gentiles, who do not have God's written Law, instinctively follow what the law says, they show that in their hearts they know right from wrong. They demonstrate that God's law is written within them." See also Chadwick, *Early Church*, 96; and Stevenson, *New Eusebius*, 183–184 (quoting Clement's *Stromata* 1.5.28, 1–3).

for a very different kind of preparation for salvation. In so doing, of course, he ran the risk of accepting some of the elitist attitudes traditionally associated with the ways of Greek philosophy in ancient culture.

In the interpretation of the Scriptures, Clement accepted allegorical exegesis in the tradition of Philo of Alexandria, thereby promoting a method also favoured by the Gnostics. Of course, he claimed the prior validity of the *literal* meaning of the text. But he went on to claim that such a literal interpretation gives believers something like "milk" for the child; they are to go further, to eat "meat," that is to seek a deeper wisdom in becoming mature Christians. Although Clement could appeal to biblical language (1 Cor 3:2, or Heb 5:12–14), in this approach we also note a reflection of the gnostic tendency to focus on wisdom as a higher truth. Indeed, as we have seen, Clement refers to the wise Christian as the "true gnostic" who seeks the deeper levels of spiritual truth in the Scriptures.

Clement was criticized already in his own time for adopting an elitist approach. We must remember, however, that he was developing a way of reading Scripture that was different from the more strictly literal approach of the Jews to the Old Testament. And his approach does reflect an attempt in the church at this time to distinguish the role of the bishop and clergy from that of the laity, with the former having greater responsibility for maintaining the faith and truth in the church.

B.3. Tertullian (ca. 160–225)

Tertullian was born in Carthage and received an excellent education in the two most prestigious subjects taught at that time: rhetoric and law. He was converted to Christianity in Rome, ca. AD 190.[88] Upon his return to Carthage (ca. 197) he became a leader in the church and, as presbyter, placed his considerable gifts of eloquence and clear expression at the service of the church. Tertullian was the first of the Christian Fathers to write at length in the Latin language, and his use of Latin terminology for the Trinity and the person of Christ made a distinctive contribution to apologetical literature and development of theological understanding. We note the application of a sharp legal mind in his refutation of heretics like Marcion as he sought to clarify the relationship between mainstream Christianity and Gnosticism.

---

88. For a useful general introduction on Tertullian's thought, see E. Ferguson, "Tertullian," 85–99. See also Chadwick, *Early Church*, 89–93; and Frend, *Rise of Christianity*, 348–351.

Tertullian was deeply affected by the wave of persecution under Emperor Septimius Severus (AD 202), and keenly aware of the strain this placed on the churches.[89] At this time he himself developed sympathies for the ascetic and rigorist mentality of the Montanists.[90] To the very end of his life, he used his eloquence to protest "worldly" inclinations among Catholic Christians.

As *Apologist*, Tertullian presented strong arguments against the state in its persecution of Christians. Since the early second-century correspondence of Pliny and Trajan, emperors had decreed that Christians were not to be hunted down; but if they were accused, and refused to repudiate the Christian confession, they were to be severely punished.[91] Tertullian argued that this practice was both unjust and two-faced; if Christians are not to be sought out, that surely indicates that they are no harm to society![92]

"Prescription" of heretics

The important arguments in responding to Gnosticism are given in Tertullian's *Praescriptio Haereticorum* (*The Prescription of Heretics*).[93] In this work he uses the word *praescriptio* as a legal term for an argument given to anticipate a case and prevent it from appearing in court. But the term has a second and perhaps even more relevant meaning, for it can be used to affirm a legal right in possessing something which has been held for a long time, like "squatters' rights." The *Praescriptio Haereticorum* applies both of these principles.

In the dispute with Gnostics on the use and interpretation of Scriptures, Tertullian claims that rightful ownership of these writings belongs with the church, because it has made use of them for a number of generations already. Like Irenaeus, Tertullian focuses on those churches which can point to an uninterrupted line of bishops going right back to the time of the apostles, especially Peter and Paul (as at Rome). Such a tradition gives the church the right to claim ownership of the Scriptures. And it means that heretics have no right to dispute with the church on them, or to use the Scriptures with

---

89. Chadwick, *Early Church*, 91.

90. On Montanism as it affected the African Church, see ch. 6, §B. For a useful introductory treatment on Montanism, as a rigorist apocalyptic movement, see Frend, *Rise of Christianity*, 253–256; also Latourette, *First Five Centuries*, 128–129; and Chadwick, *Early Church*, 52–53. Frend, "Montanism," reviews recent research on Montanism, recognizing the contribution of P. de Labriolle and W. M. Ramsay on Montanism as a social movement; see Frend, "Montanism," 521–537, especially 527–529 and 535. On Tertullian's adherence to Montanism, see also Frend, *Rise of Christianity*, 349–350; and Chadwick, *Early Church*, 92.

91. See ch. 4, §A.2

92. See Stevenson, *New Eusebius*, 157–158 (quoting Tertullian's *Apology* 1 and 5).

93. Frend, *Rise of Christianity*, 282.

their own highly idiosyncratic interpretation. Gnostics are latecomers, who are trying to change what rightfully belongs to the church by way of tradition (*Praescriptio* 37).[94] On this basis Tertullian would also claim that heretics have no right to trace their own views back to the Scriptures, for this would necessitate an interpretation which is very different from that of Christians. The argument developed by Tertullian in dealing with dissidents and heretical groups initiated an approach which would be used frequently in the subsequent history of Christianity.

One interesting feature of Tertullian's argument is the attempt to trace the views of gnostic and other heretical groups back to various *schools of philosophy*.[95] Because Christian truth is ultimate, Tertullian argued, Christians can dispense with any other school of thought in the search for truth. According to Tertullian, the pursuit of philosophical thought reflects idle speculation, which can only lead astray, as it gives rise to the fantastic tales which characterize gnostic teachings. So, all heresy has its source in the schools of philosophy.

This approach is of interest because the term "heresy" (in Greek, *hairesis*) was initially used among the philosophers to indicate different schools of thought, based on particular *choices* made by thinkers (Greek *hairein* means "to choose"). Writing at the time of Jesus, the historian Josephus used the term *hairesis* to indicate the different branches or sects in Judaism, namely, the Pharisees or Sadducees. Of course, Tertullian himself had received a legal training in logic and argumentation, as well as ethics, and his own writings reveal considerable influence of philosophical thought, especially that of Aristotle and Stoicism.[96] But in his reaction to philosophy, Tertullian demonstrates a typically Roman suspicion of speculative thought.

C. Apostolic Succession, Ecclesiastical Structures and Creeds

False and heretical teachings, such as those of the Gnostics, made a significant impact on the church. In some respects the problems of persecution may well have been easier to deal with as an "external" threat. Problems of gnostic teachings affected the church at the core of its teaching and preaching.

---

94. The passage is quoted in Stevenson, *New Eusebius*, 169–170; for Tertullian's argument on tradition and apostolic succession, see also Stevenson, 164–166.

95. The text, *Praescriptio* 7, is quoted in Stevenson, *New Eusebius*, 166–167. Hippolytus uses the same approach in his *Refutation of All Heresies*; see Frend, *Rise of Christianity*, 282.

96. This is recognized by Frend, *Rise of Christianity*, 290.

C.1. Apostolic Succession

These crises arose in the second century when all the immediate apostles and followers of Christ had already passed from the scene, and the next generation of disciples would already have been quite elderly. Who was to take over from them as primary witnesses?[97] How was the church to remain unified, as Jesus had prayed (John 17:20-21)? And how was the truth of the gospel to be preserved? The appearance of heretical teachings, docetist, gnostic or Marcionist, made these issues critical. What, precisely, was the source of authority within the church to deal with these issues, and respond decisively?[98]

The crucial issue was that of authority.[99] The church is not like a social club or even a professional association; it asks its members to be prepared to die for the faith, should that be required. As counterpart to such imposing claims on the lives of its members, it has the power to introduce them to eternal life. But what is the basis of its authority in preaching, teaching and practice? The Christian church realized that, ultimately, its authority does not rest with itself; it rests on the word of God, and more particularly, the Word as revealed in Jesus Christ.

Bishops and elders

By the end of the first century, leadership roles, or *offices* (based on the Latin *officium*, "duty"

Figure 8.4. Ignatius. With Polycarp he was a disciple of the Apostle John; he became the third bishop of Antioch and is considered as one of the Apostolic Fathers. This Byzantine portrayal is found in the Hosios Loukas Monastery (Boeotia, Greece). Photographic reproduction by Shakko, based on Chatzidakis's *Byzantine Art of Greece*. Public Domain.

---

97. On the critical importance of apostolic succession, see Frend, *Rise of Christianity*, 140-141.

98. Such questions are also addressed by Pelikan in discussing the canon and creeds (*Emergence of the Catholic Tradition*, 108-120).

99. In his discussion of Irenaeus, Frend (*Rise of Christianity*, 245) focuses on this issue, as does Chadwick, *Early Church*, 41.

or "service") in the church were fairly well-established. In one of his letters (ca. AD 110), Bishop Ignatius of Antioch speaks of the "monarchical" or ruling bishop as an established fact.[100]

In Rome the title "priest" (based on the Greek *presbus/presbuteros*, or "elder") still appeared to be interchangeable with that of "bishop" (*episkopos*, meaning "overseer"). As bishop of Rome at this time (ca. AD 95), Clement spoke of the authority of the apostles being handed down to bishops or presbyters and deacons (Greek, *diakonos*, as "one who serves").[101] According to Clement, the authority of church leaders is based on their following in the teachings of the apostles; ultimately, their exercise of leadership in the church is based on the authority which Christ had first handed on to the apostles.[102] Indeed, all second generation leaders had been ordained to their tasks by the apostles themselves.

Two important ideas are expressed here: (1) the central role of the *bishop* within the Christian congregation, and (2) the element of *apostolic succession* in the ordination of bishops or overseers in the church. These concepts are first brought together clearly in the writing of Irenaeus.[103] Only when they are joined together do these teachings serve to explain the greater authority, power and status which emerged in the second century for bishops in the congregations for which they bore responsibility; the bishop was now seen to act with *apostolic authority*. This teaching of Irenaeus is expressed clearly as

---

100. On the role of the bishop, see Latourette, *First Five Centuries*, 132.

101. The relevant passage is found in Clement's *First Letter to the Corinthians*, 42,

The apostles have preached the gospel to us from the Lord Jesus Christ; Jesus Christ [has done so] from God. Christ therefore was sent forth by God, and the apostles by Christ. Both these appointments, then, were made in an orderly way, according to the will of God. Having therefore received their orders, and being fully assured by the resurrection of our Lord Jesus Christ, and established in the word of God, with full assurance of the Holy Ghost, they went forth proclaiming that the kingdom of God was at hand. And thus preaching through countries and cities, they appointed the first-fruits [of their labours], having first proved them by the Spirit, to be bishops and deacons of those who should afterwards believe. Nor was this any new thing, since indeed many ages before it was written concerning bishops and deacons. For thus the Scriptures state in a certain place, "I will appoint their bishops (overseers) in righteousness, and their deacons (servants) in faith."

The passage refers to Isaiah 60:17, based on the Septuagint version, "I will give your rulers in peace, and your overseers in righteousness."

102. See Matthew 28:18–20,

Then Jesus came to them and said, "All authority in heaven and on earth has been given to me. Therefore go and make disciples of all nations, baptizing them in the name of the Father and of the Son and of the Holy Spirit, and teaching them to obey everything I have commanded you. And surely I am with you always, to the very end of the age."

103. Frend, *Rise of Christianity*, 249–150.

his response in the struggle with Gnostics, because they had claimed apostolic authority for their own teachings, appealing to secret teachings of Jesus and the apostles, which had also been transmitted secretly. Irenaeus responds to that position with a clear statement of the principle of apostolic succession:

> Thus it is within the power of all who in every church may wish to see the truth, to contemplate clearly the tradition of the apostles manifested throughout the whole world. And we are in a position to give an account of those who were instituted bishops in the churches by the apostles; we are also able [to demonstrate] the succession of these men, down to our own times. And we know these to have been leaders who neither taught nor knew of anything like what these [heretics] rave about. For if the apostles had known hidden mysteries, and had been in the habit of imparting these privately, apart from the rest, to "the perfect," they would have delivered them especially to those leaders whom they were also setting in authority over the churches themselves. For the apostles wished these men to be very perfect and blameless in all things, for they were also leaving them behind as their successors, delivering up their own place of government over the churches to these men. Indeed, these men, if they discharged their functions honestly, would be a great boon [to the church], but if they should fall away, the direst calamity. (*Against Heresies* 3.3.1)

Those churches and cities where the apostles had served personally thus gained in prestige; among these, the bishop of Rome gradually gained a position of first ranking, for it was the city where both Peter and Paul had served.[104] The emergence of such a status for Rome was recognized by Irenaeus (in a section following the above quote), as he indicates the importance of

> ... the tradition derived from the apostles, a tradition of the very great, the very ancient and universally known Church founded and organized at Rome by the two most glorious apostles, Peter and Paul; as ... the faith preached to men, which comes down to our time by means of the successions of the bishops. For it is a matter of necessity that every church should agree with this Church, on account of its pre-eminent authority ... inasmuch as

---

104. On Rome emerging as a leading centre for early Christianity, see Frend, *Rise of Christianity*, 130; also Latourette, *First Five Centuries*, 118–119 and 185–187.

the apostolical tradition has been preserved continuously. (*Against Heresies* 3.3.2)

Apostolic succession in Rome

The role of the bishop in guiding the church was all the more keenly appreciated in responding to the challenges of a gnostic appeal to secret, esoteric transmission of teachings, as in the early gnostic *Gospel of Thomas*, or the *Gospel of James*.[105] In response, the church put on record the transmission of teaching in a line of unbroken leadership from the time of the apostles, as witness to the teaching of Christ himself. Irenaeus gives the *apostolic succession* for the church in Rome as an important example of the principle:

> The blessed apostles, then, having founded and built up the church, committed into the hands of Linus the office of the episcopate. Paul makes mention of this Linus in the Epistles to Timothy. To him succeeded Anacletus; and after him, in the third place from the apostles, Clement was allotted the bishopric. This man had seen the blessed apostles, and had been conversant with them, and thus one might say that he had the preaching of the apostles still echoing [in his ears], and their traditions before his eyes. Nor was he alone [in this], for there were many still remaining who had received instructions from the apostles.... To this Clement there succeeded Evaristus. Alexander followed Evaristus; then, sixth from the apostles, Sixtus was appointed; after him, Telephorus, who was gloriously martyred; then Hyginus; after him, Pius; then after him, Anicetus. Sorer succeeded Anicetus, and now Eleutherius holds the inheritance of the episcopate in the twelfth place from the apostles. In this order, and by this succession, the ecclesiastical tradition from the apostles, and the preaching of the truth, have come down to us. And this is most abundant proof that there is one and the same life-giving faith, which has been preserved in the church from the apostles until now, and handed down in truth. (*Against Heresies* 3.3.3)[106]

Such heightened authority for the bishop was strengthened in the third century by Cyprian as bishop in Carthage (AD 249–258) during the wave of

---

105. For further discussion of such gospels, see ch. 9.

106. For other passages on the significance of ecclesiastical tradition, see Stevenson, *New Eusebius*, 114–118.

persecution under the emperors Decius and Valerian.[107] On the issue of the nature and motivation of acceptance back into the congregations of those who had relinquished their faith under pressure of persecution, but who later repented and wished to be readmitted, Cyprian declared that only the (local) bishop could make the ultimate decision.[108]

C.2. Apostles and Fathers

The lists of bishops and elders in the various churches start by recognizing the special place of Apostolic Fathers like Papias, Barnabas, and Clement of Rome, who had enjoyed living contact with the apostles.[109] Like the apostles themselves, the Apostolic Fathers were remembered for pastoral letters, which they circulated among sister congregations; as we have noted, many of them died a martyr's death. Thus from the third century we frequently find a double appeal to *the Apostles and the Fathers*, as the bishops and important leaders or teachers who spoke with authority on various issues. The acceptance of a number of "Fathers" of the (early) church is closely connected with their *teaching function* in resolving difficult problems faced by the church. As teachers, however, the Fathers were not speaking for themselves; their advice, considered equal to that of the apostles themselves, was given on behalf of the church, particularly when they were dealing with significant controversies on the character and work of Christ, issues which would finally receive close attention at the councils of Nicea and Chalcedon. Furthermore, the pronouncements of the Fathers carried considerably more authority to the extent that they spoke with one voice on any given issue.[110]

We note that there is no fixed list of "Fathers"; the selection of "Fathers" was flexible. Recognized as teachers, Fathers helped to maintain the unity of the church in faith and practice, especially in the face of threat from heretical groups. Fathers functioned locally, in connection with local synods, and later, with the great ecumenical councils. Their views were not always accepted immediately. Origen's work made a considerable impact almost

---

107. On Cyprian, see Patout Burns, "Cyprian of Carthage," 127–140; see also Frend, *Rise of Christianity*, 351–357, and on his role as bishop, see especially 351–353.

108. On Cyprian's role in strengthening the position of the bishop in the north African Church, see also ch. 6, §B.

109. See also ch. 7, §A.6. Frend refers to this early period (AD 70–135) as "sub-apostolic" (*Rise of the Monophysite Movement*, 120–121).

110. On the role of the *Fathers* in establishing *Patristics* as a discipline (based on the Latin *patres*, "fathers"), see appendix I.

immediately, influencing theological views of Alexandrians (like Athanasius) and the Cappadocians; but already at that time some aspects were seen to be controversial, and were definitely rejected in later centuries. Tertullian's views, on the other hand, though controversial in his own time, grew steadily in acceptance over the centuries. Similarly, not all the decisions of councils would be accepted immediately, or implemented throughout the world of the Christian church; decisions grew in authority as they were affirmed by subsequent councils.

C.3. Early Creeds

A creed is a statement of faith (based on the Latin *credo*, "I believe"). While creeds serve to express belief, they are also means of strengthening belief. It is unfortunate that some churches today do not use the creeds in worship. Islam, a major world religion, is creedal; the words of the *shahada* (confession): *La ilaha illallah Muhammadur rasulullah* (i.e. "God is one and Muhammad is his messenger") is made not only with the initiation of new converts; it is on the lips of Muslims even at the point of death.

The emergence of widely accepted creeds is a second major feature of second-century Christianity as it responded to Gnosticism.[111] The designation of the first universally accepted creed to emerge, the *Apostles' Creed*, is a good indication that apostolicity was also an important factor in the formulation of these creeds. This does not mean that the apostles themselves formulated such a creed. It does affirm the witness of the apostles as the basis for the faith expressed, as in turn, a witness to the authentic teaching of Christ himself. The form of this creed as we now have it probably dates from the fifth century.[112] But there are numerous passages in the New Testament, particularly those which focus on the Lordship of Christ, and on the meaning of his death and resurrection, which show incipient forms of such a creed, as a confession of faith.[113]

A number of creeds which emerged in the second century reflect the growing Christian understanding of Jesus. These appear to have developed from the original baptismal confession as given with the commissioning of

---

111. On the emergence of the creeds, see Frend, *Rise of Christianity*, 134–135, 250 and 399–400.

112. For the creed as used at present, see chapter appendix 8.2 at the end of chapter 8. While its core clearly dates from a much earlier period, particularly as the *Roman Symbol*, the current form may be dated as late as the sixth century; see Latourette, *First Five Centuries*, 135–136.

113. See chapter appendix 7.2 above, on Jesus as Lord.

Jesus in Matthew 28:19: "... baptizing them in the name of the Father and of the Son and of the Holy Spirit."[114] This much is clear from the early form of confession recorded in the *Apostolic Tradition* of Hippolytus (written ca. AD 215). It asks three questions: first, whether the candidate for baptism believes in God the almighty Father; second, whether the candidate believes in Christ Jesus, the Son of God, born of the Holy Spirit; and third, whether he (or she) believes in the Holy Spirit, the holy church and the resurrection of the flesh. Confession of faith at baptism was meant as a summary restatement of instruction given to new believers.[115]

The earliest baptismal confessions given in the Scriptures focus on belief in the saving work of Jesus Christ. The very first of the statements of the Apostles' Creed, affirming the work of God the Father in creation, appears to reflect second-century controversies with Gnostics on this issue. The sections affirming the Holy Spirit and the church were probably elaborated somewhat later. Even so, the section dealing with the Son remained the central and largest part of the creed.

One of the earliest well-formulated creeds emerged during the third century in Rome; called the *Old Roman Creed*, or *Roman Symbol*, it was the ancestor of the Apostles' Creed and of other eastern Christian creeds:

> I believe in God the Father almighty; and in Christ Jesus His only Son our Lord, Who was born from the Holy Spirit and the Virgin Mary, Who under Pontius Pilate was crucified and buried, on the third day rose again from the dead, ascended into heaven, and sits at the right hand of the Father, whence he will come to judge the living and the dead.[116]

At a time when Gnostics wanted to add their own writings to those accepted by the church, and to give their own distinctive interpretation of the Scriptures, such a creed would have a crucial role in safeguarding the teachings of the Christian against distortion of the truth. The confession of God the Father as Creator certainly undermined a gnostic accent on the difference between the Father of Jesus and the Creator Father of Genesis. It is clear that the creed

---

114. A similar trinitarian formulation is found in the blessing of 2 Cor 13:14, "May the grace of the Lord Jesus Christ, and the love of God, and the fellowship of the Holy Spirit be with you all." For early use of this triple invocation see also the *Didachê*, quoted in Stevenson, *New Eusebius*, 9. On the creeds, see further Kelly, *Early Christian Creeds*, a classic work on early creeds.

115. See Stevenson, *New Eusebius*, 141–143, especially 142.

116. Stevenson quotes two predecessors to this early creed (*New Eusebius*, 123).

could function both as a test of faith, and as a guide to orthodox believers on the acceptable interpretative key to the Scriptures.

C.4. Irenaeus, Tertullian, and the "Rule of Faith"

When Irenaeus responded to heretical views by appealing to the Christian faith handed down in the church from the apostles, he referred to its traditionally accepted content as the "rule of faith" or "canon" of faith.[117] He summarized his own understanding of this "rule" as follows:

> The church, though dispersed throughout the whole world, even to the ends of the earth, has received from the apostles and their disciples this faith: [She believes] in one God, the Father Almighty, Maker of heaven and earth and the sea and all things that are in them; and in one Christ Jesus, the Son of God, who became incarnate for our salvation; and in the Holy Spirit, who proclaimed through the prophets the dispensations of God, and the advents, and the birth from a virgin, and the passion, and the resurrection from the dead, and the ascension into heaven in the flesh of the beloved Christ Jesus, our Lord, and His [future] manifestation from heaven in the glory of the Father "to gather all things in one" [Eph 1:10], and to raise up anew all flesh of the whole human race, in order that to Christ Jesus, our Lord, and God, and Saviour, and King, according to the will of the invisible Father, "every knee should bow, of things in heaven, and things in earth, and things under the earth, and that every tongue should confess" [Phil 2:10-11] to Him, and that He should execute just judgment towards all; that He may send "spiritual wickednesses" [Eph 6:12], and the angels who transgressed and became apostates, together with the ungodly, and unrighteous, and wicked, and profane among men, into everlasting fire; but may, in the exercise of His grace, confer immortality on the righteous, and holy, and those who have kept His commandments, and have persevered in His love, some from the beginning [of their Christian course], and others from [the date of] their repentance, and may surround them with everlasting glory. (*Against Heresies* 1.10.1) [118]

---

117. On use of the term "canon" see ch. 9, §A.
118. See Stevenson, *New Eusebius*, 111–112.

The "rule" or "canon" of faith outlined above is more elaborate, but still close in expression to the baptismal creed widely used in the churches. Certainly, by establishing the "rule of faith," Irenaeus did not wish to go beyond the traditional affirmation of Jesus Christ as the Son of God, as it had been maintained by the Christian church, handed down from the apostles.

In his response to gnostic teachers in the *Praescriptio Haereticorum* (*The Prescription of Heretics*), Tertullian similarly refers to the "rule of faith" to affirm Christian teaching of Jesus as Son of God:

> Now, with regard to this rule of faith – that we may from this point acknowledge what it is which we defend – it is, you must know, that which prescribes the belief that there is one only God, and that He is none other than the Creator of the world, who produced all things out of nothing through His own Word, first of all sent forth; that this Word is called His Son, *and*, under the name of God, was seen 'in diverse manners' by the patriarchs, heard at all times in the prophets, at last brought down by the Spirit and Power of the Father into the Virgin Mary, was made flesh in her womb, and, being born of her, went forth as Jesus Christ; thenceforth He preached the new law and the new promise of the kingdom of heaven, worked miracles; having been crucified, He rose again the third day; [then] having ascended into the heavens, He sat at the right hand of the Father; sent instead of Himself the Power of the Holy Ghost to lead such as believe; will come with glory to take the saints to the enjoyment of everlasting life and of the heavenly promises, and to condemn the wicked to everlasting fire, after the resurrection of both these classes shall have happened, together with the restoration of their flesh. This rule, as it will be proved, was taught by Christ, and raises amongst ourselves no other questions than those which heresies introduce, and which make men heretics. (*Prescription of Heretics* 13)[119]

Tertullian here makes a strong affirmation of the distinct individual personality of the Son as God's Word. While the Word was first invisible, with the incarnation the Word entered history for our salvation. Note also that Tertullian affirms the distinction of Father, Son and Holy Spirit. He presents them as one being, one in substance, though three in person.

---

119. See Stevenson, 165.

Here we find a distinctive contribution of Tertullian, not just in terms of an answer to the Gnostics, but more positively in beginning to develop a Trinitarian theological position which would be appreciated and elaborated especially in the "golden age" of early Christian theological discussion, the fourth century. It is now clear that, while the Gnostics challenged the church to the core, the response also stimulated a lively discussion, initiating positions and policies that would make a deep impression on the life of the church for centuries to come.

Chapter Appendix 8.1
Writings of the Apostolic Fathers

I Clement	ca. AD 95
Didachê	ca. 100
The Shepherd of Hermas	ca. 100
Epistle of Barnabas	ca. 100–120
Ignatius, *Letters*	ca. 110
Polycarp, *To the Philippians*	ca. 110
[Martyrdom of Polycarp	ca. 155/160]
Fragments of Papias	ca. 130
II Clement	ca. 120–140
Epistle to Diognetus	between AD 150 and 225

Chapter Appendix 8.2
The Apostles' Creed

By the fifth century, the Apostles' Creed came to be recognized universally by Christians. As noted, it is not given this name because it was actually composed by the apostles themselves. As with the issue of *apostolic succession* in the churches, it was accepted as a statement of core beliefs of Christianity handed down from the apostles.

> ### *The Apostles' Creed*
>
> I believe in God the Father, Almighty, Maker of heaven and earth,
> And in Jesus Christ, his only begotten Son, our Lord,
> Who was conceived by the Holy Ghost, born of the Virgin Mary,
> Suffered under Pontius Pilate, was crucified, died and was buried,

He descended into hell,
The third day he rose again from the dead,
He ascended into heaven,
and sits at the right hand of God the Father Almighty,
From thence he shall come to judge the quick and the dead.
I believe in the Holy Ghost,
I believe in the holy catholic church,
The communion of saints,
The forgiveness of sins,
The resurrection of the body,
And the life everlasting. Amen.

Questions for Discussion and Review

Second-Century Gnosticism and Its Impact

1. Why is the second-century movement that emphasizes spirituality called "Gnosticism"? What is the connection of this term with "knowledge"?

2. Why is Gnosticism regarded as a "syncretistic" movement?

3. What is the most important question addressed by Gnostics?

4. How did Valentinus account for the creation of the world, and for the role of Sophia in that creative process? What is the relationship between Sophia and the Father?

5. How, according to Valentinus, are people saved, and what is the role of Jesus in salvation?

6. How did Basileides modify the views of Valentinus?

7. How did Marcion seek to modify the traditional Christian reading of the Old Testament?

8. Which are the outstanding features of gnostic teaching? Which aspects of these teachings most seriously contradict Christian beliefs?

9. What is the true Christian understanding of the relationship between what is "carnal" and "spiritual," or between what is created material/bodily, and what is spiritual?

The Response of Early Christian Fathers to Gnosticism

1. Which aspects of Gnosticism were considered unacceptable by Irenaeus? And why?

2. How did he respond to the Gnostics? Explain the meaning of the term "apostolic succession," and its role in his response to Gnostics.

3. Why was a Christian understanding of creation so important for Irenaeus?

4. What is a creed, and what is a canon?

5. How did Clement of Alexandria's response to Gnosticism differ from that of Irenaeus?

6. What did Clement mean by the term *praeparatio evangelica*? Why was this term significant in his discussion with Gnostics?

7. Why did Clement accept allegorical interpretation of Scripture?

8. How did Tertullian develop the legal argument in his attempt to undermine the claims of the Gnostics?

9. What is the significance of the term *praescriptio* in his polemics with Gnostics?

10. What is the most important aspect of Tertullian's contribution to the discussion and refutation of Gnostics?

Apostolic Succession, Ecclesiastic Structures and Creeds

1. What is the basis of the authority of the church in teaching and practice?

2. Why was the issue of apostolic succession so important in the response of the church to Gnostics?

3. What are the implications of the issue of apostolic succession for the role of bishops?

4. What was Irenaeus's contribution on the issue of apostolic succession in his response to Gnostics?

5. How did the church deal with the issue of apocryphal gospels and documents purporting to reflect the teaching of Jesus and the early church?

6. Who were recognized as "Fathers" of the early church? And on what conditions?

7. How did the universally accepted Apostles' Creed come to have that title? What is the significance of attributing this creed to the apostles?

8. Explain how the original Trinitarian baptismal formula could have served as the core for the Apostles' Creed. Why was it deemed necessary to add various sentences?

9. Why did Tertullian and Irenaeus use the term "the rule of faith"? How would you explain the relationship between this rule of faith and the creed?

Further Reading

Barnes, T. D. *Tertullian: A Historical and Literary Study*. Oxford: Clarendon, 1971.
Bauer, Walter. *Orthodoxy and Heresy in Earliest Christianity*. Translated by R. Kraft and G. Krodel. Philadelphia: Fortress, 1971.
Campenhausen, H. von. *The Fathers of the Latin Church*. London: A & C Black, 1964.
Daniélou, J., and Henri Marrou. *The First Six Hundred Years*. Translated by V. Cronin. London: Darton, Longman & Todd, 1964.
Frend, W. H. C. *Saints and Sinners in the Early Church: Differing and Conflicting Traditions in the First Six Centuries*. London: Darton, Longman & Todd, 1985.
Hanson, R. P. C. *Tradition in the Early Church*. London: SCM, 1962.
Harnack, Adolf von. *Marcion: The Gospel of the Alien God*. Durham, NC: Labyrinth Press, 1988 [*Marcion: Das Evangelium von Fremden Gott*. Leipzig: J. C. Hinrichs, 1921].
Hengel, Martin. *Judaism and Hellenism: Studies in Their Encounter in Palestine during the Early Hellenistic Period*. 2 vols. Minneapolis: Fortress, 1974.
———. *The "Hellenization" of Judaea in the First Century after Christ*. Philadelphia: Fortress, 1989.
Jonas, Hans. *The Gnostic Religion: The Message of the Alien God and the Beginnings of Christianity*. Boston: Beacon Press, 1963.
Kelly, J. N. D. *Early Christian Doctrines*. San Francisco: Harper & Row, 1978.
———. *Early Christian Creeds*. London: Longman, 1972.
King, Karen L., ed. *Images of the Feminine in Gnosticism*. Philadelphia: Fortress, 1988.
Labriolle, P. de. *The History and Literature of Christianity from Tertullian to Boethius*. London: Kegan Paul; Philadelphia: Westminster, 1956.
Layton, B. *The Gnostic Scriptures*. Garden City, NY: Doubleday, 1987.
Lilla, S. R. C. *Clement of Alexandria: A Study in Christian Platonism and Gnosticism*. Oxford: Oxford University Press, 1971.
Pagels, Elaine. *The Gnostic Gospels*. Philadelphia: Fortress Press, 1981.

Pétrement, Simone. *A Separate God: The Christian Origins of Gnosticism*. Translated by Carol Harrison. San Francisco: HarperCollins, 1990.

Prestige, G. L. *Fathers and Heretics*. London: SPCK, 1940.

Robinson, J. M., ed. *The Nag Hammadi Library in English*. 4th revised edition. Leiden: Brill; San Francisco: Harper & Row, 1996.

Rudolph, Kurt. *Gnosis: The Nature and History of Gnosticism*. Edinburgh: T&T Clark; San Francisco: Harper & Row, 1987.

Stern, S. M. "Quotations from Apocryphal Gospels in Abd Al-Jabbar." *Journal of Theological Studies* 18, no. 1 (1967): 34–57.

———. "Abd Al-Jabbar's Account of How Christ's Religion Was Falsified by the Adoption of Roman Customs." *Journal of Theological Studies* 19, no. 1 (1968): 128–185.

Turner, H. E.W. *The Patterns of Christian Truth: A Study in the Relations between Orthodoxy and Heresy in the Early Church*. London: A. R. Mowbray, 1954.

Vallée, G. *A Study in Anti-Gnostic Polemics: Irenaeus, Hippolytus and Epiphanius*. Waterloo, ON: Wilfrid Laurier University Press, 1981.

Williams, R., ed. *The Making of Orthodoxy*. New York: Cambridge University Press, 1989.

Yamauchi, Edwin M. *Pre-Christian Gnosticism: A Survey of the Proposed Evidences*. 2nd edition. Grand Rapids, MI: Baker, 1983.

9

The Biblical Canon and Alternative Gospels

> It is not possible that the gospels can be either more or fewer in number than they are. For there are four zones of the world in which we live, and four principal winds. The church, scattered throughout all the world, has as its "pillar and ground" the gospel and the spirit of life. So it is fitting that the Church too should have four pillars, breathing out immortality on every side, and giving human beings life afresh. This is the reason why the Word, through whom all things were made, who is seated on the cherubim, and holds all things together – this Word, when he was manifested to mankind, gave us the gospel under four forms, but bound together by One Spirit.
>
> Irenaeus, *Against Heresies* 3.11.8

Although there was never any serious doubt about the validity of the four canonical gospels (Matthew, Mark, Luke and John), Irenaeus was writing at the end of the second century, a time when there were many other gospels in circulation. The arguments – or perhaps better, analogies – provided by Irenaeus reflect something of the urgency of the need to have these four gospels recognized as authentic and authoritative. Then all the various other gospels could be relegated to a secondary ranking, useful perhaps, and even regarded as edifying, but not among those works designated for reading in public gatherings of the church.

This brings us to the third area in which the Gnostics and Marcion made a strong impact on the life of the church, the establishment of the "canon" of Scripture. These groups motivated Christians to agree on a list of accepted, authentic writings of Scripture, selecting those books which were considered truly inspired and "canonical," or part of the "canon" of Scripture, and therefore respected as books for which one should be prepared to die.

Such a discussion of canonical and alternative gospels is not just a matter of historical interest. A best-selling novel of recent years, Dan Brown's *The Da Vinci Code*[1] shows us that these issues have contemporary relevance. Brown's title refers to the great Renaissance artist Leonardo da Vinci, whose famous painting of the *Last Supper* appears to present the apostle John in a feminine guise; and that feminine presence is considered no less than a representation of Mary Magdalene.[2] In Brown's tale the painting affirms her as the leading apostle; even more, that Jesus was secretly married to her, and that at the time of the crucifixion she was pregnant with his child. According to the story, a medieval secret society was planning to reveal the secret marriage, and introduce worship of Mary Magdalene as a "goddess," or "sacred feminine," in a move to threaten the powerful male hierarchy of the Catholic church. The marriage is alleged to have been suppressed by the Nicene council (AD 325), which supposedly had voted on Jesus's divinity (and celibacy), knowingly fabricating these as a means of political control in the empire.

In this novel Brown has integrated themes popular in contemporary western culture: theories of conspiracy, secrecy, intrigue, feminism and political motivation in decision making. Our discussion of the Nicene council in the chapter which follows (ch. 10) will show clearly enough that the deity of Christ was indeed a central preoccupation.[3] However, that council rejected Arius's teaching on the "assumed" deity of Christ, his *becoming* God's Son because of merit. Nor was it the intention of the council to *establish* Christ's divinity, for even Arius already accepted that, as did the orthodox bishops. At issue, rather, was an explicit understanding of his divine status.[4]

---

1. The book, published in 2003 with Anchor Books and Doubleday (New York), was released as a film in 2006. For a brief synopsis of the story, see Ehrman, *Truth and Fiction in the Da Vinci Code*, xvii–xix.

2. Jesus cast out seven demons from Mary Magdalene (Mark 16:9); she also accompanied him on his travels, especially the final journey to Jerusalem. She was present at the crucifixion, and was the first to meet him after his resurrection (Luke 8:1–3; Matt 27:55–56 and 61; Mark 15:40–16:11; John 20).

3. See Ehrman, *Truth and Fiction in the Da Vinci Code*, 14–23. On the council, see also ch. 5, §B.5, and the more extended discussion in ch. 10, §A.3 and §A.4.

4. For New Testament writings that clearly reflect Jesus as Lord and God, see chapter appendix 7.2. Passages like John 1:1–18, especially 1:1, "The Word was God," indicate early acceptance of Jesus having a status equal to God, and worthy of worship as God (the gospel is dated to the mid- to late-first century). Aside from well-known first-century Jewish expulsion of Christians for worshipping Jesus as a "second God," early second-century evidence affirming

A. The "Canon"

For the current chapter we note Brown's presentation of the choice of four canonical gospels as part of the strategy of the Nicene council in establishing Christ's divinity. These four gospels were allegedly chosen from among some eighty gospel accounts extant in the fourth century. Why the choice of these four? They portrayed Jesus as divine. And the other gospels were to have been rejected for presenting Jesus as too human. This version of events was not Brown's own invention; a similar account of about eighty gospels in circulation, gradually reduced to the canonical four, is known from medieval writers, including ninth-century Muslim scholars.[5] The present chapter therefore needs to clarify how the four canonical gospels (along with other New Testament writings) were chosen, and explore reasons for the choice, as well as the reasons why other gospels were considered spurious and were not accepted as "canonical."

As a technical term in the history of Christianity, the word "canon" (from the Greek, *kanôn*) first appears in the fourth-century *Ecclesiastical History* of Eusebius (ca. AD 260–339), where it represents a list of books accepted by the church, and recommended for public reading as part of the liturgy.[6] However, the idea already functioned in the second-century *rule of faith*, affirmed by both Irenaeus and Tertullian in the controversy over gnostic teaching. As "rule of faith" (*regula fidei*), the creed functioned exactly as a *kanôn*, namely, a widely accepted standard by which to evaluate writings ("measuring" them for truth),

---

Jesus being worshipped as God also comes from the Roman governor of Bithynia, Pliny the Younger. In a letter (of AD 117) he asks Emperor Trajan what to do about Christians singing hymns to "Jesus as a god" (see ch. 4, §A.2). On second- and third-century witness to acceptance of the deity of Christ (Tertullian, Irenaeus, and Origen), see Witherington, *The Gospel Code*, 54–56. Ehrman (*Truth and Fiction in the Da Vinci Code*, 16) recognizes John 1:1–18, especially 1:1, as a key verse; see also Jesus's response to questions in Mark 14:62–65 (with parallels in other gospels); Paul in 1 Cor 8:5–6; Phil 2:9–11; Hebrews 1:3; and Revelation 1:1–7 and 4–5.

5. For the ninth-century account by the Muslim scholar Abd Al-Jabbar, affirming eighty gospels, see the discussion in this chapter §E and note 57. On Al-Jabbar, see also ch. 7, §A.4 and note 33.

6. The Greek term *kanôn* originally referred to a reed used as a measuring rod. As such, the term was already used by philosophers to refer to a collection of writings which were authoritative in presenting truth, and useful in assessing the value of other writings. Epicureans had used the term as their "rule" on acceptable teaching. Eusebius uses the term to distinguish books which are accepted, from those presented as if they were written by the apostles themselves (often with heretical intent), and therefore to be rejected as forgeries; the relevant passage, *Ecclesiastical History* 3.25, is cited below (chapter appendix 9.3).

and make judgements on acceptable teachings.[7] In this sense, the development of the canon can be understood as part of the Christian repudiation of gnostic teachings.

In the process of determining the canon of the New Testament, the church followed a pattern already established for the Old Testament.[8] Indeed, the collected set of Old Testament books had been established as a "canon" for Judaism some centuries before the New Testament period. The struggle with Gnosticism first challenged Christians to determine their own attitude to the Old Testament; would they agree with Marcion's approach, and reject the Old Testament writings as authentic and authoritative for the churches? Gnosticism also challenged them to establish the "canon" of New Testament writings.[9] We have already noted how Marcion favoured certain of the writings which circulated in the churches, giving a place of honour to the writings of Paul, and to Luke among the gospels.[10]

The following survey of the establishment of the New Testament canon begins by examining how the Christian church incorporated the Old Testament. This is followed by discussion of the process of establishing the New Testament as we now have it. Although the final decision about what was to be included was agreed on in the fourth century, even the much earlier writings of the Apostolic Fathers provide quotations which represent an incipient canon of the New Testament. As a collection it grew gradually; but from the beginning

---

7. On the "rule of faith" and early creeds, see ch. 8, §C, especially §C.3 and §C.4. On the canon as an emerging list of NT books, see Frend, *Rise of Christianity*, 250–251; and Latourette, *First Five Centuries*, 133.

8. The New Testament writings themselves refer to the Old Testament as *Scripture(s)*. See Matt 26:53–54, "But how then would the Scriptures be fulfilled that say it must happen in this way?"; also John 5:39, "You diligently study the Scriptures because you think that by them you possess eternal life. These are the Scriptures that testify about me"; and Luke 4:20–21, "Then he rolled up the scroll, gave it back to the attendant and sat down.... [H]e began by saying to them, 'Today this Scripture is fulfilled in your hearing.'" See also John 2:22, "After he was raised from the dead, his disciples recalled what he had said. Then they believed the Scripture and the words that Jesus had spoken." The divine authority of the Scriptures is affirmed in Matthew 1:22, "All this took place to fulfill what the Lord had said through the prophet." See also John 10:34–36, "Jesus answered them, 'Is it not written in your Law, "I have said you are gods"? If he called them 'gods,' to whom the word of God came – and the Scripture cannot be broken..'" For use of the term "old covenant" see 2 Cor 3:14–15, "... to this day the same veil remains when the old covenant is read.... Even to this day when Moses is read, a veil covers their hearts." Note also the term "Law," or "Torah," to refer to the entire Old Testament, in John 10:34, or 1 Cor 14:21, "In the Law it is written:'Through men of strange tongues and through the lips of foreigners I will speak to this people.'"

9. On the gnostic "canon," see Frend, *Rise of Christianity*, 208–209.

10. See ch. 8, §A.3. See also Frend, *Rise of Christianity*, 215; and Latourette, *First Five Centuries*, 127 and 133.

the core books were not in doubt: the four gospels, Acts, the Pauline Epistles and Revelation. These books were widely accepted throughout the church from the first century. Indeed, some were more favoured in particular regions of the empire. A few were held in doubt until much later. Others, like the Shepherd of Hermas, were accepted early on, but did not finally come to be included.

B. The Scriptures of the Jews

The first time we find Christian authors providing a list of Old Testament writings, giving a canon similar to what we now have, is with Melito of Sardis (ca. AD 170), the bishop who went to Palestine specifically to determine which books of the Old Testament were accepted by the Jews of that time.[11] Long before Melito we have the witness of Josephus (ca. AD 95), speaking of twenty-two books of the Old Testament Scriptures: five books of Moses, thirteen prophetic books of history from the death of Moses to the reign of Artaxerxes, and four books of hymns of praise and rules for human life.[12] The order of books is similar to that given for the Septuagint, the third-century BC Greek translation of the Old Testament into Greek.[13] Within Judaism of the time, however, the order of books was not fixed. This is because they existed as scrolls and were kept in baskets, or placed on shelves. As such they would not be designated with the more fixed order of books included in a codex, the format in which early Christian writings would soon be circulating, a format more like the books we now use, with cut pages and binding. The Septuagint

---

11. See Bruce, *Canon of Scripture*, 70–71. Melito's list does not tally completely in content or order of books with that known from the *Vulgate*, Jerome's Latin translation of the Bible (see ch. 12, §D.2).

12. Josephus, *Contra Apionem* 1.8. On the witness of Josephus, see Beckwith, "Canon of the Old Testament," 165–169. To account for the smaller total count of twenty-two books, Josephus combined various books like Ruth with Judges, and Lamentations with Jeremiah. On the threefold division of the OT into Law, Prophets and Writings, see also the prologue to Ben Sira's Ecclesiasticus, added with the Greek translation (late second century BC).

13. On the Septuagint, see ch. 1, §A.3 and §A.5. As we have noted, legend attributes the translation to the Egyptian ruler Ptolemy Philadelphus (285–246 BC) who asked the Jews to contribute a version of their writings to the great library of Alexandria. Seventy elders were brought from Jerusalem and in a short time they produced a translation on which all agreed (whence the name, *Septuagint* for *seventy*). On the significance of the Septuagint for Hellenistic Judaism, see ch. 1, §A.3 and §A.5; on the legend and alternative theories, see Ferguson, *Backgrounds*, 432–438. The order of the books follows subject matter: narrative, history, poetry and prophecy. Talmudic and rabbinic sources divided thirty-nine books into twenty-four: the Torah in five books; eight Prophets (Joshua, Judges, Samuel [2 bks.], Kings [2 bks.], Isaiah, Jeremiah, Ezekiel and twelve minor prophets); and eleven Writings (Psalms, Proverbs, Job, plus five scrolls: the Song of Songs, Ruth, Lamentations, Ecclesiastes, Esther; and three books of history: Daniel, Ezra-Nehemiah, Chronicles [2 bks.]).

translation does include books which would not eventually be included in the Christian canon for the OT; but even as it was, it proved very significant for the early growth of Christianity in the Greek-speaking section of the Roman Empire. Old Testament quotations in the gospels or letters of Paul are almost invariably based on the Septuagint.

For the most part, the books of the Old Testament as we know it were collected during the exile of the Jews in Babylon (580–538 BC). At that time the Jews could not rely on the temple, with its priesthood, festivals and sacrifices, as the focus of normal patterns of worship. As a result they valued the collected writings all the more, especially the Pentateuch, or Torah as given by Moses, examining it for direction on how to keep God's commandments. Books of the other two major sections, the "prophets" (history) and "writings" (psalms and wisdom literature) were also collected. These books together constituted the *Scriptures*, as the written word of God, to be read aloud in public worship in the *synagogue*, the venue developed during the period of exile for regular gathering of the local community.

Even though not all the books of the Old Testament were originally written in the format in which we now have them, the existence of written records does take us back to the early history of Israel. The Torah, or five books of the Law (Pentateuch), the oldest part, was never questioned as authoritative.[14] Books in the other major divisions, the Prophets and Writings, collected over a period of centuries, won authoritative standing more gradually.[15] Malachi, the last of the prophets, was written in the fifth century BC.[16] Many scholars accept a closing of the Old Testament canon around 200 BC.

---

14. These books may have been written down as early as the thirteenth century BC, a date far earlier than that generally quoted for its recognition within Judaism as such (i.e. 440 BC – the date which may reflect editing for the final format). On Moses himself seeing to the writing of the book of the covenant, see Deut 31:9, "So Moses wrote down this law and gave it to the priests . . ." Also, Deut 31:24–26, "After Moses finished writing in a book the words of this law from beginning to end . . ."

15. First included were Joshua, Judges, Samuel and Kings, writing of the Lord leading his people and shaping Israel as a nation. The prophets Isaiah, Jeremiah, Ezekiel and the twelve minor prophets were considered authoritative soon after being written, because their prophecies of the anger of God in exiling his people had come true. Note also that the scroll on which the prophecies of Isaiah were written, was called the *scroll of the Lord* (Isa 34:16).

16. In comparison we know less about *Writings*, like the Song of Songs. The teaching of wisdom was regarded as a special gift of God. On this see 1 Kgs 3:28, and 4:29–30, "God gave Solomon wisdom and very great insight, and a breadth of understanding as measureless as the sand on the seashore."

The Biblical Canon and Alternative Gospels 255

Figure 9.1. Ezra the scribe. This illustration of a medieval manuscript of the Vulgate Bible depicts Ezra "repairing" the text of the Old Testament. Photographic reproduction by Dsmdgold. Public Domain.

Both Josephus and the writer of 2 Maccabees attribute a significant role to Ezra and Nehemiah in the gathering of books.[17]

And information given in Ezra 7 and Nehemiah 8–10 supports the conclusion that these two men had a special role in the formation of the Old Testament canon, perhaps by editing the books in the form in which they would finally be accepted.[18] The Old Testament canon certainly approximated its later format by the time when 2 Esdras was written (first century BC). In

---

17. See 2 Macc. 2:13–15; the letter presented (supposedly from 165 BC) may not be authentic, but the information given appears to reflect general knowledge. The Jewish *Talmud* (ca. AD 500) attributes significant roles to Hezekiah, Ezra and Nehemiah in completing the OT books (*Baba Bathra* 14b, 15a).

18. On Ezra, as "a teacher well versed in the Law of Moses," see Ezra 7:6; also Ezra 7:10, "Ezra had devoted himself to the study and observance of the Law of the LORD, and to teaching its decrees and laws in Israel." Nehemiah 8:1 calls him "Ezra the scribe." On his explanation of the Scriptures, see Neh 8:8, "They read from the Book of the Law of God, making it clear and giving the meaning so that the people could understand what was being read." According to Josephus (*Contra Apionem* 1.8, ca. AD 95), the accounts covering the period after Artaxerxes 1 (465–425 BC) do not deserve the same respect as those on the earlier period (i.e. from the foundation of the earth). This confirms a completion of historical books in the time of Ezra.

speaking of twenty-two books which no one ventured to alter, to add, or take anything away, Josephus reflects a "closed" canon.

When the leaders of the Jewish community met as a synod in Jamnia to consider the future of Judaism after the fall of Jerusalem (AD 70), they established the canon of Old Testament books which would be normative for Jews.[19] At that time they also condemned use of the Septuagint, mainly because it had become so closely associated with Christian interpretation of the Old Testament. And they repudiated Christian interpretation of Jesus as the Messiah for its recognition of him as "a second God." At this time, too, Christians were expelled from synagogues.

B.1. Use of the Old Testament in the New

As we have noted above, Jesus presented himself as the Messiah, and his life a fulfillment of the Old Testament.[20] In his teachings he frequently quoted the Old Testament.[21] Paul too makes many references to the Old Testament in his letters, as does the Epistle to the Hebrews. Of the gospels, Matthew most often refers to the events of the life of Christ as fulfillment of the Old Testament.

A clear example of early Christian (typological) interpretation of the Old Testament can be found in Justin Martyr's *Dialogue with Trypho the Jew*. On the one hand he argues that the Old Testament belongs to the synagogue, as the New Testament belongs to the church; on the other hand, he affirms the church as the *true Israel*, as also Paul argues in the letter to the Romans (Rom 11:17–21).

---

19. If leaders of the Jews determined the canon of OT books in discussions at Jamnia (see ch. 2, §A.4), we note once more that this was not a new decision, but a confirmation of what was already accepted. For the witness of the *Mishnah Yadayim* 3.5, on books which "soil the hands," see Bruce, *Canon of Scripture*, 34.

20. See especially John 4:25–26, "The woman said, 'I know that Messiah (called Christ) is coming. When he comes, he will explain everything to us.' Then Jesus declared, 'I who speak to you am he.'" See also Matt 5:17–19, "Do not think that I have come to abolish the Law or the Prophets; I have not come to abolish them but to fulfill them."

21. Jesus's discussion with the Emmaus travelers (Luke 24:25–27) is of special interest, particularly because he explains the crucifixion as fulfillment of Old Testament prophecies, "He said to them, 'How foolish you are, and how slow of heart to believe all that the prophets have spoken! Did not the Christ have to suffer these things and then enter his glory?' And beginning with Moses and all the Prophets, he explained to them what was said in all the Scriptures concerning himself."

B.2. Christian Rejection of the Old?

We have noted the most serious challenge for Christian use of the Old Testament presented by Marcion, who arrived in Rome from Asia Minor (ca. AD 140), and proclaimed a Creator God in Genesis different from the Father of Jesus Christ.[22] Marcion wanted the Christian church to repudiate the entire Old Testament for its presentation of Jehovah God as a cruel, vengeful and jealous tyrant. Among New Testament writings he appreciated the Gospel of Luke and Letters of Paul, but even these writings were edited to highlight the themes he favoured, focusing on "spirituality" and a dualism of body and soul.

In repudiating such an approach to the Old Testament, the early church responded with renewed approval of its writings for liturgical reading. It also insisted on the unity of the two testaments, or covenants; the Old Testament represented the anticipation of the Messiah, for which the New Testament represented a fulfillment.

Figure 9.2. The Shrine of the Book (Jerusalem). This Shrine was built to house the Dead Sea Scrolls found in the Qumran caves (1947–1956). The white dome is seen; the rest of the structure, below ground, is reflected in a surrounding pool of water. It houses the oldest known manuscript of Isaiah (2nd century BC). Photo "Sons of Light at Dusk" by Ze'ev Barkan / CC BY 2.0.

---

22. On Marcion, see ch. 8, §A.3 and ch. 1, §A.1.

Christians affirmed the Old Testament prophets because these foretold the coming of the Saviour, promised from the very beginning, right from the occasion of Adam and Eve falling into sin (Gen 3:15).

B.3. Interpretation of the Old Testament

Reading of the Old Testament remained a central practice for Christian worship. The question was, how to interpret the teachings (like the laws) of the Old Testament. On this practice there were different schools of thought:

Allegorical

This approach, first represented among Christians by some works of Justin Martyr, is characteristic of biblical explanation in the Alexandrian schools of Clement and Origen. It was based on Philo of Alexandria's allegorical method of interpreting the Old Testament.[23] Philo confronted the need to adapt OT laws meant for an ancient agricultural society for the Jews of his own urban context in Alexandria. In the interpretation of the Scriptures, the allegorical method took philosophical motifs (particularly the story of the soul and its life journey) to explain events which could not be easily interpreted otherwise. Christians adopted the approach especially on the model of Paul's allegorical explanation of Abraham, Hagar and Sarah, and the birth of Ishmael and Isaac (Gal 4:21–31). Embarrassing events or texts (like Solomon's Song of Songs) could be explained as having an underlying hidden meaning, different from the text when read in a more literal fashion. Important representatives are Clement of Alexandria, Origen and Ambrose.

Historical and literal

Within Judaism itself, Philo's approach was eventually repudiated, especially because it had been adopted and adapted by Christians. For the Jews, the accepted approach in interpretation of Scripture was characterized by a historical and literal reading. Such an approach in interpretation took the words of Scripture at face-value and in their ordinary sense, without trying to read a deeper meaning into the text, and with little attention to figurative language.

Among early Christians, this approach continued to draw adherents, partly in reaction to more elaborate allegorization in biblical interpretation by writers like Origen. Most proponents of a historical and literal interpretation were associated with the Christian theological school based in Antioch. Its most

---

23. On Philo's allegorical commentaries, see ch. 7, §B.5.

famous representative was Theodore of Mopsuestia (bishop, 392–428). The literal approach is also represented in the fourth century by Cappadocian Basil (in his work on Genesis, the *Hexaemeron*), by Chrysostom of Antioch and Augustine of Hippo in North Africa, although Augustine was also influenced by Ambrose of Milan toward allegorical interpretation. In the study of Scripture, Ambrose (ca. 340–397) provided the link between Alexandria and Rome.

Typological

The typological approach is not always clearly distinguished from the allegorical method, for it also looks beneath the literal meaning of the text for a secondary meaning. However, it is particularly used to interpret events, figures or sayings in the Old Testament as an anticipation of the New Testament, with a particular focus on the life and accomplishments of Jesus Christ. Thus it recognizes the New Testament as fulfillment of Old Testament prophecy. Justin Martyr's *Dialogue with Trypho* provides a good example of this method.

C. Formation of the New Testament

Early Christianity had its beginning with the celebration of Pentecost in Jerusalem and the preaching of Peter, bringing many to repentance and faith in Jesus. Even though the apostles continued to worship at the temple, as did Paul on his return from missionary travels, the story now began to focus on the believers gathered in Jerusalem, as well as the believers in many of the communities visited by the apostles, in Antioch and throughout Palestine and elsewhere in the empire, wherever diaspora Jews had settled. In Acts 2:5–11, Luke gives a significant listing of the different places of origin for the pilgrims present in Jerusalem at Pentecost.[24] On his missionary journeys Paul visited such Jewish communities of Asia Minor, Greece and Rome. He joined the diaspora Jews in worship in their synagogues, sharing with them the story of Jesus as the fulfillment of hopes and expectations based on the Old Testament promises.[25]

---

24. Acts 2:5–11,
Now there were staying in Jerusalem God-fearing Jews from every nation under heaven.... Parthians, Medes and Elamites; residents of Mesopotamia, Judea and Cappadocia, Pontus and Asia, Phrygia and Pamphylia, Egypt and the parts of Libya near Cyrene; visitors from Rome (both Jews and converts to Judaism); Cretans and Arabs.

25. See Acts 17:2, "As his custom was, Paul went into the synagogue, and on three Sabbath days he reasoned with them from the Scriptures, explaining and proving that the Christ had to suffer and rise from the dead."

From the beginning, the Scriptures were central to Christian worship. Although Christians gathered not on the Sabbath, but on Sunday, the first day of the week (to commemorate the resurrection), the pattern of worship largely followed that of the synagogue: prayers, the reading of Scripture and the singing of psalms and hymns. While Jews made extensive use of ritual cleansing by water, the role of baptism as the sign of belief in Jesus was new, as was the eucharistic feast to commemorate Jesus's death. Justin Martyr's *Apology* provides significant information about the worship pattern of early Christian congregations, as does the *Didachê* (the *Teaching of the Twelve Apostles*).[26] But the actual writing of the New Testament, as witness to the events around the birth, death and resurrection of Jesus, came about as the first generation of his followers, the apostles, realized the need to remember and pass on these events. Moreover, the followers of Jesus grew in their understanding of his life as a fulfilment of the Old Testament; such growth in understanding is reflected especially in the New Testament books of Romans and Hebrews. Paul's prison experience was also a strong motivation for him to write to the congregations he helped to organize, because he could no longer visit them in person.

At its core the New Testament canon has a collection of "sayings of the Lord" which were treasured among early Christians; we find reference to such a collection in a number of passages throughout the New Testament, particularly with the institution of the Lord's Supper.[27] Paul's letters to new believers in Corinth were among the earliest New Testament writings to appear. Although originally written for specific congregations, the letters of Paul soon circulated among the churches, a practice which Paul himself encouraged. The Pauline letters may have been available as a collection as early as AD 85;[28] the Apostolic Fathers already referred to these Pauline letters as a group. An important second-century papyrus fragment (Chester Beatty) listing the New

---

26. On the *Didachê*, see Latourette, *First Five Centuries*, 117–118; also ch. 7, §A.6.

27. See 1 Cor 7:10, 12 and 25,
> To the married I give this command (not I, but the Lord): A wife must not separate from her husband. . . . To the rest I say this (I, not the Lord): If any brother has a wife who is not a believer and she is willing to live with him, he must not divorce her. . . . Now about virgins: I have no command from the Lord, but I give a judgment as one who by the Lord's mercy is trustworthy.

See also 1 Cor 11:23–24, "For I received from the Lord what I also passed on to you: The Lord Jesus, on the night he was betrayed, took bread . . ."

28. See 2 Pet 3:15–16, "Bear in mind that our Lord's patience means salvation, just as our dear brother Paul also wrote you with the wisdom that God gave him. He writes the same way in all his letters, speaking in them of these matters."

Testament writings in circulation also demonstrates that these letters were well-established as a collection.[29]

The Gospel of Mark was probably the first of the four gospels to appear, and it was widely circulated. We know that it was published not just as a scroll, but in codex form, more like books as we now know them. Frequent use of the gospel, and the need to refer quickly and easily to its various parts, encouraged a more convenient format for reading and citation. This was at a time when very few books were circulating in this format.

We also know of wide circulation of the gospels in the early Christian church based on numerous citations, especially from Matthew, in contemporary literature. Although Clement, the late first-century bishop of Rome, may have quoted the gospel from oral tradition and memory, Polycarp's letters (ca. AD 115), show clear acquaintance with both Matthew and Luke as written gospels.

C.1. Factors Influencing the Formation of the "Canon"

a) *The example of the Old Testament canon.* Christians had the Old Testament canon as their example. The Greek term *kanôn* (or "canon") was known among philosophers, and was used to indicate a "rule" for teaching, or the key teachings by which an author might be judged to belong to a specific group or school of thought.

b) *The challenge of Gnostics,* and especially Marcion, who forced Christians to determine how they would read the Scriptures. The Gnostics produced their own commentaries (including an early commentary on the Gospel of John), and wrote more gospels which were allegedly based on the witness of apostles like James and Thomas. To support their own interpretations they quoted Pauline letters or the gospels selectively (also taking passages out of context in the process).

c) *Use of the "rule of faith":* Tertullian argued in the *Praescriptio Haereticorum* that the Scriptures are the possession of the church; more precisely, they belong to the members of the church, namely those who have subscribed to the baptismal creed as it developed from the Great Commission of Christ as given at the end of the Gospel of Matthew. Tertullian identified this creed (in a more

---

29. Bruce, *Canon of Scripture*, 129–131.

developed form) as a "rule of faith" (*regula fidei*), and the key to the meaning of the Scriptures.

d) *Apostolicity in the transmission of faith*: Even the second-century Justin Martyr had realized that the four gospels were appreciated because they were received as the "memoirs" of the apostles themselves (*Apology* 1.66.3). These gospels were written by those who knew Jesus well, his own disciples, or those close to the disciples: Paul was confronted by Jesus en route to Damascus; Luke travelled with Paul; Mark traveled with Paul and Barnabas, and also knew Peter.[30]

In his work *Against Heresies* Irenaeus developed Tertullian's position on the "rule of faith," insisting on close association with one of the apostles who was himself a primary witness to the life of Christ, as the basic criterion for canonical status of New Testament writings. Like Tertullian, Irenaeus argued for close attention to the whole meaning of Scripture, not taking its parts or sayings out of context. In opposing the gnostic appeal to secret teachings of Jesus, supposedly handed on orally, Irenaeus pointed to the open and public transmission of the faith in the church by the apostles, Apostolic Fathers, presbyters or elders and the bishops appointed by them, in an unbroken succession from Christ to the present time.

Indeed, for second-century Christianity the most important criterion for inclusion in the "canon" was that of apostolicity, requiring that a document be written by, or have close connection with one of apostles, the same factor used in judging the teachings of the Gnostics.[31] Fourth-century decisions would also consider the factor of *widespread acceptance* and use in the churches. Inclusion of some books, like Hebrews, James, or Revelation, was delayed over uncertainty regarding authorship. But works like the Shepherd of Hermas, though widely used and recognized as valuable for devotional reading, were finally not included because the apostolic connection was lacking. If they were included in the published Scriptures, these works would be designated as "apocryphal."[32]

---

30. On the four canonical gospels as the earliest reliable accounts of the life of Jesus, see Witherington, *Gospel Code*, 38–52.

31. In his discussion of "canonicity" Bruce focuses on three criteria: *orthodoxy* (agreement with the rule of faith), *apostolicity*, and *consensus* of the churches on usage; see Bruce, *Canon of Scripture*, 251–266, especially 254.

32. On the term "apocryphal" to refer to those books which never became part of the officially accepted canon, see the discussion of alternative gospels in §E below.

C.2. Acceptance of Four Gospels

These four canonical gospels are still accepted as reliable not just because the geographical and historical details of the New Testament have been corroborated for accuracy by archaeological finds. Christians also rely on the settled view of early believers who accepted four distinct gospels long before the end of the second century, when Irenaeus attested to the fourfold gospel.

These four gospels were also used originally in widely different areas: Matthew in Palestine, Mark in Rome and John in Asia Minor; Luke was associated with the churches established by Paul.

From the beginning of Christianity numerous attempts have been made to amalgamate these accounts into a single document, as in the work of Tatian's *Diatessaron* (AD 170).[33] But such an effort to harmonize the gospels was never widely accepted; nor did it succeed in replacing the original four gospels, for these were already too well-established individually by this time. Indeed, such an amalgamation would undermine the advantage of having four distinct perspectives on the life and message of Jesus, as a portrayal more complete and interesting than is possible with only one document.

In *Against Heresies* 3.11.8 Irenaeus agrees with Justin Martyr that all four gospels should be accepted as canonical, and compares the fourfold gospel to the four corners of the earth, and four winds of heaven.[34] Later critics, like Porphyry, would mock slight differences in information given in these gospels. Even so, the church continued to accept all four accounts; cumulatively these gospels give overwhelming evidence of coincidence in what is told of Jesus, as full assurance of the truthfulness of the account.

---

33. On the *Diatesseron*, see Eusebius *HE* 4.29.6–7, quoted in Stevenson, *New Eusebius*, 125–126. For an attempt to rehabilitate Tatian in the context of second-century Christianity, see Hunt, *Christianity in the Second Century*. See also P. Foster's brief introductory essay, "Tatian," 15–35. In his account of early Syriac Christianity, Jenkins notes the significance of Tatian's testimony in assuming four, and *only four* authentic gospels in composing the *Diatesseron*, while the Syrian churches were well acquainted with many rival gospels (Jenkins, *Lost History of Christianity*, 87–88).

34. The crucial argument is given in the passage with which this chapter opens, from Irenaeus's *Against Heresies* 3.11.8. Irenaeus also quotes Acts, the Pauline epistles, Revelation and other Catholic epistles as equally authentic; he recognizes that, unlike esoteric gnostic writings, these have their authority from apostolic origin. See also Stevenson, *New Eusebius*, 117–118; and Bruce, *Canon of Scripture*, 170–177.

Figure 9.3. Christ and the four living creatures. The sculpted figures at the portal of the Church of St Trophime (Arles, France), representing Christ surrounded by four creatures, symbolize the four evangelists: Matthew shown as human but with wings of an angel (upper left); Mark as a lion (lower left); Luke as an ox (lower right); and John as an eagle (upper right). The symbolism is based on the four living creatures of Ezekiel 1, and Revelation 4:6–9. Photo "St Trophime Portal Detail" by Rolf Süssbrich / CC BY-SA 3.0.

D. The Canon in the Making

In the history of the New Testament canon, a special role must be accorded the *Muratorian fragment*, as the first strong witness to a set of New Testament books which is close to our present collection in content. The document reflects mid-second-century usage in the church in Rome.[35] It gives a list that includes the four gospels, Acts, the Pauline letters, the pastoral letters, First and Second John, Jude, and the Apocalypse. Missing from the list are: Hebrews, James, two letters of Peter and the third letter of John. But the document

---

35. This is a *fragment* from a manuscript which is usually dated to about AD 170, or at least the period AD 170–210, since it quotes the Shepherd of Hermas as recent; it is thought to be associated with Hippolytus of Rome, a contemporary of Irenaeus. Its name comes from the Italian Ludovico Muratori, who found the fragment in 1840, as part of an eighth-century theological book. See further, Bruce, *Canon of Scripture*, 158–169.

clearly differentiates the books to be read publicly in church services from those which may be used for private edification. It includes one book which was later excluded, the *Apocalypse of Peter*.³⁶

Early collections of New Testament writings also include other works which were not finally accepted for the canon: the Shepherd of Hermas, the *Didachê*, the *Epistle of Barnabas*, the *Gospel of the Hebrews*, the Wisdom of Solomon and *Acts of Paul*. Nonetheless, the Muratorian fragment is a significant indication that by the year AD 200 the collection of New Testament texts as it was used in the churches included much of what we now accept as canonical. At this time we also first hear of a distinct "Old" and "New" Testament.

Figure 9.4. Codex Sinaiticus (ca. AD 350). This is a page from the early Greek manuscript containing the oldest complete copy of the New Testament and most of the Greek Old Testament. Photographic reproduction by Maksim. Public Domain.

The late second- and third-century writings of Clement of Alexandria and Origen are helpful in reflecting this process, for they assume an acceptance of most New Testament writings of the present canon, with uncertainty about a few. These two theologians reflect a strong consensus on the books which present the core of the canon; such agreement is confirmed by the fourth-century listings of Eusebius in his *Ecclesiastical History*, where he quotes Origen's list.³⁷ They also reflect ongoing use by local churches of books like the Shepherd of Hermas (which was still included in the important early manuscript of the Bible, the Codex Sinaiticus, of AD 350), and letters of Clement (which also appear in another outstanding early manuscript, the Codex Alexandrinus, of AD 450).

Textual work on writings of the Old and New Testament owes much to the third- and fourth-century theologians Origen and Jerome. With his work on the *Hexapla*, bringing together six manuscripts of the OT, Origen laid the foundations for a critical text of the OT in Greek;³⁸ this work also led him to

---

36. On the *Apocalypse of Peter*, see Daniélou, *Theology of Jewish Christianity*, 18 and 25–26.
37. For the passage in Eusebius *HE* 6.25, see chapter appendix 9.2.
38. On Origen's contribution in theology and biblical studies, see ch. 10, §A.3.

write commentaries on books of both the Old and New Testament. For the Latin-speaking world, Jerome developed Origen's initiatives in establishing the Hebrew text of the Old Testament and gave the first uniform translation of both the Old and New Testament, the Vulgate (or "common") translation. This translation would be endorsed for liturgical reading in the western empire. When asked to explain the reasons for his translation, especially where he diverged significantly from the known versions, Jerome wrote extensive commentaries to accompany the Vulgate.

Already in the late third century Eusebius spoke confidently of a threefold distinction of New Testament writings: (1) those universally acknowledged; (2) those which are disputed, and finally (3) those which are spurious and are to be rejected.[39] The official decision on the canon of the New Testament came soon after the legal acceptance of Christianity (AD 313) under Emperor Constantine. From that time churches could worship openly, and collections of the text (or codices [plural of codex]) were needed for use in the liturgy. The three complete early Greek Bibles which have survived in excellent condition, the Codex Alexandrinus, Sinaiticus and Vaticanus, date from that time.

For the eastern and Greek-speaking church, a listing of twenty-seven New Testament books, just as we have them, was given in Athanasius's festal letter of AD 367 (at Easter); it included four gospels, Acts, the general Epistles, Pauline Epistles, and Revelation.[40] Athanasius did acknowledge some books as being useful for edification (e.g. the *Didachê* and Shepherd), but these were assigned a category distinct from canonical books intended for religious instruction. In the West, decisions of the Council of Hippo Regius (393) and of the Council of Carthage (397), where Augustine was influential, also gave an official list of twenty-seven New Testament writings to be read in church services; this list tallies exactly with the canonical list still accepted today.

From the above account it is clear that, contrary to the views promoted by Dan Brown in *The Da Vinci Code*, acceptance of the canon of Scripture as we have it was not primarily a matter of decisions of synods and their leaders. It is true that at the time of the Nicene council Constantine ordered copies of the Scriptures to be prepared for the churches of Constantinople, as partial reparation of damage for the church; providing these copies assumed consensus on the exact content of the canon. And the first complete list of the twenty-seven books of the New Testament, exactly as we have them today, is given by Athanasius in AD 367. But it is also true that of the twenty-seven books

---

39. For citation of Eusebius *HE* 3.25, see chapter appendix 9.3.
40. See Latourette, *First Five Centuries*, 134.

finally accepted, twenty-three were already regarded as canonical at least two hundred years prior to that, as attested by the Muratorian fragment (ca. AD 175); at the time of the Nicene council the only books still under debate for canonicity were the Shepherd of Hermas, and Epistles like 2 Peter, Jude, 2 and 3 John and Revelation, not the four gospels.[41]

It is therefore clear that the declarations associated with Athanasius and Augustine, respectively, simply *confirmed* what the church had already accepted for some centuries as God's Word. It was only a matter of time for the entire church, in all areas represented, to positively accept these books as the basis of public worship. This was facilitated when Christianity was legalized, and empire-wide ecumenical councils were possible. The decision on the canon at that time meant that congregations were encouraged to use the writings included in the canon for public reading and preaching; these would also function as the final criterion for faith. Apostolicity gave them authority, just as it established the authority of the bishops.

E. Alternative Gospels and Apocryphal Books

After the first four gospels were written in the first century many attempts were made to rewrite and embellish these accounts. The writing of such "gospels" was often motivated by a desire to add details of interest about Jesus's family, his boyhood, or aspects of his life not covered in the early gospels. Aiming to satisfy curiosity about this important religious figure, these gospels usually mingled fact and fiction. Some of the gospels added fantastic and unbelievable details to embellish the simply told tales of the earliest gospels.

But motives also went beyond the satisfaction of curiosity. As the church was growing in the first century after Jesus's death, we know that there were factions proclaiming teachings significantly at variance from those of approved leaders. Such groups found it useful to implement a gospel format to lend an air of authority to their teachings; they would respond to the principle of apostolicity by simply claiming that their document was written by one of the early apostles. They would even attribute pronouncements from their own teachings to Jesus himself.

A considerable number of gospels reveal a special interest in Mary and the infancy of Jesus. The *Protoevangelium Jacobi* (or *Infancy Gospel of James*) reflects early interest in Mary and in her parents (Anna and Joachim); here we find a highly embellished retelling of the nativity story. Something similar

---

41. See Witherington, *Gospel Code*, 125.

is given in the *Gospel of St Matthew*, which presents animals from the jungle, including lions, who all come to pay their respect to the infant Jesus. Some infancy narratives reappear in the *Arabic Gospel of the Infancy*, which also introduces stories found in the *Gospel of Thomas* and stories of healing not found elsewhere, like healing from leprosy by means of the water in which Jesus had bathed. The *Transitus Mariæ* (*Assumption of Mary*), also called the *Evangelium Joannis* focuses on the death of Mary. In the Greek version it has a superscript: "The Account of St. John the Theologian, on the Falling Asleep of the Holy Mother of God." One of the Latin versions of this "gospel" has a preface supposedly written by Melito, bishop of Sardis, explaining that the work was published to correct false stories about her death.

One of the earliest pseudo-gospels, the second-century *Gospel of the Twelve Apostles*, is known to have been favoured by the gnostic Ebionites. Equally well known, even in antiquity, was the (*Infancy*) *Gospel of Thomas*.[42] Both Origen and Eusebius speak of this gospel as spurious and not reliable, for it is clearly identified with gnostic heretical teachings. According to the second-century Hippolytus (ca. AD 170–235), this gospel was used by Naassene Syrian Gnostics; Cyril of Jerusalem tells us that Manicheans also favoured it. The work gives the story of the young Jesus as a miracle-worker who could form pigeons of clay and with a clap of hands have them fly away as living birds.[43] Although there are not many traces of explicit Gnosticism left in this gospel, it does reveal a docetic view of Christ, with little evidence of his true humanity. Similarly, the *Gospel of Matthias* was identified (both by Origen and Eusebius) as heretical. According to Hippolytus, followers of Basileides recognized it as an account passed along from the apostle Matthias (or Matthew), presenting teachings which he had received privately from the Lord. In this category are

---

42. This gospel should not be confused with the Coptic *Gospel of Thomas* (translated in J. Robinson, *Nag Hammadi Library*, 124–138), which is based on a Greek text (ca. AD 200) included among the Nag Hammadi documents. The latter portrays Jesus as an enlightened "wise philosopher" (*Saying* 13); see Witherington, *Gospel Code*, 97–104, especially 99. The Nag Hammadi document gives (supposedly secret) sayings of Jesus, a number of them duplicating those of the canonical gospels. A correct interpretation of such sayings carries the promise of victory over death (see *Saying* 1, quoted in Ehrman, *Truth and Fiction*, 63). The Coptic Gospel is also well-known for its statement on androgyny as a condition for entering the kingdom (*Saying* 22); and for Jesus's saying on Mary being made "male," so she can become a living spirit, like the other male apostles (*Saying* 114, on which see Ehrman, *Truth and Fiction*, 67–68; and Witherington, *Gospel Code*, 100).

43. Ehrman concludes that such stories, revealing the young Jesus as a (bad-tempered) miracle-worker (*Inf. Thom.* 3.1–3; 4.1; and 14.1–3), should not be understood as historically accurate (Ehrman, *Truth and Fiction*, 50–52). On Hippolytus of Rome, see also ch. 8, the introduction to §A, note 7.

also pseudo-gospels like the *Gospel of Gamaliel*, the *Gospel of Peter*,[44] the *Gospel according to the Egyptians*,[45] *Gospel of Philip*,[46] *Gospel of Andrew*, a *Gospel of Thaddeus*, and a *Gospel of Eve*; aside from the documents discovered at Nag Hammadi, we know little about them beyond the titles.[47] Of special interest, however, is the *Gospel of Barnabas*, which claims to have been written during the first century; it was actually written in fifteenth-century Italy by a Muslim convert from Christianity.

Some of these works were recognized in the ancient church for interesting detail, and for value as devotional reading. When written by someone other than the author to whom they are attributed (and typically written a considerable time after the event), they are properly designated as "pseudepigraphal" (i.e. written under a false name or inscription).[48] The *Sibylline Oracles*, as apocalyptic pronouncements purportedly given by the prophetic Sibyls, clearly belong to this category of writing.[49] Most of the non-canonical gospels mentioned above also fall into this category, as does Christian rewriting of Jewish apocalyptic

---

44. This gospel, discovered in the tomb of a Christian monk of upper Egypt (in 1886), is available only as a fragment. But the relevant passage is noteworthy for expression of anti-Judaism; it also presents an account of the resurrection far more detailed than the canonical gospels (see Ehrman, *Truth and Fiction*, 53–56). An *Apocalypse of Peter*, included among Nag Hammadi documents (translated in J. Robinson, *Nag Hammadi Library*, 372–378), is noteworthy for its account of substitution at Jesus's crucifixion, as he is put to death; it speaks of the "physical" Jesus taking the place of the true "spiritual" and incorporeal Jesus who is present *above* the cross, mocking those who think they have killed him (*Apoc. Pet.* 81–82; see Ehrman, *Truth and Fiction*, 56–59, especially 58–59).

45. This gospel, already known to Clement of Alexandria, is translated in J. Robinson, *Nag Hammadi Library*, 208–219. Daniélou recognized this gospel as one marked by Encratism (*Theology of Jewish Christianity*, 23).

46. Translated in J. Robinson, *Nag Hammadi Library*, 139–160.

47. On such Nag Hammadi documents, see further Witherington, *Gospel Code*, 81–85.

48. Traditionally the term has been used for significant Jewish (OT) literature which does not fit other categories. While Protestants refer to these works as "pseudepigraphal" (for false author identification), we note that among Catholics they are also designated as "apocryphal." That category includes wisdom literature (4 books of *Maccabees*), apocalypses (*1 and 2 Enoch, 2 Baruch*), edifying literature (*Jubilees, Epistle of Jeremiah*), prayers, psalms (*Psalms of Solomon*) and testaments (*Testaments of the Twelve Patriarchs, Testament of Job*), as well as the story of Joseph and Aseneth. Ferguson provides short introductions to many of these, referring the reader to the comprehensive collection in Charlesworth "Research on the New Testament Apocrypha"; see E. Ferguson, *Encyclopedia of Early Christianity*, 448–462. A number of these writings were found among the Dead Sea Scrolls (and translated in Martinez, *Dead Sea Scrolls*).

49. Sibyls were older women prophets connected with traditional oracles; they typically gave prophesy of (future) events while in a state of ecstasy. One of the famous Sibyls, identified with Cumae (Naples), is celebrated in Vergil's *Aeneid* 6. Both Jews and Christians used the Sibylline oracles, adapting them for their own interpretation; Jewish oracles promoted the sovereignty of God, and his judgment on pagan corruption and immorality. See E. Ferguson, *Encyclopedia of Early Christianity*, 461–462; and Daniélou, *Theology of Jewish Christianity*, 17–18.

works, like *The Ascension of Isaiah*, or *2 Enoch*.[50] They are properly called "apocryphal" when the account presents a vision, or an apocalyptic tale based on an inspired prophetic and esoteric document (i.e. one that is to be concealed from public use until the proper time for revelation; the term "apocryphal" comes from the Greek *apokrupha*, meaning things that are *hidden*).[51]

It is important to recognize that, as it is commonly used today, the term "apocryphal" has a wider application, and is often applied to a gospel or document that has not been included in the canon. In the history of Christianity after the Reformation, the Protestant definition of the biblical canon became more restrictive; books like the Wisdom of Solomon which were excluded from the Protestant Bible (while the Catholic Bible maintained them as canonical), came to be identified as "apocryphal." Indeed, use of the term "apocryphal" when applied to books not accepted as genuine accounts, and not included in the canon, often carries with it a negative evaluation. More properly, many of these works should be designated as deutero-canonical, to indicate that they have secondary ranking in comparison with those deemed canonical. They might also be designated as *pseudepigraphal*, especially when gospels or prophetic works claim to have been written by a well-known author, and supply details not included in the canonical Scriptures.[52]

What then of the eighty gospels which, according to Dan Brown's *Da Vinci Code*, were rejected by the Nicene council for presenting an overly human Jesus? Were there ever eighty spurious gospels?[53] If we go back to the above discussion of gospels available in antiquity, and include those found at

---

50. The *Ascension of Isaiah* (from the second century BC) refers to Isaiah's death by being sawed in two, an event alluded to in Hebrews 11:37; see E. Ferguson, *Encyclopedia of Early Christianity*, 457–458. *2 Enoch*, also called *Slavonic Enoch* (because it survived only in Slavonic recension), presents Enoch's ascent through the cosmic spheres, up to the tenth heaven and the throne of God (based on Gen 5:21–32); see E. Ferguson, *Encyclopedia of Early Christianity*, 454. See also Daniélou's discussion of such New Testament apocryphal works, examined for indications of Jewish Christianity (*Theology of Jewish Christianity*, 19–28).

51. The term "apocryphal" may well have been used originally for esoteric literature, meant for a restricted audience (as in the mystery religions, where vision was restricted to initiates). Later usage applied the term to the vision which should be revealed only at the appointed time; also for secret information, like that which the Gnostics affirmed for Jesus communicating privately with the disciples, giving details not included in the four canonical gospels.

52. E. Ferguson (*Encyclopedia of Early Christianity*, 440–448) provides a brief description of books traditionally regarded as "apocryphal" (many of them certainly qualifying also as "pseudepigraphal"): additions to Esther and to Daniel, 1 and 2 Esdras, The Prayer of Manasseh, Tobit, Judith, Wisdom of Solomon, Sirach (Ecclesiasticus), Baruch, Letter of Jeremiah and 1 and 2 Maccabees.

53. On the total number of eighty gospels, see the report of Abd Al-Jabbar, note 57 below.

Nag Hammadi, the total adds up to little more than twenty gospels.[54] As we have seen, most of them accent a docetic or gnostic understanding of Jesus, spiritualized and divine, but not fully human. This is especially clear from widespread denial of the reality of Jesus's death on the cross, as we noted from Irenaeus' account of the teaching of Basileides (*Against Heresies* 1.19.1-4): at the crucifixion Jesus was supposedly already himself in heaven laughing, because people mistakenly thought they were crucifying him.[55] Whatever we make of the eighty gospels, it is clear from rudimentary acquaintance with the gnostic gospels that we can expect these, rather, to emphasize the divine Christ, at the expense of accepting Jesus as also truly human. This factor alone undermines Brown's claim, that the four gospels were chosen to foist a divine Jesus on the church at the time of the Nicene council.

Conclusions

It is clear that completion and closure of the biblical canon in the fourth century did not represent a new decision by the church. Rather, it reflected a gradual consensus on the authenticity of those books recognized for passing on the apostolic witness to the life and work of Jesus, whether written by the apostles themselves or their close associates. Certainly, the process was motivated by the need to combat the spread of heretical teachings about Jesus (Docetism and Gnosticism), forcing the church to determine authentic writings that could be traced back to eyewitness accounts. We know that from the earliest decades of their establishment, Christian congregations treasured the gospels and the letters of Paul as the core of a New Testament canon, to be used in public worship, just as also Israel, from the very early years, treasured the Mosaic Torah as a guide to community life.

Does this gradual growth in acceptance of the canon of Scripture reflect a process which is regrettable because it allowed for error in transmission? Islamic assessment of the canon typically refers to the process as one that allowed for corruption of the original *Taurat* or *Injil*, negatively affecting the documents now accepted by Jews and Christians. They consider the original revelation of God in the Bible to have been corrupted; errors have supposedly arisen from interpolation of the words of God with the comments and interpretations of human writers, making it difficult to discern what is the true

---

54. On the titles of Nag Hammadi documents, see Witherington, *Gospel Code*, 81-92.
55. See ch. 8, §A.2 on second-century Gnosticism and notes 45 and 47.

and authentic word of God.[56] Such a position on corruption in the Christian Scriptures reflects a widely held Islamic view.[57]

An evaluation of this position must recognize first, that both the Old and New Testaments were written by numerous authors, and over a period of centuries. It is also important to be clear on the decisive difference in canon formation with respect to the Islamic *Qur'an*, for the latter resulted from revelations to one author over a period of less than thirty years. It is clear that in their judgement on the Scriptures, Islamic scholars have used the Qur'an as model, and therefore recognize as "revelation" only those statements which represent the "very words" of God, namely the words which were, as it were, "dictated" immediately by God to Moses, the prophets, or to Jesus. For Christians, on the other hand, the Scriptures are regarded as authentic not because they *contain* such statements, but because these writings witness accurately to the full-orbed story of God's saving acts of redemption, the totality of God's real involvement in human history. Christians do not limit divine revelation to passages in the Bible introduced specifically with, "Thus says the Lord." Its authority is based on a recognition that the authors were divinely inspired by the Spirit of God to write as they did.

---

56. The Qur'an, Sura 2.79.

57. On the assumption that Jesus was a prophet of God and therefore must have been given a message (book) like that given by God to Moses and Muhammad, Muslims have argued that Christians must have changed the content of Jesus's book. This position is reflected in the report (cited in Stern, "Abd Al-Jabbar's Account," 135) of ninth-century Muslim scholar, Abd Al-Jabbar, Chief Kadi of Rayy (Teheran):

> Those who had made an agreement with the Romans took counsel what to substitute for the gospels which they could not obtain, and decided to compose another gospel.... Thus some persons wrote a gospel, then afterwards other persons another gospel; thus they wrote a number of gospels. They omitted, however, a great deal of what was in the original gospel ... In that [original gospel] there was no mention of the cross or the crucifixion. They say that there were eighty gospels, which were transmitted and gradually compressed, and at the end four gospels, by four authors, remained. Each of these authors made a gospel in his own time. The one coming after him would find it insufficient and would make another gospel which he thought was more correct that the gospel of his predecessor.

The citation is part of an argument to establish the true prophetic character of Muhammad (see Stern, "Abd Al-Jabbar's Account," 128–185). According to Al-Jabbar, contact with the Roman world caused Christianity to lose its original character, and led to corruption of the ancient documents. Eighty gospels written originally from memory were gradually compressed, so that finally only four gospels, written by four different authors, were left (Stern, "Abd Al-Jabbar's Account," 135 and 137). Abd Al-Jabbar questioned whether the authors of the final four gospels were truly associates or disciples of Christ, recognizing that Luke himself writes that he never saw Christ (Luke 1:1–4). On Al-Jabbar, see also note 5, and ch. 7, §A.5 and note 33.

Copying or translating the Scriptures may have left room for "error," but for Christians the problems raised by such "errors" are nullified by the benefits in support of the spread of the gospel.

Figure 9.5. Liturgical Codex. Churches which did not have the complete Bible could use a liturgical collection of biblical readings assigned for each week of the year. This 7th-century fragment from facing pages of such a liturgical codex used in one of the monasteries of Egypt, gives readings from 2 Corinthians and 2 Peter. Photo "Fragmentary double-page from a liturgical codex" by Marie-Lan Nguyen. Public Domain.

This point can be stated more positively, for the Christian faith is rooted in pivotal events of history; and divine revelation has always actively involved human instruments. So also the central message of the Scriptures, the message of God's love and his intervention to save humankind, were never threatened by minor inconsistencies of factual data; it is all the more firmly established by a multiplicity of witnesses, and by acceptance in a multiplicity of locations as the church grew, spreading rapidly throughout the Roman Empire and beyond its borders.

Chapter Appendix 9.1

Dan Brown on Jesus, Paul and Women

Dan Brown presents Mary Magdalene as a leader among the apostles who was secretly married to Jesus. Even more, the emerging worship of Mary as "Goddess," representing the "sacred feminine" in the early church, is said to have been suppressed because the dominant male hierarchy of the time would have been threatened by such a show of feminine power.[58] So we may ask, was Jesus actually married?[59] Did the church throughout the centuries, particularly after AD 325, conspire to keep the marriage secret, to avoid scandal about his life? And would his married status truly have posed an obstacle to (emerging) belief in his divine status?

Brown claims that stories about Jesus's marriage were common knowledge at that time, circulating in what are now regarded as spurious writings. It is true that two deutero-canonical gospels mention a special relationship between Jesus and Mary Magdalene. In *The Gospel of Mary (Magdalene)*, a second-century gnostic document, Jesus allows her a special vision (on the soul and its ascent past the spheres guarded by cosmic archons); the other disciples challenge the vision she is given and its meaning (she is only a woman, after all!), even as they acknowledge her as Jesus's favourite among the disciples for, "he loved her more than us."[60] The *Gospel of Philip*, one of the (third-century) Coptic texts discovered at Nag Hammadi (1945), also mentions a special relationship between Mary and Jesus, as his "companion" or "associate" (using the Greek term, *koinônos*).[61] In a different passage, Jesus is said to have kissed Mary in public, and the disciples ask why Jesus would love her more than them (*Gospel of Philip* 63.32–36).[62]

Is this a basis for the far-reaching conclusion that Jesus was married to her? None of the gospels, canonical or heretical, give any indication of a

---

58. Ehrman, *Truth and Fiction in the Da Vinci Code*, 163–164. Dan Brown's suggestion that Christianity was originally more accepting of feminine roles, to the extent of worshipping the "sacred feminine" or even a "goddess," ties in with contemporary feminist scholarship on Gnosticism, which presents these branches of Christianity as providing a more equitable role for women (Witherington, *The Gospel Code*, 104–106). See also above ch. 8, §A.2 on Sophia, and notes 31 and 38.

59. Ehrman (*Truth and Fiction in the Da Vinci Code*, 141–142) recognizes that Dan Brown is not original in his presentation of Mary; it is based on Michael Baigent's *Holy Blood, Holy Grail*. Of course, Scorsese's film, *The Last Temptation of Christ*, also presents Jesus as married to Mary Magdalene; similar claims were made by Picknett and Prince in *The Templar Revelation* (1997). Mary's pregnancy is one of Brown's more fanciful claims. Jesus was fully human; nor do his teachings feature the negative views of sexuality which characterize Gnosticism. There is no inherent reason why he could not have been married, but there is absolutely no historical basis for his marriage, and certainly none for his being married to Mary Magdalene, or having children with her; see Witherington, *The Gospel Code*, 29–32.

60. Witherington, *The Gospel Code*, 34–35 (giving the full passage) and 89–91; see also Ehrman, *Truth and Fiction in the Da Vinci Code*, 175–176.

61. Ehrman, *Truth and Fiction in the Da Vinci Code*, 143–144 and 178.

62. Ehrman, 177–179; Witherington, *The Gospel Code*, 35–37 and 85–89, especially 87.

marriage; in fact, most assume he was not married.[63] Even feminist scholars of Gnosticism like Karen King suggest that the document refers to the chaste kiss of fellowship; indeed, the text continues by affirming that, "for this reason, we all kiss one another."[64] Had Jesus been married, the apostle Paul would almost certainly have known, and alluded to this fact in his discussion on virginity in 1 Corinthians 7–9.[65] We also note that the long tradition of celibacy for Catholic clergy typically appeals to Jesus's non-married status as an argument. And without any solid evidence of Jesus ever being married, the entire backdrop for Brown's novel collapses.

In using this theme, Brown's novel certainly does tie in with contemporary interest in the presence and role of women in early Christianity, a topic which has received much attention in current discussion on allowing women to assume the ecclesiastical offices of pastor or priest. Indeed, the gospels and the letters of Paul provide considerable evidence for the involvement of women, as they also reflect the attraction of women to Jesus and to early Christianity. The apostles had not forgotten Jesus's own attention to women: his compassion for the sinful woman at the dinner (Luke 7:36–50), healing the woman suffering from hemorrhage (Luke 8:40–56), praising the widow with her small donation (Mark 12:41–44) and engaging the Samaritan woman in profound conversation (John 4:1–42). Jesus was not afraid to touch the unclean or extend a welcome to social outcasts (Matt 15:28; Luke 1:45; and 10:42). We know that a number of women (some named and most anonymous) traveled with Jesus and provided for him from their own means (Luke 8:1–3). They accompanied him on his

---

63. Ehrman reviews the possible evidence (*Truth and Fiction in the Da Vinci Code*, 152–157 and 165). In his discussion of the relationship of Jesus and Mary reflected in John 20, Witherington affirms Jesus's reminder to Mary that she not "touch" him (John 20:17) as a simple reminder that she not "cling" to him as in the time before the crucifixion and resurrection (Witherington, *The Gospel Code*, 76–77).

64. Witherington, *The Gospel Code*, 36–37 refers to Karen King's discussion of the passage in the *Gospel of Philip* in her work, *The Gospel of Mary of Magdala*, 145–147.

65. Paul's statement about other apostles, the brothers of Jesus or Peter, being accompanied by a wife (1 Cor 9:5), is particularly striking. Witherington rightly notes that, had Jesus been married, Paul would certainly have mentioned it as an example of ministry combined with marriage (*The Gospel Code*, 31).

Figure 9.6. Pompeiian fresco celebrating literacy. This portrait from ancient Pompeii (Italy) of a couple, said to be Paquius Proculo and his wife, display them with emblems of reading and writing, to reveal their pride in the tools of literacy. It is noteworthy that the wife also holds the stylus and wax tablet commonly used for writing. Photo "Fresco representing a couple" by Jebulon / CC0 1.0.

final journey to Jerusalem,[66] and stayed with him when others fled (Mark 14:50 and 15:40). They were the first at the tomb to witness the resurrection.[67]

We also know that women played a crucial role in the early missionary work of Paul; we hear of women like Lydia, who invited Paul to stay with her and sponsored the congregation meeting in her home in Philippi (Acts 16:11–15 and 40).[68] At the conclusion of Paul's letters (as in Romans 16), he lists among those to be greeted numerous women, like Phoebe, Tryphaena and Tryphos who worked alongside Paul (Romans 16:1–2, 6 and 12) and are designated as "co-workers" for the gospel (*sunergous*, Rom 16:3).[69] Some of these women were wealthy in their own right, and acted as patrons to emerging Christian communities.[70] The significant roles taken by women can be explained in part

---

66. See Matt 15:21–29; Mark 15:40–41; Luke 8:1–3; and 10:38–42. Jesus did not neglect women in his ministry, as we know from Mark 7:24–30 and 14:3–9; also from John 4:1–42 and 12:1–8. Women were prominent especially at the crucifixion: Matt 27:55; Mark 15:40–41; Luke 23:49; and John 19:25. They were also crucial as the first to witness his resurrection: Matt 28:1–10; Mark 16:1–8; Luke 23:55–24:10; and John 20 (see Ehrman *Truth and Fiction in the Da Vinci Code*, 147–151).

67. Guy, *Introducing Early Christianity*, 170–172.

68. See also Acts 12:12, for the role of Mary, mother of John Mark.

69. Ehrman mentions the story of Paul and Thekla as added support for the assumption that Paul allowed women to teach and even to baptize (*Truth and Fiction in the Da Vinci Code*, 167–172).

70. By the late third century, and certainly the fourth century, worship was shifting to the public sphere, a move that presented greater difficulties for women taking on leadership roles (Guy, *Introducing Early Christianity*, 178). For archeological evidence from inscriptions

by the use of private homes where congregations met for worship in the early years (Acts 12:12 and 16:40; Rom 16:3-5; 1 Cor 16:19; Col 4:15). While men normally assumed public roles, the home was the basic sphere of women's presence and activities. It is not altogether surprising, then, to discover women exercising a degree of leadership in such home-based congregations.

Even so, it is only possible to appreciate the unusual nature of this phenomenon when it is examined against a more general assessment of roles of women in the Greco-Roman world of the time. Most women, and certainly those of stature, were restricted to the home; outside the home they were usually veiled. Education for women was minimal, if any was given at all. Girls were typically married at an early age; their husbands were often significantly older. The girl's father or husband maintained legal power over her. In general, daughters were considered of less value, compared to boys; the dowry which had to be provided for girls to marry could pose a significant financial burden to a family.[71] As a result, female babies were more often subject to exposure at birth and left to die. And of those who were raised and married, many women died relatively young in childbirth. Few were able to break out of the strictures of domestic concerns.[72]

In comparison with their Greek counterparts, Roman women may have had a little more access to education and freedom of motion, but patriarchal structures predominated.[73]

The lives of women in Judaic culture were not significantly different; the home was also their sphere of operation, while men were expected to do business in the market place, in the courts and in politics, or on the battlefield. In Jewish families the girls were also married while still rather young. They were expected to obey the demands of Torah as it pertained to family life, so they would participate in the public festivals and the life of the synagogue, but their presence was not counted for the quorum (of ten heads of family). Unlike the young men, girls were excluded from reading the Torah (in Hebrew); at the temple they were restricted to an outer court for the Gentiles and women.[74]

---

and artwork for women in the role of presbyter or deacon, even from that period, see Guy, *Introducing Early Christianity*, 178-179.

71. Guy, 167-168.

72. Guy, 166.

73. For a discussion of the role of women in the Christian congregations as it gave rise to criticism of pagan observers like Celsus (on whom see ch. 4, §B.3), see Helleman, *Feminine Personification of Wisdom*, 261-265.

74. Guy, *Introducing Early Christianity*, 168-169.

From this perspective the role of women in the ministry of Paul is striking indeed; among the twenty-eight friends and colleagues listed by Paul (in Rom 16:1–17), there are no less than nine women. Especially noteworthy are women like Phoebe, as *diakonos* (deacon), and Prisca, who was clearly both a leader and teacher (Rom 16:1–3; also Acts 18:26). Junia is mentioned as an *apostolos*, a significant title indicating her contribution in building the church in its ministry.[75] In another passage reflecting on roles of women in worship, Paul seems to take it for granted that women were acting as prophets, and prophesying in church meetings (1 Cor 11:2–16; Acts 2:18 and 21:9; and Rev 2:20). Even with common expectations on the subordination of women, we find a clear indication of the mutual involvement of men and women (1 Cor 11:11–12; Eph 5:21 and 25).

We know of passages where Paul does express concern for the reputation of the congregation, and a desire that Christian behaviour not give offense.[76] There are NT passages (like 1 Tim 2:11–15) where Paul appears to retract some of the freedom allowed for women in an earlier phase of his ministry, reinforcing a more traditional role of submission and subservience.[77] Compared with later periods, church worship was initially less institutionalized, and probably more charismatic; we know that when public ministry roles were more closely defined by the second century, women were routinely excluded, in part to avoid public scandal. We certainly find expression of more restrictive attitudes on the role of women in the writings of Clement of Alexandria and Tertullian.[78]

At the same time it appears that second-century Montanist and gnostic groups allowed women to hold visible and significant roles;[79] we have noted the strong role of Maximilla and Priscilla alongside Montanus.[80] Irenaeus regarded the prophetic and priestly roles assigned to women among the Gnostics a reason for repudiating them as religious groups.[81] Tertullian in particular used some strong language for women who were teaching, baptizing or taking on

---

75. Guy, 172–173.

76. Guy, 174–176.

77. On this well-known text, instructing women to learn in silence, not to teach or exercise authority over a man, Ehrman assumes that it was written not by Paul himself, but by one of his followers, in his name; this is why it is thought to reflect a more patriarchal outlook (*Truth and Fiction in the Da Vinci Code*, 171, 183). Whichever date or author one would assign to such a source, it is clear that (*contra* Dan Brown) the church did not wait for the Nicene council to restrict women's roles in the church.

78. Guy, *Introducing Early Christianity*, 177–178.

79. McKechnie, *The First Christian Centuries*, 204–206.

80. See ch. 6, §B.1, and note 27.

81. Guy, *Introducing Early Christianity*, 180.

such roles of leadership; responding to those who made an appeal to the story of Thekla, ministering openly alongside Paul, Tertullian simply questioned its veracity.[82] Yet the very strong tenor of the arguments against public roles for women itself reinforces an impression of the reality of Christian women remaining active in such roles.[83]

Rhetoric aside, we know that in the Christian congregations the proportion of women was probably greater in relationship to their presence in society at large. Christian prohibition of divorce, adultery, incest and infanticide/exposure (a high proportion among them being girls) would certainly have appealed to women; such moves would serve to strengthen their position in the family and in society. In the Christian communities widows were not pressured to remarry, as was generally expected; instead they were cared for and respected. Such factors would certainly have made Christianity attractive to women.[84] As for the roles assigned to women among Gnostics, a cautionary note is needed, for gnostic views of the body and sexuality actually encouraged women to "transcend" their gendered identity, and become "male" as a condition of salvation.[85] But we also note that gnostic views and practices, however prominent in the second century, no longer enjoyed such prominence in the fourth century under Constantine. This factor certainly undermines a central assumption in Brown's portrayal of the Nicene council, especially on the so-called emerging worship of Mary Magdalene in late antiquity.

But something further must be said. Brown seems to assume that Jesus's being married would have presented him as too human, and undermined his divinity.[86] Is that assumption really warranted? Even aside from the question of his marriage, we have already noted that Jesus was recognized fully as the Son of God on other grounds. Would a marriage have undermined his deity? We

---

82. Guy, 181.

83. Eisen's *Women Officeholders in Early Christianity* examines inscriptions which indicate women taking on active roles as presbyter or deacon, particularly before the fourth century; see McKechnie, *First Christian Centuries*, 207–208, citing Eisen, *Women Officeholders in Early Christianity*, 158–159.

84. On these factors, see also McKechnie, *First Christian Centuries*, 198–201.

85. See Ehrman, *Truth and Fiction in the Da Vinci Code*, 172–179. Ehrman realizes that, as Montanist, Tertullian used some harsh language about women as "the devil's gateway" (*Truth and Fiction*, 173–174). The gnostic *Gospel of Thomas* also presents the apostle Peter speaking of Mary as a woman "not being worthy of life" (*Gospel of Thomas*, 114; *Truth and Fiction*, 180–181). In his reply to Peter, Jesus speaks of the need for a woman to transcend her femininity to be made male, for "every woman who will make herself male will enter the kingdom of heaven." See note 42 above. See further, Ehrman, *Truth and Fiction*, 180–181 and 184; Witherington, *The Gospel Code*, 75.

86. Witherington, *The Gospel Code*, 25.

know that the church never questioned the true humanity of Jesus. Marriage might have served to affirm his humanity; but both natures, human and divine, were accepted in the fourth- and fifth-century discussion without any allusion to his possibly being married. So we may conclude that there really was no historical basis at all for what Brown's novel seeks to have us accept regarding the role of Mary Magdalene, an original "matriarchal" stage in Christianity, or an elaborate conspiracy to repress it.

Chapter Appendix 9.2

Origen's Writings on Scripture

(Based on Eusebius's *Ecclesiastical History* 6.25.1–14)
We note particularly the evidence of Origen's acquaintance with the Hebrew language of the Old Testament, shown by giving the names of Old Testament books in transliteration:

> (1) When expounding the first Psalm, he [Origen] gives a catalogue of the sacred Scriptures of the Old Testament as follows: "It should be stated that the canonical books, as the Hebrews have handed them down, are twenty-two; corresponding with the number of their letters." Further on he says: (2) The twenty-two books of the Hebrews are the following: That which is called by us Genesis, but by the Hebrews, from the beginning of the book, *Bresith*, which means, "In the beginning"; Exodus, *Welesmoth*, that is, "These are the names"; Leviticus, *Wikra*, "And he called"; Numbers, *Ammesphekodeim*; Deuteronomy, *Eleaddebareim*, "These are the words"; Jesus, the son of Nave, *Josoue ben Noun*; Judges and Ruth, among them in one book, *Saphateim*; the First and Second of Kings, among them one, *Samouel*, that is, "The called of God"; the Third and Fourth of Kings in one, *Wammelch David*, that is, "The kingdom of David"; of the Chronicles, the First and Second in one, *Dabreïamein*, that is, "Records of days"; Esdras, First and Second in one, *Ezra*, that is, "An assistant"; the book of Psalms, *Spharthelleim*; the Proverbs of Solomon, *Meloth*; Ecclesiastes, *Koelth*; the Song of Songs (not, as some suppose, Songs of Songs), *Sir Hassirim*; Isaiah, *Jessia*; Jeremiah, with Lamentations and the epistle in one, *Jeremia*; Daniel, *Daniel*; Ezekiel, *Jezekiel*; Job, *Job*; Esther, *Esther*. And besides these there are the Maccabees, which are entitled *Sarbeth Sabanaiel*.

He gives these in the above-mentioned work.

(3) In his first book on Matthew's Gospel, maintaining the canon of the church, he testifies that he knows only four gospels, writing as follows: (4) Among the four gospels, which are the only indisputable ones in the Church of God under heaven, I have learned by tradition that the first was written by Matthew, who was once a publican, but afterwards an apostle of Jesus Christ, and it was prepared for the converts from Judaism, and published in the Hebrew language. (5) The second is by Mark, who composed it according to the instructions of Peter, who in his Catholic epistle acknowledges him as a son, saying, "The church that is at Babylon elected together with you, salutes you, and so does Marcus, my son." (6) And the third by Luke, the gospel commended by Paul, and composed for Gentile converts. Last of all that by John.

(7) In the fifth book of his expositions of John's gospel, he speaks thus concerning the Epistles of the apostles: "But he who was 'made sufficient to be a minister of the New Testament, not of the letter, but of the Spirit,' that is, Paul, who 'fully preached the gospel from Jerusalem and round about even unto Illyricum,' did not write to all the churches which he had instructed, and to those to which he wrote he sent but few lines. (8) And Peter, on whom the Church of Christ is built, 'against which the gates of hell shall not prevail,' has left one acknowledged epistle; perhaps also a second, but this is doubtful."

(9) "Why need we speak of him who reclined upon the bosom of Jesus, John, who has left us one gospel, though he confessed that he might write so many that the world could not contain them? And he wrote also the Apocalypse, but was commanded to keep silence and not to write the words of the seven thunders. (10) He has left also an epistle of very few lines; perhaps also a second and third; but not all consider them genuine, and together they do not contain a hundred lines."

(11) In addition he [Origen] makes the following statements in regard to the Epistle to the Hebrews in his homilies upon it: "That the verbal style of the epistle entitled 'To the Hebrews,' is not rude like the language of the apostle, who acknowledged himself 'rude in speech' that is, in expression; but that its diction is purer Greek, any one who has the power to discern differences of phraseology will acknowledge. (12) Moreover, that the thoughts

of the epistle are admirable, and not inferior to the acknowledged apostolic writings, any one who carefully examines the apostolic text will admit." (13) Further on he adds: "If I gave my opinion, I should say that the thoughts are those of the apostle, but the diction and phraseology are those of some one who remembered the apostolic teachings, and wrote down at his leisure what had been said by his teacher. Therefore if any church holds that this epistle is by Paul, let it be commended for this. For not without reason have the ancients handed it down as Paul's. (14) But who wrote the epistle, in truth, God knows. The statement of some who have gone before us is that Clement, bishop of the Romans, wrote the epistle, and of others that Luke, the author of the Gospel and the Acts, wrote it." But let this suffice on these matters.

Chapter Appendix 9.3

Eusebius on Categories of New Testament Writings

(*Ecclesiastical History* 3.25.1–6)[87]

(1) Since we are dealing with this subject it is proper to sum up the writings of the New Testament which have been already mentioned. First then must be put the holy quaternion of the gospels; following them the Acts of the Apostles. (2) After this must be reckoned the epistles of Paul; next in order the extant former epistle of John, and likewise the epistle of Peter, must be maintained. After them is to be placed, if it really seem proper, the Apocalypse of John, concerning which we shall give the different opinions at the proper time. These then belong among the *accepted* writings.

(3) Among the *disputed* writings, which are nevertheless recognized by many, are extant the so-called epistle of James and that of Jude, also the second epistle of Peter, and those that are called the second and third of John, whether they belong to the evangelist or to another person of the same name.

(4) Among the *rejected* writings must be reckoned also the *Acts of Paul*, and the so-called Shepherd, and the *Apocalypse of Peter*, and in addition to these the extant *Epistle of Barnabas*, and

---

[87]. The passage is also given in Stevenson, *New Eusebius*, 123–124.

the so-called Teachings of the Apostles; and besides, as I said, the Apocalypse of John, if it seem proper, which some, as I said, reject, but which others class with the accepted books.

(5) And among these some have placed also the Gospel according to the Hebrews, with which those of the Hebrews that have accepted Christ are especially delighted. And all these may be reckoned among the disputed books.

(6) But we have nevertheless felt compelled to give a catalogue of these also, distinguishing those works which according to ecclesiastical tradition are true and genuine and commonly accepted, from those others which, although not canonical but disputed, are yet at the same time known to most ecclesiastical writers – we have felt compelled to give this catalogue in order that we might be able to know both these works and those that are cited by the heretics under the name of the apostles, including, for instance, such books as the Gospels of Peter, of Thomas, of Matthias, or of any others besides them, and the Acts of Andrew and John and the other apostles, which no one belonging to the succession of ecclesiastical writers has deemed worthy of mention in his writings.

Questions for Review and Discussion
The Biblical Canon and Alternative Gospels

1. How did the gnostic controversy motivate the early church to determine a canon of authoritative writings?

2. In what sense did the formation of the canon of the New Testament follow the pattern of Old Testament canon formation?

3. What is the significance of the translation of the Old Testament in the Greek Septuagint for the early Christian church?

4. How did Christians describe the relationship between the Old Testament and New? How did they answer Marcion's rejection of the Old Testament?

5. What motivated Clement of Alexandria to turn to allegorical interpretation of the Old Testament? To what extent was he following the example of Philo in doing so? What is the significant difference between historical and allegorical interpretation of the Scriptures?

6. What factors were important for early Christian formation of books as codices rather than scrolls?

7. How did liturgical practice in public worship contribute to the formation of the canon, whether the Old or New Testament?

8. Explain the four important factors for the early Christian church in determining the canon.

9. What is the significance of the Muratorian fragment as witness to the formation of the New Testament canon?

10. What important information is given in the writings of Clement of Alexandria and Origen regarding the development of the New Testament canon?

11. What is the significance of the witness of Eusebius in his *History of the Church*, regarding the establishment of the canon in the late third and the fourth century?

12. Explain the criteria that are important for a document to be included in the canon.

13. Which factors can be adduced to explain the proliferation of gospels in the second century and beyond? Which new topics are introduced in these gospels?

14. Which features of the apocryphal gospels indicate the gnostic orientation of the author?

15. Explain the difference between the various terms used to classify the gospels: canonical, deutero-canonical, apocryphal or pseudepigraphal.

16. What was the original (etymological) meaning of the term "apocryphal"? Explain why this term may well have been appropriate for many of the gospels written in the second century.

Further Reading

Bauer, Walter. *Orthodoxy and Heresy in Earliest Christianity*. Translated by R. Kraft and G. Krodel. Philadelphia: Fortress, 1971.
Bruce, F. F. *The Canon of Scripture*. Downers Grove, IL: InterVarsity Press, 1988.
Charlesworth, James Hamilton. "Research on the New Testament Apocrypha and Pseudepigrapha." *Aufstieg und Niedergang der römischen Welt*, edited by W. Haase. Part 2, Principat 25, no. 5 (1988): 3919–3968.

Daniélou, J. *The Theology of Jewish Christianity*. Translated by J. A. Baker. The Development of Christian Doctrine before the Council of Nicaea 1. London: Darton, Longman & Todd, 1964.
Guy, Laurie. *Introducing Early Christianity: A Topical Survey of Its Life, Beliefs and Practices*. Downers Grove, IL: InterVarsity Press, 2004.
Hanson, R. P. C. *Tradition in the Early Church*. London: SCM, 1962.
Helleman, W. E. "The Biblical Canon: A Response to Muhib O. Opeloye, *Building Bridges of Understanding between Islam and Christianity in Nigeria* (2001)." *TCNN Research Bulletin* 41 (2004): 31–42.
Kelly, J. N. D. *Early Christian Creeds*. London: Longman, 1972.
———. *Early Christian Doctrines*. San Francisco: Harper & Row, 1978.
Martinez, Florentino Garcia. *The Dead Sea Scrolls Translated: The Qumran Texts in English*. 2nd edition. Translated by Wilfred G. E. Watson. Leiden: Brill; Grand Rapids, MI: Eerdmans, 1996.
Metzger, Bruce M. *The Canon of the New Testament: Its Origin, Development and Significance*. Oxford: Clarendon, 1988.
Schneemelcher, W., ed. *New Testament Apocrypha*. 2 vols. Translated by R. McL. Wilson. Louisville: Westminster John Knox Press, 1991–1992.
Vallée, G. *A Study in Anti-Gnostic Polemics: Irenaeus, Hippolytus and Epiphanius*. Waterloo, ON: Wilfrid Laurier University Press, 1981.
Williams, R., ed. *The Making of Orthodoxy*. New York: Cambridge University Press, 1989.
Witherington III, Ben. *The Gospel Code: Novel Claims about Jesus, Mary Magdalene and Da Vinci*. Downers Grove, IL: InterVarsity Press, 2004.

10

Arianism and the Trinity

The Ecumenical Councils of Nicea and Constantinople (AD 325–381)

> By divine admonition I assembled at the city of Nicea most of the bishops; and I myself – as one of you, who also rejoices exceedingly in being your fellow-servant – undertook the investigation of the truth together with them. Accordingly, all the points which could produce doubt or excuse for discord have been discussed and examined accurately. And may the Divine Majesty pardon the fearful enormity of the blasphemies which some were shamelessly uttering concerning our Saviour, our life and hope, declaring and confessing that they believe things contrary to the divinely inspired Scriptures and the holy faith.
>
> Constantine's letter to the Christians of Alexandria
> – from Socrates, *History of the Church* 1.9.17–20

This letter written by the Emperor Constantine to the Christian church of Alexandria reflects vividly the enormous changes experienced by Christians under an emperor who not only decreed toleration, but had actively sought to ensure the unity of Christianity in the Empire by calling an empire-wide council, the first of many. We note how proudly Constantine reflects on his own role in assembling this first ecumenical council of more than three hundred bishops at Nicea (325). In his estimation this assembly was gathered not by human intention but in response to divine prodding. Thus Constantine portrayed himself in an important role for the church, no less than a fellow-servant among the bishops.[1] Aside from calling the council, Constantine remained on hand to guide and encourage the bishops as, with them, he sought the truth, based on the Scriptures and the tradition of faith. It is clear from the letter that he was aware of the responsibility on his own shoulders for a positive outcome, especially to refute the teaching of Arius and Arian creedal statements which he regarded as blasphemous.

Historians of the last decades are typically inclined to deplore the changes experienced by the church under this Christian emperor, and focus on the negative results, especially from the perspective of medieval "Christendom." But we should not forget that the bishops themselves at the time would have been very thankful for this turn of events. To have the emperor call himself a fellow-servant in search of the truth must have sounded like music to their ears. A new era had begun for the Christian church.

But the problems confronted were still highly contentious and difficult. Initially it seemed that the effort had paid off, for in this letter Constantine implies that the very thorough examination and discussion of all points of conflict and doubt led them to an agreement which should leave no excuse for further discord! History would prove him wrong, of course. Nor can the emperor be absolved of blame in the matter, for only a few years later Constantine himself was persuaded to recall from exile those whose teaching he had considered blasphemous for affirming what was "contrary to the divinely inspired Scriptures and the holy faith."

Of course church leaders would have to take their share of the blame, for they had approved, perhaps too hastily, what still appeared to many as an ambiguously worded creed. But the reason for these ongoing problems could also be attributed to the nature of the issues addressed. Even with clearly-worded statements, and near unanimity of support, the decisions of the ecumenical councils typically gave rise to further dissent, and had to be revisited in future gatherings, to affirm what had been agreed by previous councils.

Discussion at these initial ecumenical councils were focused especially on an understanding of the person and nature of Jesus Christ, human and divine. Christians had to defend his divinity through evidence from both the Old and New Testaments. In the process of establishing belief, they used especially the Greek language and Greek thought patterns of the time; this led them to

---

1. This role is also reflected in the letter he sent to Aelafius, cited in ch. 5, §B.5 (and quoted in Frend, *Martyrdom and Persecution*, 543). Constantine took his responsibilities seriously, and clearly sought to maintain conditions which would be approved by the "most mighty God," thereby bringing peace and prosperity in the empire and securing his imperial role.

introduce Jesus Christ as the "logos" of God incarnate (or bodily). Christians look to a divine person, where Jews and Muslims look to divine writings.

For Jews, the Torah had a divine character, for through it God revealed himself. Muslims would later have the same regard for the Qur'an. Both groups contend that human beings know God primarily through these divine books. For Christians, God has revealed himself ultimately in the person of Jesus Christ; this is the final revelation and final way of knowing God. These issues were to become a source of misunderstanding between Christianity, Judaism and Islam as monotheistic religions.

The discussions and deliberations that eventually led to a clear understanding of "who Jesus really was" took many years. Through a series of ecumenical councils with representative Christians from all the regions of the empire and beyond, the church finally came to a consensus on the matter. The decisions arrived at were considered the "orthodox" positions of the church; contrary views were anathematized, and branded as heresy. The present chapter will examine the first two of the seven ecumenical councils, the Nicene council of AD 325 and the Council of Constantinople of 381. These two councils made important decisions on the divinity of Jesus and the relationship between the three divine persons, God the Father, Jesus as God's Son, and the Holy Spirit.

A. The Nicene Council of AD 325

A.1. Background

Early Christians, for the most part, took the words and actions of Jesus for granted, accepting the gospel accounts without debate or cross-examination of key statements on Jesus as "Son of Man," or "Son of God," as "God" or "Logos." In that respect they followed the pattern of Jews who, like Muslims, rarely speculated on the nature of God, while Greek culture, on the other hand, was known for questioning religious convictions. Early Christian worship used the term *Kurios* (Lord) as a title for Jesus Christ, long before it entered the Christian creed. Again, early Christians used the term "Trinity" in the baptismal formula well before it was defined. Similarly, they accepted the designation of Jesus as Logos (as in the Gospel of John 1:1), pointing to the pre-existence of the Son with the Father; they used the term in worship and written documents long before they concerned themselves with a more precise explanation for Jesus as the Logos.

This can be demonstrated from the incorporation of early Christian hymns in New Testament passages; these hymns used expressions for Jesus which would raise sharp controversy in later years. One example is Philippians 2:6-7, "Who [Jesus], being in very nature God, did not consider equality with God something to be grasped, but made himself nothing, taking the very nature of a servant, being made in human likeness." Another from Colossians 1:15-17 speaks of Jesus's divine status even more explicitly: "He is the image of the invisible God, the first-born over all creation. For by him all things were created, things in heaven and on earth . . . He is before all things, and in him all things hold together." These hymns were written several hundred years before Arius came on the scene. In fact, we may be confident that these songs had been circulating orally in the Christian congregations before being included by Paul in his letters to the churches.

Paul's ministry throughout the Roman Empire opened the way for Christianity to become a force in a Greco-Roman context where these early statements were more likely to be questioned for specific meaning. We have already noted how Docetism and Gnosticism both forced Christians to explain their teachings and practices beyond initial assumptions. Of course, even from Paul's letters, we know of significant differences in early Christian understanding of the teaching and actions of Jesus. Such differences were probably inevitable. However painful for the church at the time, they were also helpful in forcing the church to clarify its views on critical issues.

Resolving controversy

These differences also forced the Christian church to face the question of the appropriate *method* of settling major controversies and resolving divisive issues. How can agreement be achieved when there is substantive difference in thought, in interpretation of the Scriptures, or on questions of a proper lifestyle for Christians? Organizing legitimate debate and settling controversial issues was not easy in the early years. The unity of the church was sorely tested with the rise of Gnosticism and its assumption of a tradition of secret teachings.

Before Christianity was legally recognized as a religion in the Roman Empire (with Constantine), it was virtually impossible for Christians to come together except in local assemblies or regional synods. Of course, such gatherings were called frequently enough in the life of the church, right from the beginning.[2] It was necessary to debate and determine acceptable teaching and practice, organizational matters, relationships, discipline and any other

---

2. Frend (*Rise of Christianity*) discusses a number of early councils which represented a less extended geographical area, from the earliest known council in Jerusalem (Acts 15, discussed in Frend, 91–92), the council on the date of Easter (Frend, 283–284), and the Antioch council (AD 265–268) dealing with the Christology of Paul of Samosata (Frend, 386–387).

urgent (usually local) issue. Even so, the decisions and solutions which emerged were typically shared with other congregations through exchange of letters. As a new generation of leaders and writers rose to the occasion, whether to warn of heretical teachings, or to lead Christians in a better understanding, the organization of the church was strengthened.

This process of decision-making changed significantly after AD 313, the year marking the historic turn to legal status for the Christian church; now the empire had a Christian emperor who wanted to put an end to centuries of persecution. Christianity no longer had to operate "in the dark." By this time Christianity had more members than any one other religious group; and the severity of persecution under Diocletian had resulted in considerable sympathy for Christians, even among the unconverted. It was now possible for Christians to assemble more freely, even on an empire-wide basis, without fear of having their meetings undermined.

Schism and heresy

The ending of persecution had another effect, however, for divisions in the church body, hitherto confined to local controversy, now began to come out into the open. Most problematic were the major schisms in Alexandria (with the rigorist Meletians)[3] and Carthage (the issue of the Donatists).[4] In both regions the main source of the problem was the acceptance of Christians who had capitulated in the time of persecution, especially when this involved a priest or bishop. Also at issue was the status of those members whose baptism or ordination had been conducted by clergy who had, in effect, betrayed the congregation.

But schism is different from heresy, which also arose at this time. While a *schism* represents division over practice and/or personalities in the church, *heresies* arise when there is significant difference in belief and teaching. The major divisive issue regarding teaching and belief at this time was that presented by Arius, the eloquent Libyan presbyter serving in Alexandria under bishop Alexander.[5] He had been excommunicated by his bishop for presenting Christ as Son of God but *not fully* God, relying on the fact that Jesus was "begotten"

---

3. On the Meletians, see Frend, *Rise of Christianity*, 524–526; on the origins of this group with Meletius of Lycopolis, see Frend, 493. The Meletian schism never became a major problem, as was the comparable Donatist controversy in and around Carthage.

4. On the Donatists, see ch. 6, §B.1; also Frend, *Rise of Christianity*, 488–492, 523–524, 534–535 and 572–574; and Latourette, *First Five Centuries*, 129.

5. For a brief introduction to the Arian controversy (in the context of discussion of church-state issues), see ch. 5, §B.5.

as a mere creature, and therefore liable to sin and change.[6] Arius was himself quite popular among his parishioners. After being excommunicated, he took refuge in the eastern Mediterranean with Eusebius of Caesarea and others who shared his position.[7] The controversy only grew.

The divisions which resulted came to the attention of the emperor himself. Once Constantine had secured his role as sole emperor by defeating his rival Licinius (in 324), he decided that it was necessary to call an *ecumenical council* to safeguard the unity of the church.[8] Although important church communities in cities like Antioch, Alexandria, Jerusalem or Rome each had their local archbishop or patriarch, none of these leaders had the authority to call such an empire-wide council. Only the emperor had such wide-ranging authority; and he also took a deep interest in unity of religion, as a bond to hold the empire together in that troubled era. Holding ultimate responsibility for religious affairs in his role as *Pontifex Maximus*,[9] the high priest of state religion in the empire, Constantine called the church to an empire-wide assembly to heal its divisions, and to establish what would be considered correct teaching and worship, or "orthodoxy." This council took place in June and July of 325.

A.2. The Councils: Organizational Aspects

Seven *ecumenical councils* have been recognized by all segments of the early Christian church. Bishops representing all the churches throughout (what was then recognized as) the inhabited world, the *oikoumênê*, were invited to attend these meetings. Both east and western regions had to be fully represented for a council to be designated as "ecumenical." If the bishops were not themselves present, they had to send representatives with clear documentation authorizing them to speak and make decisions on their behalf.

None of the earlier local assemblies had the power or the authority of the council in Nicea,[10] certainly not on matters of publishing creeds, making binding decisions or imposing discipline. Only with Constantine's imperial authority could trouble-makers be punished with exile, or schismatic church groups be disbanded. It was also his prerogative to invite church leaders from

---

6. For Alexander's encyclical letter on the issue, see Stevenson, *New Eusebius*, 322–324.

7. On Arius, see Frend, *Rise of Christianity*, 492–503; and Stevenson, 324–325.

8. The term "ecumenical" is based on the Greek *oikoumênê*, referring to the entire inhabited world. See also Frend, *Rise of Christianity*, 497–498.

9. See ch. 5, §B.5 on the political/historical background and context of Constantine's role as *Pontifex Maximus*.

10. See Frend, *Rise of Christianity*, 498–501.

Arianism and the Trinity   293

many different regions of the empire; and it was his grand gesture to close the council with a banquet, to celebrate with the Christian bishops his imperial power after the defeat of his rivals and enemies.

Procedures

Procedures of the council followed the formal procedures of the Roman Senate. Those present had an opportunity to make their submission to committees for prior consideration; this was typically done before the actual holding of the council, though it was not uncommon to submit material for consideration as issues arose. As the questions were raised and discussed, all those present would be given an opportunity to respond, whether for or against a decision; this was done by vocal affirmation or some other form of voting. When it came to a sharp disagreement, sides were formed and participants made their position known by actually moving to one or other side in the assembly room. Given the gravity of the issues presented, discussion was unhurried, and the councils took months, rather than weeks or days, to arrive at their conclusions.

The emperor presided over these discussions, usually with the help of special theological advisers. We know of bishop Hosius (or Ossius), the Spanish bishop who participated actively in the discussions of Nicea. Because these assemblies or councils were called by the emperors, the decisions of such councils also received state approval and enforcement. Christian leaders who promoted positions which were no longer accepted could expect exclusion, or excommunication, a process also enforced by the strong arm of the state. Dissidents might be exiled and their writings suppressed, if not actually destroyed. Today we know what many of these dissidents wrote only through the work of their opponents, the "heresiologists." On questions of teaching, however, even the emperor realized that the ultimate authority lay with the bishops; and these bishops could complain quite effectively if the emperor overstepped the bounds of what they regarded as their own jurisdiction.

The church initially welcomed imperial support for the great councils. But it also discovered that some emperors (like Theodosius II) could make life more difficult for the church, supporting causes which would not ultimately be accepted as orthodox. In some sense one could rightly say that "orthodoxy" was forced upon the church, as the great councils led to a much greater degree of uniformity (or Catholicity). The discussion at any one council was not to be disrupted until the opposing parties came to unanimity, even on matters as detailed as the difference of a letter in a word (as between the terms *homoousios* ["same in essence"] or *homoiousios* ["similar in essence"] for the relationship between the Son and the Father). Even so, it became clear, especially after the fourth ecumenical council, that these councils would experience considerable difficulty in finding a precise acceptable formulation on the nature of Jesus.

The goal: harmony and truth

While emperors were looking for unity and for religious harmony, as the basis for harmony and unity in the empire, the bishops were looking for the truth of the matter, based on scriptural authority. They wished to establish teaching in harmony with traditions going back to the time of the apostles. In fact, decisions of the councils sometimes led to even sharper division and estrangement, and it often took a subsequent council to confirm decisions of an earlier one. Nonetheless, we know that the ecumenical councils were helpful in clarifying problems by revealing what was really at issue between opposing factions within the church. Eventually, if not immediately, such discussion and face-to-face confrontation between opponents helped pave the way for a consensus.

The first seven ecumenical councils have a very special place in the history of Christianity. Of these, the first four established creedal formulations that are the most widely accepted, setting a precedent that could hardly be followed in later centuries, while serving as a model for thorough discussion of issues.[11] Never again in the history of Christianity has the entire church been able to meet in this way. Difficult political and historical circumstances, and the progressive separation of the major branches of the church, east and west, made it virtually impossible to gather a fair representation of the bishops after the fifth century. During the past century some attempts have been made to involve the entire body of the Christian community in discussion of major issues facing the church. But even the decisions agreed on at the Edinburgh Missions conference of 1910, which became the precursor of the World Council of Churches, could not carry the kind of authority wielded by the earliest ecumenical councils.

Decisions of the first four councils carried more weight than those of the last three because controversies discussed in the latter, like iconoclasm, arose primarily in the eastern branch of the church. The bishops attending the last three councils were, for the most part, from the eastern church, as the Byzantine or eastern part of (what was left of) the Roman Empire grew increasingly isolated from the West and also faced problems quite different from those of the western empire.

---

11. See chapter appendix 11.1 for a list of the seven councils and their important decisions.

The major focus of attention at all these councils concerned an understanding of the person and nature of Jesus Christ, his humanity and divinity; this inevitably involved discussion of the relationship of Jesus with the Father. And from there discussion extended to questions of a biblical understanding of the Trinity. Indeed, these councils were particularly instrumental in establishing the orthodox Christian faith as a Trinitarian faith, based on the biblical understanding of God as triune, one in three, and three in one. Discussion first centred on the role of Jesus Christ, but gradually the role of the Holy Spirit also came into focus. A Trinitarian position was affirmed by the Council of Constantinople, AD 381.

A.3. Theological Background for the Nicene Council

To fully understand the depth of the controversy raised by the position of Arius, it is necessary to provide a brief review of earlier discussions of Christology. The central question which the Christian church faced was: if Christians truly believe that Jesus is fully God, and fully divine, as well as fully human, do they then believe in two Gods? And if so, are they any better than pagans whom Christians accuse of polytheism? Has their faith in Jesus Christ taken them beyond the strict monotheism of the Jews? As we have noted, the basic complaint of Jews was that Christians worshiped the historical Jesus as a "second God"; this they regarded as blasphemy.

So, the challenge for Christians was to show that they worshipped ONE God, not two. The response to the accusation came from two directions: *monarchianism*, and *Logos theology*. Each approach will be discussed briefly, in turn.

Monarchianism

Monarchianism, as the first answer to the charge of "two Gods," represents concern for the *unity* of God as sole divine ruler (based on the Greek: *monos*, as "alone"; and *archon* for "ruling").[12] Initially, Christians had been challenged to recognize and worship Jesus as Lord and God, as *Kurios*, fully equal to the God of the Old Testament. The early church recognized him as the Christ, the Messiah, and thus, the fulfilment of OT promises. John's gospel emphasized Christ as the *Logos*, the *Word* that was with God from the creation, and the *Word* through whom everything was created. Two forms of *monarchianism* can

---

12. Latourette, *First Five Centuries*, 143; see also Chadwick, *Early Church*, 85–90, who specifies this position as a critique of Logos theology (see also note 25 below).

be identified, but it should be noted immediately that, unlike *Logos theology*, both forms of monarchianism were soon rejected by local church councils of the time.

Dynamic monarchianism or adoptionism

Dynamic monarchianism presented Jesus as *human*, born miraculously of the Virgin Mary, and only later *becoming* the Son of God when the Spirit (called the Christ) came upon him at baptism.[13] It also stressed that, throughout his earthly life, Jesus *learned* obedience, and by suffering overcame the sin inherited from Adam.

This is substantially the position of *Theodotus*, who was teaching in Rome (ca. AD 190).[14] Theodotus was excommunicated (ca. 195) by Pope Victor (AD 189–199), because the Christian understanding of salvation was based on the complete deity of the Saviour; salvation cannot be assured if Jesus is regarded as no more than human, no matter how virtuous. The followers of Theodotus, who remained more numerous in the East, were called *adoptionists* because they considered Jesus as God's Son by adoption, and that on the basis of merit, not by nature. *Adoptionists* used the names "Son" and "Spirit" to represent "grace" and "divine inspiration" respectively. Their position was also designated as "*dynamic*" *monarchianism*, because God was regarded as the sole ruler (*monos archon*), who yet revealed himself as a divine power (*dynamis*) in Jesus.

Seventy years later *Paul of Samosata* (ca. 260) represented another form of adoptionism with his teaching that Jesus was a human being who was inspired by divine wisdom to say and do all that he accomplished.[15] Born of Mary as a human being, Jesus was like any other human being, though more than usually virtuous. At his baptism the Spirit of God descended on him, giving him the power to perform miracles. The Logos of God, which dwelt in all the prophets from Moses, also dwelt in Jesus, albeit in a greater measure, making for a closer union of Jesus with the Father God. Throughout his life on earth Jesus learned obedience and, by his suffering in perfect obedience, overcame sin as we all inherit it from Adam. As a result, he was adopted by God as his Son, and deified after his resurrection.

Paul was eloquent and influential, and became bishop of Antioch (260–272).[16] His position was condemned at a local synod of Antioch (in 268), and

---

13. Latourette, *First Five Centuries*, 143–144.
14. On Theodotus, see Stevenson, *New Eusebius*, 144–145.
15. See Stevenson, 261–262; also Latourette, *First Five Centuries*, 144; and Chadwick, *Early Church*, 114–115.
16. On Paul of Samosata, see also Frend, *Rise of Christianity*, 386–387.

Paul himself was excommunicated, but he continued to find followers for his position, among them Lucian (d. 312), who in turn influenced Arius.

Modalistic monarchianism

Modalistic monarchianism is also called *patripassianism*, or *Sabellianism*, for Sabellius, its main representative.[17] "Modalism" refers to the successive *modes of appearance* of God as Father, Son and Spirit. This approach sought to protect the unity of God, while maintaining the deity of Christ; its proponents spoke of the Father, Son and Holy Spirit as three *modes* of the appearance of God. Sabellius regarded God as a "monad," or a "single unit" and the Godhead as the single source of deity. As "monad," God was said to express himself, or become projected (expanded) in three operations: in creation, redemption and the bestowal of grace. Such self-expression was compared with the sun projecting itself in bestowing warmth and light. In fact, the Father and the Son were said to be one and the same; they only *appear* or are revealed in different ways, or successive modes of functioning.[18] So God is thought to remain one and the same, while also at work (successively) in creation and redemption. The modalists took seriously biblical texts like John 17:21, which emphasized the unity of God: "I and the Father are one."[19]

Like adoptionism, Sabellianism was more popular in the East than in the West. This view had the unfortunate consequence of attributing the suffering of the Son to the Father, for which it was designated *patripassianism* (meaning that "the Father also suffers"). Sabellius was born in Asia Minor, but grew up in Rome, and spread his teachings there (ca. 200). He influenced Pope Callistus (217–222), but was finally also excommunicated by this same pope; Callistus was probably influenced by Tertullian in changing his mind.[20]

The response of Tertullian

As a lawyer of North Africa in the early third century, Tertullian is known for his opposition to the Sabellian position. He argued that, in his death, Christ represented the sacrificial lamb to atone for sin. So he questioned how the anger of the Father against human sin could be satisfied if God the Father

---

17. Latourette, *First Five Centuries*, 144–145; and Chadwick, *Early Church*, 87.

18. The succession of modes is best compared to procedures in the theatre: one actor would take on a succession of roles simply by taking on different masks, to portray different dramatic characters.

19. See also Romans 9:5.

20. On Callistus (also spelled Callixtus), see Stevenson, *New Eusebius*, 146–149 and 150–152.

himself suffered on the cross?[21] Tertullian's work *Against Praxeas* exposed this type of teaching as untenable. The person named Praxeas in the title is usually thought to represent a fictitious name for Pope Callistus of Rome, for Praxeas is presented as teaching a modalist view of the Trinity, affirming that God can be identified at one time as the Father, at another time as the Son, and later again, as the Holy Spirit.[22] In further response Tertullian asked whether the Father is thought to become his own Son? Was the Father crucified? In response Tertullian affirmed a single divine nature shared by the Father and the Son; but he affirmed them as two distinct persons.

Even so, like Justin Martyr and other adherents of Logos theology (as will be noted below), Tertullian regarded the Son as subordinate: the eternal Father became "Father" when he begot the Son, as also he became "Creator" when making the world. But even more clearly than Justin Martyr, Tertullian affirmed a distinct individual personality of the Son as God's Word. "Before" entering our history, the Word was invisible, but with the incarnation that Word became visible and was embodied for our salvation.

In response to modalist views of Christ as but one "mode" of the appearance of the Godhead (first as Creator, next as Redeemer, and third as Spirit), Tertullian formulated a position which was finally accepted as a fundamental Christian explanation of the Trinity: one substance (*substantia*), or one essence (or power), in three persons (*personae*), that is three distinct entities or forms.[23] Tertullian also gave the classic formulation on the natures of Christ: one person, but two natures or substances.

Tertullian was not really a professional philosopher; he was primarily a lawyer, and it is clear that he used these terms in a legal sense. But in his discussion of the term Logos for Christ (and in response to Gnostics), Tertullian (like Irenaeus) affirmed the full humanity of Christ, as the incarnation of the Logos. As God, Jesus Christ does not in any way differ from God the Father, Creator of heaven and earth. Yet there are not three Gods, but only one. The Logos is more like God's own thought, expressed in the Word; it is another way of speaking of the biblical Wisdom of God.[24] Tertullian explained that, inasmuch as the Son's being was *generated* from the Father, and also the Holy Spirit *proceeded* from the Father, a degree of subordination was implied. But subordination would not become a controversial issue until the next century.

---

21. On Tertullian, see also ch. 8, §B.3; and Chadwick, *Early Church*, 89–93.

22. Stevenson (*New Eusebius*, 167–168) quotes the relevant passage from Tertullian's *Against Praxeas*; see also Chadwick, *Early Church*, 87–88; and Latourette, *First Five Centuries*, 144.

23. Chadwick, 89–90; and Latourette, 145.

24. Latourette, *First Five Centuries*, 145–146.

Tertullian's work was extremely significant in developing a Latin terminology for the relationship of Father and Son. He tended toward a monarchian view of God, that is, his being one in substance. The term *substantia* here was most likely used in its legal sense, to express status or property held in common. The three persons, each in turn expressed by the term *persona*, are also represented with a legal term for parties in a legal action, each with their own role in the *oikonomia*, that is the divine administration of the creation.

Tertullian developed his use of terms in the context of terminology used by Sabellius, who was known to use the term *homoousios* for divine "sameness of essence" or "being of one substance," for Father and Son. This was a term which had unfortunate associations from its use by Gnostics (and later by Manicheans), who applied it to "sameness of essence" for human souls and the demiurge by whom they are created. In response, Tertullian used the Latin term *substantia* for the deity as a single indivisible divine power. Tertullian was also the first to use the term *trinitas* for the threefold nature of God the Father, the Son generated by the Father, and the Spirit sent forth as Comforter (or Paraclete). The single divine substance was thus "extended" to three persons who are truly distinct, one from the other, as three beings. The threefold being of God, for which Tertullian used the term *persona*, would in later theological discussion (in Greek) be expressed by the term *hypostasis*.

Logos theology

A different approach on the relationship between Jesus as Son of God, and God as his Father, characterizes Logos theology. This approach is represented by Justin Martyr, Clement of Alexandria and Origen. Numerous aspects of their teaching also turned out to be problematic.[25] But those who supported Logos theology, unlike the adherents of *monarchianism*, would not be condemned or excommunicated by the church. In the desire to affirm the unity of God they would affirm a *dependence* of the Son on the Father, or the *subordination* of the Son, as Logos, to the Father.[26]

Philosophical considerations would reinforce such a subordination. Logos theology was certainly influenced by views common in Greek philosophical reflection, particularly the strong distinction between spirit (associated with the divine) and matter (seen as worldly and lower). Where Christianity affirmed

---

25. On Christ as Logos, see Latourette, 142–143; and Pelikan, *Emergence of the Catholic Tradition*, 186–190, particularly 187–188, where he recognizes the apologetic use of Logos theology (on which see ch. 4, §B.3).

26. Pelikan (*Emergence of the Catholic Tradition*, 189) affirms this as a strategy to endow greater respectability for Christian understanding of the derivation of the Son from the Father.

God's creation of the world, the Greek way of thinking would be inclined to look for some mediating power to link the divine with that which is created. Earlier Platonists regarded the human mind, or reason, as *logos* (or the *logikos/rational* "part" of the soul), and as its most divine part; later Platonists distinguished divine Mind (*Nous*) from its logos, as its expression. The logos was understood as the image, reflection or expression of Ideas from the divine Mind (*Nous*), thus mediating between spirit and matter. Adherents of Logos theology applied this model in their understanding of Christ as mediator. However, the incarnation of God in Christ would pose a serious challenge for such an understanding of Christ as Logos.

When the Apologists spoke of Christ as Logos they understood him to be the *expression* or *revelation* of the mind (or thought) of God, revealed in creation, and more fully in the incarnate Jesus. As God, the Father represented the Godhead, or ultimate source of deity. As Logos the Son was somehow generated from the Father, both for his activity in creation, and further, as incarnate Son. To the extent that they concerned themselves with the role of the Holy Spirit, the Apologists regarded the Spirit as the inspiration of the prophets, as the wisdom of God, or the effluence (outpouring) of deity, but certainly sharing fully in that divine nature.

Justin Martyr (d. ca 165) and Logos theology

We have already noted the crucial role of Logos theology in Justin Martyr's apologetical views.[27] With his discussion of the Logos as a divine instrument, active in creation, and becoming human, in turn, for our sakes, Justin is often regarded as a key representative of Logos theology. In Christ as the Logos, Justin recognized a *full revelation* of the Father. Justin's thought on the Logos may be understood as a reflection of the work of Philo of Alexandria. As we also noted above, Philo spoke of the utterly transcendent God, who nonetheless ruled the created world through his powers, mediating between himself and the creation. He regarded the Logos as the most important among these powers.[28] Indeed, Philo referred to the Logos as a Son, "first begotten," and even as a "second God."[29] For Philo, the Logos reveals the mind of God (on a lower plane), and includes all the (Platonic) Ideas as exemplars or archetypes, which are then imaged or projected onto our world as its copy.

---

27. On Justin Martyr's apologetical use of the Logos, see also ch. 4, §B.3.
28. See ch. 7, §B.5.
29. Latourette, *First Five Centuries*, 142–143.

Justin Martyr affirmed the single nature of the Godhead before creation; but he distinguished the divine Logos as God's mind or reason, and as his agent in creative work. Like Philo, Justin understood God's work of creation through his Son or Logos, who fully represented the mind or intention of God himself. Also like Philo, Justin regarded the Logos as a "second God," numerically distinct, yet inseparable and one in essence with the Father, just as fire comes from fire, or light from the sun. And he spoke of the pre-incarnate Christ, generated as God's offspring, as a "creature," and the first-begotten of all creation (Prov 8:22).

Irenaeus (Bishop of Lyons 178–203)

Irenaeus affirmed the historical person, Jesus Christ, born of the Virgin Mary, but also pre-existent with God before creation.[30] How was he produced by the Father? Irenaeus speaks of the generation of the Son from the Father as an indescribable mystery:

> If, then, the Son was not ashamed to ascribe the knowledge of that day to the Father only, but declared what was true regarding the matter, neither let us be ashamed to reserve for God those greater questions which may occur to us. For no man is superior to his master. If any one, therefore, says to us, "How then was the Son produced by the Father?" we reply to him, that no man understands that production, or generation, or calling, or revelation, or by whatever name one may describe His generation, which is in fact altogether indescribable. (*Against Heresies* 2.28.6)

But he affirms that the Son is coeternal with the Father, and a full revelation of the Father, both truly God and truly man:

> He is the Father of our Lord Jesus Christ: through His Word, who is His Son, through Him He is revealed and manifested to all to whom He is revealed; for those [only] know Him to whom the Son has revealed Him. But the Son, eternally co-existing with the Father, from of old, yes, from the beginning, always reveals the Father to Angels, Archangels, Powers, Virtues, and all to whom He wills that God should be revealed. (*Against Heresies* 2.30.9)

---

30. Latourette, 143.

Clement of Alexandria (ca. AD 200)

In his work Clement spoke clearly of the three persons of the Trinity.[31] But he also presented them *hierarchically*, with God the Father as fully transcendent, and the ultimate source of deity. Next was his Son, generated from before the foundation of the world, without beginning and inseparable from the Father. As Son, he represents the image, or the expression of the mind of the Father, comprising his ideas (as powers for animating the world). As the third person, the Spirit was compared to light issuing forth and illuminating all, as the power of both the Father and Son.

Origen (185–254)

Origen was the outstanding representative of the Alexandrian Greek philosophical school of theology; he followed Pantaenus and Clement in teaching at the catechetical school of Alexandria, although he left Alexandria to work in Palestinian Caesarea after AD 215.[32] His approach had a deep ascetic strain; he is known to have gone so far as to castrate himself. As a theologian Origen was brilliant.[33] Among his outstanding contributions to biblical studies we note the *Hexapla* (or "six-fold"), a heroic effort to present the Old Testament in six parallel columns, comparing the Septuagint translation with the Hebrew text and other important Greek translations; the goal was to determine the most accurate text. This work led him to write numerous commentaries on the Scriptures; regrettably, only a few of these have survived. But his development of Logos theology, inherited from Justin Martyr and Clement, made a significant contribution to christological discussion in the years before the Nicene council. Severely tortured with the Decian persecution, Origen died of his wounds a few years later.

---

31. On Clement's apologetical strategy, see ch. 8, §B.2; also Latourette, *First Five Centuries*, 148.

32. On Origen, see Chadwick, *Early Church*, 100–113; and Latourette, 149. On his youth, see the account of Eusebius (in Stevenson, *New Eusebius*, 190–191).

33. Origen's brilliance in philosophical theology did not go unnoticed; on several occasions he was invited to share his insights with members of the imperial family. Through his student, Thaumaturgus, who came from Cappadocia to study law in Caesarea, Origen would exercise a strong influence on the Cappadocian theologians: Basil, Gregory of Nyssa and Gregory Nazianzen (on whom see ch. 12, §B below). Through his careful scholarly work on the Old Testament, Origen made an important contribution to early Christianity. On his use of the original texts available to him, see Stevenson, *New Eusebius*, 197; also Chadwick, *Early Church*, 102. On his relationship with the Jews, whom he consulted on the Hebrew text, see de Lange, *Origen and the Jews*. On his development of allegorical interpretation, see Chadwick, *Early Church*, 107–109, and ch. 9, §B.3.

On the Trinity, Origen worked with both a pluralist and hierarchical approach. He considered God the Father as the only true God (John 17:3), or *autotheos*, and himself without generation (*agennêtos*).[34] Before time, God had brought into being a spiritual realm consisting of angels, spirits and souls.[35] But some of these spiritual beings fell, and as a result, took on bodily form.[36] The Son of God was not created, and thus *not a creature*, but *begotten* (*gennêtos*); yet not begotten in the same way as human beings, but begotten from all eternity. This generation was outside of time.

The Son also *mediates* between the unity of God and the multiplicity of spiritual beings. Although the Son is fully divine, and fully reflects the glory of the Father, he is considered God in a "secondary" sense. The third member of the Trinity, the Holy Spirit, as chief of all spiritual beings, was brought into existence by the Father and the Son.

As Logos, Christ represents the *wisdom* of God.[37] According to Origen, he is coeternal with the Father; and his generation, as Son, is described as an eternal process.[38] But he is also the image of the Father, and in this respect dependent, or subordinate. Origen notes that as Son, Jesus was obedient to the Father. Against the Gnostics, Origen taught that Christ was truly born as a human being, the child of Mary, and that he truly suffered, died, and was

---

34. Stevenson, *New Eusebius*, 202.
35. In his understanding of the spheres and planets, Origen was clearly influenced by the Ptolemaic cosmic scheme, on which see ch. 8, §A (introduction) and §A.5.
36. Chadwick, *Early Church*, 104.
37. Latourette, *First Five Centuries*, 150 and 152.
38. See Origen's *De Principiis* 1.2.2,
    And who that is capable of entertaining reverential thoughts or feelings regarding God, can suppose or believe that God the Father ever existed, even for a moment of time, without having generated this Wisdom? For in that case he must say either that God was unable to generate Wisdom before He produced her, so that He afterwards called into being her who formerly did not exist, or that He possessed the power indeed, but – what cannot be said of God without impiety – was unwilling to use it; both of which suppositions, it is patent to all, are alike absurd and impious: for they amount to this, either that God advanced from a condition of inability to one of ability, or that, although possessed of the power, He concealed it, and delayed the generation of Wisdom. Wherefore we have always held that God is the Father of His only-begotten Son, who was born indeed of Him, and derives from Him what He is, but without any beginning, not only such as may be measured by any divisions of time, but even that which the mind alone can contemplate within itself, or behold, so to speak, with the naked powers of the understanding. And therefore we must believe that Wisdom was generated before any beginning that can be either comprehended or expressed.

also resurrected. The Holy Spirit too, for Origen, is uncreated, and equal in honour with the Father and the Son.[39]

Writing in Greek, Origen used the term *hypostasis* for the three individual aspects of deity (called "persons" by Tertullian), indicating thereby that he considered all three as eternal and ultimate divine entities.[40] The term *hypostasis* represents "that which has real existence or essence"; as such, it is used for "that which has true individuality." Indeed, each of the three *hypostases* is distinct as to individual subsistence (*hupokeimenon*). Thus Origen speaks of three persons in one: one in love, mind and will, and one in harmonious action.

Origen's presentation is especially significant for clarifying the generation of the Son as an *eternal generation*, not bound by time; later christological discussion was indebted to Origen for this contribution.[41] On the other hand, his views retained a strong degree of subordination of the Son and Spirit, as secondary and tertiary with respect to their source in the Father. We should also note the potential problem in Origen's use of the term *hypostasis* (used for the three persons); etymologically the word gives the exact equivalent of the Latin *substantia*, the term used by Tertullian for the "unity of divine essence." As a result, Latin-speaking Christians were inclined to reject Origen's explanation as not fully protecting the unity of God, falling into tritheism.

---

39. For his description of the Trinity, see Origen's *De Principiis* 1.3.7,
   Moreover, nothing in the Trinity can be called greater or less, since the fountain of divinity alone contains all things by His word and reason, and by the Spirit of His mouth sanctifies all things which are worthy of sanctification, as it is written in the Psalm: "By the word of the Lord were the heavens strengthened, and all their power by the Spirit of His mouth." There is also a special working of God the Father, besides that by which He bestowed upon all things the gift of natural life. There is also a special ministry of the Lord Jesus Christ to those upon whom he confers by nature the gift of reason, by means of which they are enabled to be rightly what they are. There is also another grace of the Holy Spirit, which is bestowed upon the deserving, through the ministry of Christ and the working of the Father, in proportion to the merits of those who are rendered capable of receiving it. This is most clearly pointed out by the Apostle Paul, when demonstrating that the power of the Trinity is one and the same, in the words, "There are diversities of gifts, but the same Spirit; there are diversities of administrations, but the same Lord; and there are diversities of operations, but it is the same God who works all in all. But the manifestation of the Spirit is given to every man to profit: withal." From which it most clearly follows that there is no difference in the Trinity, but that which is called the gift of the Spirit is made known through the Son, and operated by God the Father. "But all these works that one and the self-same Spirit, dividing to every one severally as He will."

40. Chadwick, *Early Church*, 113.

41. See Stevenson, *New Eusebius*, 204–205; also Latourette, *First Five Centuries*, 152; and Chadwick, *Early Church*, 113.

A.4. Arius and the Nicene Council

As a priest in the Alexandrian church, and thus subordinate to Alexander as bishop, Arius (AD 250–336) was eloquent and serious. As such he acquired a supportive following (from ca. 311) for his position on the subordinate status of Christ as a creature, created by God, but not sharing fully in the divine nature of the Godhead.[42] In this Arius reflected the views of Lucian of Antioch, his teacher who, as noted above, used an adoptionist theology to distinguish the Father and the Son,[43] a position influenced in turn by Paul of Samosata, whose adoptionist position had already been condemned.[44]

"There was a time when he was not"

The views of Arius were similar to those of Paul of Samosata; his starting point was the need to guard the unity of God, who alone is eternal and unbegotten (*agennêtos*), without generation and without any beginning. According to Arius, the Son had a distinct beginning, for he was begotten by the Father: "There was a time (even if this was 'before time'), when the Son was not."[45] God the Father is essentially unknowable, far removed from all creatures, and cannot share or communicate his essential being, his *ousia*, which is not subject to change or division. To attribute co-eternity to the Son would imply *ditheism* (accepting two gods).

Unlike the Father, also, the Son is begotten (*gennêtos*), and therefore alien to the essence of the Father. While the Father is *agennêtos*, the Son is *gennêtos*. The Son is not an emanation (*probolê*) of his nature, or a consubstantial part (using the Sabellian term, *meros homoousion*), but rather a creature, created or made (*ktisma*, or *poiêma*), and thus dependent on the Father's will. The Father created the Logos as his Son and agent in creating and governing the world, to mediate between himself (as unbegotten) and the creation.

As such, the Logos was the first and highest of all created beings and might even be called God, but was still essentially a *creature*.[46] According to Arius, Jesus was liable to change and sin because he had a human body; but he was lacking a human soul, for the Logos took the place of the human soul. On

---

42. For an introductory survey of Arius's career and thought, see Young, *From Nicaea to Chalcedon*, 58–64.
43. Latourette, *First Five Centuries*, 152–153.
44. On Paul of Samosata, see §A.3 above; and Frend, *Rise of Christianity*, 386–387.
45. See Stevenson, *New Eusebius*, 329 and 334–337; also Latourette, *First Five Centuries*, 153.
46. Bishop Alexander of Alexandria used an encyclical letter (of AD 319), to formulate the unacceptable position of Arius; it was recorded in the historian Socrates's *History of the Church* 1.6,

this reckoning, Jesus was not fully God, for the Logos in him was created; but neither was he fully human, since he did not have a human soul.

Such an understanding of the subordination of the Son was unacceptable for the church. Arius was first challenged by Alexander, his bishop, who used Origen's language to insist on the unity of the divine monad, while still regarding the Son as a separate person with his own nature (*phusis*) or *hypostasis*. As Logos, Christ was not simply a creature, but eternal, equally with the Father. If the Father is unbegotten (*agennêtos*), Alexander argued, the Son may be said to be begotten (*gennêtos*), but he is begotten from eternity, as image and likeness of the Father.

A local synod of Alexandria under bishop Alexander condemned Arius's teaching and deposed him (in 318).[47] Arius took refuge with Eusebius of Caesarea, a fellow student of Lucian, who was sympathetic to his position. With Arius they, in turn, accused Alexander of Sabellianism. As a poet and musician, Arius composed his own confession, gaining a degree of popularity because of the poetic form in which it was chanted, as the *Thalia*.[48] While it still appeared to honour the Son as the divine Logos, this work reveals his deep concern to protect the unity of the Godhead, separating God completely from his creation.

The controversy spread and the debate got more heated; many took sides. Hosius (or Ossius), the bishop of Cordova in Spain, visited Alexandria as a representative of the emperor. He also presided over a council at Antioch where Arius's position was once more condemned; Eusebius of Caesarea, as Arius's associate, was also asked to repent of his position.[49] The procedures of this council are of special interest in anticipating later ecumenical councils; it was the first time that a local synod produced a creed to deal with an issue of belief or doctrine.

> The dogmas they have invented and assert, contrary to the Scriptures, are these: That God was not always the Father, but that there was a period when he was not the Father; that the Word of God was not from eternity but was made out of nothing; for that the ever-existing God ("the I AM" – the eternal One) made him who did not previously exist, out of nothing; wherefore there was a time when he did not exist, inasmuch as the Son is a creature and a work. That he is neither like the Father as it regards his essence, nor is he by nature either the Father's true Word, or true Wisdom, but indeed one of his works and creatures.

47. Stevenson, *New Eusebius*, 322–324; and Latourette, *First Five Centuries*, 153.
48. For excerpts from the *Thalia*, see Stevenson, *New Eusebius*, 330–332.
49. See Stevenson, *New Eusebius*, 332–334; and Latourette, *First Five Centuries*, 153.

Arianism and the Trinity 307

Figure 10.1. The council of Nicea (AD 325). The significant role of the Emperor Constantine is clear from this icon commemorating the Nicene council. Placed centrally, the emperor is shown holding the Greek text of the creed, which would finally be ratified at the Council of Constantinople (381). He is surrounded by some of the bishops in attendance. Photographic reproduction by Dante Alighieri. "Icon depiciting the First Counicl of Nicaea." Public Domain.

Nicea, May–July 325

To settle what he regarded as no more than a battle of words, and to restore peace and unity to the church, Constantine called the first ecumenical council at Nicea, not far from the imperial residence in Nicomedia (Asia Minor), in 325; the assembly lasted from May 20 – July 25.[50]

About three hundred bishops attended, most of them from the eastern part of the empire. Those attending fell into three groups: (1) Alexander, together with his deacon, Athanasius, only twenty-five years old at the time, (2) Arius and Eusebius of Nicomedia, both diametrically opposed to Alexander, and (3) the middle group represented by Eusebius of Caesarea (the historian), who

---

50. Stevenson, *New Eusebius*, 338; and Chadwick, *Early Church*, 130–131.

was theologically a successor to Origen, and likewise opposed to Sabellianism, which inclined him to favour Arius.[51]

When Arius produced his own creed it was quickly dismissed. A Palestinian creed produced by Eusebius of Caesarea, though not very helpful in dealing with the precise issue posed by Arius, was considered sufficiently acceptable as far as it went:[52]

> We believe in one God, the Father Almighty, Maker of all things visible and invisible: and in one Lord, Jesus Christ, the Word of God, God of God, Light of light, Life of life, the only-begotten Son, born before all creation, begotten of God the Father, before all ages, by whom also all things were made; who on account of our salvation became incarnate, and lived among men; and who suffered and rose again on the third day, and ascended to the Father, and shall come again in glory to judge the living and the dead. We believe also in one Holy Spirit. (Socrates, *History of the Church* 1.8)[53]

The council agreed that the Son truly was *begotten*, not made. This creed also spoke of Jesus Christ as Logos of God, as light from light, the only-begotten Son and first-born of all creation, begotten by the Father before all ages. However, the challenge before the assembly was to state the matter in such a way that it was acceptable to the church, while excluding the interpretation given by Arius, who agreed that the Son was "begotten"; at issue was the particular interpretation of that term, and its implications for the deity of the Son.

The "homoousion" solution

At this point the emperor entered the discussion, and made an attempt to break the deadlock. He needed to clinch the anti-Arian position by defeating adoptionist subordination of Jesus Christ to the Father. Through his adviser in theological matters, Hosius, he introduced the term *homoousios* ("same in essence") for Christ, and the term *ousia* ("essence") for divine substance (as it was held in common by three divine persons).[54] Being Spanish and

---

51. Latourette, *First Five Centuries*, 154. On the life, writings and christological understanding of Eusebius of Caesarea, see Young, *From Nicaea to Chalcedon*, 1–23.
52. Latourette, *First Five Centuries*, 155.
53. Quoted in Stevenson, *New Eusebius*, 344.
54. On Christ as *homoousios*, and the controversy surrounding use and meaning of the term, see also Pelikan, *Emergence of the Catholic Tradition*, 200–210.

Latin-speaking, Hosius may have been thinking of Tertullian's terminology (*substantia*), to express the unity of divine substance for the Father and Son, though the terms were not fully equivalent. A new creed produced for acceptance spoke of Jesus Christ as the Son of God and the only-begotten of the Father, begotten *of the substance (ousia) of the Father*, as "true God of true God," begotten not made, and *of one substance (or consubstantial, homoousios) with the Father*, by whom all things were made:

> We believe in one God, the Father Almighty, Maker of all things visible and invisible: and in one Lord Jesus Christ, the Son of God, the only-begotten of the Father, that is of the substance of the Father; God of God, Light of light, true God of true God; begotten not made, *consubstantial* with the Father; by whom all things were made, both [those] which are in heaven and on earth; who for the sake of us men, and on account of our salvation, descended, became incarnate, was made man, suffered and rose again on the third day; he ascended into the heavens, and will come to judge the living and the dead. [We believe] also in the Holy Spirit.
>
> But those who say "There was a time when he was not," or "He did not exist before he was begotten," or "He was made of nothing" or assert that "He is of other substance or essence than the Father," or that the Son of God is created, or mutable, or susceptible of change, the Catholic and apostolic Church of God anathematizes. (Socrates, *History of the Church* 1.8)[55]

In this way the council affirmed Christ as begotten of the very substance of the Father.[56] The intention was to affirm that the Father and Son are exactly the same in divine nature and status; emphasis on sameness of *ousia* was meant to exclude Arius's position on the subordination of the Son. Accordingly, the creed went on to speak of the Son as (derived) from the very substance of the Father, or consubstantial. Thereby it affirmed that Jesus Christ was not God in a secondary sense of the word; nor could one legitimately speak of God the Father as *pre-existing* with respect to the Son. Unlike the rest of the creation, the Son was not "created out of nothing."

---

55. The passage is quoted in Stevenson, *New Eusebius*, 345.
56. Latourette, *First Five Centuries*, 155.

"Ousia" and "hypostasis"

With this move the council attempted to exclude the subordinationist position which is more generally characteristic of Logos theology. The term *homoousion* was used to assure that Christ was regarded as fully God, not a second or subordinate deity. Even so, it is important to recognize that the term *homoousion* did carry with it controversial associations from Gnosticism and Sabellianism. In fact, the aftermath of this first council reveals considerable ongoing confusion about the intention of the term used. While few of the bishops would have given their full support to Arius, most still maintained a subordinationist understanding, much like that of Origen. Many now thought that the Sabellian heresy had been resurrected. Some confusion stemmed also from the formulation of a declaration which specifically indicated the equivalence of the term *ousia* with *hypostasis*.[57] In the letter reporting the decision of the council, Eusebius mentions that a strong word was used to emphasize that Christ does not resemble creatures, but is altogether like the Father; negatively, this meant that Christ did not derive his being from another *ousia* or *hypostasis*.[58] Even Athanasius initially used the two terms interchangeably. The formulation of the council seemed to re-introduce as many problems as it solved.

What is noteworthy here is that both words, *ousia* and *hypostasis*, are used to refer to the self-existent being, or person of the Father (not the *divine nature* of the Father as such). As such, the term *homoousion* can have two meanings; it can refer to the full and complete sharing of one identical nature (as it was used by Sabellians and Gnostics). But it can also have a generic sense, that is referring to that which is compounded of kindred substance (as in making

---

57. See Pelikan, *Emergence of the Catholic Tradition*, 219–225.

58. The letter is reported by Socrates (*History of the Church* 1.8, writing about one hundred years after the council),

Thus also the declaration that "the Son is consubstantial with the Father" having been discussed, it was agreed that this must not be understood in a corporeal sense, or in any way analogous to mortal creatures; inasmuch as it is neither by division of substance, nor by abscission nor by any change of the Father's substance and power, since the underived nature of the Father is inconsistent with all these things. That he is consubstantial with the Father then simply implies, that the Son of God has no resemblance to created things, but is in every respect like the Father only who begat him; and that he is of no other substance (*hypostasis*) or essence (*ousia*), but of the Father. To which doctrine, explained in this way, it appeared right to assent, especially since we knew that some eminent bishops and learned writers among the ancients have used the term *homoousios* in their theological discourses concerning the nature of the Father and the Son.

On Socrates as ecclesiastical historian, see appendix II, §B; and Young, *From Nicaea to Chalcedon*, 23–28.

three rings from the same bar of gold). It is clear that introduction of the term at the council was primarily meant to oppose Arius, who denied that Christ was fully God, fully divine, or divine equally with the Father. Accordingly, those leaders in the eastern church who remained critical of the Nicene formula rightly understood its use of the term *homoousion* with the first meaning. Only later would the generic sense receive more adequate attention.

The above quote (from Socrates's *History of the Church* 1.8), concludes with the expression of anathema (or a curse) on those who disagree with the decision, to show the seriousness of the council in arriving at these conclusions.[59] In this way it wished to exclude from the Christian church those who claimed with Arius that "there was a time when the Son was not," and that "he did not exist before he was begotten," or "that he was mutable, created, and susceptible to change." As a result of such decisions, the works of Arius were burned, and Arius himself was banished, together with two immediate supporters who could not bring themselves to sign the formula of agreement.[60]

Other matters before the Nicene council

The council finished with a number of items of a more general nature, like the date for the celebration of Easter, the consecration of bishops, and the treatment of "lapsed" Christians.[61] Upon its conclusion, the emperor invited all the bishops to a great banquet to celebrate the anniversary of his accession to power; this was an occasion not to be missed by the bishops, truly a first in the context of the empire. In the years after the council, however, it would become clear that when the emperor made or confirmed decisions, he also had the power of undoing them. Some of the consequences of imperial intervention were ominous.

Aftermath of the Nicene council

Decisions of the Nicene council evoked reaction already before the death of Constantine (337). His involvement meant that acceptance of theological positions became more and more politically charged. A stormy period of some sixty years of theological debate followed. Those Arians who had connections with the Byzantine court soon managed to get the emperor's attention; they asked for a reconsideration of their fate, and were recalled. Before long even

---

59. Latourette, *First Five Centuries*, 156.

60. Latourette, 157.

61. Latourette, 156. For the resolutions, or "canons" of the council, see Stevenson, *New Eusebius*, 338–344.

Arius himself was recalled (though he died soon after). By 328 Eusebius of Nicomedia, the leading Arian theologian, became chief religious adviser to Constantine. The Arians, in turn, encouraged the exile of those who held to a strict interpretation of the Nicene agreement. As a result, Athanasius, the new bishop and patriarch of Alexandria after the death of Alexander (in 328), would be exiled no less than five times.[62] He nonetheless remained a staunch upholder of the Nicene agreement.

B. The Second Ecumenical Council of Constantinople of 381

The second ecumenical council was finally called by Emperor Theodosius to deal with continuing problems raised by Arians and Semi-Arians.[63] By now it was becoming clear how much influence the emperor could exert in doctrinal issues. A controversy which, under other circumstances, might have died out within a few years, dragged on for the better part of a century. Political connections and influence would make a strong impact on ecclesiastical decisions. After Constantine died, his sons tended to support the Arian position.[64] Although Constantine II died in 340, his brother Constantius, ruling in the East (from 337–350), tried to overturn the Nicene agreement, calling a number of synods. Only Constans, who ruled in the West (until his death in 350), supported the Nicene party. When Constantius finally remained as sole ruler (350–361), an eastern synod introduced a thoroughly subordinationist creed; the name, *Anomoian Creed*, reflects its intent, to stress the *unlikeness* of Father and Son.[65]

Serious disagreement had arisen almost immediately after the exile of Arius over use of the crucial term *homoousion*, for not allowing adequate differentiation between the Father and Son.[66] Over the years varying response to the Arian position resulted in the formation of three groups: (1) an extreme Arian group called *Anomoian*, emphasizing the unlikeness (*anomoios*) of the Son with respect to the Father; (2) at the other extreme, the Nicene party led by

---

62. Latourette, *First Five Centuries*, 158. For a critical review of Athanasius's writings, his role in the Arian dispute, and the significance of his accomplishment, see Young, *From Nicaea to Chalcedon*, 65–83.

63. On Theodosius and this council, see Frend, *Rise of Christianity*, 635–642.

64. See Latourette, *First Five Centuries*, 158–159; and Chadwick, *Early Church*, 136–145. On the role of Constantine's sons in theological debates see ch. 5, §B.6.

65. See the excerpt on the "Anomoians" from Socrates' *History of the Church*, in Stevenson, *Creeds, Councils and Controversies*, 57–58.

66. See Latourette, *First Five Centuries*, 157.

Athanasius, supporting use of the term *homoousion*; (3) a large middle group called *Homoian,* taking its lead from Eusebius of Caesarea, who considered Christ to be "like" (*homoios*), but not the "same" as the Father.

B.1. Athanasius

Athanasius (ca. 295–373) emerged as the outstanding leader and single most influential theologian in the period after the Nicene council; he continued to uphold its decision.[67] As bishop he maintained close contact with monastic groups, and enjoyed staunch support from the monks of Egypt. But his opponents managed to order him deposed at a synod of Antioch (335), sending him into exile in Gaul.

Athanasius did receive support in Rome, where a synod (of 340) opposed the noncommittal creed adopted by a synod in Antioch.[68] At this point a general council was called, to be held in Sardica (343); this council failed as an ecumenical council mainly because the bloc of representatives from the East withdrew when they saw that they were outnumbered by the western group and their supporters.[69] Constans was murdered in 350, and as sole ruler, Constantius forced the western bishops to denounce Athanasius (which some did). He then held a synod at his own residence in Sirmium, Illyria (in 357), where a resolution was passed forbidding any further use of the term *ousia* (along with *homoousios,* "of the same substance"), allowing only the term *homoios* ("similar") to affirm differentiation.[70]

B.2. Reconciliation of Nicene Supporters and Homoians

The synod of Sirmium constituted almost a complete victory for the Arians. But public acknowledgement of such an extreme position provoked its own reaction. The middle group of *Homoians,* who did accept the term *ousia* for the divine essence as a common denominator between the Father and Son, now saw that their approach was excluded. If they were not ready to affirm *sameness*

---

67. On Athanasius, see Latourette, *First Five Centuries,* 157–161. On his appointment as bishop, see Stevenson, *New Eusebius,* 357. Frend reflects modern critical appraisal of Athanasius's accomplishments (*Rise of Christianity,* 524–528 and 530–531).

68. Latourette, *First Five Centuries,* 159.

69. On this council, see Stevenson, *Creeds, Councils and Controversies,* 14–21; and Frend, *Rise of Christianity,* 528–532.

70. The creed formulated at this council is also referred to as the "Blasphemy" of Sirmium (357); see Stevenson, *Creeds, Councils and Controversies,* 45–47; also Frend, *Rise of Christianity,* 539–540; and Latourette, *First Five Centuries,* 160.

of nature, they did accept *similarity in nature*. So the outcome of Sirmium, in fact, led them to a compromise with Athanasius. *Homoians* preferred the term *homoiousion* (of similar substance), to indicate similarity in divine essence, but not a complete equality, for they also maintained distinctions of *hypostasis* for the "subsistence" of three persons, as Origen had posited. The relevant arguments were current already after the synod of Ancyra, in Asia Minor (358); but more than twenty years would pass before a lasting settlement was possible.[71]

As leader of the Nicene group, Athanasius tried to convince this large middle group that their understanding was indeed not far removed from his own position. He became even more convinced of this during the few years that he was able to return to Alexandria, under the pagan Emperor Julian (361). So Athanasius began to work hard for mutual understanding and, before being exiled once more, was able to participate in a synod of Alexandria which is noted for affirming the *homoousion* of the Son and of the Holy Spirit. This affirmation paved the way for the orthodox position on the Trinity: three hypostases, one in essence, but not without differentiation (since undifferentiated essence marked the position of Sabellians).[72]

B.3. "Ousia" and "Hypostasis" Once Again

In his arguments, Athanasius focused on *identity* of divine substance, to affirm the full deity of Christ. He affirmed God as *one in substance* (*ousia*), but also acknowledged three hypostases. Use of the latter term was complicated by misunderstanding and confusion, in part because the report of the Nicene formula of agreement appeared to present the terms *hypostasis* and *ousia* (or *substantia* in Latin) as interchangeable. Moreover, opponents of the Nicene formula accented *three hypostases*, as they focused on the three distinct persons (as an anti-Sabellian formula). Yet this approach too was unacceptable because it accented the three divine persons at the expense of their unity. In response Athanasius was ready to make some adjustments in the formula of "three hypostases"; his strategy was to encourage greater precision by restricting the term *hypostasis* as the equivalent of Tertullian's *persona*. In so doing he avoided the Greek term *prosôpon*, although it represented the exact equivalent of the word *persona*. Unfortunately, that word was used in the theatre for the *mask* which players used to identify their character; when, as was customary,

---

71. Young, *From Nicaea to Chalcedon*, 78.
72. Latourette, *First Five Centuries*, 161.

one actor would play different roles, they exchanged the mask. With that meaning, the term *prosôpon* would come dangerously close to representing the problematic Sabellian modalist understanding of the three divine persons.

Athanasius's starting point was not philosophical, but an understanding of redemption through the work of Jesus Christ.[73] The significant text for him was 2 Peter 1:4, that we "escape the corruption of this world because of passion, and become partakers of the divine nature." Christians become children of God through fellowship with Christ; they become partakers of the divine nature, that is incorruptible immortality, through faith in Jesus. This raises the question, if Christ were not himself fully *divine*, how could he impart divinity? Similarly, if he were not fully *human*, how could he remove our human sin and guilt? For Athanasius, "Christ was made man, that we might be made divine," as Irenaeus had already posited.[74] This was itself reason enough to oppose the position of Arius, who accepted neither the complete humanity nor the true divinity of Christ.

With Origen, Athanasius affirmed the "generation" of the Son as an *eternal generation*, not an act of God's will. Origen had correctly emphasized this point. Human generation occurs in time; when attributed to deity, generation is timeless. But the "generation" of the Son also points to an essential distinction, or differentiation from the Father in that he is *begotten*, and the offspring of the Father. Father and Son share a sameness, just as light and brightness share sameness. Since the divine nature or substance is immaterial, it is impossible to "separate" or divide that divine substance in any way; the Son does not constitute a "portion" of divine substance. But the Son's sharing of the same divine nature does mean that he is essentially different from the rest of what is created.

The more extreme Arians who constituted the *Anomoians* emphasized the three distinct hypostases as symbolizing three distinct ranks of divinity; the distinction was one of hierarchical order. With Anomoians and Homoians, Athanasius agreed that the distinction must be protected, while he still insisted that ultimately there must also be agreement on the unity of divine status, reflecting complete identity of substance for Father, Son and Spirit. This is why he argued for maintaining the word *ousia*, to represent that substance, reserving the word *hypostasis* for the *three* in one. A local synod of the year 359 had in fact agreed to reserve use of the word *hypostasis* for *persona*.

---

73. Young, *From Nicaea to Chalcedon*, 70.
74. See Athanasius, *On the Incarnation* 54.3.

B.4. The Cappadocian Fathers

Athanasius finally returned from exile in 365, and was able to remain in Egypt under an emperor who interfered much less in church politics; he died in his own city in 373. At this point leadership on the Arian dispute passed to the three Cappadocian theologians of Asia Minor: Basil of Caesarea (d. 379), his friend Gregory of Nazianzus (329–389), and Basil's younger brother Gregory of Nyssa (ca. 335–395).[75] These Cappadocian Fathers made a strategic contribution in resolving the controversy, by using the generic understanding of *homoousion*,[76] and introducing a distinction between *ousia* and *hypostasis* as one between the general (*koinon*) and the particular (*idion*).[77] This was in part because their approach originated with the opposite perspective, an affirmation of the *homoiousion*, to affirm three truly distinct persons, not to be confused or interchanged one with the other, each of the three persons having a distinct and inalienable role in the Godhead. But they also affirmed the co-eternity of the Logos with the Father, and accepted the three hypostases: Father, Son, and Spirit, as truly "three," yet also only "one." This left open the question of the distinguishing properties of the three persons. The Cappadocians focused on

---

75. On the Cappadocians, see Young, *From Nicaea to Chalcedon*, 92–122; also Frend, *Rise of Christianity*, 630–633; and Latourette, *First Five Centuries*, 161–163.

76. See above §A.4, "Ousia" and "hypostasis."

77. Basil clarified his understanding of the crucial terms in *Letter* 236.6,

> The distinction between *ousia* and *hypostasis* is the same as that between the general and the particular; as, for instance, between the [general class] "animal" and the particular, "man." Wherefore, in the case of the Godhead, we confess one essence or substance so as not to give a variant definition of existence, but we confess a particular *hypostasis*, in order that our conception of Father, Son and Holy Spirit may be without confusion and clear. If we have no distinct perception of the separate characteristics, namely, fatherhood, sonship, and sanctification, but form our conception of God from the general idea of existence, we cannot possibly give a sound account of our faith. We must, therefore, confess the faith by adding the particular to the common. The Godhead is common; the fatherhood particular. ... Hence it results that there is a satisfactory preservation of the unity by the confession of the one Godhead, while in the distinction of the individual properties regarded in each there is the confession of the peculiar properties of the Persons. On the other hand, those who identify essence or substance and *hypostasis* are compelled to confess only three Persons (*prosôpa*) and, in their hesitation to speak of three *hypostases*, are convicted of failure to avoid the error of Sabellius, for even Sabellius himself, who in many places confuses the conception, yet, by asserting that the same hypostasis changed its form to meet the needs of the moment, does endeavour to distinguish persons.

Part of this letter, which is often attributed to Gregory of Nyssa, is quoted by Wiles and Santer, *Documents in Early Christian Thought*, 31–35.

the mode of origin: the Father as unbegotten, the Son as eternally begotten, and the Spirit characterized by procession.[78]

The turning point came when, as bishop of Caesarea, Basil had to deal with the group called *Macedonians*, who denied the full deity of the Holy Spirit.[79] At that point Basil provided decisive leadership for the churches of Asia Minor in an attempt to unite all those who opposed the Arian and subordinationist position. He was assisted by his close friend, Gregory of Nazianzus, himself the son of a bishop and educated together with Basil in Athens.[80] Gregory was an able preacher, and after spending some time working with his father, went to Constantinople, where he used his preaching to bring the city churches back to the Nicene faith. In this he received the support of the pro-Nicene Emperor Theodosius (379). Basil died that year, before another council could be called. Although Gregory of Nazianzus became bishop of Constantinople in 381, he soon retreated to monastic life, unhappy with the pressure of politics and administrative duties.

B.5. The Council of Constantinople (381)

Of the three Cappadocians, thus, only Gregory of Nyssa participated in the Council of Constantinople of 381 when it was called by Emperor Theodosius; and Gregory made a major contribution to the discussions of this council.[81]

But the ground work had been prepared well, so that the main task left to the bishops at Constantinople was simply to reaffirm the decisions of Nicea. Gregory of Nyssa presented the three hypostases as three modes of being for one identical essence, one personal God in three modes, severally distinguishable and interpenetrating one another, and without the constraints of human individual personalities. In its affirmation of the Trinity, the council also rejected the Macedonian interpretation for its denial of the consubstantiality of the Holy Spirit.

---

78. On the contribution of the Cappadocians to the settlement of the Nicene understanding, see also Guy, *Introducing Early Christianity*, 278-282.

79. On controversy concerning the deity of the Holy Spirit, as addressed by Athanasius, Basil and Gregory of Nazianzus, see Stevenson, *Creeds, Councils and Controversies*, 92-93 and 97-100.

80. On the contribution of Gregory of Nazianzus in support of the divinity of the Spirit, see Guy, *Introducing Early Christianity*, 281.

81. Latourette, *First Five Centuries*, 164. On the council itself, see also Chadwick, *The Early Church*, 150-151.

Figure 10.2. Hagia Irene, site of the First Council of Constantinople (381).
This was the first church built in Constantinople, and seat of the patriarch before the Hagia Sophia was completed. It was seriously damaged by earthquake in the 8th century. The present structure reflects the church as it was rebuilt at that time. It is now used as a museum; the Hagia Sophia can be seen in the background. Photo "Istanbul, Hagia Irene" by Alexxx1979 / CC BY-SA 4.0.

> Thus the Council of Constantinople endorsed the creed of Nicea:
>
> We believe in one God the Father Almighty, maker of heaven and earth, and of all things visible and invisible;
>
> And in one Lord Jesus Christ, the only begotten Son of God, begotten of the Father before all worlds, that is of the substance of the Father, Light of Light, very God of very God, begotten not made, consubstantial with the Father;
>
> By whom all things were made, both in heaven and earth, who for us men and for our salvation came down from heaven, and was incarnate of the Holy Ghost and the Virgin Mary, and was made man;
>
> He was crucified also for us under Pontius Pilate, and suffered, and was buried, and on the third day he rose again according to the Scriptures, and ascended into heaven, and sits on the right hand of the Father;
>
> And from thence he shall come again with glory to judge both the quick and the dead, whose kingdom shall have no end.

And [we believe] in the Holy Ghost, the Lord and Giver of life, who proceeds from the Father,

Who, with the Father and the Son together is worshipped and glorified, who spoke by the prophets.

And [we believe] in one holy Catholic and Apostolic Church;

We acknowledge one baptism for the remission of sins;

And we look for the resurrection of the dead, and the life of the world to come. Amen.[82]

The creed now known as "Nicene" was finally established firmly at the later Council of Chalcedon (451); at that time the consubstantiality of the Holy Spirit was also given further positive affirmation. Thus we note that one council endorsed the work of the previous council, thereby giving substance and reinforcement to church decisions which had been made.

From this time, Arianism would retreat to the sidelines in most regions where it was once strong, while it did maintain a presence for some time in northern Italy and among German tribes, since these had been converted to Christianity under the Arians through the missionary work of Ulfilas (ca. 311–383), whose family had been carried off in a third-century raid of Goths on Asia Minor.[83] But even in those regions the Arian faith died out by the seventh century.

---

82. This version of the creed is given in Epiphanius of Salamis (ca. 320–403), *Ancoratus* 120, quoted in the *Nicene and Post-Nicene Fathers* 14, as "The Holy Creed Which the 150 Holy Fathers Set Forth, Which Is Consonant with the Holy and Great Synod of Nice (under: The Second Ecumenical Council, The First Council of Constantinople)," adapted slightly to modernize the language. Called the Niceno-Constantinopolitan (or simply Nicene) Creed, this creed is very close to the formulation agreed on at the council of Nicea. While this creed is thought to have been produced at the council of Constantinople, recently discovered documents indicate a more complex history. The first documented reference to "The Holy Creed Which the 150 Holy Fathers Set Forth" is from the council of Chalcedon (of 451). Pelikan (*Excellent Empire*, 18–26, especially 18–19) draws attention to its significance as the only truly "ecumenical" creed, because it has a clear statement specifying the unity, holiness, catholicity (i.e. universality) and apostolic character of the church (*unam, sanctam, catholicam et apostolicam*).

83. Ulfilas would have received the Arian faith from his grandparents, who came from Cappadocia; he was one of a delegation of Goths presented to Emperor Constantius in 341, and was consecrated as bishop by Eusebius. On his return home he sought to evangelize the Visigoths, and invented the Gothic alphabet for this purpose; he also translated the Bible into the Gothic language. The Goths themselves in turn evangelized other Germanic tribes, the Vandals, Suevi, Burgundians, Heruls, and Ostrogoths. On Ulfilas, see Chadwick, *Early Church*, 249; Stevenson, *Creeds, Councils and Controversies*, 89–90; and Latourette, *First Five Centuries*, 164.

Questions for Discussion and Review

Arianism and the Trinity: Ecumenical Councils of Nicea and Constantinople (AD 325–381)

The Nicene Council of AD 325

1. Why is the year 313 significant in terms of decision making within the Christian church?

2. What is the important difference between schism and heresy as a problem for the church?

3. Why are major assemblies like that of AD 325 called "ecumenical" councils?

4. Which political factors affected the holding of a major ecumenical council? Describe the role of Emperor Constantine at the Nicene council. What is the significance of that role for the church?

5. How were decisions achieved at these councils? Describe the respective concerns of bishops and emperors in coming to decisions.

6. Why are there only seven ecumenical councils? Why are the first four councils more significant than the last three? Describe the difference between such councils and the contemporary World Council of Churches.

7. How did Monarchians like Paul of Samosata attempt to protect the unity of God? Why is his form of Monarchianism called "adoptionism"? How did Paul understand the deity of Christ?

8. What is the main difference between adoptionist and modalist Monarchianism? How did Sabellius understand the deity of Christ?

9. Why is modalist monarchianism also labelled "patripassianism"? What was Tertullian's main complaint against the modalist position? How did he attempt to answer the question of the unity of God himself?

10. Christian theologians from Justin Martyr to Origen developed the Logos theology in understanding the deity of Christ. Briefly describe the meaning of the term Logos as it represents understanding of the deity of Christ for major representatives (Justin, Irenaeus, Clement and Origen). How did adherents of Logos theology attempt to protect the unity of God? What was the main contribution of Origen?

11. The adoptionist position of Arius had been rejected by earlier church councils. Briefly outline Arius's own views on the deity of Christ. Why did his bishop Alexander repudiate such teaching?

12. How did Arius attempt to find support for his position in Caesarea and Constantinople?

13. Why did the council come to use the *homoousion* formula to answer the Arian position? Just what does the term mean, and how was it understood by participants at the council? What is the precise relationship between the terms *homoousion* and *hypostasis*?

14. What were the implications of the Nicene council for Arius himself and his immediate supporters? How did the role of the emperor in calling and enforcing decisions of the council make this gathering different from all previous church assemblies?

15. Why were the decisions of the Nicene council so quickly overturned in subsequent years?

The Second Ecumenical Council of Constantinople (of 381)

1. What impact did imperial politics have on the aftermath of the Council of Nicea, and on the implementation of its decisions, especially after the death of Constantine?

2. Which different parties emerged as the result of confusion over the meaning of *homoousion*? Why could they not agree on the Nicene formula?

3. Why was Athanasius staunchly opposed to the Arian position? What motivated him in his opposition?

4. Which factors contributed to the growing rapprochement between the *Homoian* Arians and the party of the Nicenes under Athanasius?

5. Define the important terms: *homoios*, *homoiousios* in comparison with *homoousion*; also, *hypostasis*, *persona*, *prosôpon*.

6. How did the work of the Cappadocian Fathers contribute toward the resolution made possible in the Council of Constantinople 381?

7. What political turn of events made this council of 381 possible?

Further Reading

Dvornik, F. *The General Councils of the Church.* London: Burns & Oates, 1961.
Grant, R. M. *Gods and the One God.* Philadelphia: Westminster, 1986.
———. *Eusebius as Church Historian.* Oxford: Clarendon Press, 1980.
Hanson, R. P. C. *The Search for the Christian Doctrine of God: The Arian Controversy 318–381.* Edinburgh: T&T Clark, 1988.
Kannengiesser, C. *Origen of Alexandria: His World and His Legacy.* Notre Dame: University of Notre Dame Press, 1988.
———. *Arius and Athanasius: Two Alexandrian Theologians.* Brookfield, VT: Ashgate, 1991.
Kelly, J. N. D. *Early Christian Doctrines.* San Francisco: Harper & Row, 1978.
Norris, R. A., ed. *The Christological Controversy.* Philadelphia: Fortress, 1980.
Pelikan, J. *The Emergence of the Catholic Tradition (100–600).* The Christian Tradition: A History of the Development of Doctrine 1. Chicago: University of Chicago Press, 1971.
Quasten, J. *Patrology.* 3 Volumes. Utrecht and Antwerp: Spectrum; Westminster MD: Newman Press, 1962–1964.
Rousseau, P. *Basil of Caesarea.* Berkeley: University of California Press, 1994.
Stevenson, J. *A New Eusebius. Documents Illustrating the History of the Church to AD 337.* Revised by W. H. C. Frend. London: SPCK, 1987.
———. *Creeds, Councils and Controversies: Documents Illustrative of the History of the Church AD 337–461.* Revised by W. H. C. Frend. London: SPCK, 2012.
Widdicombe, P. *The Fatherhood of God from Origen to Athanasius.* Oxford: Clarendon Press, 1994.
Wiles, M. F. *The Christian Fathers.* London: Hodder, 1968.
Young, Frances W. *From Nicaea to Chalcedon: A Guide to the Literature and Its Background.* London: SCM, 1983.

11

The Person of Jesus

Five Ecumenical Councils (AD 431–787)

> From that beginning whereby "the Word was made flesh" in the Virgin's womb, there was never a division between the divine and human substance. Through all the bodily growth, the actions were those of one Person at all times. Still we do not confuse these very things which were done inseparably by any mixture of the divine and human. Rather, we perceive what belongs to either form through the character of the respective acts. For the divine acts do not damage the validity of the human, nor the human acts that of the divine. Both concur in such a way and for this very purpose that for neither of these substances is the distinctive character absorbed, nor is the Person doubled.
>
> Pope Leo, *Epistle* 124.6.

With this letter, Pope Leo tried to explain the theological position argued in the lengthy *Tome* on the two natures of Jesus, the human and divine; the document was foundational for the discussions and decisions of the Council of Chalcedon (AD 451).[1] The letter is addressed to the monks of Palestine, where the decisions of the council met considerable resistance and critique. Although the Chalcedonian creed put an end to controversy on the two natures of Jesus in the western parts of the empire, there was no comparable resolution of the matter in the east, where the controversy continued in heated debate over the positions of Monophysites and Monothelites. Many felt that the Chalcedonian

---

1. On this letter, see Stevenson, *Creeds, Councils and Controversies*, 423.

solution threatened the unity of Jesus Christ, as a person. Such theological division in turn fuelled political division, and eventually weakened what was left of the Roman Empire in the east, especially in Syria and Egypt.

A. The Councils of Ephesus (431) and Chalcedon (451): On the Human and Divine Natures of Christ

A.1. The Council of Ephesus

After the Council of Nicea there was general agreement on the humanity and divinity of Jesus. But significant differences were emerging on how these two aspects existed in one person. Theologians connected with Antioch typically accented the *humanity*, and the historical character of Jesus; they similarly focused on the historical aspects of the Bible as the record of his life.[2] In *Alexandria*, on the other hand, Athanasius had developed the central significance of salvation in terms of the *human becoming divine*, and this view was reflected in a greater emphasis on the divine nature of Jesus. In the *West*, Tertullian's position was maintained: the fully divine and fully human nature were united but not mixed in *one person*, Jesus Christ.

There was still considerable confusion in use of the term "person." Did this represent the Son who had existed from all eternity? Or did it reflect the human being born of the Virgin Mary? Or some combination of these? Cyril of Alexandria (Patriarch of Alexandria, 412–444) promoted the view of Athanasius by emphasizing the divine Christ, even to the point of subsuming the human in the divine nature. Nestorius, on the other hand, emphasized the human, historical Christ, following in the tradition of Antioch as it was more inclined to literal understanding of Scripture.[3]

Apollinaris (d. 390)

The discussion of the nature and person of Christ as it emerged at the Council of Ephesus (in 431), takes us back to Apollinaris, bishop of Syrian Laodicea (d. 390), an early supporter of Athanasius. Even more than Athanasius himself, Apollinaris approached doctrinal issues in terms of their implications for salvation (using the text of 2 Pet 1:4, on becoming partakers of divine

---

   2. On the theological approach characteristic of Antioch, see Frend, *Rise of Christianity*, 641–642. On difference in approach between theologians from Antioch and Alexandria, see also ch. 9, §B.3.

   3. On the encounter of Cyril and Nestorius, see Frend, *Rise of Christianity*, 752–758; and Latourette, *First Five Centuries*, 165.

nature).[4] Like Athanasius, Apollinaris emphasized the divine aspect of the nature of Christ, as crucial for human participation in divine nature.[5] Using 1 Thessalonians 5:23, where Paul assumes a tri-partite human being: body, soul and spirit, Apollinaris affirmed a human body and soul in Jesus, but not a human spirit; the Logos took the place of the reasoning spirit, or rational element. Thus for Apollinaris the highest directing principle in the historical Jesus was divine; and he used this understanding of Jesus's person to explain the absence of sin, and complete harmony of will. To assure unity of the person Jesus Christ, he claimed that his person did not have a human (i.e. fallen) mind.

Apollinaris was soon confronted by questions, whether Christ was then truly human? In some ways the position of Apollinaris, in fact, resembles that of Arius, who taught that in Jesus the Logos would replace the soul (while the body is fully human). For Apollinaris the Son was fully divine, because for him the Logos was fully divine; but he was not fully human. The Cappadocian Gregory of Nazianzus opposed Apollinaris; further opposition came from Antioch, where the reality of the human Christ, born of Mary, was affirmed.[6] We should note that the position of Apollinaris was condemned already at the Council of Constantinople in 381, where Jesus was affirmed as fully human, and having a human mind.

Diodorus of Antioch and Tarsus (d. 394)

As bishop of Tarsus (from AD 378), Diodorus also wished to protect the full humanity of Christ, claiming that Jesus had a human body, soul and spirit. As such, he was united with the Logos, who is the eternal Son of God and second person of the Trinity.[7] But it was not easy to explain how, on this model, the two natures would constitute one being. And how could one explain Jesus's suffering as a human being? Clearly, it was only the human Christ who suffered and died, although the church continued to affirm that the divine was somehow present, enabling Christ to sustain this suffering. How could one affirm clear distinctions of nature, and yet maintain the unity of person? Bishop Diodorus taught a *moral* union of the two natures, comparing the union of human and

---

4. On Apollinaris (also spelled "Apollinarius") see Stevenson, *Creeds, Councils and Controversies*, 102–103; also Young, *From Nicaea to Chalcedon*, 182–191. For the critique of Gregory of Nazianzus, see Stevenson, *Creeds, Councils and Controversies*, 103–108.

5. On Apollinaris's Christology, see Frend, *Rise of Christianity*, 634–635, 641–641 and 753–754; also Latourette, *First Five Centuries*, 165; and Chadwick, *Early Church*, 192–194.

6. See Latourette, *First Five Centuries*, 165–166.

7. On Diodorus, see Young, *From Nicaea to Chalcedon*, 191–199; Chadwick, *Early Church*, 192–193; and Frend, *Rise of Christianity*, 641–642.

divine aspects in Christ to the (hypostatic) union of soul and body, or to the union of a man and woman in marriage.

Nestorius (ca. 381–452)

Theodore of Mopsuestia (bishop, 392–428)[8] and John Chrysostom[9] also responded to Apollinaris. Both were connected with the school of Antioch, and were thus influenced by Diodorus; with him they affirmed the full presence of both a human and a divine nature in Christ.[10] Nestorius, a highly regarded preacher and presbyter, also a pupil of Diodorus of Antioch, promoted a similar position when he became patriarch of Constantinople (428).[11] But he aroused the anger of Alexandrians by emphasizing the title *Christotokos* for Mary (as the one who bears the Christ) rather than *Theotokos* (the one who bears God); for Nestorius the latter title would undermine the humanity of Christ.[12] His intention was to preserve the distinction of the human and divine nature, both of them (but particularly the human aspect) complete and real. His position raised the inevitable question concerning the Lord's suffering. Was it the human nature that suffered? Or the divine? And, can the divine suffer?

Cyril, patriarch of Alexandria (412–444)

Cyril's response to Nestorius was affected by a degree of jealousy about the influence of the school of Antioch at the court of Constantinople.[13] Even so, he accepted a widely held concept of the Logos as the determining element

---

8. For an important excerpt from Theodore's *On the Incarnation*, see Stevenson, *Creeds, Councils and Controversies*, 335–339; see further, Frend, *Rise of Christianity*, 641–642 and 752–754; also Young, *From Nicaea to Chalcedon*, 199–213.

9. On Chrysostom, see Frend, *Rise of Christianity*, 749–754.

10. Wiles and Santer (*Documents in Early Christian Thought*, 57–71) provide a translation of the few remaining fragments of Theodore's *On the Incarnation*, examining the indwelling of the divine in human beings, as neither a matter of essence (*ousia*) or activity (*energeia*), but reflecting God's "good pleasure," or will.

11. On Nestorius, see Young, *From Nicaea to Chalcedon*, 229–240; Frend, *Rise of Christianity*, 752–760; and Latourette, *First Five Centuries*, 166–167.

12. Anastasius, an associate of Nestorius, had rejected the term *Theotokos* for Mary. Some who heard of it thought this meant separating Christ's humanity from his divinity. To clarify the matter, Nestorius delivered a number of public discourses rejecting *Theotokos* as a title for her. According to Socrates (*History of the Church* 7.32), "Nestorius thus acquired the reputation among the masses of asserting the blasphemous dogma that the Lord is a mere man, and attempting to foist on the Church the dogmas of Paul of Samosata and Photinus; the contention raised so great a clamor that it was thought necessary to convene a general council to take cognizance of the matter in dispute."

13. For important citations from the correspondence of Cyril and Nestorius, see Stevenson, *Creeds, Councils and Controversies*, 339–356. On Cyril, see Young, *From Nicaea to Chalcedon*, 240–265; Frend, *Rise of Christianity*, 752–761; and Chadwick, *Early Church*, 194–200.

in the person of Christ, and affirmed the divine element as dominant, at the expense of the humanity of Jesus.[14] So he attacked Nestorius for teaching only a human Christ, and himself affirmed that Christ's divine nature also divinizes the human.

In this way Cyril's approach allowed for the human element being overshadowed, if not actually swallowed up by the divine aspect. Cyril did modify Apollinaris's position by affirming that the unity of the divine and human natures resulted from the Logos becoming incarnate, and taking on human characteristics: body, soul and spirit. A personal Logos had assumed impersonal humanity, as "one *phusis* [nature] of the Logos made flesh." Also, "from two natures – one," and this "one" dominated by the Logos. Thus, the concrete existence of Jesus as an historical person centred on the Logos. Affirming the interchange of human and divine qualities, Cyril attributed divinity to Christ's humanity. In this move Cyril was supported by the monks of Egypt, Celestine I (Patriarch of Rome, 422–432), and Emperor Theodosius II.

In his opposition to Nestorius, Cyril asserted that all Christians must refer to Mary as *Theotokos*, not just *Christotokos*; for the child she bore was "God," not just the human Christ. Use of the title *Theotokos* was to become a slogan, and a test of authentic faith in Christ.[15] Already in 430, a synod in Rome ordered Nestorius to recant his use of *Christotokos*. But among Christian leaders of the West there was also a moderating position, for Ambrose and Augustine accepted Tertullian's approach, affirming the full, complete divine nature united with the full, complete human nature in Christ, and the two natures unified in the man Jesus Christ. Even so, there was considerable confusion over terminology to express the presence of two natures as an unmixed union in one person.

The Council

Emperor Theodosius II called a council for Ephesus in 431.[16] This council began in a rather disorderly way. Cyril's party arrived first and, even before the supporters of Nestorius arrived from Antioch, they began to meet.[17] In one day they managed to pass a condemnation of Nestorius, and deposed him. When Nestorius's supporters arrived and realized what was happening they, in turn, deposed Cyril. However, when the papal legates arrived from Rome,

---

14. On Cyril's position, see also Pelikan, *Emergence of the Catholic Tradition*, 230–243.
15. See Chadwick, *Early Church*, 195; and Latourette, *First Five Centuries*, 167.
16. On the council, see Chadwick, *Early Church*, 196–197.
17. Frend, *Rise of Christianity*, 758–761; and Latourette, *First Five Centuries*, 167–168.

Figure 11.1. Palm Sunday procession of Nestorians. This 8th-century wall painting from a Nestorian Chinese church (Khocho) portrays a procession of priests for a celebratory service on Palm Sunday. Photo by Daderot / CC0 1.0.

these added weight to the party of Cyril, and even Bishop John of Antioch was excommunicated. At first Theodosius imprisoned both Cyril and Nestorius, but later he released Cyril.[18]

With Nestorius's admission of willingness to get out of the way, he was exiled and survived at least twenty years, first in a monastery of the Upper Nile region, and later in Cyrenaica. The christological issue was revisited at the next council, that of Chalcedon, where a more even-handed judgement was given. Yet Nestorius was never recalled. The Nestorian position survived in the Persian Empire, and in Syria.

By the seventh century, Nestorian missionaries had reached China, and a Nestorian faith survived there until the fourteenth century, when its adherents were persecuted under the Ming dynasty. Today Nestorian (or "Assyrian") churches survive in an area of Turkey near Iran, in northern Iraq, and in India.[19]

---

18. On this council and its decisions, see Stevenson, *Creeds, Councils and Controversies*, 357–359.

19. Latourette, *First Five Centuries*, 169–170.

Cyril was reinstated when he agreed to subscribe to the creed put forward by John of Antioch, formulated to reconcile the two parties and approved in 433: "We acknowledge one Lord Jesus Christ, complete God, complete man, with a union of two natures; we confess one Christ, and the Holy Virgin as *Theotokos*."[20] Cyril, in turn, attempted to secure his own place by introducing a condemnation of Diodorus and Theodore of Mopsuestia.

A.2. The Council of Chalcedon (451)

Rivalries continued. In fact, Cyril's position was not far from that of Apollinaris as it emphasized the divine element at the expense of the human Jesus. But this view managed to prevail, particularly through the numerous Alexandrian churchmen who were occupying posts in Constantinople, close to the emperor and leading bishops.

Dioscuros and Eutyches

After Cyril died in 444, his successor Dioscuros pushed the position further.[21] In this he was supported by the ageing abbot of a monastery of Constantinople, Eutyches, who rejected the agreement of 433 as Nestorian. In elaborating the two natures of Christ, Eutyches asserted that, before the incarnation, there were two natures, the human and the divine; but after the incarnation these two natures were so blended that there was only one fully divine nature. This is the beginning of the Monophysite (also called *Miaphysite*) position which, like so much else in early Christian controversy, grew through confusion in use of terminology. Eutyches's position was condemned by the synod of 448, held in Constantinople under Patriarch Flavian.[22]

Pope Leo's *Tome*

The matter was to have been decided at a general Council of Ephesus (449). For this council both parties, the adherents of Eutyches, as well as those supporting patriarch Flavian, appealed to Pope Leo of Rome (440–461), who prepared a

---

20. On this "formula of reunion," see Frend, *Rise of Christianity*, 761–762; Latourette, *First Five Centuries*, 168; also Pelikan, *Emergence of the Catholic Tradition*, 260–261. Cyril's letter to John of Antioch is quoted in Stevenson, *Creeds, Councils and Controversies*, 360–365.

21. On Dioscuros, see Frend, *Rise of Christianity*, 763–770; and Latourette, *First Five Centuries*, 170–171.

22. For Eutychus's admissions at the council, see Stevenson, *Creeds, Councils and Controversies*, 386; on Eutyches, see Chadwick, *The Early Church*, 201; Latourette, *First Five Centuries*, 170; and Frend, *Rise of Christianity*, 764–766 and 768–769. On the Monophysite controversy, see Frend 1972, *The Rise of the Monophysite Movement*.

substantive letter, called a "tome" (i.e. a large volume), as basis for discussion at the council (449).[23] His position went back to the work of Tertullian, affirming two natures, each full and complete, in one person; the two natures remained united, but were not mixed and not changed.[24] Including both natures in one person, Jesus Christ was both fully human and fully divine.

Figure 11.2. Ephesus, site of the Ecumenical Council of 431. Once a thriving harbour city on the west coast of Asia Minor, Ephesus now lies in ruins that are being excavated. These remains of the Fountain of Trajan (early 2nd century) had a statue of the emperor surrounded by other statues and columns, overlooking a pool. Photo "Fountain of Trajan, Ephesus" by Carole Raddato / CC BY-SA 2.0.

But Pope Leo's advice was ignored at the Council of Ephesus (449). By then Flavian had died, and Dioscuros seemed to have gained a victory in restoring Eutyches. This achievement came at the expense of support from Rome, however. While Emperor Theodosius II supported the decision of the Ephesus council, Pope Leo denounced it, and used the term "den of robbers" (*latrocinium*) for this meeting.[25]

---

23. See the lengthy quotation from the *Tome* in Stevenson, *Creeds, Councils and Controversies*, 387–396; see also Pope Leo's own explanation of the Tome in his *Ep.* 124.6, quoted in Stevenson, *Creeds, Councils and Controversies*, 423.

24. On the *Tome*, see Chadwick, *Early Church*, 201–202; Latourette, *First Five Centuries*, 171; and Frend, *Rise of Christianity*, 766–767 and 768–770.

25. Chadwick, *Early Church*, 202; and Latourette, *First Five Centuries*, 171.

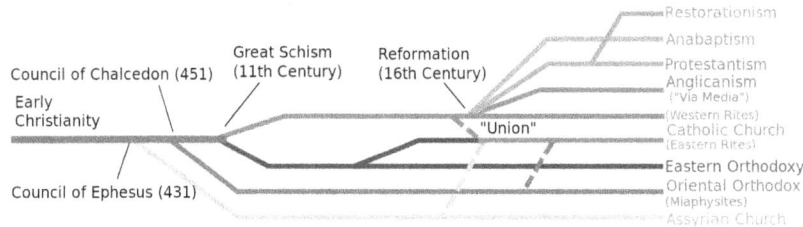

Figure 11.3. Major branches of Christianity after the Council of Ephesus (431).
The diagram is derived from "Christian lineage" by Djyang / CC BY-SA 3.0.

The Council

Theodosius II died in 450. The new emperor Marcian (spouse of Pulcheria, Theodosius's sister) called another council for Nicea in 451.[26] Before the meeting the location was changed to Chalcedon (near Nicea). The council held there would be recognized as the fourth ecumenical council, and was one of the largest ever assembled. It was also one of the most important councils ever held, for its decisions influenced the history of Christianity for centuries to come. More than five hundred bishops attended this assembly; with the exception of the papal legates, however, almost all came from the east. Leo himself was not present, but the papal legates represented him well, and his *Tome* was now given full attention. As a result, the positions of Apollinaris, Eutyches and Nestorius were all condemned. Dioscuros himself was deposed, and sent into exile. Once more a commission (which included papal legates) drew up a creed, which was ratified. It was designed to foster a compromise between Alexandria and Antioch, and closely reflected the position of Pope Leo.

The Creed of the Council of Chalcedon

The result was the *Chalcedonian Definition of the Faith*.[27] This document confessed both the perfect deity and perfect humanity of Christ, consubstantial with the Father with respect to his divine nature, and consubstantial with us human beings with respect to his human nature. In Christ there is but one person, one hypostatic union, but two natures, and these are not confused or mixed. Against the Alexandrian position, the creed affirmed that these natures

---

26. On this council, see Frend, *Rise of Christianity*, 770–773; and Chadwick, *Early Church*, 203–205.

27. For important citations from the Chalcedonian Definition of the Faith, see Stevenson, *Creeds, Councils and Controversies*, 402–407.

are not changed; nor are they divided, or separable (against the position of bishops from Antioch). The properties of each nature concur in one person: one *prosôpon*, or one *hypostasis*, the person of the Son, the only-begotten of the Father, the Lord Jesus Christ.

The crucial section of the creed, on the natures of Christ, reads as follows:

> Following the holy Fathers we teach with one voice that the Son [of God] and our Lord Jesus Christ is to be confessed as one and the same [Person], that he is perfect in Godhead and perfect in manhood, very God and very man, of a reasonable soul and [human] body consisting, consubstantial with the Father as touching his Godhead, and consubstantial with us as touching his manhood;
>
> - made in all things like unto us, sin only excepted;
>
> - begotten of his Father before the worlds according to his Godhead;
>
> - but in these last days for us men and for our salvation born [into the world] of the Virgin Mary, the Mother of God according to his manhood.
>
> This one and the same Jesus Christ, the only-begotten Son [of God] must be confessed to be in two natures, without confusion, immutably, indivisibly, distinctly, inseparably [united], and without the distinction of natures being taken away by such union, but rather the peculiar property of each nature being preserved and being united in one Person [*prosôpon*] and subsistence [*hypostasis*], not separated or divided into two persons, but one and the same Son and only-begotten, God the Word [*theon logon*], our Lord Jesus Christ, as the Prophets of old time have spoken concerning him, and as the Lord Jesus Christ has taught us, and as the Creed of the Fathers has delivered to us.[28]

Speaking of the person of Christ, the statements of the creed do have an overly negative character: no confusion and no mixture of the two natures is to be accepted, and the two natures are neither changed or divided. This was the solution of the council on the double nature of Jesus Christ. On the one hand, it dealt decisively with the problems posed by the approaches of both Alexandria and Antioch. On the other, it was incomplete in dealing with the

---

28. See Frend, *Rise of Christianity*, 771; also Latourette, *First Five Centuries*, 171–172.

issue, for it did not affirm positively *how* the natures are united in Christ. But it did establish a norm for how one can speak accurately of Christ as human and divine. It was true to the conviction of the Christian church, that in Christ we find the full revelation of God, and God revealed in human life. When the Creator becomes the creature, the immortal takes on mortality, and the eternal takes on the temporal, is it really possible to give a completely satisfying explanation?

Speaking on behalf of Pope Leo, the Roman legates also made a decisive contribution. Rome was recognized for taking a leading role in the discussion of issues central to the teaching of the church,[29] and the Alexandrian faction was reprimanded. This council also declared the church of Constantinople equal in dignity with that of Rome, alongside the other patriarchal seats of Jerusalem and Antioch.[30]

The Egyptian or Coptic church almost unanimously rejected the Chalcedonian formulation of Christ having two distinct natures, human and divine, thinking this undermined the affirmation of his divine nature. As a result of this rejection a large sector of Christianity in the Middle East and Egyptian North Africa turned to Monophysite Christology. The position of the Coptic church was echoed in both the Nubian and Ethiopian Churches, where it maintained strong ties. The Armenian church and Jacobite church in Syria also affirmed a Monophysite Christology.

B. The Last Three Ecumenical Councils: Monophysites, Monothelites, and Iconoclasm

B.1. The Fifth Ecumenical Council of Constantinople, 553

Almost immediately after the Council of Chalcedon had done its work in 451, renewed controversy broke out over the "Roman" solution. Especially in Egypt, Syria and Armenia there was confusion over the terminology, which was thought to endanger the unity of the person of Christ. Many found it difficult to distinguish between the term for "person" and that for his "nature" (*phusis*), a term also understood as representing a concrete existing being. Monophysites and their position continued to be problematic, for they preferred to speak of *one Christ, out of two natures*: the Logos and humanity, and the latter aspect fully united as one (*monos*) with the Word or Logos.

---

29. On widespread respect for the authority exercised by the church of Rome and its bishop (the pope), see Stevenson, *Creeds, Councils and Controversies*, 376–379.

30. See Stevenson, 415–417.

Justinian as emperor (527–565)

In both Egypt and Syria, religious dissent ended up becoming a vehicle for expression of local political protest. Those who were unhappy with the imperial regime used the label "Monophysite" (literally, "single nature") for themselves; in this way they appealed to the work of Cyril and his subordination of the human to the divine nature in Christ.[31] In fact, religious division added to the problems of the empire at this time. No attempt to settle the issue had any success until Justinian became emperor (527–565).[32] Justinian was a capable leader in military, cultural and religious matters. Under his rule the church in the east would be subordinated to the state far more thoroughly than was ever experienced by the church of the West; the term *caesaropapism* (affirming the "emperor" as also "pope") came to be used for this subordination of the church to the state.

Justinian supported the Chalcedonian solution.[33]

Figure 11.4. Justinian as emperor. This coin celebrates Justinian's victory over the Vandals and his reconquest of North Africa for the Byzantine Empire (ca. AD 535). Photographic reproduction from Charles Diehl (1901). *Justinien et la civilisation byzantine au VIe siècle*. Paris. Public Domain.

However, his wife Theodora had important friends among the Monophysites, and sought an end to persecution of Monophysites.[34] In an attempt to placate the latter, without undue offence to Rome, Justinian ended up interpreting the decision of Chalcedon in a Cyrillic fashion. With the

---

31. Latourette, *First Five Centuries*, 172.

32. On Justinian, see Frend, *Rise of Christianity*, 828–868; and Latourette, *First Five Centuries*, 278–284.

33. Chadwick, *Early Church*, 209.

34. On the role of Theodora, see Frend, *Rise of Christianity*, 831–832; and Latourette, *First Five Centuries*, 279.

help of his theological adviser, the monk Leontius (of Byzantium, and of Jerusalem, 485–543), he tried to break the deadlock by using Aristotelian terms to elaborate the question of two natures, speaking of a *hypostatic union* of the Word with human nature. Leontius spoke of the two natures as mingled and united in such a way that they formed only one Logos, or one hypostasis.[35] With this solution, however, the humanity of Christ was again thoroughly subordinated to the divine Logos.

The *Three Chapters*

As we have noted, the Monophysite position became a rallying cry for regional nationalism, and Monophysites increasingly represented a political threat for Justinian and the empire.[36] Especially in Egypt, Ethiopia, Armenia and Syria, Monophysites were a strong factor in distancing the people from the empire and emperor. Monophysite congregations were strengthened at this time by the itinerant preaching of Jacob Baradaeus, who became bishop of Edessa (542–578) with the support of the empress Theodora (opposing her husband on the Monophysite cause).[37]

Justinian himself took matters in hand in 544 with the edict of the *Three Chapters*, referring to three theologians connected with Antioch whose works were condemned:

1) the church historian, Theodoret of Cyrrhus, who had rejected Cyril in support of Nestorius,

2) Theodore of Mopsuestia, most important of the three, for his influence on Nestorius, and

3) Ibas of Edessa, who had also been critical of Cyril.[38]

---

35. On Leontius, see Frend, *Rise of Christianity*, 849–850.
36. On the political impact of the Monophysites, see Frend, *Rise of Christianity*, 837–848. For a more nuanced view, see his study of the Monophysites in the transition to medieval conditions in the Middle East, Frend, "Monophysites and the Transition," 339–365; and on the role of nationalism, "Nationalism as a Factor," 21–38. Frend recognizes the power of the monastic movement as fundamentally loyal to the empire, but prone to adopting popular causes which were unacceptable to authorities in Constantinople. So Frend argues that initially there was no separatist intent; and the move to accept Persian or Arab control was certainly not an aforegone conclusion ("Monophysites and the Transition," 339–340, 347 and 363–365; "Nationalism as a Factor," 36).
37. See Frend, *Rise of Christianity*, 847–848; and Latourette, *First Five Centuries*, 282–283.
38. On the "Three Chapters" see Frend, *Rise of Christianity*, 850–853; and Latourette, *First Five Centuries*, 280.

Figure 11.5. Hagia Sophia, exterior. Photo by Grzegorz Jereczek / CC BY-SA 2.0.

Figure 11.6. Justinian, Hagia Sophia and Constantinople. This mosaic located in the Hagia Sophia (southwest entrance) shows the Virgin Mary with the Christ child receiving the double offering of the cathedral (as a small model) by Emperor Justinian, and the new capital, Constantinople, as a model given by Emperor Constantine. Photo by Myrabella / CC0 1.0.

Figure 11.7. Interior of the Hagia Sophia. This painting of J. S. Sargent (1895–1925) gives some sense of the majestic scope of the cathedral church, now a museum. Photographic reproduction by SonPraises. Public Domain.

Pope Vigilius at first supported Justinian on these "Three Chapters," but later withdrew his support, for these excluded virtually any but those who took a Cyrillic interpretation of Chalcedon. And Justinian used his political authority to overrule objections from papal representatives.

The Council (553)

In 553 Justinian called the fifth ecumenical Council of Constantinople, basically to have his decree of 544 confirmed.[39] With an endorsement of the Cyrillic interpretation of Chalcedon, as it inclined to the view of Monophysites, Justinian wished to forestall the inclination of Monophysites in support of political independence in the respective regions. Not only were the "Three Chapters" condemned at this council; the theological work of Origen was also condemned as heretical.[40] Bishops of Gaul and Italy did not support Justinian in this move, however, partly because the authors condemned by him were honoured there, and they knew that these leaders

---

39. On the council, see Frend, *Rise of Christianity*, 852–853.
40. Latourette, *First Five Centuries*, 282; Frend, *Rise of Christianity*, 851.

had been respected in their own time. The pope also refused to approve the decisions of the council at first, but he was soon pressured into giving his approval.

Even so, it was not easy to find the compromise that would actually be supported by Monophysites. In this respect the Council of Constantinople failed to achieve its goal. Monophysites continued to dominate the church in Egypt and Syria. Even when persecuted within the empire, the Coptic church survived in Egypt and Ethiopia, while Jacobite followers of Baradaeus survived in Syria and in Armenia.[41] The Gregorian church also survived as a national church under the Persians.[42]

After the death of Justinian (in 565), the Roman Empire suffered major division: Italy came to be dominated by Lombards; Spain by Visigoths. Syria, Palestine and Egypt were now ruled by the Persians; and the Balkans were taken by the Slavs. Mobilized by Islam (under Muhammad, d. 632), the Arabs took Antioch (in 611), and Alexandria (by 618/19).[43] Political apathy of the Monophysites toward Constantinople was certainly a factor in these conquests.[44]

By the 620s, however, the Byzantines had reconquered much of what was lost. The Persians were defeated by Emperor Heraclius (610–642), and the eastern provinces restored to the Roman Empire under his rule. But Arabs reclaimed Damascus in 635, and both Jerusalem and Antioch were taken in 638. Alexandria fell to the Muslims in 642; the Persian Empire fell in 651. As a result, much of Asia Minor and North Africa was in Arab hands by 650. Carthage fell to the Muslims in 698; Spain was conquered by 711. Charles Martel and the Franks finally stopped the Muslim advance at Poitiers/Tours in 732. Constantinople itself resisted the attacks of 672–678 and 717–718, and would not finally fall (to Muslim Turks) until 1453.

Recent scholarly work has done much to shed light on conditions of the Syriac church in the earliest centuries under Muslim rule.[45] In part

---

41. On the sixth-century Jacobus Baradaeus, organizing the "Jacobite" church from his base in Edessa, see Jenkins, *Lost History of Christianity*, 58 and 61–62.

42. Latourette, *First Five Centuries*, 281.

43. Frend, *Rise of Christianity*, 854–856.

44. Even so, we note the cautionary approach of Frend on the transition; see note 36 above. More recent writings of M. P. Penn (*Envisioning Islam*; and *When Christians First Met Muslims*) also challenge the assumption that Christians who did not accept the Chalcedonian agreement welcomed Arab conquest of their territories. On the rise of Islam and the impact of Arab conquests, see Latourette, *First Five Centuries*, 286–291.

45. See especially Jenkins, *Lost History of Christianity*, and Isichei, *History of Christianity in Africa*, 42–44.

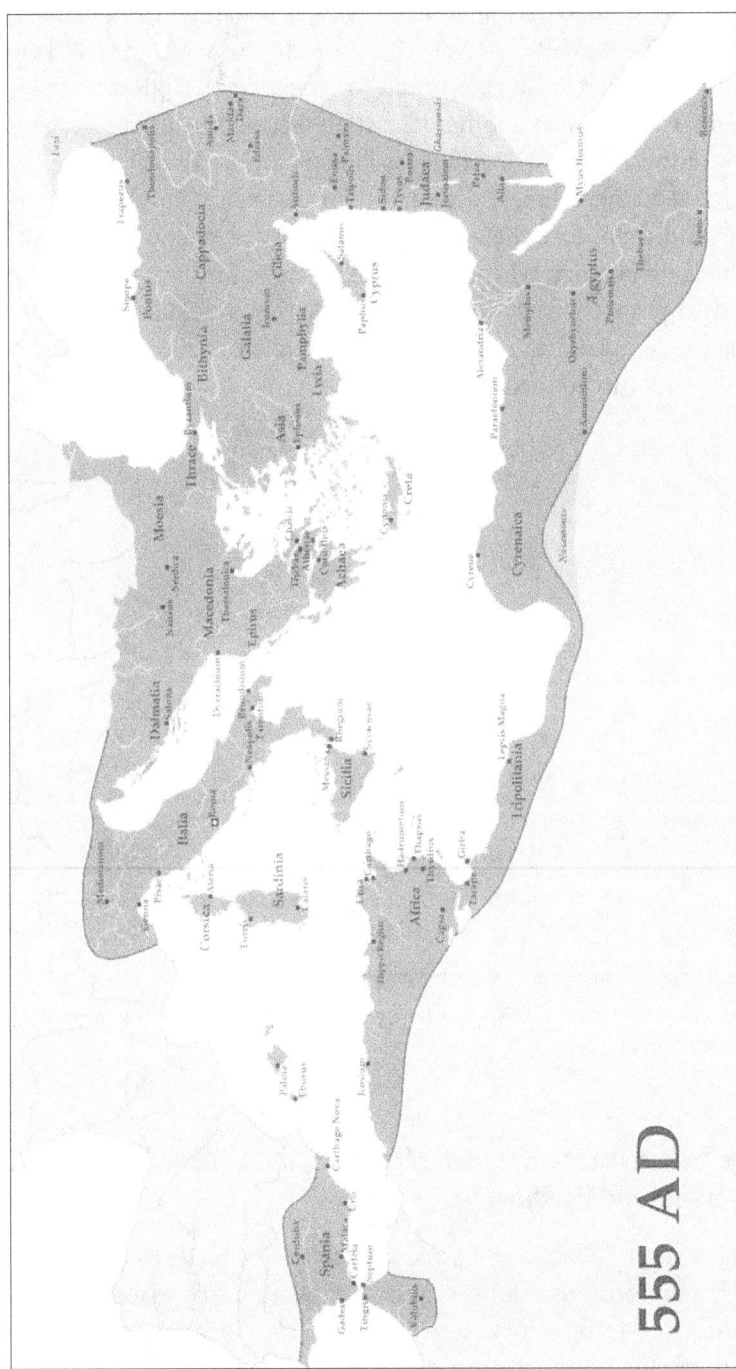

Map 11.1. Extent of the Byzantine Empire under Justinian AD 555. "The Eastern Roman Empire and its vassals" by Tatryn / CC BY-SA 3.0.

these Monophysite Christians were looking for an end to persecution by Chalcedonian "Melchite" powers. But they do not seem to have been fully aware, initially, that Arab rule would impose a new religion; they regarded the "Ishmaelites" as just another Christian faction.[46] And the Arabs initially tolerated Monophysite Christians as "People of the Book" like themselves. They charged a head tax, and valued their contribution in the civil service. The Copts did not lose their role as a majority of the population in Egypt until the tenth century, when significant waves of Muslim Arab immigration changed the proportions. Worsened conditions also resulted from the eleventh- and twelfth-century Crusades, which raised concerns about the loyalty of the Coptic community to their rulers.

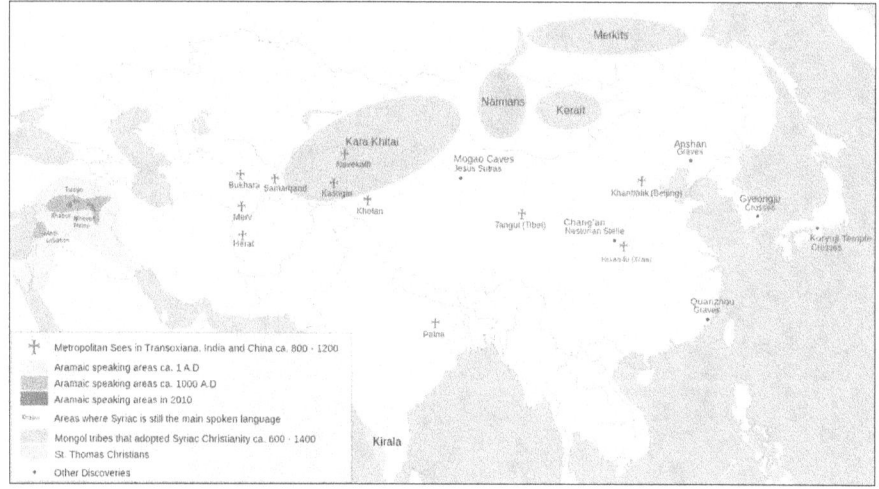

Map 11.2. Spread of Syriac Christianity to the Orient.
Map "Syriac language and Syriac Christianity in the Middle East and Asia" by Kathovo. Public Domain.

B.2. The Sixth Ecumenical Council of Constantinople (680–681): Monophysites and Monothelites

Under Emperor Heraclius renewed attempts were made to unite the empire through religion. Patriarch Sergius of Constantinople used the work of Dionysius the Areopagite in a new approach to bring the various factions closer together. Taking the Aristotelian term for "actuality" (*energeia*), he

---

46. Isichei, 43.

proposed a new understanding of the person of Christ, namely as one person performing both human and divine deeds through one divine operation, or one *energeia*. This move helped to conciliate Monophysites, but it too did not survive long, for it alienated the Roman Pope Honorius (625–638). In response, Sergius proposed a "monothelite" position, that in Christ there was only one will (*thelêma*). When the pope and two patriarchs achieved agreement on this, the emperor published an edict that forbade discussion of the *energeia* of Christ, proclaiming instead *one will*.[47]

But John IV (640–642), the next pope, condemned the *monothelite* position on Christ having but "one will."[48] And Pope Martin (649–655) also opposed it. At this time a Roman synod (of 649) affirmed two wills, human and divine, specifically to protect the complete humanity, as well as the divinity of Christ.[49] In the east, Maximus the Confessor supported this position. The emperor did not take well to this initiative, and made life pretty miserable for Maximus and for Pope Martin. As opponents of the emperor, these men were imprisoned, tortured and exiled to the Crimea. By this time, however, most of the provinces held by Monophysites were taken over by Arabs and came under Islamic control; so politically, at least, the discussion was becoming irrelevant.

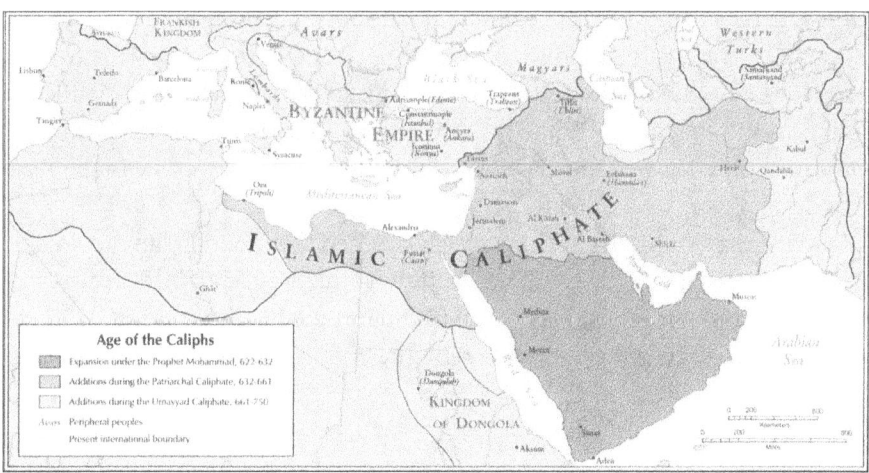

Map 11.3. Age of the Caliphs AD 622–750.
Map by Norman B. Leventhal Map Center / CC BY 2.0.

---

47. Chadwick, *East and West*, 59–60.
48. Latourette, *First Five Centuries*, 284.
49. Chadwick, *East and West*, 61.

The Council of Constantinople (680–681)

When a later emperor, Constantine IV (668–685), found himself in need of support from Italy, he tried to conciliate the current pope, Agatho (678–681), through a letter to explain the theological position taken in the east. He also decided to hold an ecumenical council in Constantinople to deal with the issue of two energies and two wills. This council, held from 680–681, affirmed the *two wills* of Christ, claiming that these wills are not contrary to one another because the human will is subject to the divine omnipotent will.[50] In this way the council would oppose the *monothelite* position, as it followed the advice of Pope Agatho and various synods of Rome that in Christ *two wills* and *two energies* were to be affirmed.[51]

The affirmation of a human will of Christ was also meant to affirm the *true freedom* of Jesus Christ, as a human being. Affirmation of a full human nature meant repudiation of any notion of the human Christ as no more than a passive tool of the divine Logos. In this respect the life of Christ would provide a model for the life of the Christian. Through faith, the divine will should work through the human will, not at its expense. In this way the decision of Constantinople completed the work of Chalcedon.

It should be noted that at this council, once again, the western explanations were taken as definitive. The council did, however, demonstrate the growing distance between east and west, for both regions of the empire (or what was left of it) were beleaguered at this time. Further distance was revealed in distinctive practices in the church. While bishops were unmarried in either sector, the eastern church allowed the marriage of priests and deacons, while in the West marriage of clergy was already being discouraged.[52]

Maronite Christians in Lebanon maintained the monothelite theological position into the twelfth century, when they finally accepted the decision of Rome. Monophysites and Nestorians also continued to live independently in the Arab world for many centuries. By the eighth century, however, Arians had disappeared.[53]

---

50. Chadwick, *East and West*, 64–65.

51. Latourette, *First Five Centuries*, 285.

52. Chadwick, *East and West*, 68. The rift between East and West continued to grow. The decision of the eastern council (of 692), allowing marriage for deacons and presbyters, was not accepted in the West. One of the later popes did sign his consent to this decision, but only in a qualified manner.

53. Latourette, *First Five Centuries*, 285.

B.3. The Seventh Council at Nicea (787)

The eighth-century Byzantine Emperor Leo III (717–740) gave new life to the empire. Leo appeared to respect the relative independence of the church in theological matters by affirming that the "material" realm would be under his own care, while the church should restrict its concern to "spiritual" affairs. Even so, his initiative in removing use of icons in worship was clearly received as a move to take control of the church as well.[54] His approach may well have been inspired by the Judaic ban on representation of God (from the second commandment), or the Islamic ban on representation of the human being. Indeed, early in the 720s, Muslim caliphs had proclaimed a strict prohibition against showing religious images in the churches under their control.[55]

Iconoclasm

Leo first forbade use of icons in public worship in 725. Among the common people and in monastic circles many resisted this move. Throughout the eastern empire, icons were venerated in homes and chapels. Destruction of beloved icons of Christ even caused riots.[56]

In the West, depictions of Christ, Mary and the saints were used as a means of instructing the illiterate in faith. A synod of Rome excommunicated the opponents of icons (731), and the popes condemned the "iconoclasts" (i.e. those destroying icons). In fact, by this time the papacy itself was dependent for political support primarily on Frankish rulers. In response, Leo's son, Emperor Constantine V called a council in Constantinople to enforce the edict condemning use of icons and denouncing what he called "adoration of the creature." But the church, and certainly its western part, was not well represented at this assembly (of 753/4). As a result, this council has not been accepted as an *ecumenical* council.

The Council of 787

A resolution finally came when Constantine V died in 780, and was succeeded by his son Constantine VI (780–797). At this point the widow Empress Irina influenced her son to remove the policy against icons, which he did.[57] After

---

54. Chadwick, *East and West*, 72.
55. Jenkins, *Lost History of Christianity*, 191.
56. On the iconoclast controversy, see Latourette, *First Five Centuries*, 292–297; and Chadwick, *East and West*, 71–82.
57. On the role of the empress, see Chadwick, *East and West*, 80; and Latourette, *First Five Centuries*, 296.

promoting Tarasius to the patriarchate, Constantine VI called the Council of Nicea in 787 to establish the rites connected with icons. Tarasius presided at this council and the Roman pope was represented.

The council endorsed the "veneration" of icons, insisting that true worship is reserved for the divine nature. Honour given to icons, or images, is meant only for that which is represented by the image, namely Christ in his humanity, (the human) Mary, or the saints, and for the historical aspects of gospel or Old Testament events.

Figure 11.8. The Council of Nicea (787). This 11th-century miniature, taken from the *Menologion* of the Byzantine ruler Basil II (976–1025), portrays the Council with Emperor Constantine VI in a central position, presiding over the decision to endorse use of icons. The prostrate figure represents one of the bishops begging forgiveness for defending iconoclasm. The *Menologion* is a liturgical calendar with short descriptions of saints to be remembered on specific days. Photographic reproduction from DigiVatLib "Menologion of Basil." Public Domain.

John of Damascus and Theodore of Studius

Those who supported the use of icons were inspired by an appreciation of the historical reality of the embodied human Christ. Outstanding among them was John of Damascus (ca. 700–753), the son of a Christian holding a high rank in the civil service under Islamic rule.[58] He later became a monk, and wrote a compendium of Christian teaching, the *Fountain of Knowledge*.[59] Clear and

---

58. Chadwick, *East and West*, 72.
59. Latourette, *First Five Centuries*, 291–292.

well-written, it would be considered a classic of patristic writings in the East. When it was translated into Latin in the twelfth century it became influential in the West as well. Also important for supporting the ongoing use of icons was Theodore of Studius, who became famous for the reform of the monastery in Constantinople, to which he gave his *Rule*.[60]

Thus icons were approved, and their role in worship regulated; they were not to be presented in sculpted form (as was later accepted in the West).[61] Those opposed to images were said to be Hellenizers, or Origenists; perhaps they were thought to represent the views of Monophysites, denying the reality of the incarnation, the true humanity of Christ. In honour of this decision, the first Sunday of Lent came to be celebrated as the "Triumph of Orthodoxy."

This was indeed a battle won by monks, who wanted to see restrictions on the dominance of the emperor over the church. To address the matter, Tarasius affirmed a significant policy on the church and state, that the church should be supreme in dogmatic discussions, while the state would retain its authority in ecclesiastical law and administration. Other decisions reached at this council include the rejection of the role of lay persons in the appointment of bishops, and support for an annual synod to be held in each province.

To conclude, it is certainly clear from our discussion of these councils that no decision on important matters in the church was taken hurriedly. Every position on an issue was thoroughly discussed. And eventually the Christian church would maintain its own authoritative role in determining teachings in accordance with the Scriptures and the traditions established in the earliest years of Christianity.

Chapter Appendix 11.1

Summary of the First Seven Ecumenical Councils

1. **Council of Nicea** (AD 325) – Repudiating the Arian view of Jesus as subordinate to the Father, this council affirmed the Son as identical in divine substance (*homoousios*) with the Father.

---

60. Latourette, 295. Theodore would suffer greatly in the ninth-century revival of iconoclasm when he opposed Emperor Leo V in religious matters (Chadwick, *East and West*, 82; and Latourette, *First Five Centuries*, 296).

61. In the West, the Franks did not understand this issue as it concerned the eastern churches, and forbade the veneration of icons. Western Christianity did not accept the decisions of this seventh ecumenical council until the eleventh century; see Chadwick, *East and West*, 82.

2. **Second Ecumenical Council of Constantinople** (381) – Along with an affirmation of the Nicene position on the relationship of Father and Son (the *homoousion*), this council affirmed a Trinitarian (threefold) distinction of divine persons, as three hypostases, or three distinct modes of being, for one identical divine essence.

3. **Council of Ephesus** (431) – This council affirmed the Lord Jesus Christ as both fully divine and fully human, two natures united in one person. Mary was assigned the title *Theotokos*, as the one who "bore God," thereby affirming the divine nature of the child to whom she gave birth.

4. **Council of Chalcedon** (451) – Jesus was affirmed as one person (one *hypostatic* union) with two natures (human and divine). But these two natures are not confused, not mixed, and not changed; nor are they divided, or separable.

5. **Fifth Ecumenical Council of Constantinople** (553) – Called by Emperor Justinian this ecumenical council confirmed his edict of 544, the *Three Chapters*, which condemned three theologians connected with the school of theology of Antioch: (1) Theodoret of Cyrrhus, who rejected Cyril of Alexandria in support of Nestorius; (2) Theodore of Mopsuestia, for his influence on Nestorius, and (3) Ibas of Edessa, who was also critical of Cyril.

6. **Sixth Ecumenical Council of Constantinople** (680–681) – In opposing Monophysites and Monothelites, and affirming the true humanity of Christ, the council affirmed *two wills*, human and divine, for Christ. It also affirmed these wills as not contrary to one another, for the human will is subject to the divine omnipotent will.

7. **Seventh Council of Nicea** (787) – This council endorsed the "veneration" of icons (images), as these represent what is human and historical; true worship is reserved for the divine nature.

Chapter Appendix 11.2

Obstacles in Understanding the Early Councils

Discussion of the seven ecumenical councils of early Christianity can pose serious difficulties for both Christian and Muslim students, especially in a context where little philosophy is taught, because many key terms in the theological debates had their roots in philosophy. So the issues almost inevitably assume some acquaintance with philosophical terminology and philosophical ways of thinking. For Muslims there is another hurdle. These councils represent the early Christian church making decisions on the deity of Christ and the Trinitarian nature of God, two crucial theological positions on which the Qur'an clearly expresses objection. Just as Judaism takes the *Shema* as fundamental, "Hear O Israel, the Lord your God, the Lord is one" (Deut 4:6), Islam has the *shahada*, "There is no God but Allah, and Muhammad is his prophet."

The Deity of Jesus

The Qur'an bestows great honour on Jesus when it refers to him as "Word of Allah," and a messenger from God.[62] Jesus is also recognized for a mediating role,[63] for he is described as an outstanding personality in this world and the hereafter; he is the son of Mary, but "close to Allah" and one of those "brought near" (Family of Imran 3:44). Acknowledging his special birth, sinlessness, miracles, ascent to heaven, and return in judgement, Jesus is regarded as a *prophet*. Indeed, Islam acknowledges characteristics of Jesus which it does not ascribe to Muhammad. Mary is highly respected as the mother of Jesus; his birth is recognized as miraculous, and his conception through divine inspiration "of Our own spirit" (Prophets 21:91; Cow 2:253). The account clearly assigns a role for a "holy spirit" breathed in at his conception.

Even so, the Christian belief that Jesus is both truly human and truly divine poses real difficulties. Muslims ask how the creature can be joined to the Creator? It is like a slave becoming a lord. But Islamic understanding of the incarnation would assume Jesus as God's son on a human analogy (with God as father and Mary as mother). So the question arises: can Allah have a son without a consort (Cattle 6:100–101)? Attributing fatherhood to Allah may be thought to imply that God is incomplete without his son, since he becomes a "father" only with the birth of a son. Speaking of God thus is thought to attribute creaturely life to the Creator, which is blasphemous (Mary 19:35). So Muslims do not accept the incarnation: *God cannot have a son.*

---

62. The term *al-Masih* is probably a derivative of the Hebrew for Messiah, *Christos* in Greek, meaning "the anointed one" (Women 4:170–171; Cow 2:253; Family of Imran 3:49).

63. That mediating role does not recognize his crucifixion and death as atonement for sin; with Docetists and Gnostics, the Qur'an denies Jesus's actual suffering, teaching that Jesus only *appeared* to have died on the cross (see ch. 8, §A.2, and notes 45 and 47). The report of his death is said to reflect boasting of Jews (Women 4:157).

Dynamic Monarchianism, Adoptionism and Arianism

This is also the reason why Muslims more readily accept the "adoptionist" approach (also called "dynamic monarchianism") as a subordinationist answer to the charge of Christians accepting "two Gods." Adoptionism stressed the human character of Jesus, born miraculously of the Virgin Mary, and later becoming the Son of God when the Spirit (the "Christ") came upon him at baptism. It relegated Jesus to the inferior role of a son – not by nature, but by adoption and through merit.

But we have seen that this attempt to protect divine unity was soundly rejected by local church councils. Theodotus of Rome was excommunicated for holding this position (ca. 195). When Paul of Samosata (bishop of Antioch, 260–272) taught a similar position seventy years later, the synod of Antioch condemned and excommunicated him (269); he nonetheless influenced Lucian of Antioch (d. 312), who in turn influenced Arius of Alexandria. This was the issue which precipitated the first ecumenical Council of Nicea.

Arius regarded Jesus as a very special person, but not fully divine. Jesus had a human body, but the Logos took the place of the human soul. Although such an attempt to protect the unity of God may resonate with Muslims, Arius's accent on the subordination of the Son was unacceptable for the Christian church. The council affirmed that as Son of God, Jesus is the image and likeness of the Father, and begotten from eternity. All that can be attributed to the Father, also belongs to the Son. The Nicene council was serious in its use of the term "equal in substance" (*homoousion*) to exclude the position of Arius.

The Triune God

Agreement on the Trinity came with the affirmation of the full deity of the Holy Spirit at the Council of Constantinople (381); this church gathering affirmed one identical divine essence, or one eternal and uncreated being in three distinct, yet also interpenetrating consubstantial beings. For Muslims, the "triune" nature of God is as problematic as the deity of the Son; as we have seen, however, this is the settled teaching of the church after the first four ecumenical councils.

Numerous passages in the Qur'an reflect the unacceptability of God as "three in one," and also appear to understand a role for Mary in the Triune God (Table Spread 5:73 and 116; Cattle 6:100–101; Women 4:171). Indeed, the Christian understanding of the Trinity (Father, Son, and Holy Spirit) does not speak of three gods; nor does it recognize Mary as a (third) member of the Trinity. In this connection it is important to recognize that the specific Trinitarian understanding to which the Qur'an objects (Table Spread 5:73, and 116; Cattle 6:101) is not the orthodox Christian expression. It is possible that Muhammad was responding to a Christian group like the Maryamiyya sect, who accepted a counterfeit Trinity which included the Father, Mary and Jesus. Adherents of this view were opposed and excommunicated by Christian authorities by the end of the seventh century.

We know that Christians of the Middle East did give considerable attention to Mary as "mother of God" already at the time of the third ecumenical council (Ephesus, 431). This was in response to Nestorius, the patriarch of Constantinople, applying only the title *Christotokos* (the one who gave birth to the Christ) for Mary, on the assumption that calling her *Theotokos* would undermine Christ's humanity. It is clear that, for Muslims, assigning Mary the title *Christotokos* would not be problematic, as it simply designates her as the one who bore the Messiah; speaking of her as *Theotokos*, however, is quite unacceptable, as it affirms the divine nature of the child she bore.

The Council of Ephesus upheld use of the title *Theotokos* for Mary (as the one who gave birth to God); Nestorius was condemned. The issue of the divine and human aspects of Jesus's person was revisited at the Council of Chalcedon (451), which gave a more evenhanded judgement, but did not reverse the condemnation of Nestorius. Nestorianism survived in the Persian Empire, and also in Syria. By the seventh century it reached China. Even today, Nestorian churches survive in Turkey near Iran, and in India.

Historical encounters: Judaism, Christianity and Early Islam
Muhammad (who died in 632) initially took a positive approach to Christianity and Judaism; Mecca was familiar with Jewish tribes and Christians visiting from East Africa. When Muhammad's followers were persecuted in the early years, Christians protected and kept them safe in Ethiopia. Consideration of the relative origins of parts of the Qur'an shows that sections written earlier, recognizing Christians as monotheist, do not denounce them as infidels (Family of Imran 3:113–114; Spider 29:46). Muhammad realized that, as "people of the book," Jews and Christians have valid revelations of their own. This is why they would not be asked to convert; and the Qur'an affirms that in matters of faith there is to be no coercion (Cow 2:256). But hostilities emerged even before Muhammad died, and the Qur'an reflects critique of the Christian Trinity (for assigning God partners and threatening divine unity); so we also find harsh criticism of Christians as polytheistic.

Muhammad had clearly anticipated cooperation from the Jewish tribes, and adopted their practice of communal prayers (on Friday), and fasting on the Day of Atonement. And friendly Jews informed him about biblical accounts.

The turning point came when Muhammad recognized the theological divide between Jews and Christians, and realized that Jews would not accept him as their prophet. Hostility intensified after the siege of Medina in 627, as Muslims routed Meccans with a ditch around Medina. Muhammad felt betrayed by the alliance of Jewish tribes with Meccan clans to oppose him, and punished the Jews. Expelled from Medina, they were massacred without mercy. During *salat* Muhammad would now direct prayers to Mecca, not to Jerusalem, showing an intent to revert to the monotheism of Abraham (Cattle 6:159 and 161). From this time a polemical note characterizes reference to Jews in the Qur'an (Table Spread 5:82). Jews, in turn, ridiculed Muhammad's version of the stories of Noah and Moses.

What then of contact with Christians? Which branches of Christianity could Muhammad have encountered? We know of Muhammad's high regard for monks. He visited some of the monasteries in Syria during the course of his travels in the area.[64] Aside from contact with other Syrian Christians, Muhammad would certainly have met Christians throughout Arabia (especially in the Najran region of Yemen);[65] and his followers taking refuge in Ethiopia reflect acquaintance with Christians there.[66] There are also reports of dialogue of a Christian leader and his companions with Muhammad in Medina.[67]

Muhammad would certainly have encountered Monophysites who did not fully accept the human nature of Christ, insisting on one fully divine nature, with the divine encompassing the human. After all, Monophysites dominated Ethiopia, Egypt, and Syria at the time of Justinian (d. 565). Political tension between Monophysite groups and Constantinople (after the council of 553) was clearly a factor in the speed with which Arabs were able to take Antioch, Jerusalem, Alexandria and Damascus between 611 and 635.

Monophysites continued to live independently in the Arab world for many centuries, as did Nestorians. A new problem arose with Monothelites (from ca. 638), who affirmed *one will* in Christ (the divine encompassing the human). Also known as Maronites, they lived in Lebanon into the twelfth century. Even aside from issues of dating, it is difficult to think of these groups as significant for Christian views that may have had an influence on Muhammad (d. 632), for he would certainly have distanced himself from their high view of the

---

64. On Muhammad's encounter with the Syrian monk Bahira when he was traveling on trade missions with his uncle Abu-Talib, see Kenny, *Early Islam*, 12–13. See also the Qur'an, Table Spread 5:82–83.

65. See the Qur'an, Family of Imran 3:61.

66. See Kenny, *Early Islam*, 31.

67. Kenny, 117.

divinity of Christ. But it is possible that Qur'anic emphasis on Mary as "mother of Jesus" reflects Nestorian disdain for the "Cyrillian" recognition of Mary as "mother of God."

Did Muhammad encounter a specific sect, or group of Judaized Christians? Scholars are not agreed on the matter, and it is difficult to trace the precise origins of earliest Muslim reaction to Christianity. At the time, Judaeo-Christians were called *nasara* by the Arabs, a designation derived from the Aramaic *nasraya*. Judaeo-Christians accepted the Torah, the Psalms and a gospel revealed to Jesus and given to their leader.[68] Such groups may well have been sensitive to the Jewish charge of "two Gods," and de-emphasized Jesus's divine character. While some groups of Judaeo-Christians denied Jesus's divinity, his virgin birth and atoning death on the cross, most considered Jesus as a prophet foretold by Moses, who fulfilled and reformed the Jewish law and was exalted as a Son of God at his baptism. Such an approach recalls elements of the Arian and adoptionist position. As noted above, it was an interpretation of Jesus's deity which Muslims could accept; indeed, similar ideas are contained in the Qur'an.

Conclusions

While the first seven ecumenical councils are undoubtedly critical for understanding the history of Christianity, and decisions taken at these early church gatherings remained a bedrock for Christian belief throughout the ages, we have noted various obstacles for Muslim understanding of those decisions. While Christians achieved a resounding affirmation on the deity of Christ and the Trinitarian nature of God, Muslims refuse to consider Jesus as truly divine, and cannot understand how God might be "three in one."

Clear recognition of differences that remain constitutes an important step toward mutual understanding; but it is important that these differences be rooted in actual positions of the Christian faith. We noted some misunderstanding among Muslims of the Trinity, as one involving God the Father, Mary as mother and Jesus as a child of this union. It is important that any disagreement should be based on the actual Christian position of "three persons in one God" (God

---

68. Identifying the leader as Elxai, Kenny identifies the group with Elkesaites (*Early Islam*, 5); on this group of Judaeo-Christians, see the introduction to ch. 2, and ch. 2, §A.4, especially notes 19 and 20.

the Father, the Son and Holy Spirit), and "one in three."[69] Where there are misconceptions or false stereotypes, these need to be cleared away.

Mary was clearly Jesus's human mother; the "fatherhood" of God needs careful explanation to differentiate this from human understanding of a father/son relationship. We need to remember, as Origen pointed out, that the divine father/son relationship existed from all eternity. Similarly, the Trinitarian nature of God as "one in three" and "three in one" needs to be differentiated from human understanding of number. The Son shares fully in the divine nature of God, yet remains truly distinct in that he is "begotten" and has his own role. So also the Holy Spirit shares fully in the divine nature, but has a distinct role in being sent forth to dwell in God's creation, and his creatures. Finally, we have to confess the mystery, and recognize that our explanations cannot really plumb the depths of that mystery. With Augustine, we recognize that our attempts to explain the matter are useful primarily to guard against false understanding of God, as Father, Son and Holy Spirit.[70]

Differences on the deity of Christ remains another obstacle. On this matter, it is important that Muslims recognize the solid rejection by various church councils of the adoptionist position of his deity. Accepting the reality of the crucifixion, death and resurrection of Jesus, Christianity teaches that only a divine person can accomplish what he did; as true God he was pure and sinless, and was able to overcome death. But the reason for his coming was precisely that he would suffer on behalf of fallen humanity. So it was important that Jesus also be truly human, and that he take on our frail humanity, our sin, and death.

We recognize the great importance of the early councils, and realize that their special contribution in the history of Christianity is all too often ignored or misunderstood. They represent the only occasions on which the entire church, east and west, was able to meet and achieve a degree of unanimity on important issues. For this reason the decisions arrived at, typically after decades of discussion, carry an authority quite unlike decisions of any later Christian councils.

At the same time we note that the important decisions of the great ecumenical councils on the two natures of Christ and the triune character of God were achieved over a number of centuries that predate the rise of

---

69. One of the best attempts to clear up misunderstanding on the Trinity and give convincing arguments that acceptance of the Trinity does not imply a rejection of monotheism, is given in Volf, "Allah and the Trinity," 20–24.

70. In spite of his voluminous treatment of the issue in the *De Trinitate*, Augustine confesses that he is faced with a mystery, and discusses it at length only because he cannot remain silent in the face of erroneous positions (see *De Trin.* 1. 3.5–6; and 5. 1.1–2).

Islam. Only discussion of icons at the seventh (and last) ecumenical council (AD 787) was affected by the Islamic ban on human representation, although Judaism had also banned representation of God as idolatry (based on the second commandment). These are the reasons why the chapters devoted to the seven ecumenical councils provide such an important link for understanding Christianity throughout the ages, and why careful study of early Christianity is essential for constructive Muslim-Christian dialogue.

Questions for Discussion and Review

The Person of Jesus: Five Ecumenical Councils (AD 431–787)

The Councils of Ephesus (431) and Chalcedon (451): On the Human and Divine Natures of Christ

1. How does the understanding of the person of Jesus Christ which was accepted at the Council of Nicea differ from that of subsequent councils?

2. Why is the question regarding the relationship between the human and divine aspects of the person of Jesus Christ important?

3. Which different views of the person of Jesus Christ had developed during the fourth century in the western empire, in Alexandria and Antioch?

4. How did Apollinaris understand the relationship of the divine and human aspects of Jesus Christ? Are his views comparable to those of Arius? How do they differ? Explain why the Council of Constantinople rejected them.

5. How did the Antiochian school of thought respond to the Alexandrian position? How did Diodorus explain the relationship between the human and divine aspects of the person of Jesus Christ?

6. Why were Christians of Constantinople upset with Nestorius? Why did he use the term *Christotokos* for Mary? Was he justified in such use? What was the weakness of his position?

7. What were Cyril's intentions in affirming Mary as *Theotokos*? Did his position on the divinity and humanity of Christ truly improve on the position of Apollinaris?

8. What was accomplished at the Council of Ephesus (431)? What were the consequences for Nestorius and his supporters? On what basis was Cyril reinstated?

9. How did Eutyches help Diodorus elaborate the position of Cyril? Why was this position not considered acceptable by Flavian of Constantinople?

10. What did Dioscuros attempt to accomplish? What actually happened at the "robbers" synod of Ephesus (449)? Why were the efforts of Dioscuros not successful?

11. How did Pope Leo attempt to mediate the positions of Flavian and Dioscuros? How would you describe the role of the Roman pope in the Council of Chalcedon? What was the effect of his *Tome* on the decision accomplished?

12. What are the strengths and weaknesses of the decision achieved at the Council of Chalcedon?

The Last Three Ecumenical Councils: Monophysites, Monothelites, and Iconoclasm

1. How do Monophysites regard the relationship of the divine and the human nature of Christ?

2. Which factors made it more difficult to resolve theological issues at this time?

3. What are the "Three Chapters" of the edict of Justinian (544)? Why was it imperative for Justinian to address concerns of Monophysites? How would this edict help Justinian to resolve the concerns of the Monophysites?

4. What was Justinian trying to accomplish in calling the Council of Constantinople in 553? How would you describe the role of the emperor at this council?

5. The issue of Monophysites was never adequately resolved; how did this impact the rule of Justinian?

6. What new issues arose in christological discussion after the Council of Constantinople?

7. What approach did Heraclius and the Patriarch of Constantinople use to bring the various factions closer together? Were they successful?

8. Why was Pope Martin so insistent on maintaining "two wills" for Christ, even at the expense of his own position and comfort?

9. Why was Emperor Constantine IV willing to reconsider the issue of the "single will" of Christ?

10. What was the role of Pope Agatho at the Council of Constantinople (680)?

11. In what sense can the Council of Constantinople in 680 be said to complete the work of Chalcedon in 451?

12. What factors motivated Emperor Leo in forbidding the use of icons in 725?

13. Which factors led to reconsideration of Leo's edict? What was the role of the widow empress in changing the policy on the role of icons?

14. What was the role of Tarasius at the council of 787? Which decisions were achieved, and how were these motivated?

15. What implications for state-church relationships emerged from this seventh council?

Further Reading

Dvornik, F. *The General Councils of the Church*. London: Burns & Oates, 1961.
Frend, W. H. C. "Nationalism as a Factor in Anti-Chalcedonian Feeling in Egypt." In *Religion and National Identity: Studies in Church History* 18, edited by Stuart Mews, 21–38. Oxford: Blackwell, 1982.
———. *The Rise of the Monophysite Movement*. Philadelphia: Augsburg Fortress, 1972.
Kelly, J. N. D. *Early Christian Doctrines*. San Francisco: Harper & Row, 1978 (1960).
McGuckin, J. A. *St Cyril of Alexandria: The Christological Controversy*. Leiden: Brill, 1994.
Norris, R. A., ed. *The Christological Controversy*. Philadelphia: Fortress, 1980.
Pelikan, J. *The Emergence of the Catholic Tradition (100–600)*. The Christian Tradition: A History of the Development of Doctrine 1. Chicago: University of Chicago Press, 1971.
Quasten, J. *Patrology*. 3 vols. Utrecht and Antwerp: Spectrum; Westminster MD: Newman Press, 1962–1964.
Sahas, D. J. *Icon and Logos: Sources of Eighth-Century Iconoclasm*. Toronto: University of Toronto Press, 1986.
———. *John of Damascus on Islam*. Leiden: Brill, 1972.
Stevenson, J. *Creeds, Councils and Controversies: Documents Illustrative of the History of the Church AD 337–461*. Revised by W. H. C. Frend. London: SPCK, 2012.
———. *A New Eusebius: Documents Illustrating the History of the Church to AD 337*. Revised by W. H. C. Frend. London: SPCK, 1987.
Widdicombe, P. *The Fatherhood of God from Origen to Athanasius*. Oxford: Clarendon Press, 1994.
Wiles, M. F. *The Christian Fathers*. London: Hodder, 1968.
Young, Frances W. *From Nicaea to Chalcedon: A Guide to the Literature and Its Background*. London: SCM, 1983.

12

The Golden Age of Early Christian Thought

Outstanding Fourth-Century Leaders

Somehow I flung myself down under a fig tree, and gave free rein to my tears.... "And thou, O Lord, how long?"... These were the words I spoke, as with a contrite and despondent spirit I wept within my heart. Suddenly from a nearby house I heard a voice like that of a boy or girl, I know not which, chanting and repeating over and over, "Take up and read. Take up and read." Instantly my feelings altered, as I began to reflect intently on the games of children, trying to remember whether I had ever heard them use such an expression, but I could not recall hearing it before. Checking the flow of tears, I got up, for I interpreted the words as no less than a divine command to open the Scripture, and read the first chapter I should come across. For I had heard how Anthony had been inspired by a reading from the gospel when he happened to attend a church service, and applied the words to himself: "Go and sell what you have and give it to the poor, and you shall have treasure in heaven, and come follow me [Matt 19:21]." By those words he was immediately converted to you.

So I hurried back to the bench where Alypius was sitting, for there I had left the copy of the letters of the apostle. I now snatched it up, opened it, and read in silence the first passage on which my eyes fell: "Not in orgies of drunkenness, not in sexual immorality and impurity, not in quarreling and envy; but clothe yourselves in the Lord Jesus Christ, and do not think about how to gratify the desire of the sinful nature." I had no need or wish to read on. As soon as I came to the end of this sentence, it seemed as if a stream of peaceful light entered my heart, and all the dark shadows of doubt fled away.

Augustine, *Confessions* 8.12.28–29

This famous passage from Augustine's *Confessions* marks the turning point in his life, his conversion to Catholic Christianity.[1] It came at a time when he enjoyed considerable fame in public life, for he was at the pinnacle of a brilliant career as teacher of rhetoric and court orator in Milan. But it was also a period of increasing inner tension and unhappiness. Old certainties had fallen away, but he could not make the transition to new convictions. Disillusioned with Manichean thought, he was finally ready to abandon the Manichean friends who had helped him to advance in his career. A degree of enchantment with mystical Neoplatonism had helped make the Christian faith more palatable. And the preaching of Ambrose had shown him how to resolve serious obstacles in understanding the Scriptures. He had come to accept Christian beliefs, first heard from his mother, Monica. But what of his personal life? Could he give up the concubine with whom he had shared many years, who had given him a wonderful son, Adeodatus? Could he give up marriage altogether, as challenged by Anthony? Such was the impact of Athanasius's *Life of Anthony* in the western empire at this time.

So it came about that one afternoon, in a state of emotional turmoil and remorse for the life he had led, Augustine entered the enclosed garden of his home in Milan, and wept bitter tears. Suddenly he heard a child's voice, *Tolle lege*! ("Take up and read!") Following the example of Anthony, whose command from God had come at an unexpected moment, and in an unexpected manner, Augustine took a daring approach, and opened up the letters of Paul in a random way. God could speak to him in that way too! As he opened the Scriptures, Augustine discovered the passage of Romans 13:11–14, encouraging him to leave behind a life of sexual immorality, and take upon himself the pattern of the Lord Jesus Christ – with no further thought of gratifying the desire of the "flesh," the natural human inclination. This was the passage which finally brought Augustine to new conviction, leading him to "cast off the works of darkness," and deny himself, especially in the demands of the body, to leave behind his old life and seek baptism. There was no turning back.

---

1. Stevenson, *Creeds, Councils and Controversies*, 247–248.

Augustine's life and work receives more extensive treatment below,[2] and at this point we note only a few of the immediate consequences from Augustine's conversion. He abandoned his profession as orator, and joined family members and friends in retreat at Cassiciacum, an estate not far from the city. There he immersed himself in devotional and theological literature, and began serious study of the Scriptures. Together with his son Adeodatus, Augustine was baptized by Ambrose in the spring of 387.[3]

Augustine's masterful telling of the event has assured the account of becoming the most well-known conversion story of early Christianity. In fact, the *Confessions* as such became one of the most beloved autobiographical accounts of Christian struggle to understand and put the faith into practice. Yet it is only one of a number of high-profile conversions to Christianity in the fourth century, a period of truly momentous change and new beginnings in the life of the Christian church, and one known for its ample share of brilliant writers, thinkers and leaders. When the century opened, persecution had been among the most fierce ever endured by the church. But with Constantine as ruler of the empire, that had all changed. Persecution targeted at Christians and the Christian church stopped.

Closely connected with this period of transition are the church historian also known for his encomium in praise of Constantine, Eusebius of Caesarea (ca. 260–340), and Lactantius (250–320), who wrote the *Institutes* and *On the Deaths of the Persecutors*. The latter work recognized and celebrated God's providence in protecting the church through a dangerous period, and raising up a Christian emperor. The present chapter will focus on the life and work of other significant leaders who helped shape Christianity in the fourth and early fifth centuries. In so doing we recognize that these theologians built on the work of the earlier periods, the foundations laid by Justin Martyr, Clement of Alexandria, Tertullian, Irenaeus, as well as Origen.

We also note the many important leaders who, like Lactantius, came from (north) Africa. It is clear enough that African thinkers made a significant contribution to the positions established for Christianity in this era. Just as the North African theologians Clement of Alexandria, Tertullian and Origen were significant for apologetics and the response to Gnosticism, so also Athanasius, Cyril of Alexandria and Augustine made an important contribution in establishing Trinitarian Christian thought, especially through their response to Arianism and other problematic groups. In summarizing their contribution,

---

2. See §D.3 below.
3. Latourette, *First Five Centuries*, 174.

it is helpful to distinguish the geographical locations and schools of thought with which they were most closely associated: Alexandrian, Cappadocian, Antiochene and finally the Latin (or western).

A. Alexandrian Theology

The Alexandrian school of theology can be traced back to Pantaenus, Clement and Origen. We have already noted the contribution of Clement of Alexandria in the second century with his understanding of both the Old Testament and Greek philosophical culture as parallel approaches in preparing the way for the New Testament (the *praeparatio evangelica*).[4] Origen also made a major contribution to Nicene theology by insisting that the "generation" of Christ, as God's Son, represented an eternal, or timeless process.[5] Although some speculative aspects of Origen's thought would remain controversial, and later adherents had to clarify the distinction between the human and divine elements in the double nature of Christ Jesus, Origen's stature in the Alexandrian tradition of theological reflection was unsurpassed.

A.1. Athanasius (ca. 295–373)

With Alexander, the bishop of Alexandria, Athanasius had attended the Nicene council of 325; when Alexander died in 328, Athanasius succeeded him as bishop. But his staunch defence of the Nicene affirmation, in collaboration with the Cappadocian Fathers, caused Athanasius considerable grief once the Arians returned from exile and tried to undermine his authority. He was frequently accused on trumped-up charges, like meddling in politics, and interfering with the supply of grain for the imperial capital, a serious charge.[6] Arian elements at court in Constantinople saw to it that he was exiled on numerous occasions during his forty years as bishop of Alexandria.[7] Only the last ten years of his life were relatively peaceful.

---

4. See ch. 8, §B.2; and for his contribution on Logos theology, ch. 10, §A.3.

5. See ch. 10, §A.3.

6. On Athanasius, see Frend, *Rise of Christianity*, 532–528 and 530–531. On Athanasius's role in these controversies, see also Latourette, *First Five Centuries*, 157–160.

7. See Stevenson, *Creeds, Councils and Controversies*, 1–2, for a letter on his behalf (preserved in Socrates's history), written by Emperor Constantine II to the church in Alexandria; Constantine II announces Athanasius's return to that city (in 337) from a period of exile in the western part of the empire. See also Stevenson, *Creeds, Councils and Controversies*, 39–41, for a letter of Athanasius on a later arrest (AD 356).

Athanasius wrote a number of valuable works against the Arians: the *Discourses*, the *History of the Arians*, *Apology against Arians*, and *The Decree of the Nicene Synod*. These writings are characterized by a pastoral and exegetical approach. As we have noted, his favourite text was 2 Peter 1:4, "[H]e has given us his very great and precious promises so that through them you may participate in the divine nature and escape the corruption in the world caused by evil desires."[8] In an important theological treatise, *On the Incarnation*, Athanasius accented the approach of Irenaeus, "He became human that we might become divine; He revealed himself in a body that we might see the invisible Father; He endured human insults that we might inherit immortality."[9]

During the various periods of exile Athanasius enjoyed the support of local monks. In gratitude for their help he wrote the treatise on the *Life of Anthony*. Appreciated as a popular statement of the monastic life, it greatly influenced the spread of monasticism, in both the east and west.[10] Aside from such writings, Athanasius is noted for the many letters he wrote. The *Festal Letter* of Easter AD 367 is of special importance for its list of those books of the Old and New Testament which were accepted for use in public worship at that time.[11]

A.2. Cyril of Alexandria (ca. 372–444)

As bishop (or patriarch) of Alexandria from 412 to 444, Cyril's work falls outside of the fourth-century context, but we note him as an important successor to Athanasius's emphasis on the deity of Christ. Cyril is called the "teacher of the incarnation" particularly because a major preoccupation of his life as bishop was to oppose Nestorius and representatives of the school of Antioch on the nature of Christ after the incarnation; in that connection he defended the title *Theotokos* for Mary.[12] Although the emergence of Monophysite theology, as such, must be credited to Eutyches,[13] Cyril's position anticipated the emerging Monophysite position, for he affirmed two natures before the incarnation, while the incarnate Christ is marked by *one nature* (Greek, *monos*, *phusis*)

---

8. See the relevant discussion on the background for the second ecumenical council at Constantinople (381) in ch. 10, §B.1 and 3.

9. Athanasius, *On the Incarnation* 54.3; see also Needham, *2000 Years of Christ's Power*, 1.210.

10. See ch. 3, §A.1.

11. See ch. 9, §D.

12. See ch. 11, §A.1.

13. On Monophysites, who claimed a single nature for Christ, with the divine overshadowing the human aspect, see ch. 11, §B.1.

dominated by the Logos. This view modifies only slightly the position of Apollinaris who taught that Christ did not have a human mind or spirit (a position condemned in 381). According to Cyril, the incarnate Logos took on a human body, soul and spirit.

Cyril's literary contributions were impressive. He wrote significant essays in biblical theology, as well as biblical commentaries and homilies.[14] In theological politics, on the other hand, Cyril is remembered for some rather unscrupulous tactics in opposing his rivals from Antioch.[15] At the Council of Ephesus in 431 he did not wait for the arrival of colleagues in support of Nestorius before initiating debate to secure condemnation and banishment of Nestorius by Theodosius II. He is also known for intolerance in dealing with non-Christians, particularly Jews and pagans. The violent death (in 415) of the female pagan philosopher, Hypatia, may be attributed at least in part to his policies.

B. The Cappadocians[16]

B.1. Basil of Caesarea (ca. 330–379)

The three Cappadocian leaders: Basil, his brother Gregory of Nyssa (ca. 335–395) and his friend Gregory of Nazianzus (ca. 330–390), came from relatively well-to-do families of Bithynia, in Asia Minor (present-day Turkey), the most Christianized area of the Roman Empire at that time. In the period leading up to the Council of Constantinople (381), these men were able to make a constructive contribution to theological disputes concerning the deity of Christ and of the Holy Spirit. All three had benefited from an excellent education in rhetoric and philosophy. All three were deeply influenced by the work and thought of Origen. In fact, Basil's grandparents had converted to Christianity under Gregory Thaumatourgos, who was trained by Origen.

With the persecution of Diocletian, Basil's family had lost all of its extensive landholdings. But in subsequent years much was recovered, and Basil was sent to Athens for his education.[17] There he became a close friend of Gregory of

---

14. Vallée, *Shaping of Christianity*, 176–177.

15. On Cyril's character, see the judgment of the historian Theodoret; he suffered at Cyril's hands, and regarded him no less than a "villain" and a "plague" (quoted in Stevenson, *Creeds, Councils and Controversies*, 367–370).

16. For a general assessment of the Cappadocians, see Vallée, *Shaping of Christianity*, 177–179; also Latourette, *First Five Centuries*, 160–163 and 165–166.

17. On Basil, see Frend, *Rise of Christianity*, 629–634.

Nazianzus his fellow-student. Gregory's father was bishop of Nazianzus.[18] Upon completing his studies, Basil planned to follow in his father's footsteps as a public orator and teacher of rhetoric. But within a few years he abandoned these ambitions, persuaded by the arguments of his older sister Macrina; together with a number of friends he made his retreat to a small corner of the estate. Here they followed a monastic regime with a literary focus; their favourite reading was the work of Origen.[19] They were especially interested in his devotional writings and made a collection of favourite passages, the *Philokalia*. At this time Basil developed a *Rule* for monastic communities which proved to be influential. Unlike many eastern monastic groups, Basil encouraged recognition of the authority of the local bishop over these communities.[20]

Events within the church did not allow Basil to remain in retreat for long. In 370 he was elected bishop of Caesarea in Cappadocia, and took on the leadership of the Nicene party in Asia Minor; his attempts to turn back the tide of Arianizing in the congregations involved him in considerable controversy. His letters leave a vivid portrayal of serious disputes dividing the church at this time. Against the *Macedonians*, who did not consider the Holy Spirit divine, he wrote *On the Holy Spirit*; his work appealed to liturgical and baptismal practice to cement the orthodox position on the Trinity. Together with his brother Gregory (of Nyssa) and his friend Gregory of Nazianzus, he affirmed use of the term *ousia* for the single divine essence of God, while the term *hypostasis* would be reserved to designate each of the three persons, Father, Son and Holy Spirit.[21] Aside from an important role as preacher, Basil was gifted as a practical church leader and administrator. He died in 379, some months before the start of the Council of Constantinople, which would benefit greatly from his preparatory work.

B.2. Gregory of Nazianzus (ca. 330–390)

As an eloquent speaker and staunch defender of the Nicene formula, Gregory of Nazianzus had been appointed bishop of Constantinople (379–381). Although he preferred the quiet life of a writer to the stormy life of theological polemics and church politics, Gregory was unable to escape interaction with the Arians,

---

18. On Gregory of Nazianzus, see Frend, *Rise of Christianity*, 630–631, 636–638 and 640–641.

19. See the introduction to ch. 3, and §B.1 of that chapter.

20. See ch. 3, §B.1; also Stevenson, *Creeds, Councils and Controversies*, 115–117; and Frend, *Rise of Christianity*, 631 and 881–882.

21. See ch. 10, §B.4; and Stevenson, *Creeds, Councils and Controversies*, 123–124.

and argued brilliantly for Trinitarian orthodoxy. But his appointment as bishop was short-lived; trumped-up charges regarding his administrative practice led to sudden retirement.[22] He was no longer in Constantinople when Emperor Theodosius called the second ecumenical council for 381.

B.3. Gregory of Nyssa (ca. 335–395)

Only Gregory of Nyssa, the most prolific writer of the three Cappadocians, actually attended the Council of Constantinople, and influenced its conclusions in reaffirming the Nicene Creed on the Son being "consubstantial" (*homoousios*) with the Father.[23]

Figure 12.1. Gregory of Nyssa. This 10th-century depiction is taken from the liturgical calendar (*Menologion*) of the Byzantine Emperor Basil II. Photographic reproduction by Shakko. Public Domain.

Of the three Cappadocians, Gregory was more inclined to philosophical reflection on the nature of the Trinity, and use of Platonic terminology. Even so, his Christology sought to remove any residual traces of Docetism. Both Basil and Gregory are known for writing on virginity and the ascetic life. The finest of these treatises are Gregory's *Life of Moses*, and his *Life of Macrina*, his memoir and tribute for his eldest sister who was instrumental in developing a

---

22. On his departure from Constantinople, see Stevenson, 129–132.

23. On Gregory of Nyssa, see Frend, *Rise of Christianity*, 630–631, 636 and 640–641. For Gregory's understanding of the Trinity, see Stevenson, *Creeds, Councils and Controversies*, 125–126.

female monastic establishment parallel to that of Basil.[24] The *Life* was used by later Christians to canonize Macrina, her mother Emelia, and grandmother Macrina the Elder.

C. Syrian Antioch

C.1. John Chrysostom (354–406)

Theologians connected with Antioch were noted for a distinctive approach in the interpretation of Scripture. Unlike Alexandrians, the Antiochenes repudiated allegorical interpretation to seek a deeper underlying meaning of the biblical text; they focused on the literal or historical meaning of passages. This also made for sharp differences in theological positions, as we have noted in the controversy between Nestorius and Cyril of Alexandria.

Chrysostom grew up in a Christian family in Antioch; although his father died early, he received an outstanding education, studying with the most prestigious public orator of the time, Libanius. This is how he acquired a reputation for eloquence and the name "Chrysostom," which means, literally, "the one with a golden mouth."[25] After baptism at about the age of twenty, Chrysostom practised an ascetic regime at home until the death of his widowed mother, Anthusa (ca. 375); at that time he made his retreat to the Syrian mountains. But the regime of fasting and restraint was too rigorous; his health suffered, and he returned to Antioch (ca. 381). Ordained a deacon and presbyter, John soon became famous throughout the Greek-speaking church for his talent in preaching.[26]

In 397 (or 398) Chrysostom was invited by the emperor to take up an appointment as court-preacher, bishop and patriarch in Constantinople.

He accepted the call, but found his work complicated by political pressure and intrigue, especially when his eloquent sermons critiqued the luxurious lifestyle of the elite at court.[27] He was equally fearless in criticizing clergy who professed celibacy while living together with "spiritual sisters." Others he accused of neglecting their duties while enriching themselves.[28] Seeking

---

24. On the role of Macrina, see the introduction to ch. 3, also §B.1 and 2 of that chapter.

25. On Chrysostom, see Frend, *Rise of Christianity*, 749–752; Young, *From Nicaea to Chalcedon*, 143–159; and Chadwick, *Early Church*, 186–191. For a recent biographical account, see Kelly, *Golden Mouth*.

26. Chadwick, *Early Church*, 186.

27. Chadwick, 187–188.

28. Chadwick, 187. In his *History* 6.21.2–6, Socrates is critical of Chrysostom for impatience and inclination to anger (see Stevenson, *Creeds, Councils and Controversies*, 322).

reform in support of the poor, Chrysostom encouraged moderation for the rich and powerful. It was only a matter of time before former supporters, including the empress, turned against Chrysostom as a troublesome preacher, and encouraged the emperor to have him exiled.[29] But on the very night of his departure there was a strong earthquake, felt significantly at the palace; the Empress Eudoxia was so frightened that she pleaded with Chrysostom to return.[30]

Figure 12.2. John Chrysostom. This depiction of the great 4th-century preacher, known for the *Divine Liturgy* named after him, is from the 11th-century mosaic at the Hosios Loukas monastery (Boeotia, Greece). Photographic reproduction by Shakko, based on Chatzidakis's *Byzantine Art in Greece*. Public Domain.

Chrysostom's return to the capital was brief. He continued to preach in the same manner, and Eudoxia had further cause to feel insulted when he compared her with Jezebel (1 Kgs 19–21). Exiled a second time, Chrysostom left for Armenia, until finally he was ordered to retreat further to the Black Sea area, became ill and died on the journey (406). In 438 Emperor Theodosius II had Chrysostom's remains brought back to Constantinople to be buried in the Church of the Apostles.

Chrysostom is remembered especially for his "liturgy," which remains the standard for the eucharistic service in the Eastern Orthodox church.[31] Many of his sermons were recorded by admirers and secretaries; they are still appreciated as models for preachers. Fifty-eight sermons on the Psalms are extant, ninety on the Gospel of Matthew, and eighty-eight on the Gospel

---

29. One of the important motivating factors for Chrysostom's exile was his endorsement of a group of monks (considered "Origenist") who rejected any anthropomorphic description of God. The many Egyptian monks who disagreed with them looked to the Patriarch of Alexandria to support their approach. Affirming them, the Patriarch used his influence to undermine Chrysostom's position in Constantinople; see Isichei, *History of Christianity in Africa*, 25.

30. Frend, *Rise of Christianity*, 750; and Chadwick, *Early Church*, 189–190.

31. Vallée, *Shaping of Christianity*, 180.

of John. Rejecting the allegorization favoured in Alexandria, Chrysostom's sermons exhibit the exegetical style representative of the school of Antioch, focused on the literal text and the historical basis for Christianity.

D. The Latin West

Theologians using the Latin language were crucial in shaping western theology, for by the fourth century fluency in the Greek language was becoming less common in the western empire, even for those who were well-educated. The most significant contribution in innovative and original theological thought was undoubtedly that of Augustine, though his accomplishment certainly rests on the work of earlier African theologians, Tertullian (ca. 160–225) and Cyprian (ca. 200–258), as well as the Alexandrian tradition (through Ambrose). We have noted the important contribution of Tertullian, along with Irenaeus, in responding to claims of Gnostics, especially in the *Praescriptio* and in his contribution on the "rule of faith."[32] Equally important was Tertullian's response on the Sabellian position in the *Adversus Praxeas*, which defended a Trinitarian understanding of God as one divine substance in three distinct persons, a formulation very close to that accepted as the standard formula at the ecumenical council of Constantinople (381).[33]

As bishop of Carthage, Cyprian is remembered especially for pastoral statements on the importance of church unity, and his strong stance on repentance and discipline for those who had lapsed under the strain of persecution; his intransigence led to a schismatic movement (in 251). But his courageous and firm profession of faith in the persecution under Emperor Valerian also made a deep impression.[34]

D.1. Ambrose (ca. 340–397)

As bishop of Milan, Ambrose had a considerable immediate influence on Augustine as a Christian thinker. Ambrose came from an influential Roman family. Before he became bishop (373), he was governor of Milan, the city which had replaced Rome as the new centre of government in the West.[35]

---

32. See ch. 8, §C.4.
33. See ch. 10, §A.3.
34. On Cyprian, see ch. 6, §B.1 above.
35. For the early account of the life of Ambrose by Paulinus the Deacon, see Hoare, *Western Fathers*, 149–188.

It was a time of serious tension between Nicene and Arian Christians. The Arian bishop of Milan, Auxentius, had died, and the threat of violence over the succession brought Ambrose to the church, to keep order. He addressed the crowd, and as he spoke a child called out, "Ambrose as bishop!"

Figure 12.3. Ambrose, bishop of Milan. The strong-minded defender of the Catholic faith against the Arians is depicted in this 10th-century miniature, from the *Menologion* of the Byzantine Emperor Basil II, as a man of prayer. Photographic reproduction by DigiVatLib. Public Domain.

Many echoed the sentiment. Although Ambrose was only a catechumen at the time, he was not able to dissuade them. After going through the required levels of church office he was consecrated bishop, and came to represent Nicene (or Catholic) Christianity in this important city.[36]

Well educated, Ambrose was an able speaker and administrator. He reminded his parishioners to support the weak and the needy, and was greatly loved by the people for his defence of the church against pagans, heretical opponents and the power of the state. When the Goths invaded, he ordered the sale of gold vessels of the church to pay the ransom for the captives.

Ambrose was also fluent in Greek, which gave him access to current literature on theological issues, especially from the Alexandrian school. Among those who appreciated his sermons was the young Augustine. Although he initially came simply to enjoy the rhetorical style of the sermons, Augustine was moved by the content of the preaching and submitted himself for baptism in the

---

36. On the career of Ambrose, see Frend, *Rise of Christianity*, 618–626.

church.³⁷ Ambrose was especially helpful for Augustine in demonstrating that troublesome and embarassing passages of Scripture (like Abraham passing off his wife Sarah as his sister, Gen 12:10–20; Gen 20:1–18) could be understood through allegorical interpretation, thereby providing Augustine useful tools in responding to tough questions from Manicheans.

Ambrose remained active politically, and showed himself fearless in a number of confrontations. When Emperor Valentinian used him as an ambassador with the rebels, Ambrose was successful in averting an invasion of Rome. When Justina, the (Arian) mother of the emperor, wanted to hold a public celebration with Arians in the central church of Milan, Ambrose had the congregation occupy the church building and continue singing hymns (many of them of his own composition); he even celebrated communion while the church was under siege.³⁸

The most celebrated confrontation resulted from Emperor Theodosius's intent to punish zealous Christians who had destroyed a synagogue. Theodosius was staunchly Nicene in commitment, having supervised the Council of Constantinople (in 381) which endorsed the Nicene Creed; but on this matter Ambrose protested his treatment of Christians. The emperor finally yielded, and withdrew the punishment.

A second incident was more serious. A Roman officer had been killed in a riot in Thessalonica. Theodosius sent an order to punish the people. Ambrose advised moderation, but the order had already been sent, and could not be recalled. Local troops invited the population into the amphitheatre and there slaughtered about seven thousand inhabitants of the city.³⁹ Ambrose responded by blocking the emperor from worshipping in the church the next time he came to Milan. While the emperor resented being excluded, he eventually granted the validity of the response and confessed his guilt. He also declared a stay of thirty days if an order of execution of citizens was to be given.⁴⁰ In the contest of will between imperial and ecclesiastical power, it became clear that Ambrose would not yield. Ambrose insisted that the church belongs to God, and cannot be assigned to Caesar. Even the emperor is within the church, not above it.⁴¹

---

37. On the relationship between Ambrose and Augustine, see Frend, 664–665.

38. See Augustine's *Confessions* 9.7.15–16. On the confrontation between Ambrose and Arians at the imperial court, see Frend, 622–623; on the role of music in these disputes, see Latourette, *First Five Centuries*, 206–208.

39. See also ch. 5, §C above.

40. Frend, *Rise of Christianity*, 623–626; see also Chadwick, *Early Church*, 167–168.

41. See Needham, *2000 Years of Christ's Power*, 172, quoting Ambrose's sermon against Auxentius, 35–36; for the passage see also Stevenson, *Creeds, Councils and Controversies*, 162–163.

D.2. Jerome (ca. 342–420)

Jerome's career is more stormy than that of any other leader of this period.[42] He possessed a brilliant mind, and was capable of providing a great service to the church. Jerome's gift for eloquence and style, together with his mastery of languages, was particularly significant for his work on the Latin translation of the Scriptures.

Born of Christian parents in Northern Italy, Jerome was given an outstanding education in classical literature. Even as he wished to adopt the monastic life, he remained torn between his love for the pagan writers and Christian literature.[43] During a time of inner turmoil, he experienced a dream in which he was confronted with the question, whether his ultimate allegiance was with Christ or with Cicero (the great Latin orator and writer of the first century BC). When he realized that an honest answer pointed to Cicero, he resolved to live even more austerely, punishing himself with fasting and ascetic restraint, and devoting himself exclusively to the Scriptures.[44]

Figure 12.4. Jerome in his study. This 15th-century painting of Jerome by the Italian Antonella da Messina (1430–1479), is a tribute to the great 4th-century teacher and Bible translator. The Yorck Project. Public Domain.

---

42. On Jerome, see Frend, *Rise of Christianity*, 715–719; and Chadwick, *Early Church*, 214–216. For a recent biographical account, see Kelly, *Jerome*.

43. For Jerome's contribution to monasticism, see ch. 3, §C.2.

44. See Chadwick, *Early Church*, 215. On the dream, recounted in a letter to Eustochium (*Ep.* 22.30), see Stevenson, *Creeds, Councils and Controversies*, 208–209; also Tierney, *Middle Ages*, 32.

After some years in Palestine, Jerome attended the Council of Constantinople (AD 381), and returned to Rome, where he became theological adviser to Pope Damasus. Noting his talents, the pope commissioned him to prepare a new translation of the Scriptures in Latin.[45] This was the project to which he devoted the rest of his life.

When Jerome left for Palestine after the death of Damasus (in 384), he was accompanied by some of the upper class women of Rome, whom he had served as spiritual adviser.[46] Establishing a monastic home parallel to that of Jerome himself in Bethlehem, Paula and Eustochium used the training he had given them in the ancient languages to help translate the Old Testament direct from the Hebrew. Jerome also found Jewish assistants well-versed in Hebrew, to assure him that his translation would be based on the original text as it had been established by scholars of Judaism.[47] The translation which emerged, the *Vulgate* (from Latin *vulgus*, meaning "common"), became the standard Bible for the Latin-speaking church.[48]

When it was ready for church use, Jerome's new translation met with considerable resistance, also from Augustine. At the time Augustine was bishop of Hippo in North Africa, and concerned about divergence from earlier well-known translations which were based on the Septuagint, not the original Hebrew text. Because most of his parishioners would have been illiterate, and their knowledge of Scripture was based on memorization, they would be puzzled by the significant differences of the newly translated text compared to the versions with which they were familiar. Clear explanation and motivation of the changes were called for.

To convince the church that his translation was based on the authentic text, verified by Hebrew scholars, Jerome wrote extensive commentaries in support of his understanding of the Scriptures. He also carried on a substantive correspondence with friends and colleagues, much of it polemical; he always

---

45. For an excerpt of Jerome's letter to Pope Damasus on the Latin translation, see Stevenson, *Creeds, Councils and Controversies*, 210–211. See also Latourette, *History of the Expansion of Christianity*, 232–234.

46. On Jerome's association with these women, see also ch. 3, §B.2 and §C.2.

47. Chadwick, *Early Church*, 214 and 216.

48. On the significance of this translation, see ch. 9, §D; also Latourette, *History of the Expansion of Christianity*, 232–233. Using the Septuagint, Jerome included what are called apocryphal books (like Maccabees), although he realized that they were different in character and level of inspiration compared with biblical books on the lists approved by the councils (see ch. 9, §D). The Roman Catholic Church accepted the apocryphal books as inspired much later, and included them among biblical books read as part of the liturgy at the time of the Reformation, with a decree at the Council of Trent (in 1546).

seemed to be quarrelling with someone.[49] In his usual manner, Jerome initially demonstrated little tolerance for Augustine's arguments and questions. But the exchange of letters between these leading fourth-century theologians reveals how Jerome gradually came to respect the theological depth of Augustine's approach. And Jerome's commentaries would remain as a significant monument to his own painstaking work and that of associates like Paula and Eustochium.[50]

D.3. Augustine of Hippo (354–430)

For western theology Augustine (Aurelius Augustinus) has the prominence which Origen posed in the east. Unlike Ambrose or Jerome, Augustine was not able to read the Greek theologians easily in the original language; but even without significant knowledge of Greek and indirect acquaintance with theological treatises in Greek, Augustine surpassed Origen in shaping global Christian theology. He has long been regarded as the greatest theologian produced by early Christianity.[51]

We know quite a bit about Augustine's early years from his own inevitably selective account in the *Confessions*, from which we quoted at the beginning of the chapter.[52] As a child Augustine had been recognized for his intellectual gifts, and his parents had provided the best possible education within their means. He was born in Thagaste, a small town in North Africa (Souk-Ahras in present-day Algeria), with parents of middling income. His father, a minor official of the Roman government, remained pagan most of his life. His mother, Monica, of Berber descent, was a devout Christian who never stopped praying for her eldest son.

Augustine first attended local schools and those of the regional centre, Madauros (now Mdaourouch). Later he pursued his education in Carthage (370–374), a centre known for its economic, cultural and political significance in that region of North Africa. Here Augustine studied rhetoric. He also got involved in the attractions and pleasures of the city, acquiring a concubine who remained his common-law wife for many years. They had one son, Adeodatus (i.e. "given by God"). Though nominally of the Catholic faith, Augustine had

---

49. Latourette, *History of the Expansion of Christianity*, 231–233.

50. On Paula's contribution, see Latourette, 232.

51. On Augustine, see Latourette, 96–97 and 173–181; Chadwick, *Early Church*, 216–236; and Frend, *Rise of Christianity*, 659–680. For the ancient account of his life by Possidius, see Hoare, *Western Fathers*, 193–244.

52. He wrote this account when he was 43 (ca. 397); for an accessible modern translation, see Wirt, *Confessions of Augustine*.

not been baptized, for this was typically postponed until the stormy years of childhood and adolescence had passed. In Carthage, however, Augustine was drawn to groups on the fringes of the Christian church, especially the Manicheans.[53]

Manicheans held teachings similar to those of the Gnostics, with a strong dualism of good and evil, or light and darkness, as virtually equal and balanced powers; they also taught a strong distinction between spirit and flesh.[54] Such dualism reflects the Persian roots of the founder, the third-century Mani (d. AD 260). Much like the Gnostics, Manicheans regarded evil as an independent principle; their approach removed the problem of reconciling human sin or suffering with the power and goodness of God. Salvation was understood as a separation of the "spiritual" from the "material" context, and as a means for the spirit to return to its true home in the spiritual realm. These teachings were supported by astrological calculations. Since bodily existence was thought to belong to the realm of evil, Manicheans dissuaded members from marriage and having children. Augustine was initially attracted by Manichean critique of the crude language of Scripture (in the Latin translation); also by Manichean presentation of evil as a force opposing the goodness of God, and as something for which God, as Creator, was not responsible.[55]

For nine years Augustine remained a "hearer," as the first step in membership. He did not progress to the higher levels, for even in Carthage he realized that Manichean arguments could not be supported. Their leaders could not satisfy his basic questions on astrological calculations. Even so, Augustine used a network of Manichean colleagues in his quest for professional promotion in Carthage and in Italy, especially in Rome (by 383), where Manichean teachings had spread among leading social groups.

But in Rome Augustine also became acquainted with Neoplatonic philosophers.[56] Already in Carthage, Augustine had read the philosophical treatises of Cicero, the first century BC master orator, especially his *Hortensius*, a "protreptic" treatise, or essay to encourage students in the pursuit of truth as a goal more worthy than the pursuit of eloquence.[57] Like most ancient students

---

53. On the Manicheans, see Frend, *Rise of Christianity*, 314–318; and Stevenson, *Creeds, Councils and Controversies*, 241–243. On Augustine and the Manicheans, see Frend, *Rise of Christianity*, 661–664.

54. On the important contrast of light and dark, see Frend, *Rise of Christianity*, 316.

55. For Augustine's critique of Manichean thought, see also Frend, 663.

56. On Augustine and the Neoplatonists, see Frend, *Rise of Christianity*, 663; and Chadwick, *Early Church*, 217–218.

57. On the impact of Cicero, see Augustine's *Confessions* 3.3.6 – 5.9; also quoted in Stevenson, *Creeds, Councils and Controversies*, 239–241.

of rhetoric, Augustine considered philosophical understanding as the true completion of his education.[58]

The Neoplatonists in Rome followed Plotinus, a mystic philosopher who had taught in Rome during the third century. His brilliant pupil and successor Porphyry had written anti-Christian treatises and participated in the last fierce round of persecution under Diocletian.[59] Porphyry's treatises had also served the anti-Christian Emperor Julian in his attempt to turn back the clock on the legal status of Christianity. However, in Augustine's time prominent Neoplatonists like Victorinus, also of African origin, and known for his Latin translation of Plotinus's treatises, had accepted the Christian faith (ca. 355). The priest Simplician's account of the conversion of Victorinus made a deep impression on Augustine.[60]

Unlike the dualism of the Manicheans, Plotinus's thought is monistic, accepting only one ultimate principle of reality.[61] His *Enneads* advocate preliminary ascetic practice, as the first step toward mystical union with the transcendent first and highest principle, the One. Such union is beyond human experience. This principle is also the undiminished divine source of all else; everything else is derived from the One in a series of emanations. To explain this, the Neoplatonists used the example of the sun, from which both rays of light and heat emanate, yet without diminishing the source. At the opposite end of the spectrum of being is multiplicity and evil. While evil is real, it has no concrete ontological status as such (as Manicheans supposed). It is simply regarded as the *absence* of good, or distance from the One; it reflects a retreat from unity into multiplicity.

While in Milan, where he held the prestigious post of court orator, Augustine gradually overcame some significant philosophical and professional hurdles to acceptance of the Christian faith. Aside from the support of Neoplatonist thought to counter Manichean dualism, he was listening to the sermons of Ambrose, whose allegorical interpretation helped him find a different way of understanding the passages of Scripture on which the Manicheans had focused their critique.[62] Augustine came to a new appreciation of the "crudeness" of Old

---

58. Chadwick, *Early Church*, 217–218.

59. On Porphyry, see ch. 4, §B.3.

60. See Augustine's *Confessions* 8.2.4–5; and Stevenson, *Creeds, Councils and Controversies*, 243–245.

61. Ferguson, *Backgrounds*, 391–392.

62. On Augustine's appreciation of Ambrose, see the excerpt from his *Confessions* 5.13.23 – 14.25, quoted in Stevenson, *Creeds, Councils and Controversies*, 241–243. On Augustine's conversion, see Latourette, *History of the Expansion of Christianity*, 96–97; and Frend, *Rise of Christianity*, 664.

Testament accounts, even in the imperfect contemporary Latin translations (before Jerome finished the Vulgate).

The remaining obstacles were personal. He had remained faithful to his concubine of many years, but his mother Monica (who had joined him in Rome) felt that his social and professional status required a proper marriage; she arranged for him to marry a young bride from a prominent family. Although the girl was still too young for marriage, Augustine had to send his concubine away; he did so with regret and tears. While he waited for his fiancée to mature, Augustine struggled with the monastic ideal. At this time he read Athanasius's *Life of Anthony*, and felt a decisive call to take up a new life.[63] And, as noted above, Anthony's example also encouraged Augustine in hearing God speak through the passage in Paul's Epistle to the Romans. The result was dramatic. Not only would Augustine abandon a life of sexual licence; he would also abandon the teaching of rhetoric. To prepare himself for baptism, Augustine withdrew to an estate outside of Rome for a time of disciplined prayer, reading and discussion with students and close friends. During these months Augustine also wrote a number of philosophical dialogues on happiness, the question of evil, and the nature of the Christian life, using a Christian perspective, albeit one deeply influenced by Neoplatonism.[64]

Monica died before he could make his way back to North Africa, to settle on the family estate (387). His son Adeodatus, only eighteen years of age, also died at this time. Back in Africa, Augustine sold most of the family possessions and, together with friends and former colleagues, assumed a semi-monastic life.[65] In the following years he was ordained as presbyter, and when he visited Hippo in 391 Augustine was conscripted to help the old and sickly bishop. When the bishop died in 396, Augustine became bishop in his place.[66] He spent the rest of his life in Hippo, addressing the issues of the day through his growing understanding of the Scriptures. Thus he dealt in turn with the challenges of the Manicheans, Donatists and Pelagians.

---

63. Stevenson, *Creeds, Councils and Controversies*, 245–247; and Frend, *Rise of Christianity*, 666.

64. These are the *Cassiciacum Dialogues*, Augustine's first attempts to elaborate a Christian understanding of the questions.

65. Frend, *Rise of Christianity*, 666–667.

66. Frend, 667; and Chadwick, *Early Church*, 218.

Figure 12.5. Augustine's conversion. This 15th-century work by the Italian artist Fra Angelico (1395–1455) depicts Augustine's prayers in the garden at the time of his conversion. Photographic reproduction by Drolexandre. Public Domain.

Against the Manicheans, Augustine emphasized the freedom of the will; our human lives are not predetermined (astrologically). We can act of our own will, even while we recognize that many conditions do serve to determine our decisions. Of course, the free will can make wrong decisions, and evil is real (though not a substance, as Manicheans maintained). As noted above, some of his opponents accused him of remaining a Manichee,[67] especially in terms of his understanding of sin and predestination, issues that became important in his opposition to the Pelagians. But unlike the Manicheans, Augustine affirmed the essential goodness of all that God has created.

Augustine recognized the Donatists as a schismatic group; this means that on doctrinal issues there was no essential difference with the Catholic church.[68] Donatists had separated over the ordination of Caecilian as bishop of Carthage, regarding that ordination as invalid because of the participation of a priest who had betrayed the faith in time of persecution. To answer the

---

67. See ch. 6, §B.1; also Isichei, *History of Christianity in Africa*, 40.

68. On the Donatists, see ch. 5, §B.5, and ch. 6, §B.1; see also Frend, *Rise of Christianity*, 653–658; and Stevenson, *Creeds, Councils and Controversies*, 257–262. On Augustine's involvement with the Donatists, see the excerpt from Possidius's *Life of St Augustine*, 9, in Stevenson, 251–252; and further, Chadwick, *Early Church*, 219–225; and Frend, *Rise of Christianity*, 668–673.

Donatists, Augustine affirmed the validity of the sacrament and the process of ordination, even when the ceremony was conducted by participants who might be considered less than worthy. Not wishing to approve of unworthy behaviour of church officers as such, he explained that the effectiveness of the sacrament lies not with the priest conducting this, but with the church which has been given authority from the time of the apostles. He reminded the Donatists not to turn to violence, as did the Circumcellions, wandering about in the countryside.[69]

More troublesome yet than either of these groups, was the teaching of Pelagius (b. ca. 355), a British monk who came to Rome, where he taught the possibility of overcoming sin by human effort.[70] If sin is a matter of the will and of bad example, while the human will itself is free, Pelagius argued, sin can be overcome. It is possible to lead a sinless life. In response, Augustine called on his own experience, his inability to control and overcome his inclinations on his own, in spite of the will to do so.[71] The will has become powerless because of ingrained sin. Freedom of choice is a relative matter. Human beings were once free not to sin, but only before the fall of humanity into sin. Once fallen, human beings need divine grace to restore true freedom.[72] Only in heaven will humanity be truly free not to sin, that is, to choose only that which is not sinful. Pelagius refused to accept the condition of original sin, or the subsequent corruption of human nature. He could not accept Adam's mistake as the root cause of the corruption of human nature and subsequent human suffering. But the Pelagian teaching was condemned in a synod held at Carthage in 416, and again in 418.[73]

A number of essential writings of Augustine have made a deep impact on the history of western Christianity. Among these the *Confessions* and the *City of God* deserve special mention. We will examine Augustine's *City of God* in the following chapter, in the discussion of the fall of the Roman Empire in the West. The *Confessions* appear to be autobiographical, but are actually written as an extended prayer and song of praise to God, through which Augustine retells the story of his pilgrimage to faith. He begins with the events of his

---

69. See Stevenson, *Creeds, Councils and Controversies*, 254–255.

70. On the Pelagians, see Chadwick, *Early Church*, 227–235; and Frend, *Rise of Christianity*, 673–679.

71. On the Pelagian controversy, and Augustine's understanding of original sin, see Stevenson, *Creeds, Councils and Controversies*, 267–275.

72. Pelikan rightly focuses on grace as the central theme for Augustine's theology (*Christian Emergence of the Catholic Tradition*, 292–318, especially 294–295).

73. Latourette, *History of the Expansion of Christianity*, 180.

earliest years, and gives details of his career up to the time of conversion. These accounts are capped with a concluding reflection on his new understanding of the world as God's creation. The most memorable quote (based on the Psalms) from the *Confessions* comes in the introductory paragraph, "Our hearts are restless until they find their rest in You."

Other memorable passages are found in the *Confessions* 10.6.8-9:

> 8. I love You, O Lord, not with doubting, but with absolute certainty. You have struck at my heart with Your word until I loved You. And now the heavens, the earth, and everything in them tell me that I should love You; nor do they stop speaking to all, "so that we are without excuse" (Romans 1:20). . . . .
>
> The heavens and earth do not tell forth Your praises to deaf ears. But what do I love when I love You? Not physical beauty, or the splendour of our existence in time, or the radiance of the light which is so pleasant to our eyes, or the sweet melodies of familiar songs, or the flagrant smell of flowers, and ointments and spices; nor is it the taste of manna and honey, or the arms with which we like to embrace one another.
>
> These are not the things I love when I love my God; and yet there is a certain kind of light, and sound, and fragrance, and food, and embracement which I love when loving my God, for it is the light, sound, fragrance, food and embracement of my inner man. There is a light that shines into my soul, in a place not contained by space. It can hear melodies which time cannot snatch away, and inhale a fragrance which no breeze of the wind can blow away. It receives a food which is not diminished by eating, and it receives a divine embrace from which it cannot be separated, and of which it never gets tired. This is what I love, when I love my God.
>
> 9. And what is this, my God? I asked the earth; and it answered, "I am not He"; and everything in it made the same reply. I asked the sea and its depth, and the creeping things that live in it, and they replied, "We are not your God, seek higher than us." I asked the gentle breezes, and the air with all its inhabitants answered me, "Anaximenes[74] was deceived; I am not God." I asked the heavens, the sun, the moon and stars: "Neither," they said, "are we the God

---

74. Anaximenes was the sixth-century BC Greek philosopher who understood *air* as the chief original and divine component of all reality.

whom you seek." And I spoke to all these things which crowd about my bodily existence, "You have told me about my God, that you are not He; then tell me something about Him." And with a loud voice they all cried out, "He made us." I questioned them further by fixing my attention on them; and their beauty was their reply.

Then I directed my thoughts within myself, and said, "Who are you?" And I answered, "A man." But in me there are both body and soul, the one external, the other within me. By which of these should I seek my God, for I have already sought him with my physical being from earth to heaven, as far as the sight of my eyes can take me? But the inner part is better for this search, for all these bodily messengers have given the answers from the heavens and earth and all that is within it, as they said, "We are not God, but He made us," addressing that inner part, as both their president and judge. My inner being knows all these things through the service of the external person; I, the inner person, know all this – I, the soul, through the senses of my body. I asked all the vast bulk of the earth about my God, and it answered me, "I am not He, but He made me."

The theme of love for God is continued in sections 27.38 and 29.40:

38. Too late I came to love You, O Beauty, so ancient, and yet so new! Too late I came to love You. For You were within me, and I remained outside and tried to seek You there; I, unlovely, rushed about wildly among the things of beauty which You made. You were with me, but I was not with You. All those things kept me far from You, although they had no real existence except in You. You called me, and cried aloud, and even forced Yourself past my deafness. You bathed me in Your light and wrapped me in your splendour to chase away my blindness. You gave such a delightful fragrance, and I drew it in and panted hard after You. I tasted, and it made me hunger and thirst. You touched me, and I burned to receive Your peace.

40. All my hopes are in Your great mercy alone. So give what You command, and command what You will. You give the order that we exercise self-control. And by self-control we are bound up and given integrity, no longer scattered abroad into multiplicity. For anyone who loves anything besides You loves You too little,

unless he loves it because of You. O love, that always burns, and is never quenched! O Love that is my God, enkindle me! You command self-control. Give what You command, and command what You will.[75]

In one of his most important theological works, *On the Trinity* (*De Trinitate*), Augustine completes the efforts of the Nicene discussions to overcome the subordinationist approach of Tertullian and Origen. He affirms the unity of God in three persons, coequal and coeternal; no one of the persons is to be considered earlier, later, inferior or superior to the other. The Son, fully God, is *begotten*, not made. The Spirit, also fully God, is sent forth and *proceeds* from the Father and Son. Augustine is the first to emphasize the "double sending" of the Spirit, for he realized that, aside from the promise given in Acts 1:4–5, in the Gospel of John 20:22 the Son is also represented as sending the Spirit. This is the origin of the *filioque* clause in the Nicene Creed (Latin, "and from the Son"), although it was not fully incorporated in this creed before the ninth century.[76] Augustine encouraged such a reading, to support mutuality and full equality of all three persons of the Trinity.

In *On the Trinity* Augustine tries to explain the divine *trinitas* by exploring a number of analogies. Such an approach was based on his understanding of creation as a reflection of its Creator; one might well expect to find traces of God's own being in that which he made. The most famous of these analogies is based on love: the Father may be regarded as the one who loves, the Son is the beloved, and the Spirit represents the love that binds them.[77] But Augustine was actually more satisfied with the analogy of the Trinity in the activities of the human mind (as image of God), with memory, understanding and love (or will), as three aspects that are one in essence, and also equal in mutual relationships.[78] The position developed in this work was acclaimed by the church east and west, for the *De Trinitate* was known in the Byzantine church

---

75. The above presents a modification of the modern translation of the *Confessions* by Wirt, *Confessions of Augustine*, 124–126.

76. The *Nicene Creed* as it is now read in western churches, has the following clause on the Holy Spirit: "And I believe in the Holy Spirit, the Lord and Giver of life; who proceeds from the Father *and the Son*." The Eastern Orthodox church, which never adopted the *filioque*, understood the procession of the Spirit from the Father, through the Son, and uses only the following: "who proceeds from the Father." See Chadwick, *East and West*, 64; and Guy, *Introducing Early Christianity*, 285.

77. *De Trinitate* 8.10.14; and 15.6.10 (*NPNF* 3.124, 204). See further on love as the essential character of God, 6.5.7 (*NPNF* 3.100). On these passages, see also Guy, *Introducing Early Christianity*, 283–284.

78. This analogy is explored in book 9 of the *De Trinitate* (*NPNF* 3.125–133); see also 10.12.19 (*NPNF* 3.143). See further Guy, *Introducing Early Christianity*, 284–285.

through a Greek translation, and influenced Gregory Palamas of Mount Athos (1296–1359) in his *One Hundred and Fifty Chapters*.[79]

Augustine died in 430 as the Vandals besieged Hippo.[80] His many and voluminous writings have remained as a treasure for the Catholic church and for universal Christianity. They have continued to exert an enormous influence on Christian faith and practice.

Questions for Discussion and Review

The Golden Age of Early Christian Thought: Outstanding Fourth-Century Leaders

1. What is the major contribution of Athanasius in the dispute with Arians?

2. In which sense did Cyril develop the approach of Athanasius in Christology? Why was Cyril so critical of Nestorius?

3. How did the Cappadocian Fathers manage to complete the work left unfinished by the death of Athanasius?

4. How did Chrysostom's monastic inclination influence his work as a pastor and preacher?

5. Why was Chrysostom exiled from Constantinople?

6. How did Ambrose become bishop? Was this a normal procedure?

7. What is the significance of the varied interaction of Ambrose with the empress mother Justina and the emperors Valentinian and Theodosius?

8. What, in your view, is Ambrose's major contribution for the history of Christianity?

9. For which contributions is Jerome chiefly remembered? Explain.

10. What is the significance of the assistance given by Paula and Eustochium for Jerome's work of translating the Bible?

---

79. See Helleman, "Christ the Wisdom of God," 276–277.

80. While many others fled the invading tribes, Augustine was one of those who elected to stay; he was already quite old and not well. For his reflections on flight in such circumstances, see his *Ep.* 228 to Bishop Honoratus, quoted in Stevenson, *Creeds, Councils and Controversies*, 425–426. See also the quote from Possidius's *Life* on his last days, in Stevenson, 280–281.

11. Why was Augustine initially so reluctant to embrace the Christian faith of his mother Monica? Which obstacles did he have to overcome before his conversion and baptism?

12. How were these various obstacles turned into aspects of strength in Augustine's work as a pastor and bishop?

13. How did Augustine refute the Manicheans?

14. Why was Neoplatonism so attractive to Augustine?

15. Why was Augustine especially troubled by the position of Pelagius?

16. How does Augustine's work on the Trinity add to the decisions of earlier councils on the Trinity?

17. What do you think is Augustine's most important contribution for the history of Christianity? Explain your answer.

Further Reading

Brown, Peter. *Augustine of Hippo: A Biography*. Berkeley: University of California Press, 2000.
Chrysostom, John. *Chrysostom and His Message: Selections from His Sermons*. Translated by S. Neill. London; New York: London Society for Christian Literature, 1962.
Clark, Elizabeth. *Jerome, Chrysostom and Friends*. New York: Mellen, 1979.
Kannengiesser, C. *Arius and Athanasius: Two Alexandrian Theologians*. Brookfield, VT: Ashgate, 1991.
Kelly, J. N. D. *Golden Mouth: The Story of John Chrysostom, Ascetic, Preacher, Bishop*. Ithaca, NY: Cornell University Press, 1995.
———. *Jerome: His Life, Writings and Controversies*. Peabody, MA: Hendrickson, 1998.
McLynn, N. B. *Ambrose of Milan: Church and Court in a Christian Capital*. Berkeley: University of California Press, 1994.
Meredith, A. *The Cappadocians*. Crestwood, NY: St Vladimir's Seminary Press, 1995.

Section III

Epilogue

13

The Disintegration of the Roman Empire

All the destruction, the slaughter, plundering, the burning and distress to which Rome was subjected in this latest calamity – these were but the result of events that are normal in time of war. But there was something quite new and unprecedented, for the savage barbarians demonstrated unexpected mercy in choosing the largest churches and setting them aside as places where refugees who were promised immunity could safely gather. In these churches none were slain or raped. An enemy who actually showed compassion led many who were to be set free into these churches. Of these none would be dragged away into slavery by a cruel foe.

It is quite obvious that this must be attributed to the name of Christ and to a Christian civilizing factor. Whoever sees this and does not acknowledge it with praise is ungrateful. And whoever stands in the way of others giving such praise is simply unreasonable. Nor should anyone with some sense credit the barbarians themselves with such mercy. Rather, God himself struck awe into their savage and bloodthirsty minds; He curbed and tamed their hearts, as long ago He spoke by the prophets, "I will punish their sins with the rod and their iniquity with stripes; but I will not remove my loving-kindness from them (Psalm 89:32–33).

Augustine, *The City of God* 1, 7

The attack of the barbarian Visigoths on the city of Rome (AD 410), described in this passage from Augustine's *The City of God*, shook the empire, east and west, Christian and pagan alike. From his monastic retreat in Bethlehem Jerome bemoaned the attack on Rome as the tragedy of a city which had once subjugated an entire world, but was now itself conquered.[1] Who could have imagined such an attack on the city that had stood as a symbol of Roman power for so many centuries? Was this truly the end of history? Was it the end of the empire?

Legends about the founding of Rome take us back to the mid-eighth century BC; the traditional date is 753 BC. Rome survived and flourished for more than ten centuries, first as a republic and then, with the rule of Caesar Augustus, as an empire. Citizens of the empire spoke of their capital as *Roma aeterna*, the eternal city, trusting that it was protected by the gods, especially by Jupiter, the most powerful among them.[2] And the citizens of Rome were encouraged to maintain public worship so they could enjoy the *pax deorum*, the peace given by the gods.

But, as Augustine recognizes, a new era had opened for the city and the empire. Those who interpreted the attack as the end of history had not recognized what was truly remarkable and novel about this attack. In the midst of a harrowing catastrophe, Augustine finds the silver lining: God's mercy was shown to his people in the unexpected compassion shown by the barbarian invaders. Indeed, the enemy actually spared many, and especially Christians who identified themselves with the churches. The largest of the churches were made available to allow Christians to escape the destruction and grant them amnesty. Here they were not killed, maimed, enslaved or raped. Augustine reminds his readers, accordingly, that it was important not to jump to unreasonable conclusions about the actual damage to the city.[3] It could have been so much worse. The ruthless attackers showed surprising compassion; was it because they had been influenced by (Arian) Christianity? Did they respect the churches as Christian establishments in Rome because they had themselves been Christianized?[4]

---

1. See Jerome's *Ep.* 127.11 and 12.
2. On the myth of "eternal Rome," see P. Brown, *World of Late Antiquity*, 120.
3. Chadwick recognizes that the impact of the sack of Rome in 410 on the Roman citizenry was especially emotional and psychological, and out of proportion to the actual damage caused by the Goths (*Early Church*, 250).
4. Arian Goths were largely responsible for the spread of Christianity to other Germanic tribes; see Chadwick, *Early Church*, 249.

It is interesting that Augustine recognizes the attackers as savage barbarians and cruel; he does not credit the barbarians, as such, with a capacity for mercy. He will not praise them at the expense of the more civilized members of the empire. Nor does he highlight the fact that they were Christianized and therefore respected the Christian presence in Rome, even if this may well have been a significant factor. As Christians, the Goths may well have intentionally avoided indiscriminate attacks on fellow Christians, fearing the just judgement of the Christian God (as promised in Ps 89). Augustine's approach is more subtle, for he credits the name of Christ, and the work of God in the hearts of the attackers, curbing and taming them, and derailing their bloodthirsty intentions into showing an uncharacteristic degree of compassion. Here we also find an indication of how Augustine will respond to the complaints of many who were only too ready to blame the sacking of Rome on its conversion to Christianity, and to the subsequent neglect of the pagan gods honoured by the Romans from the earliest days of the republic.

We return to examine Augustine's argument in greater detail below. The present chapter focuses on the reasons for the fall of the Roman Empire, especially because public acceptance of Christianity has been identified as an important cause of its demise. Even so, we remember that the fifth-century collapse affected mainly the western regions of the empire. In the east the Byzantine Roman Empire survived for another millennium. Constantinople, the eastern capital, was finally taken by the Turks in 1453.

Historians are still debating the specific watershed events and dates that mark the fifth-century decline and fall in the West. If the city of Rome received a rude awakening with the invasion of the Goths under Alaric in 410, the real end to any meaningful sense of the older imperial administration governing in the West came when Goths themselves became emperors in 476. At that time the remaining parts of the Roman Empire were distributed as barbarian kingdoms; these continued to exist as independent governing structures within the borders of the former empire.[5]

Few scholars have been convinced by the thesis of Henri Pirenne (1862–1935), expounded in his *History of Europe*,[6] and *Mohammed and Charlemagne*,[7] that the Roman Empire did not collapse in any essential way until the seventh

---

5. On the significance of the year 476, see Cary's *History of Rome*, 551.

6. Pirenne's *History of Europe* was published first in French (1939), and in the English translation of B. Miall (1955).

7. The work appeared posthumously as *Mahomet et Charlemagne* (1937); and in the English translation of Miall, *Mohammed and Charlemagne* (1939). For an appreciative review, see Brown, *Society and the Holy*, 63–79.

century, when the equilibrium of power around the Mediterranean was destroyed with the coming of Islam. Accenting the continuity of the Roman Empire in Europe right until the coming of Islam, Pirenne's position represents a significant alternative to Gibbon's famous presentation of the fall of the empire as a correlate of its becoming Christian. But Pirenne's work did serve to stimulate new studies focused on the nature of change in late antiquity. This can be noted in the work of Arnaldo Momigliano and Peter Brown, among others.

There is also no agreement on the exact reasons for the collapse of the empire in the West.[8] Scholars have accented political, military, economic, social and religious factors.[9] But historians are virtually unanimous on the military weakness of the empire in the West. We begin our discussion with this factor.[10]

A. Invasions and Other Factors in the Collapse

The survival of Rome from the eighth century BC to the fifth century AD represents a remarkable longevity for any single state. The most evident signal for the collapse of the western empire was the invasion of foreign peoples, especially the Germanic or Gothic tribes, considered "barbarian" because they could speak neither of the two main languages of the empire (Latin and

---

8. The question has attracted the attention of historians over the centuries; we mention only Edward Gibbon, Oswald Spengler, Henri Pirenne and Arnold Toynbee of those who studied the fall as a paradigm for issues of importance in their own time. By the mid-twentieth century, Kagan recognized that historians of his time were less inclined to speak of "decline" when examining issues of political allegiance and relationships, turning rather to terms like "disintegration." They now typically place a more positive accent on factors of "continuity" and "reintegration" (Kagan, *Decline and Fall*, vii). Ward-Perkins correctly notes the pivotal role of Peter Brown's, *The World of Late Antiquity*, focused not on fall or decline, but rather on transformation and ongoing lively political and cultural debate (Ward-Perkins, *Fall of Rome*, 3–4; see also Brown, *Society and the Holy*, 58–59). Arnaldo Momigliano's *The Conflict between Paganism and Christianity in the Fourth Century* also contributed to a more positive understanding of late antiquity. In the present chapter we return to the issue of the "fall of Rome" particularly because the theme was addressed on a large scale first in Augustine's *City of God*.

9. For a survey of outstanding historians who have reflected on the issue (M. I. Rostovtzeff, F. W. Walbank, J. B. Bury, F. Tenney, W. E. Heitland, etc.), see Kagan, *Decline and Fall*. M. Cary (*History of Rome*) is representative of many ancient historians in devoting a number of pages to the "end of the empire," discussing factors like exhaustion of land and mineral resources, disease, vice, losses in war, weakness of the economy, lack of political freedom, a highly centralized government and taxation (550–558). This approach on the "decline of the ancient world" can also be noted in Katz, *Decline of Rome*. Jones (*Decline of the Ancient World*, 362–370) discusses the causes of the fall of the empire in a concluding chapter, and raises issues like economic deterioration, taxation and decline in public spirit.

10. See Jones, *Decline of the Ancient World*, 362–363; and Cary, *History of Rome*, 556. In his account of the period, Peter Brown focuses on cultural, economic and social factors; he also recognizes the crucial weakness of the army (*World of Late Antiquity*, 118–120).

Greek). The border of the empire in Europe, consisting of the Rhine and the Danube rivers, held quite well until the time of Emperor Marcus Aurelius (AD 160–180), when serious losses were first suffered by soldiers stationed to protect these territories.

Such attacks increased in intensity in the latter half of the third century, as the Goths in turn felt the pressure of the Huns in westward migration, driving them further inside the empire. The Visigoths defeated Emperor Valens and his troops in battle at Adrianople (AD 378).

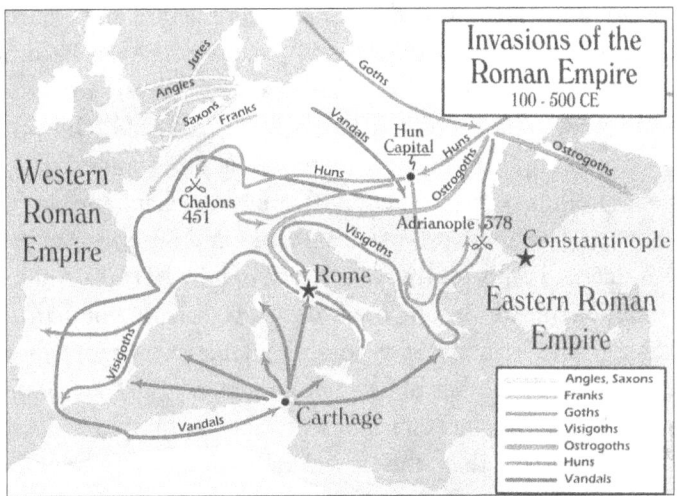

Map 13.1. Migration and invasion in the Empire, AD 100–500.
Map "Invasions of the Roman Empire" by MapMaster / CC BY-SA 2.5.

As the military situation worsened, other problems surfaced; economic distress was widespread, and we also hear of plague and pestilence wiping out entire population groups. These critical factors led Diocletian to the strategic move of dividing the administration of the empire into the eastern and western regions.[11] He also moved the imperial capital from Rome to Nicomedia, near the ancient city of Byzantium (later renamed Constantinople), in order to establish a more easily defended administrative centre not as far removed from the most troubled regions. From this time already "the eternal city" Rome was losing prestige and political significance. In Italy the imperial court moved to Milan.[12]

---

11. See discussion of these factors in ch. 5, §B.1.
12. This is the city where Augustine became court orator; see ch. 12, §D.3.

Military loss in the West cannot be disputed. But we also remember that the Germanic peoples had already been crossing the imperial borders in a more or less peaceful manner for centuries, and many of their tribes had been absorbed into the empire. By the third century these people had also been incorporated into the armies guarding the border.[13] Over the years they had adapted relatively well to Roman habits and culture. During the late third century, from about AD 370–470, this process accelerated, in part through growing pressure of the (Visi-)Goths and the Huns beyond them in a steady stream of migration from the east.[14]

The Visigoths retreated to settle in Spain after the sack and pillage of Rome in 410. Regardless of how one might assess that event, it was becoming clear that the old order was passing away. Imperial legions were too busy dealing with invading peoples to keep the borders well defended.[15] Once the Rhine-Danube border was broken through, there was no other suitable geographical line of defence in Europe to back it up. After entering Gaul, the German tribes continued on to Spain and North Africa. Franks and Burgundians established the modern state of France, taking over much of it by AD 500. Angles, Saxons and Jutes did the same for Britain, the Danes in Denmark, Lombards in North Italy, and Saxons in Germany. Slavs took the Balkans.[16] These tribes split the western empire into a number of new nation-states.[17] But the Roman Empire as such was able to retain its eastern base in Constantinople and Asia Minor.

Were military losses, then, the crucial factor in the collapse of the Roman Empire? Historians have introduced various theories to explain the fall. Most well known is the organic analogy for historical institutions espoused by the ideological historian Oswald Spengler (1880–1936).[18] He suggested that empires follow the pattern of an organism, with identifiable stages of birth, growth and maturity, illness and decay. On this model, death can be ascertained from natural causes, accident, murder, or suicide. Spengler used the fall of

---

13. Chadwick, *Early Church*, 247.
14. Chadwick, 247–248.
15. Cary, *History of Rome*, 556.
16. On these invasions, see P. Brown, *World of Late Antiquity*, 122–127.
17. With the exception of the Franks, Angles, Saxons and Jutes, who were all pagan, many barbarian tribes were Christian by this time. And even the remaining pagan tribes were Christianized under Pope Gregory the Great, when he sent Augustine (later Archbishop of Canterbury) as the first missionary to England. Clovis, ruler of the Franks, would be one of the most important converts to Christianity at this time (496).
18. Spengler's *The Decline of the West* (1918–1922, in German), with its metaphor of organic growth and decay, reflects some of the social pessimism of post-war Europe; see Pelikan, *Excellent Empire*, 10–11.

Rome as his model, and inspired a number of authors to study factors within the Roman Empire which might ultimately have caused its downfall, issues like the failure of genuine land reform, or growing disunity of its regions. Perhaps the collapse was caused simply by "the pressure of its own weight," that is, its sheer size? Other scholars examined evidence of "disease" in the prevalence of slavery as cheap labour, thereby removing incentives to develop technology and industry. Such scholarly efforts helped initiate a significant variant on the long-standing focus of Gibbon, who looked to the growing role of Christianity within the empire, the prevailing theological disputes, and Christian policies on war and violence, as determining factors for loss of morale within the empire.[19]

The chaotic conditions of the late third century did lead to significant depopulation, with consequences of real shortage of labour in areas from which the army was traditionally recruited. As a result the army came to depend on enrolment of barbarians as mercenaries; these could not be relied on to defend the empire as a patriotic duty.[20] They had to be paid to do their work. At the same time, the demands of a top-heavy administration and maintenance of a large army required heavy taxation; many peasants were paying taxes too burdensome in relation to their earnings. And tenants on the large estates of the western empire were charged rental fees so high that they could hardly feed their families. Even officials charged with tax collection regularly fled their duty because of the demands on their personal assets. The growing military threat contributed to economic breakdown and decentralization, as craftsmen and labourers fled the towns to take refuge on large estates.

Loss of border provinces along the Danube in this period accentuated the political separation between besieged western regions which were Latin-speaking, and the more wealthy and stable Greek-speaking parts of the empire in the east. Reduction of movement under such conditions, in turn, meant reduction of trade. Conditions in the western empire were on a downward spiral, and it is hard to disentangle causes from results. What makes analysis of the true causes more difficult is the fact that many of the weaknesses encountered in the West, like problems with the army, a corrupt bureaucracy, divisive theological disputes, depopulation of areas, or rigidity in social relations, were also present in the eastern part of the empire, the part which did not fall.[21]

---

19. On the eighteenth-century work of Edward Gibbon (1737–1794), see §B and §C below.

20. Chadwick, *Early Church*, 247. On the professionalization of the military, see also Cary, *History of Rome*, 556.

21. This point is recognized by Jones, *Decline of the Ancient World*, 362 and 370.

B. The Influence of Christianity

In that context we return to the factor which has held the attention of authors from the fourth century on, the (near) coincidence of the fall with the Christianizing of the empire. In modern times Edward Gibbon's *History of the Decline and Fall of the Roman Empire* (1776–1781) revived the old argument that Christianity was responsible for the collapse of the empire.[22] According to Gibbon, Christianity sapped public morale, suppressed intellectual life and undermined the unity of the empire through doctrinal controversies. After AD 381 Theodosius I closed the pagan temples, and banned worship of the traditional gods. Already at that time traditionalists in the empire argued that disaster was inevitable once the gods on whom Rome had always relied for its victories were no longer respected and worshipped.[23] By 411 the pagan opposition challenged the Christians, "When we were sacrificing to our gods, Rome was flourishing. Now our sacrifices are forbidden, and see what is happening to Rome everywhere."[24]

---

22. Characterized by Enlightenment rationalism (and in that respect comparable with the approach of Voltaire), Edward Gibbon's work would influence generations to come on the topic. Pelikan opens his discussion by citing Gibbon's oft-quoted summary of having "described the triumph of barbarism and religion" (*Excellent Empire*, 29; see also 39). Jones makes only a brief reference to the question of Christian influence as a factor in the absence of a spirit of public service (*Decline of the Ancient World*, 369–370). While earlier editions of Cary's *History of Rome* take a similar approach in discussing the causes of the fall of Rome, the third edition (with H. H. Scullard) does note the role of religion, recognizing the weakness of Gibbon's thesis (Cary's *History of Rome*, 551, 554 and 557–558).

23. Johannes Geffcken's *The Last Days of Greco-Roman Paganism* provided one of the more substantive responses to the argument on the role of Christianity in late antiquity:
No scholar of ancient history . . . will now believe the dogma of earlier days, that there is a direct connection between the coming into existence and spread of Christianity on the one hand and the decline of paganism on the other. The exact opposite is the case. The struggle of Christianity against the deep faith of the pagan multitudes . . . was incomparably harder than its conflict with the power of the Roman state (Author's preface, vii).

Proper recognition of the continued power of paganism means recognition of the victory of the new faith as the greater achievement. In this connection Geffcken alludes to Adolf von Harnack's *The Mission and Expansion of Christianity*, giving the story from the side of Christianity. His own work aims to give the comparable story for the end of paganism (from the third century), for which he claims a remarkable durability, particularly in its alliance with philosophy (*Last Days of Greco-Roman Paganism*, 307). Geffcken cites the role of economic decline, as well as political factors in the demise of the empire (*Last Days of Greco-Roman Paganism*, vii).

24. Augustine, *Sermon* 296.6; see also Frend, *Rise of Christianity*, 700.

Certainly, Christians tended to pacifism from the beginning.[25] Especially when Christianity was still persecuted, Tertullian was prominent among those making strong arguments to dissuade Christians from joining the army.[26] Christians were encouraged to support the state, rather, by praying for those in positions of power.[27] Was the biblical advice to "turn the other cheek" the real determinative in the prohibition on military service for Christians? Far more significant, actually, was the fact that participating in pagan rites was obligatory for those in the military as it was for those in political office. Even so, we hear of significant numbers of Christians serving in the army by the third century. They were recruited to help defend the frontier areas. But as long as they remained in service or held political positions they were excluded from communion in the congregations, as we know from the record of a church council in Gaul (AD 313). The popes also continued to bar from ordination those holding government posts. The reason was that such work inevitably involved them in pagan idolatrous rites, which were deemed incompatible with the Christian confession. This would be even more true for those serving in the army.[28]

But did these factors really reduce enthusiasm to resist the enemy and to defend the empire against invaders? Did Christianity really weaken the empire in this way, lending its weight to the forces of disintegration? In answering this question it is important to remember, as Augustine realized, that Christianity had already reached the German peoples before the fourth century, through the work of Ulfilas the Goth (b. ca. 310).[29] In fact, Arian Christianity was widespread among the Germanic tribes. The Goths invading Rome were certainly not oblivious to the presence of Christianity, and were reluctant to raze churches.

Political separation between East and West inevitably affected the church. Yet, both structurally and organizationally, Christianity remained united for many centuries to come.[30] The Arian crisis did not ultimately divide Christianity,

---

25. In addition, Latourette acknowledges that the social groups to which most early Christians belonged at that time would not have been recruited for the armies (*History of the Expansion of Christianity*, 242–243).

26. Latourette, *History of the Expansion of Christianity*, 243.

27. See the discussion of this issue in ch. 5, §B.3.

28. Latourette, *History of the Expansion of Christianity*, 243.

29. Chadwick, *Early Church*, 249. On Ulfilas, see ch. 10, §B.5 and note 83.

30. See Jones, *Decline of the Ancient World*, 362. Growing language barriers would exacerbate differences between Christianity, East and West, but the decisive split did not come until the eleventh century, and then it was largely due to the Crusades and behaviour of the Crusaders who were backed by western Christian rulers.

nor did the West experience the bitter theological divisions which would finally alienate Christians of Syria or Egypt in the sixth and seventh centuries. Indeed, as the political centre moved from Rome to Constantinople, the organizational capacities and prestige of the church in the West grew proportionately.

So we need to ask, if theological dispute is thought to have caused division and sapped morale, why the empire in the East did not fall earlier than the western empire? And we remember that Constantine had hoped to use Christianity to foster unity within the empire, as a powerful counterweight to factors of disintegration in the third century. There is no solid evidence to show that Christians were less ready to fight when it was necessary to defend themselves or their communities. On the contrary, Augustine of Hippo's masterpiece, *The City of God*, shows us how seriously Christians were reflecting on the demands of a time of invasion and war.

C. Augustine's Contribution in *The City of God*

Although the theme of Augustine's *The City of God* has a timeless quality, the work was specifically motivated by the sacking of Rome by the Goths in 410 (the event noted in the passage with which we opened this chapter).[31] Like other Christian writers of the time, Augustine recognized that God may use war to correct the corruption and immorality of human society. Thus he begins the work by responding to charges of traditionalists that Rome had fallen because of its conversion to Christianity and the subsequent neglect of the pagan gods honoured by the Romans from its earliest days. The work shows Augustine's superb command of ancient history, and judicious use of themes from that history to refute these accusations.

Augustine was not alone in developing this argument. His contemporary, Orosius, writing the *Historia contra Paganos* (*History against the Pagans*) focused on all the disasters which had overcome Rome while worshipping pagan deities.[32] Not long after, Salvian joined other Christian authors in giving his analysis in the *De Gubernatione Dei* (*On the Rule of God*), arguing that attacks of the barbarians on the empire were part of God's punishment for the sins of the Roman people, their oppression of the poor, public immorality and addiction to public games.[33] By comparison, the barbarians were typically austere, righteous and chaste, even if they were uncivilized. The fifth-century Latin poet, Commodian, who may have had African roots, also welcomed the

---

31. Chadwick, *Early Church*, 225.
32. Pelikan, *Excellent Empire*, 94; and Chadwick, *Early Church*, 225.
33. Chadwick, *Early Church*, 248.

barbarian onslaught as God's response to Roman pride and the greed of its wealthy citizens.[34] To answer pagan accusations in *The City of God*, Augustine used and adapted elements from both approaches.[35]

The work begins with five books giving an account of pagan cults, showing that they could not assure prosperity; nor could they avert disaster. In the next five books Augustine shows that worship of the pagan gods was not helpful in assuring happiness after death, any more than it could assure happiness in this world. After clearing away these arguments on pagan religion, the second major part (consisting of twelve books) gives a more constructive discussion, starting with four books on the origin of the two cities, the city of this world and the city of God. Augustine takes his readers right back to early biblical accounts of the creation to show that, throughout history, there have been two cities, or rather two city-states, one from God and one human.[36] Each was built on the foundation of its own kind of love, whether love of God or love of the self. In human history the two cities or kingdoms are mixed, although they are also in irreconcilable opposition; the city of God is not, however, simply to be identified with the church, nor is the city of this earth to be identified with the Roman Empire.[37] Augustine uses another four books to continue that history. He finally turns to eschatology in the last four books (19–22); discussing the respective destinies of these cities, he shows that, in the end, only the kingdom of God will remain. Human kingdoms, built on selfish aims, are doomed to pass away.

Augustine recognizes that God allowed Rome to flourish through greatness of human ability; he could certainly commend the virtues of great Roman leaders like Cato. Under pagan gods and leaders Rome had prospered, while Christian emperors had experienced many disasters.[38] But even the greatest of human achievements cannot last forever. So Augustine advises Christians of his time not to be too deeply disturbed by the disasters; they should redirect

---

34. Isichei, *History of Christianity in Africa*, 41.

35. As noted above, Augustine shows the contours of his argument already in the passage of *The City of God* 1.7 given at the opening of this chapter (see also Stevenson, *Creeds, Councils and Controversies*, 247–248). See further Latourette, *History of the Expansion of Christianity*, 175–176; and Chadwick, *Early Church*, 226–227.

36. See *The City of God* 11.1, also quoted in Stevenson, *Creeds, Councils and Controversies*, 266–267.

37. Chadwick, *Early Church*, 226.

38. Pelikan recognizes a degree of ambiguity in Augustine's analysis of the fall of Rome. Augustine avoids Eusebius's affirmation of the fall of Rome as a triumph of the Christian church (see Pelikan, *Excellent Empire*, 100). He does not praise barbarian invaders at the expense of the Romans, as does Orosius. Nor does he affirm the millennialist approach characterizing the apocalypticism of Jerome (Pelikan, *Excellent Empire*, 95–96 and 99–100).

their expectations by looking to the heavenly city. Setbacks could be welcomed as God's discipline, which is meant to purify the elect. The empire had fulfilled an important role as the context for spreading the gospel. Once this purpose was finished, God had allowed the Roman Empire, like many other human kingdoms, to decline and collapse. Only the kingdom of God endures, and it is destined for ultimate victory.[39]

How then does Augustine evaluate the Roman Empire of his day? Augustine was certainly no pacifist. His letters of advice to anguished public servants on how to act as Christians are filled with good common sense; they are to "turn the other cheek" while also fulfilling their duty as public servants. On the issue of military service, Augustine knew that the position of Christians within the state had changed since Constantine, and he recognized the need for Christian participation in war, certainly if it is based on an honourable cause.[40]

So he reminds his readers that Jesus never rejected service to the state or in the army, asking only that in these various enterprises they remain honest, and be content with fair wages. On this issue, Augustine is responsible for an initial affirmation of the "just war" approach for Christians.

Figure 13.1. St Martin leaving the imperial army to seek baptism as a Christian. This 14th-century fresco was painted by Simone Martini for the Lower Church of San Francesco (Assisi). The York Project. Public Domain.

---

39. Gibbon was certainly familiar with Augustine's *City of God*, and respected its author for a "strong, capacious, argumentative mind" (Pelikan, *Excellent Empire*, 94). According to Pelikan, Gibbon wanted to refute Augustine's celebration of the "triumph of religion over both the barbarism of the invaders and the barbarism of the Roman Empire" (*Excellent Empire*, 94–95).

40. On this question, Augustine followed the example given by Ambrose; see Latourette, *History of the Expansion of Christianity*, 244.

In conclusion, we recognize the fall of the Roman Empire as an issue that has fascinated scholars for many centuries. Even today, there is no unanimity on the specific time or event marking its demise. Scholarly analysis also demonstrates considerable variety of approach in explaining the cause of collapse. What is clear is the factor of military weakness in the western, European part of the empire. Economic and social factors made their own contribution. However, it is also clear that significant religious change, specifically the acceptance of Christianity, cannot be substantiated as the leading cause of political instability and collapse in the West. Those who hold to such a position need to demonstrate why the same change in religion did not also lead to collapse in the eastern empire. For Christianity was equally strong in the east and the Byzantine Empire survived another thousand years after the invasions in Europe.

Questions for Discussion and Review

The Fall of the (Western) Roman Empire

1. Why was Rome considered "the eternal city"? Which factors brought this prestigious role for Rome to an end?

2. What are the traditional dates for the fall of the Roman Empire, east and west? Why are these dates important?

3. Which important military events marked the downfall of the empire in Europe?

4. Which factors were responsible for the increasing weakness in defending the borders of the empire along the Rhine and Danube?

5. Which other factors, social, political and economic, contributed to the demise of the western empire?

6. Why did pagan traditionalists consider Christianity responsible for the disasters affecting the empire in the fourth and fifth centuries?

7. Which modern authors have revived this argument? What are the reasons for coming back to this dated position? What is its main shortcoming?

8. Which arguments were used by early Christian authors to answer such an accusation? Evaluate the effectiveness of their response.

9. How did Augustine answer pagan traditionalists who considered Christians responsible for the sack of Rome? Evaluate the effectiveness of the answer given in *The City of God*.

Further Reading

Brown, Peter R. L. *The World of Late Antiquity, from Marcus Aurelius to Muhammad*. London: Thames & Hudson, 1971.

———. *Society and the Holy in Late Antiquity*. London: Faber & Faber, 1982.

Geffcken, Johannes. *The Last Days of Greco-Roman Paganism* [Der Ausgang des griechisch-römischen Heidentums]. Translated by S. MacCormack. Amsterdam: North-Holland Publishing, 1978.

Hadas, Moses., ed. *Gibbon's Decline and Fall of the Roman Empire: A Modern Abridgment*. New York: Fawcett Books, Random House, 1992.

Harnack, Adolf von. *The Mission and Expansion of Christianity in the First Three Centuries*. Vol. 1 of the 1908 edition. Translated by James Moffatt, with foreword by Jaroslav Pelikan. Gloucester, MA: Peter Smith, Harper Torchbook; London: Williams & Norgate, 1972.

Hodges, R., and D. Whitehouse. *Mohammed, Charlemagne and the Origins of Europe: Archeology and the Pirenne Thesis*. London: Duckworth, 1983.

Jones, A. H. M. *The Decline of the Ancient World*. London: Longmans, Green & Co., 1966.

Kagan, D. ed. *Decline and Fall of the Roman Empire: Why Did It Collapse?* Boston: D. C. Heath, 1962.

———. *The End of the Roman Empire: Decline or Transformation?* Lexington, MA: D. C. Heath, 1978.

Katz, Solomon. *The Decline of Rome and the Rise of Mediaeval Europe*. Ithaca, NY: Cornell University Press, 1955.

MacMullen, Ramsay. *Corruption and the Decline of Rome*. New Haven: Yale University Press, 1988.

Momigliano, A., ed. *The Conflict between Paganism and Christianity in the Fourth Century*. Oxford: Clarendon Press, 1963.

Pirenne, Henri. *Mohammed and Charlemagne*. Translated by B. Miall. London: Allen & Unwin, 1939.

Spengler, Oswald. *The Decline of the West*. Translated by Charles Francis Atkinson. London: Allen & Unwin, 1926.

Toynbee, Arnold J. *Hellenism: The History of a Civilization*. London: Oxford University Press, 1959.

———. *A Study of History*. 12 vols. London: Oxford University Press, 1935–1961.

Ward-Perkins, Bryan. *The Fall of Rome and the End of Civilization*. New York: Oxford University Press, 2005.

Appendix I

From Patristics to the Study of Early Christianity

Contemporary study of early Christianity is based on a long tradition designated also by its traditional title, *Patristic Studies*, or simply *Patristics*.[1] As such, it reflects the original focus on the "Fathers" (in Latin, *patres*).[2] That title was used to designate important leaders or teachers who shaped and guided the Christian church in its early years; it reflects widespread commendation for authentic teaching and holiness of life.[3] The list typically includes leaders, preachers and theologians like Tertullian, Cyprian, Ambrose, Jerome and Augustine in the West; Clement of Alexandria, Athanasius and the Cappadocians in the East.[4]

A. Renaissance and Reformation

Patristics as we know it today came into its own with the Renaissance and Reformation. Renaissance scholars were stimulated by the influx of scholars from the east, after the fall of Constantinople (1453), bringing with them

---

1. As such *Patristics* represents an abbreviation for *Theologia Patristica* (further abbreviated as *Patrologia* or *Patrology*), the study of the writings of the early Christian Fathers, particularly because of their impact on early Christianity and the decisions made in ecclesiastic assemblies, whether at localized synods or ecumenical councils.

2. Drobner, *Fathers of the Church*, 3. Young ("Greek Fathers," 135–136) suggests that use of the term "Father" may be based on Paul calling himself "father" with respect to the church in Corinth, meaning that he took responsibility for bringing this congregation to birth. As such, the term includes an element of affection.

3. Their teaching was accepted on the basis of agreement with the traditions handed down from the apostles, on the principle of apostolic succession (on which see ch. 7, §A.6 and ch. 8, §C.1); see also Drobner, *Fathers of the Church*, 3–4.

4. For the western church the term *Patristics* includes especially Fathers of early Christianity; the Eastern Orthodox Church, however, recognizes as Fathers even bishops, teachers and martyrs of the last century.

a treasury of ancient Greek literature, Christian and pagan.[5] This meant a significant addition to works of the Latin Fathers available at the time, mostly as *Florilegia*, that is, collections of favourite passages, biblical commentaries and excerpts from papal decrees or church councils.[6] It was a time of renewed critical attention to early Christian manuscripts, especially because these were being prepared for first printed editions.

Patristic scholarship was affected deeply also by the Reformation, spearheaded by Martin Luther and the publication of his theses in Wittenberg (1517). With the birth of the Protestant churches, the reformers typically regarded the beliefs and practice in the Roman Catholic church as a corruption of an earlier pure expression of the faith; the blame for deterioration was usually assigned to a process of accommodation to pagan Greco-Roman culture in late antiquity. This explains the slogan, *ad fontes*, the call to return to the roots of Christianity, to the simplicity of worship in the early church of the apostles.[7] Appealing to the authority of Scripture, the reformers challenged the dominant argument from "tradition."[8]

These concerns motivated renewed study of patristic writings in countries dominated by the reformers, and careful examination of early Christian practice to provide a model for their churches in terms of liturgy, governance and discipline. Luther (1483–1546), Zwingli (1484–1531) and Calvin (1509–1564) all cited the Fathers in support of their own teaching and practice.[9] In the prefatory address to the king of France in the *Institutes of the Christian Religion* (1536), Calvin used the patristic witness to show that the teachings of the reformers were identical to those of the Fathers.[10]

---

5. Since Greek had become a dead language for Europeans, these scholars from Constantinople would once more teach western Christians to read NT texts for themselves; Backus, "Early Church in the Renaissance," 289–290.

6. Backus, "Early Church in the Renaissance," 300.

7. On the theme of "return to the sources," (i.e. seeking the simplicity of early Christianity), see Helleman, *Hellenization Revisited*, 429–430.

8. The Catholic historian Caesar Baronius (1538–1607) responded by publishing the 14-volume *Ecclesiastical Annals*, arguing for the Roman church as true recipient of the Christian tradition; see Lössl, *Early Church*, 34–35.

9. Backus cites the debate between followers of Zwingli and Luther on the presence of Christ in the Eucharist, with Zwingli appealing to Chrysostom (ca. 347–407) on the symbolic presence; Luther responded by debating his interpretation of the passage (Backus, "Early Church in the Renaissance," 294).

10. Calvin contends that, "if it were to our present purpose, I could with no trouble at all prove that the greater part of what we are saying today meets their [i.e. the fathers] approval (*Institutes of the Christian Religion* 1.18, citing the 1960 translation of F. Lewis Battle)." But in the next few pages Calvin recognizes issues, like the sacraments, icons or fasting, on which the fathers are not in agreement; see the *Institutes*, 1.18–32. For the "Prefatory Address" to King

At that time Roman Catholic scholars were also engaged in publication of works of the Fathers; we have only to think of the significant editorial and critical work of Erasmus (1469–1536).[11] But as a discipline, Patristics was established with the publication of the *Patrologia* by the Lutheran Johannes Gerhard (d. 1673); it was subtitled *On the Life and Work of Early Christian Church Teachers*.[12] Ongoing interest in subsequent years is evident from publication of critical editions of the Fathers alongside editions of pagan Greco-Roman authors like Virgil and Cicero.

Interest in early Christianity was also sparked by attention to manuscripts of the Bible as these became available. Particularly important was the Codex Alexandrinus, a gift from the patriarch of Constantinople to the king of England (in 1628). This famous manuscript of the Bible included an important letter of the early bishop of Rome, Clement. Equally significant was the publication of the genuine letters of Ignatius (d. ca. 115) by the Dutch scholar Isaac Voss (1646).[13]

B. Seventeenth- and Eighteenth-Century Developments

The heirs of the reformers continued to look to the Fathers for an authentic interpretation of the Scriptures. Even the seventeenth-century nonconformist John Wesley (1703–1791) can be cited for such appreciation and respect.[14] During the seventeenth century the well-established English universities, Oxford and Cambridge, had become important centres of patristic scholarship. Especially important was the work of Richard Bentley of Cambridge (1662–1742), whose acquaintance with the Fathers and expertise in emendation of

---

Francis I of France, see *Institutes*, 1.9–30. See also Backus, "Early Church in the Renaissance," 293 and 301–302.

11. The outstanding contribution of Erasmus, his preparation of the printed New Testament (1516), known as the *Textus Receptus* (i.e. the text as we have received it), was accepted for some two centuries, even though it was based on manuscripts that were less than perfect. This is especially significant because in their desire to provide the Scriptures in vernacular translation, the Reformers used the *Textus Receptus* for their translation of the NT; see Neill, *Interpretation*, 64. We also note *Acta Sacrorum*, the Bollandist project by Catholic scholars to establish a calendar of feast days for the saints; Lössl, *Early Church*, 36.

12. Drobner, *Fathers of the Church*, 5.

13. Grant, *After the New Testament*, 4–6.

14. Young, "Retrospect: Interpretation and Appropriation," 485.

classical texts was significant in developing principles for reconstructing a critical text of the New Testament.[15]

Europe, and particularly Germany, also became an important centre of scholarly study at this time, as Enlightenment scholarship demonstrated a new critical approach to historical evidence.[16] This approach certainly influenced the work of Edward Gibbon (1737–1794), whose massive history, *The Decline and Fall of the Roman Empire*, depicted Christianity in late antiquity as the triumph of corruption and barbarism.[17] Such a critical historical emphasis also represents the rise of a more professional scholarly approach at newly founded universities.[18] This was a time of new interest for the sciences, especially as the companion of industrialization, signaling a trend which would eventually serve to relegate university study of theology to the sidelines.[19]

---

15. Neill, *Interpretation*, 65. Using principles developed by Richard Bentley and J. J. Griesbach (1745–1812), scholars began critical emendation of the text of the New Testament; important in this regard are Karl Lachmann (1793–1851) and Count Tischendorf (1815–1874). Equally important was the nineteenth-century contribution on the text by Cambridge scholars Westcott and Hort, on whom see Neill, *Interpretation*, 69–75, and note 25 below.

16. The rise of German scholarship is marked by substantive contributions in philosophy by Immanuel Kant (1724–1804) and Georg W. F. Hegel (1770–1831), whose work would have a significant impact on theology and would also influence understanding of early Christianity (see Neill, *Interpretation*, 2–5). On G. B. Niebuhr's critical approach to the history of Rome and of Israel, see Neill, *Interpretation*, 7–8.

17. On Gibbon's views, see especially ch. 13. Lössl recognizes Gibbon's careful use of the reliable 16-volume work of L. S. le Nain de Tillemont (1637–1698) on the first six centuries of the church; he also used the *Ecclesiastical History* of the eighteenth-century rationalist Lutheran church historian, J. L. Mosheim. Influenced by the Enlightenment, Mosheim regarded transcendent factors irrelevant for early church history (i.e. before Constantine); see Lössl, *Early Church*, 37. Even so, Mosheim made a positive contribution through his habit of incorporating the primary sources, many of which were difficult to access at the time, except in Catholic libraries (Clark, "From Patristics," 9). By the next century this work would be replaced by J. Gieseler's *Text-Book of Church History* (1824), also noted for lengthy quotes from original sources, but more evangelical in spirit. Some decades later scholars would appreciate the massive *General History of the Christian Religion and Church* by Berlin professor A. Neander; see Clark, "From Patristics," 9.

18. According to Elizabeth Clark, "Patristics" became a discipline "in the modern sense of the word" only in the nineteenth century, when (German) universities served as a venue for developing scholarly tools, critical texts, scholarly journals and conferences (Clark, "From Patristics to Early Christian Studies," 8). She realizes that state-supported universities would not necessarily be hospitable for disciplines closely intertwined with theology. Indeed, in nineteenth-century France, anticlerical attitudes pushed Patristics out of the university, to be incorporated in the Catholic Institute; the situation was further complicated by a law of 1880 prohibiting such private institutions from granting degrees, or referring to themselves as a "university" ("From Patristics," 11–12).

19. Lössl, *Early Church*, 38.

C. The Nineteenth Century: Historical Criticism

Historical criticism and a purely historical interpretation of the Scriptures made an impact on the revolutionary work of D. F. Strauss (1808–1874), *The Quest of the Historical Jesus* (1835). Equally influential was his disciple, F. C. Baur of Tübingen (1792–1860). Baur agreed with Strauss on the supernatural (or miraculous) as mythical and essentially unknowable because it cannot be examined for historical evidence. Accordingly, he rejected historical knowledge of a transcendent, personal God who might intervene in this world; and the life of Jesus certainly would not be subject to known categories of history.[20] In his understanding of early Christianity, Baur applied an Hegelian dialectic of three stages, beginning with

- the thesis: Judaic/Petrine Christianity;
- the antithesis: Pauline/Hellenic Christianity;
- and synthesis: Catholic Christianity, the response to Gnosticism.

The approach led to absurd conclusions on classification of New Testament documents, dating these to the late second century.[21] Baur's dialectical understanding would continue to impact study of early Christianity through its use by Harnack.[22]

More constructively, the nineteenth century witnessed the massive collection of patristic sources in Greek and Latin by Jean-Paul Migne, the *Patrologiae Cursus Completus*. Although many of the manuscripts were published without adequate critical editing, the hundreds of volumes made available by this collection gave an important stimulus to the translation of patristic documents in modern languages.[23] At this time the Oxford Movement (with E. Pusey and J. Henry Newman) began publishing the Oxford Library of the Fathers (1835–1888). Their "high church" orientation was balanced

---

20. Neill, *Interpretation*, 12–16.

21. Neill attributes the serious mistakes made by Baur to his (philosophically motivated) presuppositions on the purely empirical nature of critical historical work (i.e. supposedly free of prior assumptions), and his understanding of a Hegelian dialectical process in history (Neill, *Interpretation*, 24–25 and 27–28).

22. Chesnut, "A Century of Patristic Studies," 38; and Neill, *Interpretation*, 19–21. On Harnack, see Helleman, *Hellenization Revisited*, 437, 444–445; see also the comment of Munck, "Pauline Research" (note 40 below).

23. Lössl, *Early Church*, 38. Equally important was nineteenth-century work in editing patristic texts by Benedictine Maurist fathers, who had begun to publish the works of Augustine in 1679; in the eighteenth century they continued this work with editions of John Chrysostom, Basil, Tertullian, Cyril of Jerusalem, Cyprian, Origen, and Gregory of Nazianzus. Much of their work was reprinted by Migne, who published the *Patrologia Latina* (1844–1864) in 218 volumes, and *Patrologia Graeca* (1857–1866) in 166 volumes. See Clark, "From Patristics," 8 and 10.

in Protestant Scotland by the work of A. Roberts and J. Donaldson on the Ante-Nicene Christian Library, publishing texts relevant for more "evangelical" interests.[24]

In England the response to Baur and the Tübingen school on late dating of New Testament writings focused on citation of these documents by the Fathers. Collaborating with B. F. Westcott (1825–1901) and F. J. A. Hort (1828–1892) to address the weaknesses of the German scholarly work, J. B. Lightfoot (1828–1889) examined the authenticity of the seven letters of Ignatius (recognized by Voss), and the first Epistle of Clement.[25] Because both Ignatius and Clement cite many New Testament documents as already in circulation in their own time, the end of the first century, Lightfoot disputed Baur's dating of New Testament books after AD 130.[26] Lightfoot also assigned a date at the end of the first century AD for the newly discovered *Didachê* (*Teaching of the Twelve Apostles*), of interest for its discussion of church order; although somewhat speculative, the conclusions of Lightfoot on dating are now widely accepted.[27]

Such an approach on the New Testament was affirmed by a very different type of scholarly work in archaeology. From his work on Greek inscriptions of ancient Asia Minor, Sir William Ramsay (1851–1939) was able to corroborate Luke's thorough acquaintance with relevant titles of imperial and local officials, and thereby support the authenticity and date of New Testament books like Luke/Acts.[28] Ramsay's work points ahead to the growing significance of field work and archaeology for patristic scholarship, as in the discovery of papyrus fragments at the trash heap of Oxyrynchus in the Egyptian desert (1897).[29]

---

24. Clark ("From Patristics," 13) notes the significant publication of the *Journal for Theological Studies* (from 1899), edited by Henry B. Swete, promoting moderate use of German critical scholarship.

25. On the exceptional significance of work done by these three scholars, see Grant, *After the New Testament*, 6. Their efforts to address historical weaknesses of the Baur position took the format of commentary on the New Testament; see Neill, *Interpretation*, 33–35.

26. Neill, *Interpretation*, 47–50, 53 and 57. The results of Lightfoot's work were published in *The Apostolic Fathers*, still in print in the collaborative edition of Lightfoot and Harmer (of 1891); this work was recently (1999) updated by Holmes, *The Apostolic Fathers: Greek Texts and English Translations*.

27. Neill, *Interpretation*, 60. Neill recognizes the significance of Westcott's knowledge of the Christian Fathers in establishing definitions for a dictionary of the Greek NT, since the literary context of the early Fathers was relatively close to that of the NT (*Interpretation*, 92).

28. Neill, *Interpretation*, 141–143.

29. Neill, 146. Significant work on deciphering and publishing these finds must be attributed to B. P. Grenfell and A. S. Hunt. Such work provided an entirely new evaluation of the Greek language in common Hellenistic use, the *Koiné*; the results are evident in J. H. Moulton's *Grammar of New Testament Greek* and grammar text of F. Blass and A. DeBrunner (1931), translated into English by R. W. Funk (1961); see Neill, *Interpretation*, 149.

Adolf von Harnack

In Germany the approach of Baur continued to make its impact on Albert Ritschl (1822–1889) and Adolf von Harnack (1851–1930). The historical-critical reading of the Bible remained dominant well into the twentieth century. Ritschl's approach to early Christianity was deeply influenced by contemporary epistemological rejection of the influence of Plato in patristic theology, and also by Bismarck's attack on Roman Catholicism within the German Empire (1871–1887).[30] Harnack agreed that patristic theology had wrongly subordinated Christian truth to the philosophical ideas of Plato and Aristotle.[31] Since Catholic theology (after Aquinas) was based on Aristotle, Harnack's position contributed to Protestant (anti-Catholic) suspicions that anything beyond the New Testament itself should be denigrated as "Catholicism."[32]

Although Harnack continued to highlight a contrast between Gentile and Jewish Christianity,[33] his work, *The Mission and Expansion of Christianity*, reveals a more careful approach on the historical data.[34] Harnack agreed with

---

30. On Ritschl's essay "Theology and Metaphysics" (1881), see Chesnut, "A Century of Patristic Studies," 39–40. Clark remarks that German scholars made a significant contribution with their use of historical and critical methods, but, "their sectarian and anti-Catholic prejudices, overlaid with a modified Hegelianism, obstructed the development of a more solidly 'historical' view of the early church" ("From Patristics," 9).

31. Chesnut, "A Century of Patristic Studies," 41.

32. Even within Catholic circles, scholars used early Christianity as a weapon to encourage reform – witness the 1879 papal bull of Pope Leo XIII (1878–1903), *Aeterni Patris*, with its recommendation to study Thomas Aquinas as a way of unifying Catholic thought in the face of contemporary challenges. In practice that meant the dominance of Neo-Thomism, also for the study of early Christianity, as is shown in the work of Joseph Tixeront, *Histoire des dogmes* (1905–1912). He appealed (against Harnack) to the doctrine of "substantial immutability of dogma" as revealed truth, but agreed at least in part with Harnack on the Greek philosophical form of dogma, as an inevitable development (Chesnut, "A Century of Patristic Studies," 51). Louis Duchesne (1843–1922), on the other hand, used a modernist perspective in his *Histoire ancienne de l'église* (1912), while a teleological approach characterizes his work on church development over the centuries. Rejecting rigid Thomist scholasticism, Duchesne was also critical of Platonism as it affected early Christian teaching (in Justin, Clement of Alexandria or Origen); in his support of the growing role of the bishop in antiquity, he also accented the need for collegiality (Chesnut, "A Century of Patristic Studies," 48–50; Lössl, *Early Church*, 39).

33. See Helleman, *Hellenization Revisited*, 437; also 72–73.

34. Neill, *Interpretation*, 57–58. Between 1882 and 1897, Harnack and his colleagues initiated an important series of studies on early Christian texts, *Texte und Untersuchungen*, and a series of critical editions of Christian texts, *Die griechischen christlichen Schriftsteller der ersten drei Jahrhunderte* [*Greek Christian Authors of the First Three Centuries*]. At this time a comparable series on Latin authors was begun in Vienna, *Corpus Scriptorum Ecclesiasticorurm Latinorum*; see Lössl, *Early Church*, 39. Such work was continued in the twentieth century in Belgium with the *Corpus Christianorum, Series Latina* (1954) and *Series Graeca* (1977). The French Jesuits also worked on an outstanding series of texts, the *Sources Chrétiennes*, consisting now of some 500 volumes; see Clark, "From Patristics," 8, 12.

Lightfoot on earlier dating of the New Testament; he also appreciated the significant work of Edwin Hatch (1835–1889), *The Organization of the Early Christian Churches* (1881),[35] and *The Influence of Greek Ideas on Christianity* (1889).[36] Harnack's own *The History of Dogma* (*Lehrbuch der Dogmengeschichte*, 1886–1889), presented dogma as the "work of the Greek spirit on the soil of the Gospel," based on his view that Christian belief was expressed in forms borrowed from non-Christian Greek philosophy already in the first century.[37] Pagan Greek philosophy served to transform a living faith into creeds and rituals. This is also the underlying theme of Harnack's immensely popular lectures of 1899–1900, *What Is Christianity*? (*Das Wesen des Christentums*), as it avoided the theological constraints of (Catholic) dogma by portraying Jesus as a modern Martin Luther, an advocate of spiritual freedom. Harnack's anti-Catholic rhetoric takes us back to the early post-Reformation controversy.[38]

On that theme the American scholar Philip Schaff (1819–1893), author of an eight-volume *History of the Christian Church* (1858–1890), was certainly ahead of his time, for he regarded Protestantism and Catholicism more ecumenically, as two branches growing from a common trunk.[39] But Harnack's position continued to make a deep impact throughout the twentieth century, even as scholars of early Christianity refuted or refined that position.[40] In his study of the "Greek spirit" as it influenced Cappadocian Fathers like Gregory of Nyssa, Werner Jaeger's *Early Christianity and Greek Paideia* (1962) presented patristic theology as a positive culmination of Greek thought. Thus Jaeger paved the way for more detailed studies by G. C. Stead or J. M. Dillon on the role of key philosophical terms in Greek.[41] In his biography of Augustine (2000

---

35. Harnack himself translated this work into German.

36. The work focused on the influence of Greek thought and cultural patterns on early Christianity, specifically on the role of logic, rhetoric and metaphysics, for which Harnack provided additional material when it was published in German (1892); see Neill, *Interpretation*, 137–138. It was published as a paperback in New York (1957).

37. Chesnut, "A Century of Patristic Studies," 36–38. Harnack's work on dogma was translated into English by N. Buchanan (from 1894–1899). For more recent analysis, see Rowe, "Adolf von Harnack," 69–98.

38. Neill, *Interpretation*, 131–136. Clark ("From Patristics," 12) points to Alfred Loisy, *L'Evangile et l'église*, as a response to Harnack's "essentializing" of the core of early Christianity in his *Das Wesen des Christentums* ("essence" is the English equivalent of the German *Wesen*).

39. Chesnut, "Century of Patristic Studies," 41.

40. Even in 1965 Munck complained that arguments of the Tübingen school on the Jewish/Gentile division of Christianity, especially when they have already been refuted, still continue to hinder correct understanding of early Christianity in Palestine; see Munck, "Pauline Research," 168–169.

41. Chesnut, "A Century of Patristic Studies," 41–42 and 43. See Stead (*Divine Substance*) and Dillon (*Middle Platonists*).

[1967]), Peter Brown also respected Greco-Roman antiquity as the context for his study, even as he incorporated a broadened socio-political understanding of that ancient world in scholarly examination of Augustine's life and work.[42]

One aspect of Harnack's work which has received extensive attention and correction is his understanding of Judaism in the New Testament and early Christianity. Characteristic elements like angelology and demonology, as well as an apocalyptic eschatology, had escaped Harnack's attention.[43] Already in the nineteenth century Alfred Edersheim (1825–1889), writing *The Life and Times of Jesus the Messiah* (1883), had concerned himself with that Jewish background, and introduced Rabbinic materials relevant for the gospels.[44] While H. L. Strack and P. Billerbeck provided an indispensable tool by using the Talmud and Midrash in their commentary on the New Testament,[45] the work of W. Bousset (1865–1920), *Die Religion des Judentums im neutestamentlichem Zeitalter* (*The Religion of the Jews in New Testament Times* (1903)), represented the "history of religions" school of thought on this theme.[46] More recently the Catholic scholar Jean Daniélou has called attention to the debt of early biblical study to Jewish exegetical work on the Old Testament, recognizing the significant influence of Judaism and early Jewish Christianity alongside that of Greco-Roman culture.

---

42. See P. Brown, *Augustine of Hippo*; on scholarly implementation of a methodology which takes us back to Harnack, see Chesnut, "A Century of Patristic Studies," 42–43. Certainly, not all work accomplished at this time should be attributed to the influence of Harnack. We mention the contribution of J. N. D. Kelly on creeds and doctrines (*Early Christian Creeds*; *Early Christian Doctrines*); Henry Chadwick's outstanding edition of Origen's *Contra Celsum* (1965), and his history of the early church, appearing in 1967 (updated slightly in 1993); also S. L. Greenslade, *Schism in the Early Church*. On these, see Chesnut, "A Century of Patristic Studies," 54; and Brakke, "Early Church in North America," 474.

43. On Daniélou's *Theology of Jewish Christianity*, see Chesnut, "A Century of Patristic Studies," 43–44. With Johannes Quasten, Jean Daniélou represents the outstanding contribution of post-WW II Catholic scholars (Chesnut, "A Century of Patristic Studies," 52). Equally important are French Catholic scholars Pierre de Labriolle, Pierre Courcelle, and Henri-Irénée Marrou, who were instrumental in incorporating study of early Christianity with a new focus on late antiquity, to bridge the divide between studies of ancient classical and the medieval periods (see Clark, "From Patristics to Early Christian Studies," 12). Chesnut attributes massive change in Roman Catholic theology, marked by the Second Vatican Council (1962–1965), to the shift in focus on third- or fourth-century Christianity, away from the thirteenth century (and Thomas Aquinas). In liturgical revision too, Vatican Council documents reveal clear dependence on patristic and biblical thought (rather than scholastic Thomism); see Chesnut, "A Century of Patristic Studies," 52.

44. See Alfred Edersheim, *The Life and Times of Jesus the Messiah* (1901–1907); on this work, see Neill, *Interpretation*, 294–295.

45. See Hermann L. Strack and Paul Billerbeck, *Kommentar zum Neuen Testament aus Talmud und Midrasch* (1922–1961).

46. The theme would be taken up by W. D. Davies (1948), *Paul and Rabbinic Judaism*.

D. The Twentieth Century

Jewish Christianity and the ongoing relationship between Jews and Christians continued to receive considerable attention after the dramatic discovery of the Dead Sea Scrolls in the caves of Qumran (1947). Representing the library of an ascetic community of the first century BC, these texts added significantly to our acquaintance with Hellenistic Judaism beyond the information given by Philo of Alexandria and Josephus.[47] Post-WW II studies portray Judaism with assumptions quite different from those of Harnack, incorporating international dismay at the kind of racism which led to the Holocaust. The impressive work of E. P. Sanders on Palestinian Judaism (*Paul and Palestinian Judaism*, 1977), and Jacob Neusner on the Pharisees (*The Rabbinic Traditions about the Pharisees Before 70 AD*; *From Politics to Piety*, etc.), has helped establish a new assessment of the Pharisees, Scribes and Rabbis.[48] Martin Hengel's *Judaism and Hellenism* was likewise important in arguing for the Hellenistic character of Judaism, both before and after the New Testament era.[49]

Patristic studies in the twentieth century were deeply impacted by the discovery of the Nag Hammadi library in the Upper Nile region of Egypt, not far from the location of the ancient Pachomian monastery (1945–1946).[50] As with the discovery of the Dead Sea Scrolls, the story of these thirteen

---

47. For English translation of the scrolls, see Vermes, *Dead Sea Scrolls*. Aside from OT texts, the scrolls feature a "Teacher of Righteousness," and include commentaries, a *Manual of Discipline*, and *Psalms of Thanksgiving*, as well as the apocalyptic work, *The War of the Sons of Light against the Sons of Darkness*. On the controversies surrounding these scrolls, see Neill, *Interpretation*, 297–312.

48. See White ("Adolf Harnack," 107–108) for discussion of the social realities, which include work on archaeological findings, like those of Keyers and Strange (*Archeology*), or Kraabel ("Diaspora Synagogue"), on the Diaspora synagogue.

49. On Hengel, see the appreciative discussion of Hurtado, "Martin Hengel's Impact," 70–76. A large segment of Hurtado's review of the work of Hengel (from early writing on the Zealots to more recent work on the Septuagint as Christian Scripture) is focused on his *Judaism and Hellenism*, and on significant response to this work by English scholars (Feldman, Collins, Hill). Clark ("From Patristics," 21) alerts us to important recent work on Judaism and late antiquity, beginning with the significant volume by Meeks and Wilken, *Jews and Christians in Antioch*; Wilken, *The Land Called Holy*; Kraemer on Jews among Christians and pagans in the Greco-Roman world (*Her Share of the Blessings*); Taylor's work on anti-Judaism (*Anti-Judaism and Early Christian Identity*); works of Lieu on Jews of the second century (*Image and Reality*) and on the issue of Christian identity (*Christian Identity*); Boyarin on Judaeo-Christianity ("Judaeo-Christianity Redivivus," and *Border Lines*); and Fredriksen on Augustine and the Jews ("*Secundum Carnem*," and *Augustine and the Jews*).

50. This discovery caught public attention, far more than other significant discoveries, like the *Apostolic Tradition* of Hippolytus, or Nestorius's *Bazaar of Heracleides*; on the latter, see Chesnut, "A Century of Patristic Studies," 63. On recovery of the work of Nestorius, see Bethune-Baker, *Nestorius and His Teaching*.

leather-bound volumes, with a total of forty-nine gnostic documents, has often been recounted. The treatises were finally made available for study in facsimile format; a complete translation, the *Nag Hammadi Library*, edited by James Robinson was first published in 1977.[51] This work stimulated new discussion of older gnostic documents, particularly the *Gospel of Thomas*. It was now possible to test more accurately Harnack's assessment of gnostic views as an "acute secularizing, or Hellenizing" of Christianity, with rejection of the Old Testament.[52] From the beginning Harnack had regarded Gnosticism as a product of Greek philosophical thought. There were other approaches; the position of Richard Reitzenstein (1861–1931) and Wilhelm Bousset (1865–1920), representative of the "history of religions" school, and later adopted by Hans Jonas, explained Gnosticism in terms of Near Eastern thought and beliefs.[53] This approach looked for gnostic origins in Persian (Iranian) religious dualism of light and darkness, with strong pessimism with respect to our world, balanced by a myth of redemption (for which they found support in Mandaean beliefs). This also meant dating the rise of Gnosticism much earlier than second-century Christianity.[54]

Recognizing an underlying current of anti-Judaism in many gnostic documents, German scholars have looked to pre-Christian non-Jewish *gnôsis* for the origins of Gnosticism.[55] English scholarship on the Nag Hammadi documents has, for the most part, examined gnostic origins in heterodox Judaism or groups on the outer fringes of Christianity.[56] Yet work on Platonism

---

51. The fourth revised edition was published by Brill (Leiden, 1996); the first paperback edition of the translation was published by Harper and Row, 1981.

52. Chesnut, "A Century of Patristic Studies," 62, quoting Harnack's *History of Dogma* 1.227–228 (Buchanan trans.).

53. Hans Jonas, *Gnosis und spätantiker Geist*, appeared in English translation as *The Gnostic Religion: The Message of the Alien God and the Beginnings of Christianity*. The work shows a turn to existentialism as basis for interpreting ancient Gnosticism. Jonas was evidently influenced by Martin Heidegger's view on human alienation in our world, and the challenge to assert true being in freedom from forces that would enslave. See Neill, *Interpretation*, 175–176.

54. Neill, *Interpretation*, 160–164 and 177–178.

55. See Chesnut, "A Century of Patristic Studies," 62; and Neill, *Interpretation*, 179. The Dutch scholar G. Quispel (*Gnosis als Weltreligion*) was sceptical of pre-Christian Gnosticism; he recognized that Gnostics behaved like Christian heretics, even if their views show little inner connection with events pivotal for historically based Christianity: the life, death and resurrection of Jesus (see Neill, *Interpretation*, 180).

56. For scholars looking to Judaism, particularly the development of eschatological thought after the fall of Jerusalem in AD 70, Neill cites R. McL. Wilson, *The Gnostic Problem*; R. M. Grant, *Gnosticism and Early Christianity*; and his *Gnosticism: A Source Book of Heretical Writings from the Early Christian Period*. Grant noted the absence of a redeemer figure in pre-Christian or Greco-Roman religion, and realized that the relevant model is to be found in Jesus (Neill,

and Pythagoreanism in late antiquity has led scholars like John Dillon to renewed appreciation of Harnack's approach; Dillon's *The Middle Platonists* examines Gnosticism in terms of a "Platonic underworld."[57] On these issues outstanding work was done by the American (Episcopalian) scholar R. M. Grant (*Gnosticism and Early Christianity, Gnosticism*).[58] Even so, the question of origins cannot be solved without clarity and a degree of consensus on the definition and distinctive features of Gnosticism itself.[59]

Archaeological Work

We have already noted the impact of work in archaeology on the direction of patristic studies in the twentieth century, taking the discipline well beyond a traditional focus on literary documents. Archaeological work of the past century has uncovered a wealth of materials: papyri, inscriptions and ecclesiastical architecture as well as the decoration of walls or floor mosaics, much of it supplying new information on the nature of early Christianity. As a serious discipline, archaeological excavation began in the mid-nineteenth century along the Mediterranean in countries like Algeria, where such work was made possible through the French colonial regime. Here archaeologists had amazing success in uncovering temples, triumphal arches, baths, colonnades, houses and churches, all intact. The treaty of Berlin (1878) was significant for renewed interest in Turkey, allowing Ramsay to make important discoveries from ancient Asia Minor.[60] In the twentieth century W. H. C. Frend has done outstanding archaeological work in the ancient villages of Numidia (present-day Algeria) in North Africa.[61] His efforts have been particularly significant

---

Interpretation, 180). Grant is also known for work in social history, *Early Christianity and Society*, and *Eusebius as Church Historian*.

    57. On Dillon, see Chesnut, "A Century of Patristic Studies," 62–63.

    58. Chesnut, "A Century of Patristic Studies," 55.

    59. See Neill, *Interpretation*, 175.

    60. On Ramsay, see Neill, *Interpretation*, 141–143 (referenced at note 28 above). Nineteenth-century interest in archaeology was stimulated by controversy surrounding the life of Jesus raised by writings of D. F. Strauss (1808–1874) and Ernest Renan (1823–1892); scholars sought to disprove (or prove) the biblical records. Such issues motivated W. M. Ramsay to trace the travels of Paul, to find confirmation of Luke's account; he also discovered significant Jewish inscriptions (see also Frend, "Archeology and Patristic Studies," 12).

    61. Frend realized that modern work in archaeology as it pertains to early Christianity can be dated to Renaissance archaeological exploration of the catacombs by members of the Roman Academy (Frend, "Archeology and Patristic Studies," 10). On G. B. de Rossi's nineteenth-century research on Roman catacombs, and its impact on our knowledge of early Christian practice, see Frend, "Archeology and Patristic Studies," 10–11; and Clark, "From Patristics," 8.

in uncovering evidence of groups like the Donatists who could be recognized through inscriptions from their watchword, *Deo Laudes*, even when they were excluded from the orthodox Catholic communities.[62]

Alongside increasingly careful methods of excavation there were also incidental discoveries, like the Dead Sea Scrolls and the Nag Hammadi documents. These materials have all contributed substantially to a new understanding of early Christianity, especially in North Africa where evidence of relevant socio-economic conditions have helped to integrate the study of early Christianity with the broader themes of Greco-Roman history and culture.[63] For Patristics this means that early Christianity would be examined for its contribution to the rise of (medieval) European culture.[64] It would be regarded as one more component in the emerging history of Europe.[65] Such an approach is evident in studies of Greco-Roman antiquity which note the impact of pagan culture on Christianity; works like C. N. Cochrane's *Christianity and Classical Culture*, or W. H. C. Frend, *The Donatist Church: A Movement of Protest in Roman North Africa* are examples of this. For the influence of ancient rhetoric on early Christianity, we note G. Kennedy's *Greek Rhetoric under Christian Emperors*, or his *New Testament Interpretation through Rhetorical Criticism*.[66] This approach is understandable when early Christianity is taught within the context of a "Religious Studies" program in North American universities.[67]

---

62. Frend, "Archeology and Patristic Studies," 14. Archaeological evidence on these schismatic groups has indicated socio-economic conditions which reinforced martyr cults, in defiance of Roman authorities (pagan or Christian), as significant clues to their tenacity in late antiquity.

63. Frend, "Archeology and Patristic Studies," 14–15.

64. Frend, 9–10; Clark recognizes the impact of work by historians of classical antiquity like Sir Ronald Syme, Fergus Millar, Peter Brown, John Matthews and Roger Bagnall, examining the social history of the late Republic and early Roman Empire, and influencing, in turn, study of the social milieu of early Christianity ("From Patristics," 16).

65. Lössl is candid in acknowledging that, at present, scholars who study early Christianity may not be particularly interested in the subject as such, regarding Christianity as just one of the numerous phenomena in religion of the Roman Empire; they may even operate with an underlying agenda of hostility, perhaps in reaction to negative personal experience of Christianity. Thus he cautions readers to be aware of motivation, and be prepared to deconstruct such views for a balanced understanding (Lössl, *Early Church*, 2–4).

66. Chesnut ("A Century of Patristic Studies," 60–61) also refers to the important work in the 1960s and 1970s of A. Momigliano (ed.), *The Conflict between Paganism and Christianity in the Fourth Century*; F. Dvornik, *Early Christian and Byzantine Political Philosophy*; F. E. Peters, *Harvest of Hellenism: A History of the Near East from Alexander the Great to the Triumph of Christianity*; and A. E. Cameron, *Circus Factions: Blues and Greens at Rome and Byzantium*.

67. In such a context it is clear that Christianity cannot have a privileged status; ideologically the "Religious Studies" department must treat all religious groups, whether or not they are Christian, as equal. In fact, religious phenomena are now typically understood in terms of (social/political) struggle for power and status. "Political correctness" also militates against

At the same time we note significant scholarship on early Christianity now done in the context of other academic disciplines: history, sociology or literary criticism.[68]

Patristics in the Modern University Context

In the context of nineteenth-century Protestant European universities, patristic studies typically shifted the focus away from study of the texts of the Fathers, to the study of the early church as such, or church history.[69] That focus on early Christianity was motivated especially by archaeological work like that of Frend, providing important "material" and epigraphical evidence beyond the text, while also illustrating the lives and careers of Christians through the social environment. This allowed for an attractive interweaving of literary and archaeological evidence, the one reinforcing and illuminating the other.[70] Frend capitalized on the attraction of archaeological studies at a time when Harnack's influence meant far less enthusiasm for study of the church councils

---

professing allegiance to one specific point of departure in religion. Chesnut ("A Century of Patristic Studies," 61) recognizes the difficulties in doing justice to the full spectrum of religious belief in a context where no special attention can be given to early Christianity. But this is the context motivating the new standard designation for dating BCE (i.e, before the common era) and CE (common era), versus the more traditional BC (before Christ) and AD (*anno domini*, i.e. in the year of our Lord). Lössl notes that both systems use the birth of Jesus as fixed point of departure. And neither the older or newer conventions are truly "common," since other systems of dating, like the Islamic or Chinese, are also used internationally. For these reasons Lössl maintains the traditional reference in his own work on the early church (*Early Church*, 12–13).

68. In his 1988 anniversary review, "A Century of Patristic Studies," Chesnut recognized that, aside from the older tradition still alive at universities like Oxford, early Christianity was not usually discussed in departments of Classical Studies (Greek, or Roman); since the Enlightenment, these have typically drawn a fairly sharp divide between pagan and Christian authors (see Helleman, *Christianity and the Classics*, 13–30). Recent decades have witnessed some reversal of that trend, with disappearance of older divisions between classical studies and the study of theology or religion, psychology, and sociology (Chesnut, "A Century of Patristic Studies," 61). Noting institutional developments in secular universities which have transformed Patristics into the study of "Early Christianity," Clark points to leading scholars Timothy Barnes, Peter Brown, Averil Cameron, Robin Lane Fox, Ramsay MacMullen, Robert Markus and Mark Vessey, all connected with specialized disciplines like late ancient history, literary theory, or anthropology, not with departments of religious studies as such (Clark, "From Patristics," 16; also Brakke, "Early Church in North America," 475–476).

69. Clark ("From Patristics," 9) comments on the term "Church History" as the academic discipline which subsumed "Patristics" in Protestant universities. Lössl, on the other hand, argues for retaining a focus on the "early church," even though it might be deemed partisan (i.e. favouring institutionalized Christianity, or privileging the role of bishops or theologians at the expense of "marginalized" groups, the laity, women or heretical groups); Lössl, *Early Church*, 13–14. See also the comments of Clark in note 73 below.

70. Frend, *Saints and Sinners*, 18.

or the teachings of the Fathers.[71] Archaeology made a significant contribution in establishing such studies on a non-dogmatic basis; as Frend recognized, questions of orthodoxy or heresy are not immediately relevant in assessing archaeological discoveries.[72] All of these factors contributed to the transition of the discipline from "Patristics" to "Church History" and beyond that, to the study of "Early Christianity."[73]

These transitions, in turn, have impacted the understanding of early Christianity itself. In assimilating sectarian evidence from the Dead Sea Scrolls, scholars began speaking of a plurality of *Judaisms*. Closer acquaintance with Nag Hammadi gnostic documents also led scholars to speak of a plurality of *Christianities*. For Christianity, we note such an approach in Walter Bauer's *Orthodoxy and Heresy in Earliest Christianity* (1934; English trans. 1971). In spite of Bauer's profession of impartiality and objectivity, his emphasis on diversity within early non- or pre-Catholic Christianity, as the matrix from which orthodoxy developed,[74] actually left the impression of an apology on behalf of early *hairesis*.[75] Bauer owed much of his success to support from major liberal theologians like Rudolf Bultmann and Helmut Koester, and to the timing of the English translation; it was published just when English translations of the Nag Hammadi documents provided new acquaintance with

---

71. Frend, "Archeology and Patristic Studies," 9-10.

72. Frend himself reflected on the relative freedom from constraints of "orthodoxy" he experienced in archaeological work, noting that patristic scholars, particularly when associated with theologically oriented institutions, would be far more constrained by faith-related issues (Frend, *Saints and Sinners*, 10).

73. On the transition from "Patristics" to "Early Christian Studies," with significant attention to social realities, see also Clark, "From Patristics," 7-41, particularly 14, where she mentions that the term "Patristics" has been all but abandoned because of its ecclesiastical connotations, its reflection of male concerns and those of the "orthodox" church, all aspects irrelevant for scholars pursuing work in departments of Religious Studies (i.e. at secular universities).

74. Bauer argued that "orthodox" Christianity was initially in a minority; only later was it able to impose its form of Christianity as the correct or "orthodox" interpretation; on Bauer, see Henry, "Why Is Contemporary Scholarship," 123-126. Desjardins notes critique of the "Bauer thesis" by scholars like T. Robinson (*Bauer Thesis Examined*), arguing that these heretical movements were neither early, nor as strong as Bauer alleged (Desjardins, "Bauer and Beyond," 66-68).

75. In this regard, Bauer was not original; Lössl calls attention to the Pietist scholar Gottfried Arnold (1666-1714), whose "non-partisan history of the church and its heretics" also revealed decided sympathy for heretical groups like the Gnostics (*Early Church*, 36-37).

early "heretics."[76] The more recent scholarly work of Elaine Pagels, *Gnostic Paul* and *The Gnostic Gospels*, also follows in the footsteps of Koester and Bauer.[77]

New Directions: Women in Early Christianity

In the last decades of the twentieth century, patristic studies were marked by diversity of emphasis as it borrowed a diversity of scholarly principles from disciplines like psychology, sociology, anthropology and literary criticism, and also evidenced considerable diversity of geographical areas of focus through new attention to Syriac and Coptic Christianity.[78] Also significant are new studies on the social and ecclesiastical roles of women in early Christianity.[79]

---

76. Henry argues that Bauer's demonstration of the temporal priority of heretical positions was motivated by a desire to give legitimacy to some contemporary forms of Christianity; it assumes the modern romantic notion of heretics as "authentic" but "suppressed" independent believers, and relies on a modern suspicion of those who have risen to the top (Henry, "Why Is Contemporary Scholarship," 125–126).

77. On the work of Elaine Pagels, see Chesnut, "A Century of Patristic Studies," 63.

78. Clark recognizes the significance of the late nineteenth-century introduction of "Oriental" studies for Patristic study of Syriac Fathers, particularly with the publication of Syriac, Coptic, Arabic and Ethiopic texts in the *Corpus Scriptorum Christianorum Orientalium* (Paris, 1903–). On Coptic texts, Clark cites the work of twentieth-century Belgian scholars P. Ladeuze and L. Théophile Lefort; and on Syriac (monophysite) texts, J. Lebon. This work has been admirably advanced by Sebastian Brock, with work on asceticism, biblical study, heresy and liturgy. Also important is the research of Griffith on asceticism in the Syrian church and monasteries (*Arabic Christianity*; "Asceticism"), and in early Muslim-Christian encounter (*Beginnings of Christian Theology*); see Clark, "From Patristics," 13–14.

79. Clark ("From Patristics," 18–19) mentions important recent scholarship on women in early Christianity, particularly in discussion of social history, with a focus on related topics like sexuality, gender, the "body" and power, as well as postcolonial concerns from historical, theoretical and comparative perspectives: Rosemary Ruether on asceticism ("Misogynism and Virginal Feminism in the Fathers of the Church"; and "Mothers of the Church: Ascetic Women in the Late Patristic Age"); Ross Kraemer's anthology of readings (*Maenads, Martyrs, Matrons, Monastics*), and survey on women in religion of the Greco-Roman world (*Her Share of the Blessings*); Elizabeth Clark on asceticism, Jerome, Chrysostom, and Melania (*Jerome, Chrysostom, and Friends*; *Women in the Early Church*; *The Life of Melania, the Younger*; and *Ascetic Piety and Women's Faith*); Sebastian Brock and Susan A. Harvey on Syrian women (*Holy Women of the Syrian Orient*); Karen Torjesen (*When Women Were Priests*); Gillian Clark (*Women in Late Antiquity*); K. Power (*Veiled Desire*) and Kari Børresen (*Subordination and Equivalence*) on women in the work of Augustine; Kate Cooper on womanhood in late antiquity (*The Virgin and the Bride*); Scott F. Johnson (*The Life and Miracles of Thekla*); Ruth Albrecht on Macrina (*Das Leben der heiligen Makrina*); Anne Jensen (*God's Self-Confident Daughters*); and finally, Ute Eisen (*Women Officeholders in Early Christianity*). For more specific discussion of issues like sexuality, the body, diet, medicine or power, Clark refers to work by Elizabeth Castelli ("Virginity and Its Meaning for Women's Sexuality in Early Christianity"); Gail P. Corrington on ascetic self-control ("Anorexia, Asceticism, and Autonomy"); Virginia Burrus on heretical and ascetic women (*Chastity as Autonomy*); and Teresa Shaw (*"The Burden of the Flesh": Fasting and Sexuality in Early Christianity*). For studies with a "theological" orientation, Clark refers to

Elizabeth Schüssler Fiorenza's important book, *In Memory of Her: A Feminist Theological Reconstruction of Christian Origins* (1983), with its focus on New Testament evidence for participation of women among those following Jesus, has been foundational. She also examined the role of women in house churches established by Paul, as an environment which would provide significant opportunities for leadership.[80]

Schüssler Fiorenza's work has raised the question of why Christian women who appear to be so prominent in the earliest stages of Christianity had much less important roles in later centuries. Some scholars have argued that women's roles did not necessarily diminish, but we are simply lacking the evidence because (male) writers of the second century were less interested in their role.[81] Considerable attention has been devoted to the prominence of women in gnostic circles.[82] Feminist authors have also argued that factors like the rise of asceticism, or positive appreciation of virginity and life on the fringes of traditional family structures, gave women more freedom from the dangers and constraints of marriage and child-bearing.[83] Kate Cooper (*Virgin and the Bride*) and Judith C. Stark (*Rise of Christianity: A Sociologist Reconsiders History*) have taken a different approach, arguing that Christianity was appealing to women because it rejected abortion and (female) infanticide. While this may have led to a rise in female fertility, Christianity provided the counterbalance by idealizing virginity. Stark also argues that significant recurrence in the acts of church councils of a *prohibition* on female leadership indicates that in the

---

Margaret Miles on Augustine's *Confessions* (*Desire and Delight*); and Verna Harrison on gender ("Male and Female in Cappadocian Theology").

80. See McKechnie, *First Christian Centuries*, 191–192. While Schüssler Fiorenza provided a commentary on relevant biblical texts, Luise Schottroff (*Lydia's Impatient Sisters*) addressed issues of background in social history. Important historical background in Greco-Roman society is also given by Kraemer (*Her Share of the Blessings*), explaining restriction on roles of women in the Pastoral Epistles in terms of an emergence of male clergy, and the reason, in turn, for closer connections between women's religion and heretical Christianity. On second-century roles of Christian women, see McKechnie, *First Christian Centuries*, 192–195; also E. Pagels, *Gnostic Gospels*, and K. King, *Images*.

81. See Jensen, *God's Self-Confident Daughters*; on this topic see also McKechnie, *First Christian Centuries*, 195–197.

82. On female imagery in the Nag Hammadi texts, see King, *Images of the Feminine in Gnosticism*; also Clark, "From Patristics," 22.

83. For significant bibliography on this theme, see Clark, "From Patristics," 19–20, and 22.

first five centuries opportunities for women in leadership were actually more numerous than we now assume.[84]

An important recent study of inscriptions and epigraphical evidence, Eisen's *Women Officeholders in Early Christianity*, further challenges assumptions of diminished involvement of women in the church after the first two generations. It includes inscriptions showing that before the fourth century it was not unusual for women to assume the office of deacon.[85] Among Montanists, certainly, women are known to have taken on roles as presbyter, or bishop; such titles would have been assigned to women who were themselves ordained to the position, or because they survived martyrdom (as "confessor").[86]

While historians of past centuries have typically undervalued the role of women in the history of Christianity, the pendulum now appears to have swung in the opposite direction. Bestselling novels like Dan Brown's *The Da Vinci Code* provide supposedly historical and factual accounts of a matriarchal or feminine principle, suppressed with the repudiation of Gnosticism.[87] Capitalizing on public interest in the relatively strong role of women in early Christianity, these authors resort to intrigue and conspiracy theory to criminalize the intentions of the "majority" Christian church of the time.[88]

Sociology and Anthropology Impact Early Christian Studies

Alongside the impact of archaeological work, examination of the roles of women from a feminist perspective has encouraged the use of principles from

---

84. On their work, see McKechnie, *First Christian Centuries*, 198–201. On important earlier studies of the role of women provided by Clark (*Jerome, Chrysostom, and Friends*), Gryson (*Ministry of Women*) or Laporte (*Role of Women*), see Chesnut, "A Century of Patristic Studies," 59–60.

85. McKechnie, *First Christian Centuries*, 207–208, citing Eisen, *Women Officeholders*, 158–159.

86. On the role of the "confessor," see ch. 4, §C; also McKechnie, *First Christian Centuries*, 204–206. For other important studies of women in leadership, see 79 above.

87. Dan Brown's work relies, in turn, on Michael Baigent's *The Holy Blood and the Holy Grail*; on these, see the above discussion in the introduction to ch. 9 and chapter appendix 9.1.

88. For his assessment of the factual errors which bedevil these works, Lössl (*Early Church*, 7) appeals to Ehrman (*Truth and Fiction*, 141–184). It is now widely accepted that both gnostic and anti-gnostic movements (like Montanists) made room for feminine participation in leadership. But neither of these movements can be characterized as *matriarchal*; in fact, gnostic documents typically required women to become "male," i.e. to transcend her gender, as a condition of salvation. Citing (the Montanist) Tertullian on women as the "devil's gateway," Lössl (*Early Church*, 7–8) notes that it is by no means clear whether the status of women would have been enhanced or degraded by participation in these groups; see Tertullian's essay *On the Apparel of Women* (ANF 4).

disciplines like sociology and social anthropology. This is evident in the work of Ramsay MacMullen, *Roman Social Relations*; in H. C. Kee's *Christian Origins in Sociological Perspective*; and Wayne Meeks' study of urban Christianity (*First Urban Christians*).[89] The study of Jews and Christians in Antioch by Meeks and Wilken (*Jews and Christians in Antioch in the First Four Centuries of the Common Era*) also features an emphasis on diversity of social structure and status within Christian communities. The sociological approach was already exemplified in Arnold Toynbee's *Study of History*, and more recently in J. G. Gager's *Kingdom and Community: The Social World of Early Christianity*, portraying Christianity as a sectarian movement affected by kinship ties, social status and income.[90] In his *Augustine of Hippo: A Biography* (first published in 1967; updated 2000), Peter Brown appealed to sociology of religion;[91] the articles on religious belief and power structures collected in his *Society and the Holy in Late Antiquity* also feature the perspective of social anthropology.[92] R. Lane Fox, in *Pagans and Christians*, similarly demonstrates attention to the wider religious, cultural and social context.[93] On the psychological dimension in the appeal of Christianity, we note A. D. Nock's work on conversion (*Conversion, Early Gentile Christianity*), and E. R. Dodds's *Pagan and Christian in an Age of Anxiety*.

The study of *late antiquity* as such has emerged in recent decades as a new focus for interdisciplinary scholarship embracing perspectives from literature, culture, history, art and theology.[94] Of course, Patristics has long benefited from

---

89. On the seminal work of Wayne Meeks (1970s–1980s), organizing seminars on the social world of early Christianity, see Clark, "From Patristics," 17.

90. Chesnut, "A Century of Patristic Studies," 58–59.

91. Chesnut, 57–58.

92. See Chesnut, 59; also Clark, "From Patristics," 18.

93. Clark indicates the relevant topics in the study of late antiquity: asceticism, law, slavery, literacy, the family, women, children and heresy; she also contributes an important bibliography (Clark, "From Patristics," 17). On the family, she notes the anthology of Halvor Moxnes (*Constructing Early Christian Families*); work of David Balch and Carolyn Osiek (*Early Christian Families*); and studies by Raymond van Dam (*Families and Friends in Late Roman Cappadocia*) and Brent Shaw ("Family in Antiquity"). For law she notes work by Judith Evans Grubbs (*Law and Family*), Antti Arjava (*Women and Law*), and Jill Harries (*Law and Empire*).

94. Reflecting on early Christianity as a discipline, Brakke shows awareness of special challenges for contemporary scholars of early Christianity who do not typically identify themselves as "historians of Christianity." Subtopics like "Late Antiquity" have "undermined the paradigm 'History of Christianity,' itself a recent development replacing a history of 'the early church'" (Brakke, "Early Church in North America," 475–478). See also Clark ("From Patristics," 21), on Brakke's argument for dropping the term "Christian" in favour of "late ancient studies" or "late antiquity," designations which no longer afford a privileged place to Christianity. Brakke's analysis ("Early Church in North America," 475 and 480–491) is useful in recognizing the impact of contemporary postmodern critical theory as it "calls into question the construction

interdisciplinary efforts, for its work typically overlapped with that of classical studies, history, philosophy and theology.[95] A more traditional approach is still evident in the philological work of translation and editing of texts, as well as exegetical studies. Nor has older work on church history, like that of Henry Chadwick or J. N. D. Kelly's work on the creeds, outlived its usefulness.[96] The same can be said for theological studies (Frances Young, Andrew Louth), or historical work (H. A. Drake, or T. D. Barnes on Constantine and Eusebius).[97] The ongoing challenge for contemporary study of early Christianity is to formulate a comprehensive view that embraces the multiple kinds of data being collected and studied.[98]

E. Conclusion

Patristic studies have clearly undergone substantive change over the centuries, and especially in the last five decades, as it greatly expanded the scope of interest and range of methodologies in its interpretation of relevant documents and other kinds of evidence. In his review of patristic studies of the past century (1988), G. F. Chesnut affirmed that, as an academic discipline, patristic studies are still alive and well.[99] In this positive assessment, Chesnut called special attention to the ongoing constructive role of the study of early Christianity in ecumenical efforts to bridge the divide between sectors of Christianity which have long remained distant from one another.[100] That ecumenical spirit is

---

of grand narratives of any kind by complicating the relationship between text and context . . . opening up new areas of conflict and opportunity in the field."

95. Vallée (*Shaping of Christianity*, 4–5) rightly draws attention to the interdisciplinary character of patristic studies; it was closely connected traditionally with academic disciplines like philosophy, classical philology, theology, history, biblical studies and literary theory; he notes inherent problems of definition for such a conglomerate of disciplines as these reflect on an emerging religious movement through literature and other sources.

96. See Brakke, "Early Church in North America," 474.

97. Lössl, *Early Church*, 40–41. See also Chesnut, "A Century of Patristic Studies," 61; and Clark, "From Patristics," 14.

98. This challenge was noted already by Elizabeth Clark, commenting on the journal *Zeitschrift für Antikes Christentum* (from 1997), seeking to link scholars in different countries, and to incorporate "Patristics" into scholarship on Late Antiquity, implementing new methodologies, and use of material culture. The primary goal was to keep scholars abreast of important work done in areas closely related to their own (Clark, "From Patristics," 10).

99. Chesnut, "A Century of Patristic Studies," 64.

100. Chesnut ("A Century of Patristic Studies," 46) compares the Enlightenment-oriented perspective of Harnack with contemporary ecumenical consciousness, as in work on Christian doctrine by J. Pelikan (*Christian Tradition*), see also Outler "The Idea of 'Development.'" For a similar comment on ecumenical implications of interest in early Christianity, see Vallée, "By looking together at ancient witnesses, scholars of all confessional backgrounds take a firm step

still embodied in the international Patristics conferences inaugurated by F. L. Cross at Oxford in 1951, and held at four-year intervals since that time. These conferences have done much to stimulate study of early Christianity across denominational and national boundaries, attracting more than seven hundred scholars at week-long conferences. The spirit of cooperation from different theological and denominational perspectives gives a living testimony for the potential of Christian unity, and demonstrates concretely that the polemical spirit of nineteenth-century scholarship is no longer the dominant approach.

---

toward overcoming Christian divisions. The discovery of the lush diversity that characterized the early centuries is conducive to greater tolerance and mutual understanding" (Vallée, *Shaping of Christianity*, 6).

Appendix II

Four Important Early Church Historians

A. Eusebius of Caesarea

The most important place among ancient historians of Christianity must be assigned to Eusebius Pamphilus (ca. AD 260–340), or Eusebius of Caesarea.[1] His ten-volume *Ecclesiastical History* covers about three hundred years, from the beginning of Christianity until the year 324, just prior to the Nicene council. The work closes with a eulogy of Constantine and his son Crispus. Since Crispus was suspected of treason and put to death in 326, we may assume that the *History* was completed before that event.

Much of what we know about the life of Eusebius is based on information passed on in his works. Probably a native of Palestine, Eusebius was acquainted with both Syriac and Greek, but not familiar with Latin. He appears to have come from a prominent family; this may be the reason why he was not harmed in the persecution of Diocletian. The persecution under Licinius was not as severe, though it did continue until 323, when Licinius was finally defeated by Constantine. Eusebius's social status may also explain why he rose to considerable prominence at the imperial court of Constantine. Not long after the end of persecution (313), Eusebius became bishop of Caesarea in Palestine, a position he held until his death.

Eusebius's support for the Arian cause is clear from his involvement with the Nicene council. Along with Asterius, Eusebius of Nicomedia and Arius, Eusebius was influenced by theological views of Lucian at the school of

---

1. For a useful recent scholarly assessment of Eusebius, with an introduction to his life and works, see T. D. Barnes, "Eusebius of Caesarea," 173–193.

Antioch. Even though he was condemned for his position on the humanity of Christ, Lucian was once more in communion with the church when he died a martyr (312/313). At the Nicene council Eusebius attempted to maintain an "orthodox" approach on the deity of Christ when he produced the creed of Caesarea. He did support Arius initially, and did not support the introduction of the *homoousion*; nonetheless, he was not among those exiled with Arius after the council.

What motivated him to write the *Ecclesiastical History*? When he began the work late in the third century, he may have sensed that the church was entering a new phase, that the era of persecution was actually coming to an end. The work is still presented as a type of apology for Christianity. Such an intent clearly determined Eusebius's method in presenting the early centuries of the church and the kind of material included. The work focuses on the struggle with persecution and controversies with heretics who tried to undermine the faith.[2] Two significant accounts of persecution are noteworthy, the trial and martyrdom of Polycarp, and the second-century persecution in Lyons and Vienne.[3] These accounts, given in full detail, become representative of the many other occasions when Christians suffered for the faith.

The historical coverage of the period includes important descriptions of the figures and events marking these early centuries. If Eusebius was not a particularly creative thinker like Origen or Augustine, he was certainly conscientious in using his sources as he tells the story, and providing considerable illustrative detail. The *History* is particularly valuable for its quotation of numerous otherwise unknown documents. Eusebius clearly benefited from the excellent library in Caesarea, developed by Origen and Pamphilus.[4] This means that he had access to basic chronologies, the previous historical work of second-century Hegesippus and the universal history of Julius Africanus (ca. AD 180–250); these writers, in turn, had used the chronicles of the second-century Hippolytus of Rome.

As Apologist for Christianity, Eusebius is also recognized for following the approach of Josephus's apologetic work for Judaism in his *Jewish Antiquities*.[5]

---

2. Lössl, *Early Church*, 25–26.

3. On the death of Polycarp, see the introduction to ch. 4. Highlights of Eusebius's account of the persecution in Lyons and Vienne are given in chapter appendix 4.1.

4. Among key historians of Christianity Guy (*Introducing Early Christianity*, 11) gives first position to Lactantius (ca. AD 250–320); he was born in North Africa, and became an orator in Nicomedia and tutor to Constantine's son, Crispus. Lactantius's work *On the Deaths of the Persecutors* is an important source on the persecution which began in 303; it was written before the end of persecution. On Lactantius, see ch. 5, §B.3 and §B.4.

5. Lössl, *Early Church*, 27.

While noting emperors who persecuted Christians, Eusebius wanted to show that the empire provided a positive context for the growth of the church, particularly when viewed in retrospect from the time of Constantine.[6] In presenting the various heresies, like Ebionism, Gnosticism, or Montanism, Eusebius was mostly content to relate information at second hand. There are some problems in the chronology presented, particularly because he confused the various Antonine emperors. Of course, Eusebius was not the only historian who had a problem keeping them straight. More regrettable, however, is his ignorance of the Latin language and consequent failure to give adequate coverage of events in western Christendom.

In the original Greek, Eusebius's *History* was published in numerous editions; a number of manuscripts remain available. Numerous translations were made, beginning with an early translation into ancient Syriac and a Latin translation by Rufinus in the early fifth century. Rufinus translated nine books, and then himself added two to take the account up to the demise of Theodosius the Great. As such it was readily accessible to Augustine (354–430), and helpful in his work on *The City of God*.[7] On the issue of church and state, however, we realize that Augustine took a rather different approach. Eusebius praised the emperor and came to regard the church as an integral factor in the Roman Empire; Augustine's *City of God* took a far more critical approach on Roman political reality, recognizing that the agenda of church and state would not necessarily coincide.[8] And the significant impetus for Augustine's work came from the tragic events of the attack on Rome in 410.[9] Accordingly, Augustine did not regard the rule of Constantine as the beginning of a new era, as many thought. But he did agree with Eusebius in rejecting millenarian views of those who expected the imminent return and thousand-year reign of Christ.[10]

None of the next generation of historians, Socrates (ca. 379–440), Sozomen (d. ca. 450) and Theodoret (ca. 393–460) duplicated Eusebius on the period covered. All of them began their accounts of the church at the point where he stopped, with Constantine; and all three covered the period from Constantine to the mid-fifth century. Their respect for Eusebius's accomplishment is evident

---

6. Lössl, 29. On this theme we also note his *Life of Constantine*.

7. For discussion of the *City of God*, see ch. 12.

8. As Lössl admits, Augustine went so far as to regard the state and its political leaders as a band of criminals (*Early Church*, 31).

9. Lössl, *Early Church*, 30.

10. These include the Donatist theologian Tyconius (d. ca. 400), whose commentary on Revelation influenced his view of history; but Tyconius realized that the millenarian views should be interpreted allegorically.

from the fact that none of them thought it necessary to write another historical account of that earlier period. It is a pity, nonetheless, that all three wrote in Greek; like Eusebius, these historians were ignorant of the Latin language, and not one of them was able to fill the gap in Eusebius's account on the western church.

B. Socrates (ca. 379–440)

Socrates Scholasticus, a lawyer in Constantinople, wrote an important *History of the Church* covering the period 305–439. His work, like that of Eusebius, is particularly useful for the original documents which are cited and included as evidence.[11]

We do not know much about Socrates as a person; our information comes almost entirely from his own work. He was born and appears to have spent his entire life in Constantinople. He was familiar with the outstanding features of the city, the amphitheatre, baths, hippodrome and churches, all of them proudly mentioned in the *History*. Socrates clearly received a good education in rhetoric; his surname, *Scholasticus*, indicates that he would have worked as a lawyer. Although Socrates, like Eusebius, did not know Latin, he was aware of the Latin translation of Eusebius's *History*, and refers to Rufinus. Also like Eusebius, Socrates restricts his focus to the church in the east, with little attention for the western church. While Socrates was probably a member of the Catholic church, scholars of his work have noted a remarkable fairness and balance in his accounts of heretical groups: Arians, Macedonians, Eunomians, and Novatians. He even treats Julian the Apostate with some sympathy.[12]

Socrates states explicitly at the beginning of the work that he intends to continue the history of the church from where Eusebius finished, though he does mention a desire to review issues which have not received adequate treatment in the earlier work. The period covered by him, approximately 130 years, is critical in the history of Christianity. Three important councils of the church were held: those of Nicea (325), of Constantinople (381), and the first Council of Ephesus (431). Socrates includes the second Council of Ephesus (449), also designated as the "Council of Robbers" (*Latrocinium*). The significant Council of Chalcedon was held not much later (451). During these

---

11. Guy, *Introducing Early Christianity*, 11.

12. For Socrates's defence of Origen, at a time when the great theologian was under attack, see Stevenson, *Creeds, Councils and Controversies*, 193–194.

years the position of the church became well-established within the empire, but the period also witnessed many contentious issues and heresies.

Socrates's work is divided chronologically into seven books according to ruling emperors, beginning with the accession of Constantine the Great (306–337), when the persecution of Diocletian was ending. The second book covers the reign of Constantius II (337–360). The next two emperors, Julian (361–363) and Jovian (363–364), reigning for very short periods each, are combined in one book. The fourth book presents Valens (364–378); the fifth, Theodosius the Great (379–395); the sixth, Arcadius (395–408); and the final seventh book is devoted to the reign of Theodosius the Younger (408–439). Socrates closes with a eulogy of Theodosius the Younger in his seventeenth consulship.

What motivated Socrates to write? Aside from his own love for the historical account, it appears that he wanted to imitate the narrative of Eusebius, whose work he greatly respected, and to bring the account up to date. The work was commissioned by a certain Theodorus, and is dedicated to him. As in Eusebius's work, there are mistakes in chronology, dating and other detail; for example, he reports on two others exiled with Arius, not five. But in comparison with other historical coverage of this period, we note his careful incorporation of relevant data. On the whole, Socrates was impartial in evaluating biographical detail for bishops, emperors or monks. His work includes reference to important ancillary persons, like Ulfilas and Hypatia, and also momentous events, like the conversion of people groups to Christianity: the Saracens, Goths, Burgundians, Persians and Jews.[13] Socrates's work remains important for its inclusion of significant documents, letters, public decrees and official accounts, and for his attention to oral tradition, eyewitness accounts and other primary sources crucial in the life of the church.

C. Sozomen (d. ca. 450)

Sozomen (or Salamanes Hermias Sozomenus) also wrote an *Ecclesiastical History* covering the period 324–439. His work was evidently written after that of Socrates; it borrows from Socrates, and at various points seeks to embellish considerably on the available account. Like Socrates, Sozomen begins his work with the rule of Constantine, and ends with the seventeenth consulate of Theodosius the Younger.

---

13. On Ulfilas, see ch. 10, §B.5, and Stevenson, *Creeds, Councils and Controversies*, 76–77. On Hypatia, see the quote from Socrates given in Stevenson, 284–285; also ch. 12, §A.2.

Sozomen was born and educated in Gaza (Palestine), and shows considerable familiarity with a lifestyle based on the "monastic philosophy" of the region, and also with the monastic fathers (or founders) and their disciples in Egypt, Syria, Palestine, Pontus and Armenia (bk. 12). He went to Phoenician Berytus (modern-day Beirut) to attend the well-known school of law in the city and eventually practised law in Constantinople (bk. 2.3).

In terms of rhetorical style and elegant expression, Sozomen's work surpassed that of Socrates, but did not improve on his balanced evaluation of the materials covered. Sozomen was evidently ready to accept and include legendary materials of dubious origin. Even so, his *History* is valuable for its inclusion of original documents omitted by Socrates.

D. Theodoret (ca. 393–460)

Syrian by birth, Theodoret also wrote an *Ecclesiastical History* in five books. It covers a period somewhat shorter than that of Sozomen, the years 323–428, that is, from the overthrow of Licinius by Constantine, and the origin of the Arian controversy, to the death of Emperor Honorius (423) and of Theodore of Mopsuestia (429).

Theodoret was clearly active in the church and the controversies of the time, both as the bishop of Cyrrhus in Syria and as a supporter of the Antiochenes in the fifth-century debates, sympathizing with Theodore of Mopsuestia and Nestorius on the person and nature of Christ.[14] Accordingly, we have considerable information on the life of Theodoret. At the age of twenty-three, after a relatively traditional education, he entered the monastery of Nicerte, just a few miles from Apamea, and remained there for seven years. At that time (423) he was consecrated bishop of Cyrrhus (or Cyrus) in eastern Syria, not far from the Euphrates, and for some twenty-five years he devoted himself to improving the Christian community, focusing on the conversion of non-Christian peoples and Jews, and winning over heretics to the orthodox faith. This was quite a challenge, since the region was known for the presence of heretical groups: Arians, Marcionites, Eunomians and Judaizers. Aside from ecclesiastical concerns, Theodoret is known for commissioning public buildings, adorning the city with porticoes, two great bridges, baths and an aqueduct. He also had a reputation for using his skill in medicine and surgery, and providing competent practitioners in these skills.

---

14. Guy, *Introducing Early Christianity*, 11.

His troubles began when he supported Nestorius in the conflict with Cyril of Alexandria.[15] As a result, Theodoret would himself be included among those condemned and removed from his position as bishop at the "Robbers Council" of 449 (Pope Leo's *Latrocinium*). At that point he appealed to Pope Leo in Rome to help justify his position,[16] and with the support of the western church he was acquitted at Chalcedon. It is not clear whether he then returned to Cyrrhus or retired to a monastery.

Theodoret later renounced the specific teaching of Nestorius on the two natures of Christ, but he never renounced his friendship with Nestorius, begun probably when Nestorius was a monk in the convent just outside Antioch. He also remained friends with Diodorus of Tarsus and respected Theodore of Mopsuestia as one of the great teachers of theology in the school of Antioch as well as being bishop in Mopsuestia (in Cilicia Secunda, AD 392–428). It was unfortunate that Justinian included the writings of Theodoret against Cyril when he condemned the Nestorian "Three Chapters"; this was his attempt to reconcile opponents of Chalcedon and thus resolve the Monophysite issue (at the fifth ecumenical Council at Constantinople, 553). So it turned out that even though his writings in defence of Nestorius did not prevent Theodoret being reinstated at Chalcedon, he would still be anathematized at the Council of Constantinople in 553.

Theodoret's *History* covers the same period as that of Socrates and Sozomen, but his work is noted for wider familiarity with the Greek, Syriac, and Hebrew languages. If he did not know Latin well, he was much better informed about western Catholic theology. We are particularly indebted to Theodoret's work for elaborating on the role of Pope Leo of Rome in the controversies leading up to the Council of Chalcedon.

---

15. Theodoret's position on the person of Christ is quoted in Stevenson, *Creeds, Councils and Controversies*, 332–333.

16. See the quotation from Theodoret's letter to pope Leo (*Ep.* 113), in Stevenson, 347–349.

Appendix III

Historiography of Early Christianity in Africa

Groves: *The Planting of Christianity in Africa*

The Planting of Christianity in Africa in four volumes by C. P. Groves (1948–1964) can be cited as an important exception among twentieth-century historians of Christianity in Africa, most of whom devote little attention to the earliest phase. The first four chapters of the first volume (68 pages) discuss early Christianity in Africa as part of the Roman Empire, from the apostolic age in Egypt. Groves then turns to missionary efforts beyond Egypt itself in Nubia and Ethiopia, as regions where Christianity was able to survive for a long time before succumbing to Islamic forces.

For North Africa proper, Groves examines the organization of Roman provinces and development of the Christian church prior to the fifth-century Vandal invasions. Although Byzantine rulers regained control for some two centuries, the Arab invasions significantly impacted the viability of Christianity here. Indeed, Groves notes explicitly that for early North African Christianity we know of no attempts to evangelize (southward) beyond the borders of the empire, although Islamic forces did invade Sub-Saharan West Africa from the north.[1]

Postcolonial Studies of African Christianity

During the period following on independence, African scholars were much preoccupied with questions of autonomy and a non-Western identity,

---

1. Groves, *Planting of Christianity in Africa*, vii–viii.

specifically in repudiating colonialism.² They sought to indigenize the faith, to address properly African concerns, and reflect authentic African experience.³ The recovery of earliest Christianity would eventually play an important role in efforts to write the history of Christianity from a non-Western (and post-missionary) point of view.⁴

An important early publication, *Christianity in Independent Africa* (1978), raised the question of whether Christianity can be adapted to address African realities.⁵ More specific attention to the significance of an early strong Christian presence in North Africa is given by one of the African authors contributing to this work, the Gambian Lamin Sanneh, in his *West African Christianity* (1983); the introductory pages note the importance of Alexandria, Simon of Cyrene, the Ethiopian eunuch, and Apollos, as well as the traditional link of Mark with Egypt, and the apostle Thomas with "India."⁶

Equally important is the work of Ogbu U. Kalu, editor of *African Church Historiography: An Ecumenical Perspective* (1986). More recently he edited a substantive work (of more than 500 pages), which also presents an ecumenical perspective, *African Christianity: An African Story* (2007). Here Kalu uses the terms, "power, poverty and prayer" to characterize "an identifiable African Christianity," with an ongoing presence from antiquity to modern African Christianity (xi, 36). For early Christianity in Africa, he affirms the African identity of its leaders; Tertullian and Augustine (of the Maghreb) were African, not Italian (24). After AD 274 Egypt held a large majority of Christians. On the question of indigenization of Christianity in the Maghreb, Egypt, Ethiopia

---

2. On this theme, see Bediako, *Christianity in Africa*. See also the work of Ogbu U. Kalu, who edited proceedings of a conference on African church history (Nairobi, August 1986), *African Church Historiography: An Ecumenical Perspective*; his introduction (9–27) outlines the ecumenical perspective which was to guide discussion.

3. Such Afrocentric concerns are reflected by the Liberian Nya Kwiawon Taryor, *The Impact of the African Tradition on African Christianity*. Focused on biblical references to Africans, Ethiopians and Nubians, the work argues that Christianity is indigenous to Africa. A similar Afrocentric approach characterizes Keith Augustus Burton's *The Blessing of Africa*.

4. On the call for Africans to take pride in their Christian roots, see Daughrity, "Assessing Christianity in Africa's Transforming Context," 359–360. Bediako's *Theology and Identity*, also reflects initiative on this theme, but the need for further discussion of early Christianity in Africa remains.

5. E. Fasholé-Luke et al. eds., *Christianity in Independent Africa* is based on the 1974 conference (in Jos, Nigeria) of the Society for African Church History (established in 1962). Most of the contributors bear African names; see Verstraelen, *History of Christianity in Africa*, 4–5.

6. On ambiguity in use of the term "India" for ancient sites of Ethiopia, Nubia, the coastal area of Yemen as well as the continent now identified by the term, see ch. 6, note 1. For the significance of Lamin Sanneh's position on Christianity as a "transcontinental, intercultural and panoramic" faith, not to be owned by either the East or West, see Daughrity, "Assessing Christianity," 360–361.

and Nubia, Bible translation was only the beginning, for "traditional Egyptian religion contained much that resonated with the new: notions of salvation, eschatology, ethics and liturgy could find parallels in the Osiris-Horus myths" (25).[7]

Verstraelen on Historiography of Christianity in Africa

Recognition of Christianity as essentially "non-Western" is further reflected in varying degrees by four historians of Christianity in Africa reviewed by Frans Verstraelen in 2002: Adrian Hastings, John Baur, Elizabeth Isichei and Bengt Sundkler.[8] None of these authors can be designated "indigenous Africans," but all bring significant African experience to their work, and are conscious of the need to interpret the history of Christianity from within the African setting.

Although not indicated in the title, Hastings's *The Church in Africa 1450-1950* (1997), opens with a chapter on the Ethiopian church in the fifteenth century, the time of Zara Ya'iqob (3-45). In this context he devotes some pages to the foundations of the Ethiopian church in Judaic traditions.

Affirming Christianity as neither a "western" product of colonial history, nor a recent phenomenon in Africa, Baur's *Two Thousand Years of Christianity in Africa* (published 1994) begins in AD 62, the date when, according to tradition, the gospel writer Mark became the first bishop of Alexandria (17, 20). Passing rapidly over early Christianity in Egypt and North Africa, he devotes some attention to Nubians and Ethiopians (21-39),[9] especially the Amharic Ethiopians of the Aksumite kingdom and the influence of Judaism evidenced in the fourteenth-century legends of the *Kebra Nagast*.[10]

---

7. These quotes are taken from Kalu, "African Christianity," 25-44. Two other articles in this collection focus on early Christianity: Kenneth Sawyer and Youhana Youssef, "Early Christianity in North Africa," 45-74; and Anderson and Kalu, "Christianity in Sudan and Ethiopia," 76-104.

8. Verstraelen's *History of Christianity in Africa in the Context of African History* was published in Zimbabwe, 2002. Previews and surveys of these and other works on Christianity in Africa can be accessed at the website, "Christianity in Africa," https://www.questia.com/library/religion/christianity/christianity-in-africa/.

9. For Nubians, Baur recognizes the significant discoveries made by UNESCO-sponsored archaeological expeditions (1959-1969) to uncover the ruins of earlier civilizations, before these would permanently disappear under the lake resulting from a new dam on the Nile. They discovered impressive centres of Nubian Christianity, with cathedrals like that of Faras, and beautiful wall paintings.

10. These relate the visit of the Queen of Sheba with Solomon, from which she returned pregnant with a son, Menelek I. This Menelek is said to have gone back to Solomon to bring the "Ark of the Covenant" home with him, so that his people too would belong to the "chosen" ones (Baur, *Two Thousand Years*, 35-37).

Verstraelen appreciates the first chapter of Isichei's *A History of Christianity in Africa: From Antiquity to the Present* (1995) for the range and depth of her treatment of early African Christianity, and for the quality of sources used (13–44).[11] Her discussion begins with the Jewish diaspora and developments in the Egyptian church from the Gnostics to Athanasius, Cyril and the Monophysites. After brief discussion of Nubia and Aksum, she returns to the "Maghreb" to note the significance of Augustine and the Donatist struggles, the Vandal invasions (AD 429), repossession by Justinian (533), and final conquest by the Arabs (from 670–705). Isichei notes the extinction of Christianity here as one of the great mysteries of African history, though she alludes to some factors: the urban character of Christian culture, and its weakening through sectarian division and invasions of Vandals and Berber nomads.[12]

Beginning with Christianity in Egypt, Sundkler's massive work, *A History of the Church in Africa* (2000), recognizes the significant influence of Philo of Alexandria, as well as important legends honouring Mark as its first bishop (and his martyrdom of AD 68). Aside from Clement and Origen, Sundkler notes Athanasius for opposing Arians, and consecrating Frumentius as first bishop of Aksum, thus establishing a lasting link between the Coptic and Ethiopian Christian church. For the Coptic separation from imperial "Byzantine" or Melchite Christianity, Sundkler highlights the watershed decision of Chalcedon (AD 451), solidifying a nationalist movement as it embraced the Unionite (Monophysite) position.[13] And the Coptic church survived the Arab conquests; of the original one hundred episcopal sees, twenty-five remain. As proud descendants of the Pharaohs, the Copts showed themselves able to adapt to new circumstances.[14]

For North Africa, Sundkler notes the strategic role of Tertullian in the transition from use of Greek to Latin for the church,[15] before moving on to discuss Cyprian, and Augustine as the great preacher and polemicist, with a fateful role in implementing the imperial policy on the Donatists (after the debates of 411). On the demise of Christianity in this region, Sundkler recognizes crucial differences between the Coptic and North African church

---

11. For affirmation of the quality of her work, see also Jegede, "Academic Works on the History, Growth and Development of Christianity in Africa," 209–211.
12. Isichei, *History of Christianity*, 43–44.
13. Sundkler, *History of the Church in Africa*, 16.
14. Sundkler, 18.
15. Sundkler, 22.

in terms of geography, especially in relating to the (Sahara) desert and in the use of local languages.[16]

Nubian and Ethiopian Christianity maintained strong links with the Coptic church; Sundkler recognizes the important Ge'ez translations of treatises of Cyril of Alexandria in the text *Qerilos* (i.e. Cyril) (37). For acquaintance with ancient Nubia, Sundkler mentions the recent UNESCO excavations, revealing impressive buildings and monuments, noted as evidence of a royal church and court religion (30–32). He finishes this section with brief discussion of the fifteenth-century king Zar'a Ya'qob (or Ya'iqob) who used the legendary connection with Solomon to unite the church with the throne (39–40).

Finneran: The Archaeological Contribution

In the year that Verstraelen published his review (2002), Neil Finneran published *The Archaeology of Christianity in Africa* to compile archaeological evidence for the earliest Christianity in North Africa, the Copts of the Nile valley, and the Orthodox church of Nubia and Ethiopia. Like Sundkler, the author consciously rejects the "diffusionist" Eurocentric perspective as he seeks to assume a native African perspective on developments in religion for the discussion of artefacts, archaeological evidence and church architecture.

After an introductory survey of Christianity in the Roman Empire, and the contribution of archaeology for our knowledge of the churches (especially after the significant work of W. H. C. Frend), Finneran focuses on North Africa as granary for the city of Rome, evidence for the Donatist struggle, martyrdom and the Vandal invasion. For churches and monasteries in Egypt, he cites Coptic texts and archaeological discoveries. For Nubia, he notes the contribution of archaeology in supplying remarkable additions to our knowledge of an otherwise lost history, using helpful maps and ground plans to illustrate the significance of its monasteries and cathedrals, as at Faras.

Four Recent Authors on Early Christianity in Roman North Africa

It is impossible, and unnecessary in the present context, to give an exhaustive survey of recent work on early Christianity in Africa, whether in article or book form. With internet capacity it is not difficult to construct bibliographies on specialized topics, like the North African Donatists, or newly uncovered

---

16. Sundkler, 29.

evidence of Christianity in ancient Nubia or Ethiopia.[17] The four authors introduced here are significant for a wider scope of geography (of Roman North Africa, now the Maghreb) and extended chronology in topics covered. For the present study, it is useful to note a few substantive general works on the subject, leaving aside for now the scholarly publications focused on more specialized aspects of early Christianity in North Africa.

Joseph Cuoq

Joseph Cuoq's *L'Eglise d'Afrique du Nord du IIe au XIIe siècle* (*The North African Church from the Second to the Twelfth Century*), a historical account focused on Christian North Africa, appearing in 1984, about two decades before Verstraelen's survey, is focused on the Maghreb and covers the period up to the Arab conquests and Islamic rule through the twelfth century. Cuoq begins with the pre-Christian history, turning to the early years of persecution and apologetics, Cyprian and his emphasis on unity, the years of the Donatist controversy, and the towering figure of Augustine. As Arians, the Vandal invaders persecuted the Catholic church, until Justinian recovered that part of the former empire for a little more than a century. For the Arab conquests from AD 649, Cuoq notes the importance of Berber participation in the Arab army. And Arabs ruled the region with assistance of Islamized Berbers.[18] But Cuoq recognizes that, aside from these warrior tribes, there were initially no large-scale conversions of the tribes to Islam.

Christianity remained culturally dominant for the first century of Islamic rule, but its leadership was weakened as many priests fled to Italy. This exodus continued from the eighth to the twelfth century.[19] Cuoq emphasizes that Christianity was not obliterated, citing archaeological indications of its presence

---

17. Along with Kalu's *African Christianity: An African Story* (on which see note 7 above), one could rightfully include the recent work of Bongmba as editor of *The Routledge Companion to Christianity in Africa*, since a number of articles in this collection are also devoted to the earliest period. Bongmba himself provides an introduction on "Christianity in North Africa," focused on the Donatist controversy (45–60). This is followed by Youhanna N. Youssef's "Christianity in Egypt: The Coptic Church," discussing gnostic and monastic emphases (up to the fourteenth century) (61–78). Gerhard van den Heever's "Early Christian Discourses and Literature in North African Christianities in the Context of Hellenistic Judaism and Graeco-Roman Culture," surveys significant literature (biblical, apocryphal, historical or exegetical), with special attention to Philo and Origen (61–78).

18. Cuoq, *L'Eglise d'Afrique du Nord*, 176.

19. Maureen Tilley confirms weakness of leadership as a significant factor; she notes persecution by Arian Vandals, Justinian's attacks on the bishops in the controversy over the "Three Chapters," and finally, the erosion of authority of the North African bishops in their territories through interference from Rome (Tilley, "Collapse of a Collegial Church," 17–21).

in the tenth and eleventh centuries. In addressing the question why the vibrant faith of the third to the sixth centuries finally disappeared, Cuoq reminds us that the decline after the Arab conquests was spread over five hundred years. At first, Islam was relatively tolerant of the "Peoples of the Book," even though it imposed a ghetto existence.[20] But allegiance to the church of Rome and use of the Latin language exacerbated that isolation.[21]

Robin Daniel

Robin Daniel's *This Holy Seed* (1993) is also focused on earliest Christianity in the North African provinces. From discussion of the martyrdom of Perpetua and Felicitas (AD 203), placed in its cultural/religious, geographic and historical context, he proceeds to discuss Tertullian, the Montanists, and Cyprian. He then takes an indepth look at the fifth-century church of Augustine, finishing with the Vandal and Arab invasions. Although he notes the subordinate role of the indigenous Berber population (properly, the *Imazighen*), he does recognize that, just as Islam was slow to take hold of the people, Christianity was slow to disappear, remaining for at least another five centuries after the Arab conquests of the seventh century.[22]

On the causes of this disappearance, Daniel notes Christian identity through use of the Latin language, but puts more emphasis on significant departure from an original simplicity. Throughout the work (of some 500 pages), Daniel writes in an engaging and accessible style, at times bordering on devotional language in an attempt to draw out the contemporary relevance of questions faced in the early church.

François Decret

Another work on early Christianity of the imperial North African provinces (present-day Algeria, Tunisia and Libya), Decret's *Early Christianity in North Africa* appeared first in French (1996), and then in English translation (2009). After surveying the geography and political background, Decret turns to evidence of Christianity from the second century with the martyrs of Scilli (AD 180). This is followed by chapters on Tertullian and Cyprian, bridged by a transitional discussion of third-century crises, a period critical to ecclesiastical

---

20. Cuoq, *L'Eglise d'Afrique du Nord*, 174.
21. Cuoq, 178–179.
22. Daniel, *This Holy Seed*, 417.

development. Analysis of church organization at this time gives helpful background for the Donatist schism, a major focus of the book. The next two chapters examine conditions in the fourth century, preparatory to presenting the role of Augustine. The book finishes with a discussion of the Vandal and Arab conquests in the fifth and seventh centuries respectively.

The book is valuable for its introductory presentation of major figures; in this respect it serves as a companion to reading their original works. The important controversies are discussed: Montanist, Donatist, Manichean and Pelagian. Intended for students, the work does not pretend to provide significantly new insight or cover new ground; nor was the bibliography updated from the original French publication (of 1996). Indeed, it has been criticized for passing too quickly over sensitive issues and details, and assuming as settled some interpretations that remain controversial, as on Tertullian and the Jews. But for students of early Christianity, Decret has provided an important service with this well-written, comprehensive, and accessible work in its English translation.

J. Patout Burns Jr (et al.)

Burns's impressive work, *Christianity in Roman Africa: The Development of Its Practices and Beliefs*, published in 2014, is focused on Christian Roman Africa (ancient Libya, Tunisia, Algeria, and Morocco), and the contributions of Tertullian, Cyprian and Augustine to a church known for its strong ecclesiology and concern for purity and holiness. The book represents a multidisciplinary collaborative effort, and is written at a more sophisticated scholarly level, compared with the work of Daniel or Decret.[23] The authors begin with a survey of Christianity in Roman Africa from the second century to the Arab conquests, discussing relevant factors like geography and political history, especially the impact of persecution and of invasions in late antiquity. Further chapters explore specific features of worship in the churches, much of it based on architectural evidence.

Chapters 5 through 12 constitute the substance of the book. Here the authors review theological discussion from Tertullian to Augustine, with special attention to issues like rebaptism (accepted by the Donatists, but repudiated by the Catholic church). The focus is on issues of church leadership and liturgical practice, rites of baptism, penitence and the Eucharist. But the everyday life of

---

23. The five authors of this publication, in addition to Burns, are: Robin M. Jensen, Graeme W. Clarke, Susan T. Stevens, William Tabbernee and Maureen A. Tilley.

Christians, their customs of marriage, death and burial also receive attention. The work makes a major contribution in discussing these topics in relation to the relevant architectural features known from archaeological sites, whether church buildings, martyr shrines or cemeteries, connecting what is known of Christian practice and belief in the various periods with relevant archaeological, epigraphic, iconographical and literary evidence.

Shaw: The Kingdom of God in Africa

In *The Kingdom of God in Africa: A Short History of African Christianity*, published in 1996, Mark Shaw, like Finneran, dismisses the "Eurocentric" (or missionary) approach, as well as the nationalist emphasis on the indigenous factor, as the clue to church growth. For both of these factors he is concerned about triumphalism. This publication is of special interest for its attention to the earliest years in Egypt, North Africa, Ethiopia and Nubia.[24] The author, a Westerner (lecturing in Nairobi), struggled significantly with the historiographical issue of taking a definite perspective and providing an appropriate scholarly framework for the history of Christianity in Africa.[25]

With an allusion to Augustine's "City of God," Shaw suggests the concept of the "kingdom" of God, as a mixed world of the city of God and of humanity. On this basis he approaches the history of African Christianity through themes characteristic for each of its major periods,[26] characterizing early Christianity as "theocratic." Such identification is based on the dominant monastic emphases of Egypt and the Nile civilizations;[27] concern for the sovereignty of God in Augustine's *City of God*;[28] and the theocratic character of Christianity in the Nubia and Ethiopia.[29]

Dominique Arnauld: The First Seven Centuries of Christianity in Africa

Dominique Arnauld's *Histoire du Christianisme en Afrique: Les sept premiers siècles* [*A History of Christianity in Africa: The First Seven Centuries*], published in 2001, is similarly important for assuming a broader scope; alongside

---

24. Shaw, *Kingdom of God*, 11–72.
25. Shaw, 12–20.
26. Shaw, 20.
27. Shaw, 39.
28. Shaw, 58.
29. Shaw, 72.

treatment of Roman North Africa, he discusses Coptic, Nubian and Ethiopian Christianity. For the earliest period Arnauld accents the syncretist nature of religion in Egypt and "Africa" as part of the Mediterranean base under Roman rule. After brief discussion of Jews and Greeks, Gnostics and early Christian leaders like Clement of Alexandria and Origen, he moves on to Libya and Nubia, noting evangelization here even before AD 313, and the establishment of monastic life.[30] Turning to North "Africa" proper, he notes the Latin character of its church, and the contribution of Tertullian and Cyprian in discipline, language, liturgy and theological literature.[31]

The second section (on the period AD 313–451) discusses growth in church life and the politics of religion. For Egypt, he profiles Athanasius's leadership in a stormy time of christological discussion. For Christian North Africa, Arnauld rightly notes Augustine's struggles with Manichees, Donatists and Pelagians before the Vandal invasion. For the last period (up to AD 642), Arnauld notes Byzantine attempts to recover lost territory, and the effect of the Monophysite conviction on the Egyptian Christian church. For Ethiopia, we hear of the Nine Saints, and influence of the Coptic Monophysites on the Aksumite church.

Like other historians, Arnauld addresses the question of the complete disappearance of vibrant Christianity in North Africa.[32] He acknowledges a complexity of factors, including the contradictions of Roman occupation and the decline of Roman municipalities. But he rejects current answers regarding the church as an alien imposition on a subject people (and thus disappearing when the conqueror disappears), or its weakening through Vandal and Arab conquests. Arnauld contends that the population groups of the eastern and western sectors of the empire were diverse, and Romanization was always partial.

Oden: How Africa Shaped the Christian Mind

Thomas Oden's *How Africa Shaped the Christian Mind: Rediscovering the African Seedbed of Western Christianity*, published in 2007 as a relatively small work discussing the first five centuries of Christianity in Africa, belongs in a class of its own. Questioning the long-standing European perspective on African Christianity, Oden takes a bold approach in arguing for Africa as the

---

30. Arnauld, *Histoire du Christianisme en Afrique*, 55.
31. Arnauld, 91–93.
32. Arnauld, 307–309.

true "cradle" of Christianity. The work has its flaws, as reviewers have noted, but it can certainly be appreciated in the present context as a testimony to recent historiographical work on Christianity in Africa.

As he recognizes the intellectual achievements associated with major North African cultural centres like Alexandria and Carthage, Oden argues that the Christian world owes a debt to Africans. Significant theological discussion of the early centuries of Christianity originated in North Africa, and was transmitted from there to Europe and Asia. Oden implements this vision by challenging contemporary African Christians to take ownership of that legacy, inspiring them to make their own contribution in the context of global Christianity. He encourages them to recover the treasures of the church lost with the Arab conquests and use new historical insight to reshape the relationship between Christianity and Islam.[33]

Oden affirms African origins particularly in matters like the development of rhetorical and dialectical skills for the church and its liturgy, Christian biblical exegesis, ecumenical and conciliar methods of decision-making, organizational patterns of monasticism, and the categorization of Christian teaching and heresy. In so doing, he draws on significant work in related publications like the *Ancient Christian Commentary on Scripture*.[34] In this way he seeks to reverse age-old perceptions of the inferiority of work associated with the African culture and its peoples. In the final chapters, however, he shows that the book has a more concrete aim in outlining ongoing research, to examine all the necessary evidence for achieving a more balanced perception of earliest African Christianity, to rediscover its lost history and establish a new syllabus of church fathers and mothers as its earliest witnesses.[35] This project demands disciplined research, acquaintance with ancient languages and study of relevant textual or archaeological data. To accomplish these goals, Oden clearly envisions an international team of academics, linking their work with the help of modern computer technology.[36]

---

33. Oden, *How Africa Shaped*, 134.

34. Thomas Oden is the general editor for this multi-volume ecumenical project of commentaries on Bible books, based on works of early Christianity; the series has been published by InterVarsity Press (Downers Grove, IL) since 1998. Full-length commentaries from various patristic authors on books of the Bible are now being made available through the *Ancient Christian Texts* series. Featuring commentaries on the Psalms and Romans, the website, http://www.ivpress.com/accs/, also mentions patristic commentary on the Nicene Creed (in five vols.) as part of the *Ancient Christian Doctrine* series.

35. Oden, *How Africa Shaped*, 135–153.

36. Oden, 148, 150.

In 2011, Oden authored two publications that further implement the vision and research indicated in *How Africa Shaped the Christian Mind*, encouraging Africans to reclaim their Christian heritage. The first, *Early Libyan Christianity: Uncovering a North African Tradition*, emerged from a series of lectures in 2008 given at the Da'wa Islamic University (Tripoli). The work discusses six centuries of early Christianity in ancient Tripolitania and Cyrenaica (modern Libya), regions all but neglected in historical study of early Christianity to date. Here we find the origins of important Christians leaders, Simon of Cyrene, Arius and Bishop Synesius of Cyrene. While the significance of relevant evidence may be contested and conclusions are necessarily speculative, Oden provides substantive analysis of the relevant literature, from the New Testament to the work of Synesius. He also examines archaeological remains, from mosaics and baptisteries to the impressive imperial architectural structures of Leptis Magna.

In a work published that same year, *The African Memory of Mark: Reassessing Early Church Tradition*, Oden provides a new look at Mark, the gospel writer and close associate of the apostles, as he is known and respected in African tradition. The book brings together many stories about Mark based on hagiography, oral legends, historical documents, archaeological evidence and liturgical practice in the ancient churches, with special attention to traditions of the Coptic church.

The Center for Early African Christianity

Thomas Oden's vision, outlined in *How Africa Shaped the Christian Mind*, also motivated the research centre, *The Center for Early African Christianity*, now anchored at Yale University (New Haven, CT, USA) with its important website (http://www.earlyafricanchristianity.com). Before his death in 2017, Thomas Oden himself functioned as Director and Editor of the works of early African Christianity, working closely with Michael Glerup as Executive Director and Associate Editor of these works. The centre is served by an advisory board representative of the best of contemporary African scholarship, among whom we note the late Lamin Sanneh, former Professor of History and also Professor of Missions and World Christianity at Yale University.

The mission statement also closely reflects the goals affirmed in Oden's 2007 publication (noted above):

> To educate African leadership in the depth of African intellectual literary achievements, especially those from the Christian tradition of the first millennium ... using classic African sources. ... The resources are already there, waiting to be discovered. The

resources are in Africa. The wisdom is in the texts of Africa. The matrix is the soil of Africa. We desire to make these classic sources available in order to equip 21st century Africans to become the leaders of 21st century Christianity, even as they were leaders of early Christianity.... The implications of that provenance for 21st century global Christianity have not been adequately explored or appreciated.

The site provides an invaluable source of maps, photos and illustrations, access to relevant seminars and podcasts, notes on new publications and links to authors and texts through sites like the *Patrologia Latina*, *Thesaurus Linguae Graecae*, the *Perseus Project*, and the *Dictionary of African Christian Biography*, to name but a few.

Glossary of Important Terms

abbot – (from Aramaic *abba*, father) the head or superior in the monastery.

adoptionism – the belief that Jesus was a perfect human being, who was adopted by God as his Son. This adoption is usually thought to have occurred when the Holy Spirit descended on Jesus at his baptism.

aeon – (from Greek *aiôn*, for age, lifetime or eternity) eternal beings, or an eternal period of time, thousands of years.

allegory – (from Greek *allos*, other, and *agorein*, to speak publicly) a text or speech which has a meaning beyond (i.e. underlying, or hidden beneath) that which is said openly and literally about people, things or events, as in a parable. The text refers to one thing symbolized or imaged by another. The term is also used for an *interpretation* of a text to mean something different from the immediate literal or surface meaning. That other meaning may involve the relationship of the soul to God.

Anomoian – (from Greek *anomoios*, unlike) a christological view stressing the unlikeness of the Son with respect to the Father; it was one of the positions taken in the Arian controversies.

anchorite – (from Greek *anachorein*, to retreat, or retire) a hermit, or a solitary ascetic who withdraws from the world and society to allow for meditation and to achieve spiritual perfection.

apocalyptic – a body of literature which reveals secret knowledge about events of the future, or the end of time; this frequently involves messianic expectations.

apocryphal – (from Greek *apokrupha*, hidden or obscure) originally a term for fourteen books included in the Septuagint translation, but not accepted in Judaism for the canon of the Hebrew Scriptures. Books designated *Apocryphal* in Protestant Bibles are called deutero-canonical (i.e. of secondary rank in the canon) in Roman Catholic Bibles. The term has wider use for writings (like the secret gospels, or infancy gospels) which are considered not genuine or authentic.

Apologist – (from Greek *apologia*, a public defence) second-century Christian writers who gave a reasoned explanation and defence of Christianity for (hostile) non-Christian audiences.

apostate – (from the Greek *apostasia*, for defection or revolt) the term refers to the formal renunciation of belief or affiliation; it was used for the Emperor Julian (AD 331–363) to indicate his public rejection of Christianity as the prominent religious affiliation of the Roman Empire at that time.

Apostolic Fathers – a group of Christian teachers and writers especially from the late first and second century. They are regarded as "Fathers" of the church in succession to the apostles.

apostolic succession – the teaching that religious authority conferred on the apostles by Jesus was passed on to bishops of the Catholic Christian church in unbroken succession.

apostle – (from Greek *apostellein*, to send) designation of the first twelve students or disciples of Jesus, sent out by him on a special mission to preach the gospel.

archetype – (from Greek *archon*, leading, and *tupos*, imprint) the original pattern, or model from which other things are made, as a prototype.

archimandrite – (from Greek *archon*, leader, and *mandra*, enclosure or monastery) the head of a monastery, or series of monasteries, especially in the Eastern Orthodox church.

Arian – a supporter of Arius, who considered Christ, as the word of God, a created being, and thus not fully God.

Asceticism – (from Greek *askein*, to train or exercise, as for athletic contests) a life and practice based on rigorous, disciplined self-denial, with the aim of achieving spiritual perfection.

baptism – the rite or sacrament of entry to the Christian church, using water as a symbol of cleansing from a life of sin, dying with Christ to the old, and beginning a new life, or rising again with him. Early Christianity practised total immersion where feasible.

Bible – the sacred book containing authoritative writings for Jews (the First Covenant, or Old Testament) and Christians (both Old and New Testaments).

caesaropapism – (literally, the "emperor" is also "pope") a term for subordination of the church to the state in government and administration and even in doctrine.

canon – (from Greek *kanon*, ruler) a list of biblical books regarded as authoritative.

catacombs – underground cemeteries in and around Rome, with vaulted sepulchres, as areas used by early Christians in gathering for worship.

catechetical school – (from Greek *katechein*, to teach) a school teaching basic principles of the faith, typically with a question-and-answer method. Such instruction was an important part of preparation for baptism. Those enrolled in the school were called *catechumens*.

Catholic – (based on the Greek *katholon*, literally, that of the whole, or universal) the term refers not only to the Roman Catholic church, but reflects the church *as a whole*, throughout the world, in contrast with the church of its parts, or groups which have separated, as heretical or schismatic.

cenobitic monasticism – (from Greek *koinos bios*, a common life) refers to ascetic discipline in a communal setting, and living under a rule for the community.

Christology – that part of theology which studies the person and work of Christ, particularly his relationship to God the Father, and to humanity.

church – (based on the Greek *kuriakon*, [house] of the Lord) the assembly of Christian believers as those "called together" for worship, instruction and edification. It may also refer to the building set apart for public worship. The equivalent term (as adjective) is "ecclesiastical" (from Greek *ekklêsia*, assembly, or literally, "those called out") relating to the church as the gathering of God's people.

codex (pl. codices) – a volume of a manuscript from the Scriptures or an ancient classical text, composed of numerous pages cut to size, and bound by sewing at one edge (while the scroll has pages pasted end to end, joined together and rolled up).

Compline – last hour of prayer for the day in the divine office, that is the daily liturgical schedule of prayers and readings, especially in a monastic community.

confessor – one who has suffered for the faith in a time of persecution, confessing the faith publicly under duress, but not to the point of death. As survivors, confessors were given a special status in the congregation.

convent – a monastic establishment, usually for women as nuns, but possibly also for monks who live together under strict religious vows.

creed – (from Latin *credo*, I believe) a concise statement of the faith.

deacon – (from Greek *diakonos*, a servant) one who serves in the church (as layman or clergy), usually with a ranking just below that of elder or priest.

demiurge – (from Greek *dêmiourgos*, craftsman) the craftsman creator of the world (in Platonism), who does his best to apply the forms to matter.

Deutero-canonical – see "apocryphal."

dhimmi – a term use by Muslims to designate the status of non-Muslims under Muslim protection. Until they convert to Islam, they remain second class citizens.

diaspora – the scattering of the (Jewish) people from the land of Israel, especially after the exile.

ditheism – a teaching which accepts two ultimate deities.

divinization – (in Greek, *theôsis*) an understanding of salvation characteristic of the Eastern Orthodox tradition, emphasizing the believer's union with Christ as human partaking in the divine nature (based on 2 Pet 1:4).

Docetism – (from Greek *dokein*, to appear) a belief that the physical body of Jesus was not real; he only seemed to have a body and thus was not really human.

dogma – term for a well-reasoned position, used for a teaching or doctrine authoritatively defined by the church.

Donatism – the position of the schismatic church of North Africa, based on the role of the fourth-century leader Donatus. This group hardly differed from the Catholic Christian church in teaching, but was more rigorous on issues arising from persecution.

dualist – the acceptance of two ultimate principles at the origin of all things, usually focused on the distinction of matter and spirit (or body and soul) as opposing principles. As a radical position, it designates a split in the divine between the true God and the creator (or between good and evil).

duophysite – (from Greek *duas*, two, and *phusis*, nature) a christological position attributing two natures, human and divine, to the person of Jesus Christ.

dynamic monarchianism – (from Greek *monos*, single; *archon*, ruling; *dunamis*, power) a type of monarchianism (see below) stressing the unity of God, who yet revealed his divine power in Jesus, as a unique person who is divinely energized by God's power.

ecclesiastical – (from Greek *ekklêsia*, assembly, literally "those called out") see above on "Church."

eclecticism – (from Greek *eklegein*, choosing, picking out) a principle of selection using materials gathered from a variety of systems, sources, or doctrines.

ecumenical councils – (from Greek, *oikoumênê*, the entire inhabited world) those councils which are recognized by all segments of the early Christian church, and so called because the bishops in attendance represented the entire Christian church as existing throughout what was then recognized as the inhabited world.

emanation – a flowing out or coming forth of what arises from another source.

Encratism – a practical and doctrinal rigorist approach in asceticism, typically reflecting a low estimation of bodily reality.

epigraphical – (from Greek *epigraphein*, to inscribe, or write on) term for evidence from engraving on grave stones, plaques or other kinds of statuary.

esoteric literature – writings meant for a restricted audience, an inner circle or chosen few.

eschatology – (from Greek *eschaton*, last) teaching about the last things, the end of time.

Essenes – members of an ascetic Jewish sect from the second century BC, who separated themselves from Judaism as it was practised in Jerusalem.

episcopal – (from Greek *episkopos*, overseer, or bishop) referring to churches governed by a bishop, or matters having to do with the bishop of the church.

eucharistic liturgy – (from Greek *eucharistia*, thankfulness, gratitude) Holy Communion, or the Lord's Supper; the Christian sacrament commemorating the death of Jesus, with his body and blood symbolized in bread and wine respectively.

Gnosticism – religious movements, typically from the second century, characterized by a dualistic teaching of salvation through *gnôsis*, as secret knowledge. Many of these groups had links with Christians, and/or borrowed ideas and terminology from them.

Godhead – the ultimate source of deity; early Christians typically used the term for God the Father.

gospel – the story of salvation in Jesus, typically from the first four books of the New Testament (Matthew, Mark, Luke and John); the word comes from the early English *godspell*, a good story, or good news, the English translation of the Greek *euangelion*, good news, or a good message.

hagiography – biographical accounts of the life and deeds of holy persons, or saints, often idealized according to a formula (with some embellishment).

Hasidim – the pious ones (from Hebrew *hasayya*), a term used for Essenes or Zealots, and also applied to a later tradition in Jewish mystical thought.

Hasmonean – rulers of second- and first-century BC Jews, originating with the Maccabees who initiated the intervening period between Syrian and Roman rule; this was a time when the Jews in Palestine achieved a degree of independence.

Hebrew Bible – the authoritative Scriptures of the Jews, consisting of the Torah, the Prophets and Writings.
Hellenism – (from *Hellenes* as a term for the Greek people) that which belongs to Greek culture, language and literature.
Hellenization – the process of acquiring Hellenic culture, or being influenced by Greek culture.
heresy – (from Greek *hairein*, to choose, and *hairesis*, as a sect, party, or group whose allegiance is based on specific choices made, not imposed externally) the term was used initially among the philosophers to indicate different schools of thought, based on choices made regarding particular views; eventually it acquired the meaning of alignment based on wrong choice, or wilful deviation from established, orthodox belief.
hermit – (from Greek *erêmos*, solitary, desolate) an ascetic who withdraws from society, typically to spend time in the desert.
Herodians – group of Jews who supported Herod as king of the Jews in the time of Jesus.
Hexapla – set of six Hebrew OT manuscripts available to Origen, published with parallel columns of text for purposes of comparison, to establish OT textual readings.
hierarchy – a system of church government by clergy or priests in graded ranking from lower to higher positions of responsibility.
Homoians – (from Greek *homoios*, similar) those taking a position on the divinity of Christ in the Arian controversies, to support the *similarity* or likeness of the Son with the Father; they rejected the Nicene *homoousion* as it affirmed *sameness* of nature between Father and Son.
hypostasis – (from Greek *hupostasis*, a real existence or substance) a term for that which has true individuality; it came to be used for each of the three persons of the Trinity taken individually.
hypostatic union – the union of Christ, the Word, with human nature; and the teaching of the consubstantial union of the divine and human natures of Christ in one person.
iconoclasm – (from Greek *eikonoklastês*, one who breaks images) an eighth- and ninth-century movement in the Eastern Orthodox church forbidding use of icons, and actively destroying these icons.
Idumeans (or Edomites) – a tribe tracing its ancestry back to Esau, Jacob's brother.
Incarnation – (from Latin *incarnatus*, made of human flesh [*caro*]) belief that the Son of God took on human flesh, implying that the historical Christ is fully human as well as fully divine.
logos – Greek term for thought, reason or word. For Platonists, the logos represented the expression of the divine mind (*Nous*), and is subordinate to that mind. For Stoics the term represented the rational principle ruling the world, as a principle in which all human life shares. Christians used the term to represent Christ as the outstanding Logos/Word of God, as in God's speaking creation into being.

For Justin Martyr the term represented a cultural bridge with non-Christian understanding. Logos theology focused on Jesus as *Word of God*, typically representing Christ in a position subordinate to the Father.

liturgy – (from Greek *leitourgia*, service) the public worship of the church, or prescribed pattern of worship, especially when it includes the Eucharist; in the Eastern Orthodox tradition this is the *Divine Liturgy*, and for the Roman Catholic tradition, the *Mass*.

Mahdi – Islamic term for the one expected, as one who will save the Muslim community; the term is used in the same sense that Christians refer to Christ as the one who is expected to return, to save them in the second coming.

Manichean – a semi-gnostic and dualistic system of belief going back to the third-century Mani.

Marcionism – teaching based on the second-century teacher, Marcion, known for preaching a radical discontinuity between the OT and NT, and also between the God of the OT and the Father of Jesus.

Maronite – Christians (in Lebanon) who adhere to the Monothelite position (see below) on the person of Jesus.

martyr – (based on the Greek *martus*, witness) a term for those who suffer and/or are put to death for adherence to the faith.

Messiah – (from the Hebrew *mashiah*, the anointed one; in Greek, the *Christos*) the saviour or liberator who was promised in the OT to bring deliverance for Jews under oppression. A messianic belief typically affirms the coming/return of a messiah or saviour, to bring deliverance at the end of history.

Modalism – in theology this refers to the successive *modes* of appearance of God in turn as Father, as Son and Spirit; the three persons of the Trinity are regarded as successive modes of expression of one God. Modalistic monarchianism, thus, stresses the unity of God, to the extent of denying essential distinctions in the Godhead. This approach has also been referred to as *patripassianism*, for it seems to attribute Jesus's suffering on the cross to the Father; and it was called *Sabellianism*, after the second century Sabellius, a main proponent of this approach.

monad – (from Greek *monos*, single, alone) a single unit or entity, simple and indivisible; also the ultimate or most elementary entity, and thus the term used for the Godhead as the single source of deity.

monarchianism – (from Greek *monos*, single, and *archon*, ruling) a theological position stressing the unity of God as ultimate ruler (on "dynamic monarchianism," see above).

monarchical bishop – the ruling bishop.

monasticism – a way of life characterized by withdrawal from the world (as hermit or anchorite), with the aim of attaining to personal sanctification and perfection. As an ascetic practice this lifestyle is also pursued communally (see "cenobitic"), typically with structured and disciplined use of time in work and prayer.

Monophysite – (from Greek *monos*, single and *phusis*, nature) a theological position focused on the one nature of Christ. This means that Christ has a single composite nature, with the human nature typically subsumed under the divine nature. This view still characterizes Coptic churches, among others.

monothelite – (from Greek *monos*, single, and *thelêma*, will) a theological position focused on a single will in Christ. This may also refer to a single will incorporating the two wills, human and divine; but the human will is subsumed under the divine.

Montanism – Christian movement originating in second-century Phrygia (Asia Minor), with a strong emphasis on the revelation of the Holy Spirit, and the imminent advent of the new Jerusalem.

mujaddid – (*Mujadadi* in Hausa) an Islamic (Arabic) term for a revivalist, one who would have a role like that of Martin Luther or Billy Graham for Christianity.

mystery religion – a religious group or cult, distinguished from public or civic religious practice in the ancient world in that it maintains "secret" beliefs and practice; adherents were initiated into these groups through rites of purification.

New Testament (NT) – the canonical books for the Christian church.

Nicene – (from Nicea [also spelled Nicaea], the city not far from Constantinople, and site of the first ecumenical council) referring to the first great ecumenical council of the Christian church called by the Emperor Constantine in 325; also the creed established by that council, and ratified by the subsequent Council of Constantinople (AD 381).

orthodoxy – (from Greek *orthos*, right, correct, and *doxa*, thought or praise) belief and practice in agreement with the rule of faith, or ecumenical creeds and confessions; it may also represent correct belief and worship. As such the term embraces more than a reference to the Eastern Orthodox church, which is based on the four patriarchs (of Constantinople, Antioch, Alexandria and Jerusalem) who deny the supreme authority of the Pope. The break with the Roman church came finally in 1054.

Old Testament (OT) – canonical books of the Jews, which the Christian church shares with the synagogue.

ousia – Greek term for essential being, also translated as "substance."

pagan – (from Latin *paganus*, peasant or civilian) originally this referred to people of the countryside, preserving local custom; it came to designate all (polytheistic) people who were not converted to Christianity.

patriarch – (from Greek *pater*, father, and *archon*, ruling) the bishop as "first Father" of an important city like Rome, Constantinople, Antioch, Alexandria and later also Jerusalem; from the fourth century the term was used for those holding the highest ecclesiastical office and exercising wide supervision in these cities and their surrounding districts.

patripassianism – (from Latin *pater*, father, and *passio*, suffering) another term for modalistic monarchianism, attributing to the Father the suffering of the Son on the cross.

patristic – (from the Latin *patres*, fathers) referring to theologians, teachers and writers of the early Christian church, as its "Fathers."

Paraclete – (from Greek *para*, alongside, and *klêtos*, called) a term for the Holy Spirit, who is sent forth as Comforter after the ascension of Jesus.

Pax Romana – Roman peace, established by the Julio-Claudian emperors, especially with the supremacy of Augustus Caesar as emperor after the long period of civil war in the first century BC; this meant the end of the Republic.

Pentateuch – (from Greek *penta*, five) the first five books of the Bible, also called Torah, or Law.

person – (based on Latin *persona*) the term first used by Tertullian for the three members of the Trinity; later discussion in Greek would use the term *hypostasis*.

Pharisees – (probably based on the Hebrew *parush*, separated) teachers of the law in post-exilic Judaism, portrayed in the New Testament as those concerned for the letter more than the spirit of the law. Aside from a strict, if not self-righteous observance of the written law, Pharisees also accepted and enforced oral tradition in law based on popular usage.

Pleroma – (based on Greek *plerôma*, fullness) the spiritual realm, including all spiritual beings, especially the angels.

polytheism – (from Greek *polus*, many, and *theos*, god) belief in a plurality of divine beings.

Pontifex Maximus – originally the highest priestly office in ancient Roman religion. With the rule of Caesar Augustus the title was attached to the emperor, and later also taken on by the bishop of Rome.

presbyter – (from Greek *presbutês*, elder) office of elder, or supervisory and pastoral task in the Christian congregation.

pseudepigrapha – (from Greek *pseudês*, false, and *epigraphein*, to inscribe) Jewish religious texts similar to biblical writings, but written under a false name or inscription, and thus not recognized as part of the Bible or the Apocrypha. Typically these were written some considerable time after the event.

Ptolemies – Hellenistic rulers of Egypt, installed after the conquests of Alexander the Great.

publicans – (from Latin *publicani*, tax collectors) tax collectors on behalf of the Roman Empire.

Qumran – a religious establishment in the desert near the Dead Sea, arising under Hasmonean rulers and functioning outside Judaism under the high priest in Jerusalem.

rabbi – a respectful Hebrew title for teacher or master, one ordained to teach Jewish and authorized to decide on matters of law and ritual.

recapitulation – a concept developed by Irenaeus for Christ as the second Adam, recapitulating, or "gathering up into himself" all the experience of humanity up to that time, and thereby inaugurating the new redeemed humanity.

religio illicita – legal term in the Roman Empire for a religion or religious group not regarded as legitimate, or legal.

resurrection – Jesus's rising to new life on the third day after his death on the cross and burial.

revelation – the process by which God discloses his plan for humankind, manifesting his person and will; this is also the name of the last book of the NT, indicating an unveiling or uncovering of what is to happen (in the future), as a comfort to those undergoing persecution.

rule of faith (*regula fidei*) – a brief summary of essential aspects of apostolic preaching, normative for Christians; this was later formulated as a creed, as in the Apostles' Creed.

rule – a collection of regulations, guidelines and directives governing the spiritual and administrative life of monasteries, like the Benedictines.

sacrament – (from Latin *sacer*, sacred, or consecrated, set apart; translation of the Greek *mustêrion*, a symbol or token, and solemn oath) the rites or ritual acts instituted by Jesus himself as a means of communicating his grace, especially through baptism and the Eucharist (Lord's Supper). The Roman Catholic church also accepts as sacraments: confirmation, penance, holy orders (ordination), matrimony and extreme unction. The term is also used for the bread and wine consecrated for Eucharist.

Sadducees – a sect of Judaism in the time of Jesus; in opposition to the Pharisees, the Sadducees denied resurrection from death, existence of angels and the binding character of law handed down by oral tradition.

Samaritans – Jews of Samaria, the ancient capital of the ten separated tribes of Israel, the northern part of Palestine, wedged between Judea and Galilee.

Sanhedrin – (from Greek *sunedrion*, assembly) the ruling body of Jews under the Romans, and highest court for religious and civil questions; it was presided over by the high priest. The Sanhedrin was abolished with the destruction of Jerusalem in AD 70.

schism – a formal division in an established group, as in a deliberate break with the church, usually based not on issues of teaching, but on personalities or practice.

scribes – (from Latin *scribere*, to write) a professional group devoted to writing, or careful copying of manuscripts; in Judaism they were also teachers of written law.

Scripture – the normative books of the Bible, the Old Testament for Jews, and the New Testament along with the Old for Christians.

Septuagint (or LXX) – the Greek translation of the OT produced in Egypt, ca. 270 BC.

Shema – the central expression of Jewish monotheism, found in Deuteronomy 6:4, "Hear O Israel. The Lord our God, the Lord is one."

Sol Invictus – the Unconquered Sun, a Roman god promoted in the third century to bring unity in Roman pagan religion.

Soteriology – (from Greek *sôtêr*, saviour) a part of theology devoted to understanding of salvation.

Subordinationism – teaching concerning Jesus as inferior in ranking, thus subordinate to the Father (as in Logos theology).

synagogue – (from Greek *sunagôgê*, bringing together, assembly) the institution established by post-exilic Jews for worship and study of Torah; establishment was based on a quorum of ten heads of families.

syncretism – (from Greek *sunkretismos*, union of two parties) term for amalgamation or reconciliation of two or more groups of religious belief, teaching and practice, usually with the sense of one being compromised in favour of the other.

synoptic – (from Greek *sunopsis*, oversight, or summary) accounts given from the same point of view, revealing interdependence. The term is used specifically for the first three NT gospels, Matthew, Mark, and Luke, since these contain a considerable amount of material in common, and can be read in parallel fashion.

testament – (from the Latin *testari*, to testify or make a will) for the Bible this refers to a convenant or agreement between God and mankind; in this sense it is used for either of the two parts, the Old or New Testament.

theology – (from Greek *theos*, god) the systematic study of God and his self-revelation in word and deed.

Theotokos – (from Greek *theos*, god, and *tokos*, one giving birth) the fifth-century title for Mary, as bearer of God in Christ.

Therapeutae – (from Greek *therapeutês*, a worshipper of God, or healer) name of a monastic group in Upper Egypt which may have had contact with the Essenes. They are known from the time of Philo of Alexandria, from whom we have a description of their life.

Torah – taken strictly, this refers to the first five books of the OT, the Pentateuch, or written law given to Moses. The term is also used to include the entire Hebrew Bible, or even more widely, the Talmud, on the assumption that the oral law was given to Moses along with written law.

Trinity – teaching of God as one in three, and three in one. The Nicene and later ecumenical councils established three coequal persons in God: Father, Son, and Spirit, all fully sharing one and the same divine substance.

typology – a school of biblical interpretation, particularly for the OT, regarding events and persons of the OT as "types" of Christ, and specifically foreshadowing or anticipating the NT.

Ulama – (Arabic) term for the council of Islamic clerics who are versed in Islamic jurisprudence, and thus guide and supervise application of Shari'ah law in an Islamic state; the role of the Council of Ulama is comparable to that of the Jewish Sanhedrin.

Umma – (Arabic) term for the Muslim community of the faithful, both local and global, or international.

Vulgate – (from Latin *vulgatus*, popular, or common) name of the revised Latin translation of the Bible prepared by Jerome and his associates, including two women, Paula and Eustochium. The Vulgate was the authorized translation in the Latin-speaking Western church.

Yan Izala – the Hausa name for a modernist Islamic sect in Nigeria, founded in 1987; the full name in Arabic is *Jama'atu Izala al-Bid'a wa Iqamat al-Sunna*.

Yan Tauri – (literally, "the invincible") an Islamic group in Northern Nigeria armed with weapons, like knives, which they are prepared to use in defence of Islam.

Bibliography

Aland, B. "Marcion: Versuch einer neuen Interpretation." *Zeitschrift für Theologie und Kirche* 70, no. 4 (1973): 420–447.

Aland, Kurt. "The Relation between Church and State in the Early Times: A Reinterpretation." *Journal of Theological Studies* 19, no. 1 (1968): 115–127.

Albrecht, Ruth. *Das Leben der heiligen Makrina auf dem Hintergrund der Thekla-Traditionen: Studien zu den Ursprüngen des weiblichen Mönchtums im 4. Jahrhundert in Kleinasien*. Göttingen: Vandenhoeck & Ruprecht, 1986.

Allen, P. *Evagrius Scholasticus: The Church Historian*. Louvain: Spicilegium Sacrum Lovaniense, fasc. 41, 1981.

Ancient Christian Commentary on Scripture. [See "Annotated Guide," §A.]

Ante-Nicene Fathers. [See "Annotated Guide," §A.]

Arjava, Antti. *Women and Law in Late Antiquity*. Oxford: Clarendon, 1996.

Armstrong, A. H. *An Introduction to Ancient Philosophy*. London: Methuen; Totowa, NJ: Rowman & Allanheld, 1983.

Arnauld, Dominique. *Histoire du Christianisme en Afrique: Les sept premiers siècles* [A History of Christianity in Africa: The First Seven Centuries]. Paris: Éditions Karthala, 2001.

Athanasius. *The Coptic Life of Anthony*. Translated by Tim Vivian. London: International Scholars Publications, 1995.

Augustine. *The City of God*. Edited by H. Bettenson. London: Penguin Classics, 1984.

———. *Confessions*. Edited by R. Pine-Coffin. London: Penguin Classics, 1961.. *The Life of St Anthony*. Translated by R. T. Meyer. New York: Newman Press, 1978.

Augustine. *The City of God*. Edited by H. Bettenson. London: Penguin Classics, 1984.

———. *Confessions*. Edited by R. Pine-Coffin. London: Penguin Classics, 1961.

Backus, Irena. "The Early Church in the Renaissance and Reformation." In *Early Christianity: Origins and Evolution to AD 600: In Honour of W. H. C. Frend*, edited by Ian Hazlett, 291–303. Nashville: Abingdon, 1991.

Bagnall, R. *Egypt in Late Antiquity*. Princeton: Princeton University Press, 1993.

Baigent, Michael, Richard Leigh, and Henry Lincoln. *The Holy Blood and the Holy Grail*. London: Corgi, 1982.

Bainton, R. H. *Early Christianity*. Malabar, FL: Robert E. Krieger, 1984.

Balás, David L. "Marcion Revisited: A Post-Harnack Perspective." In *Texts and Testaments: Biblical and Intertestamental Texts*, edited by G. E. March, 95–108. San Antonio: Trinity University Press, 1980.

Balch, D. L., and C. Osiek, eds. *Early Christian Families in Context: An Interdisciplinary Dialogue*. Grand Rapids, MI: Eerdmans, 2003.

Banks, Robert. *Going to Church in the First Century*. Auburn, ME: Christian Books, 1980.

Barnard, L. W. *Athenagoras: A Study in Second Century Apologetics*. Paris: Beauchesne, 1972.

———. *Justin Martyr: His Life and Thought*. Cambridge: Cambridge University Press, 1967.

Barnes, T. D. *Athanasius and Constantius*. Cambridge, MA: Harvard University Press, 1993.

———. *Constantine and Eusebius*. Cambridge, MA: Harvard University Press, 1981.

———. "Eusebius of Caesarea." In *Early Christian Thinkers: The Lives and Legacies of Twelve Key Figures*, edited by Paul Foster, 173–193. Downers Grove, IL: IVP Academic, 2010.

———. "Legislation against the Christians." *Journal of Roman Studies* 58 (1968): 32–50.

———. *The New Empire of Diocletian and Constantine*. Cambridge, MA: Harvard University Press, 1982.

———. *Tertullian: A Historical and Literary Study*. Oxford: Clarendon, 1971.

Bartlett, John R. *Jews in the Hellenistic World*. Cambridge: Cambridge University Press, 1985.

Bauer, Walter. *Orthodoxy and Heresy in Earliest Christianity (Rechtgläubigkeit und Ketzerei im ältesten Christentum)*. Translated by Robert A. Kraft and Gerhard Krodel. Philadelphia: Fortress, 1971.

Baur, John. *Two Thousand Years of Christianity in Africa*. Nairobi: Paulines Publications Africa, 1994.

Baynes, N. H. *Constantine the Great and the Christian Church*. London: Oxford University Press, 1972.

Beckwith, R. T. "Canon of the Old Testament." In *The New Bible Dictionary*, edited by James D. Douglas, N. Hillyer and D. R. Woods, 165–169. Downers Grove, IL: InterVarsity Press, 1996. [See also "Annotated Guide," §C.]

Bediako, Kwame. *Christianity in Africa: The Renewal of a Non-Western Religion*. Maryknoll, NY: Orbis Books; Edinburgh: Edinburgh University Press, 1995.

———. *Theology and Identity: The Impact of Culture upon Christian Thought in the Second Century and Modern Africa*. Oxford: Regnum Books, 1992.

Benko, Stephen. "Pagan Criticism of Christianity during the First Centuries AD." *Aufstieg und Niedergang der römischen Welt*, edited by W. Haase. Part 2, Principat 23, no. 2 (1980): 1055–1118.

———. *Pagan Rome and the Early Christians*. London: Batsford, 1984.

Bethune-Baker, J. F. *Nestorius and His Teaching: A Fresh Examination of the Evidence*. Cambridge: Cambridge University Press, 1908.

Bickerman, Elias J. *The Jews in the Greek Age*. Cambridge, MA: Harvard University Press, 1988.

Blyden, E. Wilmot. *Christianity, Islam and the Negro Race*. Edinburgh: Edinburgh University Press, 1959.

Bongmba, Elias Kifon, ed. *The Routledge Companion to Christianity in Africa*. New York: Routledge; London: Taylor & Francis, 2016.

Borgen, Peder. *Early Christianity and Hellenistic Judaism.* Edinburgh: T&T Clark, 1998.
Børresen, K. E. *Subordination and Equivalence: The Nature and Role of Woman in Augustine and Thomas Aquinas.* Translated by C. H. Talbot. Washington DC: University Press of America, 1981.
———, ed. *Image of God and Gender Models in Judaeo-Christian Tradition.* Oslo: Solum Forlag, 1991.
Bowers, Paul. "Nubian Christianity: The Neglected Heritage." *Africa Journal of Evangelical Theology* 4, no. 1 (1985): 3–23.
Bowersock, G. W. *Julian the Apostate.* London: Duckworth, 1978.
Boyarin, D. *Border Lines: The Partition of Judaeo-Christianity.* Philadelphia: University of Pennsylvania Press, 2004.
———, ed. "Judaeo-Christianity Redivivus." *Journal of Early Christian Studies* 9 (2001): 417–419.
Brakke, David. "The Early Church in North America: Late Antiquity, Theory and the History of Christianity." *Church History* 71, no. 3 (2002): 473–491.
Brock, Sebastian P. *A Brief Outline of Syriac Literature.* Kottayam: St Ephrem Ecumenical Research Institute, 1997.
———. "The Development of Syriac Studies." In *The Edward Hincks Bicentenary Lectures,* edited by K. J. Cathcart, 94–113. Dublin: University College Department of Near Eastern Languages, 1994.
———. *Studies in Syriac Christianity: Collected Studies.* London: Variorum, 1992.
———. *Syrian Perspective on Late Antiquity.* London: Variorum, 1984.
———, and S. Ashbrook Harvey, eds. *Holy Women of the Syrian Orient.* Berkeley: University of California Press, 1998.
Brown, Dan. *The Da Vinci Code.* New York: Anchor Books; New York: Doubleday, 2003.
Brown, Peter R. L. *Augustine of Hippo: A Biography.* Revised with epilogue. Berkeley: University of California Press; London: Faber & Faber, 2000.
———. *The Body and Society: Men, Women and Sexual Renunciation in Early Christianity.* New York: Columbia University Press, 1988.
———. *The Cult of the Saints: Its Rise and Function in Latin Christianity.* Chicago: Chicago University Press, 1981.
———. *The Making of Late Antiquity.* Cambridge, MA: Harvard University Press, 1978.
———. *Power and Persuasion in Late Antiquity: Toward a Christian Empire.* Madison, WI: University of Wisconsin Press, 1992.
———. *Society and the Holy in Late Antiquity.* London: Faber & Faber; Berkeley: University of California Press, 1982.
———. *The World of Late Antiquity from Marcus Aurelius to Muhammad.* London: Thames & Hudson, 1971.
Bruce, F. F. *The Canon of Scripture.* Downers Grove, IL: InterVarsity Press, 1988.
———. *Israel and the Nations: The History of Israel from the Exodus to the Fall of the Second Temple.* Revised by David F. Payne. Grand Rapids, MI: Eerdmans, 1997.
———. *Paul: Apostle of the Heart Set Free.* Grand Rapids, MI: Eerdmans, 2000.

Burkert, W. *Ancient Mystery Cults*. Cambridge, MA: Harvard University Press, 1989.

Burns Jr., J. Patout. "Cyprian of Carthage." In *Early Christian Thinkers: The Lives and Legacies of Twelve Key Figures*, edited by Paul Foster, 127–140. Downers Grove, IL: IVP Academic, 2010.

———, and Robin M. Jensen, with Graeme W. Clarke, Susan T. Stevens, William Tabbernee, and Maureen A. Tilley. *Christianity in Roman Africa: The Development of Its Practices and Beliefs*. Grand Rapids, MI: Eerdmans, 2014.

Burrus, Virginia. *Chastity as Autonomy: Women in the Stories of the Apocryphal Acts*. Lewiston: Mellen, 1987.

Calvin, John. *Institutes of the Christian Religion*. 2 vols. Translated by Ford Lewis Battles. Edited by John T. McNeil. Library of Christian Classics, vols. 20 and 21. Philadelphia: Westminster Press, 1960.

Cameron, Averil E. *Christianity and the Rhetoric of Empire: The Development of Christian Discourse*. Berkeley: University of California Press, 1991.

———. *Circus Factions: Blues and Greens at Rome and Byzantium*. Oxford: Clarendon Press, 1976.

Cary, M., and H. H. Scullard. *A History of Rome Down to the Reign of Constantine*. 3rd revised edition. London: Macmillan; Houndmills, Basingstoke, UK and New York: Palgrave Publishers, 1996.

Castelli, E. "Virginity and Its Meaning for Women's Sexuality in Early Christianity." *Journal of Feminist Studies in Religion* 2, no. 1 (1986): 61–88.

Celsus. *On True Doctrine: A Discourse against the Christians*. Translated by R. Joseph Hoffmann. New York: Oxford University Press, 1987.

Chadwick, H. *Early Christian Thought and the Classical Tradition*. Oxford: Oxford University Press, 1966.

———. *The Early Church*. London: Penguin, 1993.

———. *East and West: The Making of a Rift in the Church. From Apostolic Times until the Council of Florence*. Oxford: Oxford University Press, 2003.

———, trans. *Origen, Contra Celsum*. Cambridge: Cambridge University Press, 1965.

Chesnut, Glenn F. "A Century of Patristic Studies, 1888–1988." In *A Century of Church History: The Legacy of Philip Schaff*, edited by Henry W. Bowden, 36–73. Carbondale: Southern Illinois University Press, 1988.

———. *The First Christian Histories: Eusebius, Socrates, Sozomen, Theodoret and Evagrius*. Macon, GA: Mercer University Press, 1986.

Chidester, David. *Christianity: A Global History*. London: Penguin, 2000.

Chitty, D. J. *The Desert a City*. Crestwood, NJ: St Vladimir's Seminary Press, 1966.

Chrysostom, John. *Chrysostom and His Message: Selections from His Sermons*. Translated by S. Neill. London: London Society for Christian Literature, 1962.

Clark, Elizabeth A. *Ascetic Piety and Women's Faith: Essays on Late Ancient Christianity*. Lewiston, NY: Mellen, 1986.

———. "From Patristics to Early Christian Studies." In *The Oxford Handbook of Early Christian Studies*, edited by Susan A. Harvey and David G. Hunter, 7–41. Oxford: Oxford University Press, 2008. [See also "Annotated Guide," §C.]

———. *Jerome, Chrysostom and Friends: Essays and Translations*. Lewiston, NY: Mellen, 1979.

———. *The Life of Melania the Younger: Introduction, Translation and Commentary*. Lewiston, NY: Mellen, 1984.

———. *The Origenist Controversy: The Cultural Construction of an Early Christian Debate*. Princeton: Princeton University Press, 1992.

———, ed. *Women in the Early Church*. Wilmington, DE: Michael Glazier, 1983.

Clark, Gillian. *Women in Late Antiquity: Pagan and Christian Lifestyles*. New York: Oxford University Press, 1993.

Cloke, G. *"This Female Man of God": Women and Spiritual Power in the Patristic Age, AD 350–450*. London: Routledge, 1995.

Cochrane, Charles Norris. *Christianity and Classical Culture: A Study of Thought and Action from Augustus to Augustine*. London: Oxford University Press, 1944.

Cooper, Kate. *The Virgin and the Bride: Idealized Womanhood in Late Antiquity*. Cambridge, MA: Harvard University Press, 1996.

Corrington, Gail P. "Anorexia, Asceticism and Autonomy: Self-Control as Liberation and Transcendence." *Journal of Feminist Studies in Religion* 2, no. 2 (1986): 51–61.

Cox, P. *Biography in Late Antiquity*. Berkeley: University of California Press, 1983.

Cuoq, Joseph. *L'Eglise d'Afrique du Nord du IIe au XIIe siècle* [*The North African Church from the Second to the Twelfth Century*]. Paris: Editions du Centurion, 1984.

Daniélou, J. *The Development of Christian Doctrine before the Council of Nicaea, vol. 1: The Theology of Jewish Christianity*. Translated by John Austin Baker. London: Darton, Longman & Todd, 1964.

———. *The Development of Christian Doctrine before the Council of Nicaea, vol. 2: Gospel Message and Hellenistic Culture*. Translated by John Austin Baker. London: Darton, Longman & Todd; Philadelphia: Westminster Press, 1973.

———. *The Development of Christian Doctrine before the Council of Nicaea, vol. 3: The Origins of Latin Christianity*. Translated by David Smith and John Austin Baker. London: Darton, Longman & Todd, 1977.

Daughrity, Dyron B. "Assessing Christianity in Africa's Transforming Context." *International Review of Mission* 103, no. 2 (2014): 348–362.

Davies, W. D. *Paul and Rabbinic Judaism: Some Rabbinic Elements in Pauline Theology*. 4th ed., with new preface. London: SPCK; Mifflintown, PA: Sigler Press, 1998.

Davis, A. J. "Coptic Christianity." *Tarikh* 2, no. 1 (1967): 43–52.

———. "The Orthodoxy of the Ethiopian Church." *Tarikh* 2, no. 1 (1967): 62–69.

Decret, François. *Early Christianity in North Africa* (*Le christianisme en Afrique du Nord ancienne* [1996]). Translated by Edward L. Smither. Cambridge: James Clarke, 2011.

Desjardins, Michel. "Bauer and Beyond: On Recent Scholarly Discussions of *Hairesis* in the Early Christian Era." *The Second Century* 8 (1991): 65–82.
Digeser, Elizabeth DePalma. *A Threat to Public Piety: Christians, Platonists, and the Great Persecution*. Ithaca, NY: Cornell University Press, 2012.
Dillon, John. *The Middle Platonists: Study of Platonism 80 BC to AD 220*. London: Duckworth, 1977.
Dix, G., and H. Chadwick. *The Treatise on the Apostolic Tradition of St Hippolytus of Rome*. London: SPCK, 1968.
Dodd, C. H. *The Interpretation of the Fourth Gospel*. Cambridge: Cambridge University Press, 1953.
Dodds, E. R. *Pagan and Christian in an Age of Anxiety: Some Aspects of Religious Experience from Marcus Aurelius to Constantine*. Cambridge: Cambridge University Press; New York: Norton, 1970.
Donner, F. M. *The Early Islamic Conquests*. Princeton: Princeton University Press, 1981.
Douglas, James Dixon, N. Hillyer, and D. R. Woods, eds. *The New Bible Dictionary*. 3rd revised ed. Grand Rapids, MI: Eerdmans; Downers Grove, IL: InterVarsity Press, 1996.
Drake, H. A. *In Praise of Constantine: A Historical Study and New Translation of Eusebius' Tricennial Orations*. Berkeley: University of California Press, 1976.
Dvornik, Francis. *Early Christian and Byzantine Political Philosophy: Origins and Background*. Washington: Dumbarton Oaks Center for Byzantine Studies, 1966.
———. *The General Councils of the Church*. London: Burns & Oates, 1961.
Edersheim, Alfred. *The Life and Times of Jesus the Messiah*. 2 vols. London: Longmans, Green Co., 1901–1907.
Edwards, David L., and John Stott. *Essentials*. London: Hodder & Stoughton, 1988.
Edwards, M. J., ed., *Apologetics in the Roman Empire: Pagans, Jews and Christians*. Oxford: Clarendon, 1999.
Ehrman, Bart. *Truth and Fiction in the Da Vinci Code*. Oxford: Oxford University Press, 2004.
Eisen, Ute E. *Women Officeholders in Early Christianity: Epigraphical and Literary Studies*. Translated by L. M. Maloney. Collegeville, MN: Liturgical Press, 2000.
Ellis, Ieuan. "In Defence of Early North African Christianity." In *New Testament Christianity for Africa and the World*, edited by Mark Glasswell and Edward Fasholé-Luke, 157–165. London: SPCK, 1974.
Elm, Susan. *Virgins of God: The Making of Asceticism in Late Antiquity*. New York: Oxford University Press, 1994.
Eusebius of Caesarea. *Ecclesiastical History: The History of the Church from Christ to Constantine* (*Historia Ecclesiastica*, abbrev. *HE*). Translated by G. Williamson. Harmondsworth: Penguin, 1965.
Faraji, Salim. *The Roots of Nubian Christianity Uncovered: The Triumph of the Last Pharaoh: Religious Encounters in Late Antique Roman Africa*. Trenton, NJ: Africa World Press, 2012.

Ferguson, Everett. *Backgrounds of Early Christianity*. 3rd edition. Grand Rapids, MI: Eerdmans, 2003.

———. *Church and State in the Early Church*. New York: Garland, 1993.

———. *Early Christianity and Judaism*. New York: Garland, 1993.

———, ed. *Encyclopedia of Early Christianity*. New York: Garland, 1990.

———. "Tertullian." In *Early Christian Thinkers: The Lives and Legacies of Twelve Key Figures*, edited by Paul Foster, 85–99. Downers Grove, IL: IVP Academic, 2010.

Ferguson, John. "Aspects of the Early Christianity in North Africa." *Tarikh* 2, no. 1 (1967): 16–27.

———. *Clement of Alexandria*. New York: Twayne, 1974.

Finneran, Neil. *The Archaeology of Christianity in Africa*. Stroud: Tempus, 2002.

Foster, John. *The First Advance*. Delhi: SPCK, 2004.

Foster, Paul, ed. *Early Christian Thinkers: The Lives and Legacies of Twelve Key Figures*. Downers Grove, IL: IVP Academic, 2010.

———. "Tatian." In *Early Christian Thinkers: The Lives and Legacies of Twelve Key Figures*, edited by Paul Foster, 15–35. Downers Grove, IL: IVP Academic, 2010.

Fredriksen, Paula. *Augustine and the Jews*. New York: Doubleday, 2006.

———. "'Secundum Carnem': History and Israel in the Theology of St Augustine." In *The Limits of Ancient Christianity: Essays on Late Antique Thought and Culture in Honor of R. A. Markus*, edited by W. E. Klingshirn and M. Vessey, 26–41. Ann Arbor: University of Michigan Press, 1999.

Frend, W. H. C. *Archeology and History in the Study of Early Christianity*. London: Variorum, 1988.

———. "Archeology and Patristic Studies." In *Studia Patristica* 18, edited by E. A. Livingstone, 9–21. Kalamazoo, MI: Cistercian Publications, 1985.

———. "Church and State, Perspectives and Problems in the Patristic Era." In *Studia Patristica* 18, edited by E. A. Livingstone, 38–54. Oxford: Pergamon Press, 1982.

———. *The Donatist Church: A Movement of Protest in Roman North Africa*. Oxford: Clarendon, 1971.

———. "The Donatist Church – Forty Years On." In *Window on Origins: Essays on the Early Church*, edited by C. Landman and D. P. Whitelaw, 70–84. Pretoria: University of South Africa, 1985.

———. "Early Christianity and Society: A Jewish Legacy in the Pre-Constantinian Era." *Harvard Theological Review* 76 (1983): 53–71 (reprinted in Frend 1988 section V).

———. *The Early Church*. London: Hodder & Stoughton; Philadelphia: Fortress Press, 1982.

———. *Martyrdom and Persecution in the Early Church: A Study of Conflict from the Maccabeees to Donatus*. Oxford: Basil Blackwell, 1965.

———. "The Monophysites and the Transition between the Ancient World and the Middle Ages." In *Atti dei Convegni Lincei* 45, 339–365. Rome: Accademia Nazionale dei Lincei, 1980.

———. "Montanism: Research and Problems." *Rivista di storia e letteratura religiosa* 30 (1984): 521–537.
———. "Nationalism as a Factor in Anti-Chalcedonian Feeling in Egypt." In *Religion and National Identity: Studies in Church History* 18, edited by Stuart Mews, 21–38. Oxford: Blackwell, 1982.
———. "Prelude to the Great Persecution: The Propaganda War." *Journal of Ecclesiastical History* 38 (1987): 1–18.
———. *The Rise of Christianity*. London: Darton, Longman & Todd, 1984.
———. *The Rise of the Monophysite Movement*. Cambridge: Cambridge University Press, 1972.
———. *Saints and Sinners in the Early Church: Differing and Conflicting Traditions in the First Six Centuries*. London: Darton, Longman & Todd, 1985.
Fux, Pierre-Yves, Jean-Michel Roessli, and Otto Wermelinger, eds. *Augustinus Afer: Saint Augustin, africanité et universalité: actes du colloque international, Alger-Annaba, 1–7 avril 2001*. Fribourg: Editions Universitaires, 2003.
Gager, John G. *Kingdom and Community: The Social World of Early Christianity*. Englewood Cliffs, NJ: Prentice-Hall, 1975.
———. *The Origins of Anti-Semitism: Attitudes toward Judaism in Pagan and Christian Antiquity*. New York: Oxford University Press, 1985.
Geffcken, Johannes. *The Last Days of Greco-Roman Paganism* [*Der Ausgang des griechisch-römischen Heidentums*]. Translated by S. MacCormack. Amsterdam: North-Holland Publishing, 1978.
Gersh, S. *Middle Platonism and Neoplatonism. The Latin Tradition*. 2 vols. Notre Dame: University of Notre Dame Press, 1986.
Gibbon, Edward. *The Decline and Fall of the Roman Empire*. A modern abridgment by Moses Hadas. 8th print. New York: Fawcett Books, Random House, 1992.
Glasswell, Mark, and Edward Fasholé-Luke, eds. *New Testament Christianity for Africa and the World*. London: SPCK, 1974.
Gonzalez, Justo L. *The Early Church to the Dawn of the Reformation*. The Story of Christianity 1. San Francisco: Harper & Row, 1984.
Grant, Robert M. *After the New Testament*. Philadelphia: Fortress, 1967.
———. *Augustus to Constantine: The Rise and Triumph of Christianity in the Roman World*. Louisville: Westminster John Knox, 1970.
———. *Early Christianity and Society: Seven Studies*. San Francisco: Harper & Row, 1977.
———. *Eusebius as Church Historian*. Oxford: Clarendon, 1980.
———, ed. *Gnosticism: A Source Book of Heretical Writings from the Early Christian Period*. New York: Harper; AMS Press, 1978.
———. *Gnosticism and Early Christianity*. New York: Columbia University Press, 1966.
———. *Gods and the One God: Christian Theology in the Greco-Roman World*. Philadelphia: Westminster Press, 1988.
———. *Greek Apologists of the Second Century*. Philadelphia: Westminster Press, 1988.

———. *Irenaeus of Lyons*. New York: Routledge, 1997.
Greenslade, S. L. *Early Latin Theology*. Library of Christian Classics 5. London: SCM; Philadelphia: Westminster, 1956.
———. *Schism in the Early Church*. London: SCM Press, 1964.
Gregg, R. C., and D. E. Groh. *Early Arianism: A View of Salvation*. London: SCM Press, 1981.
Griffith, S. H. *Arabic Christianity in the Monasteries of Ninth-Century Palestine*. Aldershot: Variorum, 1992.
———. "Asceticism in the Church of Syria: The Hermeneutics of Early Syrian Monasticism." In *Asceticism*, edited by Vincent L. Wimbush and Richard Valantasis, 220–245. New York: Oxford University Press, 1995.
———. *The Beginnings of Christian Theology in Arabic: Muslim-Christian Encounters in the Early Islamic Period*. Aldershot: Ashgate, 2002.
Griggs, C. W. *Early Egyptian Christianity*. Coptic Studies 2. Leiden: Brill, 1990.
Groves, C. P. *The Planting of Christianity in Africa*. 4 vols. London: Lutterworth, 1948–1964.
Grubbs, Judith Evans. *Law and Family in Late Antiquity: The Emperor Constantine's Marriage Legislation*. Oxford: Clarendon, 1994.
———. "'Pagan' and 'Christian' Marriage: The State of the Question." *Journal of Early Christian Studies* 2, no. 3 (1995): 361–412.
Gryson, R. *The Ministry of Women in the Early Church*. Translated by J. LaPorte and M. L. Hall. Collegeville, MN: Liturgical Press, 1976.
Guy, Laurie. *Introducing Early Christianity: A Topical Survey of Its Life, Beliefs and Practices*. Downers Grove, IL: InterVarsity Press, 2004.
Hadas, Moses. *Hellenistic Culture: Fusion and Diffusion*. New York: Columbia University Press, 1959.
———, ed. *Gibbon's Decline and Fall of the Roman Empire: A Modern Abridgment*. New York: Fawcett Books, 1992.
Hagendahl, H. *Latin Fathers and the Classics: A Study on the Apologists, Jerome and Other Christian Writers*. Göteborg: Almqvist & Wiksell, 1958.
Hahneman, G. M. *The Muratorian Fragment and the Development of the Canon*. Oxford: Clarendon, 1992.
Hanson, R. P. C. *The Search for the Christian Doctrine of God: The Arian Controversy 318–381*. Edinburgh: T&T Clark, 1988.
———. *Tradition in the Early Church*. London: SCM, 1962.
Harnack, Adolf von. *The Expansion of Christianity in the First Three Centuries*. 2 vols. Translated by James Moffatt (German edition 1902). London: Williams & Norgate; New York: G. P. Putnam's Sons, 1904–1905.
———. *History of Dogma* [*Lehrbuch der Dogmengeschichte*. (1894–1899) 3rd ed.] Translated by N. Buchanan et al. 4 vols. New York: Dover Publications, 1961.
———. *Marcion: The Gospel of the Alien God*. Durham, NC: Labyrinth Press, 1990.

———. *The Mission and Expansion of Christianity in the First Three Centuries*. Vol. 1 of the 1908 edition. Translated by James Moffatt, with foreword by Jaroslav Pelikan. Gloucester, MA: Peter Smith, Harper Torchbook; London: Williams & Norgate, 1972.

———. *What Is Christianity?* [*Das Wesen des Christentums*]. Translated by Thomas Bailey Saunders, with introduction by Rudolf Bultmann. Philadelphia: Fortress Press, 1986.

Harries, Jill. *Law and Empire in Late Antiquity*. Cambridge: Cambridge University Press, 1999.

Harrison, Verna. "Male and Female in Cappadocian Theology." *Journal of Theological Studies* 41, no. 2 (1990): 441–471.

Hastings, Adrian. "150–550." In *A World History of Christianity*, edited by Adrian Hastings, 25–65. Grand Rapids, MI: Eerdmans, 1999.

———. *The Church in Africa 1450–1950*. Oxford: Clarendon, 1997.

———, ed. *A World History of Christianity*. Grand Rapids, MI: Eerdmans, 1999.

Hatch, Edwin. *The Organization of the Early Christian Churches*. London: Rivingtons, 1881.

———. *The Influence of Greek Ideas on Christianity*. New York: Harper, 1957.

Hazlett, Ian, ed. *Early Christianity: Origins and Evolution to AD 600: In Honour of W. H. C. Frend*. London: SPCK; Nashville: Abingdon, 1991.

Helleman, W. E. "The Biblical Canon: A Response to Muhib O. Opeloye, *Building Bridges of Understanding between Islam and Christianity in Nigeria* (2001)." *TCNN Research Bulletin* 41 (2004): 31–42.

———. "'Christ the Wisdom of God': The Logic of Attribution in Augustine's *De Trinitate* 5–7." *Studia Patristica* XLIV–XLIX (2010): 271–277.

———, ed. *Christianity and the Classics: The Acceptance of a Heritage*. Lanham, MD: University Press of America, 1990.

———. *The Feminine Personification of Wisdom: A Study of Homer's Penelope, Cappadocian Macrina, Boethius' Philosophia, and Dante's Beatrice*. Lewiston: Mellen, 2009.

———, ed. *Hellenization Revisited: Shaping a Christian Response within the Greco-Roman World*. Lanham, MD: University Press of America, 1994.

Hemer, Colin J. "Archaeological Light on Earliest Christianity." In *The History of Christianity*, edited by Tim Dowley, 53–58. Oxford: Lion Publishing, 1990.

Hengel, Martin. *The 'Hellenization' of Judaea in the First Century after Christ*. Philadelphia: Fortress, 1989.

———. *Judaism and Hellenism: Studies in Their Encounter in Palestine during the Early Hellenistic Period*. 2 vols. Minneapolis: Fortress, 1974.

Henry, P. "Why Is Contemporary Scholarship so Enamored of Ancient Heretics?" *Studia Patristica* 17, no. 1 (1982): 123–126.

Hevbare, J. A. "Christianity in Nubia." *Tarikh* 2, no. 1 (1967): 53–61.

Hick, John. *Death and Eternal Life*. New York: Harper & Row, 1976.

Hill, Jonathan. *The New Lion Handbook: The History of Christianity*. Oxford: Lion, 2007.
Hodges, R., and D. Whitehouse. *Mohammed, Charlemagne and the Origins of Europe: Archeology and the Pirenne Thesis*. London: Duckworth, 1983.
Holmes, Michael W., ed. and rev. *The Apostolic Fathers: Greek Texts and English Translations*. Updated edition of *The Apostolic Fathers*, 2nd ed., edited and translated by J. B. Lightfoot and J. R. Harmer (London: Macmillan, 1891). Grand Rapids MI: Baker Books, 1999.
Humphries, M. *Early Christianity*. London: Routledge, 2006.
Hunt, Emily J. *Christianity in the Second Century: The Case of Tatian*. London: Routledge, 2003.
Hurtado, Larry W. "Martin Hengel's Impact on English-Speaking Scholarship." *Expository Times* 120, no. 2 (2008): 70–76.
Isichei, Elizabeth. *A History of Christianity in Africa: From Antiquity to the Present*. London: SPCK, 1995.
Jaeger, W. *Early Christianity and Greek Paideia*. Cambridge, MA: Harvard University Press, 1962.
Jefford, Clayton N., with Kenneth J. Harder and Louis D. Amezaga, Jr. *Reading the Apostolic Fathers: An Introduction*. Peabody, MA: Hendrickson, 1996.
Jegede, Gabriel Gbenga. "Academic Works on the History, Growth and Development of Christianity in Africa: A Retrospective and Perspective Appraisal." *International Journal of Humanities and Social Science* 3, no. 1 (2013): 208–215.
Jenkins, Philip. *The Lost History of Christianity: The Thousand-Year Golden Age of the Church in the Middle East, Africa and Asia*. New York: HarperCollins, 2008.
Jensen, A. *God's Self-Confident Daughters: Early Christianity and the Liberation of Women*. Translated by O. C. Dean Jr. Louisville: Westminster John Knox Press, 1996.
Johnson, S. F. *The Life and Miracles of Thekla: A Literary Study*. Cambridge, MA: Harvard University Press, 2006.
Jonas, Hans. *The Gnostic Religion: The Message of the Alien God and the Beginnings of Christianity* (*Gnosis und spätantiker Geist*. Göttingen: Vandenhoeck, 1954). Boston: Beacon, 1963.
Jones, A. H. M. *Constantine and the Conversion of Europe*. Toronto: University of Toronto Press, 1978.
———. *The Decline of the Ancient World*. London: Longmans, Green & Co., 1966.
Kagan, D. *Decline and Fall of the Roman Empire: Why Did It Collapse?* Boston: D. C. Heath, 1962.
———, ed. *The End of the Roman Empire: Decline or Transformation?* Lexington, MA: D. C. Heath, 1978.
Kalu, Ogbu U., ed. *African Christianity: An African Story*. Trenton, NJ: Africa World Press, 2007.

———, ed. *African Church Historiography: An Ecumenical Perspective*. Papers presented at a Workshop on African Church History held at Nairobi, August 3–8, 1986. Bern: Evangelische Arbeitsstelle Oekumene Schweiz, 1988.

———. "The Golden Age of Christianity in Africa? Early Christianity in North Africa Revisited." *Nsukka Journal of Religious Studies* 1, no. 1 (1996): 34–49.

Kane, Ousmane. *Muslim Modernity in Postcolonial Nigeria*. Leiden: Brill, 2003.

Kannengiesser, C. *Arius and Athanasius: Two Alexandrian Theologians*. Brookfield, VT: Ashgate, 1991.

———. "Fifty Years of Patristics." *Theological Studies* 50 (1989): 633–656.

———. "The Future of Patristics." *Theological Studies* 52 (1991): 128–139.

———. *Origen of Alexandria: His World and His Legacy*. Notre Dame: University of Notre Dame Press, 1988.

Kastfelt, Niels. "Religion, State and Politics: The Case of the Government House Mosque in Yola, 1988–1993." In *Religion and Politics in Africa and the Islamic World*, edited by Niels Kastfelt and Jessie Tvillinggaard, 41–59. Copenhagen: University of Copenhagen, 1997.

Katz, Solomon. *The Decline of Rome and the Rise of Mediaeval Europe*. Ithaca, NY: Cornell University Press, 1955.

Kee, H. C. *Christian Origins in Sociological Perspective*. Philadelphia: Fortress, 1980.

———. *Medicine, Miracle and Magic in New Testament Times*. Cambridge: Cambridge University Press, 1986.

Kelly, J. N. D. *Early Christian Creeds*. 3rd ed. London: Longman, 1972.

———. *Early Christian Doctrines*. 5th rev. ed. San Francisco: Harper & Row, 1978.

———. *Golden Mouth. The Story of John Chrysostom, Ascetic, Preacher, Bishop*. Ithaca, NY: Cornell University Press, 1995.

———. *Jerome: His Life, Writings and Controversies*. London: Duckworth; Peabody, MA: Hendrickson, 1998.

Kennedy, George A. *Greek Rhetoric under Christian Emperors*. Princeton, NJ: Princeton University Press, 1983.

———. *New Testament Interpretation through Rhetorical Criticism*. Chapel Hill: University of North Carolina Press, 1984.

Kenny, Joseph. *Early Islam*. Ibadan: Dominican Press, 1997.

Keyers, E. M., and J. F. Strange. *Archeology, the Rabbis and Early Christianity*. Nashville: Abingdon, 1981.

King, Karen L. *The Gospel of Mary of Magdala*. Santa Rosa, CA: Polebridge, 2003.

———, ed. *Images of the Feminine in Gnosticism*. Philadelphia: Fortress, 1988.

Knipfling, J. R. "The Libelli of the Decian Persecution." *Harvard Theological Review* 16, no. 4 (1923): 345–390.

Kovacs, Judith L. "Clement of Alexandria." In *Early Christian Thinkers: The Lives and Legacies of Twelve Key Figures*, edited by Paul Foster, 68–84. Downers Grove, IL: IVP Academic, 2010.

Kraabel, A. T. "The Diaspora Synagogue: Archeological and Epigraphic Evidence." *Aufstieg und Niedergang der römischen Welt*, edited by H. Temporini and W. Haase. Part 2, Principat 19, no. 1 (1979): 477–510.

Kraemer, Ross Shepard. *Her Share of the Blessings: Women's Religions among Pagans, Jews and Christians in the Greco-Roman World*. New York: Oxford University Press, 1992.

———, ed. *Maenads, Martyrs, Matrons, Monastics: A Sourcebook on Women's Religions in the Greco-Roman World*. Philadelphia: Fortress, 1988.

———. "Women and Gender." In *The Oxford Handbook of Early Christian Studies*, edited by Susan Ashbrook Harvey and David G. Hunter, 465–492. Oxford: Oxford University Press, 2008.

Kraft, R. A., and Geo. W. E. Nickelsburg. *Early Judaism and Its Modern Interpreters*. Philadelphia: Fortress, 1986.

Lacroix, W. F. G. *Africa in Antiquity: A Linguistic and Toponymic Analysis of Ptolemy's Map of Africa*. Saarbrücken, Germany: Verlag für Entwicklungspolitik Saarbrücken GmbH, 1998.

Lane Fox, R. *Pagans and Christians*. Harmondsworth: Penguin; New York: Knopf, 1987.

Lange, N. R. M. de. *Origen and the Jews*. Cambridge: Cambridge University Press, 1976.

Laporte, J. *The Role of Women in Early Christianity*. Lewiston: Mellen, 1982.

Latourette, K. S. *The First Five Centuries*. Vol. 1 of *History of the Expansion of Christianity*. Rev. ed. London: Eyre & Spottiswoode; New York: Harper & Row, 1975.

Layton, B., ed. *The Rediscovery of Gnosticism: Proceedings of the International Conference on Gnosticism* (at Yale, New Haven, CT, March 1978). 2 vols. Leiden: Brill, 1980–1981.

Leon, Harry J. *The Jews of Ancient Rome*. Philadelphia: Jewish Publication Society of America, 1960.

Levine, A. J., ed. *"Women Like This": New Perspectives on Jewish Women in the Greco-Roman World*. Atlanta: Scholars Press, 1991.

Levine, L. I. *The Synagogue in Late Antiquity*. Philadelphia: The American Schools of Oriental Research, 1987.

Lieu, Judith. *Christian Identity in the Jewish and Graeco-Roman World*. Oxford: Oxford University Press, 2004.

———. *Image and Reality: The Jews in the World of the Christians in the Second Century*. Edinburgh: T&T Clark, 1996.

Lilla, S. R. C. *Clement of Alexandria: A Study in Christian Platonism and Gnosticism*. Oxford: Oxford University Press, 1971.

Loisy, Alfred. *L'Evangile et l'église*. Paris: A. Picard, 1902.

Lonergan, Bernard. *The Way to Nicea: The Dialectical Development of Trinitarian Theology*. London: Darton, Longman & Todd, 1976.

Lossky, V. *The Vision of God*. London: Faith Press, 1963.

Lössl, Josef. *The Early Church: History and Memory*. London: T&T Clark, 2010.

Louth, A. *The Origins of the Christian Mystical Tradition: From Plato to Denys*. Oxford: Clarendon, 1981.

Lutzer, Erwin W. *The DaVinci Deception*. Wheaton, IL: Tyndale House, 2004.

Lyman, Rebecca. "Origen." In *Early Christian Thinkers: The Lives and Legacies of Twelve Key Figures*, edited by Paul Foster, 111–126. Downers Grove, IL: IVP Academic, 2010.

MacMullen, Ramsay. *Corruption and the Decline of Rome*. New Haven: Yale University Press, 1988.

———. *Enemies of the Roman Order: Treason, Unrest and Alienation in the Empire*. Cambridge, MA: Harvard University Press; London: Routledge, 1992.

———. *Paganism in the Roman Empire*. New Haven: Yale University Press, 1981.

———. *Roman Social Relations: 50 BC to AD 284*. New Haven: Yale University Press, 1974.

Maier, H. O. *The Social Setting of the Ministry as Reflected in the Writings of Hermas, Clement and Ignatius*. Waterloo, ON: Wilfrid Laurier Press, 1991.

Markus, R. A. *Christianity in the Roman World*. London: Thames & Hudson, 1975.

———. "Church History and Early Church Historians." In *The Materials, Sources and Methods of Ecclesiastical History: Studies in Church History*, edited by D. Baker, 1–17. Oxford: Oxford University Press, 1975.

Marshall, David. *The Devil Hides Out: New Age and the Occult: A Christian Perspective*. Hagerstown, MD: Autumn House, 1994.

Martin, L. H. *Hellenistic Religions*. Oxford: Oxford University Press, 1987.

Martinez, Florentino Garcia. *The Dead Sea Scrolls Translated: The Qumran Texts in English*. 2nd ed. Translated by Wilfred G. E. Watson. Leiden: Brill; Grand Rapids, MI: Eerdmans, 1996.

Mason, Steve. *Josephus, Judea, and Christian Origins: Methods and Categories*. Peabody, MA: Hendrickson, 2009.

Mayerson, P. "A Confusion of Indias: Asian India and African India in the Byzantine Sources." *Journal of the American Oriental Society* 113, no. 2 (1993): 169–174.

McGuckin, J. A. *St Cyril of Alexandria: The Christological Controversy*. Leiden: Brill, 1994.

McKechnie, Paul. *The First Christian Centuries: Perspectives on the Early Church*. Leicester: Apollos, 2001.

McLynn, N. B. *Ambrose of Milan: Church and Court in a Christian Capital*. Berkeley: University of California Press, 1994.

Meeks, Wayne. *The First Urban Christians: The Social World of the Apostle Paul*. New Haven: Yale University Press, 1983.

———, and Robert L. Wilken. *Jews and Christians in Antioch in the First Four Centuries of the Common Era*. Missoula, MT: Scholars Press, 1978.

Merahi, Kessis Kefyalew. *Christianity in Ethiopia*. Addis Ababa: Merahi (self-) publication, 2007.

Meredith, A. *The Cappadocians*. Crestwood, NY: St Vladimir's Seminary Press, 1995.

Merton, T., ed. *The Wisdom of the Desert: Sayings from the Desert Fathers of the Fourth Century*. London: Hollis & Carter, 1961.

Metzger, B. M. *The Canon of the New Testament: Its Origin, Development and Significance*. 2nd ed. Oxford: Clarendon, 1988.

———. "Considerations of Methodology in the Study of the Mystery Religions and Early Christianity." *Harvard Theological Review* 48 (1955): 1–20.

Meyer, Marvin W., ed. *The Ancient Mysteries: A Sourcebook*. San Francisco: Harper & Row, 1987.

Milburn, R. L. P. *Early Christian Art and Architecture*. Aldershot, UK: Scholar Press, 1988.

Miles, M. R. *Desire and Delight: A New Reading of Augustine's Confessions*. New York: Crossroad, 1992.

Minns, Denis. "Irenaeus." In *Early Christian Thinkers: The Lives and Legacies of Twelve Key Figures*, edited by Paul Foster, 36–51. Downers Grove, IL: IVP Academic, 2010.

Momigliano, A., ed. *The Conflict between Paganism and Christianity in the Fourth Century*. Oxford: Clarendon, 1963.

Moxnes, Halvor, ed. *Constructing Early Christian Families: Family as Social Reality and Metaphor*. London: Routledge, 1997.

Munck, Johannes. "Pauline Research Since Schweitzer." In *The Bible in Modern Scholarship*, edited by P. Hyatt, 166–177. Nashville: Abingdon, 1965.

Musurillo, Herbert. *The Acts of the Christian Martyrs. Introduction, Text and Translations*. Oxford: Clarendon, 1972.

Needham, N. R. *2000 Years of Christ's Power, Part One: The Age of the Early Fathers*. Darlington, UK: Evangel Press, 2002.

Neill, Stephen. *The Interpretation of the New Testament*. London: Oxford University Press, 1964.

Neusner, Jacob. *From Politics to Piety: The Emergence of Pharisaic Judaism*. Englewood Cliffs, NJ: Prentice-Hall, 1973.

———. *The Rabbinic Traditions about the Pharisees before 70 AD*. 3 vols. Leiden: Brill, 1971.

———. "The Rabbinic Traditions about the Pharisees before 70 CE: An Overview." In *In Quest of the Historical Pharisees*, edited by J. Neusner and Bruce D. Chilton, 297–312. Waco, TX: Baylor University Press, 2007.

Nock, A. D. *Conversion: The Old and the New in Religion from Alexander the Great to Augustine of Hippo*. London: Oxford University Press, 1933.

———. *Early Gentile Christianity and Its Hellenistic Background*. New York: Harper & Row, 1964.

Noll, Mark A. *Turning Points: Decisive Moments in the History of Christianity*. Grand Rapids, MI: Baker, 1997.

Norris, R. A., ed. *The Christological Controversy*. Philadelphia: Fortress, 1980.

Oden, Thomas C. *The African Memory of Mark: Reassessing Early Church Tradition*. Downers Grove, IL: InterVarsity Press, 2011.

———. *Early Libyan Christianity: Uncovering a North African Tradition.* Downers Grove, IL: InterVarsity Press, 2011.

———. *How Africa Shaped the Christian Mind: The African Seedbed of European Christianity.* Downers Grove, IL: InterVarsity Press, 2007.

Old, H. O. *The Patristic Roots of Reformed Worship.* Zürcher Beiträge zur Reformationsgeschichte 5. Zürich: Theologischer Verlag, 1975.

Orlandi, T. "Coptic Literature." In *The Roots of Egyptian Christianity*, edited by B. A. Pearson and J. E. Goehring, 51–81. Philadelphia: Fortress, 1986.

Osborn, E. *Tertullian: First Theologian of the West.* Cambridge: Cambridge University Press, 1997.

Outler, A. C. "The Idea of 'Development' in the History of Christian Doctrine: A Comment." In *Schools of Thought in the Christian Tradition*, edited by Patrick Henry, 7–14. Philadelphia: Fortress Press, 1984.

The Oxford Handbook of Early Christian Studies. [See "Annotated Guide," §C.]

Pagels, Elaine H. *The Gnostic Gospels.* New York: Vintage Books; Random House, 1981.

———. *The Gnostic Paul: Gnostic Exegesis of the Pauline Letters.* Philadelphia: Fortress, 1975.

Parkes, James. *The Conflict of the Church and the Synagogue.* New York: Atheneum, 1969.

Parvis, Paul. "Justin Martyr." In *Early Christian Thinkers: The Lives and Legacies of Twelve Key Figures*, edited by Paul Foster, 1–14. Downers Grove, IL: IVP Academic, 2010.

Parvis, Sara. "Perpetua." In *Early Christian Thinkers: The Lives and Legacies of Twelve Key Figures*, edited by Paul Foster, 100–110. Downers Grove, IL: IVP Academic, 2010.

Pearson, Birger A. *Gnosticism, Judaism and Egyptian Christianity.* Minneapolis: Fortress Press, 1990.

Pelikan, J. *The Emergence of the Catholic Tradition (100–600).* Vol. 1 of *The Christian Tradition: A History of the Development of Doctrine.* Chicago: University of Chicago Press, 1971.

———. *The Excellent Empire: The Fall of Rome and the Triumph of the Church.* San Francisco: Harper & Row, 1987.

Penn, Michael Philip. *Envisioning Islam: Syriac Christians and the Early Muslim World.* Philadelphia: University of Pennsylvania Press, 2015.

———. *When Christians First Met Muslims: A Sourcebook of the Earliest Syriac Writings on Islam.* Philadelphia: University of Pennsylvania Press, 2015.

Perkins, Judith. "The Apocryphal Acts of the Apostles and the Early Christian Martyrdom." *Arethusa* 18, no. 2 (1985): 211–230.

Peters, F. E. *Harvest of Hellenism: A History of the Near East from Alexander the Great to the Triumph of Christianity.* New York: Simon & Schuster, 1970.

Petersen, J. M. *Handmaids of the Lord: Holy Women in Late Antiquity and the Early Middle Ages.* Kalamazoo, MI: Cistercian Publications, 1996.

Pétrement, Simone. *A Separate God: The Christian Origins of Gnosticism.* Translated by Carol Harrison. San Francisco: HarperCollins, 1990.

Picknett, L., and C. Prince. *The Templar Revelation: Secret Guardians of the True Identity of Christ.* London: Bantam, 1997.
Pirenne, Henri. *A History of Europe: From the Invasions to the XVI Century.* Garden City, NY: Doubleday Anchor Books, 1958.
———. *Mohammed and Charlemagne.* Translated by B. Miall. London: Allen & Unwin, 1939.
Power, K. *Veiled Desire: Augustine's Writing on Women.* London: Darton, Longman & Todd, 1995.
Prestige, G. L. *Fathers and Heretics.* London: SPCK, 1940.
Quispel, G. *Gnosis als Weltreligion.* Zürich: Origo, 1951.
Qur'an, The Holy. Text, translation and commentary by Abdullah Yusuf Ali. 3rd edition. New York: Hafner Publishing, 1946.
Rahner, H. *Church and State in Early Christianity.* Translated by L. D. Davis. San Francisco: St Ignatius, 1992.
Renan, Ernest. *The Life of Jesus.* Translated by Charles Edwin Wilbour (based on *Vie de Jésus* 1864). New York: Carleton; Paris: Michel Lévy Frères, 1891.
Richardson, P. *Israel in the Apostolic Church.* Cambridge: Cambridge University Press, 1969.
Rist, J. M. *Augustine: Ancient Thought Baptized.* Cambridge: Cambridge University Press, 1994.
———. *Stoic Philosophy.* Cambridge: Cambridge University Press, 1969.
Robinson, J. M., ed. *The Nag Hammadi Library in English.* 4th rev. ed. Leiden: Brill; New York: Harper & Row, 1996.
Robinson, T. *The Bauer Thesis Examined: The Geography of Heresy in the Early Christian Church.* Lewiston: Mellen, 1988.
Rousseau, Philip. *Ascetics, Authority and the Church in the Age of Jerome and Cassian.* Oxford: Oxford University Press, 1978.
———. *Basil of Caesarea.* Berkeley: University of California Press, 1994.
———. *Pachomius: The Making of a Community in Fourth-Century Egypt.* Berkeley: University of California Press, 1985.
Rowe, Wm. V. "Adolf von Harnack and the Concept of Hellenization." In *Hellenization Revisited: Shaping a Christian Response within the Greco-Roman World*, edited by W. E. Helleman, 69–98. Lanham, MD: University Press of America, 1994.
Rowland, Christopher. *Christian Origins: From Messianic Movement to Christian Religion.* London: SPCK; Minneapolis: Augsburg, 1985.
Rudolph, Kurt. *Gnosis: The Nature and History of Gnosticism.* Edinburgh: T&T Clark; San Francisco: Harper & Row, 1987.
Ruether, Rosemary R. "Misogynism and Virginal Feminism in the Fathers of the Church." In *Religion and Sexism: Images of Women in the Jewish and Christian Traditions*, edited by R. R. Ruether, 150–183. New York: Simon & Schuster, 1974.

———. "Mothers of the Church: Ascetic Women in the Late Patristic Age." In *Women of Spirit: Female Leadership in the Jewish and Christian Traditions*, edited by R. R. Ruether and E. McLaughlin, 71–98. New York: Simon & Schuster, 1979.

Sahas, D. J. *Icon and Logos: Sources of Eighth-Century Iconoclasm*. Toronto: University of Toronto Press, 1986.

———. *John of Damascus on Islam*. Leiden: Brill, 1972.

Sanders, E. P. *Jesus and Judaism*. London: SCM, 1985.

———. *Judaism: Practice and Belief 63 BCE – 66 CE*. London: SCM Press, 1992.

———. *Paul and Palestinian Judaism*. Philadelphia: Fortress, 1977.

Sanneh, Lamin. *West African Christianity: The Religious Impact*. London: C. Hurst & Co., 1983.

Sarkissian, K. *A Brief Introduction to Armenian Christian Literature*. London: Faith Press, 1960.

Sawyer, Kenneth, and Youhanna Youssef. "Early Christianity in North Africa." In *African Christianity: An African Story*, edited by Ogbu Kalu, 44–74. Trenton, NJ: Africa World Press, 2007.

Scholer, D. M., ed. *Women in Early Christianity*. New York: Garland, 1993.

Schottroff, Luise. *Lydia's Impatient Sisters: A Feminist Social History of Early Christianity (Lydias ungeduldige Schwestern)*. Translated by Barbara and Martin Rumscheidt. Louisville: Westminster John Knox Press, 1995.

Schüssler Fiorenza, Elizabeth. *In Memory of Her: A Feminist Theological Reconstruction of Christian Origins*. New York: Crossroad, 1983.

Segal, A. *Rebecca's Children: Judaism and Christianity in the Roman World*. Cambridge, MA: Harvard University Press, 1986.

Seland, Eivind Heldaas. "Early Christianity in East Africa and Red Sea/Indian Ocean Commerce." *African Archaeological Review* 31, no. 4 (2014): 637–47.

Shaw, Brent. "The Family in Antiquity: The Experience of Augustine." *Past & Present* 115 (1987): 3–51.

Shaw, Mark R. *The Kingdom of God in Africa: A Short History of African Christianity*. Grand Rapids, MI: Baker Books, 1996.

Shaw, Teresa. *"The Burden of the Flesh": Fasting and Sexuality in Early Christianity*. Minneapolis: Fortress Press, 1998.

Simon, Marcel. *Verus Israel: A Study of the Relations between Christians and Jews in the Roman Empire (135–425)*. Oxford: Oxford University Press, 1986.

Smallwood, E. Mary. "The Jews in Egypt and Cyrenaica during the Ptolemaic and Roman Periods." In *Africa in Classical Antiquity: Nine Studies*, edited by L. A. Thompson and John Ferguson, 110–131. Ibadan: Ibadan University Press, 1969.

———. *The Jews under Roman Rule*. Leiden: Brill, 1976.

Spengler, Oswald. *The Decline of the West (Der Untergang des Abendlandes* [1918–1922]). Translated by Charles Francis Atkinson. London: Allen & Unwin, 1926.

Stark, R. *The Rise of Christianity: A Sociologist Reconsiders History*. Princeton: Princeton University Press, 1996.

Stead, G. C. *Divine Substance*. Oxford: Clarendon, 1977.
———. *Philosophy in Late Antiquity*. Cambridge: Cambridge University Press, 1994.
———. "The Valentinian Myth of Sophia." *Journal of Theological Studies* 20, no. 1 (1969): 75–104.
Stern, S. M. "Abd Al-Jabbar's Account of How Christ's Religion Was Falsified by the Adoption of Roman Customs." *Journal of Theological Studies* 19, no. 1 (1968): 128–185.
———. "Quotations from Apocryphal Gospels in Abd Al-Jabbar." *Journal of Theological Studies* 18, no. 1 (1967): 34–57.
Stevenson, J., ed. *Creeds, Councils and Controversies: Documents Illustrative of the History of the Church AD 337–461*. Revised by W. H. C. Frend. Grand Rapids, MI: Baker Academic; London: SPCK, 2012.
———. *A New Eusebius: Documents Illustrating the History of the Church to AD 337*. Revised by W. H. C. Frend. London: SPCK, 1987.
Stewart, C. *Cassian the Monk*. New York: Oxford University Press, 1998.
Strauss, David Friedrich. *The Life of Jesus Critically Examined*. Translated by George Eliot (from 4th German ed.). London: Sonnenschein, 1892.
Sundkler, Bengt, and Christopher Steed. *A History of the Church in Africa*. Cambridge: Cambridge University Press, 2000.
Tafla, Bairu. "The Establishment of the Ethiopian Church." *Tarikh* 2, no. 1 (1967): 28–42.
Taylor, Miriam S. *Anti-Judaism and Early Christian Identity: A Critique of the Scholarly Consensus*. Leiden: Brill, 1995.
Tennent, Timothy C. "The Challenge of Churchless Christianity: An Evangelical Assessment" *International Bulletin of Missionary Research* 29, no. 4 (2005): 171–177.
Tenney, M. *New Testament Times*. Grand Rapids, MI: Eerdmans, 1964.
Thompson, L. A. "Christianity in Egypt before the Arab Conquest." *Tarikh* 2, no. 1 (1967): 4–15.
Tilley, Maureen A. "The Collapse of a Collegial Church: North African Christianity on the Eve of Islam." *Theological Studies* 62, no. 1 (2001): 3–22.
Torjesen, K. J. *When Women Were Priests: Women's Leadership in the Early Church and the Scandal of Their Subordination in the Rise of Christianity*. San Francisco: Harper, 1993.
Toynbee, Arnold J. *Hellenism: The History of a Civilization*. London: Oxford University Press, 1959.
———. *A Study of History*. 12 vols. London: Oxford University Press, 1935–1961.
Turner, H. E. W. *The Pattern of Christian Truth*. London: Mowbray, 1954.
Ullendorff, Edward. *The Ethiopians: An Introduction to Country and People*. London: Oxford University Press, 1965.
Vallée, Gérard. *The Shaping of Christianity*. New York: Paulist Press, 1999.

———. *A Study in Anti-Gnostic Polemics: Irenaeus, Hippolytus and Epiphanius.* Waterloo, ON: Wilfrid Laurier University Press, 1981.

VanDam, Raymond. *Families and Friends in Late Roman Cappadocia.* Philadelphia: University of Pennsylvania Press, 2003.

VanderKam, J. C. *The Dead Sea Scrolls Today.* Grand Rapids, MI: Eerdmans, 1994.

Vermès, Geza. *The Dead Sea Scrolls in English.* Harmondsworth, Baltimore: Penguin, 1965.

———. *The Dead Sea Scrolls: Qumran in Perspective.* Cleveland, OH: Collins & World, 1978.

Verstraelen, Frans J. *History of Christianity in Africa in the Context of African History: A Comparative Assessment of Four Recent Historiographical Contributions.* Gweru, Zimbabwe: Mambo Press, 2002.

Volf, Miroslav. "Allah and the Trinity." *The Christian Century* 128, no. 5 (2011): 20–24.

Volp, Ulrich. "Hippolytus of Rome." In *Early Christian Thinkers: The Lives and Legacies of Twelve Key Figures*, edited by Paul Foster, 141–153. Downers Grove, IL: IVP Academic, 2010.

Walls, Andrew F. *The Cross-Cultural Process in Christian History.* New York: Orbis, 2002.

Ward, Kevin. "Africa." In *A World History of Christianity*, edited by Adrian Hastings, 192–237. Grand Rapids, MI: Eerdmans, 1999.

Ward-Perkins, Bryan. *The Fall of Rome and the End of Civilization.* New York: Oxford University Press, 2005.

White, L. Michael. "Adolf Harnack and the 'Expansion' of Early Christianity." *Second Century* 5, no. 2 (1985/86): 97–127.

Widdicombe, P. *The Fatherhood of God from Origen to Athanasius.* Oxford: Clarendon, 1994.

Wiles, M. F. *The Christian Fathers.* London: Hodder, 1968.

Wilken, R. L. *The Christians as the Romans Saw Them.* New Haven: Yale University Press, 1984.

———. *The Land Called Holy: Palestine in Christian History and Thought.* New Haven: Yale University Press, 1992.

Williams, Rowan, ed. *The Making of Orthodoxy.* New York: Cambridge University Press, 1989.

Wilson, R. McL. *The Gnostic Problem: A Study of the Relations between Hellenistic Judaism and the Gnostic Heresy.* London: A. R. Mowbray, 1958.

Wimbush, V. L., and R. Valantasis, eds. *Asceticism.* New York: Oxford University Press, 1995.

Wirt, Sherwood E. *The Confessions of Augustine in Modern English.* Grand Rapids, MI: Zondervan, 1997.

Witherington III, Ben. *The Gospel Code: Novel Claims about Jesus, Mary Magdalene and Da Vinci.* Downers Grove, IL: InterVarsity Press, 2004.

———. *Women in the Earliest Churches.* Cambridge: Cambridge University Press, 1988.

Yamauchi, Edwin M. *Pre-Christian Gnosticism: A Survey of the Proposed Evidences*. 2nd ed. Grand Rapids, MI: Baker Books, 1983.

Young, Frances W. *Biblical Exegesis and the Formation of Christian Culture*. Cambridge: Cambridge University Press, 1997.

———. *From Nicaea to Chalcedon: A Guide to the Literature and Its Background*. London: SCM, 1983.

———. "The Greek Fathers." In *Early Christianity: Origins and Evolution to AD 600. In Honour of W. H. C. Frend*, edited by Ian Hazlett, 135–147. London: SPCK; Nashville: Abingdon, 1991.

———. "Retrospect: Interpretation and Appropriation." In *The Cambridge History of Early Christian Literature*, edited by Frances Young, Lewis Ayres and Andrew Louth, 485–494. Cambridge: Cambridge University Press, 2004.

Annotated Guide to Sources for Studies in Early Christianity

A. Sources of the Christian Fathers and Relevant Texts in English

Ancient Christian Commentary on Scripture. 1998–. A multi-volume ecumenical project of commentaries for Bible books, based on the work of early Christian authors, and published by InterVarsity Press (Downers Grove, IL), with Thomas C. Oden as general editor. The series is described as "a postcritical revival of the early commentary tradition known as the *glossa ordinaria*." See the website: http://www.ivpress.com/accs/ for details of Bible commentaries published to date and respective editors.

Ancient Christian Doctrine. 2009–. Thomas C. Oden, ed. A five-volume discussion of the Nicene Creed, giving phrase-by-phrase commentary based on patristic authors in Greek, Latin, Coptic and Syriac. The work includes biographical sketches, a survey of ancient sources meant to elucidate key theological concepts and teachings. See the website: http://www.ivpress.com/series/acd/index2.php?531-8-1721%20ACD/.

Ancient Christian Texts. 2009–. Thomas C. Oden and Gerald L. Bray, series editors. A multi-volume series providing new translations of full-length commentaries on biblical books, written by early Christian leaders and representative of early Christian thought. See the website: http://www.ivpress.com/series/acd-act/index2.php?531-WB-1556%20ACDACT/.

Ancient Christian Writers: The Works of the Fathers in Translation. 1946–. J. Quasten and J. C. Plumpe, eds. 61 vols. Westminster MD, New York: Newman Press; London: Longmans Green. An excellent translation series with extensive footnotes and valuable citation of primary sources.

The Ante-Nicene Fathers: Translations of the Writings of the Fathers down to A. D. 325 (ANF). 1994. A. Roberts and J. Donaldson, eds. 10 vols. Peabody MA: Hendrickson. Published originally as *Ante-Nicene Christian Library* in Edinburgh: T&T Clark (1867–1872), with an additional volume published in New York: Christian Literature (1879). A revised American edition was published in Buffalo NY: Christian Literature Pub. Co. (1885–1903). More recent reprints have appeared in 1950–1951 and 1978 from Grand Rapids, MI: Eerdmans, and as the "Early Church Fathers" on the *Christian Classics Ethereal Library*, a CD prepared at Calvin College (Grand Rapids, MI), now available online at: http://www.ccel.org/fathers.html.

The Apostolic Fathers: Greek Texts and English Translations. 2006 (1992). J. B. Lightfoot, trans., edited and completed by J. R. Harmer, with further revision by Michael W. Holmes. 3rd ed. Grand Rapids, MI: Baker Academic. This work revises Lightfoot and Harmer, *The Apostolic Fathers: Revised Texts with Short Introductions and English Translations* (1891), published originally by Macmillan in London, UK.

Christian Classics Ethereal Library. Online collection of the *Ante-Nicene, Nicene and Post-Nicene Fathers* in translation. See above, *The Ante-Nicene Fathers*. Available at: http://www.ccel.org/fathers.html.

Early Christian Writings is an online collection of texts, translations, and commentary from the first three centuries AD. It contains the New Testament, Apocrypha, documents of the Gnostics, and church fathers, at: http://www.earlychristianwritings.com/.

The Fathers of the Church: A New Translation. 1947–. 84 vols. Washington DC: Catholic University of America Press. See also *Fathers of the Church* published in New York: Fathers of the Church Inc., 1949–60; now online as "The Fathers of the Church (New Advent)," www.newadvent.org/fathers. The collection provides an impressive series of reliable translations, but without the notes available in *Ancient Christian Writers*.

The Gnostic Scriptures. 1987. B. Layton, ed. Anchor Bible Reference Library. Garden City, NY: Doubleday. An extensive and useful collection of texts.

Library of Christian Classics. 1953–1969. J. Baillie, J. T. McNeill and H. P. van Dusen, eds. Philadelphia: Westminster; London: SCM.

Loeb Classical Library. 1912–. Cambridge, MA: Harvard University Press; London: Heinemann.

The Nag Hammadi Library, 1996 (1977). J. Robinson, ed. 4th revised edition. Leiden: Brill.

New Testament Apocrypha. 1991–1992 (1989). W. Schneemelcher, ed. R. McL. Wilson, trans. 2 vols. Cambridge: James Clark & Co.; Louisville: Westminster John Knox. A useful basic collection, including introduction, notes and references to other primary sources.

The Nicene and Post-Nicene Fathers (NPNF). First series (with writings of Augustine and Chrysostom, in fourteen volumes). 1994. H. Wace and Ph. Schaff, eds. Peabody MA: Hendrickson. The collection was first published in 1867–1872 by T&T Clark in Edinburgh. There have been numerous reprints with the Christian Literature Company in New York/Buffalo (1886–1890); Grand Rapids, MI: Eerdmans (1956); Edinburgh: T&T Clark (1989–1994). The collection is also available as the "Church Fathers" on the *Christian Classics Ethereal Library*, a CD prepared at Calvin College, Grand Rapids, MI, and available online: http://www.ccel.org/fathers.html.

The Nicene and Post-Nicene Fathers (NPNF). Second series (with writings of numerous later Fathers, in fourteen volumes). 1994. H. Wace and Ph. Schaff, eds. Peabody MA: Hendrickson. The collection was also published in 1867–72 by T&T Clark in Edinburgh. It was reprinted in New York: Christian Literature Company (1890-1900); Oxford/London: Parker & Co. (1890-1900); Grand Rapids, MI: Eerdmans (1974-1983); Edinburgh: T&T Clark (1989-94). It is also available as the "Church Fathers" on the *Christian Classics Ethereal Library*, a CD prepared at Calvin College, Grand Rapids, MI, and available online: http://www.ccel.org/fathers.html.

The Old Testament Pseudepigrapha. 1983-1985. James Hamilton Charlesworth, ed. 2 vols. Garden City, NY: Doubleday; London: Darton, Longman & Todd. The first volume includes apocalyptic literature and testaments; the second includes expanded parts of the Old Testament, legends, wisdom and philosophical literature, prayers, psalms, odes and fragments of Judeo-Hellenistic works otherwise lost.

Oxford Library of the Christian Fathers. 1838-1881. M. Dods, ed. Edinburgh: T&T Clark; New York: Eerdmans.

Translations of Christian Literature. 1919-. S. Simpson and L. Clarke, eds. London; New York: SPCK.

B. Writings of the Fathers in the Original Languages

Corpus Christianorum: Series Apocrypha. 1983-. Turnhout: Brepols. The *Corpus Christianorum* series supplements Migne's collection (the *Patrologiae Cursus Completus*), with improved and new critical texts.

Corpus Christianorum: Series Graeca. 1977-. Turnholt: Brepols. *Corpus Christianorum: Series Latina*. 1954-. Turnhout: Brepols.

Corpus Scriptorum Christianorum Orientalium (CSCO). 1903-. Louvain: various imprints.

CSCO: *Scriptores Aethiopici*. 1903-12. Paris, etc.; and 1926. Louvain.

CSCO: *Scriptores Coptici*. 1906-49. Paris, etc.; and 1949-. Louvain.

Corpus Scriptorum Ecclesiasticorum Latinorum (CSEL). 1866-. Vienna: various imprints.

Graecorum Corpus Scriptorum (GCS). 1897-. Berlin.

The Oxyrhynchus Papyri. 1898-. Bernard P. Grenfell and Arthur S. Hunt, eds. Multi-volume set. London: Egypt Exploration Society.

Patrologiae Cursus Completus. 1844-1880. Jacques-Paul Migne, ed. Paris: Garnier. The collection includes the *Series Graeca* (abbrev. *PG*) in 162 vols., with Greek texts also presented in Latin translation. The electronic form of *Patrologia Graeca* has been digitized in image format at: http://patristica.net/graeca/. For links to PDF downloadable files see: http://www.roger-pearse.com/weblog/patrologia-graeca-pg-pdfs/. See also: http://www.documentacatholicaomnia.eu/25_20_25-_Rerum_Conspectus_Pro_Auctoribus_Ordinatus.html. The *Series Latina* (abbrev. *PL*) has 224 vols. For more recent volumes: *Patrologiae Latinae Supplementum*. 1958-70. A. Hamman ed. 5 vols. Paris: Garnier. As with the *PG*, *PL* is complete but dependent upon old editions. Electronic database for the

Patrologia Latina is available through Ann Arbor: Proquest Information and Learning Company, New York (1996). A complete electronic version of Migne's first edition is available at: http://patristica.net/latina/, http://pld.chadwyck.co.uk/, and http://www.documentacatholicaomnia.eu/1815-1875,_Migne,_Patrologia_ Latina_01._Rerum_Conspectus_Pro_Tomis_Ordinatus,_MLT.html. Though some manuscript texts are inferior in quality, this still provides the most comprehensive collection of the Fathers.

Sources chrétiennes. 1942–. Paris: Éditions du Cerf. These volumes give a French translation alongside the text in the original language.

C. Handbooks and Dictionaries

Atlas of the Early Christian World. Edited by F. van der Meer and C. Mohrmann. London: Nelson, 1958.

Biographical Dictionary of Christian Theologians. Edited by P. Carey and J. Lienhard. Peabody, MA: Hendrickson, 2002.

Blackwell Companion to Eastern Christianity. Edited by Ken Parry. Malden, MA: Blackwell, 2007.

Blackwell Dictionary of Eastern Christianity. Edited by Ken Parry and J. Hinnells. Oxford: Blackwell, 2000. Contains articles on geographical areas, persons, theological issues and liturgy.

The Cambridge History of Early Christian Literature. Edited by F. Young, L. Ayres and A. Louth. Cambridge: Cambridge University Press, 2004.

The Catholic Encyclopedia. 1905–1922. New York: Encyclopedia Press. Available online: http://www.newadvent.org/cathen/. Though dated, this work remains useful for indepth articles and emphasis on historical information. The *New Advent* website as such http://www.newadvent.com, also provides a collection of the Ante-Nicene, Nicene and Post-Nicene Fathers in translation; it presents the lives of the saints and a wide range of general information about Christian History.

Church History: An Introduction to Research, Reference Works and Methods. James E. Bradley and Richard A. Muller. Grand Rapids, MI: Eerdmans, 1995.

The Dictionary of African Christian Biography (DACB). This dictionary consists of an online database (http://www.dacb.org/) documenting the history of African Christianity from both oral and written sources. The website allows access to recent issues of the *Journal of African Christian Biography*, and other valuable resources from World Council of Churches archives. For early Christianity in Africa, see "Ancient Christian World to approximately AD 650" (http://www.dacb.org/stories/ancientchristw.html). Clicking on maps of ancient and modern Africa allows one to discover biographies relevant to a particular region or country (http://www.dacb.org/stories/ancient-africa.html and http://www.dacb.org/stories/dacbmap.html). While some biographies are rather short, others are longer, and many include useful bibliographies.

A Dictionary of Early Christian Beliefs. David W. Bercot. Peabody, MA: Hendrickson, 1998. This work includes excerpts from Ante-Nicene patristic writings, organized by theological, historical and ethical topics.

Dictionary of Early Christian Literature. Siegmar Döpp and Wilhelm Geerlings, eds. New York: Crossroads, 2000. Contains alphabetically arranged essays on the Fathers with bibliographical information of important editions, translations and critical studies.

The Early Church: An Annotated Bibliography of Literature in English. 1993. Thomas A. Robinson. Metuchen, NJ: American Theological Library Association and Scarecrow Press. This bibliographic work is a helpful and detailed source, although inevitably such books are soon dated.

The Ecole Initiative. Online at: http://ecole.evansville.edu/. A scholarly cooperative effort to establish an online encyclopedia of the history of Christianity up to the Reformation. The collection contains translations of Jewish, Christian and Islamic primary sources, short and long essays and a geographical timeline with a geographical cross-index. Useful for articles of various lengths and links to online images.

Encyclopedia of Early Christianity. Everett Ferguson ed. with M. McHugh and F. Norris associate eds. 2 vols. 2nd ed. New York: Garland Publishers, 1997. Contains short, useful summaries of important facts, with bibliographies.

The Fathers of the Church: A Comprehensive Introduction. Hubertus R. Drobner. Peabody MA: Hendrickson, 2007. A chronological guide to the Fathers, with bibliographical information updating the earlier volumes of Quasten's *Patrology*.

The Fathers of the Greek Church. H. von Campenhausen. London: Adam & Charles Black, 1963.

The Fathers of the Latin Church. H. von Campenhausen. London: Adam & Charles Black, 1964.

A Grammar of New Testament Greek. James Hope Moulton, ed. Edinburgh: T&T Clark, 1908–1976.

Guide to Early Church Documents. This hypertext index, managed by the Institute for Christian Leadership, has pointers to (1) New Testament Canonical Information; (2) Writings of the Apostolic Fathers; (3) Patristic Texts; (4) Creeds and Canons; (5) Later Documents and Miscellaneous Texts; and (6) Relevant Internet Sites. http://www.iclnet.org/pub/resources/christian-history.html.

Handbook of Patristic Exegesis: The Bible in Ancient Christianity. Charles Kannengiesser. 2 vols. Leiden: Brill, 2004.

Late Antiquity: A Guide to the Postclassical World. G. W. Bowersock, Peter Brown and Oleg Grabar, eds. Cambridge, MA: Belknap Press/Harvard Press, 1999. The work introduces the European and Middle Eastern world from AD 250–800, and includes essays on issues like Islam, or war and violence.

The New Bible Dictionary. James Dixon Douglas and N. Hillyer eds. with D. R. Woods revision ed. 3rd revised ed. Grand Rapids, MI: Eerdmans; Downers Grove, IL: InterVarsity Press, 1996 (1961).

The Oxford Classical Dictionary. S. Hornblower and A. Spawforth, eds. 3rd ed. Oxford: Oxford University Press, 1996. A thoroughly revised edition of the 2nd ed. (1970) with N. G. L. Hammond and H. H. Scullard, eds.

The Oxford Dictionary of Byzantium. Alexander P. Kazhdan, ed. 3 vols. New York: Oxford University Press, 1991. Includes major articles on a range of topics for the Byzantine Empire, from the 4th to 15th centuries.

The Oxford Dictionary of the Christian Church. F. L. Cross and E. A. Livingstone, eds. 3rd ed. rev. London, New York, Toronto: Oxford University Press, 2005. Contains short pieces on people, movements and Christian teachings, with concise bibliographies.

The Oxford Handbook of Early Christian Studies. Susan Ashbrook Harvey and David G. Hunter, eds. Oxford: Oxford University Press, 2008. Particularly useful is the section by Joseph F. Kelly and Jeanne-Nicole Saint-Laurent, "*Instrumenta Studiorum*: Tools of the Trade" (ch. 46, 957–977).

Patrology. 5 vols. Johannes Quasten, ed. (with Angelo di Berardino, ed. for vols. 4 and 5). Vol. 1, *The Beginnings of Patristic Literature*; Vol. 2, *The Ante-Nicene Literature after Irenaeus*; Vol. 3, *The Golden Age of Greek Patristic Literature from the Council of Nicaea to the Council of Chalcedon*; Vol. 4, *The Golden Age of Latin Patristic Literature from the Council of Nicaea to the Council of Chalcedon*; Vol. 5, *The Eastern Fathers from the Council of Chalcedon (451) to John of Damascus (750)*. Utrecht/Antwerp: Spectrum Publishers; Westminster MD: Newman (and for vol. 5, Cambridge: James Clarke & Co), 1951–2006. A basic tool with chronologically arranged essays on the Fathers, lists of major writings and bibliographies of important editions, translations and critical studies. The earlier volumes are somewhat dated for secondary sources and methodological approaches.

The Perseus Digital Library. G. Crane, editor-in-chief, Tufts University, 2006. Accessed at: http://www.perseus.tufts.edu. Contains Greek and Latin dictionaries, and morphological analysis of words.

Theological Dictionary of the New Testament. Gerhard Kittel and Geoffrey W. Bromiley, eds. and trans. 10 vols. Grand Rapids, MI: Eerdmans, 1964–1976.

The Westminster Handbook to Patristic Theology. J. McGuckin, ed. Louisville: Westminster John Knox, 2004.

D. Basic Texts in the History of Early Christianity

Atiya, Aziz Suryal. *A History of Eastern Christianity*. Notre Dame: University of Notre Dame Press; Millwood, NY: Kraus Reprint, 1980.

Barrett, C. K., ed. *The New Testament Background: Selected Documents*. Rev. ed. New York: Harper & Row, 1987.

Bickerman, Elias J. *The Jews in the Greek Age*. Cambridge, MA: Harvard University Press, 1988.

Brock, S. P., and S. A. Harvey, eds. and trans. *Holy Women of the Christian Orient*. Berkeley: University California Press, 1998.

Brown, Peter R. L. *The World of Late Antiquity from Marcus Aurelius to Muhammad*. London: Thames & Hudson, 1971.

Bruce, F. F. *Israel and the Nations: The History of Israel from the Exodus to the Fall of the Second Temple*. Revised by David F. Payne. Grand Rapids, MI: Eerdmans, 1997.

Cameron, A., Bryan Ward-Perkins and Michael Whitby, eds. *Late Antiquity: Empire and Successors, A.D. 425–600*. Vol. 14 of *The Cambridge Ancient History*. Cambridge: Cambridge University Press, 2005.

Chadwick, H. *The Early Church*. London: Penguin, 1993.

Charlesworth, James Hamilton. *The Old Testament Pseudepigrapha and the New Testament: Prolegomena for the Study of Christian Origins*. Cambridge: Cambridge University Press, 1985.

———. "Research on the New Testament Apocrypha and Pseudepigrapha." *Aufstieg und Niedergang der römischen Welt*, edited by W. Haase. Part 2, Principat 25, no. 5 (1988): 3919–3968.

Daniélou, J., and Henri Marrou. *The First Six Hundred Years*. Vol. 1 of *The Christian Centuries*. Translated by V. Cronin. London: Darton, Longman & Todd; New York: McGraw-Hill, 1964.

Davis, Leo Donald. *The First Seven Ecumenical Councils (325–787)*. Wilmington, DE: Michael Glazier, 1987.

Deissmann, A. *Light from the Ancient East: The New Testament Illustrated by Recently Discovered Texts of the Graeco-Roman World*. 4th ed. Grand Rapids, MI: Baker Book House, 1965.

Ehrman, B., and A. Jacobs. *Christianity in Late Antiquity, 300–450: A Reader*. New York: Oxford University Press, 2004. An outstanding collection with helpful introductions.

Eusebius of Caesarea. *The History of the Church from Christ to Constantine (Ecclesiastical History)*. Translated by G. Williamson. Harmondsworth: Penguin, 1965.

Ferguson, Everett. *Backgrounds of Early Christianity*. 3rd ed. Grand Rapids, MI: Eerdmans, 2003.

Frend, W. H. C. *The Rise of Christianity*. London: Darton, Longman & Todd.

Gonzalez, Justo L. *The Early Church to the Dawn of the Reformation*. Vol. 1 of *The Story of Christianity*. San Francisco: Harper and Row, 1984.

Harnack, A. von. *The Mission and Expansion of Christianity in the First Three Centuries*. London: Williams & Norgate; Gloucester, MA: Peter Smith, 1963.

Hazlett, Ian. *Early Christianity: Origins and Evolution to AD 600. In Honour of W. H. C. Frend*. London: SPCK, 1991.

Hengel, Martin. *Judaism and Hellenism: Studies in Their Encounter in Palestine during the Early Hellenistic Period*. 2 vols. Minneapolis: Fortress Press, 1974.

Hoare, F. R. trans. and ed. *The Western Fathers.* New York: Harper & Row, 1965. Gives early biographies of Martin of Tours, Ambrose, Augustine of Hippo, Honoratus of Arles and Germanus of Auxerre.

Kelly, J. N. D. *Early Christian Creeds.* London: Longman, 1972.

———. *Early Christian Doctrines.* London: A & C Black, 1960.

Labriolle, P. de. *The History and Literature of Christianity from Tertullian to Boethius.* London: Kegan Paul; Philadelphia: Westminster, 1956.

Latourette, K. S. *The First Five Centuries.* Vol. 1 of *History of the Expansion of Christianity.* Rev. ed. London: Eyre & Spottiswoode; New York: Harper & Row, 1975.

MacMullen, R., and E. N. Lane, eds. *Paganism and Christianity, 100–425 CE: A Sourcebook.* Minneapolis: Fortress Press, 1992.

Metzger, B. M. *The Canon of the New Testament: Its Origin, Development and Significance.* Oxford: Clarendon, 1988.

Musurillo, Herbert. *The Acts of the Christian Martyrs.* With Introduction, Text and Translations. Oxford: Clarendon, 1972.

Neusner, J. *The Rabbinic Traditions about the Pharisees before 70 AD.* 3 vols. Leiden: Brill, 1971.

Pelikan, J. *The Emergence of the Catholic Tradition (100–600).* Vol. 1 of *The Christian Tradition: A History of the Development of Doctrine.* Chicago: University of Chicago Press, 1971.

Penn, Michael Philip. *Envisioning Islam: Syriac Christians and the Early Muslim World.* Philadelphia: University of Pennsylvania Press, 2015.

———. *When Christians First Met Muslims: A Sourcebook of the Earliest Syriac Writings on Islam.* Philadelphia: University of Pennsylvania Press, 2015.

Schaff, Philip. *History of the Christian Church.* 8 vols. New York: Scribner, 1907–1914. Published originally 1858–1890.

Schürer, E. *The History of the Jewish People in the Age of Christ (175 BC – 135 AD).* G. Vermès et al. eds. (trans. and rev.). 3 vols. Edinburgh: T&T Clark, 1973–1987. Especially helpful as introduction to primary sources.

Stevenson, J. *Creeds, Councils and Controversies: Documents Illustrative of the History of the Church AD 337–461.* W. H. C. Frend revision. London: SPCK, 2012.

———. *A New Eusebius. Documents Illustrating the History of the Church to AD 337.* W. H. C. Frend revision. London: SPCK, 1987.

Strack, Hermann L., and Paul Billerbeck. *Kommentar zum Neuen Testament aus Talmud und Midrasch.* 6 vols. München: Beck, 1922–1961.

Tcherikover, V. *Hellenistic Civilization and the Jews.* Translated by S. Applebaum. Philadelphia: Jewish Publication Society of America, 1959.

Tierney, B. *The Middle Ages: Sources of Medieval History.* New York: A. A. Knopf, 1978.

Vallée, G. *The Shaping of Christianity: The History and Literature of Its Formative Centuries (100–800).* New York: Paulist Press, 1999.

Wiles, M., and M. Santer. *Documents in Early Christian Thought.* Cambridge: Cambridge University Press, 1975.

Wimbush, V. L., ed. *Ascetic Behavior in Greco-Roman Antiquity: A Sourcebook.* Minneapolis: Fortress, 1990.
Young, F. M. *From Nicaea to Chalcedon: A Guide to the Literature and Its Background.* Philadelphia: Fortress Press, 1983.

E. Historiography of Early African Christianity

Arnauld, Dominique. *Histoire du Christianisme en Afrique: Les sept premiers siècles* [*A History of Christianity in Africa: The First Seven Centuries*]. Paris: editions Karthala, 2001.
Baur, John. *Two Thousand Years of Christianity in Africa.* Nairobi: Paulines Publications Africa, 1994.
Bediako. Kwame. *Christianity in Africa: The Renewal of a Non-Western Religion.* Maryknoll: Orbis Books; Edinburgh: Edinburgh University Press, 1995.
Burton, Keith Augustus. *The Blessing of Africa: The Bible and African Christianity.* Downers Grove, IL: IVP Academic, 2007.
Cuoq, Joseph. *L'Eglise d'Afrique du Nord du IIe au XIIe siècle* [*The North African Church from the Second to the Twelfth Century*]. Paris: Editions du Centurion, 1984.
Daniel, Robin. *This Holy Seed.* Harpenden, UK: Tamarisk, 1993.
Fasholé-Luke, E., R. Gray, A. Hastings, and G. Tasie, eds. *Christianity in Independent Africa.* London: R. Collins, 1978.
Finneran, Neil. *The Archaeology of Christianity in Africa.* Stroud: Tempus, 2002.
Groves, C. P. *The Planting of Christianity in Africa.* 4 vols. London: Lutterworth, 1948–1964.
Hastings, Adrian. *The Church in Africa 1450–1950.* Oxford: Clarendon, 1997.
Isichei, Elizabeth. *A History of Christianity in Africa: From Antiquity to the Present.* London: SPCK, 1995.
Kalu, Ogbu U., ed. *African Christianity: An African Story.* Trenton, NJ: Africa World Press, 2007.
Oden, Thomas C. *How Africa Shaped the Christian Mind: Rediscovering the African Seedbed of Western Christianity.* Downers Grove, IL: IVP Books, 2007.
Sanneh, Lamin. *West African Christianity: The Religious Impact.* London: C. Hurst & Co., 1983.
Shaw, Mark R. *The Kingdom of God in Africa: A Short History of African Christianity.* Grand Rapids, MI: Baker Books, 1996.
Sundkler, Bengt, with Christopher Steed. *A History of the Church in Africa.* Cambridge: Cambridge University Press, 2000.
Taryor, Nya Kwiawon. *The Impact of the African Tradition on African Christianity.* Chicago: Strugglers' Community Press, 1984.
Verstraelen, Frans J. *History of Christianity in Africa in the Context of African History: A Comparative Assessment of Four Recent Historiographical Contributions.* Gweru, Zimbabwe: Mambo Press, 2002.

F. Research Centres and Other Online Resources

Churches of the North African Orthodox tradition have (English language) websites; for the Egyptian Coptic Orthodox Church: www.coptic.net/EncyclopediaCoptica, and for the Ethiopian Orthodox Tewahedo Church: www.ethiopianorthodox.org/english/indexenglish.html.

For a website with links to previews and surveys of numerous valuable works on Christianity in Africa, see: https://www.questia.com/library/religion/christianity/christianity-in-africa/.

For ongoing research on Early Christianity in Africa and links to valuable resources check the website of *The Center for Early African Christianity* (based at Yale University in Connecticut, USA): http://www.earlyafricanchristianity.com.

The above website provides an important link for the *Christian History Magazine* devoted to "Early African Christianity" (Issue 105), https://www.christianhistoryinstitute.org/magazine/issue/christianity-in-early-africa/, with a further introduction to relevant and important literature, https://www.christianhistoryinstitute.org/magazine/article/north-africa-recommended-resources/. This issue has numerous articles on early North African leaders, from Tertullian and Anthony to Augustine, and important cities like Carthage and Alexandria, issues of martyrdom and monasticism, Ethiopian traditions or the witness of archaeology.

Students are also advised to check back issues of the online *Christian History Magazine* for discussion of Augustine (vols. 15 and 67), Eastern Orthodoxy (54), Gnostics (96) or Christians and Muslims (74): www.christianhistorymagazine.org.

Index of Subjects

A
abba 64
abbot 64, 79
Acts (N) 40, 86, 185, 253, 264, 266
Acts of Paul (apocryphal) 265
Adonai 185
adoptionism 296
Adversus Praxeas (Tertullian) 367
Aeon (aeon) 208, 213, 214, 222
Africa 44, 146, 147, 151, 429, 431
Aksum xix, 44, 66, 167, 432
Aksumite
　church 438
　court 146
　kingdom 146, 431
　rulers 146
Aksumite Ethiopians 170
Alexandria 10, 37, 42, 46, 47, 50, 57, 78, 159, 160, 161, 167, 197–199, 207, 214, 217, 229, 253, 259, 287, 291, 292, 302, 306, 312, 314, 324, 331, 332, 338, 350, 360, 361, 367, 430, 431, 439
Algeria 151, 158, 372, 410, 435, 436
Allah xxiii, 5, 347
Amharic language 164, 165
anchorite 58, 66, 71
Ancient Christian Commentary on Scripture 439
Anomoian 139, 312, 315
Ante-Nicene Christian Library 404, 475
antinomian 221
Antioch 37, 72, 74, 227, 258, 259, 292, 296, 306, 313, 324–327, 331–333, 335, 338, 348, 350, 361, 362, 365, 417, 422, 427
apocalyptic 15, 269, 407
apocryphal 45, 181, 219, 262, 269, 270, 371
apologetic 100

Apologist 46, 96, 98, 99, 101–103, 117, 131, 132, 229, 232, 300, 422
Apology (Plato) 99, 105, 194
Apology (Tertullian) 97, 100–102, 132, 232
Apology (Justin Martyr) 85, 100, 102, 104, 105, 108, 260, 262
Apology (Athanasius) 361
apostle 36, 38, 47, 135, 190, 281, 357
Apostles' Creed 239, 240, 243
apostolic 235, 236, 262, 271, 282, 309, 429
Apostolic Fathers 177, 190, 191, 228, 238, 243, 252, 260, 262
apostolicity 239, 262, 267
apostolic succession 227, 235–237, 243, 399
Arab
　Christians 50
　conquests xix, 159, 171, 432, 434–436, 438, 439
　invasions xx, xxii, 429, 435
　Muslims 172
　rule 340
　world 350
Aramaic 10, 68, 351
archimandrite 64
archon(tes) 209, 212, 218, 221, 274, 295, 296
Arian xxii, 59, 60, 135–139, 157, 188, 311–313, 315–317, 319, 342, 345, 351, 360, 361, 363, 368, 369, 386, 393, 421, 424, 426, 432, 434
Arianism xxi, 140, 163, 192, 319, 348, 359
aristocracy 16, 56
Armenia 48, 333, 335, 426
ascetic 18, 55–64, 68–71, 74–76, 79, 85, 114, 221, 232, 302, 364, 365, 370, 374, 408

asceticism 56, 62–64, 69–71, 74, 75, 414, 415, 417
Asia Minor 10, 29, 45, 47, 49, 68, 69, 86, 91, 92, 112, 115, 124, 130, 139, 153, 177, 193, 225, 257, 259, 263, 297, 307, 314, 316, 317, 319, 338, 362, 363, 390, 404, 410
Assyrian 328
atheism 91, 98, 105
Athens 6, 21, 24, 27, 229, 317, 362
authoritative 249, 251, 252, 254, 345
authority 10, 20, 22, 26, 41, 59, 64, 66, 70, 79, 114, 122, 153, 154, 162, 179, 182, 183, 207, 234–239, 263, 267, 272, 292–294, 337, 345, 352, 360, 363, 377, 400

B
Babylon(ian) 6, 8, 13, 14, 131, 254, 281
baptism 18, 57, 73–76, 111, 133, 135, 154, 155, 165, 200, 211, 227–229, 240, 260, 291, 296, 319, 348, 351, 358, 365, 368, 375, 436
baptismal confession 239, 240
barbarian 76, 141, 386–388, 390, 395
Berber 147, 149–151, 155, 156, 372, 432, 434, 435
Bithynia 45, 46, 92, 124, 220, 362
blasphemy (blasphemous) 183, 186, 187, 288, 295, 326, 347
Books of Jeu 210
Byzantine 163
  Africa 157
  church xxii, 380
  court 311
  rulers 429
Byzantine Empire xix, xxii, 65, 124, 141, 294, 387, 397

C
Caesarea 14, 42, 86, 97, 302, 422
canon 220, 241, 249, 251–256, 260–262, 265–267, 270–272, 281

canonical 4, 49, 181, 182, 219, 224, 249, 250, 262, 263, 265, 266, 269, 270, 280, 283
Cappadocia 49, 56, 72, 302, 319, 363
carnal 215, 217, 224
Carthage 21, 94, 96, 97, 137, 138, 147–154, 222, 231, 237, 266, 291, 338, 367, 372, 373, 376, 377, 439
catechetical school 147, 161, 229, 302
catechumen 133, 368
Catholic church 5, 34, 137, 152, 155, 162, 376, 381, 400, 424, 434, 436
Catholicity 293
celibate 57, 69
cenobitic 62
Chalcedon (council) 49, 67, 168, 169, 170, 238, 319, 323, 324, 328, 329, 331, 333, 334, 337, 342, 346, 349, 424, 427, 432
Chalcedonian Creed 323, 331, 332
chastity 63, 79
China 49, 50, 68, 80, 328, 349
Christendom
  medieval 288
  western 423
Christianity
  Arab 50, 51
  Coptic 146, 148, 158, 162, 171, 414, 438
  Ethiopian 158, 438
  Jewish 41, 405, 408
  Nubian 171, 438
  Orthodox (orthodox) xxii, xxiii, 60, 136, 138, 152, 171, 216, 241, 250, 289, 293, 323, 314, 349, 363, 411, 413, 422, 426, 433
  Syriac 414
christological 148, 302, 304, 328, 438
Christology 49, 290, 295, 333, 364
Christotokos 326, 327, 349
church and state xxii, 96, 97, 121–124, 126, 129, 133, 136, 137, 139–141, 232, 334, 345, 368, 393, 423
circumcision 12, 33, 34, 37, 38, 40, 42, 43, 45, 87, 199

Index of Subjects 487

City of God (Augustine) 377, 385, 386, 394–396, 423, 437
codex 253, 261
Codex Alexandrinus 265, 266, 401
Codex Sinaiticus 265
colonial xix, 410
colonization xix, 16
Confessions (Augustine) 69, 358, 359, 372, 377, 378
confessor 113, 114, 207, 153, 154, 416
consensus 262
Constantinople xxii, xxiii, 23, 68, 74, 75, 131, 134, 140, 163, 170, 171, 266, 317, 326, 329, 333, 335, 338, 340, 342, 345, 349, 350, 360, 363, 365, 366, 387, 389, 390, 394, 400, 401, 424, 426
consubstantial (consubstantiality) 137, 138, 305, 309, 310, 317–319, 331, 332, 348, 364
Coptic 159, 162
 calendar 165
 Christians 49, 57
 church xxii, 34, 47, 64, 148, 159, 162, 163, 169, 333, 338, 432, 433, 438, 440
 community 340
 language 63, 147, 163
 literature 162
 manuscripts 211
 texts 433
Coptic Orthodox Church xxii
Copts 163, 340, 432
Corinth 21, 57, 103, 191, 260, 399
Corpus Christianorum, Series Apocrypha 477
Corpus Christianorum, Series Graeca 405, 477
Corpus Christianorum, Series Latina 405, 477
Corpus Scriptorum Christianorum Orientalium 414, 477
Corpus Scriptorum Ecclesiasticorurm Latinorum 405
cosmos 197–199, 213, 217, 221

Council of Chalcedon 49, 67, 168–170, 238, 319, 323, 324, 328, 329, 331, 333, 334, 337, 342, 346, 349, 424, 427, 432
Council of Constantinople 55, 287, 289, 295, 312, 317, 318, 325, 333, 337, 338, 340, 342, 343, 346, 348, 362–364, 367, 369, 371, 424, 427
Council of Ephesus 67, 324, 327, 329, 330, 346, 349, 362, 424
Council of Nicea xxii, 30, 34, 52, 114, 136, 137, 238, 266, 267, 270, 271, 279, 287, 289, 292, 293, 295, 302, 305, 307, 311, 313, 317, 324, 331, 343–346, 348, 360, 421, 422, 424
covenant 40, 165, 178, 254
creation 106, 199, 215–218, 222–225, 227, 240, 290, 295, 297, 299, 300, 301, 305, 306, 308, 309, 352, 378, 380, 395
creed 239, 288, 289, 306, 308, 309, 313, 319, 329, 331
 Anomoian 139
 baptismal 242, 261
 creed of Caesarea 422
crucifixion xxiii, 20, 178, 184, 186, 209, 218, 219, 220, 256, 269, 271, 347, 352
Cyrene (Lybia) 149, 183, 208, 218, 219, 259, 430, 440

D
Damascus 350
deacon 75, 115, 307, 365, 416
Dead Sea Scrolls 17–19, 57, 200, 269, 408, 411, 413
deity 55, 185–187, 191, 192, 296, 297, 308, 310, 314, 331, 347, 348, 351, 352, 361, 362, 422
demonic 24, 58, 101
Desert Fathers 61, 64, 69
Desert Mothers 61, 64
deutero-canonical 216, 270
dhimmi 158
Dialogues (Plato) 194, 195

Dialogues (Cassiciacum) (Augustine) 375
Dialogue with Trypho the Jew (Justin Martyr) 103, 192, 256, 259
diaspora 8, 26, 36, 37, 39, 40, 259, 432
Diatessaron (Tatian) 263
Didachê 191, 260, 265, 266, 404
discipline 58, 59, 62–64, 79, 80, 290, 292, 367, 396, 400–402, 410, 413, 418, 438
divine
   conception 347
   favour 76, 122
   grace 377
   Holy Spirit 363
   humanity 230
   law 136
   liturgy (service) 80, 366
   messenger 212
   nature 298–300, 305, 309, 310, 315, 324–327, 329–331, 333–334, 344, 346, 349, 350, 352, 361
   origin (source) 212, 374
   person(s) 289, 304, 308, 314, 315, 340, 346, 352
   power 27, 224, 296
   realm (as spiritual) 189, 197, 208, 224, 299
   revelation (inspired) 113, 272, 273, 287–289
   Roman emperor 23, 26
   Son (God's, Christ Jesus) 137, 148, 171, 178, 185–190, 192–193, 208, 250, 251, 271, 274, 288, 290, 295, 301, 311, 315, 323–327, 329, 331, 333, 334, 347–349, 351, 360
   soul 300
   spark 212
   substance (essence) 299, 304, 308, 309, 313–315, 323, 345, 346, 348, 363, 367
   will 341, 342, 346
   Word/Logos 46, 106, 134, 191–192, 197, 300, 301, 306, 325, 335, 342
divinity 50, 137, 163, 178, 187, 188, 195, 208, 225, 288, 289, 295, 304, 315, 324, 326, 327, 341, 351
Docetism 177, 188, 208, 271, 290, 364
Donatist (Donatism) xxi, 111, 137, 138, 140, 148, 151–156, 159, 162, 291, 375, 376, 377, 411, 432, 433, 436, 438
Dongola 170, 172
dualist (dualistic) 195, 209, 222–224
dynamic monarchianism 296

E
early Christian xxi, xxiii, 20, 33, 57, 85, 149, 161, 181, 185, 192, 209, 225, 243, 253, 256, 260, 261, 289, 290, 292, 329, 347, 400, 405, 438, 475
early Christianity xix, xxi–xxiv, 4, 15, 19, 65, 86, 109, 148, 150, 161, 178, 192, 225, 275, 346, 353, 359, 372, 399, 401–403, 405–407, 410–414, 416–418, 429, 430, 431, 433, 435–437, 440, 441
early Christianity in Africa xx, 147
early church 19, 37, 45, 85, 145, 184, 190, 257, 295, 351, 400, 412, 435
East Africa 349
Eastern Orthodox 34, 70, 72, 366
Ebionites (Ebionism) 33, 34, 42–44, 221, 268, 423
ecclesiastical (offices) 64, 75, 114, 138, 234, 237, 275, 283, 312, 345, 369, 410, 414, 426, 435
Ecclesiastical History (Eusebius) 112, 115, 251, 280, 282, 421
ecumenical council(s) xxi, 67, 187, 238, 267, 287–289, 292, 294, 306, 307, 312, 313, 331, 342, 343, 345, 346, 348, 351, 352, 364, 367, 399
Edessa 48, 49, 66, 68, 335
Edict of Milan 130, 131, 138
Edict of Toleration (Galerius) 128–130
Egypt xix, xxii, 8, 10, 22, 26, 29, 37, 47, 49, 57, 58, 61, 62, 64–66, 69, 75, 76, 94, 139, 148, 149, 159–163,

165, 168–171, 211, 217, 313, 316, 324, 327, 333–335, 338, 340, 350, 394, 408, 426, 429–433, 437, 438
Elkesaite 33, 43, 351
emperor 22, 23, 26, 29, 30, 108, 122, 123, 127, 129, 138, 140, 141, 155, 287, 288, 291–293, 306, 308, 311, 312, 329, 334, 335, 341, 345, 359, 36
   as Pontifex Maximus (chief high priest) 29, 30, 133, 139, 292
   deified 25, 37, 84, 88, 111
   worship 13, 22, 25–26, 87, 88, 92, 93, 99–102, 126, 132
empire 22–27, 46, 294, 295
   and Christianity 47, 49, 84, 85, 87, 95, 96, 98, 123, 133, 138, 139–141, 155, 267, 289, 291–293, 311, 391, 392, 394, 395, 423
   and invasion 95, 140, 141, 151, 389, 390, 393, 394
   and Jews 42
   and Monophysites 335
   and peace 44, 45, 132, 288
   and religion 96, 122, 123, 126, 132, 135, 334, 340, 343
   and reorganization 124, 125, 389
   Byzantine (see Byzantine Empire)
   disintegration 385, 386, 391, 397
   fall 387, 388, 390, 394, 397
   Islamic 168, 169
   Roman (see Roman Empire)
Encratites 221
encyclical 5, 305
Enlightenment 85, 392, 402, 412, 418
Enneads (Plotinus) 374
Ephesus 38, 103, 227
Epicureans 251
Epistle of Barnabas 45, 265
eschatology 395, 407, 431
esoteric 211, 212, 216, 223, 237, 263, 270
Essenes 8, 15–19, 36, 41, 44, 57, 71, 199

Ethiopia (Ethiopian[s]) xix, xxii, 47, 49, 51, 65, 66, 146–148, 164, 165, 167–170, 229, 335, 338, 349, 350, 429–431, 434, 437, 438
Ethiopian Orthodox Church 146, 165, 169, 432
Eucharist 217, 400, 436
excommunication 154, 293
exile 6, 8, 13, 91, 98, 137, 139, 160, 254, 288, 292, 312, 313, 316, 331, 360, 361, 366

F
Falasha 164
feminist
   authors 415
   perspective 416
   scholars 216, 275

G
Ge'ez 65, 146, 165, 168, 433
gender 216, 414, 416
Genesis 199, 216, 224, 240, 257
Gentiles 15, 33, 34, 37, 38, 40, 41, 43, 45, 84, 87, 121, 178, 183, 230
Georgia 48
gnôsis 211, 212, 223, 230, 409
gnostic (Gnostic) xxii, 46, 111, 188, 207, 221, 222, 240, 243, 367, 438
   and Docetism 178, 188, 208, 225, 271, 290
   communities 208
   documents 210, 211, 217, 409, 413, 416
   dualist 222
   gospels 237, 268, 271, 274, 279, 409, 413
   interpretation of Scripture xxii
   Manichean 156, 189, 373
   Marcion 4, 220, 221
   redemption (salvation) 212, 213, 215
   serpent 221, 224
   Sophia 214–217

490 Early Christianity

Gnosticism xxi, xxiii, 47, 109–192, 207, 208, 210, 226, 230, 232, 239, 252, 274, 275, 359, 409, 416
  Alexandrian 161, 229
  and allegorical interpretation 223, 231
  and astronomy 209
  and canon of Scripture 249, 250, 261
  and creation 223, 224, 227, 240
  and crucifixion (of Jesus) 178, 208, 218, 219, 347
  and Hellenization 161, 409
  and *homoousion* 299, 310
  and Jewish Christianity 43, 409
  and Old Testament 230
  and philosophy 209, 224, 230, 233, 409, 410
  and secret teaching 227, 236, 237, 262, 270
  and syncretism 24, 209, 223
  and women 275, 278, 279, 415, 416
  as heresy 210, 232–234, 268, 409, 423
  leaders 161, 209, 213, 225
  origin 209, 409
God-fearers 39, 45
gospel 37, 39, 46, 47, 57, 58, 65, 76, 86, 161, 162, 180, 181, 185, 214, 219, 220, 223, 225–227, 230, 234, 249, 261, 263, 267, 268, 270, 273, 281, 289, 295, 344, 351, 357, 396
Gospel of Philip 274
Gospel of the Hebrews 265
Gospel of Thomas 237, 268, 409
Gothic
  language 319
  tribes 97, 388
government 16, 44, 101, 103, 122–124, 136, 140, 145, 152, 153, 156, 159, 200, 236, 367, 372, 393
governor 20, 92, 93, 115, 116, 183, 367

H
Hadiths xxiii
Hasidim 11
Hasmonean 12, 13, 16, 19
Hebrew Bible 5
Hegelian (Hegelianism) 147, 148, 403, 405
Hellenism (Hellenistic) 3–5, 10, 21, 26, 50, 70, 139, 148, 192, 198, 199, 404, 408
Hellenization 5, 6, 9, 11, 12, 15, 16, 161, 162, 198
heresy 56, 60, 140, 152, 156, 208, 233, 289, 291, 310, 413, 414, 417, 439
hermit 58, 62, 68, 73, 74, 78, 79
Herodians 17
Hexaemeron 259
Hexapla 265
hierarchy 194
high priest 12, 30, 133
hijra 169
Himyar Kingdom of Yemen 50
history 5, 15, 133, 228, 242, 253, 272, 273
  African 432
  ancient 392, 394
  biblical 395
  church 402, 412, 418, 424
  colonial 431
  Greco-Roman 411
  Nubian 433
  of African Christianity 437, 439
  of Christianity 4, 121, 122, 147, 188, 233, 251, 270, 294, 331, 351, 352, 402, 416, 424, 430, 431
  of early African Christianity 152
  of Ethiopia 146, 170
  of Europe 411
  of Israel 254
  of Nubia 170
  of religions 407, 409
  of the canon 264
  of theology 195
  of western Christianity 377
  political 436
  pre-Christian 434
  social 415

Index of Subjects   491

Holy Spirit 39, 153, 163, 184–186, 215, 224, 229, 240–242, 272, 289, 295–300, 302–304, 308, 309, 314–317, 319, 348, 352, 362, 363, 380
Homoian 313
homoios 313
homoiousios (*homoiousion*) 293, 314, 316
homoousios (*homoousion*) 139, 293, 305, 308, 310, 312, 314, 316, 346, 348, 422
human
  being(s) 199, 208, 215, 217, 219, 224, 225, 227, 249, 289, 303, 324, 325, 331, 343, 377
  Christ (Jesus, God's Son) 107, 178, 188, 189, 208, 230, 251, 270, 271, 274, 279, 288, 290, 295, 296, 300, 303, 305, 306, 315, 323–327, 329–331, 333, 334, 344, 346–350, 352, 360, 361
  evil 189
  generation 315
  history 272, 395
  imperfection 199
  kingdom 396
  knowledge 230
  nature 107, 171, 180, 193, 280, 324, 326, 327, 331, 335, 342, 346, 377
  person 340
  race 90, 91, 133, 136, 241
  reason 107
  sacrifice 156
  sin 75, 183, 184, 224, 297, 315, 373
  soul (mind) 50, 189, 195, 299, 300, 305–306, 325, 348, 362, 380
  suffering 37
  understanding 352
  will 341, 342, 346, 376, 377
  writers 271
humanity 199, 211, 216, 224, 227, 228, 230, 327, 352, 377, 437

  of Jesus 180, 188, 221, 225, 280, 295, 298, 315, 324, 325–327, 331, 333, 335, 341, 344, 345, 346, 349, 422
hypostasis (hypostases) 299, 304, 306, 310, 314–317, 332, 335, 346, 363
hypostatic union 326, 331, 335, 346

I
iconoclasm xxii, 294, 345
Idumean(s) 12, 13, 17
immortality 84, 133, 194, 241, 249, 315, 361
Imperator 22
incarnation 50, 209, 221, 225, 228, 242, 298, 300, 329, 345, 347, 361
India xix, 47, 52, 68, 80, 146, 229, 328, 349, 430
indigenization xix, 158, 430
initiation 28, 212, 223, 227, 239
interdisciplinary 138, 417, 418
interpretation
  allegorical 198, 199, 220, 223, 259, 365, 369, 374
  literal 231, 258
Islam xxiii, 158, 163, 168, 172, 187, 188, 239, 289, 338, 347, 349, 353, 388, 434, 435, 439

J
Jamnia (Jabneh) 41, 42, 256
Jerusalem 6, 13–17, 19, 20, 33, 36, 37, 39, 41, 42, 44, 68, 79, 86, 87, 134, 181, 253, 256, 259, 281, 292, 333, 335, 338, 350
Jerusalem Council 34, 37, 40, 41
Jerusalem, temple 6, 14, 41, 165
Jewish
  Christians 33, 39, 41, 43, 44, 87
  community 13, 164, 256, 259
  context 34
  culture 40, 41
  custom 4
  exiles 146
  feasts 42
  festal calendar 12

law(s) 4, 38
leaders 36, 183
rebellion 19
religion 13, 16, 35, 45
resistance 12, 41
Sabbath 88
Scriptures 37
society 11
synagogue 45
tradition(s) 19, 41
worship 161
writers 186
Jewish Antiquities (Josephus) 422
Judaism
  Babylonian 14, 15
  Diaspora 14, 15, 45
  Hellenistic 223
  Palestinian 14, 16
  Rabbinic 41
Judaizers 39, 178, 426
Judea 8, 9, 14, 41, 90, 190

K

Kurios 37, 83, 88, 100, 109, 185, 208, 289, 295

L

Lake Chad 171, 172
late antiquity 388, 392, 400, 402, 407, 410, 411, 417, 436
law of Moses 3
Libya 149, 435, 436, 438
Life of Macrina (Gregory of Nyssa) 56, 72, 364
Life of Moses (Philo of Alexandria) 364
literacy 417
literal (meaning, interpretation) 185, 231, 258, 259, 324, 365, 367
logos (reason) 106, 107, 193, 197, 208, 289, 299, 300
Logos (Word, Jesus) 106–108, 134, 191, 192, 197–199, 208, 214, 216, 217, 223, 224, 230, 289, 295, 296, 298–303, 305, 306, 308, 310, 316, 325–327, 333, 335, 342, 348, 362

Logos theology 295, 296, 299, 300, 302, 360
Luke, Gospel of 220, 252, 261
Lyons 93, 109, 112, 115, 116, 216, 225, 422

M

Maccabean (people, rulers) 12, 16, 20, 42, 88, 138
Maccabees (books of) 3, 4, 88, 255, 269, 270, 280, 371
Macedonian 9, 21, 317
Maghreb xix, xxiv, 149, 158, 430, 432, 434
Manichaeism 33, 43
Manichean(s), Manichee(s) 156, 222, 268, 299, 369, 373–376, 436, 438
manuscript(s) 210, 265, 401
Mark, Gospel of 261
Maronites 342, 350
marriage 24, 55, 57, 61, 71, 85, 153, 221, 326, 342, 358, 373, 375, 415, 437
martyr(s) (martyrdom) xxii, 51, 59, 84–88, 91, 93, 94, 98, 109–114, 116, 150, 151, 153, 154, 157, 177, 178, 191, 238, 411, 416, 422, 433, 435, 437
Masada 41
Matthew, Gospel of 261
meaning
  historical 365
  literal 191, 259, 365
Mediterranean xix, 8, 21, 26, 45, 47, 148, 150, 160, 292, 388, 410, 438
Melechite 163
Meletian (schism) 162, 291
Meroe 167, 170
Mesopotamia 47, 50, 68
Messiah (messianic) 14, 16, 18, 19, 34–37, 40, 43, 44, 86, 103, 178, 179, 180, 183, 185, 186, 200–202, 219, 228, 256, 257, 295, 349
Milan 125, 358, 367, 369, 374, 389

missionary xix, xxii, 40, 45, 47, 76, 80, 86, 87, 124, 158, 259, 319, 390, 429
Mithras 29, 126
Modalism (modalist) 297, 298, 315
monarchian(ism) 295–297, 299
monastic
  calling 74
  communities 18, 61, 73, 75, 79, 80, 211
  developments 70
  discipline 62
  education 66
  establishment(s) 55, 69, 72, 78, 158, 365, 371
  fellowship 59
  groups 313, 343
  ideal 69, 375
  life 57, 58, 64, 65, 70, 72, 74, 75, 78, 80, 317, 361, 370, 375, 386, 438
  model 56, 63, 66
  movement 56, 162, 335
  orders 80
  philosophy 426
  practice 72, 75, 76
  rule 68, 363, 434, 437
  tradition 78
monasticism xxii, 56, 62, 63, 66, 70, 72, 74, 76, 78, 79, 114, 162, 361, 439
  Byzantine 70
monk 65, 66, 67, 75, 76, 335, 344, 377, 427
Monophysite(s) (Monophysitism) xxi, 49, 163, 168, 170, 171, 329, 332–335, 337, 338, 340, 345, 346, 350, 361, 427, 432, 438
monotheism 20, 197, 199, 295, 350
monothelite 341, 342
Montanist (Montanism) 46, 153, 232, 278, 416, 432, 435, 436
Morocco 436
Mosaic laws 87, 199
Muratorian fragment 264–266
Muslim 169, 186, 351
  advance 338
  caliphs 343
  dominance xxi
  invaders 157, 158, 171
  invasion xxii
  jihadists 156
  rule 338
  scholars 85, 187, 219
  traders 44
Muslim Arabs 172
mysteries (gnostic) 213, 236
mystery religions (mysteries) 27–29, 126, 189, 223, 270

N
Naassenes 221, 222
Nag Hammadi library (documents, scrolls) xxiii, 159, 161, 209–211, 214, 215, 222, 268, 269, 271, 274, 408, 409, 411, 413, 415
nationalism 16, 36, 152, 335
Nazarene 43
Neoplatonism 358, 375
Neo-Thomism 405
Nestorian 50, 52, 328, 329, 349, 351, 427
New Testament 4, 5, 8, 15, 20, 22, 49, 57, 70, 84, 86, 106, 131, 179, 203, 220, 239, 252, 256, 257, 259, 260, 262, 263, 265, 266, 271, 281, 282, 289, 360, 361, 402–408, 415, 440
Nicene Creed 163, 318, 319, 364, 369, 380, 475
Nigeria 5, 19, 98, 123, 172
Nile (civilizations) xix, 50, 58, 61, 63, 158, 159, 161, 162, 171, 211, 328, 408, 431, 433, 437
Nisibis 66, 78
North Africa(n) (Maghreb) xix–xxii, xxiv, 21, 139, 147, 149, 151, 152, 154, 162, 259, 297, 372, 375, 390, 410, 429, 432–435, 437, 438
  bishop of 238, 371, 434
  Christianity xxiv, 47, 85, 111, 150, 151, 154, 158, 411, 429, 431, 433–435, 438, 439

Christians xxi, xxiv, 6
church(es) xxi, xxii, 145, 152, 156, 157
Circumcellions in 162
Donatists in 111, 137, 138, 153–156, 159, 411, 433
Egyptian 159, 333
martyrs 47, 147, 153
monasticism 69
Muslim invasion 157, 338
puritan 155
theologians 359, 422
Nubia (Nubian) xix, xxii, 49, 148, 165, 167, 170–172, 333, 429, 431–434, 437, 438
Numidia 150, 151, 154, 410

O

Odes of Solomon 211
offices (of monastic worship) 76
Old Testament 5, 10, 37, 38, 40, 43, 103, 106, 161, 179, 180, 184, 191, 198, 200, 215, 220, 222, 227, 230, 231, 252–261, 266, 280, 295, 302, 344, 360, 371, 375, 407, 409
On the Trinity (Augustine) 380
orthodoxy 229, 262, 292, 293, 364, 413
ousia (Greek: essence) 305, 308–310, 313–316, 326, 363
Oxford Library of the Fathers 403
Oxford Movement 403

P

pacifism 393
pagan(s) 110
and persecution 110, 116
gods 95, 102, 105, 133, 188, 192, 193, 387, 394, 395
Greek culture 9, 400, 401, 411
historian 140
idolatry 18
philosophers (philosophy) 106, 362, 406
priests 121, 134
rites 11, 92, 393, 395
sacrifice 140, 392
teachings 107, 199
temples 65
tribes 390
worship (prayers) 74, 96, 134
Palestine 5, 9–17, 20, 22, 26, 34, 40, 41, 47, 50, 68, 72, 74, 75, 134, 139, 165, 199, 226, 253, 259, 263, 323, 338, 371, 406, 421, 426
papal 5, 327, 331, 337, 400
papal bull 405
papyrus (papyri) 58, 260, 404, 410
patriarch (patriarchate) 47, 64, 292, 312, 326, 329, 344, 349, 361, 365, 401
patristic 5, 148, 345, 400, 401, 403–407, 410, 412, 414, 418
Patrologia 399, 401
Patrologiae Cursus Completus 403, 477
Patrologia Graeca 403, 477
Patrologia Latina 403, 441, 478
Pax Romana 14, 23
Pelagian 375, 377, 436, 438
Pentateuch 37, 164, 198, 254
Pentecost 44, 165, 184, 259
persecution xxii, 4, 12, 27, 44, 58, 86, 89, 92–98, 105, 131, 132, 147, 151, 161, 163, 167, 186, 190, 228, 229, 233, 302, 421, 422, 423
and lapsed Christians 110, 111, 135, 153, 238, 291, 367, 376
and martyrdom 86, 109
by Nero 23, 46, 89, 91
by Persian rulers 49
by Vandals 434
causes 85, 89, 99–102, 122, 126, 131, 178
ending 130, 131, 359, 421, 422
goals 114
"great persecution" (under Diocletian) 56, 59, 86, 121, 123, 124, 126–129, 154, 159, 162, 193, 291, 362, 374, 421, 425
in Lyons 94, 109, 112, 115–117, 422
in Rome 23, 91

Index of Subjects   495

of Athanasius 163
of Christians 47, 50, 51, 85, 87
of Donatists 137, 138, 140, 155–157
of heretics 140
of Jews 33, 45
of Monophysites 168, 170, 334, 338, 340
of Muslims 169, 349
of Nestorians 328
of Perpetua 94
response (Apologists) 98, 104, 114, 232, 393
response (Galen) 108
response (Celsus) 108
result of 100, 109, 110, 127, 151, 154, 157, 162, 291, 436
types 86
Persia 48, 49, 52, 68, 126, 140
person 141, 167, 184, 208, 211, 212, 231, 242, 260, 288, 289, 295, 298, 301, 302, 306, 310, 324, 325, 327, 330–333, 340, 346, 348, 349, 352, 424, 426
persona 299, 314, 315
personality 242, 298, 347
Peshitta (Syriac Bible) 49
Pharisees 12, 15, 16, 19, 20, 36, 38, 41, 183, 186, 233
Philokalia 69, 363
philosophical xxii, 71, 103, 108, 189, 192, 199, 209, 213, 222, 224, 225, 230, 233, 258, 299, 302, 315, 347, 360, 364, 373–375, 405, 406, 409
philosophy 6, 27, 55–57, 60, 77, 78, 103, 107, 109, 161, 192, 193, 198, 209, 230, 233, 346, 362, 406, 418
pillar saints 68
Pistis Sophia 210
Platonism 108, 189, 195, 209, 405, 409
Plato's Ideas 194–197, 199, 300
Pleroma 213, 215, 216
pneuma (*pneumatikoi*) 215, 216, 218
polytheistic 24, 349
Pontifex Maximus 30, 133, 134, 292

Praeparatio evangelica (Clement of Alexandria) 230, 360
Praescriptio Haereticorum (Tertullian) 6, 217, 232, 233, 242, 261, 367
pre-creation fall 224
presbyter 75, 225, 231, 291, 326, 365, 375, 416
priest 11, 16, 17, 64, 74, 154, 180, 235, 291, 292, 305, 376
prophets 37, 40, 103, 106, 107, 191, 199, 241, 242, 254, 258, 272, 296, 300, 319
pseudepigraphal 269, 270
psychic 208, 215, 217, 224
Ptolemies (Ptolemaic) 10, 22, 26, 47, 160, 209, 223
publican 281
Punic (language) 21, 147, 150, 151, 156
purify 396
puritanical 151, 162
purity 59, 151, 152, 191, 195, 436

Q
Qumran 18, 19, 41, 57, 71, 200, 408
Qur'an xxiii, xxiv, 51, 187, 219, 272, 289, 347–351

R
reading, literal 258
rebaptism. *See also* baptism
Redeemer 189, 212, 213, 298
Red Sea xix, 50, 146, 165, 167
Reformation xxiii, 270, 371, 399, 400, 406
religio illicita 88, 118, 130
religion(s) 26, 101, 130, 148, 411
  African xix, 433
  Berber 156
  Catholic 136
  Christianity 34, 47, 49, 88, 123, 130, 140, 167, 229, 290
  Egyptian 431
  Ethiopian 51
  Greek 4, 24
  Islam 122, 239, 340

Jewish 4, 42, 87
Nubian 171, 433
pagan 76, 395
Persian 209
politics of 438
polytheistic 192
practice of 16
Roman 4, 24, 30, 96
sociology of 417
unity of 292
Zoroastrian 49, 189, 209, 223
Renaissance xxiii, 399, 410
republic 21, 22, 386, 387
revelation 68, 106, 113, 199, 223, 270–273, 289–301, 333
Roman Empire xix, xxii, 5, 20, 21, 27, 29, 41, 45, 46, 49, 68, 74, 85, 109, 121, 122, 124, 130, 133, 136, 138, 146, 147, 160, 179, 186, 192, 193, 197, 254, 273, 290, 294, 324, 338, 362, 387, 390, 395, 396, 411, 423, 429, 433
fall of xxi–xxiii, 377, 385, 387, 397
Rome 24, 45, 114, 124, 125, 131, 140, 150, 160, 333, 367, 388, 389
asceticism in 71, 74, 371
centre of empire 20–23, 389, 394
Christianity in 45, 46, 88–90, 100, 148, 154, 227, 231, 232, 235–238, 264, 313, 327, 329, 330, 333, 334, 342, 343, 386, 387, 401, 427, 434
creed of 240
fall of xxii, 96, 385, 388, 390, 392, 394, 395
founding of 386
fire in 89, 124
Gnostics in 207, 214, 217, 220, 222, 225, 257
invasion of 369, 385–387, 390, 393, 394, 423
Jewish community in 13, 23
Manicheans in 373
persecution (and martyrdom) in 91, 93, 94, 177
religion in 26, 27, 29, 123, 192, 386, 392, 394
students in 151
teachers in 4, 296, 297, 373, 374, 377
Rule (monastic) 68, 70, 78–80, 345, 363
Rule of Faith 228, 241, 242, 251, 252, 261, 262, 367
Rule of the Holy Pachomius 63, 64, 69, 75, 79
Russia 47, 80, 141

S
Sabaea 146, 165
Sabellianism (Sabellius) 297, 299, 306, 308, 310, 316
sacrifice(s) 11, 26, 29, 44, 83, 85, 88, 92, 93, 96–99, 101, 112, 121, 122, 127, 217, 254, 392
human 156, 157
Old Testament 34
pagan 127, 140
Sadducees 8, 12, 16, 17, 19, 186, 233
Sahara xix, 158, 433
Sanhedrin 16, 26, 37, 41, 42
Satan 112, 122, 132, 228
Saviour 178, 179, 185, 186, 189, 208, 215, 241, 258, 287, 296
schism (schismatic) 111, 137, 138, 140, 153, 154, 155, 162, 291, 292, 367, 376, 411, 436
scholastic 407
school of theology
Alexandrian 302, 360
Antioch 346
Scillium (Scilli) 93, 132, 147, 150, 435
scribe 63
Scripture 4, 61, 63, 69, 78, 109, 168, 199, 223, 225, 231, 249, 252, 258, 260, 262, 266, 271, 280, 324, 357, 365, 369, 371, 373, 374, 400
scroll 17, 252, 254, 261
Second Jewish Commonwealth 8
Second Temple Judaism 6, 15, 16, 19
Seleucid 3, 4, 10

Semitic 164, 165
Septuagint 10, 15, 103, 198, 235, 253, 256, 302, 371
Shema 45, 347
Shepherd of Hermas 43, 243, 253, 262, 264, 265, 267
Sibyls 269
slave(s), slavery 13, 15, 56, 87, 124, 132, 152, 172, 391, 417
Smyrna 83, 84, 190, 227
Sol Invictus 29, 126, 127, 129, 133
Song of the Pearl 211
Sophia 210, 214–216, 224, 274
Sources chrétiennes 478
spiritual 189, 212, 221, 224, 343
 adviser 371
 beings 303
 freedom 406
 life 79
 reality 194, 196, 197
 realm 214, 223, 303
 truth 231
spiritual vs. material 217, 222, 373
Stoic (Stoicism) 6, 87, 93, 106, 197–199, 229, 233
subordinate 138, 197, 298, 303, 305, 310, 345, 435
subordination 138, 141, 298, 299, 304, 306, 308, 309, 334, 348
substantia 298, 299, 304, 309, 314
synagogue 10, 41, 186, 254, 256, 260, 369
syncretism 24, 26, 111, 223
synod 50, 256, 296, 306, 312–315, 327, 329, 341, 343, 345, 348, 377
Syriac
 church(es) 34, 68, 72, 338
 language 49, 52, 68, 421, 423, 427
Syriac Fathers 414
Syrian 11, 12, 35, 37, 39, 47, 49, 66, 68, 74, 78, 168, 268, 350, 365, 426

T
Talmud 255, 407
tax (collectors) 20, 160, 183, 340, 391

Textus Receptus 401
The Gospel of Mary 274
theôsis 148
Theotokos 326, 327, 329, 346, 349, 361
Therapeutae 57, 71
The Wisdom of Solomon 265
Thomism 407
Three Chapters 335, 337, 346, 427, 434
toleration 139, 140, 287
Tome 323, 331
Torah 12, 20, 41, 88, 184, 199, 220, 230, 254, 271, 277, 289, 351
traditor (traitor) 111, 153
transcendent 197, 199, 212, 214, 216, 217, 300, 302, 374, 402, 403
Transjordan 33, 42
Trinitarian (Trinity) 148, 187, 231, 243, 287, 289, 295, 298, 302–304, 314, 317, 325, 346–348, 351, 352, 359, 363, 364, 367, 380
trinitas 148, 299, 380
triune 295, 348, 352
true philosophy 56, 103, 193
Tübingen 403, 404, 406
Tunisia 147, 149, 157, 158, 435, 436
Turkey 10, 47, 328, 349, 362, 410
Turks (Muslim) 141
typological (interpretation) 103, 256, 259

U
Ukraine 47
Ulama 16
understanding, literal 324
unity 5, 123, 126, 135, 137, 152, 153, 167, 191, 238, 257, 287, 290, 292, 294, 295, 297, 299, 303–307, 309, 314, 315, 324, 325, 327, 333, 348, 349, 367, 374, 380, 392, 394, 419, 434
university(ies) 80, 197, 401, 402, 412

V
Vandal(s)
 Arian 434

Gothic 157
invasions xx, xxii, 156, 381, 429, 432–436, 438
Vienne 93, 115, 422
virginity 55, 72, 75, 112, 364, 415
virtue 55, 56, 193, 197, 208, 230
Visigoths 319, 338, 386, 389, 390
Vulgate 253, 266, 371, 375

W

West Africa 429
wisdom 57, 60, 61, 103, 192, 197, 216, 224, 231, 254, 296, 300, 303
women 71, 72, 87, 150, 183, 371, 412, 414–417
  education 277
  in the church 279, 416
  leadership 46
  monasticism 64, 70–72, 74, 75, 80
  role of xxiii, 277, 278, 414, 416
world religions 34

Y

Yemen xix, 50, 51, 146, 165, 350

Z

Zealots 19, 36

Index of Names

A

Abba Pantalewon 66
Abgar of Edessa, King 48
Abraham (OT) 48, 68, 178, 223, 258, 350, 369
Abraham of Kashkar 68
Abu Bolos 58
Adam 179, 180, 186, 228, 258, 296, 377
Adeodatus (son of Augustine) 358, 359, 375
Aedesius 145, 146, 167
Agatho (seventh-century pope) 342
Akiba, Rabbi 42
Alexander, bishop of Jerusalem 96
Alexander of Alexandria, bishop 291, 292, 305–307, 312, 360
Alexander the Great 9, 10, 21, 26, 197
Al-Jabbar, Abd xxiii, 85, 188, 219, 272
Ambrose, bishop of Milan 140, 258, 259, 327, 358, 359, 367–369, 374
Ammianus Marcellinus (historian) 140
Amun, Egyptian monastic 61, 71
Anastasius (sixth-century emperor) 326
Anthony, Egyptian monastic 56, 58–61, 63, 67, 71, 76, 358
Antigonus, Hasmonean king 13
Antiochus III 11
Antiochus IV Epiphanes 3, 4, 11, 12
Antoninus Pius, Emperor 104
Apollinaris (fourth-century bishop) 324–327, 329, 331, 362
Aristides of Athens, Apologist 117
Aristotle 196, 197, 233, 405
Arius 137, 148, 187, 188, 290, 291, 295, 297, 305–312, 315, 325, 348, 421, 425, 440
Arnauld, Dominique xxi, 159, 437, 438
Athanasius xxii, 58, 59, 61, 69, 71, 137, 139, 140, 147, 148, 159, 162, 167, 239, 266, 267, 307, 310, 312–316, 324, 358–361, 375, 432, 438
Athenagoras of Athens 118
Augustine (AD 354–430) xxi, xxii, 147, 155, 266, 267, 327, 352, 367, 372, 399, 406–407, 408, 417, 422, 423, 430, 432, 434–436
  and allegorical interpretation 259
  and Ambrose 367, 368
  and Donatists 155, 156, 376, 377
  and attack on Rome 386, 387, 393–395
  and Manichees 156, 222, 369, 373, 374, 376, 377
  and military service 396
  and monasticism 69, 375
  and Neoplatonists 373, 374
  and trinitarian thought 359, 380
  as bishop 375, 377
  baptism 359, 372, 373
  conversion 61, 357, 358, 374, 375, 377
  death 381
  education 372
Augustine of Canterbury 80
Augustus Caesar 13, 14, 21–23, 25, 29, 125, 127, 129, 170, 198, 386

B

Babyllas, bishop of Antioch 96
Baradaeus, Jacob 335
Bardaisan of Edessa 49
Barnabas (companion of apostle Paul) 40, 262
Barnabas of Alexandria 191, 238, 243
Basileides (gnostic) 161, 213, 217–219, 221, 268, 271
Basil of Caesarea 55, 56, 66, 69, 70, 72, 79, 259, 302, 316, 317, 362–364
Baur, F. C. 403–405

Baur, John 431
Bediako, Kwame xx
Benedict of Nursia 64, 70, 79
Bentley, Richard 401
Blyden, Wilmot 158
Brown, Dan 266, 270–274, 279, 416
Brown, Peter 67, 152, 388, 407, 417
Bultmann, Rudolf 148, 212, 413
Burns Jr., J. Patout 436

C

Caecilian, bishop of Carthage 137, 154, 155, 376
Carpocrates (gnostic) 221
Cassian, see John Cassian
Cassiodorus 78, 79
Celestine I (fifth-century patriarch of Rome) 327
Celsus 108
Chrysostom, see John Chrysostom
Cicero 131, 370, 373, 401
Claudius, Emperor 23
Clement (early bishop of Rome) 91, 190, 191, 235, 237, 238, 243, 261, 401, 404
Clement II 190, 243
Clement of Alexandria 47, 148, 161, 225, 229–231, 258, 265, 269, 278, 299, 302, 359, 360, 405, 438
Clovis 390
Constans 138, 139, 312, 313
Constantine 30, 42, 45, 47, 85, 86, 122, 123, 127, 129–141, 155, 266, 287, 288, 290, 292, 307, 311, 312, 359, 394, 396, 421, 423, 425, 426
Constantine IV 342
Constantine V 343
Constantine VI 343
Constantius II (son of Constantine) 138, 139, 312, 313, 319, 341, 425
Constantius Chlorus (father of Constantine) 127, 129
Crispus (son of Constantine) 421
Cuoq, Joseph 434

Cyprian 96–98, 102, 110, 112, 114, 147, 151–154, 237, 367, 432, 434–436, 438
Cyriacus of Alodia 171
Cyril of Alexandria 324, 326, 327, 329, 334, 335, 346, 359, 361, 362, 365, 427, 432, 433
Cyril of Jerusalem 268
Cyrus (Persian ruler) 6

D

Daniel, Robin 435
Decius, Emperor 58, 86, 87, 94–97, 100, 110, 124, 132, 153, 238
Decret, François 435
Demetrius of Alexandria 47, 161
Didymus the Blind 147
Diocletian 23, 59, 86, 98, 121, 122, 124–127, 129, 131, 154, 159, 162, 193, 291, 362, 374, 389, 421, 425
Diodorus, Bishop of Antioch 325, 326, 329
Dionysius the Areopagite 340
Dioscuros (fifth-century patriarch of Alexandria) 329, 330, 331
Domitian, Emperor 91, 101, 131
Donatus of Carthage 137, 151, 152, 154, 155, 162

E

Erasmus 401
Eusebius of Caesarea (Pamphilus) 42, 47, 50, 71, 86, 94, 112, 113, 115, 121, 129, 130, 133–135, 137, 161, 162, 217, 251, 263, 265, 266, 268, 280, 282, 292, 302, 306–308, 310, 313, 359, 395, 410, 418, 421–425
Eusebius of Nicomedia 134, 137, 141, 307, 312, 319, 421
Eustochium (fourth-century associate of Jerome) 71, 72, 371, 372
Eutyches (fifth-century archimandrite of Constantinople) 329–331, 361
Evagrius (fourth-century ascetic theologian) 74

Index of Names 501

Eve 179, 224, 228, 258
Ezana, King 145, 167, 170
Ezra 8, 14, 255

F
Fabian (third-century bishop of Rome) 96
Felicitas (servant of Perpetua) 93, 94, 113, 150, 435
Finneran, Neil 433
Flavian, Patriarch of Constantinople 329, 330
Frend, W. H. C. 74, 79, 126, 152, 155, 158, 410–412, 433
Frumentius 145, 146, 167, 432

G
Gaius Caligula, Emperor 23
Galen 108, 110
Galerius (fourth-century Roman emperor) 121, 122, 126, 127, 129
Gallus (third-century emperor) 97
Gibbon, Edward 85, 388, 391, 392, 396, 402
Gregory (Armenian prince) 49
Gregory of Nazianzus (Nazianzen) 74, 147, 226, 302, 316, 317, 325, 362, 363, 403
Gregory of Nyssa 55, 56, 72, 302, 316, 317, 362–364, 406
Gregory Thaumatourgos 362
Gregory the Great (sixth-century pope) 70, 80, 226, 390
Groves, C. P. 429

H
Hadrian, Emperor 13, 41, 93, 117, 134
Harnack, Adolf von xxiii, 5, 35, 148, 161, 403, 405–410, 412, 418
Hastings, Adrian 431
Hecataeus (historian) 9
Hegel, Georg W. F. 402
Helena (mother of Constantine) 42, 129, 134

Hengel, Martin 408
Heracleon (gnostic) 221
Heraclius, Emperor (seventh-century) 338, 340
Hermas of Rome 191
Herod (the Great) 13, 14, 17, 20, 161
Hilary (fourth-century theologian) 73
Hippolytus of Rome 111–113, 209, 217, 218, 233, 240, 264, 268, 408, 422
Homer 198
Hosius, Bishop 134, 137, 293, 306, 308, 309

I
Ibas of Edessa 335, 346
Ignatius of Antioch 87, 93, 177, 178, 190, 191, 235, 401, 404
Irenaeus 33, 34, 44, 84, 99, 208, 210, 214, 216, 218, 220, 221, 225–230, 232, 235–237, 241, 242, 249, 251, 262, 263, 271, 278, 298, 301, 315, 359, 361, 367
Isichei, Elizabeth 172, 431, 432

J
James, apostle 45, 261
James, brother of Jesus 38, 40
Jerome 33, 43, 63, 64, 69, 71, 74, 75, 155, 253, 265, 370–372, 375, 386, 395
Johanan ben Zakkai 41
John, apostle 52, 85, 91, 98, 180, 185, 226, 234, 250, 263, 264, 281–283, 295
John Cassian 64, 70, 75, 76, 78, 79
John Chrysostom 72, 226, 326, 365–367, 403
John Hyrcanus 8, 12
John IV, Pope 341
John of Antioch 328, 329
John of Damascus 344
John the Baptist 36, 57, 165, 180, 182, 185, 200
Josephus 18, 71, 233, 253, 255, 408, 422

Joshua (OT) 36, 179, 253
Jovinian (fourth-century theologian) 75
Judas Iscariot 184, 219
Judas Maccabaeus 3, 12
Julian, Emperor (the Apostate) 139, 140, 314, 374, 424, 425
Julius Africanus (third-century historian) 422
Julius Caesar 23
Junia (associate of apostle Paul) 278
Justinian, Emperor 78, 136, 141, 158, 170, 334, 335, 337, 338, 346, 350, 427, 432, 434
Justin Martyr 33, 46, 49, 56, 85, 99–104, 106–108, 117, 192, 225, 229, 256, 258–260, 262, 263, 298–302, 359

K
Kalu, Ogbu U. 430
Kant, Immanuel 402
King, Karen 275

L
Lactantius 101, 121, 122, 126, 130–132, 147, 359, 422
Leo III, Emperor 343
Leontius (sixth-century Byzantine monk) 335
Licinius (fourth-century Augustus of the East) 130, 292, 421, 426
Lucian of Antioch 297, 305, 306, 348, 421
Luke, apostle 36, 226, 262, 404
Lydia (companion of apostle Paul) 46, 276

M
Macarios, Egyptian monastic 61
Macrina 55, 56, 69, 72, 363
Marcian, Emperor 331
Marcion 4, 5, 220, 221, 224, 225, 231, 249, 252, 257, 261

Marcus Aurelius 93, 101, 117, 118, 125, 132, 197, 389
Mark, apostle 47, 161, 185, 226, 262, 281, 430–432
Martin Luther 400, 406
Martin of Tours 73, 74
Mary Magdalene 184, 273, 274, 279
Mary, mother of Jesus 75, 161, 165, 177, 180, 185, 186, 228, 229, 240, 242, 267, 296, 301, 303, 318, 324, 326, 327, 332, 343, 346–349, 351, 352, 361
Matthew, apostle 165, 226, 268
Maximilla (Montanist leader) 278
Maximin (fourth-century emperor) 129, 130, 162
Maximus the Confessor 341
Melito of Sardis 101, 117, 253, 268
Menander (gnostic) 217, 221
Menelik I 165
Meropius of Tyre 146
Migne, Jean-Paul 403
Minucius Felix 118
Momigliano, Arnaldo 388
Monica (mother of Augustine) 358, 372, 375
Montanus 153, 278
Moses (OT) 3, 4, 8, 15, 34, 37, 39, 40, 42–44, 50, 164, 179, 183, 184, 199, 223, 253, 254, 256, 272, 296, 350, 351, 364
Muhammad xxiii, 51, 68, 169, 219, 239, 272, 338, 347, 349–351

N
Nehemiah 8, 14, 255
Nero 23, 46, 83, 86, 87, 89–91, 101, 124, 131
Nestorius 324, 326–328, 331, 335, 346, 349, 361, 362, 365, 426, 427

O
Oden, Thomas xxi, 147, 149, 438–440

Origen xxi, xxii, 50, 146, 147, 236, 302, 337, 345, 359, 360, 362, 363, 372, 422, 432, 438
  and allegorical interpretation 258
  and biblical canon 265, 280–281
  and Celsus 108–109, 407
  and Logos theology 299
  and Palestinian Caesarea 42
  and persecution 94, 97, 302
  and Philokalia 69
  and pseudo-gospels 268
  and trinitarian thought 303, 304, 306, 308, 310, 314, 315, 352, 380
  as Greek scholar 74
  Hexapla (OT manuscripts) 265, 302
  teacher in Alexandria 161, 258, 302, 360
Orosius (historian) 394, 395
Osius (Ossius). *See also* Hosius

P

Pachomius 62, 64, 69, 76, 79
Palladius (historian) 62
Pamphilus (third century) 42, 422. *See also* Eusebius
Pantaenus of Alexandria 46, 229, 302
Patrick of Ireland 76, 78
Paula (fourth-century monastic) 71, 72, 75, 371, 372
Paul, apostle 13, 38, 40, 44–46, 57, 71, 86, 87, 91, 101, 124, 178, 185, 186, 217, 220, 224, 232, 236, 237, 252, 256–260, 262, 263, 275, 278, 281, 282, 290, 296, 325, 358, 415
Paul of Samosata 290, 296, 305, 326, 348
Pelagius (British monk) 377
Perpetua 93, 94, 113, 150, 435
Petilian of Constantine (North Africa) 155
Philo of Alexandria 57, 71, 160, 198, 229, 231, 258, 300, 408, 432
Phoebe (companion of apostle Paul) 278
Pirenne, Henri 387

Plato 6, 99, 105–107, 192, 194, 195, 199, 209, 405
Pliny (the Younger) 88, 92, 93, 100, 232
Polycarp 83, 84, 87, 93, 100, 177, 190, 191, 225, 261, 422
Pompey 13, 20, 23
Pontius Pilate 14, 20, 177, 178, 180, 183, 229, 240, 318
Pope Callistus 297, 298
Pope Damasus 74, 75, 371
Pope Honorius 341
Pope Leo (fifth century) 323, 329–331, 333, 427
Pope Leo XIII 405
Pope Martin 341
Pope Victor 147, 296
Porphyry 108, 126, 139, 193, 263, 374
Prisca (associate of apostle Paul) 278
Priscilla (Montanist prophetess) 278
Ptolemaeus (gnostic) 221
Ptolemy I 10

Q

Quadratus (Apologist) 117
Queen of Sheba 146, 165, 431

R

Ramsay, Sir William 404, 410
Rufinus (fifth-century historian) 69, 145, 146, 423, 424

S

Sabellius 297, 299, 316
Sanneh, Lamin xx, 430, 440
Saturninus of Antioch 221
Schaff, Philip 406
Schüssler Fiorenza, Elizabeth 415
Septimius Severus, Emperor 94, 147, 232
Sergius (Patriarch of Constantinople) 340, 341
Shaw, Mark 437
Silko (Nubian king) 170
Simon ben Kochba 33, 42, 43
Simon Magus 221

Simon of Cyrene 149, 184, 208, 218, 219, 430, 440
Simon the Samaritan 217
Socrates 99, 101, 105–107, 192–194, 423–427
Socrates (historian) 287, 305, 308, 309, 326, 360, 365
Solomon (king of Israel) 6, 12, 146, 165, 180, 216, 254, 258, 280, 431, 433
Sozomen 66, 423, 425, 426, 427
Spengler, Oswald 390
Sundkler, Bengt 431–433
Symeon the Stylite 66–68
Synesius of Cyrene 440

T
Tacitus (historian) 89, 90, 124
Tatian (Apologist) 49, 117, 263
Telesphorus, bishop of Rome 93
Tertullian xxi, xxii, 6, 85, 147, 151, 278, 359, 367, 399, 430, 432, 435, 436
   and asceticism 56
   and baptism 111
   and emperors 102, 232
   and Gnostics 207–209, 225, 231–233, 242, 251
   and military service 393
   and natures of Christ 298, 330
   and persecution (martyrdom) 101, 111, 132, 150, 231
   and philosophy 233
   and "rule of faith" 242, 261–262
   and trinitarian thought 242, 243, 297–299, 304, 380
   and women 278, 279
   Apologist 99, 100, 232
   Montanist 153
Theodora, Empress (wife of Justinian) 170, 171, 334, 335
Theodore of Mopsuestia 259, 326, 329, 335, 346, 426, 427
Theodore the Studite (of Studius) 70, 344, 345
Theodore of Sykeon 68
Theodoret of Cyrrhus 335, 346, 423, 426, 427
Theodosius I, the Great (fourth-century emperor) 123, 140, 312, 317, 364, 369, 392, 423, 425
Theodosius II, the Younger (fifth-century emperor) 140, 293, 327, 328, 330, 331, 362, 366, 425
Theodotus of Rome 348
Thomas, apostle 52, 184, 261, 430
Tiberius, Emperor 101
Trajan, Emperor 88, 92, 93, 100, 232

U
Ulfilas (the Goth) 319, 393, 425

V
Valentinus (gnostic) 161, 207, 214, 216, 217, 221, 225
Valerian, Emperor (third century) 83, 86, 95, 98, 238
Verecundus (sixth-century African bishop) 147
Verstraelen, Frans xx, 431, 432, 434
Victorinus (fourth-century theologian) 374
Voss, Isaac 401

W
Wesley, John 401

Y
Yared 66, 168

Langham Literature and its imprints are a ministry of Langham Partnership.

Langham Partnership is a global fellowship working in pursuit of the vision God entrusted to its founder John Stott –

> *to facilitate the growth of the church in maturity and Christ-likeness through raising the standards of biblical preaching and teaching.*

Our vision is to see churches in the majority world equipped for mission and growing to maturity in Christ through the ministry of pastors and leaders who believe, teach and live by the Word of God.

Our mission is to strengthen the ministry of the Word of God through:
- nurturing national movements for biblical preaching
- fostering the creation and distribution of evangelical literature
- enhancing evangelical theological education

especially in countries where churches are under-resourced.

Our ministry

Langham Preaching partners with national leaders to nurture indigenous biblical preaching movements for pastors and lay preachers all around the world. With the support of a team of trainers from many countries, a multi-level programme of seminars provides practical training, and is followed by a programme for training local facilitators. Local preachers' groups and national and regional networks ensure continuity and ongoing development, seeking to build vigorous movements committed to Bible exposition.

Langham Literature provides majority world preachers, scholars and seminary libraries with evangelical books and electronic resources through publishing and distribution, grants and discounts. The programme also fosters the creation of indigenous evangelical books in many languages, through writer's grants, strengthening local evangelical publishing houses, and investment in major regional literature projects, such as one volume Bible commentaries like *The Africa Bible Commentary* and *The South Asia Bible Commentary*.

Langham Scholars provides financial support for evangelical doctoral students from the majority world so that, when they return home, they may train pastors and other Christian leaders with sound, biblical and theological teaching. This programme equips those who equip others. Langham Scholars also works in partnership with majority world seminaries in strengthening evangelical theological education. A growing number of Langham Scholars study in high quality doctoral programmes in the majority world itself. As well as teaching the next generation of pastors, graduated Langham Scholars exercise significant influence through their writing and leadership.

To learn more about Langham Partnership and the work we do visit **langham.org**